BEYOND THE RED, WHITE, AND BLUE

A Student's Introduction to American Studies

12/25/94
To Gregory, Bryce, A.G., + Ann.
Look for Mom on page 41.
Best wishes from
Grandpa Lew

Lewis H. Carlson
James M. Ferreira

Western Michigan University

KENDALL/HUNT PUBLISHING COMPANY
2460 Kerper Boulevard P.O. Box 539 Dubuque, Iowa 52004-0539

Credits

Page 26	Excerpt from BABBITT, copyright 1922 by Harcourt Brace & Company and renewed 1950 by Sinclair Lewis, reprinted by permission of the publisher.
Page 40	Copyright © 1990 by Harper's Magazine. All rights reserved. Reprinted from the August issue by special permission.
Page 49	"Little Boxes" by Malvina Reynolds. Copyright © 1962, 1963 by Schroder Music Company. Copyright renewed 1990 by N. Schimmel. Reprinted with permission.
Page 68	Reprinted by permission of the author.
Page 149	From THE PASSION OF CLAUDE MCKAY by Wayne Cooper. Copyright © 1973 by Wayne Cooper. Reprinted by permission of Schocken Books, published by Pantheon Books, a Division of Random House, Inc.
Page 150	Reprinted by permission of Harold Ober Associates Incorporated. Copyright © 1953 by Langston Hughes. Copyright renewed 1981 by George Houston Bass.
Page 153	I Am a Black Woman, published by Wm. Morrow & Co., 1970, by permission of the author.
Page 154	"The Ethics of Living Jim Crow" from UNCLE TOM'S CHILDREN by Richard Wright. Copyright 1936 by Richard Wright. Copyright renewed 1964 by Ellen Wright. Reprinted by permission of HarperCollins Publishers.
Page 172	Pages 46-50, 53-59 from BLACK RAGE by William H. Grier and Price M. Cobbs. Copyright © 1968 by Basic Books, Inc. Reprinted by permission of Basic Books, a division of HarperCollins Publishers.
Page 186	From DIE NIGGER DIE by H. Rap Brown. Copyright © 1969 by Lynne Brown. Used by permission of Doubleday, a division of Bantam Doubleday Dell Publishing Group, Inc.
Page 188	Reprinted with permission from The New York Review of Books. Copyright © 1971 Nyrev, Inc.
Page 192	"New Space/The Growth of Black Consciousness in the Sixties" by Larry Neal from The Black Seventies. Copyright © 1970 by Floyd B. Barbour for Porter Sargent Publisher, Boston, MA. Reprinted by permission.
Page 196	From INVISIBLE MAN by Ralph Ellison. Copyright 1947, 1948, 1952 by Ralph Ellison. Reprinted by permission of Random House, Inc.
Page 203	From THE AUTOBIOGRAPHY OF MALCOLM X by Malcolm X with Alex Haley. Copyright © 1964 by Alex Haley and Malcolm X. Copyright © 1965 by Alex Haley and Betty Shabazz. Reprinted by permission of Random House, Inc.
Page 213	From RED SCARE, 1919-1920: A STUDY IN NATIONAL HYSTERIA by Robert K. Murray, published by the University of Minnesota Press. Copyright © 1964 by the University of Minnesota Press. Reprinted by permission.

This edition has been printed directly from camera-ready copy

ISBN 8403-8816-0

Printed in the United States of America
10 9 8 7 6 5 4 3 2 1

Page 217 Bud Schultz; Ruth Schultz. It Did Happen Here, pages 237-248, published by the University of California Press. Copyright © 1989 The Regents of the University of California.

Page 227 From The Man Who Cried Genocide: An Autobiography by William Patterson. Pp. 7-13, 75-90. Copyright © 1971 by International Publishers. Reprinted with permission.

Page 260 From ONE LONELY NIGHT by Mickey Spillane. Copyright 1951 by E. P. Dutton. Renewed © 1979 by Mickey Spillane. Used by permission of the publisher, Dutton, an imprint of New American Library, a division of Penguin Books USA Inc.

Page 261 "The Cold War as Entertainment in 'Fifties Television" by J. Fred MacDonald. Copyright © 1978 by the Journal of Popular Film and Television. Reprinted with permission of the author and publisher.

Page 270 "The Triumph of the Egghead" by Louis Bromfield from The Freeman, Dec. 1, 1952. Copyright © 1952 by The Freeman. Reprinted with permission of Freeman Magazine.

Page 287 Reprinted by permission of the author. From the LAFAYETTE COLLEGE ALUMNI QUARTERLY, Fall, 1985, pp. 21-25.

Page 305 Adapted from Lady Borton, from Harper's Magazine, June 1973.

Page 317 "Change and Continuity in American Foreign Policy Since 1930" by John Garry Clifford. Copyright © by John Garry Clifford. Reprinted by permission of the author.

Page 329 Reprinted by permission of Donadio & Ashworth, Inc. Copyright © 1969 Michael Arlen.

Page 334 By Ron Weber. Copyright © 1978 by Ron Weber. Reprinted by permission of the author.

Page 335 By Horace Coleman. Copyright © by Horace Coleman, Reprinted by permission of the author.

Page 335 By Horace Coleman. Copyright © by Horace Coleman, Reprinted by permission of the author.

Page 336 By W. D. Ehrhart. Copyright © 1984 by W. D. Ehrhart. Reprinted by permission of the author.

Page 336 By W. D. Ehrhart. Copyright © 1984 by W. D. Ehrhart. Reprinted by permission of the author.

Page 337 By W. D. Ehrhart. Copyright © 1984 by W. D. Ehrhart. Reprinted by permission of the author.

Page 338 By D. F. Brown. Copyright © 1984 by D. F. Brown. Reprinted by permission of the author.

Page 339 By John Balaban. Copyright © 1974, 1980 by John Balaban. Reprinted by permission of the author.

Page 340 By John Balaban. Copyright © 1974, 1980 by John Balaban. Reprinted by permission of the author.

Page 341 By John Balaban. Copyright © 1974, 1980 by John Balaban. Reprinted by permission of the author.

Page 342 By Steven Ford Brown. Copyright © by Steven Ford Brown. Reprinted by permission of the author.

Page 347 Reprinted by permission of Bradford Lyttle.

Page 359 Excerpt is from Why We Were in Vietnam by Norman Podhoretz. Copyright © 1982 by Norman Podhoretz. Reprinted by permission of Georges Borchardt, Inc. for the author.

Page 363 Reprinted by permission of the authors, William L. Griffen and John Marciano, and the editor, John Fiske of Rownan & Littlefield, publisher.

Page 374 "Censored! An Overview of the History of Banned and Censored Records in America" by Peter Melton. From Goldmine, Feb. 22, 1991, pp. 113-116. Copyright © 1991 by Goldmine. Reprinted with permission of the author and Goldmine.

Page 383 "Censorship Yesterday and Today-As American As Apple Pie?" by Gillian G. Gaar. From Goldmine, Feb. 22, 1991, pp. 48, 50. Copyright © 1991 by Goldmine. Reprinted with permission of the author and Goldmine.

Page 388 "The Censorship Debate: Four Opinions" by Jeff Tamarkin. From Goldmine, Feb. 22, 1991, pp. 52-54, 112, 126. Copyright © 1991 by Goldmine. Reprinted with permission of the author and Goldmine.

Page 400 Copyright © 1958 by Harper's Magazine. All rights reserved. Reprinted from the January issue by special permission.

Page 404 Copyright 1957 Time Inc. Reprinted by permission.

Page 406 From NEWSWEEK, 7/16/56, © 1956, Newsweek, Inc. All rights reserved. Reprinted by permission.

Page 408 "The Vicksburg Ghost" by Sue Hubbell. From The New Yorker, Sept. 25, 1989, pp. 106-117. Copyright © 1989 by Sue Hubbell. Reprinted by permission of The Darhansoff & Verrill Literary Agency.

Page 419 Copyright © SAN FRANCISCO CHRONICLE. Reprinted by permission.

Page 430 "The Great Kid-Con" by Susan Huck. From Review of the News, Feb. 11, 1970. Pp. 17-24. Copyright © 1970 by Review of the News. Reprinted with permission of the John Birch Society.

Page 435 "Country Music and American Values" by John Buckly. From Popular Music and Society, Vol. 6, No. 4, 1978. Pp. 293-301. Copyright © 1978 by Popular Music and Society. Reprinted with permission.

Page 444 "Frankenchrist versus the State: The New Right, Rock Music, and the Case of Jello Biafra" by David Kennedy. From Journal of Popular Culture, Summer 1990, Vol. 24. Pp. 131-147. Copyright © 1990 by Journal of Popular Culture. Reprinted with permission.

TABLE OF CONTENTS

Page

PREFACE

ACKNOWLEDGEMENTS

PART I - THE AMERICAN DREAM 1

Ben Franklin, *POOR RICHARD'S ALMANAC* 3

Ralph Waldo Emerson, *SELF-RELIANCE* 9

Henry David Thoreau, *LIFE WITHOUT PRINCIPLE* 13

and *CIVIL DISOBEDIENCE* 16

Sinclair Lewis, BABBITT 26

Helen Stephens, *OLYMPIC CHAMPION* 31

Tom Monaghan, *THE THRILL OF POVERTY* 40

Ann Thomas, *DISILLUSIONED IDEALIST* 41

Patricia Cutler, *FROM CADILLACS TO HEALTH CARE* 45

Malvina Reynolds, *LITTLE BOXES* 49

Lew Carlson, *RONALD REAGAN AND AMERICAN POPULAR CULTURE* 50

James Ferreira, *JOHN WAYNE: AMERICAN HERO* 59

Lewis Easterling, *OBSERVATIONS OF AN AGING, UNEMPLOYED, MIDDLE-CLASS, WHITE MAN* 68

PART II - RACE AND ETHNICITY 91

Lew Carlson, *JIM JEFFRIES VERSUS JACK JOHNSON* 93

Lew Carlson and George Colburn, *IN THEIR PLACE* 105

Eva Martinez, *THE WHITENING OF AMERICA* 138

Frederick Douglass, *MY BONDAGE AND MY FREEDOM* 142

W. E. B. Du Bois, *SONG OF THE SMOKE* 146

Paul Dunbar, *WE WEAR THE MASK* 148

Claude McKay, *IF WE MUST DIE* 149

Langston Hughes, *DEAR DR. BUTTS* 150

Mari Evans, *BLACK JAM FOR DR. NEGRO* 153

Richard Wright, *THE ETHICS OF LIVING JIM CROW* 154

Archie Williams, *OLYMPIC CHAMPION* 163

William H. Grier and Price M. Cobbs, *BLACK RAGE* 172

Henry Vance Davis, *AN AFRICAN-AMERICAN PERSPECTIVE ON THE REAGAN-BUSH YEARS AND BEYOND* 179

H. Rap Brown, *DIE NIGGER DIE* 186

James Baldwin, *AN OPEN LETTER TO MY SISTER, MISS ANGELA DAVIS* 188

Larry Neal, *NEW SPACE/THE GROWTH OF BLACK CONSCIOUSNESS* 192

Ralph Ellison, *PROLOGUE FROM THE INVISIBLE MAN* 196

AUTOBIOGRAPHY OF MALCOLM X 203

PART III - ANTI-COMMUNISM 210

Robert K. Murray, *RED SCARE* 213

Jack Miller, *THE EVERETT MASSACRE, 1916* 217

BOL-SHE-VEEK 226

William Patterson, *THE MAN WHO CRIED GENOCIDE* 227

Lew Carlson, *THE HOLLYWOOD HEARINGS* 240

Richard Nixon, *ALGER HISS AND THE COMMUNIST CONSPIRACY IN WASHINGTON* 252

Senator Joe McCarthy, *WHEELING WEST VIRGINIA SPEECH* 258

Mickey Spillane, *ONE LONELY NIGHT* 260

J. Fred MacDonald, *THE COLD WAR AS ENTERTAINMENT IN 'FIFTIES TELEVISION* 261

Louis Bromfield, *THE TRIUMPH OF THE EGGHEAD* 270

Ronald Reagan, *EVIL EMPIRE SPEECH* 274

PART IV - THE VIETNAM WAR 276

Walter LaFeber, *AMERICA, RUSSIA, AND THE COLD WAR* 279

President Lyndon B. Johnson, *PEACE WITHOUT CONQUEST* 283

James Quay, *LIFE, LIBERTY, AND THE RIGHT TO PROTEST* 287

Brian "Doc" Koss, *MEDIC* 293

Lynda Van Devanter, *HUMP DAY* 296

WOMEN POETS OF THE VIETNAM WAR

DUSTY 303

Sharon Grant, *THE BEST ACT IN PLEIKU, NO ONE UNDER 18 ADMITTED* 304

Lady Borton, *A BOOM, A BILLOW* 305

Penny Kettlewell, *THE COFFEE ROOM SOLDIER* 306

Mary Pat O'Connor, *SEVENTEEN SUMMERS AFTER VIETNAM* 307

Marilyn McMahon, *KNOWING* 308

John Erdos, *GRUNT* 310

John Garry Clifford, *CHANGE AND CONTINUITY IN AMERICAN FOREIGN POLICY SINCE 1930* 317

President Richard M. Nixon, *A CONVERSATION WITH THE PRESIDENT ABOUT FOREIGN POLICY* 324

Michael Arlen, *THE LIVING-ROOM WAR* 329

SOLDIER POETS OF THE WAR

Ron Weber, *A CONCISE HISTORY OF THE VIETNAM WAR: 1965-1968* 324

Horace Coleman, *A BLACK SOLDIER REMEMBERS* 335

Horace Coleman, *A DOWNED PILOT LEARNS HOW TO FLY* 335

W. D. Ehrhart, *TIME ON TARGET* 336

W. D. Ehrhart, *MAKING THE CHILDREN BEHAVE* 336

W. D. Ehrhart, *THE INVASION OF GRENADA* 337

D. F. Brown, *STILL LATER THERE ARE WAR STORIES* 338

John Balaban, *AFTER OUR WAR* 339

John Balaban, *THOUGHTS BEFORE DAWN* 340

John Balaban, *IN CELEBRATION OF SPRING* 341

Steven Ford Brown, *AFTER THE VIETNAM WAR* 342

Students for a Democratic Society, *THE PORT HURON STATEMENT* 343

Bradford Lyttle, *THE DEMOCRATIC CONVENTION DEMONSTRATIONS, 1968* 347

MAYOR RICHARD DALEY AND THE CITY OF CHICAGO DEFEND THEIR POLICE, 1968 356

Norman Podhoretz, *WHY WE WERE IN VIETNAM* 359

William L. Griffen & John Marciano, *TEACHING THE VIETNAM WAR* 363

PART V - THE STRUGGLE OVER POPULAR MUSIC 369

Peter Melton, *CENSORED* 374

William G. Gaar, *CENSORSHIP YESTERDAY AND TODAY* 383

Jeff Tamarkin, *THE CENSORSHIP DEBATE - FOUR OPINIONS* 388

James & Annette Baxter, *THE MAN IN THE BLUE SUEDE SHOES* 400

THE ROCK IS SOLID 404

John Lardner, *DEVITALIZING ELVIS* 406

Sue Hubbell, *THE VICKSBURG GHOST* 408

Ralph J. Gleason, *LIKE A ROLLING STONE* 419

Susan Huck, *THE GREAT KID-CON* 430

John Buckley, *COUNTRY MUSIC AND AMERICAN VALUES* 435

David Kennedy, *FRANKENCHRIST VERSUS THE STATE* 443

PREFACE

This book presents the American Studies student with a multi-disciplinary approach to five, arbitrarily chosen, historical topics: the American Dream, Race, Anti-Communism, the Vietnam War, and the Struggle Over Popular Music. The intent is not to present a comprehensive, historical treatment of each of these topics or to persuade the student that one interpretation is more credible than another; rather, the editors want to expose students to as many kinds of source materials and contrasting viewpoints as is possible within the limited space of this book. Above all, they want to make students feel more comfortable using a multi-disciplinary and cross-disciplinary approach when examining and evaluating the myriad themes, movements, and personalities which make up our American past.

Students will examine how social scientists and humanists differ in their research and writing; more specifically, given a precise historical problem, how might political scientists, historians, economists or sociologists differ from each other, as well as from poets, novelists, artists or composers in their analyses and presentations? Students will determine whether different kinds of criteria apply when evaluating an essay, article, or monograph rather than a poem, a work of fiction, or a musical composition. In short, the student will learn how to recognize and authenticate a document before judging its historical value.

Students will also confront the common American whose views are so often overlooked. Should his or her opinions receive equal consideration with those of the so-called experts? And what of minorities and women? Do they bring a different perspective to the study of the American experience, and are their interpretations less or more objective than those of the white males who so long have been the dominant storytellers in our culture?

Students will find the source materials in this book represent what is commonly called high and low culture, but how does one qualitatively and quantitatively evaluate such sources? Most chroniclers of the American experience give far greater credence to the works of recognized arbiters of good taste and to professional scholars than they do to those who create for mass or popular audiences. Many of the selections in this book will test such assumptions, and we ask readers to examine how their own likes and dislikes affect their acceptance or rejection of the works and conclusions of others.

Several of the selections in this book, such as the excerpts by Franklin, Thoreau, Emerson, and Douglas, are American classics. Also originally published elsewhere are those contributions by prominent novelists, historians, poets, and essayists. However, several original essays were written especially for this reader. In addition, there are a number of oral histories which represent common Americans. Most readers assume the more important the writer, the more credible and relevant the selection. Students, however, should decide for themselves if this is always the case.

ACKNOWLEDGEMENTS

We would like to thank Ms. Alberta Cumming for her cheerful help in typing parts of this manuscript and for her frequent and enlightening instructions on computer applications. Lew Carlson would also like to thank Western Michigan University's Faculty Research Grant for support during the initial stages of research.

PART I - THE AMERICAN DREAM

This land is your land
This land is my land
From California to the New York Island
From the redwood forest
To the gulf stream waters
This land was made for you and me

Woody Guthrie, folksinger

Whenever Richard Cory went down town,
We people on the pavement looked at him:
He was a gentleman from sole to crown,
Clean favored, and imperially slim.

And he was always quietly arrayed,
And he was always human when he talked;
But still he fluttered pulses when he said,
"Good morning," and he glittered when he walked.

And he was rich--yes, richer than a king--
And admirably schooled in every grace:
In fine, we thought that he was everything
To make us wish that we were in his place.

So on we worked, and waited for the light,
And went without meat, and cursed the bread;
And Richard Cory, one calm summer night,
Went home and put a bullet through his head.

Richard Cory, 1897
Edwin Arlington Robinson

The thing most well-fed people want above all else from their government is, figuratively speaking, the right to shoot craps with loaded dice.

Kurt Vonnegut, novelist, 1991

It is no slogan to say America will always occupy a special place in God's heart.

President George Bush, 1992

We believe in this country that man was created in the image of God, that he was given talents and responsibilities and he was instructed to use them to build a better place in which to live. And this is the really great thing about America. And this is where it contrasts with what Russian and other Godless societies are trying to do.

Richard DeVos, President of the AMWAY Corporation

INTRODUCTION

The following selections make it clear there are as many interpretations of the American Dream as there are Americans, but over the years most have stressed economic factors. Ben Franklin anticipated many later proponents of the traditional American Dream with his thrifty, nose-to-the-grindstone work ethic and his moralistic preachments that promised to make practitioners "healthy, wealthy, and wise." But with his myriad interests and accomplishments, Franklin's own life more closely resembled that of Renaissance man rather than the lives of later business giants who so often extolled his writings as moral beacons for those seeking to accumulate economic riches. In the nineteenth century, dissident voices such as Ralph Waldo Emerson and Henry David Thoreau countered the traditional views of Franklin and his would-be followers when they extolled an inner understanding of the natural world that transcended the expanding materialistic society that surrounded them.

Throughout our history, most Americans have held onto the simple hope that somehow their children and their children's children would realize a better economic life. The fact that as late as 1920, fully 80 per cent of American families did not reach even a minimum standard of living, makes it easier to understand why most people have been more concerned with earning their daily bread than with lofty notions of what constitutes "the good and worthwhile life." Critics of the economic Dream, such as Sinclair Lewis, Patricia Cutler, and Malvina Reynolds may have sympathized with those struggling for their daily existence, but are sharply critical of the materialistic excesses of men like George Babbitt, Tom Monaghan, and Richard DeVos who quantify themselves, their religion, and their country in terms of accumulated wealth.

Helen Stephens, Ann Thomas, and Lewis Easterling are examples of individuals whose American Dreams were shattered by forces over which they had little or no control. For reasons of gender, economics, or age their lives were inexorably changed.

Some Americans seek vicariously to fill voids in their own lives through such recognized folk heroes as Ronald Reagan and John Wayne, but what then is the true American Dream? Is it definable, and, if so, who should do the defining? Or, as citizens of an open and democratic society that extols individual freedoms above all else, are such definitions better left unstated?

Ben Franklin, *POOR RICHARD'S ALMANAC (1758)*

Every school child knows about Franklin "inventing" electricity. The brighter ones can even tell their teacher about the first library, fire station, etc. But Benjamin Franklin's fame would not have endured had he not set down on paper his ideas for living the successful and admirable life. Franklin has been called the epitome of the Enlightenment, the versatile, practical embodiment of rational man in the eighteenth century." Franklin believed that an appeal to reason would provide solutions for all human problems, and he was most anxious to share his views. Poor Richard's Almanac *is filled with those aphorisms meant to help future generations become "healthy, wealthy, and wise." The following excerpts are taken from* The Way To Wealth: Preface to Poor Richard, *1758.*

It would be thought a hard Government that should tax its People one tenth Part of their *Time*, to be employed in its Service. But *Idleness* taxes many of us much more, if we reckon all that is spent in absolute *Sloth*, or doing of nothing, with that which is spent in idle Employments or Amusements, that amount to nothing. *Sloth*, by bringing on Diseases, absolutely shortens life. *Sloth, like Rust, consumes faster than Labour wears, while the used Key is always bright,* as *Poor Richard* says. But *dost thou love Life, then do not squander Time, for that's the Stuff Life is made of*, as *Poor Richard* says. -- How much more than is necessary do we spend in Sleep! forgetting that *The sleeping Fox catches no Poultry, and that there will be sleeping enough in the Grave*, as *Poor Richard* says. If Time be of all Things the most precious, *wasting Time* must be, as *Poor Richard* says, *the greatest Prodigality*, since, as he elsewhere tells us, *Lost Time is never found again*; and what we call *Time-enough, always proves little enough*: Let us then up and be doing, and doing to the Purpose; so by Diligence shall we do more with less Perplexity. *Sloth makes all Things difficult, but Industry all easy*, as *Poor Richard* says; and *He that riseth late, must trot all Day, and shall scarce overtake his Business at Night. While Laziness travels so slowly, that Poverty soon overtakes him, as we read* in *Poor Richard*, who adds, *Drive thy Business, let not that drive thee; and Early to Bed, and early to rise, makes a Man healthy, wealthy and wise.*

So what signifies *wishing* and *hoping* for better Times. We may make these Times better if we bestir ourselves. *Industry need not wish*, as *Poor Richard* says, and *He that lives upon Hope will die fasting. There are no Gains, without Pains*; then *Help Hands, for I have no Lands,* or if I have, they are smartly taxed. And, as *Poor Richard* likewise observes, *He that hath a Trade hath an Estate, and He that hath a Calling, hath an Office of Profit and Honour*; but then the *Trade* must be worked at, and the *Calling* well followed, or neither the *Estate*, nor the *Office*, will enable us to pay our Taxes. -- If we are industrious we shall never starve; for, as *Poor Richard* says, *At the working Man's House* Hunger *looks in, but dares not enter*. Nor will the Bailiff or the Constable enter, for *Industry pays Debts, while Despair encreaseth them*, says *Poor Richard*. -- What though you have found no Treasure, nor has any rich Relation left you a Legacy, *Diligence is the Mother of Good luck*, as *Poor Richard* says, and *God gives all Things to Industry*. Then *plough deep, while Sluggards sleep, and you shall have Corn to sell and to keep*, says *Poor Dick*. Work while it is called To-day, for you know not how much you may be hindered To-morrow, which makes *Poor Richard* say, *One To-day is worth two To-morrows*; and farther. *Have you somewhat to do To-morrow, do it To-day*. If you were a Servant, would you not be ashamed that a good Master should catch you idle? Are you then your own Master, *be ashamed to catch yourself idle*, as *Poor Dick* says. When there is so much to be done for yourself, your Family, your Country, and your gracious King, be up by Peep of Day; *Let not the Sun look down and say, Inglorious here he lies*. Handle your Tools without Mittens: remember that the *Cat in Gloves catches no Mice*, as *Poor Richard* says. 'Tis true there is much to be done, and perhaps you are weak handed, but stick to it steadily, and you will see great Effects, for *constant Dropping wears away Stones*, and by *Diligence and Patience the Mouse ate in two the Cable*; and *little Strokes fell great Oaks*, as *Poor Richard* says in his Almanack, the year I cannot just now remember.

Me thinks I hear some of you say, *Must a Man afford himself no Leisure?* -- I will tell thee, my Friend, what *Poor Richard* says. *Employ thy Time well if thou meanest to gain Leisure*; and *since thou art not sure of a Minute, throw not away an Hour*. Leisure is Time for doing something useful; this Leisure the diligent Man will obtain, but the lazy Man never; so that, as *Poor Richard* says, a *Life of Leisure and a Life of Laziness are two Things*. Do you imagine that Sloth will afford you more Comfort than Labour? No, for as *Poor Richard* says, *Trouble springs from Idleness, and grievous Toil from needless Ease. Many without Labour, would live by their wits only, but they break for want of Stock*. Whereas Industry gives Comfort, and Plenty, and Respect: *Fly Pleasures, and they'll follow you. The diligent Spinner has a large Shift*; and *now I have a Sheep and a Cow, every Body bids me Good morrow*; all which is well said by *Poor Richard*.

But with our Industry, we must likewise be *steady, settled* and *careful*, and oversee our own *Affairs with our own Eyes*, and not trust too much to others; for, as *Poor Richard* says,

I never saw an oft removed Tree,
Nor yet an oft removed Family,
That throve so well as those that settled be.

And again, *Three Removes is as bad as a Fire*; and again, *Keep thy Shop, and thy Shop will keep thee*; and again, *If you would have your Business done, go; If not, send*. And again,

He that by the Plough would thrive,
Himself must either hold or drive.

And again, *The Eye of a Master will do more Work than both His Hands*; and again, *Want of Care does us more Damage than Want of Knowledge*; and again, *Not to oversee Workmen, is to leave them your Purse open*. Trusting too much to others Care is the Ruin of many; for as the *Almanack* says, *In the Affairs of this World, Men are saved, not by Faith, but by the Want of it;* but a Man's own Care is profitable; for, saith *Poor Dick*, *Learning is to the Studious*, and *Riches to the Careful*, as well as *Power to the Bold*, and *Heaven to the Virtuous*. And farther,

If you would have a faithful Servant, and one that you like, serve yourself. And again, he adviseth to Circumspection and Care, even in the smallest Matters, because sometimes *a little Neglect may breed great Mischief*; adding, *For want of a Nail the Shoe was lost; for want of a Shoe the Horse was lost; and for want of a Horse the Rider was lost*, being overtaken and slain by the Enemy, all for want of Care about a Horse shoe Nail.

So much for Industry, my Friends, and Attention to one's own Business; but to these we must add *Frugality*, if we would make our *Industry* more certainly successful. A Man may, if he knows not how to save as he gets, *keep his Nose all his Life to the Grindstone*, and die not worth a *Groat* at last. A *fat Kitchen makes a lean Will,* as *Poor Richard* says; and,

Many Estates are spent in the Getting,
Since Women for Tea forsook Spinning and Knitting,
And Men for Punch forsook Hewing and Splitting.

If you would be wealthy, says he, in another Almanack, *think of Saving as well as of Getting: The* Indies *have not made Spain rich because her Outgoes are greater than her Incomes.* Away then with your expensive Follies, and you will not have so much Cause to complain of hard Times, heavy Taxes, and chargeable Families; for, as *Poor Dick* says,

Women and Wine, Game and Deceit,
Make the Wealth small, and the Wants great.

And farther, *What maintains one Vice, would bring up two Children.* You may think perhaps, That a *little Tea*, or a *little* Punch now and then, Diet a *little* more costly, Clothes a *littler* finer, and a *little* Entertainment now and then, can be no *great* Matter, but remember what *Poor Richard* says, *Many* a Little *makes a Mickle*; and farther, *Beware of* little *Expenses; a small Leak will sink a great Ship*; and again, *Who Dainties love, shall Beggars prove*; and moreover, *Fools make Feasts, and wise Men eat them.*

Here you are all got together at this Vendue of *Fineries and Knicknacks.* You call them *Goods*, but if you do not take Care, they will prove *Evils* to some of you. You expect they will be sold *cheap*, and perhaps they may for less than they cost; but if you have no Occasion for them, they must be *dear* to you. Remember what *Poor Richard* says, *Buy what thou hast no Need of, and ere long thou shalt sell thy Necessaries.* And again, *At a great Penny-worth pause a while*: He means, that perhaps the Cheapness is *apparent* only, and not *real*; or the Bargain, by straitning thee in thy Business, may do thee more Harm than Good. For in another place he says, *Many have been ruined by buying good Penn-worths.* Again, *Poor Richard* says, *'Tis foolish to lay out Money in a Purchase of Repentance*; and yet this Folly is practised every Day at Vendues, for want of minding the Almanack. *Wise Men, as Poor Dick says, learn by others Harms, Fools scarcely by their own*; but *Felix quem faciunt aliena Pericula cauturn.* Many a one, for the Sake of Finery on the Back, have gone with a hungry Belly, and half starved their Families; *Silks and Sattins, Scarlet and Velvets*, as *Poor Richard* says, *put out the Kitchen Fire.* These are not the Necessaries of Life; they can scarcely be called the *Conveniences*, and yet only because they look pretty, how many *want to have them.* The *artificial* Wants of Mankind thus become more numerous than the *natural*; and, as *Poor Dick* says, *For one* poor *Person, there are an hundred indigent*. By these, and other Extravagancies, the Genteel are reduced to Poverty, and forced to borrow of those whom they formerly despised, but who through *Industry* and *Frugality* have maintained their Standing; in which Case it appears plainly, that a *Ploughman on his Legs is higher than a Gentleman on his Knees*, as *Poor Richard* says. Perhaps they have had a small Estate left them which they knew not the Getting of; they think *'tis Day, and will never be Night;* that a little to be spent out of *so much*, is not worth minding; (*a Child and a Fool*, as *Poor Richard* says, *imagine* Twenty Shillings *and Twenty Years can never be spent*) but, *always taking out of, the Mealtub, and never putting in, soon comes to the Bottom*; then, as *Poor Dick* says, When *the Well's dry, they know the Worth of Water*. But this they might have known before, if they had taken his Advice; *If you would know the Value of Money, go and try to borrow some*; for, *he that goes a borrowing goes a sorrowing*; and indeed so does he that lends to such People, when he goes *to get it in again*. -- *Poor Dick* farther advises, and says,

Fond Pride of Dress is ure a very Curse;
E'er Fancy you consult, consult your Purse.

And again, *Pride is as loud a Beggar as Want, and a great deal more saucy*. When you have bought one fine Thing you must buy ten more, that your Appearance may be all of a *Piece*: but *Poor Dick* says, *'Tis easier to suppress the first Desire, than to satisfy all that follow it*. And 'tis truly Folly for the Poor to ape the Rich, as for the Frog to swell, in order to equal the Ox.

Great Estates may venture more,
But little Boats should keep near Shore.

'Tis however a Folly soon punished; for *Pride that dines on Vanity sups on Contempt*, as *Poor Richard* says. And in another Place, *Pride breakfasted with Plenty, dined with Poverty, and supped with Infamy*. And after all, of what Use is this *Pride of Appearance*, for which so much is risked, so much is suffered? It cannot promote Health, or ease Pain; it makes no Increase of Merit in the Person, it creates Envy, it hastens Misfortune.

What is a Butterfly? At best
He's but a Caterpillar drest.
The gaudy Fop's his Picture just,

as *Poor Richard* says.

But what Madness must it be to *run in Debt* for these Superfluities! We are offered, by the Terms of this Vendue, *Six Months Credit*; and that perhaps has induced some of us to attend it, because we cannot spare the ready Money, and hope now to be fine without it. But, ah, think what you do when you run in Debt; *You give to another, Power over your Liberty*. If you cannot pay at the Time, you will be ashamed to see your Creditor: you will be in Fear when you speak to him; you will make poor pitiful sneaking Excuses, and by Degrees come to lose your Veracity, and sink into base downright lying; for, as *Poor Richard* says, *The second Vice is Lying, the first is running in Debt*. And again, to the same Purpose, *Lying rides upon Debt's Back*. Whereas a freeborn *Englishman* ought not to be ashamed or afraid to see or speak to any

Man living. But Poverty often deprives a Man of all Spirit and Virtue; *T'is hard for an empty Bag to stand upright,* as *Poor Richard* truly says. What would you think of that Prince, or that Government, who should issue an Edict forbiding you to dress like a Gentleman or a Gentlewoman, on Pain of Imprisonment or Servitude? Would you not say, that you are free, have a Right to dress as you please, and that such an Edict would be a Breach of your Privileges, and such a Government tyrannical? And yet you are about to put yourself under that Tyranny when you run in Debt for such Dress! Your Creditor has Authority at his Pleasure to deprive you of your Liberty, by confining you in Goal [*sic*] for Life, or to sell you for a Servant, if you should not be able to pay him! When you have got your Bargain, you may, perhaps, think little of Payment; but *Creditors, Poor Richard* tells us, have *better Memories than Debtors*; and in another Place says, *Creditors are a superstitious Sect, great Observers of set Days and Times*. The Day comes round before you are aware, and the Demand is made before you are prepared to satisfy it. Or if you bear your Debt in Mind, the Term which at first seemed so long, will, as it lessens, appear extremely short. *Time* will seem to have added Wings to Heels as well as Shoulders. *Those have a short Lent*, saith *Poor Richard, who owe Money to be paid at Easter*. Then since, as he says, *The Borrower is a Slave to the lender, and the Debtor to the Creditor,* disdain the Chain, preserve your Freedom; and maintain your Independence: But *industrious* and *free*; be *frugal* and *free*. At present, perhaps, you may think yourself in thriving Circumstances, and that you can bear a little Extravagance {*sic*] without Injury;

For Age and Want, save while you may;
No Morning Sun lasts a whole Day,

as *Poor Richard* says--Gain may be temporary and uncertain, but ever while you live, Expense is constant and certain; and *'tis easier to build two Chimnies than to keep one in Fuel*, as *Poor Richard* says. *So rather go to Bed supperless than rise in Debt.*

Get what you can, and what you get hold;
'Tis the Stone that will turn all your Lead into Gold,

as *Poor Richard* says, And when you have got the Philosopher's Stone, sure you will no longer complain of bad Times, or the Difficulty of paying Taxes.

This Doctrine, my Friends, is *Reason* and *Wisdom*; but after all, do not depend too much upon your own *Industry*; and *Frugality*, and *Prudence*, though excellent Things, for they may all be blasted without the Blessing of Heaven; and therefore ask that Blessing humbly, and be not uncharitable to those that at present seem to want it, but comfort and help them. Remember *Job* suffered, and was afterwards prosperous.

And now to conclude, *Experience keeps a dear School, but Fools will learn in no other, and scarce in that*; for it is true, *we may give Advice, but we cannot give Conduct*, as *Poor Richard* says: However, remember this, *They that won't be counselled, can't be helped*, as *Poor Richard* says: And farther, That *if you will not hear Reason, she'll surely rap your Knuckles*.

Thus the Old Gentleman ended his Harangue. The people heard it, and approved the Doctrine and immediately practised the contrary, just as if it had been a common Sermon; for the Vendue opened, and they began to buy extravagantly, notwithstanding all his Cautions, and their own Fear of Taxes.--I found the good Man had thoroughly studied my Almanacks, and digested all I had dropt on those Topicks during the Course of Five-and-twenty Years. The frequent Mention he made of me must have tried any one else, but my Vanity was wonderfully delighted with it, though I was conscious that not a tenth Part of the Wisdom was my own which he ascribed to me, but rather the *Gleanings* I had made of the Sense of all Ages and Nations. However, I resolved to be the better for the Echo of it; and though I had at first determined to buy Stuff for a new Coat, I went away resolved to wear my old One a little longer. *Reader*, if thou wilt do the same, thy Profit will be as great as mine.

Ralph Waldo Emerson, *SELF-RELIANCE* (1841)

Every other writer of his era and beyond had to come terms with this giant of 19th-century literature and philosophy. Optimistic and inspirational, Emerson used his eloquent prose to urge Americans to break away from European styles and to develop their own art, literature, and philosophy. Emerson and his fellow Transcendentalists rejected the restrictive nature of Puritan theology and urged Americans to emphasize their individuality; hence, totally unacceptable for an Emerson or a Henry David Thoreau was the popular quest for financial riches and social conformity. In this selection from Self-Reliance *Emerson pleads with his fellow Americans to retain their individual uniqueness.*

I read the other day some verses written by an eminent painter which were original and not conventional. The soul always hears an admonition in such lines, let the subject be what it may. The sentiment they instil is of more value than any thought they may contain. To believe your own thought, to believe that what is true for you in your private heart is true for all men--that is genius. Speak your latent conviction, and it shall be the universal sense; for the inmost in due time becomes the outmost, and our first thought is rendered back to us by the trumpets of the Last Judgment. Familiar as the voice of the mind is to each, the highest merit we ascribe to Moses, Plato and Milton is that they set at naught books and traditions, and spoke not what men are, but what *they* thought. A man should learn to detect and watch that gleam of light which flashes across his mind from within, more than the lustre of the firmament of bards and sages. Yet he dismisses without notice his thought, because it is his. In every work of genius we recognize our own rejected thoughts; they come back to us with a certain alienated majesty. . . .

Trust thyself: every heart vibrates to that iron string. Accept the place the divine providence has found for you, the society of your contemporaries, the connection of events. Great men have always done so, and confided themselves childlike to the genius of their age, betraying their perception that the absolutely trustworthy was seated at their heart, working through their hands, predominating in all their being. And we are now men, and must accept in the highest mind the same transcendent destiny; and not minors and invalids in a protected corner, not cowards fleeing before a revolution, but guides, redeemers and benefactors, obeying the Almighty effort and advancing on Chaos and the Dark. . . .

Society everywhere is in conspiracy against the manhood of every one of its members. Society is a join-stock company, in which the members agree, for the better securing of his bread to each shareholder, to surrender the liberty and culture of the eater. The virtue in most request is conformity. Self-reliance is its aversion. It loves not realities and creators but names and customs.

Whoso would be a man, must be a nonconformist. He who would gather immortal palms must not be hindered by the name of goodness, but must explore if it be goodness. Nothing is at last sacred but the integrity of your own mind. Absolve you to yourself, and you shall have the suffrage of the world. I remember an answer which when quite young I was prompted to make to a valued adviser who was wont to importune me with the dear old doctrines of the church. On my saying, "What have I to do with the sacredness of traditions, if I live wholly from within?" my friend suggested--"But these impulses may be from below, not from above." I replied, "They do not seem to me to be such; but if I am the Devil's child, I will live then from the Devil." No law can be sacred to me but that of my nature. Good and bad are but names very readily transferable to that or this; the only right is what is after my constitution; the only wrong what is against it. A man is to carry himself in the presence of all opposition as if every thing were titular and ephemeral but he. I am ashamed to think how easily we capitulate to badges and names, to large societies and dead institutions. . . .

What I must do is all that concerns me, not what the people think. This rule, equally arduous in actual and in intellectual life, may serve for the whole distinction between greatness and meanness. It is the harder because you will always find those who think they know what is your duty better than you know it. It is easy in the world to live after the world's opinion; it is easy in solitude to live after your own; but the great man is he who in the midst of the crowd keeps with perfect sweetness the independence of solitude.

The objection to conforming to usages that have become dead to you is that it scatters your force. It loses your time and blurs the impression of your character. If you maintain a dead church, contribute to a dead Bible-society, vote with a great party either for the government or against it, spread your table like base housekeepers--under all these screens I have difficulty to detect the precise man you are: and of course so much force is withdrawn from your proper life. But do your work, and I shall know you. Do your work, and you shall reinforce yourself. A man must consider what a blindman's-bluff is this game of conformity. If I know your sect I anticipate your argument. I hear a preacher announce for his text and topic the expediency of one of the institutions of his church. Do I not know beforehand that not possibly can he say a new and spontaneous word? Do I not know that with all this ostentation of examining the grounds of the institution he will do no such thing? Do I not know that he is pledged to himself not to look but at one side, the permitted side, not as a man, but as a parish minister? He is a retained attorney, and these airs of the bench are the emptiest affectation. Well, most men have bound their eyes with one or another handkerchief, and attached themselves to some one of these communities of opinion. This conformity makes them not false in a few particulars, authors of a few lies, but false in all particulars. . . .

The other terror that scares us from self-trust is our consistency; a reverence for our past act or word because the eyes of others have no other data for computing our orbit than our past acts, and we are loth to disappoint them.

But why should you keep your head over your shoulder? Why drag about this corpse of your memory, lest you contradict somewhat you have stated in this or that public place? Suppose you should contradict yourself; what then? It seems to be a rule of wisdom never to rely on your memory alone, scarcely even in acts of pure memory, but to bring the past for judgment into the thousand-eyed present, and live ever in a new day. In your metaphysics you have denied personality to the Deity, yet when the devout motions of the soul come, yield to them heart and life, though they should clothe God with shape and color. Leave your theory, as Joseph his coat in the hand of the harlot, and flee.

A foolish consistency is the hobgoblin of little minds, adored by little statesmen and philosophers and divines. With consistency a great soul has simply nothing to do. He may as well concern himself with his shadow on the wall. Speak what you think now in hard words and to-morrow speak what to-morrow thinks in hard words again, though it contradict every thing you said to-day.--'Ah, so you shall be sure to be misunderstood.'--Is it so bad then to be misunderstood? Pythagoras was misunderstood, and Socrates, and Jesus, and Luther, and Copernicus, and Galileo, and Newton, and every pure and wise spirit that ever took flesh. To be great is to be misunderstood. . . .

The magnetism which all original action exerts is explained when we inquire the reason of self-trust. Who is the Trustee? What is the aboriginal Self, on which a universal reliance may be grounded? What is the nature and power of that science-baffling star, without parallax, without calculable elements, which shoots a ray of beauty even into trivial and impure actions, if the least mark of independence appear? The inquiry leads us to that source, at once the essence of genius, of virtue, and of life, which we call Spontaneity or Instinct. We denote this primary wisdom as Intuition, whilst all later teachings are tuitions. In that deep force, the last fact behind which analysis cannot go, all things find their common origin. . . . Here is the fountain of action and of thought. Here are the lungs of that inspiration which giveth man wisdom and which cannot be denied without impiety and atheism. We lie in the lap of immense intelligence, which makes us receivers of its truth and organs of its activity. When we discern justice, when we discern truth, we do nothing of ourselves, but allow a passage to its beams. If we ask whence this comes, if we seek to pry into the soul that causes, all philosophy is at fault. Its presence or its absence is all we can affirm. . . .

The relations of the soul to the devine spirit are so pure that it is profane to seek to interpose helps. It must be that when God speaketh he should communicate, not one thing, but all things; should fill the world with his voice; should scatter forth light, nature, time, souls, from the centre of the present thought; and new date and new create the whole. Whenever a mind is simple and receives a divine wisdom old things pass away--means, teachers, texts, temples fall; it lives now, and absorbs past and future into the present hour. All things are made sacred by relation to it--one as much as another. All things are dissolved to their centre by their cause, and in the universal miracle petty and particular miracles disappear. If therefore a man claims to know and speak of God and carries you backward to the phraseology of some old mouldered nation in another country, in another world, believe him not. Is the acorn better than the oak which is its fullness and completion? Is the parent better than the child into whom he has cast his ripened being? Whence then this worship of the past? The centuries are conspirators against the sanity and authority of the soul. Time and space are but physiological colors which the eye makes, but the soul is light: where it is, is day; where it was, is night; and history is an impertinence and an injury if it be any thing more than a cheerful apologue or parable of my being and becoming. . . .

This should be plain enough. Yet see what strong intellects dare not yet hear God himself unless he speak the phraseology of I know not what David, or Jeremiah, or Paul. We shall not always set so great a price on a few texts, on a few lives. . . . When we have new perception, we shall gladly disburden the memory of its hoarded treasures as old rubbish. When a man lives with God, his voice shall be as sweet as the murmur of the brook and the rustle of the corn.

And now at last the highest truth on this subject remains unsaid; probably cannot be said;

for all that we say is the far-off remembering of the intuition. That thought by what I can now nearest approach to say it, is this. When good is near, when you have life in yourself, it is not by any known or accustomed way; you shall not discern the foot prints of any other; you shall not see the face of man; you shall not hear any name; the way, the thought, the good, shall be wholly strange and new. It shall exclude example and experience. . . .

HENRY DAVID THOREAU

Henry David Thoreau urged his contemporaries to guide their lives by one simple dictum: "Simplicity, simplicity, simplicity." Thoreau insisted that most men lived lives of quiet desperation, in large part because their lives were controlled by the material objects they so diligently pursued. During his two years at Walden Pond, Thoreau reduced life to its bare essentials. This left him ample time to sample the beauty of nature and to contemplate how best to live in harmony with his natural surroundings. His essays Life without Principle *and* Civil Disobedience *are as relevant today as they were when he wrote them*

LIFE WITHOUT PRINCIPLE (1863)

At a lyceum, not long since, I felt that the lecturer had chosen a theme too foreign to himself, and so failed to interest me as much as he might have done. He described things not in or near to his heart, but toward his extremities and superficies. There was, in this sense, no truly central or centralizing thought in the lecture. I would have had him deal with his privatest experience, as the poet does. The greatest compliment that was ever paid me was when one asked me what *I thought*, and attended to my answer. I am surprised, as well as delighted, when this happens, it is such a rare use he would make of me, as if he were acquainted with the tool. Commonly, if men want anything of me, it is only to know how many acres I make of their land,--since I am a surveyor--or, at most, what trivial news I have burdened myself with. They never will go to law for my meat; they prefer the shell. A man once came a considerable distance to ask me to lecture on Slavery; but on conversing with him, I found that he and his clique expected seven eighths of the lecture to be theirs, and only one eighth mine; so I declined. I take it for granted, when I am invited to lecture anywhere,--for I have had a little experience in that business,--that there is a desire to hear what *I think* on some subject, though I may be the greatest fool in the country,--and not that I should say pleasant things merely, or such as the audience will assent to; and I resolve, accordingly, that I will give them a strong dose of myself. They have sent for me, and engaged to pay for me, and I am determined that they shall have me, though I bore them beyond all precedent.

So now I would say something similar to you, my readers. Since *you* are my readers, and I have not been much of a traveler, I will not talk about people a thousand miles off, but come as near home as I can. As the time is short, I will leave out all the flattery, and retain all the criticism.

Let us consider the way in which we spend our lives.

This world is a place of business. What an infinite bustle! I am awaked almost every night by the panting of the locomotive. It interrupts my dreams. There is no sabbath. It would be glorious to see mankind at leisure for once. It is nothing but work, work, work. I cannot easily buy a blank-book to write thoughts in; they are commonly ruled for dollars and cents. An Irishman, seeing me making a minute in the fields, took it for granted that I was calculating my wages. If a man was tossed out of a window when an infant, and so made a cripple for life, or scared out of his wits by the Indians, it is regretted chiefly because he was thus incapacitated for--business! I think that there is nothing, not even crime, more opposed to poetry, to philosophy, ay, to life itself, than this incessant business.

There is a coarse and boisterous money-making fellow in the outskirts of our town, who is going to build a bank-wall under the hill along the edge of his meadow. The powers have put this into his head to keep him out of mischief, and he wishes me to spend three weeks digging there with him. The result will be that he will perhaps get some more money to hoard, and leave for his heirs to spend foolishly. If I do this, most will commend me as an industrious and hard-working man; but if I choose to devote myself to certain labors which yield more real profit, though but little money, they may be inclined to look on me as an idler. Nevertheless, as I do not need the police of meaningless labor to regulate me, and do not see anything praiseworthy in this fellow's undertaking any more than in many an enterprise of our own or foreign governments, however amusing it may be to him or them, I prefer to finish my education at a different school.

If a man walk in the woods for love of them half of each day, he is in danger of being regarded as a loafer; but if he spends his whole day as a speculator, shearing off those woods and making earth bald before her time, he is esteemed an industrious and enterprising citizen. As if a town had no interest in its forests but to cut them down! . . .

The ways by which you may get money almost without exception lead downward. To have done anything by which you earned money *merely* is to have been truly idle or worse. If the laborer gets no more than the wages which his employer pays him, he is cheated, he cheats himself. If you would get money as a writer or lecturer, you must be popular, which is to go down perpendicularly. Those services which the community will most readily pay for, it is most disagreeable to render. You are paid for being something less than a man. The State does not commonly reward a genius any more wisely. . . .

The aim of the laborer should be, not to get his living, to get "a good job," but to perform well a certain work; and, even in a pecuniary sense, it would be economy for a town to pay its laborers so well that they would not feel that they were working for low ends, as for a livelihood merely, but for scientific, or even moral ends. Do not hire a man who does your work for money, but him who does it for love of it.

It is remarkable that there are few men so well employed, so much to their minds, but that a little money or fame would commonly buy them off from their present pursuit. I see advertisements for *active* young men, as if activity were the whole of a young man's capital. Yet I have been surprised when one has with confidence proposed to me, a grown man, to embark in some enterprise of his, as if I had absolutely nothing to do, my life having been a complete failure hitherto. What a doubtful compliment this to pay me! As if he had met me halfway across the ocean beating up against the wind, but bound nowhere, and proposed to me to go along with him! If I did, what do you think the underwriters would say? No, no! I am not without employment at this stage of the voyage. To tell the truth, I saw an advertisement for able-bodied seamen, when I was a boy, sauntering in my native port, and as soon as I came of age I embarked.

The community has no bribe that will tempt a wise man. You may raise money enough to tunnel a mountain, but you cannot raise money enough to hire a man who is minding *his own* business. An efficient and valuable man does what he can, whether the community pay him for it or not. . . .

Perhaps I am more than usually jealous with respect to my freedom. I feel that my connection with and obligation to society are still very slight and transient. Those slight labors which afford me a livelihood, and by which it is allowed that I am to some extent serviceable to my contemporaries, are as yet commonly a pleasure to me, and I am not often reminded that they are a necessity. So far I am successful. But I foresee that if my wants should be much increased, the labor required to supply them would become a drudgery. If I should sell both my forenoons and afternoons to society, as most appear to do, I am sure that for me there would be nothing left worth living for. I trust that I shall never thus sell my birthright for a mess of pottage. I wish to suggest that a man may be very industrious, and yet not spend his time well. There is no more fatal blunderer than he who consumes the greater part of his life getting his living. All great enterprises are self-supporting. The poet, for instance, must sustain his body by his poetry, as a steam planing-mill feeds its boilers with the savings it makes. You must get your living by loving. But as it is said of the merchants that ninety-seven in a hundred fail, so the life of men generally, tried by this standard, is a failure, and bankruptcy may be surely prophesied. It is remarkable that there is little or nothing to be remembered written on the subject of getting a living; how to make getting a living not merely honest and honorable, but altogether inviting and glorious; for if *getting* a living is not so, then living is not. One would think, from looking at literature, that this question had never disturbed a solitary individual's musings. Is it that men are too much disgusted with their experience to speak of it? The lesson of value which money teaches, which the Author of the Universe has taken so much pains to teach us, we are inclined to skip altogether. As for the means of living, it is wonderful how indifferent men of all classes are about it, even reformers, so called,--whether they inherit, or earn, or steal it. I think that Society has done nothing for us in this respect, or at least has undone what she has done. Cold and hunger seem more friendly to my nature than those methods which men have adopted and advise to ward them off.

The title *wise* is, for the most part, falsely applied. How can one be a wise man, if he does not know any better how to live than other men?--if he is only more cunning and intellectually subtle? Does Wisdom work in a treadmill? or does she teach how to succeed *by her example*? Is there any such thing as wisdom not applied to life? Is she merely the miller who grinds the finest logic? It is pertinent to ask if Plato got his living in a better way or more successfully than his contemporaries,--or did he succumb to the difficulties of life like other men? Did he seem to prevail over some of them merely by indifference, or by assuming grand airs? or find it easier to live, because his aunt remembered him in her will? The ways in which most men get their living, that is, live, are mere make-shifts, and a shirking of the real business of life,--chiefly because they do not know, but partly because they do not mean, any better.

The rush to California, for instance, and the attitude, not merely of merchants, but of philosophers and prophets, so called, in relation to it, reflect the greatest disgrace on mankind. That so many are ready to live by luck, and so get the means of commanding the labor of others less lucky, without contributing any value to society! And that is called enterprise! I know of no more startling development of the immorality of trade, and all the common modes of getting a living. The philosophy and poetry and religion of such a mankind are not worth the dust of a puff-ball. The hog that gets his living by rooting, stirring up the soil so, would be ashamed of such company. If I could command the wealth of all the worlds by lifting my finger, I would not pay *such* a price for it. Even Mahomet knew that God did not make this world in jest. It makes God to be a moneyed gentleman who scatters a handful of pennies in order to see mankind scramble for them. The world's raffle! A subsistence in the domains of Nature a thing to be raffled for! What a comment, what a satire, on our institutions! The conclusion will be, that mankind will hang itself upon a tree. And have all the precepts in all the Bibles taught men only this? and is the last and most admirable invention of the human race only an improved muck-rake? Is this the ground on which Orientals and Occidentals meet? Did God direct us so to get our living, digging where we never planted,--and He would, perchance, reward us with lumps of gold?

God gave the righteous man a certificate entitling him to food and raiment, but the unrighteous man found a facsimile of the same in God's coffers, and appropriated it, and obtained food and raiment like the former. It is one of the most extensive systems of counterfeiting that the world has seen. I did not know that mankind were suffering for want of gold. I have seen a little of it. I know that it is very malleable, but not so malleable as wit. A grain of gold will gild a great surface, but not so much as a grain of wisdom.

CIVIL DISOBEDIENCE (1848)

I heartily accept the motto, "That the government is best which governs least"; and I should like to see it acted up to more rapidly and systematically. Carried out, it finally amounts to this, which also I believe,--"That government is best which governs not at all"; and when men are prepared for it, that will be the kind of government which they will have. Government is at best but an expedient; but most governments are usually, and all governments are sometimes, inexpedient. The objections which have been brought against a standing army, may also at last be brought against a standing government. The standing army is only an arm of the standing government. The government itself, which is only the mode which the people have chosen to execute their will, is equally liable to be abused and perverted before the people can act through it...

But it is not the less necessary for this; for the people must have some complicated machinery or other, and hear its din, to satisfy that idea of government which they have. Governments show thus how successfully men can be imposed on, even impose on themselves, for their own advantage. It is excellent, we must allow. Yet this government never of itself furthered any enterprise, but by the alacrity with which it got out of its way. **It** does not keep the country free. **It** does not settle the West. **It** does not educate. The character inherent in the American people has done all that has been accomplished; and it would have done somewhat more, if the government had not sometimes got in its way. For government is an expedient by which men would fain succeed in letting one another alone; and, as has been said, when it is most expedient, the governed are most let alone by it....

But to speak practically and as a citizen, unlike those who call themselves no-government men, I ask for, not at once no government, but **at once** a better government. Let every man make known what kind of government would command his respect, and that will be one step toward obtaining it.

After all, the practical reason why, when the power is once in the hands of the people, a majority are permitted, and for a long period continue, to rule, is not because they are most likely to be in the right, nor because this seems fairest to the minority, but because they are physically the strongest. But a government in which the majority rule in all cases cannot be based on justice, even as far as men understand it. Can there not be a government in which majorities do not virtually decide only those questions to which the rule of expediency is applicable? Must every citizen even for a moment, or in the least degree, resign his conscience to the legislator? Why has every man a conscience, then? I think that we should be men first,and subjects afterward. It is not desirable to cultivate a respect for the law, so much as for the right. The only obligation which I have a right to assume, is to do at any time what I think is right....

Law never made men a whit more just; and, by means of their respect for it, even the well disposed are daily made the agents of injustice....

The mass of men serve the state.. not as men mainly, but as machines, with their bodies. They are the standing army, and the militia, jailers, constables, *posse comitatus*, etc. In most cases there is no free exercise whatever of their judgment or of the moral sense; but they put themselves on a level with wood and earth and stones; and wooden men can perhaps be manufactured that will serve the purpose as well. Such command no more respect than men of straw or a lump of dirt. They have the same sort of worth only as horses and dogs. Yet such as these even are commonly esteemed good citizens. Others, such as most legislators, politicians, lawyers, ministers, and office holders, serve the state chiefly with their heads; and, as they rarely make any moral distinctions, they are as likely to serve the Devil, without **intending** it, as God. A very few, as heroes, patriots, martyrs, reformers in the great sense, and **men,** serve the state with their conscience also, and some necessarily resist it for the most part; and they are commonly treated as enemies by it....He who gives himself entirely to his fellow-men appears to them useless and selfish; but he who gives himself partially to them is pronounced a benefactor and philanthropist.

How does it become a man to behave toward this American government today? I answer that he cannot without disgrace be associated with it. I cannot for an instant recognize that political organization as **my** government which is the **slave's** government also.

All men recognize the right of revolution; that is, the right to refuse allegiance to, and to resist, the government, when its tyranny or its inefficiency are great and unendurable....

When a sixth of the population of a nation which has undertaken to be the refuge of liberty are slaves, and a whole country is unjustly overrun and conquered by a foreign army, (Thoreau is referring to the men who were in pursuit of fugitive slaves) and subjected to military law, I think that it is not too soon for honest men to rebel and revolutionize. What makes this duty the more urgent is the fact that the country so overrun is not our own, but ours is the invading army....[ed. note: the country referred to is Mexico during the Mexican-American War]

Practically speaking, the opponents to a reform in Massachusetts are not a hundred thousand politicians at the South, but a hundred thousand merchants and farmers here, who are more interested in commerce and agriculture than they are in humanity, and are not prepared to do justice to the slave...**cost what it may.** I quarrel not with far-off foes, but with those who, near at home, co-operate with, and do the bidding of, those far away, and without whom the latter would be harmless. We are accustomed to say, that the mass of men are unprepared; but improvement is slow, because the few are not materially wiser or better than the many. It is not so important that many should be as good as you, as that there be some absolute goodness somewhere; for that will leaven the whole lump. There are thousands who are **in opinion** opposed to slavery and to war, who yet in effect do nothing to put an end to them; who esteeming themselves children of Washington and Franklin, sit down with their hands in their pockets, and say that they know not what to do and do nothing...They will wait, well disposed, for others to remedy the evil, that they may no longer have it to regret. At most, they give only a cheap vote and a feeble countenance and God-speed to the right, as it goes by them. There are nine hundred and ninety-nine patrons of virtue to one virtuous man. But it is easier to deal with the real possessor of a thing than with the temporary guardian of it.

All voting is a sort of gaming, like checkers or backgammon, with a slight moral tinge to it, a playing with right and wrong, with moral questions; and betting naturally accompanies it. The character of the voters is not staked. I cast my vote, perchance, as I think right; but I am not vitally concerned that that right should prevail. I am willing to leave it to the majority. Its obligation, therefore, never exceeds that of expediency. Even voting for the right is doing nothing for it. It is only expressing to men feebly your desire that it should prevail. A wise man will not leave the right to the mercy of chance, nor wish it to prevail through the power of the majority. There is but little virtue in the action of masses of men. When the majority shall at length vote for the abolition of slavery, it will be because they're indifferent to slavery, or because there is but little slavery left to be abolished by their vote. They will then be the only slaves. Only his vote can hasten the abolition of slavery who asserts his own freedom by his vote....

His vote is of no more worth than that of any unprincipled foreigner or hireling native, who may have been bought. O for a man who is a **man**, and, as my neighbor says, has a bone in his back which you cannot pass your hand through. Our statistics are at fault: the population has been returned too large. How many **men** are there to a square thousand miles in this country? Hardly one....

It is not a man's duty, as a matter of course, to devote himself to the eradication of any, even the most enormous wrong; he may still properly have other concerns to engage him; but it is his duty, at least, to wash his hands of it, and, if he gives it no thought longer, not to give it practically his support. If I devote myself to other pursuits and contemplations, I must first see, at least, that I do not pursue them sitting upon another man's shoulders. I must get off him first that he may pursue contemplations too....

Action from principle, the perception and the performance of right, changes things and relations; it is essentially revolutionary, and does not consist wholly with anything which was. It not only divides states and churches, it divides families; ay, it divides the individual, separating the diabolical in him from the divine.

Unjust laws exist: shall we be content to obey them, or shall we endeavor to amend them, and obey them until we have succeeded, or shall we transgress them at once? Men generally, under such a government as this, think they ought to wait until they have persuaded the majority to alter them. They think that, if they should resist, the remedy would be worse than the evil. But it is the fault of government itself that the remedy **is** worse than the evil.

It makes it worse. Why is it not more apt to anticipate and provide for reform? Why does it not cherish its wise minority? Why does it cry and resist before it is hurt? Why does it not encourage its citizens to be on the alert to point out its faults, and **do** better than it would have them? Why does it always crucify Christ, and excommunicate Copernicus and Luther, and pronounce Washington and Franklin rebels?

As for adopting the ways which the State has provided for remedying the evil, I know not of such ways. They take too much time, and a man's life will be gone. I have other affairs to attend to. I came into this world, not chiefly to make this a good place to live in, but to live in it, be it good or bad. A man has not everything to do, but something; and because he cannot do **everything**, it is not necessary that he should do **something** wrong. It is not my business to be petitioning the Governor or the legislature anymore than it is theirs to petition me; and, if they should not hear my petition, what should I do then? But in this case the State has provided no way: its very Constitution is the evil. This may seem to be harsh and stubborn and unconciliatory; but it is to treat with the utmost kindness and consideration the only spirit that can appreciate or deserves it. So is all change for the better, like birth and death, which convulse the body.

I meet this American government, or its representative, the State government, directly, and face to face, once a year--no more--in the person of the tax gatherer; this is the only mode in which a man situated as I am necessarily meets it; and then says distinctly, Recognize me; and the simplest, the most effectual, and, in the present posture of affairs, the indispensable mode of treating with it on this head, of expressing your little satisfaction with and love for it, is to deny it then....I know this well, that if one thousand, if one hundred, if ten men who I could name,--if ten **honest** men only,--ay, if **one honest** man, in this State of Massachusetts, **ceasing to hold slaves,** were actually to withdraw from this copartnership, and be locked up in the country jail therefore, it would be the abolition of slavery in America. For it matters not how small the beginning may seem to be: what is once well done is done forever. But we love better to talk about it: that we say is our mission. Reform keeps many scores of newspapers in its services, but not one man....

Under a government which imprisons any unjustly, the true place for a just man is also prison. The proper place today, the only place which Massachusetts has provided for her freer and less desponding spirits, is in her prisons, to be put out and locked out of the State by her own act, as they have already put themselves out by their principles....It is there that the State places those who are not **with** her, but against her,--the only house in a slave State in which a freeman can abide with honor. If any think that their influence would be lost there, and their voices no longer afflict the ear of the State, they would not be as any enemy within its walls, they do not know by how much truth is stronger than error, nor how much more eloquently and effectively he can combat injustice who has experienced a little in his own person. Cast your whole vote, not a strip of paper merely, but your whole influence. A minority is powerless while it conforms to the majority; it is not even a minority then; but it is irresistible when it clogs by its whole weight. If the alternative is to keep all just men in prison, or give up war and slavery, the State will not hesitate which to choose. If a thousand men were not to pay their tax-bills this year, that would not be a violent and bloody measure, as it would be to pay them, and enable the State to commit violence and shed innocent blood. This is, in fact, the definition of a peaceful revolution, if any such is possible....Is there not a sort of bloodshed when the conscience is wounded? Through this wound a man's real manhood and immortality flow out, and he bleeds to an everlasting death. I see this blood flowing now.

I have contemplated the imprisonment of the offender, rather than the seizure of his goods,--though both will serve the same purpose,--because they who asset the purest right, and consequently are most dangerous to a corrupt State, commonly have not spent much time in accumulating property. To such the State renders comparatively small service, and a slight tax is wont to appear exorbitant, particularly if they are obliged to earn it by special labor with their hands. If there were one who lived wholly without the use of money, the State itself would hesitate to demand it of him. But the rich man,--not to make any invidious comparison,--is always sold to the institution which makes him rich. Absolutely speaking, the more money, the less virtue; for money comes between a man and his objects, and obtains them for him; and it was certainly no great virtue to obtain it. It puts to rest many questions which he would otherwise be taxed to answer; while the only new question which it puts is the hard but superfluous one, how to spend it. Thus his moral ground is taken from under his feet. The opportunities of living are diminished in proportion as what are called the "means" are increased. The best thing a man can do for his culture when he is rich is to endeavor to carry out those schemes which he entertained when he was poor....

When I converse with the freest of my neighbors, I perceive that, whatever they may say about the magnitude and seriousness of the question, and their regard for the public tranquility, the long and short of the matter is, that they cannot spare the protection of the existing government, and they dread the consequences to their property and families of disobedience to it. For my own part, I should not like to think that I ever rely on the protection of the State. But, if I deny the authority of the State when it presents its tax bill, it will soon take and waste all my property, and so harass me and my children without end. This is hard. This makes it impossible for a man to live honestly, and at the same time comfortably, in outward respects. It will not be worth the while to accumulate property; that would be sure to go again. You must hire or squat somewhere, and raise but a small crop, and eat that soon. You must live within yourself, and depend upon yourself always tucked up and ready for a start, and not have many affairs....It costs me less in every sense to incur the penalty of disobedience to the State, than it would to obey. I should feel as if I were worth less in that case....

I have paid no poll-tax for six years. I was put into a jail once on this account, for one night; and as I stood considering the walls of solid stone, two or three feet thick, the door of wood and iron, a foot thick, and the iron grating which strained the light, I could not help being struck with the foolishness of that institution which treated me as if I were mere flesh and bones, to be locked up. I wondered that it should have been concluded at length that this was the best use it could put me to, and had never thought to avail itself of my services in some way. I saw that, if there was a wall of stone between me and my townsmen, there was a still more difficult one to climb or break through, before they could get to be as free as I was. I did not for a moment feel confined, and the walls seemed a great waste of stone and mortar. I felt as if I alone of all my townsmen had paid my tax. They plainly did not know how to treat me, but behaved like persons who are underbred. In every threat and in every compliment there was a blunder; for they thought that my chief desire was to stand on the other side of that stone wall. I could not but smile to see how industriously they locked the door on my meditations, which followed them out again without let or hinderance, and **they** were really all that was dangerous.

As they could not reach me, they resolved to punish my body; just as boys, if they cannot come at some person against whom they have a spite, will abuse his dog. I saw that the State was half-witted, that it was timid as a lone woman with her silver spoons, and that it did not know its friends from its foes, and I lost all my remaining respect for it, and pitied it.

Thus the State never intentionally confronts a man's sense, intellectual or moral, but only his body, his senses. It is not armed with superior wit or honesty, but with superior physical strength. I was not born to be forced. I will breathe after my own fashion. Let us see who is the strongest. What force has a multitude? They only can force me who obey a higher law than I. They force me to become like themselves. I do not hear of **men** being **forced** to live this way or that by masses of men. What sort of life were that to live? When I meet a government which says to me, "Your money or your life," why should I be in haste to give it my money? It may be in a great strait, and not know what to do: I cannot help that. It must help itself; do as I do. It is not worth the while to snivel about it. I am not responsible for the successful working of the machinery of society. I am not the son of the engineer. I perceive that, when an acorn and a chestnut fall side by side, the one does not remain inert to make way for the other, but both obey their own laws, and spring and grow and flourish as best they can, till one, perchance overshadows and destroys the other. If a plant cannot live according to its nature, it dies; and so a man....

The night in prison was novel and interesting enough. The prisoners in their shirt-sleeves were enjoying a chat and the evening air in the doorway, when I entered. But the jailer said, "Come, boys, it is time to lock up;" and so they dispersed, and I heard the sound of their steps returning into the hollow apartments. My room-mate was introduced to me by the jailer, as "a first-rate fellow and a clever man." When the door was locked, he showed me where to hang my hat, and how he managed matters there. The rooms were whitewashed once a month; and this one, at least, was the whitest, most simply furnished, and probably the neatest apartment in town. He naturally wanted to know where I came from, and what brought me there; and, when I had told him, I asked him in turn how he came there, presuming him to be an honest man, of course; and as the world goes, I believe he was. "Why," said he, "they accuse me of burning a barn; but I never did it." As near as I could discover, he had probably gone to bed in a barn when drunk, and smoked his pipe there; and so a barn burnt. He had the reputation of being a clever man, had been there some three months waiting for his trial to come on, and would have to wait as much longer; but he was quite domesticated and contented, since he got his board for nothing, and thought that he was well treated.

He occupied one window, and I the other; and I saw, that, if one stayed there long, his principal business would be to look out the window. I had read all the tracts that were left there, and examined where former prisoners had broken out, and where a grate had been sawed off, and heard the history of the various occupants of that room; for I found even here there was a history and a gossip which never circulated beyond the walls of the jail. Probably this is the only house in the town where verses are composed, which are afterward printed in a circular form, but not published. I was shown quite a long list of verses which were composed by some young men who had been detected in an attempt to escape, who avenged themselves by singing them.

I pumped my fellow-prisoner as dry as I could, for fear I should never see him again; but at length he showed me which was my bed, and left me to blow out the lamp.

It was like travelling into a far country, such as I had never expected to behold, to lie there for one night. It seemed to me that I never had heard the town-clock strike before, nor the evening sounds of the village; for we slept with the window open, which were inside the grating. It was to see my native village in the light of the Middle Ages, and our Concord was turned into a Rhine stream, and visions of knights and castles passed before me. They were the voices of the old burghers that I heard in the streets. I was an involuntary spectator and auditor of whatever was done and said in the kitchen of the adjacent village-inn, a wholly new and rare experience to me. It was a closer view of my native town. I was fairly inside of it. I never had seen its institutions before. This is one of its peculiar institutions; for it is a shire town. I began to comprehend what its inhabitants were about.

In the morning, our breakfasts were put through the hole in the door, in small oblong-square tin pans, made to fit, and holding a pint of chocolate, with brown bread,and an iron spoon. When they called for the vessels again, I was green enough to return what bread I had left; but my comrade seized it, and said that I should lay that up for lunch or dinner. Soon after he was let out to work a haying in a neighboring field, whither he went every day, and would not be back till noon; so he bade me good-day, saying that he doubted if he should see me again.

When I came out of prison,--for some one interfered, and paid that tax,--I did not perceive that great changes had taken place on the common, such as he observed who went in a youth, and emerged a tottering and gray-headed man; and yet a change had to my eyes come over the scene,--the town, and State, and country,--greater than any that mere time could effect. I saw yet more distinctly the State in which I lived. I saw to what extent the people among whom I lived could be trusted as good neighbors and friends; that their friendship was for summer weather only, that they did not greatly propose to do right; that they were a distinct race from me by their prejudices and superstitions, as the Chinamen and Malays are; that, in their sacrifices to humanity, they ran no risks not even to their property; that, after all, they were not so noble but they treated the thief as he had treated them, and hoped, by a certain outward observance and a few prayers, and by walking in a particular straight though useless path from time to time, to save their souls. This may be to judge my neighbors harshly; for I believe that many of them are not aware that they have such an institution as the jail in their village.

It was formerly the custom in our village, when a poor debtor came out of jail, for his acquaintances to salute him, looking through their fingers, which were crossed to represent the grating of a jail window, "How do ye do?" My neighbors did not thus salute me, but first looked at me, and then at one another, as if I had returned from a long journey. I was put into jail as I was going to the shoemakers to get a shoe which was mended. When I was let out the next morning, I proceeded to finish my errand, and having put on my mended shoe, joined a huckleberry party, who were impatient to put themselves under my conduct; in half an hour,--for the horse was soon tackled,--was in the midst of a huckleberry field, on one of our highest hills, two miles off, and then the State was nowhere to be seen.

This is the whole history of "My Prisons."...

I have never declined paying the highway tax, because I am as desirous of being a good neighbor as I am of being a bad subject; and, as for supporting the schools, I am doing my part to educate my fellow-countrymen now. It is for no particular item in the tax-bill that I refuse to pay it. I simply wish to refuse allegiance to the State, to withdraw and stand aloof from it effectually. I do not care to trace the course of my dollar, if I could, til it buys a man or a musket to shoot one with,--the dollar is innocent,--but I am concerned to trace the effects of my allegiance. In fact, I quietly declare war with the State, after my fashion, though I will still make what use and get what advantage of her I can, as is usual in such cases.

If others pay the tax which is demanded of me, from a sympathy with the State, they do but what they have already done in their own case, or rather they abet injustice to a greater extent than the State requires. If they pay the tax from a mistaken interest in the individual taxed, to save his property, or prevent his going to jail, it is because they have not considered wisely how far they let their private feelings interfere with the public good.

This, then, is my position at present. But one cannot be too much on his guard in such a case, lest his action be biased by obstinacy, or an undue regard for the opinion of men. Let him see that he does only what belongs to himself and to the hour.

I think sometimes, Why, this people mean well; they are only ignorant; they would do better if they knew how: why give your neighbors this pain to treat you as they are not inclined to? But I think again, this is no reason why I should do as they do, or permit others to suffer much greater pain of a different kind. Again I sometimes say to myself, When many millions of men, without heat, without ill will, without personal feelings of any kind, demand of you a few shillings only, without the possibility, such is their constitution, of retracting or altering their present demand, and without the possibility, on your side, of appeal to any other millions, why expose yourself to this overwhelming brute force? You do not resist cold and hunger, the winds and the waves, thus obstinately; you quietly submit to a thousand similar necessities. You do not put your head into the fire. But just in proportion as I regard this as not wholly a brute force, but partly a human force, and consider that I have relations to those millions as to so many millions of men, and not of mere brute or inanimate things, I see that appeal is possible, first and instantaneously, from them to the Maker of them, and secondly, from them to themselves. But, if I put my head deliberately into the fire, there is no appeal to fire or to the Maker of fire, and I have only myself to blame. If I could convince myself that I have any right to be satisfied with men as they are, and to treat them accordingly, and not according, in some respects, to my requisitions and expectations of what they and I ought to be, then, like a good Mussulman and fatalist, I should endeavor to be satisfied with things as they are, and say it is the will of God. And, above all, there is this difference between resisting this and a purely brute or natural force, that I can resist this with some effect; but I cannot expect, like Orpheus, to change the nature of rocks and trees and beasts.

I do not wish to quarrel with any man or nation. I do not wish to split hairs, to make fine distinctions, or set myself up as better than my neighbors. I seek rather, I may say, even an excuse for conforming to the laws of the land. I am but too ready to conform to them. Indeed, I have reason to suspect myself on this head and each year, as the tax gatherer comes round, I find myself disposed to review the acts and position of the general and State governments, and the spirit of the people, to discover a pretext for conformity.... I believe that the State will soon be able to take all my work of this sort out of my hands, and then I shall be no better a patriot than my fellow-countrymen. Seen from a lower point of view, the Constitution, with all its faults, is very good; the law and the courts are very respectable; even this State and this American government are, in many respects, very admirable and rare things, to be thankful for, such as a great many have described them; but seen from a point of view a little higher, they are what I have described them; seen from a higher still, and the highest, who shall say what they are, or that they are worth looking at or thinking of at all?

However, the government does not concern me much, and I shall bestow the fewest possible thoughts on it. It is not many moments that I live under a government, even in this world. If a man is thought-free, fancy-free, imagination-free, that which **is not** ever for a long time appearing **to be** to him, unwise rulers or reformers cannot fatally interrupt him.

I know that most men think differently from myself; but those whose lives are by profession devoted to the study of these or kindred subjects, content me as little as any. Statesmen and legislators, standing so completely within the institutions, never distinctly and nakedly behold it. They speak of moving society, but have no resting-place without it. They may be men of a certain experience and discrimination, and have no doubt invented ingenious and even useful systems, for which we sincerely thank them; but all their wit and usefulness lie within certain not very wide limits. They are wont to forget that the world is not governed by policy and expediency....Truth is always in harmony with herself, and is not concerned chiefly to reveal the justice that may consist with wrong-doing....

They who know of no purer sources of truth, who have traced up its steam no higher, stand, and wisely stand by the Bible and the Constitution, and drink at it there with reverence and humility; but they who behold where it comes trickling into this lake or that pool, gird up their loins once more, and continue their pilgrimages toward its fountain-head.

No man with a genius for legislation has appeared in America. They are rare in the history of the world. There are orators, politicians, and eloquent men, by the thousand; but the speaker has not yet opened his mouth to speak, who is capable of settling the much vexed questions of the day. We love eloquence for its own sake, and not for any truth which it may utter, or any heroism it may inspire. Our legislators have not yet learned the comparative value of free-trade and of freedom, of union, and of rectitude, to a nation. They have no genius or talent for comparatively humble questions of taxation and finance, commerce and manufacturers and agriculture. If we were left solely to the wordy wit of legislators in Congress for our guidance, uncorrected by the seasonable experience and the effectual complaints of the people, America would not long retain her rank among the nations. For eighteen hundred years, though perchance I have no right to say it, the New Testament has been written; yet where is the legislator who has wisdom and practical talent enough to avail himself of the light which it sheds on the science of legislation?

The authority of government, even such as I am willing to submit to,--for I will cheerfully obey those who know and can do better than I, and in many things even those who can do better than I, and in many things even those who neither know or can do so well,--is still an impure one: to be strictly just, it must have the sanction and consent of the governed. It can have no pure right over my person and property but what I concede to it. The progress from an absolute to a limited monarchy, from a limited monarchy to a democracy, is progress toward a true respect for the individual. Even the Chinese philosopher was wise enough to regard the individual as the basis of the empire. Is a democracy, such as we know it, the last improvement possible in government? Is it not possible to take a step further towards recognizing and organizing the rights of man? There will never be a really free and enlightened State, until the State comes to recognize the individual as a higher and independent power, from which all its own power and authority are derived and treats him accordingly. I please myself with imagining a State at last which can afford to be just to all men, and to treat the individual with respect as a neighbor; which even would not think it inconsistent with it own repose, if a few were to live aloof from it, not meddling with it, nor embraced by it, who fulfilled all the duties of neighbors and fellow-men. A State which bore this kind of fruit, and suffered it to drop off as fast as it ripened, would prepare the way for a still more perfect and glorious State, which also I have imagined but not yet anywhere seen.

Sinclair Lewis, *BABBITT (1922)*

Sinclair Lewis was the first American to win the Nobel Prize for literature. When he published "Babbitt" in 1922, he so indelibly defined his main character that the word "Babbitt" has remained in our dictionary to describe "a self-satisfied person who conforms readily to conventional, middle-class ideas, especially of business and material success." The following is George Babbitt's unforgettable speech to the Zenith Real Estate Board.

Gentlemen, it strikes me that each year at this annual occasion when friend and foe get together and lay down the battle-ax and let the waves of good-fellowship waft them up the flowery slopes of amity, it behooves us, standing together eye to eye and shoulder to shoulder as fellow-citizens of the best city in the world, to consider where we are both as regards ourselves and the common weal.

It is true that even with our 361,000 or practically 362,000 population, there are, by the last census, almost a score of larger cities in the United States. But, gentlemen, if by the next census we do not stand at least tenth, then I'll be the first to request any knocker to remove my shirt and to eat the same, with the compliments of G. F. Babbitt, Esquire! It may be true that New York, Chicago, and Philadelphia will continue to keep ahead of us in size. But aside from these three cities, which are notoriously so overgrown that no decent white man, nobody who loves his wife and kiddies and God's good out-o'-doors and likes to shake the hand of his neighbor in greeting, would want to live in them--and let me tell you right here and how, I wouldn't trade a high-class Zenith acreage development for the whole length and breadth of Broadway or State Street!--aside from these three, it's evident to any one with a head for facts that Zenith is the finest example of American life and prosperity to be found anywhere.

I don't mean to say we're perfect. We've got a lot to do in the way of extending the paving of motor boulevards, for, believe me, it's the fellow with four to ten thousand a year, say, and an automobile and a nice little family in a bungalow on the edge of town, that makes the wheels of progress go round!

That's the type of fellow that's ruling America to-day; in fact, it's the ideal type to which the entire world must tend, if there's to be a decent, well-balanced, Christian, go-ahead future for this little old planet! Once in a while I must naturally sit back and size up this Solid American Citizen, with a whale of a lot of satisfaction.

Our Ideal Citizen--I picture him first and foremost as being busier than a bird-dog, not wasting a lot of good time in day-dreaming or going to sassiety teas or kicking about things that are none of his business, but putting the zip into some store or profession or aft. At night he lights up a good cigar, and climbs into the little old 'bus, and maybe cusses the carburetor, and shoots out home. He mows the lawn, or sneaks in some practice putting, and then he's ready for dinner. After dinner he tells the kiddies a story, or takes the family to the movies, or plays a few fists of bridge, or reads the evening paper, and a chapter or two of some good lively Western novel if he has a taste for literature, and maybe the folks next-door drop in and they sit and visit about their friends and the topics of the day. Then he goes happily to bed, his conscience clear, having contributed his mite to the prosperity of the city and to his own bank-account.

In politics and religion this Sane Citizen is the canniest man on earth; and in the arts he invariable has a natural taste which makes him pick out the best, every time. In no country in the world will you find so many reproductions of the Old Masters and of well-known paintings on parlor walls as in these United States. No country has anything like our number of phonographs, with not only dance records and comic but also the best operas, such as Verdi, rendered by the world's highest-paid singers.

In other countries, art and literature are left to a lot of shabby bums living in attics and feeding on booze and spaghetti, but in America the successful writer or picture-painter is indistinguishable from any other decent business man; and I, for one, am only too glad that the man who has the rare skill to season his message with interesting reading matter and who shows both purpose and pep in handling his literary wares has a chance to drag down his fifty thousand bucks a year, to mingle with the biggest executives on terms of perfect equality, and to show as big a house and as well a car as any Captain of Industry! But, mind you, it's the appreciation of the Regular Guy who I have been depicting which has made this possible, and you got to hand as much credit to him as to the authors themselves.

Finally, but most important, our Standardized Citizen, even if he is a bachelor, is a lover of the Little Ones, a supporter of the hearthstone which is the basic foundation of our civilization, first, last, and all the time, and the thing that most distinguishes us from the decayed nations of Europe.

I have never yet toured Europe--and as a matter of fact, I don't know that I care to such an awful lot, as long as there's our own mighty cities and mountains to be seen--but, the way I figure it out, there must be a good many of our own sort of folks abroad. Indeed, one of the most enthusiastic Rotarians I ever met boosted the tenets of one-hundred-percent pep in a burr that smacked o' bonny Scutlond and all ye bonny braes o' Bobby Burns. But same time, one thing that distinguishes us from our good brothers, the hustlers over there, is that they're willing to take a lot off the snobs and journalists and politicians, while the modern American business man knows how to talk right up for himself, knows how to make it good and plenty clear that he intends to run the works. He doesn't have to call in some highbrow hired-man when it's necessary for him to answer the crooked critics of the sane and efficient life. He's not dumb, like the old-fashioned merchant. He's got a vocabulary and a punch.

With all modesty, I want to stand up here as a representative business man and gently whisper, "Here's our kind of folks! Here's the specifications of the Standardized American Citizen! Here's the new generation of Americans: fellows with hair on their chests and smiles in their eyes and adding-machines in their offices. We're not doing any boasting, but we like ourselves first-rate, and if you don't like us, look out--better get under cover before the cyclone hits town!"

So! In my clumsy way I have tried to sketch the Real He-man, the fellow with Zip and Bang. And it's because Zenith has so large a proportion of such men that it's the most stable, the greatest of our cities. New York also has its thousands of Real Folks, but New York is cursed with un-numbered foreigners. So are Chicago and San Francisco. Oh, we have a golden roster of cities--Detroit and Cleveland with their renowned factories, Cincinnati with its great machine-tool and soap products. Pittsburg and Birmingham with their steel, Kansas City and

Minneapolis and Omaha that open their bountiful gates on the bosom of the ocean-like wheat-lands, and countless other magnificent sister-cities, for, by the last census, there were no less than sixty-eight glorious American burgs with a population of over one hundred thousand! And all these cities stand together for power and purity, and against foreign ideas and communism--Atlanta with Hartford, Rochester with Denver, Milwaukee with Indianapolis, Los Angeles with Scranton, Portland, Maine, with Portland, Oregon. A good live wire from Baltimore or Seattle or Duluth is the twin-brother of every like fellow booster from Buffalo or Akron, Fort Worth or Oskaloosa!

But it's here in Zenith, the home for manly men and womanly women and bright kids, that you find the largest proportion of these Regular Guys, and that's what sets it in a class by itself; that's why Zenith will be remembered in history as having set the pace for civilization that shall endure when the old time-killing ways are gone forever and the day of earnest efficient endeavor shall have dawned all round the world!

Some time I hope folks will quit handing all the credit to a lot of moth-eaten, mildewed, out-of-date, European dumps, and give proper credit to the famous Zenith spirit, that clean fighting determination to win Success that has made the little old Zip City celebrated in every land and clime, wherever condensed milk and pasteboard cartons are known! Believe me, the world has fallen too long for these worn-out countries that aren't producing anything but boot-blacks and scenery and booze, that haven't got one bathroom per hundred people, and that don't know a loose-leaf ledger from a slip-cover; and it's just about time for some Zenithite to get his back up and holler for a show-down!

I tell you, Zenith and her sister-cities are producing a new type of civilization. There are many resemblances between Zenith and these other burgs, and I'm darn glad of it! The extra ordinary, growing, and sane standardization of stores, offices, streets, hotels, clothes, and newspapers throughout the United States shows how strong and enduring a type is ours.

I always like to remember a piece that Chum Frink wrote for the newspapers about his lecture-tours. It is doubtless familiar to many of you, but if you will permit me, I'll take a chance and read it. It's one of the classic poems, like "If" by Kipling, or Ella Wheeler Wilcox's "The Man Worth While"; and I always carry this clipping of it in my note-book:

> *When I am out upon the road, a poet with a peddlers load, I mostly sing a hearty song, and take a chew and hike along, a-handing out my samples fine of Cheero Brand of sweet sunshine, and peddling optimistic pokes and stable lines of japes and jokes to Lyceums and other folks, to Rotarys, Kiwanis' Clubs, and feel I ain't like other dubs. And then old Major Silas Satan, a brainy cuss who's always waitin', he gives his tail a lively quirk, and gets in quick his dirty work. He fills me up with mullygrubs; my hair the backward way he rubs; he makes me lonelier than a hound, on Sunday when the folks ain't round. And then b' gosh, I would prefer to never be a lecturer, a-ridin' round in classy cars and smoking fifty-cent cigars, and never more I want to roam; I simply want to be back home, a-eatin' flap-jacks, hash, and ham, with folks who savvy whom I am!*
>
> *But when I get that lonely spell, I simply seek the best hotel, no matter in what town I be--St. Paul, Toledo, or K.C., in Washington, Schenectady, in Louisville*

or Albany. And at that inn it hits my dome that I again am right at home. If I should stand a lengthy spell in front of that first-class hotel,that to the drummers loves to cater, across from some big film theater; if I should look around and buzz, and wonder in what town I was, I swear that I could never tell! For all the crowd would be so swell, in just the same fine sort of jeans they wear at home, and all the queens with spiffy bonnets on their beans, and all the fellows standing round a-talkin' always. I'll be bound,the same good jolly kind of guff, 'bout autos, politics and stuff and baseball players of renown that Nice Guys talk in my home town!

Then when I entered that hotel, I'd look around and say, "Well, well!" For here would be the same news-stand, same magazines and candies grand, same smokes of famous standard brand, I'd find at home, I'll tell! And when I saw the jolly bunch come waltzing in for eats at lunch, and squaring up in natty duds to platters large of French Fried spuds, why then I'd stand right up and bawl, "I've never left my home at all!" And all replete I'd sit me down beside some guy in derby brown upon a lobby chair of plush, and murmur to him in a rush, "Hello, Bill, tell me, good old scout, how is your stock a-holdin' out?" Then we'd be off, two solid pals, a-chatterin' like giddy gals of flivvers, weather, home, and wives, lodge brothers then for all our lives! So when Sam Satan makes you blue, good friend, that's what I'd up and do, for in these States where'er you roam, you never leave your home sweet home.

Yes, sir, these other burgs are our true partners in the great game of vital living. But let's not have any mistake about this. I claim that Zenith is the best partner and the fastest-growing partner of the whole caboodle. I trust I may be pardoned if I give a few statistics to back up my claims. If they are old stuff to any of you, yet the tidings of prosperity, like the good news of the Bible, never become tedious to the ears of a real hustler, no matter how oft the sweet story is told! Every intelligent person knows that Zenith manufactures more condensed milk and evaporated cream, more paper boxes, and more lighting-fixtures, than any other city in the United States, if not in the world. But it is not so universally known that we also stand second in the manufacture of package-butter, sixth in the giant realm of motors and automobiles, and somewhere about third in cheese, leather findings, tar roofing, breakfast food, and overalls!

Our greatness, however, lies not alone in punchful prosperity but equally in that public spirit, that forward-looking idealism and brotherhood, which has marked Zenith ever since its foundation by the Fathers. We have a right, indeed we have a duty toward our fair city, to announce broadcast the facts about our high schools, characterized by their complete plants and the finest school-ventilating systems in the country, bar none; our magnificent new hotels and banks and the paintings and carved marble in their lobbies; and the Second National Tower, the second highest business building in any inland city in the entire country. When I add that we have an unparalleled number of miles of paved streets, bathrooms, vacuum cleaners, and all the other signs of civilization; that our library and art museum are well supported and housed in convenient and roomy buildings; that our park-system is more than up to par, with its handsome driveways adorned with grass, shrubs, and statuary, then I give but a hint of the all-round unlimited greatness of Zenith!

I believe, however, in keeping the best to the last. When I remind you that we have one motor car for every five and seven-eighths persons in the city, then I give a rock-ribbed practical indication of the kind of progress and braininess which is synonymous with the name Zenith!

But the way of the righteous is not all roses. Before I close I must call your attention to a problem we have to face, this coming year. The worst menace to sound government is not the avowed socialists but a lot of cowards who work under cover--the long-haired gentry who call themselves "liberals" and "radicals" and "non-partisan" and "intelligentsia" and God only knows how many other trick names! Irresponsible teachers and professors constitute the worst of this whole gang, and I am ashamed to say that several of them are on the faculty of our great State University! The U. is my own Alma Mater, and I am proud to be known as an alumni, but there are certain instructors there who seem to think we ought to turn the conduct of the nation over to hoboes and roustabouts.

Those profs are the snakes to be scotched--they and all their milk-and-water ilk! The American business man is generous to a fault, but one thing he does demand of all teachers and lecturers and journalists: if we're going to pay them our good money, they've got to help us by selling efficiency and whooping it up for rational posterity! And when it comes to these blab-mouth, fault-finding, pessimistic, cynical University teachers, let me tell you that during this golden coming year it's just as much our duty to bring influence to have those cusses fired as it is to sell all the real estate and gather in all the good shekels we can.

Not till that is done will our sons and daughters see that the ideal American manhood and culture isn't a lot of cranks sitting around chewing the rag about their Rights and their Wrongs, but a God-fearing, hustling, successful, two-fisted Regular Guy, who belongs to some church with pep and piety to it, who belongs to the Boosters or the Rotarians or the Kiwanis, to the Elks or Moose or Red Men or Knights of Columbus or any one of a score of organizations of good, jolly, kidding, laughing, sweating, upstanding, lend-a-handing Royal Good Fellows, who plays hard and works hard, and whose answer to his critics is a square-toed boot that'll teach the grouches and smart alecks to respect the He-man and get out and root for Uncle Samuel, U.S.A.!'"

HELEN STEPHENS, *OLYMPIC CHAMPION*

Perhaps because she came earlier and certainly because she deserved them, the plaudits went to Babe Didrikson, but Helen Stephens stands equally tall in the annals of women's track and field. A Missouri farm girl, she was dubbed the "Fulton Flash" when she won the 100-meter dash and anchored the 400-meter relay at Berlin in 1936. She was also the only American athlete invited to meet Hitler personally. Helen Stephens thrived on all kinds of competition. In a period of just two and a half years of amateur competition, she never lost a scratch race while winning fourteen national AAU championships in a variety of track and field events. Yet, Helen Stephens American Dream was over when she was still in her teens. In those days there were no scholarships for young women; in fact, she was treated more like a female freak than a great athlete. She had to hustle her living anyway she could. On five occasions she raced Jesse Owens, and in the 1940s, while barnstorming with a girls' basketball team, she entertained audiences during half-time by challenging anyone in the stands to come down and race her. In 1986, at the age of 68, Helen Stephens entered twelve events in the regional Senior Olympics in St. Louis and won medals in each, seven of them gold. Although, she never achieved economic success , Stephens is a positive and delightful storyteller whose sharp humor and blunt manner belie a warm and sensitive nature.

I'll have to tell you a story about my meeting up with Hitler. Well, before I had gone over to Germany, I had read quite a bit about him. I had read *Mein Kampf* and I figured that somehow or another I was going to meet him. I just felt it was in the cards. After I won the 100-meter dash, a German messenger came running up and asked me to come up to Hitler's box. Der Fuehrer wanted to meet me. My Olympic coach, Dee Beckman, was with me and she said, "No, she can't go now. She's made an agreement to broadcast back to America. As soon as we get through, we'll be available." Well, this messenger says, "I can't go back and tell the Fuehrer that. He'll shoot me." But Beckman told him, "Aw, he won't shoot you. It'll be all right."

He was a little undecided, but he took off. When we came out of the broadcast booth, he was there dancing up and down, ready to take me to meet Hitler. So the two of us went down, and they ushered us into a glass-enclosed room behind Hitler's box in the stadium. In a few minutes the doors opened and about fifteen black-shirted guards came in, lined up, and stood at attention. They had those big German Lugers on their belts, and they unsnapped them. Why, it looked like an assassination squad. Then Hitler came in with his interpreter. He gave me a little Nazi salute, and I thought, "I'm not going to salute you." So I extended my hand and gave him a good ol' Missouri handshake.

Well, immediately Hitler goes for the jugular vein. He gets ahold of my fanny and he begins to squeeze and pinch and hug me up, and he said, "You're a true Aryan type. You should be running for Germany." So after he gave me the once over and a full massage, he asked me if I'd like to spend the weekend in Berchtesgaden. I thought that must be the name of a big track meet down there. But Dee Beckman told him that I was in training. He said he could understand that because he had to be in shape to run the country. I then asked him for his autograph. Right when he was giving me his autograph some little tiny guy slipped in there and snapped a picture. Well, that Hitler he jumped right straight up. Dee Beckman whispered to me, "Hey, he just set a world standing high jump record." But it wasn't funny. He was spouting German, and he began to hit and kick that photographer. Then he motioned for his guards to come and get him. They shook him and his camera fell out on the floor, and they kicked that around like a soccer ball. Then a couple of them grabbed him and gave him a one, two, three and threw him out the door and the camera out after him. Then everything returned to normal. I had heard that Hitler could chew carpet and stuff like that. I thought, "What are you going to do for an encore after this?" Anyway, he wished me well. The next morning that picture was on postcards and sold at the stadium. I got six of them.

I grew up on a farm outside of Fulton, Missouri. My father's mother's name was Snow, which I think was English. The name Stephens has been claimed by the English and even by the Germans. My mother was Pennsylvania Dutch. So I'm sort of a duke's mixture, plus on my grandfather's side I have Cherokee Indian. Even as a kid I think I related to that although I didn't know it. I only knew this maybe ten years ago because, when they used to show me the old family album, here was this big woman sitting in a chair and I'd say, "Well, that's an Indian." And they'd say, "No, no, no!" The family tried to conceal this. It was something they didn't talk about. But she was a full-blooded Cherokee Indian.

I didn't discover my athletic talents myself. It came about when I was fifteen and a sophomore in high school. My coach, W. B. "Burt" Moore, who doubled as athletic director, track and football coach, gym teacher, and what not, was holding spring tryouts for a Missouri State Letter. One of the requirements was to run the 50 yard dash in seven seconds. Well, we were just running on a cinder path. We knew nothing about form and ran in tennis shoes and floppy clothes and all that sort of thing. But I remember; I could run! I could outrun the boys! So I took off and finished that distance and then the coach looked at his watch and said, "I don't believe I got your time right. I think it was six something." Then he says, "That'll be all." He took off and went to the local jewelry store and had his watch checked to see if it was okay. What had happened was I ran the first race in 5.8 seconds and the second one in 5.9, both of which would have been world records. Well, my coach leaked the story to the newspapers, and it made the Associated Press and got carried around the country. That's how my speed was discovered.

I learned to put the shot on the farm. I couldn't afford two dollars and a half for a shot-put, but my dad had broken a sixteen-pound anvil pounding something or other on it. So I started throwing one of the pieces. My brother and I spent a couple of years readying me for my shot-put debut. He always says that he should get some credit for this because he was my retriever.

My coach gradually worked with me and taught me something about technique and so forth. Oh, he was a lovely man. Handsome man. I secretly admired him and probably was infatuated with him. Probably loved him, and he'd like me to say that, too. He's still living. He's in Ames, Iowa. We correspond all the time.

At that time our opportunities were very limited. There was no competition back in those days. There was nothing in high school. Nothing in college. But in March of 1935 my coach found out that they were going to have the National A.A.U. Championship in St. Louis. So, for about two or three weeks he had me running, staking starts, and tossing the shot-put around. I was then seventeen. I also did some broad jumping because that was one of the events. So he entered me in the 50 meter dash, the standing broad jump, and the eilght-pound shot-put. As I recall, the superintendent of schools wasn't too keen on us going, and he told my coach for us to leave town very quietly and he hoped that we'd come back the same way and that we'd have this foolishness out of our systems. They didn't think too much of that stuff back in those days.

Well, I had absolute confidence in myself. All I wanted was an opportunity because I knew I had the stuff. So we came down to St. Louis. The coach's wife came along, too; she was one of my greatest supporters. And Stella Walsh, the 1932 Olympic champion in the 100 meters, was there. I had had her picture on my wall for a couple of months, sticking pins in it every day; I really had her wounded. Anyway, we had this 50 meter race. We all lined up. I may have been nervous. I wore a little ol' blue gym suit my mother had made for me and a pair of shoes borrowed from one of the boys on the Fulton track team and a pair of ol' grey sweat pants from another boy. And, boy, I was really ready to go! When that gun went off, Helen Stephens went off. And when that tape came up, I was there with it. Stella didn't think too much of that. She didn't like it. Burned her up. She called me a "greenie from the sticks," and that really made me mad. Stella said I'd jumped the gun. And I said, "Come to Fulton, and I'll run you over plowed ground and give you an even break." Then I told the reporters that I had never even heard of her.

I never got another opportunity to run against her again until we met in Berlin. If she had been agreeable to run against me, we could have been on an awful lot of programs around the country, even after the Olympics. We'd even have been at the big men's meets. She always got a lot of money in advance before she'd run. A lot of people have told me that, but I was one of those simon-pure amateurs, you know, trying to play it all by the rulebook.

So, anyway, that was how I got started. And once I had beaten her, I made national news and from then on they had to pay attention to me. I was then seventeen and a senior in high school. That same night in the A.A.U. meet I went on and won the standing broad jump and the shot-put. So I won three National A.A.U. titles in my first track meet, but I had worked hard with that stuff although I certainly wasn't a finished product by any means.

It was a lot of fun. I remember an ol' gal from St. Louis who was on the *Post Dispatch* there. She came down and wrote an article and did a lot of pictures. She had me dressed up in overalls and carrying a shotgun with my brother's hunting dog. The caption read, "From farm to fame in 6.6 seconds."

Two things happened before I tried out for the Olympics. Some Fulton businessmen formed the Fulton Athletic Club which sort of defrayed my expenses and those of my coach and chaperon. Back in those days you had to have chaperons. They saw that I got to a few meets. Then the other thing was I enrolled at a local college. I had one year there before the Olympics. I trained with the boys, and I took a lot of starch out of some of them. I did a lot of long distance running like 400 and 800 meters. It's a crying shame that they didn't have those events for girls back in those days. They didn't have them because they didn't think the women could run them. When they ran that 800 meter race in 1928, the gals fainted because they were trained to run 50 yards, and it just killed them when they ran that longer race. But I would've loved to run those longer races because, when I ran 100 meters, my coach taught me to run 120 meters. When that tape comes up, everyone stops. I always went through that bugger like it was never there. I think a lot of these runners today don't drive through the finish line. It's like they're not going to waste an extra step. I've watched a lot of top-class people and they're always ready to collapse.

Back in those days you qualified through the A.A.U.. It was the only thing that was going back then. I qualified in a local A.A.U. Ozark District meet in St. Louis. I broke the world record in the qualifying, and then they found out the track was a foot short and all that sort of thing. It went on like that back in those days. They always had to have so many officials present of a certain stature and qualification and so many watches that were checked properly. And every time I'd run I'd break a record. But when I got through, it was always somebody who had made a mistake. And they always gave an excuse, "Oh, well, you'll beat that some day."

I never lost a race from scratch in my entire amateur career of two-and-a-half years leading up to the Olympics. I think I may have lost a handicapped race somewhere along the line when they used to give these girls fifteen or twenty yards on me. But I never lost a scratch race.

It also used to burn me up that in the official meets you could only enter three events because, shoot, I could have done more. Well, when I went to any track meet I was not overly friendly with anyone. And, of course, there was my appearance and my deep voice. I was going to kill them, you know, let them know it right off the bat. Of course later on, after you get to know people, they become your life-long friends. But my coach was partly responsible for that. He didn't want me to become friendly with anyone. Stay aloof from them. Don't associate with them. Just go out there and run away from them. There's a little psych in all this.

Babe Didrikson was a bit like that. She could not stand another woman. I've heard many stories about her. Back when she was on the Olympic team in '32, she was a tobacco chewing, cursing, spitting, regular ol' tomboy and hellcat who couldn't stand anyone, and nobody could stand her. I'll tell you a little story about my first meeting with her. It was after I returned from Berlin in 1936, and I was down in Washington, D.C. to run in a track meet. Babe, of course, knew my Olympic coach, Dee Beckman, and several of the other girls. And she came over to the hotel that night to say hello to them and confided that she wanted to see me. Well, during the course of the evening, she suggested that she and I don swimming suits and take a little swim. We weren't trying to beat each other swimming, but after we got out of the hotel pool, she suggested that we throw some of these life preservers, which were filled and rather heavy. She said, "Let's toss a few of these out on the water." I felt right away that she was testing me, but I said, "Okay, lead off." We tossed a few out, and she said, "Let's go for some distance." And I said, "All right; just head right out there." Well, what happened was we threw a few and I decided that I could probably use a spin like a discus thrower, and I wound up and threw that thing clear across the pool up against a chainlink fence. And the Babe says, "It's time to go in. I've got a golf date tomorrow, and it's getting chilly."

I played one season with the All-American Redheads, a women's basketball team, and we toured all around the country. Eventually I had a team called the Helen Stephens Olympic Co-Eds, which was similar to the Redheads. We were booked around the country. One summer I got involved in a promotion with a baseball team similar to the House of David. These were called the House of Davidites. No, I know what you're thinking--that it was some ol' gals with beards or something. I may be on tape, and I may not be, but it doesn't make any difference. I'm going to tell you this story. I think it's good. You know, Babe Didrikson toured the country with the House of David at one time. Yes, she did. Well, one time in some town or other some old haughty gal looked over her eye glasses at Babe when the Babe was throwing a few balls with these bearded guys and said, "Babe, where's YOUR beard?" And the Babe looked her over and said, "I'm sitting on it, sister, just like you are."

My first boat ride was going over to the Olympics, but a funny thing happened even before we pulled out of the dock in New York. I discovered two or three boxes of literature and letters in my cabin about the Jewish people wanting us to take a stand against competing against the Germans in the Olympics. They were wanting us to stage a protest of some type. I turned this material over to my coach, and I think she turned it over to the Olympic officials. That was the first, but more came later in Berlin--letters, telegrams--where people would write and tell you to get down on your mark and then refuse to run and say that you wanted prisoner so-and-so released from the concentration camps. I never could understand how those telegrams got through to Germany at that time. That was always amazing to me.

Well, on the boat the most famous incident was the champagne party and Eleanor Holm Jarrett. We all thought Eleanor was very outgoing--a hell of a nice girl. Actually, I didn't know too much about her. She was living a different life than mine. She was out in the world, singing in a band, traveling around, and I was fresh off the farm. She was used to drinking champagne for breakfast, and I'd never had any of that stuff. But anyway, I remember the officials talking and saying that Eleanor was acting up. They tried to warn her that she was going to get in trouble, and a few days later she evidently did.

She and some reporters were playing cards, poker, or whatever, and she just drank too much and got seen by the wrong person--a very straight-laced ol' gal who turned her in. Avery Brundage decided to show his authority and made an example of her before somebody else got out of hand. Back in those days those Olympic officials were authority figures to all of us athletes. They expected discipline, and by and large they got it. Call it fear, intimidation, whatever. I remember the morning after this incident--and I was embarrassed to be a party to it--they paraded all the gals through Eleanor's cabin to see her. I think she had already received her admonishment. She was going to be kicked off the team. We all went down there in a group, and this kid had a hangover. We thought she was sick, and I guess she was.

I remember her when we landed in Germany. We were going to take a train, but she wasn't with us. I remember seeing her out of uniform with her suitcases off boarding another train. I thought it was sort of pathetic in a way. As she has said, Hitler told her that he would never have kicked her off the German team; first he would have let her swim, win a gold medal, and then kicked her off the team.

I think she would probably have won, too. That was one of those things. It made a lot of history. I can't say whether it was wrong or right. If we have rules, you got to stick to the rules, but she was a free spirit and used to living a different lifestyle than the other athletes did. She didn't think any more about drinking champagne than anyone else would think about drinking water.

There were three heats in the 100 meter race in Berlin. I ran the first heat, I believe, in 11.4, which was a world record, but they claimed that there was a cross wind. I never heard of a cross wind ever hurting anyone. They weren't ready to accept my speed at that time.

In my semifinal heat I ran an 11.5, which was also a world record, and then in the finals I did it again to get the Olympic and world record of 11.5. But there were some people there who were timing it by hand and they claimed that I ran that thing in anywhere from 11.1 up. Some said 11.3. There was quite a debate. My Olympic coach was there when they decided to set that record at the meeting afterwards. They just didn't feel it was possible for anyone to run that fast and cut the record down that much. Stella Walsh's time had been 11.9 in 1932. My time probably should have been better than 11.5. You got to realize that I was strong! I was really strong and I had a nine-foot stride. And I might have been even better a few years later if I had kept it up.

My coach was always working on my start. I had a slow start because I wanted to take a big stride on that first step. By taking that big first stride I was moving right away, getting into that long stride immediately. Of course, they had the idea back in those days that you had to get those little ol' choppy steps to pick that up. I think some of these athletes today get a pretty good long first stride and then a lot of them keep their rear up pretty high. We used to be crouched down, coming out on an angle. I think they've learned a lot about technique. I was a natural runner. I could run like a deer. I had speed. I just had it.

We'll never really know what would have happened in that relay race if that German girl hadn't dropped the baton when she was about ten yards ahead. She received it all right, but then dropped it when she exchanged it from one hand to the other. You didn't have to do that if you were running last, but she was used to running first. I saw that happening out of the corner of my eye, but I couldn't wait to appreciate it at the time. In any case, I felt that I would have made up the difference because the Germans had their slowest runner going last. I felt that I could have chewed her up. But in retrospect, as the years pass, maybe I wasn't as fast as I thought I was, but at the time I thought it would have been a close finish.

Our quarters over there were spartan. We had a dormitory that was a nice, new, modern building. We had a bed in there but not a real mattress. It was just a cotton or kapok-filled thing. There was also a little stand and a light hanging from the ceiling. There was a community bath and showers. On the first floor we had a lounge which was nicely furnished to use if you had guests or if the press came. There wasn't any luxury connected with it. The dining room was nearby, and I remember they started out by feeding us green apples for breakfast and that heavy black bread that most of us had never eaten. So we raised a lot of Ned with them until we got some bacon and eggs and some American cereal in there. I think they were trying to weaken us.

Those German girls who were attached to us as English-speaking guides could speak good English, and they were telling us that the German people were going to treat us nice while we were there, but that didn't mean that they necessarily liked us. They said they were going to beat the hell out of us come the next war, and in that very stadium there were tunnels underneath for air raid shelters. We weren't used to hearing all this. And all those training fields adjacent to the stadium were filled with thousands of German school children marching around with broomsticks and swords--the Hitler Youth, the Boy Scouts.

I met Hermann Goering before I met Hitler. I think I drank my first glass of beer with him. He offered me some, and I looked at my Olympic coach, Dee Beckman, and wondered, "Is this going to be all right? Should I do this or not?" She gave me the motion to go ahead and drink it--you know, you're in good company or something. Of course, he was playing footsie under the table. He was an ol' rascal, I can tell you that.

I remember that after the Olympics all of the gold medalists were invited to Goebbels' estate along with the upper Four Hundred of Berlin society and the top people of the German army, navy, and air force. They threw a big garden party there for us. They had about seven outdoor dance pavillions and bars with champagne running freely. There were soldiers all over, standing at attention. During the course of the evening, a messenger came up to me and said, "Hermann Goering wants to see you upstairs." Harriet Bland, a relay runner from St. Louis, and I said, "Hey, this'd be a fun experience to go up there. We won't tell anybody." Well, we went up, and there was a soldier in uniform standing before the door. Now this party was later written up by the press as one of those orgies, and that's what it was. We get inside the door and there's Goering sitting on a great big divan and a couple of gals sitting there in dubious attire. He had a table in front of him, and I knew things weren't according to Hoyle when one of those girls slithered up from under the table. Then I realized this black thing he had on was his kimona and he was sitting there in his shorts. And, of course, he gives me the Heil Hitler sign and congratulations. He told me to have a drink and brought the wine over. Well, I thought, "I'm not drinking anything here." So I took the wine and toasted with it and set it back, just ceremonial like. So he says, "You and your friend make yourself comfortable and everything, and if you would like to be more comfortable, I'll have you shown into an adjacent room, and I'll be in to see you later."

I thought, "Oh, my God." And Harriet, she's over there talking to somebody. Just then Goering got a phone call, and a good-looking German officer came up and said, "Would you like to come over with me and meet so and so?" So we did and he says, "I don't think you young people should be here. This is not a proper place, and things will get out of hand before the evening's over. If you'll bear with me, I'll introduce you to several well-known officers who are here." And he introduced me to old World War I generals, and then he said, "I think you all will be uncomfortable here. We'll gradually work over to the door, if it's all right with you." He told us that he didn't approve of what was going to take place there. We had a hard time catching Harriet and getting her going because she couldn't get it through her head what was going on. As I got ready to go out the door ol' Hermann Goering was still on the phone, and he jumps up and says, "Auf Wiedersehen, Fraulein Stephens." And then he blew me a kiss--and that's the last I ever saw of him. I later thought, "Gee, I wonder what I missed out on. I could have had even a bigger story to tell."

After the Olympics I came back and ran for my college and wore their colors. I ran in the 1937 indoor A.A.U. meet in St. Louis and won the fifty, the shot- put, and the standing broad jump for the third time. The last race I ever ran as an amateur athelete was in Chicago. That was in August of 1937.

I lost my amateur standing, I guess, because I signed an agreement with a fellow to represent me. We made ourselves available for offers. I endorsed Quaker Oats and another breakfast cereal similar to Wheaties called Huskies, out of New York. Then I started touring the country with the All-American Redheads, a women's basketball team that played only men.

You really didn't have to be a redhead. You could put a rinse on it if you wished. I did it once for kicks. Thought it would put some life in it. At the half of the game I would challenge the fastest man in town to run the 20 yard dash across the floor, and then maybe I'd do a standing broad jump, and then they'd put pads down, and I'd toss the shot. There was many a man who said I beat him in this country. I run into a lot of them in this Midwest area. They come up and say, "Remember that little ol' skinny kid you ran against about forty years ago or so? Well, that's me. Now I weigh 200 and I'm baldheaded and walk with a cane."

I even ran five races against Jesse Owens--100 yards on ball diamonds--and he gave me eight to ten yards, based on our fastest times. We usually wound up with practically a photo finish. I ran him in Chicago at Wrigley Field; Muskegon, Michigan; Toledo and Columbus, Ohio; and Louisville, Kentucky. I guess you never heard of anybody getting a broken finger in a foot race, but when we were running at Wrigley Field in Chicago during World War II, the race was so close that Jesse threw his arms back to his left and he caught my right hand as it came up and broke my little finger.

I had a lot of fun with that stuff. It was like the broad jump. I won three national championships in the standing broad jump, but that was not an Olympic event. I used to jump eight feet, eight inches or something. Many a time I had an exhibition in gyms with my basketball team, and I used to jump nine feet, eleven inches. Now that's a pretty fair country jump. That was from a standing position.

I got good in the shot-put later on when I put on a little weight. I remember one time, in 1952 I guess it was, the Russians were doing something with the shot-put in the Olympics. I think they had set a record of fifty-some feet. (Editor's note: Galina Zibina of the USSR set a world record of 50 feet, 1 1/2 inches at the Helsinki Games in 1952). At the time I was giving an exhibition in a ballpark up in Rhinelander, Wisconsin, and I told them to mark out the United States record, the Olympic record, and the world record. I said, "I'm going to break the world record." I weighed 195 pounds then. I was pretty muscular, and I had worked on that shot; it was just a baby to me. I knew just what to do, and I tossed that sucker out there close to 55 feet--54 feet, 11 inches or something. It was better than the record that had been set just a couple of days before.

I once had a meeting in Chicago about going into golf. Sam Snead was there, and he was going to be my advisor. They were going to send me to Florida for two years, and I wasn't going to have to worry about expenses. They'd take care of everything. They were going to get me the finest coaches and teach me the game. I may have blown it. But there wasn't any money then. In 1937 there wasn't any money in golf. They said that they felt that there was a future in that game and they would gamble if I would. Well, I'll tell you, I needed to get ahold of some money. I needed money for my folks so I could buy them a farm. I just couldn't gamble that they were going to feed me for two years. I figured I was going to eat one way or another.

You know, in recent years many girls have got into problems with this sex bit. Avery Brundage asked me what to do about it. I'd been pestered around the world on this question. So I met him in Chicago. I was then the President of the Midwest Chapter of Former Olympians. I said, "I'm going to tell it to you in two words." He said, "What's that?" I said, "Examine them." He said, "How are we going to do that?" I said, "That's for you and your crew to figure out." And then they came up with all those chromosome and sex tests. After that on national television he gets up and says it was all my idea. I later learned that there were a lot of people who hated my guts. They just hated my guts.

They had some pretty good examples of that back in my day. The Germans had a gal who was a high jumper and she was really a man. There were no ifs, ands or buts about it. He placed about fourth or fifth so it didn't do him any good. After the Olympics were all over, I understand that he went to Holland and fathered two children. They used to ask him, "Gee, you must have had a great time running around in those girls' dressing rooms masquerading as a woman." And he said, "Aw, it wasn't so hot."

I've stayed pretty active in sports my whole life. I bowl and play a little golf. I did pretty well in the Senior Olympics this year. Anybody can enter from fifty-five on up. They have different age classes. Well, I ran the 50, the 100, and the 200 meter dashes, the standing broad jump, the running broad jump, threw the discus, put the shot and threw the javelin. That's eight events. And I won every one of them. I'd never even thrown a javelin before.

When people ask me how I rate my career, I tell them a little story that Dizzy Dean used to tell. Dizzy was one of the most unforgettable characters I ever met in sports. He was one of the great, great characters and a butcher of the king's English. I always liked what he said when he was being inducted into the Baseball Hall of Fame. Some smart-assed reporter asked, "Well, Dizzy, how do you rate yourself?" And Dizzy said, "I wasn't the greatest, but I was amongst 'em."

I kind of feel the same way.

Thomas Monaghan, *THE THRILL OF POVERTY* (1990)

Tom Monaghan is best known as the founder and multi-millionaire owner of Domino's Pizza and as president and owner of the Detroit Tigers baseball team. Below is an excerpt from a speech he gave to a group business executives in Detroit, as reported in Harper's Magazine, *August 1990.*

To me one of the most exciting things in the world is being poor. Survival is such an exciting challenge. There was a study done about twenty years ago, I think at Harvard, which said that the average family of four could live on $68 a year. That's a balanced diet--everything they need for a year. Now today that might be $250 or $300, but when we see these people in lines in supermarkets with all these food stamps, buying potato chips and snack foods and ice cream, I mean, give me a break! That's poverty?

Now you're probably wondering how you can live on $68 a year. The first thing you do is go to the Farm Bureau and buy a hundred-pound bag of powdered milk, like they feed the calves--there's nothing wrong with it; it tastes just like regular milk when you put a little water in it. That would probably last you the better part of a year. While you're at the Farm Bureau you buy yourself a bushel of oats or wheat or corn, and you mash that stuff up. What you're eating isn't all that tasty--it kind of tastes like cornmeal mush--but it's healthy. And you grow some vegetables and you get a few vitamin pills to supplement your diet. And I think that's exciting.

You ought to really explore the cheapest ways to live. Living in a house trailer--my gosh, that was the greatest living I ever did. We bought a used house trailer for $1,400, and we paid about $30 a month for the lot. Now you can get a lot for $175 and you can buy a used house trailer for maybe $5,000. And you're building some equity in something; you're not paying rent. Oh gosh, I'd love to talk to all these people who say they can't get by.

Ann Thomas, *DISILLUSIONED IDEALIST*

Ann Thomas is a twenty-nine-year-old former journalist who is presently raising a three-year-old son and working part-time. Her husband is a former Air Force officer who is presently laid off fromhis job as a commercial pilot with one ofAmerica's leading airlines. A typically idealistic university student. Thomas lost her idealism during the Reagan years. She particularly deplores the way Reagan was able to exploit the shallowness of television to project an image that was neither accurate nor helpful for the long-range health of the country.

When I was eighteen, I was sure the world was there for me to take. After my university studies, I knew I would find a good job with unlimited upward mobility, and that I would also undoubtedly exceed my parents' middle-class standard of living. I also had visions of becoming a lawyer, going to Washington, D.C., and working to make this country a better place to live.

It's funny how a single event can change things. One day in 1979 I was helping the local Democratic Party prepare to welcome Vice President Walter Mondale who was coming to my hometown for a speaking engagement. He never arrived. That was the day President Jimmy Carter's attempted rescue of the American hostages in Iran ended in death and disaster. That failed attempt probably cost Carter the election, and it certainly changed the course of American history and my own as well. I just quit my participant's role in politics after the election of Reagan.

I remember the whole hostage crisis with considerable bitterness. Every night TV newscasters would announce the number of days the hostages had then been held in captivity. The fact that the hostages were eventually released on Reagan's Inauguration Day made it obvious to me that Reagan's people had cut a secret deal with Iran's Ayatollah Khomeini to hold the hostages until after the election. In return, Reagan allowed arms shipments to Iran, the very country that had been holding our men hostage.

Carter did have other political problems. He told the American people the truth, that there was "a malaise" in the land that we would have to work very hard to cure. He was especially referring to our social and educational ills. Reagan told us just the opposite, that there was nothing basically wrong with America, that everything would be fine if we just bought into his political philosophy.

I was a university student between 1981-1985, precisely the years of Reagan's first administration. Although I personally thought Reagan was a bad joke. I did understand why so many young people supported him. Most students, then and now, equate the American Dream with their own economic opportunities. That was the era of the "Yuppies", but even students in the liberal arts were planning to go into business and make their fortunes. Reagan certainly did much to create such an attitude with his simplistic notions of an unfettered economy restoring America's greatness. If a few of those students had studied the 1920s, they would have known much the same thing had been said back then by Presidents Harding, Coolidge, and Hoover.

Reagan was a knee-jerk conservative of obviously limited intelligence who always appeared too glib and superficial to be real. He was an actor who could deliver his lines but who had no depth or sincerity. He knew when to get a tear in his eye, but it was first and foremost his speechwriters who knew how to write his lines for him. There was the famous Lebanon truck-bombing incident in which more than 240 American Marines lost their lives. Someone showed Reagan a photograph of a badly wounded soldier pointing to the Marine motto "semper fidelis" on his helmet. According to one of his aides, Reagan rehearsed telling this story over and over until he could deliver it with a genuine tear in his eye. It became a movie scene that left audiences gasping, "What a wonderful hero that young boy is who so willingly offers his life to his country!" Instead, they should have been demanding an explanation for the policies that got this boy wounded and 240 of his fellow soldiers killed.

Reagan reassured America that after the defeat in Vietnam and after the hostage crisis, he would take us back to the 1940s and '50s when America, like the classic gunfighter, stood tall and unchallenged in her military might. Reagan even announced that his dream Cabinet would have included John Wayne as Secretary of State and Clint Eastwood as Secretary of Defense. He was probably thinking of the time John Wayne told the Veterans of Foreign Wars, "We only take up arms to make this country what it is supposed to be, God's guesthouse on earth." This image of a divinely inspired, just, and all-powerful America showing off its giant gun became a kind of masculine fertility symbol for those testosterone-starved males who always voted for Reagan in much larger numbers than did females.

Reagan also played very effectively on Americans' fear of Communists. Because our intentions were always noble, any evil had to come from without. He labeled Russia the "evil empire," borrowing again from a movie line. Such tactics appeal to those Americans who maintain that through violence we will be redeemed. If Reagan had been President during the Vietnam War, we probably would have stayed the course because he would have played into all that beloved mythology much more convincingly than Johnson and Nixon were able to do. He would have had Americans believing Vietnam was "the final showdown at the O.K. Corral."

Working on a small-town, Texas newspaper helped me understand how the media could distort Americans' perception of reality. We are not independent thinkers. More and more, it is the 6:30 television news that forms our opinions, and, unfortunately, it is less and less the newspapers that influence us. And the media were generally very unfair to Carter while going overboard for Reagan.

One has to understand that the media not only influence popular perceptions but also tend to go along with what they perceive as popular or unpopular issues. In other words, if the polls show a President to be unpopular with the people, the media are much more likely to feature negative stories about the President--and vice versa. In the 1980 election the polls told us well before we voted, who would be President, and this can be an influencing factor for a people trained to take their cues from the media. Polling today is even more sophisticated. Computers tell us what the people are thinking, or are supposed to be thinking, then the politicians decide where they should stand on the issue.

Americans did not see their boys killing or being killed during Reagan's brief attacks on Libya and Grenada and during Bush's Panama invasion and his Gulf War because the media were now allowed to be there to record the horrors of war. Military families were told during the Gulf War that if a family member happened to be killed, there would be no formal military burial ceremony. There would be no ceremony to greet the returning bodies. This was a political decision to keep the reality of war away from the American people. And, of course, the authorities also hid the tens of thousands of dead Iraqis. The media were controlled by the White House as if the war was some big Nitendo Game. We were shown specific footage from the cockpit of an F-15 to show us that our so-called "smart bombs" hit only military targets. At the time Americans overwhelmingly supported the Gulf War, but now more and more of us realize the war was another example of duplicitous government leadership.

I married a military pilot shortly after I graduated from the university. To be in the military in the mid-1980s was to step back in time--to the 1950s--and the height of the cold war. During the Reagan Years the military was one of America's fastest growing industries. Whatever the military wanted, it got. Reagan's announced cuts in government spending never applied to the military. He spent more on the military during his eight years than all the previous peacetime presidents combined and the national debt under Reagan exceeded that of all previous Presidents combined. He tripled the defense budget, and those of us in the military reaped the benefits. It is a far different story today. What Reagan did not understand, or refused to admit, was that the money had to come from somewhere. He thought those billions of dollars were somehow separate from the rest of the economy. He could not admit that expenditures are expenditures regardless of what they are spent for, and that the economy simply could not grow fast enough to absorb the runaway defense budget. George Bush called this "voodoo economics back in 1980 before he became Reagan's running mate, and he was right. We couldn't cut taxes, triple the defense budget, deregulate essential industries and still have a healthy economy. So today the money and resources are not there for the military or for anyone else. We overbuilt the military preparing for a threat that never really existed.

The average American did not mind the dismantling of American social programs until he himself was affected. But now Reaganomics has come home to roost, and we have to pay the piper, except we have no money to do so. We are attempting to pay our debts through the loss of jobs, a crumbling infrastructure, a disastrous school system, and a health system that is a national disgrace. While Reagan deregulated industry and allowed jobs to go south, Japan and Germany built-up their economies. While we were spending over seventy-five per cent of our national research money on military projects, Germany and Japan were spending less than five per cent. Bush seems to ignore all this, and now the American people are ignoring him. They know he comes from money, was born with a silver spoon in his mouth, and is an elitist. Reagan was able to play up the myth that he was just a good ol' boy from a small town in the Middle West, that he was really one of the people. Bush is incapable of playing such a role. Americans also know that Bush has no domestic policy so they have turned on him. Americans generally are concerned about the environment, better schools, national health care, the homeless, and the poor, and they want a leader who can either make them forget about all this, as Reagan was able to do, or they want the kind of action Bush is apparently incapable of providing.

Before Perot withdrew, I would not have been surprised if the 1992 election had been thrown into the House of Representatives because no candidate had been able to win an electoral majority. I thought it not beyond the realm of possibility that Perot could actually have won in November. In some ways Perot was Reagan incarnate. He was again that outsider riding in to save the country. He made wonderful television sound bites because, like Reagan, he had great one-liners that seemed to reduce complex issues to just common sense. The idea that America can only be saved by "throwing the rascals out" is so pervasive now that someone like Perot has a real chance.

My husband could see the handwriting on the wall so he got out of the air force in June of 1990 to become a commercial pilot; unfortunately, that was not such a good decision. He began flying for U.S. Air, but after six months he was laid off, and he still is. This meant we lost his full-time salary, and also our health benefits. It is a very scary thing to be without health benefits when you have a young child. But I remain an optimist. I've said repeatedly that I think my husband will be back to work in six months. Of course, I've said this three times, but I still believe it. I have to. I still buy into the view that the future will be better than the present. The history of America has been marked by optimism, but we are going to have to find someone who can use our government to implement creative social and economic changes. Clearly, Bush was not the person to do so. Perhaps Clinton will surprise us. God knows, we could certainly use a nice surprise.

Patricia Cutler, *FROM CADILLACS TO HEALTH CARE*

Patricia Cutler is a thirty-year-old former advertising copywriter who switched from selling Cadillacs for General Motors to promoting good health care for the people in a small rural county. Having been recently diagnosed with a form of cancer called Hodgkin's disease only reinforced her belief that the selling of illusions is deleterious to everyone's health in a society pledged to the conspicuous onsumption of material objects. Especially troubling to Cutler is how television and advertising producers increasingly perceive of children as "consumer trainees."

Whoever tells the stories in a society controls that society. In ancient times the elders in the tribe told the stories that instructed the people on how to live. With the invention of the alphabet, those who could write also began to tell the stories; and with the eventual invention of the printing press publishers joined authors in transmitting messages to the people. But over the past half century television has taken over the storytelling function for most Americans, and especially for children, and television often means hard-selling advertising. The average American watches more than four hours of television a day, including some forty ads an hour, and many children--especially pre-schoolers and those in dysfunctional families--watch more than that. In fact, by the time the average young person turns eighteen, he or she will have spent more time in front of a television set than in school. We have to ask ourselves what are the stories that television is telling our children. If they are learning only to be consumer trainees, television has become a very dangerous force for future generations.

Traditionally, parents, schools, and religious institutions were the primary social conditioners. These are, of course, three very different institutions, but essentially they could agree on how a child could best be raised into adulthood. Today these institutions are competing with countless mass-mediated images in what many of us feel is an unfair competition. It is very difficult, for example, for parents to be heard over the constant bombardment of electronic signals that seek to program the child into accepting commercial products as the key to happiness.

The child learns at a very early age what kind of sugar-coated cereal to eat, which plastic toys are supposed to bring him joy, and even what kind of people to like. This is not reality but what the television and advertising producers have substituted for reality, and it conditions youngsters to want more and more rather than aspiring to be more and more.

I can take my small nephew for a walk in the woods and show him the beauties of nature, but this experience cannot compete with what he has already seen on television. If you give a youngster a choice between nature according to Disneyland and real nature, it is strictly no contest. But how does one achieve internal peace in a mass-mediated world that's based on such artificial truths? Can children, as well as grownups, find peace in such a world? We accumulate all of these things, looking for the one magical product that's finally going to click it all into place, and advertisers play ruthlessly on this search for the quick external fix.

And what happens to the child who has been conditioned to expect someone or something else to entertain him when he learns that the real world is quite different from that projected daily by television? Writer Jerzy Kosinski has pointed out that when the television child goes to school he is placed into an environment that, unlike his television world, he can no longer control. If something on television seemed threatening or made him unhappy, he could simply change the channel. But that doesn't work in school where he has to learn to get along with others and to absorb information over which he has little or no control.

Of course, children are so resilient that most adjust to a changing environment. But why should a child's most precious years be stolen from him by the one-eyed monster that certainly does not have his best interests at heart? I know that when I have children, I will strictly limit their television watching. My father did this with me, and I still much prefer books to television. But my husband is a heavy television watcher, so when we have kids I'll have to limit his TV watching as well.

Television does more than simply condition us to be consumers. Its programs and advertisements create such a seemingly appealing and attractive world that our own drab existence seems somehow diminished in comparison. What is real is that we do live on this planet and we live in a country where we have so much more than do most other countries. But we don't quite see it that way. We think we desperately need the material products our economy produces. We are conditioned to believe we need the biggest boat when in reality maybe we just need to look at the water. We need to realize we can't manufacture trees. We end up cutting them down to make the paper to produce the brochures we environmentalists distribute to tell the rest of the people to save the forests.

I spent six years working for an advertising agency that marketed cars for General Motors, and I can assure you that advertising does spur us on to consume. It is the motor that makes our economy run. Our health as a nation is almost entirely predicated on how much we consume, and what we consume are products that are made from diminishing natural resources. We need to realize that something is being left out of this equation--that what we consume is not real--that our people are real--and are our most precious natural resource.

Advertisers defend their work by pointing out that they help people make choices. They argue that people really do need deodorants to smell good and tooth paste to keep their teeth clean and their breath fresh. They insist selling such products is a necessary service. In reality, of course, they are not selling tooth paste and deodorants, but an image of happiness, satisfaction, success, and even romance. This is nonsense, except advertisers know that many Americans desperately seek such illusions. Advertisers also prey on our insecurities and fears. If you don't buy this product, you never are going to be a lovable, normal, and desirable human being.

Of course, one has to have money to participate in this entire process. The poor can only watch in frustration and bitterness, as we saw last summer in Los Angeles when residents took matters into their own hands during the riots. The looters had also been conditioned by advertisers, and they stole the goods they perceived would bring them the good life.

Advertising can do some positive things. Unquestionably public service ads have played a primary role in getting young people either to stop smoking or not to start at all. There's simply no question about this. Very rarely will you see an educated young man smoking, and comparatively few young women. The poorer classes still seem to smoke so perhaps they ignore the ads or perhaps their lives are so bad they just don't care. But positive advertisements make up a very small percentage of those we see, including those that urge us to keep on smoking.

When we allow ourselves to be rational, our conscious mind dismisses advertising as nonsense. But our subconscious mind is not capable of rational thought; instead, it absorbs subliminal messages that can then dictate conscious behavior. For example, heavy television watchers--those who watch more than four hours a day--are further removed from reality than those who are light or non-watchers. And this has nothing to do with gender, race, class, or education. The more we watch TV the less we knows about the reality of the world around us. For example, heavy watchers believe that this world is much more violent than in reality it is. They think that the majority of women stay home taking care of their men. They are much more likely to believe that people are happiest only when with their own race or ethnic group. And they think old people are simply feeble imbeciles bearing milk and cookies for their young charges while they themselves are troubled by halitosis and irregularity. They simply cannot perceive of what reality is. I live in a neighborhood where there has not been a serious crime in thirty years; yet, one of my neighbors locks her door every night and takes a gun to bed with her. Where does she get such ideas? The mass-mediated world pushes us farther and farther away from what we empirically understand as reality.

During the time of the Gulf War, heavy television watchers were much less likely to understand the real issues. The majority of heavy TV watchers thought we were fighting that war to preserve democracy in Kuwait and Saudi Arabia. You have to wonder what it was that was being shown them over the tube. People who read were much more likely to understand that in reality the war was being fought over who would control the source of oil in the Middle East.

The Gulf War was sold to us like any other product. It was antiseptic: no dirt, no mess, no smells, and no death, and it promised us a safer, more secure future. It was a fascinating, vicarious experience for viewers, but it had nothing to do with reality. Its portrayal was decidedly different than the Vietnam War, which, even though it was on television, gave us a slice of reality. We did see American boys coming home in body bags. We saw badly hurt young men. We saw some of the horrors of war, and we didn't like what we saw. This should have warned us not to be so ready to accept another unnecessary war. But this was a new generation, trained by television and incapable of seeing reality. And what is even more remarkable is that the older generation also bought into the romance of the Gulf War which indicates that television had re-educated them into accepting its illusions as reality. Our government realized this and as a result forbade any film of the horrors of the war being shown to the American people. Our reporters were not even allowed near the front lines.

The conditioning we've received from television and advertising helps explain why the average American was unable to see through Ronald Reagan. He was sold to us as one more product, only this time the product happened to be the presidency. He acted like we thought a president should; he looked like one; and thus it didn't matter that he was ill-prepared for the realities of the world in which we are all forced to survive. Ronald Reagan was an actor, and he did a good job of acting like the president. He was a product that we thought we had to have. It's no accident that many of his closest campaign advisers came from Madison Avenue. Of course, this now applies to all our major candidates. We've gone beyond the discussion of political issues; we now simply try to ascertain which candidate appears to be the better package, rather than who is best qualified to be a statesman.

When I was diagnosed with Hodgkin's disease, I realized more than ever that we humans must comes to grips with reality if we are to cope with our existence. I had long rejected advertising's false promise of a better life, but now there was no question that I had to find peace and fulfillment from within. I thought about my old boss as someone who apparently had everything--except an understanding of life. She was successful in business, had all the money she could ever want, a good education, a fine family, good social standing, but was one of the most unhappy persons I have ever known. I mean, truly unhappy. Then I thought about myself. At the time I had almost no money, was not yet married, no real business success, and a life-threatening disease; yet, I felt I was wonderfully happy, especially in comparison to her. She had all the trappings but none of the essence of life. I had the essence but none of the trappings.

I am no longer selling products but services. I am in the health field, and this helps me feel internally at peace. I previously did ads for Cadillacs, the car that supposedly represents the ultimate in successful living--the ultimate dream. I was selling an image of success and prestige. The car itself was inconsequential for our ads. It was what we substituted for the car. You can simply count the number of times the words "prestige" and "style" are used in a Cadillac advertisement. What we were trying to sell was a feeling, not a car. But in the health care business I help people cope with illnesses or handicaps or I simply sell them on improving their everyday health, and this gives me tremendous satisfaction. I never had this feeling when I saw someone drive off in a Cadillac. I somehow experienced a feeling of sadness. That individual had just spent $60,000 on something he was really not going to get.

So I now gain my happiness from the fact that I am helping people and that I am alive and have hope. I hear so many stories from other people who were diagnosed with the same kind of cancer. Someone will say, "Oh, my aunt had that and she died. People actually say that. In fact, I had one person say, "Oh, my uncle died of that." When I told him, "Oh, that must have been some time ago because it's quite curable now," he said, "No, that was only about five years ago." It may be insensitive, but it makes me realize that just being on this earth gives me happiness. I understand that adversity makes us stronger human beings. Unlike the promises of advertising, delirious and unceasing happiness are impossibilities; we must learn to seize the moment and be decent human beings doing decent and relevant things for those we love and cherish.

Malvina Reynolds, ***LITTLE BOXES (1962)***

Inspired by the quickly emerging suburbs of the fifties and the fear that America was submerging itself in mediocre and sterile uniformity, Malvina Reynolds wrote the words and music to Little Boxes *in 1962.*

Little boxes on the hillside
Little boxes made of ticky tacky,
Little boxes on the hillside,
Little boxes all the same.
There's a green one and a pink one
And a blue one and a yellow one,
And they're all made out of ticky tacky
And they all look just the same.
And the people in the houses
All went to the university,
Where they all were put in boxes,
Little boxes all the same.
And there's doctors and lawyers
And business executives,
And they're all made out of ticky tacky
And they all look just the same.

And they all play on the golf course
And they drink their martinis dry,
And they all have pretty children
And the children go to school,
And the children go to summer camp
And then to the university,
Where they all get put in boxes
And they all come out the same.

And the boys go into business
And marry and raise a family,
And they all live in boxes
Little boxes all the same.
There's a green one and a pink one
And a blue one and a yellow one,
And they're all made out of ticky tacky
And they all look just the same.

Lew Carlson, *RONALD REAGAN AND AMERICAN POPULAR CULTURE*

Ronald Reagan was the perfect political candidate for a people trained to believe it is their inalienable right to be happy. Always cheerful, always optimistic, America's oldest President successfully promised Americans they could have it all: a past untroubled by problems, security from Godless Communists, a balanced Federal budget, economic riches for themselves and their children, and all to be accomplished with less government and lower taxes for everyone. The fact it was impossible to fulfill such promises did not concern most Americans. For them, Reagan was the kindly grandfather who told the stories they so badly wanted to hear. After all, our popular culture had conditioned both them and the President to believe there are simple answers to all problems if we would just retain our faith in America's greatness.

Everyone sees what you seem to be, few perceive what you are, and those few don't dare oppose the general opinion, which has the majesty of the government backing it up.

Machiavelli, *The Prince*, 1513

Ronald Reagan is an anthology of the worst of American popular culture, edited for television.

Mark Crispin Miller, *New Republic*, 1989

We have seen the future and it is Disneyland

Gary Wills, author of *Reagan's America*

I'd really like to go down in history as the President who made Americans believe in themselves again.

Ronald Reagan

During the early years of the Reagan Administration, the *Washington Post* published a column by Richard Cohen entitled "The Big Picture Show," in which Cohen incisively analyzed the singular relationship that existed between Ronald Reagan and the American people:

> *Once there was man who believed in movies. He thought they were truth. For this man, there were two kinds of reality. There was real-life reality and then there was a greater reality. This was movies. When this man thought about war, he thought about war films. When this man thought of poverty, he thought about films about the Great Depression. To him, war was about heroism and sacrifice and not about carnage and waste and gross stupidity. And he did not see poverty as a social pathology. He saw it as a temporary state, a little setback that could be rectified by hard work. Movies ran through this man's head all the time. In his off hours he talked about them. He was a movie actor and in his mind, his roles and his life became fused. He could no longer tell the difference between the two and so even one day when he was shot, he talked like John Wayne in a Western. It was charming and you could not find anyone who did not envy him his wit and his courage, but the whole thing nevertheless seemed to take place in black and white. Only the popcorn was missing....*
>
> *The man who believed in movies became a very successful politician. At first this may not make much sense, but you have to remember that he was not the only one who believed in movies. WE ALL DID! And so when he talked about the Depression the way he did, and when he talked about poor people as if they were just people with coal smeared on to dirty their faces, we all nodded in recognition because we had seen the same movies.*
>
> *In his political speeches, the man who believed in movies just flipped a switch in the minds of his audience and a movie played in their heads. He talked of courage and spirit and war. And when he talked, he sometimes choked up and got teary because he believed very much in what he had seen, even though he had seen it only in the movies.*

In 1970, Jerzy Kosinski, the superb writer who emigrated to the United States from Poland after World War II, published a novel entitled *Being There*. It was the story of a semi-retarded man named Chance who for all of his 40-some years had never been allowed to leave the house in which he lived. The reality of the outside world came to him only through his color television set. Then one day he was forced to leave the mass-mediated images of his isolated sanctuary. For the first time in his life he had to go out into the real world, and the only experience he had to fall back on was what he had seen on his color television set. He applied these lessons very well, so well, in fact, that within a matter of weeks there was talk of running him for President of the United States. You see, it was not only Chance who had taken his cues from television. We all had.

When Ronald Reagan left the presidency in January of 1989, he enjoyed a personal popularity unmatched since presidential polls began during the Eisenhower years in the early 1950's. Yet, throughout Reagan's eight years in the White House, many, if not most, of his policies and programs were not supported by a majority of the American people. His cuts in environmental, educational, health, and welfare spending, retrenchment on civil rights, "Star Wars" expenditures, financial and military support of the Contras, and heating up of the Cold War usually ran some 15 to 25 points behind his personal popularity in public opinion polls. Then, too, more than 100 of his political appointees had to depart under an ethical cloud;

nevertheless, the American people believed him to be a man of unshakable principles and exemplarary character. This apparent contradiction between the President's policies and his personal popularity is not new in American history. Presidents Harding and Eisenhower are other 20th-century examples, but never before has this contrast been so striking. Harding and Eisenhower were not known for public policy pronouncements, Reagan was. The late Marshall McLuhan insisted it is the messenger rather than the message that is all important, or perhaps one of the characters in Kosinski's *Being There* put it best: "As for his thinking," mumbles one of the power brokers who would make Chance President, "he appears to be one of us." Edward J. Rollins, Reagan's 1984 campaign manager, put it somewhat differently: "Ronald Reagan is the perfect candidate," announced Rollins. "He does whatever you want him to do. And he does it superbly well."

Otis Pike, a prominent syndicated columnist, suggested that "Ronald Reagan is liked by Americans because he is so much a member of the family. He isn't a fatherly figure, for it is the role of fathers to scold and discipline as well as provide. He is a grandfatherly figure, always telling us how good we are, never telling us we're bad, always comforting us, giving us gifts and generally spoiling us more than our parents would." According to Pike, "We want to believe that the United States is the best, the bravest, the most beautiful, the strongest, the richest, the wisest and the most honorable. He told us all those things."

Political biographers Jane Mayer and Doyle McManus agree with Pike: "Part of Reagan's success as a leader lay in the fact that most of the myths he created were preferable to reality. He told an affluent country beset by stubborn social ills that we could lower taxes, increase defense spending, fight terrorism, roll back communism, and end the threat of nuclear war all without risking American lives." Reagan appeared blissfully oblivious to serious problems. He loved to tell staffers, "Don't bring me problems--bring me solutions." Back in his 1980 presidential campaign, he had announced, "There are no big problems, just big government." His ability to reduce complex issues to simple one-liners played well on television where the ten-second sound bite and the snappy joke work better than lengthy discussions of complex issues.

Most Americans believed that Reagan was sharply curtailing Big Government in spite of the fact that during his first administration he gave us the largest Federal budget--and deficit--in our history. In fact, during the Reagan years our Federal government grew so large that we reached one government-paid employee for every fifteen citizens, which was precisely the same ratio as in the Soviet Union. One of President Reagan's own favorite stories illustrates this frequent contradiction between his political policies and his idealistic pronoucements. Reagan always took sharp issue with those who insisted his policies were inimical to African Americans, despite the fact that during his eight years in office blacks lost significant ground both educationally and economically. Reagan vetoed the 1988 civil rights bill, dismissed three prominent members of the Civil Rights Commission, supported tax exemptions for private schools, tried to weaken provisions in the Voting Rights Act, and refused to meet with prominent black leaders, explaining that many of them were not sincere in their quest for civil rights. But when confronted with accusations of racism, he fondly recalled a childhood during which his parents taught him to be tolerant of everyone. His favorite story concerned two blacks who played football with him at Eureka College in Illinois. When his two teammates were denied hotel accommodations, Reagan brought them home where both were evidently welcomed by his parents.

Just before he left office, Reagan told millions of viewers of *Sixty Minutes*, another of his favorite stories to illustrate why charges of racism were so unfair: "As a sports announcer," explained Reagan, "when blacks were denied the right to play major league baseball, I was one of the little group in the nation that editorialized constantly that they should be let in." Several years earlier Reagan had also insisted that he had helped integrate baseball years before it had actually occurred. The fact that neither story was true is almost beside the point as both illustrate Reagan's extraordinary ability to reduce a complicated institutional and cultural problem to a matter of personal experience with which the common man could readily identify.

Naturally, intellectual critics found such simplistic tactics maddening, particularly Reagan's penchant for ignoring facts, ideas, and substance while manifesting his cheery optimism that good principles and an indomitable will could triumph over all. But Ronald Reagan also possessed considerable warmth, a self-deprecating sense of humor, and great personal confidence; and even his most severe critics agree he had mastered the ceremonial and symbolic functions of office so well that he always appeared presidential. Former Speaker of the House of Representatives Tip O'Neill put it best when he exclaimed, "He'd have been a lousy prime minister, but he'd have been a great king."

Newsweek, which often praised Reagan's leadership abilities while attacking his policies, duly described the President's last round of speeches before leaving Washington:

> *As he saddled up to leave town, Washington's self-described 'old sheriff' bid farewell to his posse last week. For one last time as president, Ronald Reagan recited his credo of cowboy conservatism. In valedictory speeches he likened himself to the Western heroes he once portrayed and the capital to the dusty outposts of villainy he pacified on celluloid. After eight years in Dodge City, he said, his Outsider's vision was undimmed. Washington was the problem, not the solution. 'Stop putting faith in the false god of bureaucracy,' he said, summarizing his philosophy. 'Trust the genius of the American people again. Return to the principles of the Founders...limited government, free enterprise and respect for family, community and faith.'*

One of Reagan's aids was even precise. After cautioning the listener not to laugh, he explained: "When push comes to shove, when Ronald Reagan has to make a big decision--and he doesn't make any small ones--he asks himself one question and one question only. He asks himself, 'What would John Wayne have done?'"

John Wayne and Ronald Reagan, like most Americans, have long embraced simple answers for life's problems--indeed, Ronald Reagan's charm and not a little of his success stems from the fact he never met a problem he couldn't defuse with an appropriate one-liner. He once dismissed a question about our runaway national debt with the line: "The deficit is big enough to take care of itself". And during his 1984 campaign against Walter Mondale he constantly asked voters, "Are you for April 15 or the Fourth of July?"

But who is this man with whom so many Americans enthusiastically identified? What was there in his own life that might help us understand his vast popular appeal? *Where's the Rest of Me?*, written with Richard C. Hubler, is a campaign autobiography which came out in 1965 just before Reagan ran for his first term as governor of California. The title itself is an interesting choice as it comes from a scene in the movie *King's Row.* Actor Reagan wakes up in a hospital after an accident, only to discover that he has lost both his legs. "Where's the rest of me?" was his movie line which he then adopted to describe his own life story.

The autobiography contains the usual kind of political pap, but there is little question that Reagan believed his life really was as he described it, just as he believed, as he once put it, that "God has a special plan for me." He began his story appropriately with a description of his early nursing practices: "I must say, my breast feeding was the home of the brave baby and the free bosom." After describing his favorite infant colors as "red, white, and blue," he suggested his childhood had been "one of those rare Huck Finn-Tom Sawyer idylls," but Reagan most likely never read Twain's greatest novel, *The Adventures of Huckleberry Finn*, which took place almost exclusively at night and is the story of superstition, racism, crime, hypocrisy, cruelty, and woeful ignorance.

Reagan recreated a Norman Rockwell, Andy Hardy, *Saturday Evening Post,* small-town romantic vision of his youth that so many Americans recognize and love, even though they know it primarily through countless hours spent reading favorite books and magazines, listening to popular music, and watching movies and television.

In reality, Reagan's childhood came closer to the experiences Twain described in *The Adventures of Huckleberry Finn* than he ever realized. Just a few years before Reagan was born in 1911 in Tampico, Illinois, the local newspaper described, with great enthusiasm, a nearby lynching in which one of the black victims was roasted alive. Reagan's own father had a drinking problem not too dissimilar to Huck Finn's Pap. When he had drunk too much, he was not above beating young Ron and his brother, and he had great difficulty holding a job. In fact, between the ages of six and ten Ron attended a different school each year. Hence, his serene, peaceful childhood existed only in his mind. But we Americans dote on a past invented by Walt Disney, Henry Ford, and the creators of Williamsberg, where Main Street exists as a series of moral sketches where friendly, warm people live in perfect harmony under skies that are not cloudy all day.

It is a picture of America that even our youngest citizens have firmly entrenched in their minds, although they can only know such a past from the whimsical stories of their elders or through the even more fanciful recreations of television or film. Most young people insist that it was better to live in the good ol' days because people and families were much nicer then. Such thinking helps explain why our youngest voters were among the most enthusiastic supporters of our oldest president.

Garry Wills, whose 1987 *Reagan's America: Innocents at Home* is a superb biography of Reagan, tells his readers, "We regained our youth by electing the oldest President in our history....Reagan not only represents the past, but resurrects it as a promise of the future....He is the sincerest claimant to a heritage that never existed, a perfect blend of an authentic America he grew up in and of that America's own fables about its past. Americans' early days are spent playing cowboys and Indians--as Huck Finn's days were spent enacting Tom Sawyer's adventure-book fantasies. Fake Huck-Finnery is the real American boyhood, one that Reagan never had to give up. And now, through him, neither do we."

Where's the Rest of Me? describes Reagan's teenage years spent as a lifeguard in Dixon, Illinois, where he was supposed to have saved over 70 individuals from a watery grave and his undergraduate years at Eureka College where he had fond memories of playing football, swimming, cheerleading, being president of the Booster Club and the Student Senate, and giving ten cents to the first poor person he saw each morning, but he made no mention of any class or professor he encountered. By his own admission, he took the easiest classes, getting by with mediocre grades, and a good memory; yet, he insisted that his education at Eureka was much better than that experienced by those attending the University of California, Berkeley. Perhaps he was right. He once accused universities like Berkeley of "subsidizing intellectual curiosity".

Americans have seldom been bothered by what outsiders might consider anti-intellectualism. For example, when defending his Administration against cuts in education, Reagan himself once said, "My grade school didn't have any books and look how I turned out".

Reagan always put strong emphasis on family values, but no where in *Where's the Rest of Me?* did he mention his first two children and very little about his divorce from Jane Wyman. Actually, Reagan and his second wife, Nancy, had many problems with their children and were never particularly close to them or their grandchildren. But, again it was what Reagan said that was important, and his speeches were peppered with calls for the kinds of family virtues that he insisted characterized the America of his youth.

Like most Americans, Reagan also had a romantic vision of American history. It is the history visitors can find in Henry Ford's Greenfield Village or Walt Disney's Disneyland. This, of course, is the past of our imagination, without the contradictions, ambiguities, and bunk. Of his youth, Reagan wrote, "I was a 'cavalry-Indian' buff. I thought then, and think now, that the brief post-Civil War era when our blue-clad cavalry stayed on a wartime footing against the plains and desert Indians was a phase of Americana rivaling the Kipling era for color and romance."

As an actor, Reagan always wanted to star in Western epics but he had to wait for television's *Death Valley Days* to do much of that. His favorite movie role, however, was not in a Western, but in a maudlin football film called *The Knute Rockne Story*. Reagan played George Gipp, a legendary all-American football star who tragically died during his senior year at the University of Notre Dame. In its most unforgettable scene, Gipp lies dying but summons up enough strength to whisper to his beloved Knute Rockne, "Coach, when in some future game the going gets tough, maybe you could just ask the boys to win one for the Gipper." In reality, the real Gipp smoked, drank, gambled on games in which he played, attended practice irregularly, attended classes and exams even less often, and was dismissed from Notre Dame for misconduct. He then made his living hustling pool until pressure from fans forced his readmittance to the university. The entire "Win one for the Gipper" deathbed scene was actually invented eight years after Gipp's death by Coach Rockne who used it to inspire one of his mediocre teams on to victory, but the true story affected neither Reagan, breathless movie fans, nor Notre Dame University, which in 1981 gave Reagan an honorary doctorate.

Like Americans generally, Reagan believed that sports had great lessons to impart. In his 1981 Notre Dame speech he insisted that *The Knute Rockne Story* said much about America--that it was the story of an immigrant who "became so American that...he became an All-American in a game that is still to this day uniquely American. As a coach, he did more than teach young men how to play a game. He believed truly that the noblest work of man was building the character of man. No man connected with football has ever achieved the stature or occupied the singular niche in the nation that he carved out for himself, not just in sport, but in our entire social structure."

Reagan was also very fond of citing an incident from his own playing days at Dixon High to illustrate the values to be gleaned from competitive athletics. He claimed that in a game against neighboring Mendota he had called a penalty on himself which the game officials had missed, thereby causing his team to lose by a single touchdown. Unfortunately, a check of the records indicates that during Reagan's playing days Mendota only defeated Dixon once and that by a 24 to 0 score.

The Hollywood of Reagan's formative years reinforced notions of simplicity, permanence and individuality. Gary Wills, who called "Reagan the perfect Hollywood chastity symbol, one whose innocence became indistinguishable from ignorance," wrote, "Hollywood works at sustaining the illusion that a world totally altered in its technology need not touch or challenge basic beliefs. We are allowed to dream the wildest things, so long as we do not think anything new."

It was no accident that Reagan so often invoked Hollywood plots to illustrate how he imagined life to be; after all, in this cinematic world of make-believe it is always the heroic individual who proves capable of solving life's problems, regardless how complicated or entrenched these may be. Again, the problem of race is a case in point. Just as Reagan believed his own racial attitudes were solidified by an incident with a couple of football players so too did he insist it was individuals rather than governmental decree that had ended segregation in the Armed Forces:

> *When the first bombs were dropped on Pearl Harbor, there was great segregation in the military forces. In World War II this was corrected largely under the leadership of generals like MacArthur and Eisenhower....One great story...was when the Japanese dropped the bomb [sic] on Pearl Harbor there was a Negro sailor whose total duties involved in kitchen-type duties....He cradled a machine gun in his arms, which is not an easy thing to do, and stood on the end of a pier blazing away at Japanese airplanes that were coming down and strafing him and [segregation] was all changed.*

When informed by reporters that integration in the Armed Forces had first occurred in 1948, seven years after Pearl Harbor, Reagan responded, "But I remember the scene. It was very powerful." What he remembered was a movie scene--or perhaps a couple of them. He spent his World War II military service making propaganda films. In one of them the film-makers were told to include a few black soldiers. More likely, however, Reagan was thinking of a movie called *Home of the Brave*, in which a black sailor does exactly what Reagan described.

Heroic individuals do not need government help, whether it is some businessman saving a corporation or some black woman who cares for children without parents. When Nancy Reagan was going around the country visiting drug centers, her husband said, "These centers were started not by government but by people." But it is not just Reagan who believed in the supremacy of the individual--the vast majority of Americans do, just as the vast majority of Americans believe that government--and especially big government--is their enemy.

There was no evil in Reagan's movie roles. His only villainous role was in the made-for-tv film *The Killers* that he later regretted making. There could be no dark side to Reagan--indeed, to Americans. We had to be the children of light. When as governor of California Reagan refused to visit a mental hospital to see the results of his budget cuts, a psychiatrist suggested that the governor was under strain. Reagan replied, "When I get on that couch, it will be to take a nap." For Reagan, there was no need to excise or even to recognize the dark side of our nature. We were the good, and evil was an external demon to be destroyed. Consider Reagan calling the Soviet Union "The Evil Empire" or insisting "the Soviet Union was the mother lode, the center, which controlled subversives around the world."

Reagan saw the world through his Hollywood haze. He knew what happened to the Townies when the Baddies had all the weapons. They could be saved only when the hero rode into town with his giant six-shooter to crush the evil interlopers, and never did a Hollywood hero have to do this through negotiations. One cannot imagine John Wayne sitting down at the table for serious peace talks. If we could just walk tall enough, the rest of the world would have to respect us. And, of course, our tremendous arms buildup was supposed to accomplish that goal.

But reality does not always square with its Hollywood facsimile. The bombing of Libya was an interesting case in point. Reagan had apparently been told my his military advisers that they could perform a surgical strike on Qadhafi and his family. When innocent women and children were killed by the bombing, Reagan was very upset; such misfortunes did not happen in the movies. And even when his policies resulted in the loss of American lives, such as the killing of 241 Marines in Lebanon, Reagan could not confront the political realities that underlay the tragedy. When reporters asked him if their deaths were not proof of the bankruptcy of his policy, Reagan, with tears in his eyes, answered, "Why don't you ask their mothers."

Reagan's popularity can also be tied to popular religion. Most fundamentalists warmly embraced him, and he them. He had been raised by his mother in the fundamentalist Disciples of Christ sect, although she had promised her Irish husband to raise the two boys as Catholics. But the adult Reagan showed little interest in religion until he decided to run for office. His convenient rediscovery of a practical Christianity bothered most reporters not at all, although many of them were very disturbed by Jimmy Carter's born-again religion. Carter's religion, of course, was about man's fall, of the need for repentance, of humility. Carter talked about a malaise in the land. Reagan ran against Carter's "doom-and-gloom, and talked about feeling good and promised his listeners that "America was back."

This is certainly religion as popular culture in which sadness replaces sin as the real enemy of human nature. We Americans believe in our inalienable right to happiness, just as Ronald and Nancy Reagan believed in their lucky stars, reenforced, in their case, by a daily scrutiny of the astrological charts. This mystical sense of destiny, if not astrology, is so very American; indeed, the true religion of America is America, as President Calvin Coolidge made clear when he claimed that the perfection of our history proved that God had personally invented America.

Reagan's extraordinary success in using television is also noteworthy. Arguably, a single televised speech gave him the credibility that catapulted him onto the national scene. The year was 1964, and Republican candidate Barry Goldwater was running, as one pundit put it, like a dry stream. Shortly before the election, Reagan gave a 30-minute address that electrified the viewers. The *Washington Post's* David Browder called it "the most successful political debut since William Jennings Bryan's *Cross of Gold* speech in 1896."

It was essentially the speech he had been giving for years for General Electric, but his delivery stood out in sharp contrast to that of either Barry Goldwater or Lyndon Johnson. It was the speech he continued to give during eight years in the statehouse in California and eight more years in the White House. The speech did not read particularly well, but it played as well on television as it had to General Electric salesmen. Basically, it was standard anti-communism, anti-tax, anti-big government, pro-free enterprise fare. But it reassured Americans what they already half believed--that nothing was essentially wrong with them or their country that a tougher stand against the Russians coupled with a return to homespun virtues and the entrepreneurial spirit could not correct. It called for no sacrifices, no individual or community commitment to bettering society--just a return to the imaginary past of our popular culture.

In November of 1988, *Newsweek* editorialized that "Reagan's greatest impact on the presidency had less to do with concrete accomplishments than the personal aura he brought to the job....Reagan legitimized politics as theater, where sound bites, body language and stage skills counted more than command of facts." *Newsweek* and other critics accused his presidency of ushering in the era of the packaged candidate where everything was choreographed for the cameras, right down to the dog that eagerly greeted his helicopter homecomings. All true enough, but equally important was the fact that we all wanted to believe.

Gary Wills concluded his biography of Reagan with the observation, "Visiting Reaganland is very much like taking children to Disneyland." I think that's a bit unfair to our children. Wills overlooked the fact that two out of every three visitors to Disneyland are adults--the kids could care less about the historical themes--they just want to get on the rides. It is the adults who insist that we can be nostalgic about the future, and Ronald Reagan knew it all the time.

James Ferreira, *JOHN WAYNE: AN AMERICAN HERO*

During his five-decade film career, John Wayne was America's favorite movie hero; yet, as Ferreira points out below, his fame was based not on real accomplishments but on an image carefully nurtured by the actor himself. Born Marion Morrison, Wayne became much bigger than life, but only because he so well understood what Americans expected of their heroes.

John Wayne was the most American of heroes. He was admired everywhere as a folk hero and a living legend. Only Abraham Lincoln's face and name were more familiar to Americans. Without question, he was his country's most popular cultural icon. When he died in 1979, he was recognized as an international symbol of America. Yet in his lifetime, Wayne never did a thing that could be called heroic. He saved no lives, uttered no memorable phrases, performed no extraordinary deeds, nor made any scientific discoveries that might have contributed to the spiritual or material well being of his countrymen. And despite his identification with the military, he never saw combat in any American war. He was too young for World War I and too old for the Second World War. Once when on a tour of Vietnam, a stray round hit a few yards away from where Wayne was signing autographs. According to eyewitnesses, the Duke ignored the danger and kept on signing his name for the admiring grunts. It is the only recorded instance of John Wayne facing an enemy firing real bullets.

Nevertheless, Americans persist in worshipping the heroic John Wayne. When asked to name an authentic American hero, college students inevitably identify the Duke. His face is on postcards, posters, and books. There are four biographies and a number of studies of his films. Only the florid faces of Elvis Presley and the Aryan Jesus of Protestant America grace more velvet paintings in the parking lots of abandoned gas stations. The King and the Duke are immortalized in glowing masonite portraits at flea markets everywhere. These two examples of American nobility adorn decoupage clocks and stools sold at mall craft shows. There are also expensive commemorative dishes decorated with Wayne in the cavalry hat he wore in his Westerns, his steel pot from World War Two films and his Green Beret of the U.S. Special Forces. There's a bronze statue of Wayne as Rooster Cogburn and another of him standing in front of Orange County's John Wayne Airport. A special John Wayne Winchester rifle and a single action Frontier Model Colt .45 revolver are available to his fans. One advertisement for a reproduction of a U. S. mint commemorative medal claims the Duke "exemplified the American spirit." The medal's purpose, the ad assures us, is that "he may live in the hearts of Americans forever." And the videos of his films, especially the classic Westerns, guarantee Wayne's continued exposure for years to come. Yet despite all the relics and tributes, John Wayne was not a real person; he was a film character who was developed by an a man named Marion Morrison.

The most decorated American soldier of the Second World War was Audie Murphy, an authentic warrior, who has been all but forgotten by post-World War II generations. Soon he will share the same historical fate as Sergeant Alvin York, the great American hero of World War I. Real heroes have proven to be less enduring in our national memory than are symbolic creations. At the time of his death in 1971, Murphy was accorded none of the recognition given Wayne, in large part because the real hero didn't fit the cinematic image of a hero. Murphy was too short--only 5'5--and possessed a baby face. Murphy spent his career in Hollywood as the *boy* to Wayne's *man*. The movie version of Murphy's actual war adventures, *To Hell and Back*, is regarded critically as an inferior film to Wayne's *Sands of Iwo Jima*. Reality is always less interesting than myth.

John Wayne never actually lived. There was Marion Morrison, the actor, who invented a character millions of people around the world believed was authentic. The only thing shared by Marion Morrison and John Wayne was their body. Morrison was 6'4", with the ideal lanky, muscular body that is the stereotype of the "American" physique made popular by such other Hollywood heroes as James Stewart, Gary Cooper, Randolph Scott, Henry Fonda, and Ronald Reagan.

The character of John Wayne is an ingenious composite of elements borrowed from a variety of sources. Morrison imitated the drawl, squint and self-assurance of a native American cowboy who worked in his films as a stuntman. Director John Ford gave him the rolling gait. Howard Hawks taught him the trick of looking the other person in the eye and speaking quietly but with authority. The wrinkled forehead was a gesture he added to produce an open and guileless face. He added his personality and speech from the best selling novels of Zane Grey whose Westerns were the basis of hundreds of silent and sound movies. The costume and appearance were imitations of the cowboys in the widely reproduced paintings of Frederic Remington and the illustrations of Harvey Dunn and Matt Clark. Even the name John Wayne came from Revolutionary War hero Mad Anthony Wayne, although studio executives substituted John because Anthony sounded too Italian. But the determining factor in John Wayne's development was the subtle and intelligent reading of the kind of hero movie audiences demanded. Morrison presented an image Americans could embrace as an idealized fantasy of themselves as Americans. He became their magic mirror, a reflection of what popular culture told them they should be, and they made Marion Morrison rich, famous and politically influential beyond any rational reason.

John Wayne's pronouncements on the menace of communism, his unwavering support of the war in Vietnam, and his shameless flag-waving made him a hero of the radical right and a champion of nativist causes. Such politics only enhanced his popularity with middle America. To the fathers and sons of Main Street, whom Nixon once labeled the silent majority, Wayne was the quintessential patriot. As long as he was believable in his role as hero, what he had to say about history and politics, however extreme, made perfect sense. Image is everything, and truth becomes the sincerity a person can project. Not even those who disagreed with Wayne's position on Vietnam questioned his sincerity, nor did they suggest he might intentionally be advancing a position that had more to do with preserving his popularity at the box office than with keeping the world safe for democracy.

Marion Morrison gave the generation that survived the Depression, defeated World War II fascists, and created the righteous Empire a character that embodied their best sense of themselves. How he did this reveals a great deal about the mind and temperament of modern America. If John Wayne personifies the generation that has ruled America since the end of the World War, his fictional character embodies the attitudes and opinions that have defined this generation's self-image and perception. In thought and deed, John Wayne was the spokesman for a society that saw itself as the product of a pioneer heritage ritualized and idealized in the Western, morally triumphant in a good War, but which then lost its innocence in Southeast Asia. The disillusionment that followed the withdrawal from Vietnam gave us a tragic hero who was the victim of his own illusions. John Wayne died two deaths: one on film and another of cancer. His deaths should have liberated the younger generation from the debts owed to its predecessor and an opportunity to discover itself in a world in which John Waynes are anachronisms. But the emergence of such contenders for his crown as Clint Eastwood and Sylvester (Rocky-Rambo) Stallone suggest the symbolic Wayne is still alive.

Wayne's generation of actors grew up in the Hollywood star system. The school of acting that adapted itself to motion pictures was different than the style that came from the legitimate theater. They invented and perfected what is known as the natural style of acting. Their films survived on action, not dialogue. The characters they developed did not demand great emotional depth or range. To become a "star" the actor had to invent a "personality" that would draw at the box office. The secret was unself-consciously to portray a genuine character who projected an image of honesty and sincerity. When well done, the actor created a figure who gave the illusion of being "real." The criticism that these film stars always played themselves is wrong. They played characters people would pay to see play "themselves." Morrison did this so well with John Wayne that he did indeed become John Wayne, and his life became an endless movie.

There is something all too American about the career of John Wayne. He was, of course, an amazing success story, a genuine tale of rags to riches. He earned millions of dollars during his most productive years. He believed in the American dream, in upward mobility through hard work, ambition, and will power. He projected the image of the strong family man, although three marriages ended in divorce. Wayne's self-reliance and rugged individualism were achieved without a past, making it all up as he moved along, and in this he closely paralleled America's notion of itself..

There is, however, the darker side of John Wayne--and America. It is the right-wing paranoia, the suspicion of conspiracy, the reducing of complex issues to simple dogma, and the distrust of academics, intellectuals and liberals. In politics there was no apparent disparity between John Wayne and Marion Morrison. In fact, Morrison often used John Wayne as a spokesman for views that compensated for their lack of rationality by their sheer emotional and honest intensity. Morrison's John Wayne was a true believer. His more extreme views were kept off the screen, but in public and in interviews he did not hesitate to make the most outrageously irresponsible statements. His patriotism was of the simple "love-it-or-leave-it" school. A simple dualism characterized his political and moral pronouncements. As he put it, "They tell me everything isn't black and white. Well, I say, why the hell not?" General Douglas MacArthur and Wayne were friends and mutual admirers. Both were obsessed with communism as an ideological threat to the country. Wayne thought that Joseph McCarthy was a misunderstood hero and admired the Senator's efforts at purging the government of communists. McCarthy, Wayne believed, was ruined by the Eastern Establishment press and "murdered by leftists." He repeatedly stated his belief in the domino theory. He disdained intellectuals and academics and derided them as "theorists" who thought they knew how to run the world. He believed Ho Chi Minh was an agent of international communism and the Vietnam War another effort by the Soviets to extend their empire through surrogates. War protests and demonstrations on college campuses were caused by "immature professors who have encouraged activists."

For most of his life John Wayne was a power in the Hollywood anti-communist establishment. He was one of the founding fathers and the first president of the politically conservative Motion Picture Alliance for the Preservation of American Ideals. The MPAPAI invited the House Committee on Un-American Activities to investigate the film industry for communist subversion. Wayne was a close friend and ally of Ronald Reagan in the future President's crusade against Reds in the Screen Actors Guild. Wayne's friends in MPAPAI organized a vigilante group called the Hollywood Hussars, dedicated to driving communists out of Hollywood. Members included Victor McLagen and Ward Bond. In the film *Big Jim McClain*, Wayne played a HUAC investigator in Hawaii looking for a ring of communists. The initials of the lead character were JMC as were Senator McCarthy's. Wayne made the picture while president of MPAPAI, and it enhanced his image as a hard-core right winger and anti-communist. Although one critic panned it as a "gangster action film" equating communism with terrorism in an attempt to "reinforce the feelings of the very simple minded," *Big Jim McClain* was one of the most commercially successful anti-communist movies of the 1950's, and Wayne later claimed that the film's release in 1952 helped reelect McCarthy to a second term.

In 1960, John Wayne became a member of the John Birch Society, an organization of extreme right wingers pledged to save America from communists. Among their favorite conspiracies was Eisenhower as a dupe of the communists and the fluoridation of water as a Soviet plot to weaken the American will to resist. Democrats were traitors, FDR's New Deal had been a pro-Soviet conspiracy, and General George Marshall was an agent of the Kremlin. The Birchers favorite Americans were General Douglas MacArthur, Joseph McCarthy, J.Edgar Hoover, and actor John Wayne.

The right wingers' admiration for macho loners, the rough-tough Marlboro man, is a form of nostalgia. They mourn the passing of the 19th century rugged individuals and loath the inept bureaucrat and the power of red tape. All of John Wayne's film career was spent playing gutsy, mean, no-nonsense individualists who broke the rules whenever the situation required. Ultimately, Wayne became the symbol for American manliness and the need to redeem a world made uninhabitable by fuzzy-minded, overly sensitive, left-wing conspirators. Those extolling such views see themselves as having the divine right to exert their will over the will of others. This is racism disguised as biological nationalism justified as God's will. Imperialism is rationalized as manifest destiny, the belief that Americans have a divine right to other people's land. Whether biological nationalism or social darwinism, the words justify the killing and subjugation of people of color.

One of the few critics with the courage to state the obvious, was black New York film critic Clayton Riley. Writing in *Ebony* in 1972, Riley said the unspoken message in Wayne's movies is that "non-white people are by definition the villains of the world." The public's approval of Wayne's actions on the screen and as a model for American virility and courage helped "create and maintain the nation's myth of the supreme male primitive." Riley concluded that the long term purpose of the public's idealization of Wayne was to make "racism a legitimate and acceptable emotion" in the United States. As the "Great White Father" figure, Wayne protected Middle America's sense of moral superiority from doubt and guilt, thereby denying any need for reform in the system.

As a symbol of the idealized American male, Wayne is ultimately less important as a specific character than as the legitimizer of a state of mind. As Riley says, "Reagan, Agnew *et al.* often do just as well. All play the same charade, the contemporary version of the benevolent plantation master, always responsive to the needs of the niggers who knows how to behave themselves." If Marion Morrison as John Wayne could rationalize a racist position without shame or guilt, Riley asks, what does that tell us about a country that treats him as an object of national admiration?

In the notorious 1971 *Playboy* interview, Wayne discussed his beliefs, fears and prejudices. He argued for the maintaining of white supremacy until a sufficient number of blacks were adequately educated to accept political and social responsibility. He dismissed social security and medicare as socialism. As a reliable explanation of the causes for urban disorders, Wayne cited Fred Schwarz's Christian Anti-Communist Crusade's newsletters. He rationalized the seizure of Indian lands during the settlement of the country as a matter of survival of the fittest. The Indians weren't using the land anyway, argued Wayne. He urged threatening the Soviets with nuclear war to stop them from aiding North Vietnam. The loss of China, and the Korean and Vietnamese wars, proved the validity of the domino theory. Traitors in the State Department were responsible for national disasters. When asked the difference between the country he grew up in and the America of 1971, Wayne's answer was right out of the far right's book of conspiratorial fantasies. The fundamental difference Wayne saw was the existence in 1971 of an "enemy within our borders fighting with propaganda and coloring events in a manner that belittles our country."

Wayne had become the most famous and candid spokesman for old-fashioned American imperialism, the manifest destiny of the 19th century. He could rationalize imperialism when it was devoted to the pursuit of a higher good. Consequently, dispossessing Native Americans was totally justified. "But," Wayne lamented, "the do-gooders had to give it back to the Indians. Now Americans are forced to live in the cities." White culture, Wayne argued, is "progressive and we were doing something that was for the good of everyone." None of Wayne's public utterances or their ideological assumptions stand up to logical scrutiny. Myth rarely does. The rationale for grabbing Indian land, he saw as applicable to other "empty" countries. In 1961, after making the safari film *Hatari*, Wayne urged the colonization of Tanganyika "where young people could go and get a fresh start." According to Wayne, the frontier experience still existed in the thinly populated African country, and imperialism was not imperialism if the savages occupying the land did not know how to develop it. It was the logic of 19th century American settlers who redeemed the land from savagery, and now Tanganyika could become the new frontier for the youth of America and Europe.

One of the most compelling elements in the Wayne's persona is its identification with a kind of paternal authority. Film critic Molly Haskell and author Joan Didion have both written about Wayne's appeal to women and men as a sort of American father figure. To Didion, Wayne possessed a sexual authority even a "child could perceive." In his films, Wayne often plays a tamer of wild women, someone who gives the heroine the spanking she deserves. Women are children who need a beating the way a horse needs to be broken. There is no question that in the Duke's relationship with women he is the authority figure who finally shows "Miss Scarlett" who is boss.

During the Vietnam War, Harvard invited Wayne to speak to the student body. He went at a time when the anti-war movement had branded him one of the country's leading Hawks. The hostile Harvard students were charmed by Wayne and ended the evening applauding him. He explained his success by saying that he gave them the father figure they never had. In many of his films he played a teacher and authority figure who helped men and boys pass through a rite of initiation. In *The Green Berets*, he tells the orphaned Vietnamese boy the sacrifices the Americans are making are for him. When the boy dons the green beret of his dead benefactor, he is accepting Wayne's explanation for the tragedies of his life.

This innate authority the actor projected, the credibility Americans never questioned, was enhanced by age. The older Wayne became, the more he seemed to embody the best of the American past. In a sense, he became interchangeable with Uncle Sam, an old man's face on a powerful and virile body. Yet, it was largely history as fiction, a mythic version of a nostalgic and imagined past. To those obsessed with a vision of the American male becoming effete, Wayne was the ideal role model. In reality, he was a walking anachronism in the modern world, a combination of the "eternal Knight errant to a national audience of Walter Mitty" and the "pristine man of 19th century virtues fearing God but little else." Whether Wayne played a loner, a scout or a gunfighter who cannot be reconciled with advancing civilization, or the soldier, lawman or rancher helping others to create order on the frontier, is not as important as the general impression he left with audiences. He was simply the man on horseback, the symbol of American power, determination, and rectitude.

Two adulatory biographies describe Wayne as the descendant of Scotch-Irish pioneer stock, the ethnic group that the right insists "created democracy in America." His films glorify the "indomitable spirit that sent his Scotch-Irish ancestors West to help created from a harsh wilderness the prosperous and democratic civilization America became." Wayne epitomizes the "national virtues." With his great "American face," described as "tough," "friendly," "completely masculine," "simple," "clean-cut and virile," he was the "tall, rugged man of the West," the man director John Ford described as typically American. Admirers of Wayne admit that his attractiveness as a screen image was a mixture of nostalgia, a longing for self reliance and rugged individualism and a romantic sensibility that reduced moral issues to a simple right and wrong. The West and World War II, Wayne's most familiar cinematic settings, were arenas of action unclouded by moral ambiguity and relativism. Those who mock Wayne and his films, his sympathetic biographers tell us, are "basically vacuous individuals who, in the slick, soft and affluent world of today, disdain the courage and earthiness of the men who were the backbone of America."

The contention that the Scotch-Irish built the United States is a familiar part of nativist beliefs. It is sheer hyperbole. The point does, however, serve the interests of biological nationalists who ignore the contributions of other ethnic groups to the development of the country. Making the pioneer and the Westward movement the only national experience that produces the true American, is the familiar doctrine of Social Darwinism. The superior American endured the privations of frontier life. The strong survived and the weak died. The ethnic Americans who did not undergo the process of racial purification in the West are not complete or 100% Americans.

To make the West the authentic testing ground of the Nordic hero is to reduce if not eliminate the role played by other immigrant and ethnic stock. American heroes physically resemble the racial stock of Northern Europe. To be in the American grain the hero must have the All-American look of Marion Morrison and the other film heroes of the thirties who invented the type. The Aryan leading man has wavy hair, square jaws, cleft chins, broad shoulders, deep chests and wasp-like waists. The image is a literary convention that began in the literature of Cooper, passed through the Aryan hero of Owen Wister's celebrated *The Virginian,* and persisted through the film and television representation of the American type. Conversely, anyone can play a villain: Indians, Latins and swarthy Eastern and Southern Europeans were all interchangeable in the Hollywood which invented the Nordic hero and the mythology of the West.

In the world of the John Wayne Western, evil is any force that opposes the spread of American civilization. It is a world of order replacing the chaos of savagery and primitivism. The land must be made safe for private property, commerce, and rugged, self-reliant individuals. The collectivist, tribal communities of Indians and Mexicans represent not only a practical but a theoretical obstacle to this expansive and generous imperialism. Hence, the men and women who people the wilderness must be dehumanized for the silver screen. Their deaths and the extinction of their cultures make possible the growth of Christian civilization. Politicians, scientists, and other national leaders accepted the racial stereotype of Indians as noble but cunning savages and Mexicans as shiftless, lazy and treacherous greasers well before the Civil War. The spread of scientific racism quickly led to the division of humanity into a subhuman, inferior species too biologically degenerate to redeem by the superior Nordics who were destined to rule the world. The slaughter of the anonymous and faceless Indians, Mexicans and Asians is done without guilt. In Wayne's last films his victims fall to an increasingly powerful and destructive technology. The six gun of the Western becomes the helicopter gunship of *The Green Berets*, but the cruelty and fanaticism of the enemy still excuses the violence of enemy deaths. Not coincidentally, the elimination of the males also permitted the liberation of their exotic, passionate, and eager women whom the American hero always found irresistible.

The two most revealing film treatments of Wayne's vision of Americanism are *The Alamo* and *The Green Berets*. They are the only two films Wayne directed and produced. *The Green Berets* was a financial success but a critical flop; *The Alamo* was a failure critically and financially, in spite of receiving the enthusiastic endorsement of the John Birch Society.

Both are siege films of the block-house-under-attack variety. It is one of the oldest plot devices in American literature and popular culture. Wayne had been fascinated for years with the story of the Alamo. He managed to convince a few wealthy Texas to bankroll part of the film's high cost, although later he was criticized by them for portraying the Mexicans too sympathetically.

One of Wayne's long-time associates in the MPAPAI blamed the communists for *The Alamo's* bad reviews. East Coast critics were particularly harsh and confirmed Wayne's belief they were out to get him for his work on behalf of the MPAPAI and other right-wing causes. Since the film was a tribute to "Americanism," Wayne believed the critics decided to pan it and silence him at the same time.

In reality, the reviews in the Eastern press barely mentioned politics. Bosley Crother and Brendan Gill criticized the film for its excessive length, its sentimentality, and for a script that was described as a "model of distortion and vulgarization." The most common complaint was the film was too didactic. The critics who saw it as another expression of "better dead than red" rewritten as "better dead than Mexican," missed the point Wayne was trying to make. The Alamo was America itself under siege by a faceless, anonymous enemy.

Life magazine of July 4, 1960 contained a one-page ad paid for by Batjac, Wayne's production company, entitled, "There Were No Ghost Writers at the Alamo." "Nobody should come to see this movie," Wayne warned, "unless he believes in heroes." *The Alamo* is a call for unity of political and cultural differences in the face of a common enemy. The hero unifies the country, defends property and restores the nation's virility by reviving the "honest, courageous, clear cut standards of frontier days--the days of America's birth and greatness--the days when the noblest utterances of a man came unrehearsed." The sincere and spontaneous heroes of the Alamo needed no one to put words into their mouths. Their martyrdom for Texas independence was an example for all those who "prize freedom above tyranny, individualism above conformity." To recapture the heroism of the defenders of the Alamo, Wayne called for a revival of the moral and political values of the West. Ironically, in 1960 John Kennedy was the hero on horseback--and he did not come riding out of the West but out of the Harvard Yard.

The conduct of the war in Vietnam and the discord on the home front, confirmed for Wayne and his fellow crusaders on the right their belief that the country needed a revival of the frontier ethos to counter the corruption from within. The softies and do-gooders were responsible for the defeat in Vietnam. Wayne was an aggressive proponent of the belief that intellectuals and liberals in the media had stabbed the nation in the back. After a trip to Southeast Asia in 1967, Wayne was as eager to combat the Viet Cong on film as he was to blast "Bobby Kennedy and Fulbright and all those goddam let's-be-sweet-to-our-dear-enemies guys. All they're doing is helping the Reds and hurting their country." Anyone carrying a Viet Cong flag on the streets of this country he wanted shot. He was sure the Vietnam War was part of the international communist conspiracy orchestrated by the Kremlin. "*The Alamo*," said Wayne, "was to remind people not only in America but everywhere that there were once men and women who had the guts to stand up for the things they believed. The defenders of the Alamo and of the Green Beret camp in the film were such men."

The reviews of *The Alamo* were exemplars of generosity compared to those given *The Green Berets*. One critic ripped Wayne for creating a "glorification...of a wholly vicious war." Renata Adler in the *New York Times* called the film the "right-wing extremist's ideal of what we ought to be." *Time* dismissed it as a movie "strictly for the hawks." It was panned in *Variety* as a "prime example of anomalies and anachronism compounding credibility gaps and generation gaps." The reviewers were correct in seeing the film as the right wing's argument for the war. And Wayne confirmed the critics' case by blaming the negative reviews on "radic-lib Eastern critics." He seemed blissfully unaware that the film's depiction of the Viet Cong made them indistinguishable from savage Indians, treacherous Mexicans, cunning Japanese, and other past villains from Wayne's films. At a time when Americans were making their apologies to Native and African Americans, and were struggling to liberate themselves from a long history of racism, Wayne made a movie that pitted the Green Beret cowboys against the Viet Cong Indians.

Ironically, in his final role in *The Shootist*, Wayne played an old, dying gunfighter who has no place in a world of automobiles and electricity. If *The Shootist* is Morrison's epitaph, it is a curious one. He plays an anachronism dying of cancer who deliberately allows himself to be killed in a gunfight. The boy whom Wayne teaches how to use a gun revenges his fallen teacher but throws the pistol on the saloon floor in a clear rejection of that kind of violence. Whether or not it was a message Wayne chose to send, and he did have complete control over the script, makes for interesting speculation.

In the years before Morrison died of cancer, he devoted himself to helping President Jimmy Carter get the Panama Canal treaty through Congress. He was savagely attacked by his allies on the right for supporting Carter's treaty and broke with Ronald Reagan over the issue. Morrison had been married to three Latin women and had been in business in Panama. He attacked Reagan who was using the issue to try and wrest the Republican presidential nomination away from Ford. In an open letter Wayne wrote to Reagan, he criticized his old friend for distorting the truth for political expediency. Reagan's position compromised the American tradition of justice and fair play, and Wayne was angry with Reagan for so blatantly playing politics.

It is tempting to think that in his final years Morrison was liberating himself from John Wayne, that the real man wasn't the nativist and political extremist he played all his life. John Wayne's last public appearance was at the Oscar ceremonies of 1977. He came on stage to present the award for best picture. His body was ravaged by cancer, and it was obvious he was a dying man. Yet he persisted to the end in playing the role that had made him rich and famous. He told the audience he was just ambling out on stage when in reality he had spent over two weeks of painful exercises strengthening himself so he could walk out on the stage alone. It was a genuine act of courage that fit the John Wayne image.

In an editorial in *The Saturday Review*, Norman Cousins pondered the meaning of John Wayne as an American hero. "Wayne," Cousins heard a radio announcer say, "represented the essence of Americanism: he shot first and asked questions afterward." Similar tributes to the movie gunslinger troubled Cousins. Why, he asked, must American heroes be men of "casual violence?" To Cousins, honoring violence and random brutality at the expense of the rule of law was not a sign of strength but of weakness. Such admiration leads, Cousins insisted, "to self-destruction as surely as it leads to a cheapening of life itself." If we choose a gunman as a national hero, we choose to exalt violence over reason. Cousin concluded, "One should not be shocked that mindless violence should be a familiar feature of our daily lives." Indeed, we should not.

Lewis Easterling,
OBSERVATIONS OF AN AGING, UNEMPLOYED, MIDDLE-CLASS WHITE MAN

A former junior college instructor who left the teaching profession in the 1970's, Lewis Easterling was a 54-year-old, middle-management executive in 1986 when he was terminated by a small, Midwestern manufacturing company, just two years before he would have been eligible for the company's retirement plan. He spent the next several years looking for work, only to discover that a middle-aged male has few options. After his marriage dissolved in 1990, he moved south to San Antonio, Texas, where he now tries to stretch his meagre savings doing substitute teaching. He has no health insurance and is grimly hoping that his body gives out before his money does. What follows are excerpts from what he calls his "Ghetto Journal" which he began keeping after moving into a low-income housing project in San Antonio in August of 1990.

August 12, 1990:

I have begun anew. At the age of 58 I have begun another voyage in life, a voyage in which I have no planned destination. My travels have taken me from the cool, rock strewn shores of Lake Michigan to the hot, wilted prairies of Texas; taken me from family and friends to strangers and solitary confinement; taken me from no hope of employment in Michigan to meagre possibilities in Texas.

As I sit here watching my new neighbors, I am confused. I still wonder what has happened, why I'm here, where I'm going. I am an old man without a job. Back in the fifties, I was young, inexperienced, under-qualified and unemployed. Now I am old, experienced, over-qualified, and unemployed. What goes around comes around.

It is now more than four years since I was cashiered by the company I worked for. At first I joked about my situation, telling others my dismissal was congenital. My father had been laid off by a company that moved its plant to the South. He had worked there for over a quarter of a century and was in his late fifties when they let him go. He was unable to find a job, and he died before collecting his social security pension. Thirty years later the same thing is happening to me. Like father, like son.

I no longer joke about my situation.

August 19, 1990:

Trying to acclimate myself to Texas heat, culture, cuisine, and speech as I try to reconstruct my past.

July 15, 1986 was the date of the Wednesday afternoon massacre, when the Kysor Company cut some 20% of its management personnel. It had been a great place to work. I had accomplished a lot for the company, and I planned to stay until retirement. My wife and I had bought a home on a lake, a nice fishing boat, and we had settled in for what we considered would soon be a pleasant retirement. But then the Chief Executive Officer retired and an outside CEO was brought in from a larger firm. He brought along his own people, and the working environment was transformed from a "family" atmosphere to one of fear and distrust. They began weeding out the old employees and replacing them with younger imports. By the time I was "axed" I was one of the oldest employees there, both in terms of age and length of service. I had mixed emotions at the time. I had never been laid off before and telling my wife was the most difficult part of it. I put off telling her for three days.

I was given eight weeks' pay and that was that. But I wasn't really worried; in fact, I rather looked forward to finding a new job with new challenges. I had an extensive portfolio and lots of confidence in my abilities, but that didn't seem to impress the frumpy woman at the Employment Security Commission who announced, "It's going to be difficult finding a job at your age." I had gone to the Commission to register for unemployment benefits and to learn of job opportunities in the area. Today, four years later, I can still picture that woman's face and hear her words, and now I certainly understand her message.

August 25, 1990:

My asylum is an orbiting planet called Earth. I live in the building called North America, in the United States wing, the Texas ward, the San Antonio corridor, and my room is in the ghetto. As I stare out the window of my cell I can see men breaking off dead branches of gnarled mesquite trees to build a fire, and I am reminded of James Thurber who sat by his window and watched men cut down elm trees--to clear a site--to build an institution--to house people who had been driven insane by the cutting down of elm trees.

I write because I'm bored, and I send my thoughts to people I consider my friends because the only friend I have in San Antonio is the mailman.

I'm learning redneck and espanol. I've also tried to fit into the gastronomic culture of the city but this has been difficult. I have no appetite and eat little. I only leave the apartment early in the morning when the temperature is still in the low 80's. I did try some Texas made Salsa and cried all night. My eyes are still misty this morning. And it was only "medium." I can't imagine what hot would be, but I'll learn.

My apartment complex is a low-income project (for which I now qualify). I am surrounded by blacks and Hispanics. I did see one Caucasian a few days ago. I suspect that many of my neighbors are members of Bush's Unemployed Brigades.

During the past week, in separate incidents, two drunk Hispanics fell asleep on the railroad tracks and were run over by a train. Last night a three-year-old boy was killed in a drug-related, drive-by shooting.

September 1, 1990:

It's estimated that a quarter of San Antonio's school kids are on drugs or booze, and as high as 60% in some schools. I hope to begin subbing soon, so I'll check it out. Subbing only pays $40 a day, but this will help conserve my savings and, hopefully, give me a chance for something more permanent.

I have seen an armadillo and killed a cockroach. Does this qualify me as a Texan?

You can't believe the size of the boom-boxes in my apartment complex.

September 9, 1990:

It's been four weeks since I arrived in San Antonio; that's over .14% of my entire life. If I survive until New Year's Day, I'll have spent .7% of my life in San Antonio. That's depressing. I'm plagued with morning sickness. I have difficulty acclimating to the new day. Perhaps it's because I'm forced back to reality by the light. By noon my biological and psychological clocks are in sync once again, and I feel better; I feel like any other 58-year-old unemployed ghetto resident.

Adjusting to a new world and a new way of life is difficult for anyone, but it is especially difficult for the old, and it is compounded if one is trying to adjust alone or without a crutch. I am old, alone, and adjusting without booze, so it's "muy dificil".

September 10, 1990:

Feeling a little indigo for not having children. When I go, my branch of the family tree drops off and will soon be forgotten; my name will never be discussed by future generations seeking their roots. But having no family and few friends limits the scope of my depression. Writing my thoughts on paper does lift the depression for at least an hour or two.

George Washington was born in Texas. One day his father went outside to water his favorite cactus plant and when he saw that it was chopped down, he roared, "Who cut down my favorite cactus?" "It was I," said little George. "I cannot tell a lie, it was I who chopped it down." Mr. Washington thought about little George all night and decided if George couldn't tell a lie, they couldn't continue to live in Texas--so they moved to Virginia.

Four killed in separate incidents last night.

I've noticed that most television advertisements are for lawyers or voc-tech schools. Either you successfully sue someone or you learn a trade.

September 18, 1990:

Pulling myself out of my abyss of despair, my mind scales the cliffs of hope, gazing upwards to the peaks of what may be. I need a woman!

Wanted! Rich woman to save mature raconteur from self-abuse.

September 20, 1990:

San Antonio is having a flea infestation, and the apartment complex is being sprayed. This is the most exciting thing that's happened to me during the past week.

Tomorrow I start visiting schools where I'd like to sub. Maybe then I can start living instead of merely surviving. Surviving is a cruel word, implying the lowest form of existence. You hear of someone surviving three years as a prisoner of war or surviving six weeks drifting at sea in a rubber raft. You never hear of someone living in a POW camp or on a life raft. Survival is not living.

September 23, 1990:

Just completed my Texas Teachers' Test to prove that I can read and write.

I'm feeling alive. I subbed today, and that has done wonders for my psyche. It was a suburban school and the kids were great.

October 10, 1990:

28,000 burglaries in San Antonio last year. That's about one for every 25 people.

175 murders in San Antonio so far this year. We need only 15 more for a new record.

There was a murder in our apartment complex last night, the first one since I've been here. The victim was a 31-year-old unemployed veteran. The suspect was his friend.

It is difficult living in a strange city with strange people, strange customs, and strange weather.

It is difficult living on a poverty budget: no frills and no treats.

It is difficult living without hope for the future.

It is difficult being an observer of the problems of life, but being unable to participate in finding a solution for such problems is the most difficult aspect of my life.

October 12, 1990:

Bad night! My neighbors, Boom Box Moogie and his girl friend Mattie were fighting until the wee hours. I would hear the door slam and Moogie would walk out to the parking lot. The door would slam again and Mattie would holler at him, and then shuffle out to the lot where they would holler at each other. Then they'd return to the apartment, close the door, and start hollering again.

October 20, 1990:

The life of the ghetto nomad. A rusty, broken down car has replaced the camel. This modern nomad packs all his possessions into his steel steed and moves on. A lifetime of belongings and memories cramped into the back seat of General Motor's finest. And when there is no further place to move, and his steed dies, he takes to the streets to become one of the permanently homeless.

We waste the first twenty years of most of our people; we waste the last twenty years of many of our people; and we waste the middle thirty years of some of our people. That's a lot of waste.

October 22, 1990:

The will to survive is directly influenced by hope, and hope is influenced by poverty. As poverty increases, hope decreases, as does the will to survive. This may account for the high crime rate and the violence of the ghetto. These people "live on the edge," taking chances and engaging in implicitly dangerous behavior that often results in violence and even death.

But, as one of our former politicians said, "If you want security, join the army or go to jail."

October 23, 1990:

I taught in a school today that offers classes in basketball, baseball, and other sports-related courses, but which doesn't have enough money for a decent science lab.

An irate mother shot an assistant principal in one of the San Antonio schools yesterday because she didn't like the way he was treating her son.

It must be autumn. The mesquite trees are changing colors, changing from a dull green to a dull yellow, and our apartment landlord told us to flush our toilets once an hour when the temperature falls below freezing. We call this modern ghetto technology.

November 1, 1990:

Just got back from a day with fourth grade students. I'm beginning to wonder if I made the right decision when I selected Texas as my teaching state. The schools are run like a boot camp for marines: no talking, no questioning, and when I attempt to stimulate thought and discussion an assistant principal comes in and tells the children to behave. Kids are still paddled. Maybe it's the military influence. San Antonio is filled with retired military personnel, and a lot of them have gone into education.

"For more than 100 years much complaint has been made of the unmethodical ways that schools are conducted. It is in the last thirty that we have tried to find a solution for this state of affairs, and with what result? Schools remain exactly as they were."

John Amos Comenius said those words in 1632. That's 360 years ago, and nothing much has changed.

Maybe I'll feel better tomorrow; then, again, maybe I won't.

November 2, 1990:

No work today so I sit here, watching television reruns.

Four convicts, two of them murderers, escaped from our San Antonio jail, and it was 14 hours before anyone noticed they were missing. Makes one feel good about the criminal justice system in Texas.

November 12, 1990:

The state lottery is another step closer to becoming a reality, and the ghetto people are beginning to celebrate. Poor people love the lottery, although, in reality, it's another tax they pay for being poor. The lottery provides hope and builds dreams, at least for a couple of days. It allows one to believe in destiny. Then comes renewed depression when they learn they didn't have the winning numbers, but with the next ticket the process begins anew. So the poor forego a loaf of bread or a carton of milk and buy a ticket--a chance. Man does not live by bread alone.

November 13, 1990:

San Antonio has long had many German immigrants, and I've noticed their influence on the Mexican community where many of the Hispanic girls have a reddish sheen to their coal-black hair and are thinner and finer boned than the other Mexican girls who have no "deutsch" blood.

November 14, 1990

An old man is prowling the parking lot early this morning before the huge garbage trucks arrive to empty the dumpsters. He's old and wrinkled with cheeks and jowls hanging down in a series of accordion pleats. His bony fingers clutch a broom handle with a wire hanger twisted on its end. He shuffles along in mismatched tennis shoes, peering inside the dumpsters, using his make-shift tool to fish through the trash of the night before.

I do not know his name or his story, but he is one of a growing army of homeless and hungry who haunt the city's streets. It is pathetic to watch the old and impoverished members of society in their quest for survival. We cannot explain the "old-poor" by any measure other than fate and an uncaring society. They are a hodge-podge of education, experience, race, and religion. Some have spent their entire lives scratching for survival while others have found poverty to be a more recent curse. Except for a couple of thousand dollars and a few subbing jobs I could be there with them.

November 15, 1990:

Just returned from the Robert E. Lee High School which features a 20 by 30 foot Confederate flag painted on one of the buildings. Many smaller versions hang in the classrooms. 95% of the students are Hispanic. I subbed for the history teacher whose main job is to coach football. His students knew nothing and cared less.

November 16, 1990:

I have reached the age where one begins to look back and assess the impact of his life. My biological clock is running down, and I feel the need to quantify and qualify my existence. I have little to show for my years of riding spacecraft earth. Mumps prevented any new shoots on the ol' family tree, and a mistrust learned from experience prevented the accumulation of many friends.

Good night. Dream time.

November 21, 1990:

It's the day before the Thanksgiving, the holiday of feasting and rejoicing for all the good things that have happened to us. I bought a pumpkin pie and some shaved ham for sandwiches, and that's as close to Thanksgiving as I'm going to get. Home for the holidays.

Went for a walk. Saw a man in his thirties or early forties, with matted hair, sunken eyes, and a drawn face. He wore a pair of soiled jeans and a tattered denim shirt with boots that made him appear taller than he was. He stood on the sidewalk near the entrance of a grocery store holding up his cardboard sign: "Will work for food."

November 25, 1990:

Three days after Thanksgiving. I awoke with a stranger in my bed. I had never considered him strange before; I thought I knew him well, but the more I think of him, the more alien he becomes. I was the stranger in my bed--the stranger in my life.

I hoard my emotions and do not share them with others. I cry inwardly. I have a secret laugh. I used to use alcohol as the solvent to release these emotions, but alcohol is at best a temporary reprieve.

November 27, 1990:

Professional wrestling is big in Texas but that doesn't surprise me. Anything big with a beer belly and lots of bullshit would be big in Texas.

November 29, 1990:

Over 200 people participated in the Third Annual Hill Country Machine Gun Shoot near Helotes, Texas, firing over 100 automatic weapons and shredding countless old refrigerators and other strange targets. One of the shooters explained, "Can you think of a better way to spend a holiday weekend? Soldiers died so we'd have the right to shoot all we want."

That brings a whole new meaning to the word "patriotism", but I'm not sure the four kids who were gunned down in San Antonio last night would agree.

New record of 202 murders in San Antonio. We broke the old record by twelve and still have five weeks to go in the year. Most are black or Hispanic, many are gang related or involve family or friends. There's very little "Gringo" blood spilled in San Antonio. I suspect the same could be said for Detroit, Chicago, or any other major city that contains large minority populations. The San Antonio police estimate that the "Mexican Mafia" accounts for over one-third of the homicides, and these are usually drug related.

There's an obvious correlation between the increase in crime and the growth of the police state. As crime increases, citizens demand more and more protection until the added protection results in fewer and fewer freedoms. People will always choose security over freedom.

November 30, 1990:

I've become a coupon clipper! Saved 85 cents on my last shopping "spree," including 15 cents on a four-pack of Charmin. Wouldn't Ben Franklin be proud of me.

A San Antonio girl just gave birth to a baby, stuffed it in a bowling bag and put it in the closet so her parents wouldn't find out.

December 4, 1990:

My spirits sank last week when a crown fell off one of my teeth and my car radio died. Knowing that bad things always happen in threes, I spent the week waiting for the third shoe to fall.

Today it did when my car battery died, but seven years of service is no cause for complaint. I feel better now that all three have occurred, but I'm still not jolly even though that season is quick upon us.

December 5, 1990:

Freedom spawns the most inefficient form of government because consensus is so difficult to achieve. This means that small, well-organized, and well-financed interest groups can exert inordinate influence and power. I'm thinking of the tobacco lobby that manages, year after year, to have the U.S. Government spend millions of the taxpayers money to support tobacco farmers, at the same time another branch of the government is spending more taxpayer money to research and warn against the dire effects of smoking.

December 6, 1990:

I'm filled with solutions today. AIDS? Infect one of President Bush's children with the virus or those of a top senator or congressman, and within weeks there would be limitless funds appropriated for AIDS research.

Racism? No sweat. Have Congress and the National Basketball Association trade personnel for a season.

December 7, 1990:

San Antonio is having problems with panhandlers who are not only begging money but demanding it. These panhandlers run up to a car at a stop light, rub a dirty rag across the windshield and demand $5 for cleaning. Some are getting violent if the "customer" doesn't want to pay. This is capitalism at its worst--or best--depending on your political bent.

Just went across the patio and asked if they would turn down the volume on their boom box. This is the third apartment that I've done this to, and all have been courteous and complied with my request. Maybe I'll shape up the housing project after all.

December 12, 1990:

If I make it through the holidays and into '91, I'll have to change my modus operandi to remain sane in this asylum. I'm sure the pending holidays are responsible for my present state of mind; Maybe I'll leave Spring Hills; maybe I'll leave San Antonio; maybe I'll leave Texas; maybe I'll leave.

Maybe I'll go to Iraq--or Iran. Some place where they haven't heard of "rap." Somewhere where the men work and the women stay home. Down here the women go to work and the men stay home, play rap music and drink beer from those big gallon containers--or dribble basketballs on the sidewalks.

On top of all this, I now find that I'm officially a tenant of the United States Government which has taken possession of Spring Hills as a result of the Savings and Loan fiasco. Where will my rent money now go? Will it go for bullets or butter.

Housing and Urban Development folks just came by and did a maintenance inventory on my apartment and pronounced everything in excellent shape. They gave a code number to everything, ignored me completely, and left.

December 13, 1990:

Nothing destroys the human mind and body faster than inactivity. This afternoon and tomorrow I'll be active in a high school biology class, and my mind and body will feel great. It's the days when the phone doesn't ring and there is nothing to do that I feel myself slipping into the abyss.

December 14, 1990:

I'm back, and I feel good. I feel useful. Most of the kids were attentive and a joy to be around. Today we studied the various means of reproduction, and tomorrow we'll be studying sexually transmitted diseases. I'm well versed in both of these subjects.
I've got a good memory.

December 16, 1990:

I have worked the past three days! As a reward, I've indulged myself each day with a Mexican meal at three different cantinas. Two were great, and one was Tex-Mex and not so good. It's the little things that count when you don't have much.

December 17, 1990:

A San Antonio elementary teacher was shot by a student when he attempted to break up a fight. And this was in *elementary school!*

Eviction Day. The women in the next apartment were given the boot. Spring Hill employees, accompanied by two sheriff's deputies, moved all their furniture out on the front weeds, and there's now a convoy of rattletrap cars loading up and moving out. One of the women is sitting behind her ironing board shielding herself from the sun. The other one is carrying the aquarium out, sloshing water over the sides--surfing fish. What a nice Christmas present.

December 18, 1990:

Only 13 more days! What will 1991 bring? Will I survive the year? Will the world survive? It's a bizarre life and world.

Speaking of bizarre, the San Antonio police have accused a cat of killing its master with a .22 rifle. The feline allegedly shot him in the head by accident, according to one of the police detectives. I think it's a bizarre police force.

December 21, 1990:

1000 people a day are going into the bathroom of a gas station in a small Texas town because the Virgin Mary has appeared on the floor in the form of a stain.

In Dekalb, Texas, a police officer and his wife were arrested for a series of burglaries and for drug trafficking.

The homeless increased by nearly one-third in San Antonio this year, and 44% of these are families.

December 31, 1990:

The five men Americans most admired in 1990, in descending order, were George Bush, Mikhail Gorbachev (he probably belongs), Ronald Reagan, Pope John Paul II, and Billy Graham. No wonder we're in trouble.

1,000,000 new jobs were created in 1990, but there were 7,300,000 unemployed, and at least another 7 million people such as myself who are either not registered with the government or are underemployed.

Happy New Year!

1,400,000,000 tons of carbon dioxide were released into the air and 522,000,000,000 cigarettes were smoked. End result: 157,000 new cases of lung cancer in the U.S. in 1990.

154 banks and 190 savings and loan institutions went bankrupt in the first eleven months of 1990. Our President says that all is well.

San Antonio had 218 homicides in 1990--a new record--but less than a tenth New York City's total and about 40% of the City of Brotherly Love (Philadelphia).

January 2, 1991:

A brand new year and a brand new roll. I have just begun my seventh roll of toilet paper since moving into Spring Hills, an average of 3.02 weeks per roll. Life hasn't been as shitty as I thought.

January 9, 1991:

The Stealth fighter plane contract is cancelled on the national level, but it is flourishing in Texas.

"Stealth Condoms, Inc." of Taylor, Texas, are producing and selling red, white, and blue condoms, and using the advertising slogan, "They'll never see you coming."

Maybe I'll apply for a job as "A War Starter." It's the only job where old age is actually an advantage.

January 12, 1991:

I've just finished my seventh roll of Texas toilet paper, and this one only took 1.7 weeks to consume. Perhaps it's because the "dead"line is approaching. Only three more days until we go after Saddam. I've spent the last three days watching and listening to our elected representatives debating the "Catch 22" of 1991.

As long as the world's industrial nations depend upon oil, and as long as Israel is surrounded by Arab states, we will find the Middle East a major source of problems.

If the Jews are God's chosen people how come He gave the Arabs all the oil?

January 15, 1991:

I'm beginning to babble as the bewitching hour approaches. Only seven hours left for Saddam. I purchased a bottle today in preparation for increased hopelessness.

I predict the fireworks will begin at 11:00 tomorrow morning when darkness arrives in the Mideast, and the spectre of John Wayne begins his nightly trek across the desert.

The Koran, Talmud, and Bible all going to war. God must be proud.

January 16, 1991:

I was wrong! It's now past noon and all's quiet. I don't like being wrong.

I was six hours off. "Desert Storm" just replaced "Desert Shield."

January 18, 1991:

Insanity! Madness! Lunacy! Dementia! If Kuwait did not have oil, no one would have given a tinker's damn about her fate, and rightly so. But Kuwait has oil. The entire Middle East has oil, and we want it.

Some of the inmates in my asylum are revolting; others are getting rich; some are dying; but the head crazy in our wing of the asylum has a new approval rating . 86% of the crazies believe he's doing a great job.

Bush is trying to "teach" Saddam a "lesson." Do you suppose that's what he meant when he said he wanted to be known as the "education" Prez?

January 20, 1991:

Desert Storm is already passé. After three days of nonstop news coverage of the carnage, San Antonio TV has returned to its usual weekend menu of cartoons, sports, and "I Love Lucy" reruns.

But passé is not past, and the problems spilling out of "Saddam's Box" will out-pandora Pandora. Saddam will be replaced by another bully boy--in Syria or Iran, it makes no difference. This will continue as long as we depend on their oil and as long as the Jews and the Arabs cannot find a way to live together in peace.
We will always be "The Great Satan" to the "Saddamites."

Oil money! The price of crude went down a third and the stock market went up 114 points. Our economic engine runs on the price of oil, as do the engines of all industrialized countries. Desert Storm is the price we pay for the lack of an energy policy. It is what we are doing to insure that the economies of Japan and Germany do not falter.

January 22, 1991:

Texans are buying every gas mask in sight, preparing for the day when those "God-damn Air-rabs" bring their terrorism to the Lone Star State. 'Tis a great time to own a military surplus store--or flag shoppe--or to be selling yellow ribbons.

I imagine it's a bad time to be managing a 7-11 store in Detroit or driving a cab in Washington, D.C. where the majority of these people are Arabs. I wouldn't like to be an Arab living in Texas. I don't even want to be me living in Texas.

January 26, 1991:

I remember the rows of books in the dimly lit room of Hackley Public Library, where our eyes strained in the dim light to gaze upon the exotic breasts in the *National Geographic*. I remember the *Sears and Roebuck Catalog* and the first issue of *Playboy*. I can remember my first opportunity and my first inability to perform. They were one and the same. Her name was Marlene, and we parked by Lake Michigan in my Chevy Power Glide. I didn't, couldn't, wouldn't. I am now reliving my youth.

My dreams continue. In the past I used a bottle to induce sleep and fermented grains and grapes twisted the cords of my brain, choking off any remembrance of the visions that sleep portrayed. Now I've replaced the bottle with a bed. I dream in 3-D, color, and total recall in the morning. I can travel, meet the rich and famous and have sex when, where, and with whom I wish.

But I'm awake now and reality is a cruel taskmaster. Desert Storm is now in its second week and shows no sign of letting up--or of accomplishing much. Prez Bush, speaking before an organization of religious broadcasters, called it "a just war." I think he should leave out the "a".

A Baptist church in San Antonio features a big sign: "Keep Bombing Sad Dam Hussein." Which Commandment is that?

Television evangelist Pat Robertson just announced, "This is not a war; it's a revival." He's pushing his "The Armor of God" sales package to rake in money for his own revival.

February 1, 1991:

There are no wars in my dreams; no crime; no discrimination; no politicians.

Freud defined dreams as "the imaginary gratification of unconscious wishes." My wishes are conscious.

Just had a Salsa break and my mouth's aflame, a male "hot lips" for all the wrong reasons. Since I'm eating Mexican every day, I've noticed a marked improvement in my physical feelings, but, then, I've also given up cigars and that may have something to do with it. No cigars, booze, coffee, sex, or religion. I've given them all up. Some were easier than others.

February 8, 1991:

In a small town outside of Houston a Lone Star mom so wanted her daughter to be selected to the cheerleading squad that she hired a "hit man" to waste the mother of the girl against whom her daughter was competing for the final spot on the squad. She reasoned that the other girl would be so distraught by her mother's death that she would drop out of the competition. The hit man turned out to be an undercover policeman who accepted a pair of diamond earrings as a down payment. Mom originally wanted both mother and daughter done in but could only afford the mother. Perhaps she only had one set of earrings.

February 12, 1991:

Feast or famine. I worked one half day in January, but today is the first day I've had off in February. Elementary, junior high, high school, I've had them all. This increased activity has lifted my spirits in spite of the rainy weather.

Have you ever been hugged by a little black boy? Not a fag dwarf but a first grader who wanted to bond after only five hours together.

February 14, 1991:

Valentine's Day, the day for lovers. Just returned from the store where I watched customers buying cards, flowers, candy, condoms, etc. to celebrate this day with their loved ones. I bought some yogurt, pretzels, and distilled water.

Even unpleasant experiences have their value.

I'm trying to find the value of my present experience.

February 25, 1991:

Our nothing who art in nothing,
nothing be thy nothing
Thy nothing come, thy nothing done,
On nothing as it is in nothing.

I'm in my nothingness period, a hollow man in a wasteland. I identify with the old waiter in Hemingway's "A clean, well-lighted place" when he used the "prayer" quoted above.

Just received a phone call, and tomorrow I'll be teaching math in a junior high--not my favorite level but my favorite subject so things may wash out. Last Friday was a great day. Spent it with honor students in a Shakespeare class in which I got my chance to recite Hamlet.

February 28, 1991:

Bush's approval rating will now climb to 90%--maybe even 95%. Why do Americans get so stirred up by such a nasty, one-sided little war? I'm again in the minority.

I broke even in February. My subbing income matched my housing and food expenses for the first time since I came to Texas.

March 1, 1991:

Just got back from five hours of "reading improvement" classes, but I had no problems. The kids were quiet and well behaved. Stopped and had my Mexican dinner #2 and a bottle of Dos Equis to celebrate the week's end. Then I bought a liter of vodka for $4.99 to celebrate the beginning of the weekend.

Bush's approval rating only went up to 85%, not the 90% I predicted yesterday. He's at 99% in San Antonio.

"Stormin' Norman" for vice-president in 1992--and for president in '96 and 2000. And then Colin Powell in 2004 and 2008. Quayle is Ka-put. Violence is in. Pacificism is "wimpy."

Thought for the day: "Congress" must be the opposite of "Progress."

Second thought for the day: How come we can make "Smart Bombs" but not "Smart Kids?"

Now that we've thrashed Saddam, perhaps we can turn our attention to more pressing problems at home. We might begin with our own sorry educational system. A 1983 report ("A Nation at Risk") concluded: "If an unfriendly power attempted to impose on America the mediocre educational performance that exists today, we might well have viewed it as an act of war. As it stands, we have allowed this to happen to ourselves....We have, in effect, been committing an act of unthinking, unilateral disarmament."

Now that's language any Hawk can understand.

April 8, 1991:

I'm chucking education. I came to Texas because of their system of education and because they desperately needed competent teachers. I hoped I could help, but my hopes have been dashed. I had an interview for a permanent teaching job, but at its conclusion the professional-educator-interviewer informed me they didn't hire anyone without a teaching certificate. The fact that I had taught for twelve years at a junior college evidently didn't count for anything. I did make the mistake of mentioning some ideas I had for teaching kids. Ideas are always a dangerous thing to the educational establishment.

I'm now told that I will have to pay some $10,000 for a piece of paper saying that I'm qualified to teach and that there is no possibility without a certificate of being hired by a decent school district--and there's no guarantee that an indecent district would hire me. Perhaps I'm not meant to work anymore. Perhaps I'm meant to move on to Mexico.

April 16, 1991:

Yesterday was tax day, and I mailed in my contribution to "smart bombs" and the Savings and Loan bailout. God, it's great to be a tax-paying citizen who is able to see where his money is going.

April 18, 1991:

I subbed in a fourth grade class yesterday. When I walked the class to recess, this little black girl grabbed my hand for the journey. At the end of the day I got about a dozen hugs. I must confess that my emotions are mixed about this "bonding." It does massage my ego as a teacher, but I fear that if I hug too long or too hard, I'll be accused by some frightened administrator of excessive fondling or sexual depravity.

We can now buy a Desert Storm video for less than $20.

The war was easy. The peace will be the difficult part.

Tis a depressing time, filled with depressing thoughts, events, and predictions for the future.

The "farm" is sounding better and better with each depressing day. I am tired of life--of living. I would like to buy the farm.

May 21, 1991:

I've shaved my beard in an attempt to appear younger, to appear not to have "a low energy level" to the three-piece suited state educational official who assessed my potential for teaching. I'm still pissed about that, pissed that he would equate old age with a low energy level. What I know and the help I can give kids have nothing to do with age or certification.

While the U.S. Congress debates the Brady anti-gun bill, the Texas legislature is debating a bill that would allow Texans to wear handguns concealed on their person.

There's a story circulating about a teacher who assigned his students to do some library research on euthanasia. A couple of days later, one of the students said he had been told by the librarian that the subject was too broad, that he would at least have to specify where in Asia the youths live and what exactly he needed to know about them.

Recently in New York City a homeless man, a train maintenance worker, and a dog were killed on the subway tracks. Ninety people telephoned the Transit Authority to express concern about the dog, but only three called about the worker and no one about the homeless man.

June 5, 1991:

Whom should I blame for my present predicament? I can blame old teachers, former employers, current politicians, short-sighted businessmen, dead parents, or even myself. There are many who have contributed to my demise as a contributing member of our economy, but I am awarding "major responsibility" to one Ronald Wilson Reagan. This broadcaster, actor, governor, president taught corporate America that "leaner and meaner" should be their motto for the 1980's. He taught this at the same time he was "ballooning" the Federal budget, making it "fatter" in debt, "leaner" on domestic spending, and "meaner" for all of us.

We saw many businessmen follow Reagan's advice and reduce their work force. Some moved their "work" to "forces" overseas to reduce their expenses. Ripples grew on our economy, becoming waves and then breakers under the Bush regime. Reagan had the bullshit ability to make people "feel good" about whatever

condition they found themselves in, but Bush's talent for bullshitting matches his inability to identify a principle.

I am a Reagan remnant who has been "Bushwhacked."

June 8, 1991:

Not in a mood to write. I've been down here for ten months, and things look no better than they did when I arrived.

Robert Louis Stevenson once wrote, "To travel hopefully is more enjoyable than the arrival." I am still traveling, but the hope is decreasing. I used to worry about my retirement, but that's all academic now because I'm not planning on reaching retirement.

June 15, 1991:

I'm feeling that uncontrollable urge again. I haven't killed any of them for a long time, but once more I'm beginning to feel homicidal. I've killed millions--perhaps billions--of them in the past. I've never felt guilty about doing them in. Most of the time I laughed while doing it. I've used a variety of weapons, primarily scotch and vodka in my later years, beer and wine earlier. The urge is upon me, spawned by anger and frustration, by hopelessness and helplessness. I'm going to kill some more brain cells.

June 20, 1991:

I've just saved six dollars by cutting my own hair, and it doesn't look too bad. I have no one to impress so my appearance is of no consequence. I remember the days when I had my hair styled, when I spent as much on my appearance as I now spend on sustenance. I remember the days when I "tooled" around town in my Corvette convertible; now I "limp" around in my rusted-out Buick, pausing periodically to administer needed repairs caused by 130,000 miles of hard traveling. I remember when I ate "Surf and Turf"; now it's "Tacos and Tamales". I remember when I drank Scotch for $3.00 a shot; now I buy Vodka for $4.99 a liter. I remember when....

July 1, 1991:

I miss my dogs. I miss Wolfie and Liebchen. I miss their love and companionship. It is difficult existing by oneself, without someone, or something, to talk to--to love.

July 10, 1991:

I'm still in the dumps. Texas is the slag heap of humanity, the cesspool of thought, the garbage of greed, violence, and crime.

I have a homicidal pancreas that is choking my urinary tract, constricting the tubes and impeding the flow of my precious bodily fluids, requiring that I relieve myself at two-hour intervals, making a sound night's sleep improbable.

Sleeping has been my favorite Texas activity because I could dream. Now I lay awake, tossing and tinkling. I arise to watch the TV "girly" ads that plead with viewers to call them at their 900 number for oral sex. The alternatives are limited in the early a.m., but I like Judy Canova, the Marx Brothers, and old cowboy flicks.

Old age is real. I leak from both ends. Spittle runs from my mouth at the most inopportune moments, and I am making my own Pampers, packing my jockey shorts with super absorbent handiwipes.

Tomorrow we have an eclipse of the sun and it will be my last one. I've seen two or three of them before, and that just about sums up my life. My epitaph will read: "He survived many periods of gloom."

July 12, 1991:

I've got a new neighbor! A woman moved in across the hall. She's by herself with only a little grey in her hair but with a trim body and fantastic legs. I asked her yesterday for a urine and blood sample, but she refused so I crossed her off my list.

July 13, 1991:

It's now 1:30 a.m., and sleep will not come. Perhaps it's the weather. It doesn't drop below 80 degrees until 3 or 4 in the morning. I can't afford to run my air conditioner.

The National Center for Policy Analysis, an Austin-based think tank, reported that in Texas the benefits of crime outweigh the costs. The average time behind bars for murder is two years and for rape only 5.3 months.

Early morning TV is worse than ever. There's a new program called "Amazing Love Stories." One episode featured a Civil War soldier whose left testicle was torn off by a bullet which then penetrated the ovary of a young unmarried woman living nearby. Nine months later she gave birth to a baby boy whose body contained the bullet.

And they are still advertising oral sex on TV. Just call a 900 number and talk dirty for only $3 a minute. If I save the $3 and talk dirty to myself would that be considered masturbating?

July 24, 1991:

Life stinks! I've just heard that Pee Wee Herman was arrested in an adult moviehouse for cuffing his cucumber. This brings new meaning to the term "Pee Wee's Playhouse." Now if we can pin something on Mr. Rogers and Big Bird, we can really screw up a lot of kids. What's happening to all my heroes? Bring back Soupy and Buffalo Bob.

August 14, 1991:

It's been a bad month for me. I can't sleep because of the heat, and I'm drained. I've always considered my body a garage rather than the proverbial temple, and now I'm paying for it. My body's northern regions are feeling a little better. I've put
the southern regions in drydock.

It's also been a bad week for Texas politicians. A judge in San Antonio died of a heart attack during "ze grande embrace"--at one of the local hotels--with a woman who was not his wife--during afternoon recess.

A state senator also died from a drug overdose, but he continued to vote for two days--until his body was found.

August 27, 1991:

Another steaming day, another sleepless night. School has started but teachers do not get sick during the first week of school. I'm bored--and very tired.

The late Judge Roy Bean was known throughout Texas as "The Hanging Judge." Today we have a judge in Houston that is giving sex offenders the option of serving a prison term or being surgically castrated. He will probably go down in history as "The Nothing's Hanging Judge."

Last weekend 20 people were shot in San Antonio, and today one of our citizens killed 22 people and wounded 20 others. The National Rifle Association still insists that guns don't kill people, but a Texan has a better chance of being killed by a bullet than by an automobile.

The mother and brother of San Antonio's mayor were found murdered in Fort Worth.

Why am I in this Bubba State? What am I doing in a town where many of the good burghers think Manual Labor is the President of Mexico. What am I doing in a world filled with greed, violence, and sex?

I'm not a happy camper!

December 2, 1991:

Many years ago when I was still teaching in junior college, my black students challenged me to live as they were forced to do. I've often thought about that challenge since I've been here in Texas. It's impossible to understand hopelessness until your own life is hopeless; no one really comprehends poverty unless he has no money; and discrimination is an abstract concept unless you have been its victim. Anyone who says this is not the case is either ignorantly presumptuous or a sociologist.

December 31, 1991:

153 elderly San Antonians died of starvation last year. How can that happen in Bush's "kinder, gentler" America. 153 dead oldsters.

I do understand what happens to these folks. My experiences being rejected for job after job lowered the confidence I had in myself--and the confidence I had in the American system. I once believed in competition, but the system will no longer let me compete so I too have dropped out of the market. The most popular bumper sticker in Texas is "1-800-EAT SHIT." I'm thinking of putting one on my ol' Buick or maybe it should go on my forehead.

January 1, 1992:

New Year's Day. Had myself a Denny's Grand Slam Breakfast. This was my second New Year's Day in Texas and the second time I spent it at Texas Denny's. They're the only place open on the morning after the Eve.

We're off to a good year. Our sheriff, when told that one of his deputies had exposed himself to a child, replied, "What he does on his own time is up to him."
Some researchers have played Rock-n-Roll music backwards to see if they could hear demonic messages. They tried playing country and western music backwards and they got back their dogs, girls, wives, horses, and pickups.

January 10, 1992:

The nation's in a recession; I'm in a depression. It has rained for forty days and forty nights in Texas. I think I'll build an ark and sail away.

January 15, 1992:

I now understand Shakespeare's "For in that sleep of death what dreams may come, when we have shuffled off this mortal coil..." Dreams are the best part of my day. I look forward to the night when I can escape, through dreams, to other lives and fantasies. The next best part of the day is breakfast at Cristen's Tacos or lunch at the Taco Kitchen. The third best part of my day is thinking about the first two. Not a very eventful life. With my luck, death will not be very eventful either.

I'm committing suicide. But not like Hemingway--not by putting a shotgun in my mouth. I'm doing it the Christian Science way--by not seeing a doctor. I haven't been to a doctor since I was let go in 1986. No preventive maintenance for my Buick or my body. When they quit running, I quit running.

January 20, 1992:

Being of sound mind but disintegrating body, I hereby declare this to be my last will and testament. I have nothing to will but a great deal to testify about. There shall be no "Code Blue" or anything that will prolong my life in the event that I am incapacitated. After my demise I shall be cremated (Burn, Baby, Burn!) and my ashes thrown to the winds along Washington, D.C.'s Pennsylvania Avenue.

There's plenty of wind at both ends of this street.

January 21, 1992:

I'm falling, and I can't get up.

PART II - *RACE AND ETHNICITY*

It is a terrible, inexorable law that one cannot deny the humanity of another without diminishing one's own.

James Baldwin, writer

In the process of tearing Indians off their land, of enlaving blacks, of exploiting great numbers of human beings, besides blacks and Indians, or raping the land itself--through this whole destructive process a proud civilization has been built, replete with the highest ideals and cultural achievements.

Joel Kovel, *White Racism: A Psychohistory*

The most vicious cowboy has more moral principle than the average Indian.

President Theodore Roosevelt

The Nordics propagate themselves successfully. With other races, the outcome shows deterioration on both sides. Quality of mind and body suggests that observance of ethnic law is as great a necessity to a nation as immigration law.

President Calvin Coolidge

The life story of any negro growing up in America is the story of what has been done to him and how he reacts to that.

H. Rap Brown, *Die Nigger Die*

Free at last! Free at last! Thank God almighty, we are free at last!

Old Negro Spiritual

INTRODUCTION

This second section is not an overview of race and ethnicity; that subject is simply too great and demands a much lengthier treatment; rather, this section employs a multidisciplinary approach to the question of race and ethnicity. Some selections illustrate the historical contradictions that have existed between American ideals and practices. Using Native Americans and African Americans as examples, these materials document the tremendous differences between how whites have defined certain ethnic groups and how these same ethnic groups have defined themselves. In the latter sense, the inclusion of representative African-American writers illustrates the rich cultural diversity that exists in this nation.

Psychohistorian Joel Kovel suggests that racism is so deeply implanted in the white psyche that it is part of the culture rather than some external or individual aberration. He points to the hypocrisy of the country professing the highest ideals of freedom and human dignity reducing subject minorities to pure nothingness. The essay on Jack Johnson illustrates many of the white fears and fantasies that Kovel explores. The selections on Native Americans taken from Lew Carlson and George Colburn's *In Their Place* exemplify how white historians, novelists, journalists, politicians, and other cultural leaders have supported, rationalized, or explained their treatment of Indians. Eva Martinez suggests that such writers, as well as most other technologically-driven but alienated human beings, have much to learn from Native Americans about serenity, tolerance, and harmony with nature.

African Americans such as Frederick Douglass, W. E. B. Du Bois, Paul Dunbar, Claude McKay, Langston Hughes, Mari Evans, Richard Wright,, H. Rap Brown, Ralph Ellison, and Malcolm X speak to the importance of blacks defining themselves rather than allowing the white power structure to do so for them. They clearly think of themselves as subjects rather than as the objects most whites considered them to be. Olympic gold medalist Archie Williams uses humor to defuse the racism that surrounded his life. Henry Davis describes the loss of the African-American male as a much needed role model for young blacks, and William H. Grier and Price M. Cobb analyze the rage felt by powerless black males. Novelist James Baldwin writes of the history lessons whites and blacks have too long ignored, and essayist Larry Neal calls for the growth of black consciousness.

Many of the overtly racist selections in Part II are shocking, disgusting, and incomprehensible in a country whose most noble document, the *Declaration of Independence*, professes "that all men are created equal, that they are endowed by their Creator with certain unalienable rights, that among these are life, liberty, and the pursuit of happiness." Clearly, Americans must recognize this contradiction if they are ever to implement and practice their ideals rather than just talking or writing about them. Then, too, the writings of the victims of such racial attacks can serve to remind all Americans of the need for an on-going commitment to human decency and of the advantages of living in a multi-cultural society.

Lew Carlson, *JIM JEFFRIES VERSUS JACK JOHNSON: A STUDY IN MEDIA PSYCHOHISTORY*

The essay below examines the controversial 1910 world heavyweight boxing match between "The Great White Hope," Jim Jeffries, and Jack Johnson, the first black champion. The bout was clearly about race and racial fantasies, with Johnson triggering white America's worst nightmares: a world turned topsy-turvy with blacks now doing to whites what blacks had so long done to them. Johnson's perceived arrogance and his affairs and marriages with white women so infuriated the white press that it forced a reluctant Jeffries out of retirement and demanded he restore the title to its proper owner.

The variations of the human figure are actual marks of the degeneracy in human form; and we may consider the European figure and color as standards to which to refer all other varieties, and with which to compare them.

Oliver Goldsmith, historian

Boxing is a sport that belongs uniquely to the English-speaking race and that has taken centuries for the race to develop.

Jack London, novelist

Joel Kovel's 1970 *White Racism: a Psychohistory* divided American racial attitudes into three historical eras: 1) the dominative period when whites controlled blacks through the closed system of slavery; 2) the aversive stage, beginning after slavery legally ended, in which whites either ignored blacks or thoroughly dehumanized them into some type of non-threatening buffoon or mammy character; 3) the metaracism of the post-civil rights era when the working culture attempted to turn everyone into nonassertive, non-individualistic grey (for example, several years ago when a reporter asked Henry Jordan, a black tackle for the Green Bay Packers, if Coach Vince Lombardi was a racist, he laughed and replied, "Hell no, he treated us all like shit").

According to Kovel, the dominative racist used slavery to fulfill his "illusion of complete and direct control over the natural and human world around him." In his mind, and often in reality, the slave owner reduced blacks to servile objects to be used as he saw fit. This need for total control also determined the perverse dynamics of interracial sex. White males made the rules, but, as with slavery in general, their own hypocrisy prevented any clear understanding of the tortured relationships they were trying to define. Incapable of confronting their own fantasies, white males projected their repressed desires onto blacks. Thomas Jefferson was typical. It was not poor ol' Tom who lusted and proved uncontrollable, but his slaves on the back forty. After every trip to their quarters, Jefferson returned to the Big House, sat down at his desk, and described what he considered to be the rampant sexuality of black women.

The more white males denigrated black women as wanton, sexual partners, the more they elevated their white wives and daughters to positions of isolated and lofty purity. Winthrop Jordan, Lillian Smith, Calvin Hernton, Eldridge Cleaver, among others, have written about the placing of white women on pedestals--to be worshipped as beautiful objects but never to be sullied or violated by wanton or lascivious actions. But what if these sanctified ice maidens also found attractive that which was forbidden? What if they decided to climb down from their pedestals--nay, leaped--into, say, waiting black arms? For white males, tormented by their own sexual hypocrisies, this became the ultimate nightmare.

The fears of interracial sex became even greater after the end of slavery when white America, faced by the constitutional and social possibility of equality between the races, sought new controls over African Americans. Previously it had been the physical control of slavery; now it was what Kovel called aversion that would confine blacks to second-class citizenship. When confronted by this new contradiction of equality versus racism, white America could only direct its rage outward--toward the object--and that object had to exhibit all the traits worthy of such aversion. What emerged was the hapless but happy, non-threatening darky found in American popular culture at the turn of the twentieth century. Three decades later this dim-witted, lazy, shuffling child-man had become the chicken-stealing, prevaricating, crap-shooting, procrastinating, watermelon-loving Amos and Andy of radio fame or Hollywood's Stepin Fetchit. Such stereotypes, of course, did much to reassure white Americans that here was something less than a man.

When whites denied the concept of "self-hood" to African Americans (consider the titles of black-written novels such as *Nobody Knows My Name*, *The Invisible Man*, *The Outsider*, or *The Man Who Cried I Am*), they again contradicted their own sacred ideals. "Consequently," writes Kovel, "the nation that pushed the idea of freedom and equality to the highest point yet attained was also the nation that pulled the idea of degradation and dehumanization to the lowest level ever sounded--to pure nothingness."

Jack Johnson was never troubled by negative notions of self-hood. He was the very antithesis of everything whites expected of blacks, and the more they sought to bend him to their collective will, the more openly he flaunted their taboos. He verbally assaulted his white opponents outside the boxing ring, then physically destroyed them within it. Worse yet, he openly took white women as his own. In the parlance of the day, he was the quintessential "crazy nigger," whose lack of respect for place posed a terrifying threat to a society incapable of granting, or even recognizing, racial equality. For tortured white psyches it was, as historian Winthrop Jordan put it, "a topsy turvy world of black over white." What whites had done to blacks would now be done to them, and Jack Johnson stood at the center of this nightmarish maelstrom....

Jack Johnson was in his fighting prime when he met Jim Jeffries on July 4, 1910. He was thirty-two years old and had easily knocked out several minor white hopes after winning the championship two years earlier from Tommy Burns. Both whites and blacks admitted that Johnson usually fought just well enough to win and to give hope to his next victim. Not frightening the white boxing establishment had been part of Johnson's strategy in order to get a shot at the heavyweight title, an opportunity not given to other great black fighters of his day such as Peter Jackson and Sam Langford. Johnson was the first black heavyweight champion, and the last, until Joe Louis knocked out James J. Braddock in 1937.

After Johnson's easy knockout of Burns in Australia in 1908, novelist Jack London sounded the clarion call for readers back home. Covering the fight for the New York *Herald*, London wrote, "No Armenian massacre could compare with the hopeless slaughter that took place in the Sydney stadium today." It had been a battle between a "colossus and a toy automaton," between "a playful Ethiopian and a small and futile white man." According to London, "But one thing now remains. Jim Jeffries must now emerge from his alfalfa farm and remove that golden smile from Jack Johnson's face. Jeff, it's up to you. The White Man must be rescued."

Other members of the press also appealed to the fat and contented Jeffries who did not welcome the prospect of paring his 300-pound body into fighting trim. But Johnson's taunting and the pleading press made it clear he had little choice. As biographer Randy Roberts described it, Johnson was increasingly portrayed as a threat to everything white America held dear:

> *Starting in 1909 the American public began to see the Bad Nigger in Jack Johnson. They saw his flashy clothes and his brightly colored, fast automobiles. They saw the way in which he challenged white authority in his numerous brushes with the law. They heard stories of his night life, the lurid tales of his sexual bouts were also told, and his shaved head came to symbolize the sexual virility of the black male. But most shocking of all were the times he appeared in public with white women.*

Someone had to put down this uppity black man. John Lardner wrote, "Well-muscled white boys more than six feet tall were not safe out of their mother's sight." Johnson himself fueled the fires by mercilessly putting on members of the fourth estate. "I ain't goin' ter chal'nge Mistah Jeff," he allegedly told a reporter from *Harper's Weekly*, "an' 'sides, he's so old an' fat he cain't fight anyway" (incidently, old phonograph recordings make it clear that Johnson spoke with perfect diction and grammar when that was his purpose). But it was a cute little blonde girl in the *Chicago Tribune* who put it most succinctly: "Please, Mr. Jeffries," she said, pointing a finger right at the reader, "are you going to fight Mr. Johnson?"

On April 19, 1910 Jeffries finally agreed to fight Johnson for the title he had given up five years before. White fans everywhere rejoiced, confident that Jeff would put the upstart Johnson in his place. Jeffries had enjoyed tremendous success in the ring. A huge hulk of a man, he had never lost, or even been knocked off his feet. After running out of worthwhile opponents, he had last defended his title in 1903 and formally retired from the ring two years later. But could he come back? He had to. The hope of the race was resting on his broad shoulders.

George Lewis "Tex" Rickard won promotional rights after giving Jeffries and Johnson each $10,000 for signing and guaranteeing them another $100,000 and two-thirds of the movie rights. Rickard announced the fight would be held on July 4, 1910 in a 30,000-seat arena he would erect in Reno and that he would serve as referee.

As fight day neared, reporters stepped up their attacks on Johnson. For a white supremacist such as Jack London, who had earlier written that "boxing is a sport that belongs uniquely to the English-speaking race and that has taken centuries for the race to develop," a possible Johnson victory was too painful to contemplate. His journalistic brethren agreed, and their pre-fight stories viciously denigrated Johnson. Such attacks had little effect on the supremely confident Johnson, but they undoubtedly put tremendous pressure on Jeffries.

On the day of the fight an editorial writer for the *Chicago Tribune* proclaimed, "The white man's hope and the abysmal Beast, otherwise known as the Grizzly and the Cinder, the White Mountain and the Big Smoke, will meet in what we are assured will be the last great fight for ten years." In a related article the unabashedly racist *Tribune* assessed Johnson's motivation: "Disliking work, Johnson takes up fighting to get money...because he is too lazy to do anything else." As for Jeffries, the *Tribune* reported, "It has taken a lot of pressure and a promise of a big price to get Jeff in the mood to assume the white man's responsibility."

The *San Francisco Chronicle's* Waldeman Young tried to reassure his readers--and himself--that all would go well. He meticulously described "watermelon feasts" at the Johnson camp and the way "the Big Smoke smiled at white men and women as if that were his joyous duty of the day." Young concluded that Jeffries was "mothered of a race which has dominated the world...[whereas] Johnson is in every feature and dimension the colored man."

Former heavyweight champion James J. Corbett not only helped train Jeffries but also covered the fight for several newspapers. For Corbett it was "a contest between two men of not only entirely different races but of different traditions...[and] Johnson, because of original principles and inborn characteristics..., will bow down to worship and fear the white man."

Tommy Burns, whom Johnson had so thoroughly outclassed for the crown in Australia, agreed that Jeffries would easily win, but he put it in cruder terms for the July 2 New York *Sun*: "No lazy nigger who boxes flat-footed like any bounding kangaroo is going to get away with it in any fight to the finish." And a New York *Herald* reporter described Johnson as "a real Southern darky, with most of the mannerisms of that lazy but amiable person."

So imbued were most white reporters with their own fanciful notions of racial superiority they seldom realized when Johnson deliberately "cooned" for them, even to the extent of eating watermelon or chasing chickens in front of the movie cameras that covered his training. According to one member of his retinue, he further inflamed the racial fantasies of the working press by wrapping his penis with several layers of gauze before going through his daily workout in the ring. Johnson also knew that such publicity would create greater interest in the bout itself.

A few writers became uneasy because Johnson never showed any of the fear they assumed blacks had of whites. Others, such as novelist Alfred Henry Lewis, who covered the fight for William Randolph Hearst's San Francisco *Examiner*, concluded that Johnson was just too simple to realize the magnitude of the occasion. Lewis insisted that Johnson would fight like a child because he "is without imagination" and "incapable of anticipation. The Battle of the Fourth," wrote Lewis, "is as much lost on him as though a century away." An editor for *Harper's Weekly* agreed, explaining that Johnson smiled and laughed so much because "Negroes have the mind of a child."

Quite naturally the black press saw Johnson quite differently. The *Chicago Defender* reported, "Nowhere in prize ring history is there recorded an incident of pluck, patience and perseverance that compares favorably with Johnson's quest for the championship." The

Defender recognized that Johnson was waging his battle not only against Jeffries but against "Jim Crow delegations, race prejudice, and American public insane sentiment," and it advertised an 18-inch statue of "the first Negro to be admitted the best man in the world."

The white press ridiculed such notions. Several papers printed accounts of black prayer meetings and songfests and made fun of blacks' willingness to bet on their favorite. Black bettors, on the other hand, feared only that the fight might be fixed. On June 30, a group of Chicago African Americans wired Johnson requesting his assurance that the fight would be on the level. Based on what they read in their newspapers, white bettors not surprisingly heavily backed Jeffries.

All roads led to Reno, or so it appeared as fight day neared. The July 2 *Chicago Tribune* front-page headline boldly declared, **"RED BLOODED MEN THRONG RENO; AMERICANS OF KIND THAT MAKE NATIONS ARE WAITING FOR GREATEST FISTIC BATTLE OF THE AGE."** Such support was particularly good news for the railroad companies which cleared $176,000 on ticket sales alone.

Excursion trains came from everywhere, but especially the West Coast. From San Francisco more than 5,000 fans bought their round-trip tickets for only $11.15. Decidedly more exclusive was the Millionaires Special, every passenger on which allegedly could sign his personal check for one million dollars.

Other special fight trains came from Seattle, Los Angeles, Chicago and points east. One train left Chicago with 200 aboard, including ten women. All planned to live on board while in Reno and then return by the same train. An estimated 2,000 fans made the transcontinental trek from New York. The National Sporting Club of London sent a delegation of fifty aboard the *Lusitania* and by special train from New York. Other foreign visitors came from Spain, France, Germany, Brazil, and Australia. From Ogden, Utah, came a fourteen-car train filled with Mormons who, upon arriving in Reno, announced they had come not to proselytize but to see the fight.

One train that failed to reach Reno was the *Clysmic Special* out of Cleveland. According to the *Cleveland Plain Dealer*, the promoter had sold twenty tickets for prices ranging from ten cents to $150 and then skipped town leaving the disgruntled fans at the station.

When two Jim Crow trains arrived from Chicago and Oklahoma respectively, the press had its usual fun. The New York *Sun* chortled, "There were Negroes aplenty--porters who've jumped their jobs on the Southern Pacific for a chance to wager their last five-cent piece on Johnson, sportive barbers from Los Angeles, and the plain railroad 'cinder' who has hoboed himself from Omaha and Denver." The *San Francisco Chronicle* announced, "Fully a Thousand Dusky Sports Expected."

Housing and food were a problem for black arrivals because Reno's existing hotels and restaurants drew the color line. Rickard had to arrange for blacks to be housed in storerooms and to eat in several of the newly opened restaurants. The *Chicago Tribune* praised such efforts and assured black travelers they would find rest "at billiard table rates," while the San Francisco *Examiner* announced there would be "cozy nooks where the sons of Ham can buck the tiger or take a whirl at craps and roulette."

Most disturbing to the white press were the great numbers of white women who were planning to attend the fight. Jack Johnson's preference for white women was usually not mentioned, but considerable coverage was given the ladies. Tex Rickard, ever the promoter, announced that he was building a row of booths around the top of the arena, replete with privacy curtains. He also announced that children over the age of ten would be welcome to join the ladies. "I don't want any lady or gentleman to stay away from the fight," said Rickard, "because they don't care to leave their kids unprotected."

Harper's Weekly later estimated that more than 1,000 women were among the 15,000 fans who witnessed the fight, and announced that many were there without their husbands' permission. Rex Beach, the Western writer who covered the fight for several papers, expressly ordered his wife to stay home, but she demurred, saying, "I shall see everything there is to see." Mrs. Jeffries did uphold the honor of her more traditional sisters, stating that she considered a wife's place to be at home. But a day later, the *Reno Evening Gazette* proudly announced that Mrs. Jeffries had consented to follow the progress of the fight from the *Gazette*'s building in downtown Reno.

The *Gazette* gave considerable attention to the female interest. On July 3 it reported that Mrs. D. Fritz of Reno had dreamed that a big black hand had reached through the transom of her bedroom and had written the number fifteen in red on her wall. Just below the number were the words, "Bet your whole heart." At 100 to 1 odds she did just that, betting that Johnson would knock out Jeffries in the fifteenth round. The next day her dreams, if not her fantasies, were answered.

The most bizarre case of an overly-zealous female fan featured one Kate Blancke, a well-known Cleveland actress, who had taken out an ad in her local newspaper asking for transportation to the fight. After sending several telegrams begging Rickard to send for her, she was arrested and committed to the state asylum for the insane.

The *San Francisco Chronicle* sent women's fashion expert Helen Dane to cover the fight "from a woman's perspective." Actually, Dane paid less attention to fashion than she did to the facial contours of the two fighters. She coldly described Jeffries' "set face with drawn brow and projecting chin," while finding Johnson to be "singularly Nubian in type with his flat nose, head going straight up in the back, and slanting down to the eyebrows." Even in disgust, it was Johnson who fascinated the white women who attended the fight and the thousands more who flocked to see him when he went on tour after his defeat of Jeffries.

The press coverage of the fight was unsurpassed in American sporting annals. Rickard received 3,000 requests for press seats, and the 124 working reporters sent over 150,000 words daily over the wire in the days leading up to the fight. The *San Francisco Chronicle* alone sent thirteen reporters to cover the fight, including such well known novelists as Jack London and Rex Beach, each of whom also covered the fight for other papers. Both the *Chronicle* and its hated rival, the *Examiner*, rented buildings in Reno and invited visiting fans to pick up their mail in care of their respective paper. There was also the daily competition to see which of the two papers would be first to get its afternoon edition from San Francisco to Reno. The train was too slow so each had an automobile meet the train half-way, then race over the mountains to Reno.

Both the *Chronicle* and the *Examiner* arranged theater showings of the fight for their San Francisco readers, a half century before anyone thought of closed-screen television. The *Chronicle* published full-page advertisements announcing 16,000 seats free to its readers in Blot's Arena and the Dreamland Rink. To gain admission a reader simply clipped a coupon out of the paper. The *Chronicle* ran a special telegraph wire from ringside to these arenas for a "blow-by-blow" transcription of the fight. Not to be outdone, Hearst's *Examiner* announced, **"LIVING MOVING PICTURES OF JEFFRIES-JOHNSON FIGHT."** Using local fighters dressed to represent Jeffries and Johnson, the *Examiner* promised its 17,000 fans at the Valencia Theater and the Auditorium that "every move in the real ring at Reno, every blow struck, every detail will be reproduced instantaneously from telegraphic descriptions." In addition, the *Examiner* erected a huge stage outside its building at Third and Market Streets where two additional fighters reenacted their own version of the fight for a throng of spectators that the *Examiner* estimated at 80,000.

On fight day, big crowds gathered outside newspaper offices in all major American cities and in many foreign cities as well. The *Cleveland Plain Dealer* ran its own direct wire from ringside to its Cleveland offices. The *Chicago Tribune* announced the fight round-by-round via megaphone to an estimated crowd of 10,000, including, reported the *Tribune*, many white women. Chicago's county jail planned to receive its own fight bulletins because one of its inmates was a telegraph operator, while Jack Johnson paid for a private wire to be run directly to his mother's house on the south side. Other black Chicagoans were invited to the Chicago Coliseum where the Northern Amusement Company promised a "symo-cast" using giant electrical figures flashing on a 15 by 24-foot screen. William Vanderbilt, Jr. and his friends enjoyed a private wire at their Edgemore Club on Long Island, and Booker T. Washington, who had often criticized Johnson's public behavior, set up a special room at Tuskegee Institute to get the results.

Even from far off Paris, where betting favored Jeffries five to one, came the announcement that leading restaurants were planning to provide their customers with special bulletins on the progress of the fight. The "truants and incorrigibles" of a Jersey City high school presented arguably the most bizarre reenactment when they held a mock battle between one Bruno Hasse, who was white, and Marshall Biddle, who was black. The time keeper, Bessie Clements, was the boys' English teacher. The *San Francisco Chronicle* reported that although Johnson's stand-in clearly had the better of the scrap, the bout was declared a draw.

On the eve of the fight each boxer issued his final statement. For once the press reported Johnson's words without its usual attempt to reduce them into pidgin English:

> *When I go into the ring tomorrow to fight Mr. Jeffries, I will do so with full confidence that I am able to defeat him at the game of give and take. I honestly believe that in pugilism I am Jeffries' master and it is my purpose to demonstrate this in the most decisive way possible. I think I know Jeffries thoroughly as a fighter, and with this knowledge reassuring me I am more willing to defend the title of champion against him.*

After a few thoughts on his conditioning and strategy, Johnson presented his views on sportsmanship with uncharacteristic humility:

> *Every fighter on the eve of his fight declares that he hopes the best man wins. I am quite sincere when I say that I do. If Mr. Jeffries knocks me out or gains a decision over me I will go into his corner and congratulate him as soon as I am able. My congratulations will be no fake. I mean it. If Mr. Jeffries has it in him*

> *to defeat me I think that I can modestly say he is entitled to all the congratulations he may receive....Let me say in conclusion that I believe the meeting between Mr. Jeffries and myself will be a great test of strength, skill, and endurance.*

The tone of Jeffries' remarks was strikingly different. As the fight approached, Jeffries became increasingly sullen. He was never comfortable with reporters, and he clearly found training, and particularly sparring, to be distasteful. He much preferred fishing to boxing, and he certainly felt the pressure of carrying the white man's burden. "When the gloves are knotted on my hands tomorrow afternoon," said Jeffries in his final statement, "and I stand ready to defend what is really my title, it will be at the request of the public which forced me out of retirement." He did, however, seek to reassure whites that he would win:

> *I realize full well just what depends on me, and I am not going to disappoint the public....That portion of the white race that has been looking to me to defend its athletic superiority may feel assured that I am fit to do my very best.*

On the morning of the Fourth a long stream of humanity wound its way out of Reno for the seven-mile journey to Tex Rickard's newly complete arena. The gates opened at noon and within the hour the 15,000 seats were filled. Tickets were scaled from $50 down to $10, for a total gate of $250,000. Nine motion picture cameras in rows of three lined one side of the ring. Shortly after one o'clock, the Reno Military Band began to play patriotic favorites. An hour later Johnson made his way into the ring. The band had planned to play *All Coons Look Alike to Me*, but, fearing inflaming racial tensions, switched instead to *Dixie*.

In the ring Johnson smiled and waved merrily to the predominantly white crowd, many of whom responded with a variety of racial slurs. When Jeffries followed a few minutes later, the same fans burst into tremendous applause. It was probably just as well. They would have little to cheer about for the rest of the day.

The fight itself proved disappointing. Jeffries' seven-year layoff had clearly finished him as an effective fighter. Although Johnson was only three years younger than Jeffries, he had been boxing regularly and was in peak fighting trim. The outcome was never in doubt after the first couple of rounds. Johnson toyed with Jeffries, assaulting him both verbally and physically, before turning to the fans and reporters to inquire how he was doing. Mercifully the end came in the fifteenth round when it was apparent the battered Jeffries could not go on. It was over, and the hopes of white America lay crumpled in Jeffries' corner.

Within minutes, another contest began. Eager reporters competed with one another to be the first to get their story and photographs back to the home paper. Four San Francisco *Examiner* men rushed from ringside carrying over 100 photographic plates into a waiting car, and then onto a special train for which "every other train, though it had been the private car of the President, had to give way." A dark room was constructed in the baggage car to ready the negatives for the enlarging plant in Oakland. As a hedge against railroad failure, the *Examiner* had also leased twenty-two carrier pigeons to carry small pictures in capsules attached to their legs. These films, proudly announced the *Examiner*, were the size of postage stamps. Of the twenty-two birds, five made it back to San Francisco with their precious cargo.

In the race to be first, the *Reno Evening Gazette* had an obvious advantage. Almost immediately it hit the streets with its banner headline: **"SLUGGISH WHITE GIANT IS TERRIBLY BEATEN BY THE CLEVERNESS OF THE ETHIOPIAN."** "No more tragic story was ever written," began its lead story. The *Gazette*, as did most other papers, admitted the better fighter had won. Jeffries himself agreed. The San Francisco *Examiner* quoted the vanquished champion as saying, "What will mother say when she hears that I have been licked by a nigger." More plausible were his words in the New York *Sun*: "The colored fellow beat me fair and square. I thought I would get to him before he got to me. In this I found I was mistaken."

Several reporters sowed their sour grapes. Unwilling to equate fistic supremacy with superior mental abilities, Rex Beach insisted that "Johnson demonstrated further that his race has acquired full stature as men, but whether they will ever breed brains to match his muscles is yet to be proven." An editorial in the *Cleveland Plain Dealer* suggested that Jeffries had lost because "his Caucasian mind was overwhelmed by stage fright," resulting in a complete loss of confidence. "Johnson had no such problem," stated the *Plain Dealer*, "because he is a child, with the mind of a child....He laughed and clapped his hands naively and fought as a boy." The *Chicago Tribune* admitted, **"NO YELLOW IN BLACK,"** before labeling the fight "a pitiful tragedy," and dismissing Johnson's victory with its usual racist levity:

> *The late Mr. Jeffries seems to have been unable to suppress what might be called the Smoke Nuisance....Little Arthur Johnson, a perfect specimen of smokedAmerican...has made it necessary for us to look to intellectual employments for intellectual superiority.*

Such crude comments stand in sharp contrast to the gracious words Johnson used to describe his victory:

> *He is the most gentlemanly fellow I ever battled. I could see in the early rounds he was out. I felt sorry for him. When I saw him bleeding and gradually sinking it made my heart ache. I could see no unusual honor in victory over a wreck. I wished then that I had faced him when he was at his best.*

White America's inordinate fear of self-assured, independent blacks and the very real celebration African Americans enjoyed across the country led to widespread rioting and violence in the days following Johnson's victory. On the day of the fight the *Chicago Tribune's* headline anticipated trouble if Johnson should happen to win: **"JOHNSON VICTORY BAD FOR NEGROES...IF BLACK MAN WINS FIGHT IGNORANT MEMBERS OF RACE MAY FEEL LIKE CONQUERORS."** Pittsburgh's police chief was also apprehensive, announcing that if Johnson won, there would be "no jollification parade" in Pittsburgh.

On July 5, the riots began, at least in the nation's newspapers. A New York *Herald* banner screamed, **"MOB HOLDS TOWN,"** and a few days later, again in a front-page headline, the *Herald* urged, **"TAKE THE RAZORS FROM THE BLACKS--POLICE HEAR STORIES THAT THE NEGROES MEAN TO GREET JOHNSON WITH AN OUTBREAK."** Police

Inspector Russel announced that he had it "on good authority" that a "razor war" was imminent because blacks wanted to take over New York for at least a day and a night. The *Cleveland Plain Dealer* reported blacks had shot up Mound City, Illinois, and were in possession of Keystone, West Virginia, and Columbus, Ohio. In most cases it was simply a matter of blacks conducting victory parades, but for white reporters this was that topsy turvy world with blacks now on top, and underneath the surface lurked the unspoken fears that blacks, like Johnson himself, might now go after white women.

The New York *Sun*, which blamed celebrating blacks for riots in Atlanta, Norfolk, and various Northern cities, warned that rioting would soon be spreading to the nation's capital. "Washington has a negro population of more than 100,000," reported the *Sun*, "and most of them are aroused to a high point of excitement. The streets are populated with dancing darkies all of whom have a package on."

The *Cleveland Plain Dealer* was delighted when whites took matters into their own hands. **"NEGRO CALLS HIS DOG JEFFRIES AND IS GIVEN THOROUGH BEATING FOR IT,"** blazed its headline. "The yellow cur," reported the *Plain Dealer*, "cowered at its owner's feet." When its owner was asked why he didn't call his dog Johnson, he replied, "Johnson is black; this dog is yellow."

Never shy about inflaming public opinion, Hearst's San Francisco *Examiner* reported "race riots in nearly every city of size in the U.S." However, the *Examiner,* obviously wishing to warn African Americans against taking matters into their own hands, reported that blacks were the main victims of the violence, with "thousands of Negroes beaten and several dead or dying."

The black press naturally saw matters differently, even the dying. The *Chicago Defender's* William Pickens concluded that even the sacrifice of black lives in the riots was a worthy price to pay for self-respect. "It is better for us to succeed, though some die," wrote Pickens, "than for us to fail, though all live."

African Americans everywhere hailed Johnson's easy victory, and especially in the doggerel verse of a song appearing in several black newspapers just days after the fight:

Amaze an' Grace, how sweet it sounds,
Jack Johnson knocked Jim Jeffries down.
Jim Jeffries jumped up an' hit Jack on the chin,
An' then Jack knocked him down agin.

The Yankees hold the play,
The White Man pull the trigger;
But it makes no difference what the white man say;
The world champion's still a nigger.

The press coverage of the fight and the ensuing riots died down after a few days, but a new controversy began over whether or not the fight films should be shown nationally. Well before the fight Tex Rickard, Jim Jeffries, and Jack Johnson had formed a partnership with W. T. Rock, the President of the Vitagraph Company of America, to market the films to 400 theaters across the country. Perhaps because he anticipated future difficulties, Johnson sold his rights several days before the fight for $50,000. The remaining investors naturally hoped that Jeffries would be the victor. *Harper's Weekly* estimated the films would be worth $1,000,000 if Jeffries won, but very little if Johnson emerged victorious.

Had Jeffries won, the films would have been shown without incident. Actually, movies of Johnson defeating Burns and Stanley Ketchel had circulated, but now public sentiment, whipped to a frenzy by the yellow press, demanded that the films be totally banned. Many whites thought the films would further inflame blacks and give them false ideas about equality. New Jersey Supreme Court Justice Francis J. Swayze declared his court would call a grand jury to indict anyone showing the fight films because they "pander to the vicious and disorderly elements of society." Cardinal Gibbons of Baltimore said simply, "The children have to be protected," while for San Francisco Mayor Pat McCarthy it was a question of "preserving pubic morals."

Even more precise in her objections was Mrs. James H. Crawford, the Vice President of the California Club:

> *The Negroes are to some extent a child-like race, needing guidance, schooling and encouragement. We deny them this by encouraging them to believe that they have gained anything by having one of their race as champion fighter.*

Mrs. Crawford further warned that "race riots are inevitable when we superior people allow these people to be deluded and degraded by such false ideals."

William Shaw and his Boston-based United Society of Christian Endeavor spearheaded the national campaign against showing the fight films. Shaw sent a petition to every governor warning that the films would "stimulate race hatred." Mayors in Cincinnati, Baltimore, Boston, Milwaukee, and Atlanta agreed, adding that such films would "encourage crime" and be "a detriment to public morals." In an interesting twist, blacks in Covington, Kentucky, objected to showing the films because they feared it would be whites becoming inflamed and threatening their safety.

Standing in sharp contrast to most of his fellow mayors was Brand Whitlock of Toledo who pointed out the hypocrisy of pretending to worry about children and possible violence when these same critics ignored the fact that half the kids in New York's tenements died before reaching the age of six and that 500,000 men were killed or maimed each year in industrial accidents. Whitlock also pointed out the speciousness of the race issue. "What does it prove," he asked, "that Jeffries could pummel Booker T. Washington or that Jack Johnson could do the same to Tolstoy or, perhaps, even to Colonel Roosevelt?"

Whitlock was a voice crying in the wilderness. Dire warnings were heard even abroad, and especially in the British Commonwealth. South Africa banned the films lest they "cause outbreaks of latent racial antipathies." The white press in Calcutta suggested that it would be best simply to destroy the films. The clergy in New South Wales petitioned Australian Premier Andrew Fisher to ban the pictures. Home Secretary Winston Churchill admitted in the House of Commons that although he'd certainly like to, the Government was powerless to prohibit showing the films.

The films were banned in Manila, but not in Mexico City where Governor Landan Escandon said he would welcome the fight pictures because "we have no Negro question here."

The controversy surrounding the films naturally encouraged some unscrupulous promoters.

Seven hundred eager fans entered New York's Savoy Theater to see what had been advertised as the official fight films. All the viewers got were a few photographic stills and a couple of hours of vaudeville. The crowd finally became impatient and rioted, throwing the cashier and her ticket booth out into 34th Street. Eventually, the actual fight films were shown without incident in such cities as Detroit, Hoboken, Jersey City, St. Louis, Kansas City, and New York.

In the meantime, Johnson was traveling around the country to mixed receptions. On July 5, he left Reno by private pullman car to return to Chicago. Newspapers reported a disgruntled bettor trying to shoot him in Omaha, but for the most part the crowds were friendly. In Chicago, Police Chief Leroy T. Steward issued an order forbidding any formal celebration to welcome Johnson back to his adopted city. Nevertheless, 7,000 fans were at the Northwestern Station on Wells Street. One paper reported Johnson stepped off the train and greeted his mother with, "Mommy, I sure brung home the bacon." Permit or not, the crowd, one-third of which were white with the usual conspicuous number of well-dressed females, moved on to a further celebration in front of Johnson's house at 3344 Wabash.

A couple of days later Johnson traveled to New York to honor some night club engagements and to get ready for the world tour that usually accompanied winning the heavyweight championship. He arrive on July 11 to be greeted by cheering fans and the New York *Herald's* ridicule of how it imagined he would spend his first night in Gotham:

> *The chocolate champion, who made extensive alterations to Mr. Jim Jeffries main entrance, laid his kinky head on the pillow to wade through dreams inlaid with gold certificates, moistened by oceans of wine and bounded on the north, south, east, and west by watermelon and fried chicken.*

The New York *Sun* took particular issue with the way Johnson's black fans dressed and their "amusingly formal" English. Clearly, blacks in the welcoming crowd did not speak the fractured molasses-and-grits English they did on the pages of the *Sun* and most other white newspapers of the day.

Johnson's New York fans were well behaved, although the *Cleveland Plain Dealer* called it "a charging mob" that contained "a number of well dressed white women." The *Plain Dealer* also reported that there was a move by a group of Washington, D. C. clergymen to ban Johnson himself from coming to the nation's capital. "If pictures incite race riots," reasoned the good pastors, "the presence of Johnson surely will do worse."

After a few weeks everything quieted down, Johnson left for Europe, and white America renewed its search for a new White Hope. But from where would he come? Jim Corbett, who had helped train Jeffries, now talked of training Frank Gotch, the reigning wrestling champion. An even more unlikely choice was the winner of Harvard University's intermural boxing championship who volunteered his services. In truth, there was no one. The search would continue, but for the moment Jack Johnson was king, and white America had to look outside of boxing for proof of its alleged racial superiority.

Lew Carlson and George Colburn, *IN THEIR PLACE*

Every American youngster learns about the professed glories of the melting pot, an illusory process in which each new wave of immigrants arriving on our shores was somehow "stirred" in with the earlier settlers to form the American people. Of course, there were those groups who, for one reason or another, the founding fathers and their descendants insisted would spoil the broth. Blacks, Orientals, Hispanics, and Native Americans had to be kept out of the pot and safely "in their place" to preserve another illusion: the superiority and purity of "the white race." What follows is the Preface *and* Chapter One *from Lew Carlson and George Colburn's* In Their Place: White America Defines Her Minorities, 1850-1950 *(John Wiley & Sons, 1971).*

PREFACE

This book is a historical perspective on white racism that examines the roots of current racial views in America. However, it is neither a definition nor a summary of contemporary racism in American society, and it is not designed to serve the ethnic needs of America's various minority groups. Instead, it attempts to document the pervasiveness of white racism in the United States from the post-Revolution era to the years immediately following World War II. Therefore, this anthology is directed to white America, because until whites understand why this country put its minorities "in their place," there will be no escape from that "place" by those still outside society's mainstream.

In recent years, a great many books have been written on American minorities in an attempt to recover and correct their lost or distorted past. The reasons for this outpouring, however, have been infrequently explored. Underlying these reasons is the fact that the minorities themselves almost always have been viewed as the problem; indeed, social reformers continually have tried to solve the "Negro problem" or the "Indian problem" or the "Mexican problem." As a result, well-meaning whites, living within society's mainstream, never mounted a serious attack on white racism itself. The oppressing majority never has endured a searching examination of the "white problem." Whites have seldom realized that it is impossible to stereotype another human being unless they first stereotyped themselves.

The term "white racism" only recently has been added to the basic American vocabulary. Previously, Americans had admitted that "prejudice" and "discrimination" existed, but these terms generally implied shortcomings on the part of individuals. But times have changed. Those involved in the post-World War II civil rights movement, urban disorders, confrontation politics, and the young people's revolt speak of a national responsibility from which no white American escapes. Our examination of the century prior to these events of the past few years leads us to the same conclusion. It is not individuals alone, nor a specific region, that bears responsibility for the treatment of America's minorities; our institutions, indeed, our very culture, must bear primary responsibility.

We did not have to search far to find convincing evidence of racism in the most influential sectors of mainstream American society during the 1850-1950 period. The sources utilized here illustrate this fact very well. We have included addresses by American Presidents, speeches by Congressmen and Senators, decisions by the U.S. Supreme Court, and articles in prestigious scholarly journals, popular fiction, mass-circulation magazines, and major newspapers. Therefore, this book focuses on popular and scholarly ideas that make possible the continued flourishing of mainstream and institutional racism. In our treatment of racism we have ignored society's extremist fringe, where blatant racist attitudes are to be expected.

From the end of Reconstruction until sometime after World War II, popular and scholarly conclusions about the inferiority of ethnic minorities nicely merged, producing an overwhelming climate of opinion that greatly influenced the average American. To illustrate this, only the most widely read publications and books (both popular and scholarly), the leading public officials, and the outstanding scientists are quoted in our collection. In selecting each document, we attempted to determine the prestige or popular following of the author or publication.

Finally, we must admit that the selections in this book are only a start in resurrecting a deplorable aspect of America's past that has been obscured by inspirational stories of the melting pot and opportunity under a democratic government. It is not pleasant or satisfying to find that our Presidents, Supreme Court Justices, leading scholars, respected scientists, and literary luminaries actually contributed to the "white problem" with their racist thoughts and actions. We feel this unfortunate chapter in American history has been hidden from view too long. Removal of this veil is painful because, underneath, we find overt racism practiced by our leaders and generations of American citizens accepting this racism. But not only America's minorities demand removal of the veil; so do increasing numbers of white youths in America's mainstream.

As teachers at two large public universities we know that these young people are greatly disturbed by the racism they see about them. Yet, we have seen that only when they examine the source material itself are they ready to accept the historical fact that racism has been rampant in all sectors of American society and that it has been directed at all nonwhite or otherwise "foreign" people within the society. Hopefully, this book of historical documents will create a greater understanding of the dimensions of our present-day problems.

CHAPTER 1 - NATIVE AMERICANS

I suppose I should be ashamed to say that I take the Western view of the Indian. I don't go so far as to think that the only good Indians are the dead Indians, but I believe nine out of every ten are, and I shouldn't inquire too closely into the case of the tenth. The most vicious cowboy has more moral principle than the average Indian.

Theodore Roosevelt, 1889

INTRODUCTION

"It is the fate of the American Indians that they exist in the national consciousness mainly as figures in a myth of the American past, claims Professor John R. Howard. The question is, of course, how did this myth develop? The evidence shows that not only are the frontiersmen and early governmental officials to blame for our distorted image of the Indian, but that historians, scientists, novelists, and journalists must also share in the responsibility; and their views reached a far greater audience.

For most Americans, Indians served to fulfill a historical function: they provided the challenge that whites successfully overcame in their march across the continent. Thus, in the words of Professor Daniel Boorstin, the Indian was considered little more than "sand in the smoothly oiled gear of American progress."

As early as the mid-1600s, the pattern of America's treatment of the Indian was being established by English colonists. Indians were either forced off coveted land or placed on reservations. When the reservation land was later desired, treaties were ignored and threats or force were used to convince the Indians to move on. By the time of the American Revolution, white attitudes toward Indians had been well formed. The Constitution of the United States ignored the Indians other than to classify the tribes as autonomous foreign nations. Few of the nation's leaders believed that the Indians had a right or a title to the land they had inhabited for so many centuries. It was felt that title to the land could only belong to those who cultivated it. In effect, it was the beginning of a constant and unwavering policy that sought to transform the Indian from hunter to farmer. Nevertheless, even if Indians understood and wanted to comply, they could not. The Northwest Ordinance of 1787, which stated that "the utmost good faith shall always be observed toward the Indians, their lands and property shall never be taken from them without their consent," was typical of the promises made but not kept.

In 1825, this pledge was revoked when the federal Government decided that Indian land was far too valuable to leave under Indian control. Thus, a policy of forcing the movement of all Indians to new reservations across the Mississippi River was begun. The general belief at the time was that the Plains of the West were unsuitable for human life; a "final solution" had apparently been reached. The new policy even applied to 17,000 Cherokees of Georgia who had decided years before to adopt the ways of their white conquerors. They farmed their land, sent their children to school, edited a newspaper, and elected officials as called for in a written constitution. Any hope the Cherokees or any tribe had of remaining on their land was dashed in 1830 when Congress passed the Indian Removal Act, authorizing the President to resettle any Eastern tribe regardless of existing treaties.

It was not long before Indians realized their new "homes" was also in jeopardy. The Mexican War and the discovery of gold in California promoted interest in the lands beyond the Mississippi. An immediate result was that California Indians lost most of their land, which had been guaranteed under treaties made with the Bureau of Indian Affairs in 1851.

Within a decade, the Indians were being referred to as the "vanishing race." They were disappearing for many reasons: killing of Indians was never considered a crime, the barren land often could not support a family, and disease and the lack of proper medical care devastated some tribes. The usual rationalization for the declining numbers was that the Indian could not adjust to civilization.

As white settlers moved relentlessly westward, the Indians were forced onto more barren and confining reservations. Their alternatives were few: they could either accept their treatment peacefully, or fight the settlers and the U.S. Army. As the second half of the nineteenth century progressed, more and more Indians chose to fight. The majority of whites denounced these Indians as incorrigible savages, and the wars served to reinforce their prevailing notions of superiority. Inflamed by tales of massacres in the popular press, the public encouraged the conquering of the West through the destruction of its native inhabitants.

By the end of the century, the virulent hostility of the white man toward the Indian was diminishing. Racism had not disappeared; Americans no longer considered the Indians a threat or their land to be valuable. Many Americans, therefore, felt it was time to take up the "white man's burden" and care for this vanquished foe.

As early as 1887, Congress had acted to provide the Indians with the apparent means to become "worthy" residents of the nation. With the passage of the Dawes Severalty Act in 1887, the Indian tribes were dissolved as legal entitles, and tribal land was divided up among individual members. The liberal reformer who still believed in the civilizing magic of private property and the Indian-hater who wanted the surplus Indian land both favored the measure. In the end, however, it was the whites, not the Indians, who profited. As Indian authority William T. Hagan pointed out, "Severalty may not have civilized the Indian, but it definitely corrupted most of the white men who had any contact with it."

Attempts to plug the loopholes in the Dawes Act produced few discernible changes in the end result; Indian life remained much the same. It was not until the New Deal era that the government's basic attitude toward the Indian changed. Between the Dawes Act of 1887 and the Wheeler-Howard Act of 1934, approximately 90 of the 138 million acres of land held by Indians passed into white ownership. By the mid-1920s, when the government finally granted citizenship to Indians, the Indians' death rate was exceeding their birth rate. Moreover, it was clear that they were not being assimilated. Under the leadership of John Collier, Commissioner of Indian Affairs, the New Deal government repudiated the severalty policy and called for the allotted lands to be consolidated for tribal use. With significant Federal aid, the death rate gradually declined, but even in the 1960s the life expectancy of an Indian was only 47 years.

Government policy toward the Indian, including the ill-conceived "termination" of Federal control over the Indians suggested by the Eisenhower Administration during the 1950s, could not have been carried out without the acquiescence of the American people, who either ignored

Native Americans or were conditioned to dismiss them as an inferior people. In the mid-nineteenth century the American Government had virtually practiced genocide, but there was barely a murmur of protest from the public. Sharing the blame must be the schools, the newspapers, the publishing companies, and the missionaries; for, in the end, it was they who first prepared and dispensed the information received by the American people about the continent's original inhabitants. These impressions, more than anything else, enabled the government utterly to disregard basic human rights in America's brutalizing march to the Pacific Coast. As Grover Cleveland facetiously noted in 1887, "The hunger and thirst of the white man for the Indian's land is almost equal to his hunger and thirst after righteousness." The white man, however, was conditioned to believe that he had a right to that land.

I - THE GOVERNMENT AND THE INDIAN

Indians are America's most impoverished minority. The reason for their tragic circumstances is directly traceable to the policies of the Federal Government beginning in the early nineteenth century. The brutal physical elimination of the Indian came to an end with the close of the century, and a more patronizing attitude toward him was adopted. Much of the sympathy for the Indian's plight was inspired by the publication in 1881 of Helen Hunt Jackson's *A Century of Dishonor* and a few years later by her more widely read novel, *Ramona*.

When Indian reservations were discovered to rest on valuable lands, Congress still did not hesitate to appropriate them, but the possibility of such lands being in Indian possession after 1880 appeared remote; thus the government could listen to reformers and humanitarians. As it developed, this changing attitude resulted in new programs with the well-being of the Indians in mind, but the Indians themselves were rarely consulted, and once a program was instituted, the Indians were forced to comply. In spite of the well-meaning reforms of the period between 1890 and 1930, Indians lost almost two thirds of their land. This statistic--along with their abject poverty and declining population--stood in testimony of the bankruptcy of the Government's Indian policies. The Indians were never considered in terms of their own culture. Reformers who sought to end the brutal practices of the past were, nevertheless, convinced that the Indian could be saved only if he adopted the white man's style of living. The policy of "termination" introduced during the Eisenhower years and still being debated, is the logical conclusion of such policies. By closing the Bureau of Indian Affairs and ending Governmental programs, Indians would once and for all be forced to join the system that for over three centuries had rejected them.

A. INDIANS FORCED OFF THEIR LAND BY "THE ADVANCING TIDE OF CIVILIZATION," 1880

When Congress discovered in 1880 that the Ute reservation in Colorado was the site of a rich mineral field, it moved quickly to buy the land "at a very small price" but "a very good price for the Indians." It was to be an oft-repeated tactic. The alternative, said Representative Dudley C. Haskell of Kansas, was the extermination of the Indians by those in the "on-rushing tide of civilization." In the same congressional debate, Colorado's James B. Belford endorsed the efforts to oust an idle and thriftless race of savages" from the "treasure vaults of the nation."

Congressional Record, 46th Cong., 2nd Sess., June 7, 1880.

Rep. Haskell. Mr. Speaker, if there is no other member of the House who desires to speak against this bill, I wish to present to the House as briefly as I am able the causes that have led to this Ute agreement, and the main features of the bill.

It will not be necessary for me to enter into any description of the Ute outbreak, and the conflict between the Indians and the troops out of which this agreement grew. It is a well-known fact that our policy of maintaining large Indian reservations immediately in front of the advancing tide of civilization has been found to be a poor policy, and one which we cannot sustain. It has been found thus with this Ute reservation. A large territory embracing over twelve millions of acres of the richest mineral lands of Colorado has been allowed to be occupied exclusively by less than four thousand Utes. Within twenty miles of the eastern boundary of this reservation is a city of forty thousand inhabitants. Looking longingly across the borderline of that reservation are hundreds and thousands of venturous miners who desire to secure possession of the immense mineral wealth that it contains, and this is what led to the conflict originally between the United States and the Indians. The Interior Department became well advised that it would be utterly impossible to prevent a conflict between the Indians and the miners desiring to enter upon these lands for the sake of prospecting for minerals, and in view of the fact that an outbreak had occurred they sent for and brought on here the head chiefs of the Ute Nation, in order that a peaceful conference could be had which might avert the impending danger of an Indian war and bring about a peaceful settlement of the difficulty....

The bill is made up essentially of two parts: one an agreement between the Indians and the Government to sell their lands, and the other the simple legislation necessary to carry into effect the terms of that agreement. The amount of money appropriated in the bill is $422,000. That is to provide for the payment of the first annuity, to provide for the expenses of the commission, to provide for the survey of the lands, to provide for the payment to the Indians of the improvements they have made, and to provide further that schools shall be established and school-houses built, and also to furnish more or less of subsistence, as may be needed....

There are, Mr. Speaker, before this Congress of the United States, in my judgment, but two roads open. One is to accept this bill...or we are to abandon this bill and undertake to maintain in that rich mineral district of Colorado a great Indian reservation of twelve millions of acres, against the on-rushing tide of civilization and of adventurous miners....There is no other course open. Already the miners are clustered on the borders of the reservation ready to enter. It is a mountainous country that would require three times the force the United States has at its disposal to protect and defend. It is a mountainous country, in which if we went to war there would be simply a reproduction on a larger scale of those terrible scenes in the lava-beds when we captured the Modocs. In other words, it means the absolute extermination of the Indian at a great cost of blood and treasure to the United States, or it means the peaceable solution of the question by which the Government buy their land, pay them year by year a fair stipend, care for their little ones in school, protect them under the laws of the land, put whites and Indians side by side, under the same law, and teach the red men the arts of civilization by actual contact with the civilized man himself....

Mr. Belford. If you pass this bill you at once open up a tract of country almost as large as New England; a country abounding in great material wealth, and fitted to become the home of a million active and enterprising citizens. You give the sanction of the Government to the act of the miner in taking up a claim; you open a way by which he can acquire title to land; and you apprise the Indian that he can no longer stand as a breakwater against the constantly swelling tide of civilization. The passage of this bill is the reclamation of eleven millions of acres of land from the domain of barbarism. It enlarges the possible achievement of the white man by enlarging the field in which he can labor. It settles for all time the doctrine which has received illustrations in the past that an idle and thriftless race of savages cannot be permitted to guard the treasure vaults of the nation which hold our gold and silver, but that they shall always be open, to the end that the prospector and miner may enter in and by enriching himself enrich the nation and bless the world by the results of his toil.

B. THE DAWES SEVERALTY ACT: SAVING THE UNCIVILIZED, 1887

For a number of reasons, Federal officials had been attracted by the concept of "severalty" long before it was implemented in 1887. First of all, scholars seemed to agree that private property is the basis of civilization. Secondly, turning the land over to individuals would break up the reservations and reduce the power of the chiefs. Critics of the policy were few; on this issue, both the sympathetic reformers and the most rabid Indian-hater could agree, with the latter usually being interested in the sale of "surplus" Indian land. Senator Henry L. Dawes of Massachusetts, a Yale graduate, lawyer, and sponsor of the Severalty Act, explained in the following article the need to transform the "lawless savage" to a *"civilized" American.*

Atlantic Monthly, *August 1899*

Have we failed the Indians? The present Indian policy of the government is of comparatively recent date. It is hardly yet twenty-five years since the first step was taken. The beginning was small and tentative, but the policy has steadily grown in the public confidence and in the enlargement of effort, until, judged by results, it now stands justified. Before its adoption the attitude of the government toward the different tribes was in general that of kind, patient care. There were exceptional cases in this treatment--instances of hardship, injustice, and wrong--not to be defended; traceable, however, almost always to unfit stewards and unfaithful public servants, and not to the deliberate act of the government itself. The prevailing idea was that of guardianship of an uncivilized race among us, incapable of self-support or self-restraint, over which public safety as well as the dictates of humanity required the exercise of a constant, restraining care, until it should fade out of existence in the irresistible march of civilization. It very soon became apparent that under this treatment the race did not diminish, but, by reason of protection from the slaughter of one another in wars among themselves and from diseases inseparable from savage life, it increased in number....

What was to become of the untutored, defenseless Indian, when he found himself thus pushed out of the life and home of the reservation, and cut off from the hunting and fishing which furnished the only and scanty supply of his daily wants? It was plain that if he were left alone he must of necessity become a tramp and beggar with all the evil passions of a savage, a homeless and lawless poacher upon civilization, and a terror to the peaceful citizen.

It was this condition which forced on the nation its present Indian policy. It was born of sheer necessity. Inasmuch as the Indian refused to fade out, but multiplied under the sheltering care of reservation life, and the reservation itself was slipping away from him, there was but one alternative: either he must be endured as a lawless savage, a constant menace to civilized life, or he must be fitted to become a part of that life and be absorbed into it. To permit him to be a roving savage was unendurable, and therefore the task of fitting him for civilized life was undertaken.

This, then, is the present Indian policy of the nation--to fit the Indian for civilization and to absorb him into it. It is a national work. It is less than twenty-five years since the government turned from the policy of keeping him on reservations, as quiet as possible, out of the way of civilization, waiting, with no excess of patience, for the race to fade out of existence....

This recognition of the home and family as a force in Indian civilization became a part of the present policy of dealing with the race only twelve years ago....

We are at peace with the Indian all along the border, and the line between the Indian and the white settlements is fast fading out. The pioneer goes forth to trade and barter with the red man as safely as he does with his white neighbor, and returns at night to his defenseless home with less apprehension of peril to those within than when scouts and sentinels mounted guard over it. This change has come quite as much from causes at work among the Indians themselves as from the influence of those who have been shaping our policy. During these twelve years, families and adult Indians without families, in all more than 30,000 have found homes of their own on Indian lands, and are maintaining themselves by farming, stock-raising, and other pursuits to which peace is essential, and have themselves become peacemakers....

But let it ever be kept in mind that, after all, the civilization of the Indian cannot be enacted. The function of the law in this work is little more than the clearing of the way, the removal of disabilities, the creation of opportunities, and the shelter and protection of agencies elsewhere vitalized. The one vitalizing force, without which all else will prove vain, is the Indian's own willingness to adopt civilized life. Until this is quickened into activity, everything else will wilt and perish like a plant without root. Every effort must recognize this cardinal principle. Much can be done to kindle in him a desire for a better life and to nurse its beginnings, building it up to an aggressive force; but until this exists, any attempt, through legislation or in any other way, to impose civilization upon the race will prove a failure. When that desire and hope for a better life shall begin to prevail over savage instincts, if the law shall then have made the way clear and the path plain, and, cooperating with outside efforts to strengthen and mature the new impulses, shall have made sure the rewards of civilization and the immunities of citizenship, it will have fulfilled its purpose. This is the endeavor of the Indian policy of today. Opening up so wide a field, and imposing an obligation for increased effort on every friend of the race, whatever may be his theory, it may calmly await the first stone from any of those who can claim Scriptural authority for casting it.

C. THE SUPREME COURT DECIDES THAT RESERVATION INDIANS HAVE NO PROPERTY RIGHTS, 1902

On June 6, 1901, Lone Wolf, on behalf of members of the Kiowa, Comanche, and Apache tribes of Fort Hall (Idaho) Indian Reservation sued Ethan Allen Hitchcock, the Secretary of the Interior. Lone Wolf claimed that an 1892 treaty with the government fraudulently deprived the Indians of two million acres of reservation land granted them in 1867. The controversy, which had begun soon after the 1892 treaty signing, prompted Congress in 1900 to pass legislation designed to give legal effect to the treaty, even though the Secretary of the Interior confirmed Indian charges that less than the minimum number of adult males had signed the treaty. In the following selection, Justice Edward D. White explains why the U.S. Supreme Court believed that Congress was justified in ignoring its treaty obligations when dealing with Indians.

Lone Wolf v. Hitchcock,
U.S. Supreme Court Reports, 187 U.S. 563, 1902)

The appellants base their right to relief on the proposition that by the effect of the article just quoted the confederated tribes of Kiowas, Comanches, and Apaches were vested with an interest in the lands held in common within the reservation, which interest could not be devested by Congress in any other mode than that specified in the said twelfth article, and that as a result of the said stipulation the interest of the Indians in the common lands fell within the protection of the 5th Amendment to the Constitution of the United States, and such interest--indirectly at least--came under the control of the judicial branch of the government. We are unable to yield our assent to this view.

The contention in effect ignores the status of the contracting Indians and the relation of dependency they bore and continue to bear towards the government of the United States. To uphold the claim would be to adjudge that the indirect operation of the treaty was to materially limit and qualify the controlling authority of Congress in respect to the care and protection of the Indians, and to deprive Congress, in a possible emergency, when the necessity might be urgent for a partition and disposal of the tribal lands, of all power to act, if the assent of the Indians could not be obtained....

The power exists to abrogate the provisions of an Indian treaty, though presumably such power will be exercised only when circumstances arise which will not only justify the government in disregarding the stipulations of the treaty, but may demand, in the interest of the country and the Indians themselves, that it should do so. When, therefore, treaties were entered into between the United States and a tribe of Indians it was never doubted that the power to abrogate existed in Congress, and that in a contingency such power might be availed of from considerations of governmental policy, particularly if consistent with perfect good faith towards the Indians....

The act of June 6, 1900, which is complained of in the bill, was enacted at a time when the tribal relations between the confederated tribes of Kiowas, Comanches, and Apaches still existed, and that statue and the statutes supplementary thereto dealt with the disposition of tribal property, and purported to give an adequate consideration for the surplus lands not allotted among the Indians or reserved for their benefit. Indeed, the controversy which this case presents is concluded by the decision in *Cherokee Nation v. Hitchcock*...decided at this term, where it was held that full administrative power was possessed by Congress over Indian tribal property. In effect, the action of Congress now complained of was but an exercise of such power, a mere change in the form of investment of Indian tribal property, the property of those who, as we have held, were in substantial effect the wards of the government. We must presume that Congress acted in perfect good faith in the dealings with the Indians of which complaint is made, and that the legislative branch of the government exercised its best judgment in the premises. In any event as Congress possessed full power in the matter, the judiciary cannot question or inquire into the motives which prompted the enactment of this legislation. If the injury was occasioned, which we do not wish to be understood as implying, by the use made by Congress of its power, relief must be sought by an appeal to that body for redress, and not to the courts. The legislation in question was constitutional, and the demurrer to the bill was therefore rightly sustained.

D. INDIAN COMMISSION SEEKS TO END INDIANS' "PECULIAR RACE TRAITS," 1905

Although few in this country then believed that the Native American could be assimilated, the Bureau of Indian Affairs always claimed that it was striving toward that goal. The following 1905 Report of the Board of Indian Commissioners is especially revealing because it typifies the prevailing attitude of the overnment for the half-century preceding the New Deal and because of its extraordinary ethnocentrism.

Annual Reports of the Department of the Interior,
House Document, Vol 20, 59th Cong.,
1st Sess., June 30, 1905

We believe that the strength of our American life is due in no small part to the fact that various and different race elements have entered into the making of the American the citizen of the United States in the twentieth century. No one racial stock is exclusively in control in our land. The typical modern American is a fine "composite," with race elements drawn from many sources. We do not believe that the Government of the United States in dealing with its Indian wards would act righteously or wisely if it were to attempt to crush out from those who are of Indian descent all the racial traits which differentiate the North American Indian from the other race stocks of the world. Certain conceptions of physical courage, a certain heroic stoicism in enduring physical pain, an inherited tendency to respect one's self, even if that tendency shows itself at times in unwarrantable conceit, are race traits which have value, if the people who have them become civilized and subject themselves to the laws of social morality and to the obligation of industrial efficiency, which are essential if any race stock or any group of families is to hold its own in the modern civilized world.

But the facts seem to us to be that good results are to be hoped for not by keeping the North American Indians peculiar in dress or in customs. We think that the wisest friends of the Indian recognize with great delight and value highly the art impulse in certain Indian tribes, which has shown itself in Indian music, in Indian art forms--such as the birch bark canoe, in Indian basketry, and more rarely in Indian pottery. But we firmly believe that the way to preserve the best of what is distinctively characteristic in the North American Indians is to civilize and educate them, that they may be fit for the life of the twentieth century under our American system of self-government. Because we value the elements for good which may come into our American life through the stock of North American Indians, we wish to see children of Indian descent educated in the industrial and practical arts and trained to habits of personal cleanliness, social purity, and industrious family life. We do not believe that it is right to keep the Indians out of civilization in order to be within reach of the traveler and the curious, or even of the scientific observer. In the objectionable "Indian dances" which are breaking out afresh at many points we see not a desirable maintenance of racial traits, but a distinct reversion toward barbarism and superstition. We believe that while the effort should never be made to "make a white man out of an Indian," in the sense of seeking to do violence to respect to parents or a proper or intelligent regard for what is fine in the traits and the history of one's ancestors, it is still most desirable that all the Indians on our territory should come as speedily as possible to the white man's habits of home-making, industry, cleanliness, social purity, and family integrity.

Precisely as all intelligent American patriots have seen danger to our national life in the attempt, wherever it has been made, to perpetuate in the United States large groups of foreign-born immigrants who try to keep their children from learning English and seek to perpetuate upon our territory (at the cost of true Americanism for their children) what was characteristic in the life of their own people on other continents and in past generations, precisely as in such cases we feel that the hope of our American system lies in the public schools and such educational institutions as shall maintain standards of public living that inevitably bring the children of foreign-born immigrants into the great body of English-speaking, home-loving, industrious, and pure-minded Americans--precisely so does it seem to us that all the efforts of the Government, and far more of distinctive missionary effort on the part of the Christian people of this country than has ever yet been used with this end in view, should be steadily employed in the effort to make out of the Indian children of this country intelligent, English-speaking, industrious, law-abiding Americans. We believe that the breaking up of tribal funds as rapidly as practical will help toward this end. Even if many of the Indians do for a time misuse money while they are learning how to use it properly, even if some of them squander it utterly, we believe that there is hope for the Indians in the future only as by education, faith in work, and obedience to Christian principles of morality and clean living, their children shall come to have the social standards and the social habits of our better American life throughout the land.

Our task is to hasten the slow work of race evolution. Inevitably, but often grimly and harshly by the outworking of natural forces, the national life of the stronger and more highly civilized race stock dominates in time the life of the less civilized, when races like the Anglo-Saxon and the Indian are brought into close contact. In our work for the Indians we want to discern clearly those influences and habits of life which are of the greatest advantage in leading races upward into Christian civilization; and these influences and habits we wish to make as strongly influential as possible, and as speedily as possible influential upon the life of these American tribes. It is not unreasonable to hope that through governmental agencies and through the altruistic missionary spirit of one of the foremost Christian races and governments of the world much can be done to hasten that process of civilization which natural law, left to itself, works out too slowly and at too great a loss to the less-favored race. We want to make the conditions for our less-favored brethren of the red race so favorable that the social forces which have developed themselves slowly and at great expense of time and life in our American race and our American system of government shall be made to help in the uplifting of the Indians and to shorten that interval of time which of necessity must elapse between savagery and Christian civilization.

E. PRESIDENT ROOSEVELT ADVISES INDIANS TO WORK AND SAVE, 1905

When dealing with Indians, Theodore Roosevelt usually reflected the Western viewpoint. During his presidency, Roosevelt somewhat toned down his "cowboy philosophy," but there were no basic changes from his earlier attitude about the "weaker race," which he had expressed in his four-volume The Winning of the West. *In the following letter to Chief No Shirt, Roosevelt handled the complainant like a patient father would a "headstrong child" who does not know right from wrong. The "strong friend of the red people" in the Indian Office referred to by Roosevelt in the letter was Francis E. Leupp, a New York City journalist, who employed a paternalistic approach toward the Indians. Leupp's boss, however, Interior Secretary Ethan Allen Hitchcock, was no friend of the Indians. Hitchcock was a McKinley-appointed businessman who had served as president of several mining and railway companies before coming to Washington as Secretary of the Interior in 1897. The following selection is from Elting E. Morison, Ed.,* The Letters of Theodore Roosevelt, *Vol. IV, Cambridge, Mass.: Harvard Uni. Press, 1951.*

Washington, May 18, 1905

It is true, as you say, that the earth is occupied by the white people and the red people; that, if the red people would prosper, they must follow the mode of life which has made the white people so strong; and that it is only right that the white people should show the red people what to do and how to live right. It is for that reason, because I wish to be as much a father to the red people as to the white, that I have placed in charge of the Indian Office a Commissioner in whom I have confidence, knowing him to be a strong friend of the red people and anxious to help them in every way.

But I am sorry to learn that when you sent the Commissioner word that you wished to come to Washington and he sent you a message not to come then but to send your complaints in writing, you followed your own will, like a headstrong child, instead of doing what the Commissioner advised. That is not the way to get along nicely in your new mode of life, and is not a good example to set to your people. You see, also, what the result was: you traveled three thousand miles across the country, at considerable expense, to see me, and then had to go back without seeing me. If you had done what the Commissioner wished you to, you would have avoided all this. I hope that you and your people will lay this lesson to heart for the future....

This brings me to another point in your letter where you give your reason for wishing your leases to be so arranged that you will have two payments every year instead of one. You say: "I have to have money to make my living...and of course I want my money whenever I need it." I suppose you realize that you will get only the same amount of money, whether you get it in one payment or in two. In other words, if a white lessee is going to give you $100 a year for the use of a piece of land, he will either give you the whole $100 in one payment or only $50 if he makes two payments. Now, if your lessee pays you $100 all at one time, it is not necessary that you should spend it all at one time; you can just as well spend $50 of it and keep the other $50 for six months, if that is what you wish to do. If he pays you only $50 at one time, the other $50 remains in his pocket until the next payment; surely, it ought to be just as safe in your pocket as in his. Besides, the lesson in saving would be of great value to you. No matter how much the Government or the white people do for the Indian, he will always remain poor if he foolishly spends his money just as fast as he gets it. The white man grows rich by learning to spend only part of his money and lay the other part aside till it is absolutely necessary to use it. Then he finds that he can be just as happy and do without a great many things which formerly he supposed he absolutely must have....

Indians...who wish to lease their own lands only for the purpose of shirking work, will not be permitted to do so. I wish you to tell this to your people very plainly, and say to them that the President intends to support the Commissioner in every way in insisting that able-bodied Indians shall earn their own living, just as able-bodied white men do....

Now, my friend, I hope that you will lay what I have said to heart. Try to set your people a good example of upright and industrious life, patience under difficulties, and respect for the authority of the officers I have appointed to care for your affairs. If you try as hard to help them as you do to find something in their conduct to censure, you will be surprised to discover how much real satisfaction life holds in store for you.

F. THE AMERICAN INDIAN: "A CONTINENT LOST--A CIVILIZATION WON," 1937

J. P. Kinney, who labored for 25 years in the Bureau of Indian Affairs, in 1937 published a justification of the government's Indian policy entitled, A Continent Lost, a Civilization Won. *Kinney felt himself to be enlightened on matters concerning Indians, but he placed much of the blame for the Bureau's failure on Indians themselves who lacked certain qualities conducive to intellectual, moral and economic progress." Thus, concluded Kinney, "The future of the race as a whole is in the hands of the individuals of the race." The following selection is from J. P. Kinney,* A Continent Lost, A Civilization Won, *John Hopkins Press, Baltimore, 1937.*

Those who are accustomed to condemn in unmeasured terms the conduct of the whites toward the Indians have failed to view the relationship between the races from a sufficiently detached viewpoint. If one considers only individual instances of misfortune and injustice in any society his sympathy may lead him to a distorted view of the wrongs suffered by individuals; and the same is true as to groups of individuals....

Passionate feelings must be accompanied by, or followed by, sustained and well-directed effort toward alleviation of the unfavorable conditions. In most instances it will be found that one of the difficulties encountered will be the awakening of the unfortunate as to the possibilities of a fuller life; and the zealous advocate of an enriched life for the poverty-stricken and suppressed members of society may experience many a disappointment because of the failure of the objects of his solicitude to react to the stimuli of improved economic and moral conditions. In an attempt to appraise the success attained, or the failure experienced, in efforts to improve the conditions of life among the Indians, either in the past of in the future, one must not overlook the fact that certain qualities conducive to intellectual, moral and economic progress are lacking or strangely dormant in many Indians; and that the best of intentions, carried into execution with zeal and intelligence, frequently produce mediocre results.

Furthermore, students of the Indian problem must not confine their view to the present. The people of the United States have been wrestling with this problem for nearly a century and a half. In that time there have been many changes in the economic and social order, changes that could not have been foreseen even one decade in advance in many instances. Those of previous generations should not be too harshly judged for the adoption of methods and plans that later developments have shown to be unwise or poorly suited for the accomplishment of the results desired. In preparing a schedule of the wrongs that the present generation of Indians have suffered at the hands of the whites, a double- entry system should be used and there should be entered upon the balance-sheet the advantages that such a generation has enjoyed. In listing the wrongs and misfortunes that their ancestors suffered, one should also set down on the opposite side of the sheet the wrongs and the sufferings that such ancestors inflicted upon the whites.

II - POPULAR IMAGES OF THE INDIAN

Until the Red Power movement began to shatter white America's illusions, Native Americans had been neatly stereotyped through innumerable novels, films, and television scripts. Although these white-created Indians might appear as courageous and noble savages who provided a worthy adversary for the early pioneers, they also exhibited the barbaric traits that contrasted nicely with the quiet strength and admirable character of the typical Western hero. In real life, Indians did not exist for most Americans--or, if they did, it was in some kind of human zoo, where they painfully went through the motions of a lost past for the benefit of white onlookers.

The traditional image of the Indian began not long after the first white settlers confronted him. The Puritans were only anticipating future actions when they decided Indians could not be saved, and since they were "devils," one was only doing God's bidding by eliminating them. As Americans moved westward, this basic view was reinforced by returning frontiersmen and missionaries, and soon it was so popular that Eastern writers, who had never left home, could inform their readers on the travails of frontier life. Although such stories appeared early, it was not until the post-Civil War period and the emergence of the so-called "dime novel" that an increasingly literate public could be reached in great numbers.

Favorite tales were those concerning whites who had lived among the savages and who, presumably, could then describe them with accuracy. Also popular were the eye-witness accounts of battles with the Indians, usually written by military men, who convincingly contrasted the brutal cruelty of the Indian with the cool courage of their own troops. Even after the fighting stopped, the Indian did not fare much better in the popular press. He was no longer the savage, albeit sometimes noble, adversary, who could bring out the best in our early settlers; now he became an inferior, downtrodden object who needed the help and leadership of a superior people. However, when Indians did not respond favorably to their patrons' attention, dismay, anger, cynicism, and, finally, silence resulted. Thus, in the popular mind the Indian evolved from a troublesome heathen to a mortal enemy to an unfortunate ward of the state to a non-person.

A. DESCRIBING THE HORRORS OF INDIAN CAPTIVITY, 1859

Throughout the last half of the nineteenth century, the American public was treated to numerous personal accounts of Indian captivity. These spine-tingling adventures usually thrilled their readers but did little to foster understanding between whites and Indians. The stories were filled with vivid descriptions of strange rituals, shocking tortures, and unsavory living habits, all of which helped convince readers of the Indians' innate barbarism. One of the more significant books of this genre was Three Years among the Comanches: the Narrative of Nelson Lee, the Texas Ranger. *First published pulished in 1859, it was reissued by the Western Frontier Library of the University of Oklahoma Press in 1957. The selection that follows is a typical description of an Indian torture ritual.*

There were Aikens, Martin, and Stewart, stripped entirely naked, and bound as follows: strong, high posts had been driven in the ground about three feet apart. Standing between them, their arms had been drawn up as far as they could reach, the right hand tied to the stake on the right side and the left hand to the stake opposite. Their feet, likewise, were tied to the posts near the ground. Martin and Stewart were thus strung up side by side. Directly in front of them, and within ten feet, was Aikens, in the same situation. A short time sufficed to divest me of my scanty Indian apparel and place me by the side of the latter, and in like condition. Thus we stood, or rather hung. Aikens and myself facing Stewart and Martin, all awaiting in tormenting suspense to learn what diabolical rite was now to be performed.

The Big Wolf and a number of his old men stationed themselves near us, when the war chief, at the head of the warriors, of whom there were probably two hundred, moved forward slowly, silently, and in single file. The pace was peculiar and difficult to describe, half walk, half shuffle, a spasmodic, nervous motion, like the artificial motion of figures in a puppet show. Each carried in one hand his knife or tomahawk, and in the other a flint stone, three inches or more in length and fashioned into the shape of a sharp pointed arrow. The head of the procession, as it circled a long way round, first approached Stewart and Martin. As it passed them, two of the youngest warriors broke from the line, seized them by the hair, and scalped them, then resumed their places and moved on. This operation consists of cutting off only a portion of the skin which covers the skull, of the dimensions of a dollar, and does not necessarily destroy life, as is very generally supposed; on the contrary, I have seen men, resident on the borders of Texas, who had been scalped and yet were alive and well. In this instance, the wounds inflicted were by no means mortal; nevertheless, blood flowed from them in profusion, running down over the face, and trickling from their long beards.

They passed Aikens and myself without molestation, marching round again in the same order as before. Up to this time there had been entire silence, except a yell from the two young men when in the act of scalping, but now the whole party halted a half-minute, and slapping their hands upon their mouths, united in a general and energetic war whoop. Then in silence the circuitous march was continued. When they reached Stewart and Martin the second time, the sharp flint arrowheads were brought into requisition. Each man, as he passed, with a wild screech, would brandish his tomahawk in their faces an instant, and then draw the sharp point of the stone across their bodies, not cutting deep, but penetrating the flesh just far enough to cause the blood to ooze out in great crimson streams. By the time the line had passed, our poor suffering companions presented an awful spectacle. Still they left Aikens and myself unharmed; nevertheless, we regarded it as a matter of certainty that very soon we should be subjected to similar tortures. We would have been devoutly thankful at that terrible hour--would have hailed it as a grateful privilege--could we have been permitted to choose our own mode of being put to death. How many times they circled round, halting to sound the war whoop, and going through the same demoniac exercise, I cannot tell. Suffice it to say, they persisted in the hellish work until every inch of the bodies of the unhappy men was haggled, and hacked and scarified, and covered with clotted blood. It would have been a relief to me, much more to them, could they have only died, but the object of the tormentors was to drain the fountain of their lives by slow degrees.

In the progress of their torture, there occurred an intermission of some quarter of an hour. During this period, some threw themselves on the ground and lighted their pipes, others collected in little groups, all, however, laughing and shouting, and pointing their fingers at the prisoners in derision, as if taunting them as cowards and miscreants. The prisoners bore themselves differently. Stewart uttered not a word, but his sobs and groans were such as only the intensest pain and agony can wring from the human heart. On the contrary, the pitiful cries and prayers of Martin were unceasing. Constantly he was exclaiming, "Oh,God have mercy on me!" "Oh, Father in heaven pity me!" "Oh, Lord Jesus, come and put me out of pain!" and many other expressions of like character.

I hung down my head and closed my eyes to shut out from sight the heart-sickening scene before me, but this poor comfort was not vouchsafed me. They would grasp myself, as well as Aikens, by the hair, drawing our heads back violently, compelling us, however unwillingly, to stare directly at the agonized and writhing sufferers.

At the end of, perhaps, two hours, came the last act of the fearful tragedy. The warriors halted on their last round in the form of a half-circle, when two of them moved out from the center, striking into the war dance, raising the war song, advancing, receding, now moving to the right, now to the left, occupying ten minutes in proceeding as many paces. Finally, they reached the victims, for some time danced before them, as it were, the hideous dance of hell, then drew their hatchets suddenly, and sent the bright blades crashing through their skulls.

B. CUSTER TELLS WHY CIVILIZATION WILL DESTROY THE INDIAN, 1874

As the white man moved across the Mississippi, he drove the Indian further West, or isolated him on remote reservations. Because not all Indians peacefully submitted to the white man's encroachments, the U.S. Army acted as "peacemaker" for several decades. Prominent army officers often became heroes to the public, and their views were solicited on the subject of Indians. Many of those achieving success on the battlefield later wrote their memoirs, thereby supplying movie-makers of a later day with a vast, albeit one-sided, reservoir of information about life on the frontier. One such military hero was General George A. Custer. Despite a limited career on the Plains, the flamboyant Custer published his recollections in 1874, two years before his total defeat and death in the Battle of the Little Big Horn. My Life on the Plains *provides the reader with an interesting example of a military man's thoughts on the Indian.*

Stripped of the beautiful romance with which we have been so long willing to envelop him, transferred from the inviting pages of the novelist to the localities where we are compelled to meet with him, in his native village, on the war path, and when raiding upon our frontier settlements and lines of travel, the Indian forfeits his claim to the appellation of the "noble red man." We see him as he is, and, so far as all knowledge goes, as he ever has been, a savage in every sense of the word; not worse, perhaps, than his white brother would be similarly born and bred, but one whose cruel and ferocious nature far exceeds that of any wild beast of the desert. That this is true no one who has been brought into intimate contact with the wild tribes will deny. Perhaps there are some who, as members of peace commissions or as wandering agents of some benevolent society, may have visited these tribes or attended with them at councils held for some pacific purpose, and who, by passing through the villages of the Indian while at peace, many imagine their opportunities for judging of the Indian nature all that could be desired. But the Indian, while he can seldom be accused of indulging in a great variety of wardrobe, can be said to have a character capable of adapting itself to almost every occasion. He has one character, perhaps his most serviceable one, which he preserves carefully, and only airs it when making his appeal to the Government or its agents for arms, ammunition, and license to employ them. This character is invariably paraded, and often with telling effect, when the motive is a peaceful one. Prominent chiefs invited to visit Washington invariably don this character, and in their "talks" with the "Great Father" and other less prominent personages they successfully contrive to exhibit but this one phase. Seeing them under these or similar circumstances only, it is not surprising that by many the Indian is looked upon as a simple-minded "son of nature," desiring nothing beyond the privilege of roaming and hunting over the vast unsettled wilds of the West, inheriting and asserting but few native rights, and never trespassing upon the rights of others. This view is equally erroneous with that which regards the Indian as a creature possessing the human form but divested of all other attributes of humanity, and whose traits of character, habits, modes of life, disposition and savage customs disqualify him from the exercise of all rights and privileges, even those pertaining to life itself. Taking him as we find him, at peace or at war, at home or abroad, waiving all prejudices, and laying aside all partiality, we will discover in the Indian a subject of thoughtful study and investigation. In him we will find the representative of a race whose origin is, and promises to be, a subject forever wrapped in mystery; a race incapable of being judged by the rules or laws applicable to any other known race of men; one between which and civilization there seems to have existed from time immemorial a determined and unceasing warfare--a hostility so deep-seated and inbred with the Indian character, that in the exceptional instances where the modes and habits of civilization have been reluctantly adopted, it has been at the sacrifice of power and influence as a tribe, and the more serious loss of health, vigor, and courage as individuals....

Nature intended him for a savage state; every instinct, every impulse of his soul inclines him to it. The white race might fall into a barbarous state, and afterwards, subjected to the influence of civilization, be reclaimed and prosper. Not so the Indian. He cannot be himself and be civilized; he fades away and dies. Cultivation such as the white man would give him deprives him of his identify. Education, strange as it may appear, seems to weaken rather than strengthen his intellect....

He can hunt, roam, and camp when and wheresoever he pleases, provided always that in so doing he does not run contrary to the requirements of civilization in its advancing tread. When the soil which he has claimed and hunted over for so long a time is demanded by this to him insatiable monster, there is no appeal; he must yield, or, like the car of Juggernaut, it will roll mercilessly over him, destroying as it advances. Destiny seems to have so willed it, and the world looks on and nods its approval.

C. SOLVING THE INDIAN PROBLEM WITH "REAL OLD-FASHIONED" INDIAN HUNTS, 1885

In 1885, several Arizona and New Mexico counties paid a high price for Indian scalps. Significantly, a major Eastern newspaper reporting this news from the frontier was unperturbed, and willing to rationalize the policy. The following article on the legalized scalping of Indians appeared on page one of the October 11, 1885 New York Times. *Its tone leans heavily toward justification of scalping and tends to discredit "Northern and Eastern sentimentalists" who might decry murder-for-money.*

MONEY FOR INDIAN SCALPS

Arizona and New Mexico Settlers Propose to Destroy the Savages

It has been recently telegraphed that the pioneer settlers in the border counties of Arizona have brought to light an old law in several counties offering a reward of $250 each for Indian scalps. Under this law, which is nothing more than an order made by the Country Commissioners, the ranchmen and cowboys in Cochise, Pima, and Yavapai Counties are organizing in armed bodies for the purpose of going on a real old-fashioned Indian hunt, and they propose to bring back the scalps and obtain the reward. Word now comes from Tombstone, the county seat of Cochise County, that the reward in that county has been increased to $500 for a buck Indian's scalp. The authorities in Pima and Yavapai Counties have taken steps to increase their reward to $500, and it is said Yuma, Apache, and Maricopa Counties will follow suit.

This reward system, while it may seem savage and brutal to the Northern and Eastern sentimentalists, is looked upon in this section as the only means possible of ridding Arizona of the murderous Apaches. The settlers of New Mexico and Arizona are aroused on this question, and propose to act henceforth independent of the military authorities. From time immemorial all border counties have offered rewards for bear and wolf scalps and other animals that destroyed the pioneer's stock or molested his family. Why, therefore, asks the Arizona settler, should not the authorities place a reward upon the head of the terrible Apache, who murders the white man's family and steals his stock like the wolves? "Extermination" is the battle cry now, and the coming winter will witness bloody work in this section.

D. CIVILIZING THE INDIAN WITH A GOOD AMERICAN EDUCATION, 1887

On the fast-vanishing frontier of the 1880s, a few young Indians still resisted the advance of the paleface's civilization. Far more, however, were being introduced to the white man's values and principles in numerous government boarding schools. The following article in the February 15, 1887 New York Times *indicated that such Indian schools might very well be successful in transforming the savage into someone who really understood that work and education were "civilizers."*

EDUCATED INDIANS

The Carlisle School's Way of Solving the Indian Problem

Over 100 young Indians of various tribes, now being educated at the Carlisle Indian School, gave an extremely interesting entertainment in the Academy of Music last evening before a large audience. The boys wore a light blue military uniform, trimmed with red, and the girls wore dark blue flannel costumes, consisting of a plain skirt and a basque buttoned in front with brass buttons. Their long black hair was done up in single braids tied with neat bows of ribbon. Some of the girls were very bright-faced and pretty, while others had the Indian features too strongly marked to be handsome.

Probably the most interesting thing in the entertainment was the "first lessons," illustrated by half a dozen Chiricahua Apache boys who have been in the school three months. They were supplied with long slips of paper with which they performed simple operations in arithmetic, answering in halting but grammatical English. At the request of the instructor they named and described objects, and one of the lads put the others through a similar course. Another interesting feature was a recitation by half a dozen boys and three girls, under the direction of an Indian girl, on the Constitution of the United States. The boys and girls answered intelligently questions as to the powers of the three branches of the Government, the methods of election, terms of office, Presidential succession, and duties of citizens. An Arapahoe boy said a citizen's duty was to pay his taxes and to vote.

Joshua Given, a Kiowa, told the story of his life from wild Indian boyhood up to the status of theological student. He said he wanted to be a citizen of the United States, but was told he could not without a special act of Congress. Carlos Montezuma, an Apache, who is a college graduate, a drug clerk and a medical student, was presented by invitation and narrated his experience. He was taken captive by hostile Indians 15 years ago and sold for $30 to a gentleman who was collecting curiosities, as he humorously put it, and who educated him. Samuel Townsend, a Pawnee, delivered an original speech on "Work a Civilizer," and Jemima Wheelock, an Oneida, spoke on "Education a Civilizer." There was singing by the school choir and music by the school brass band, and an interesting exhibition of boys working at type setting, cobbling, tailoring, blacksmithing, carpentering, and tinsmithing, and girls at sewing, washing, ironing, crocheting, and other feminine occupations....

E. AN UNFLATTERING PORTRAIT OF THE OIL-RICH OSAGE INDIANS, 1920

In 1915, oil was discovered on the barren reservation of the Osage

Indians of Oklahoma, and overnight many Indians became wealthy. William G. Shepherd, the author of the following article in Harper's Magazine *(November 1920) and later Professor of Economics at the University of Michigan, estimated that each family had an income of $25,000 four years after the first strike. The picture of Indians with money was evidently humorous to Shepherd, and he called his article "Lo, the Rich Indians," a parody on the time-honored phrase by which whites indicated their alleged concern for the plight of the country's original settlers. A similarly negative view of the Osage Indians can be found in Edna Ferber's* Cimarron, *the number one best-selling novel for 1930. Shepherd makes it quite clear that the Indians were better off when they were attempting to cultivate the barren soil of the Oklahoma dust bowl than when squandering their money on material goods, since in those days, at least, they were not able to afford mescal, "the cocaine, the heroin, the alcohol, all rolled into one, of the American Indian!"*

A huge car of expensive make comes up to the curb. An unshaven young man, coatless, wearing a greasy golf cap and no collar, is at the wheel. Before long you will see many of his type; he is a well-paid chauffeur for a rich Indian family. He brings the car to a stop with a suggestion of a flourish. He does not descend to open the rear door; instead he begins to roll a cigarette. From the back seat steps a huge Indian woman; she is blanketed, and her glistening hair is parted in the middle and brushed back above her ears. She has a bead necklace and a beaded bag, but you catch a flash of a silk stocking and you see that instead of moccasins she is wearing heelless, patent-leather slippers, attached to her feet with an ankle strap. Marie Antoinette, in her empire gowns, was shod like this. Behind her descends a huge red man. His garb is Indian to the last observable stitch, except for his hat. His blue trousers are edged here and there with beads and are of a soft and glistening broadcloth. A gayly colored blanket is about his shoulders. His companion has not waited for him to alight. She strides off through the entrance of a store; he follows; fifteen feet behind her. They both "Toe in," she in her empire slippers and he in his soft, beaded moccasins. The chauffeur settles back in his seat to smoke, with one leg crossed high over his knee. In other cities men of his calling, with masters not so rich by far as his, have far more dignity than he. When in distant places you heard of these Indians with their chauffeurs, you expected to see liveried autocrats at the wheels of glistening limousines, but you soon discover, in Pawhuska, that a chauffeur does not even keep a car glistening, much less wear a livery. Mud and dust on a car's sides do not affect its speed....

Not all their spending is selfish indulgence; gentler emotions often come into play.

"I want to buy best baby-carriage," said a proud young Indian mother to a storekeeper.

"But your mother bought a carriage for the baby today," said the storekeeper. "She said she wanted him to ride in his grandmother's carriage."

"All right. But he's my baby and I want him to ride in his mother's carriage sometimes, too," said the mother, as she selected a carriage, twin of the one her mother had bought....

There is one other gift that Bacon Rind wishes to show you. He draws forth a chamois-skin bag, of incredible softness, and empties its contents onto the sofa. You see a heap of what look at first glance like dried apricots, a double-handful. Bacon Rind's great brown fingers toy with the small treasure.

"Mescal," he says, importantly.

The cocaine, the heroin, the alcohol, all rolled into one, of the American Indian!

"Do you drink it?" you ask.

"No, no, no!" says Bacon Rind. "Eat four, five! Then you come very close to God!" He raises his gaze to the ceiling and lifts one huge hand. "You put some in water; they get very large, like apple. Then eat, slowly, like tobacco. Throw water away; never drink mescal; very bad."

Mr. McGuire explains. "Mescal is a drug, but the Indians don't know it. They believe that it is a gift of God to bring them closer to Him. The effect is very quick and very strong; it gives them a dreamy, happy feeling and they think it is religion."

Bacon Rind talks rapidly to your interpreter and then Mr. McGuire tells you:

"Bacon Rind says that he is going to talk about God in the meeting house Sunday. It will be a mescal ceremony. Everyone will eat a little mescal and then he will talk about the Great Spirit. It will make everyone there happy, Bacon Rind says."

"Yes, yes!" rumbles Bacon Rind, raising a hand above his head. "Me talk God, Sunday. That very good."...

There are 265,000 Indians in the United States; their race is not dying out. But, of them all, it is not improbable that these Osage Indians, with their wealth, are the unhappiest. You have that impression as you leave Pawhuska; it is not a happy town.

A blight of gold and oil and greed is on it, as heavy a curse as Indians have ever had from their wickedest medicine man.

F. THE "PAGANISM" OF THE NEW DEAL'S INDIAN POLICY, 1934

When Franklin D. Roosevelt came into office in 1933, Native Americans were on the road to extinction, with a death rate that exceeded their birth rate. As with so many other problems, New Deal officials decided some changes had to be made. John Collier, unquestionably the most sensitive Commissioner of Indian Affairs, brought to a close the Government's attempt to "civilize" and "assimilate" the Indian. Indians were again allowed freely to resume old practices, including their own religious ceremonies. For those who felt the Indian's salvation lay through Christianity, this "reversion" came as a profound shock. In the following selection from the Christian Century *(August 8, 1934), Elaine*

Goodale Eastman criticizes the Government's decision.

Not only are the elders of the tribe to be officially invited to resume their archaic rites, but in the most recent orders promulgated by the Indian office we read the following: "Any denomination or missionary, including any representative of a native Indian religion, may be granted...the use of rooms or other conveniences in boarding schools....Any child at any Indian service day school, upon written request of his or her parents...shall be excused for religious instruction, including instruction in the native Indian religion, if any, for not more than one hour each week."

It is to be clearly understood that the native religions thus affirmatively sanctioned, certainly for the first time in our history, have no sacred books or formal theology which may be taught by word of mouth. Their priests, if any, are medicine-men or shamans, dispensing wisdom and healing through the medium of songs and incantations. We never went so far as to give them our blessing, but apparently we were wrong. At all events, Mr. Collier's new order definitely "supersedes any former regulation, instruction, or practice."

Now that two full generations of Sioux and other northwestern groups have grown up in the atmosphere of Christian teaching and more or less scientific medical and hospital care under government auspices, the official re-entry of the primitive medicine-man in all his glory, handsomely panoplied in paint, furs and feathers, armed with his sacred rattles, his skins of totemic beasts, his dried bodies of lizards or snakes, hair, entrails, and other bodily detritus, will be observed with profound interest--whether as an aid to religious meditation or as a sanitary precaution. Naturally, a strip of red flannel tied to a stick must hereafter be recognized by all Indian school superintendents as an official prayer, on an exact equality with the most eloquent invocation that may be pronounced by a bishop!...

To drop all speculation and return to the solid ground of contemporaneous fact, we find rain dances and alligator dances and other esoteric or curious rites still celebrated from time to time in village or pueblo, partly "for excitement and fun," as we are told, but principally, one gathers, as tourist attractions and commercial enterprises. This may be financially profitably, but is it spiritually edifying?

However, the "native religion" most in vogue today is obviously the so-called "Peyote church," introduced from Mexico about thirty years ago, of which I quote a brief account from the well-known report of the Institute for Government Research: "The Indians assemble for meetings in churches, so-called, where they fall into trance-like stupor from the use of peyote. The organization is of no practical value to the community, and peyote addiction is probably harmful physically as well as socially. The 'Shakers' and the Peyote church are both reported to be growing."

This drug is the dried button of a small cactus found along the Rio Grande and southward into Mexico. Mrs. Flora Warren Seymour, in her "Story of the Red Man," describes the Peyote addict thus: "In a house bestrewn with a disorderly litter of rubbish, a stalwart Ute sits cross-legged on the floor. His glazed eyes stare before him, unseeing. His right arm beats upon the skin drum, as a monotonous droning chant issues from his throat. Soon he will pass entirely into the Peyote dream he is wooing with his incantations, and will see beatific visions of ineffable delight."

Indians given to the practice of this "religion" strenuously uphold their sacred right under the Constitution of the United States to continue and extend it. It is, however, forbidden by state law in South Dakota and elsewhere. Shall we soon see it introduced into tax-supported schools, under the present regime?

III. THE SCIENTISTS AND THE INDIAN

No single group did more to legitimatize race stereotyping than did American scientists. Through their supposedly objective studies of craniology, physiognomy, eugenics, ethnology, intelligence, and social behavior, these scholars, operating from a basically Anglo-Saxon norm, attempted to prove that popular images of minorities were scientifically correct. Their work on behalf of Anglo-Saxon superiority, however, only proved their own racism was stronger than their scientific dedication. J.A. Rogers, a long-ignored black anthropologist, once observed, "If the kind of science that is in ethnology went into engineering, no automobile would ever run, no air ship would ever leave the ground, in fact not even a clock would run." Unfortunately, Americans traditionally have worshipped at the shrine of scientific objectivity and few persons questioned the validity of the scientists' conclusions on race. In reality, often scientists, like novelists, historians, journalists, and politicians, reflect their personal biases and those of the society about them.

Although it was not too surprising to find frontiersmen and generals in agreement that Indians could best serve the nation in a deceased state, early scientists were scarcely less harsh. As early as 1839, Dr. Samuel George Morton, an authority on craniology, insisted that Indians were inherently savage and intractable. Two decades later, his student in anthropology at Harvard, Josiah Clark Nott, concluded that there was no such thing as a "civilized full-blooded Indian." If such derogatory assessments lessened by the end of the nineteenth century, it was as much because the Indian had ceased to be a threat as it was because of any fundamental change on the part of the scientists. To be sure, many scholars were beginning to take a genuine interest in studying Native Americans, but seldom did this interest result in conclusions that might gain him racial parity.

The scientific arguments used to assess the Indian were familiar ones. From his physiognomy to his inability to score well on intelligence tests, the Indian was clearly of a lesser race. One prominent Yale geographer went so far as to suggest that Native Americans' mental weaknesses could be explained by "Siberian Hysteria," a disease Indians were supposed to have contracted during their migration from Asia some 10,000 years before.

A. THE INDIAN ANATOMY: PROOF OF INFERIORITY, 1891

Scientists in the twentieth century could turn to Dr. Daniel G. Brinton's 1891 study, The American Race *for evidence on the superiority of the white race. Brinton, a Yale graduate who served as medical director of the Eleventh Army during the Civil War and later taught at the University of Pennsylvania, made a careful study of the Indian's anatomy and came away convinced of his inferiority.*

A special feature in Native American skulls is the presence of the epactal bone, or *os Incae,* in the occiput. It is found in a complete or incomplete condition in 3.86 per cent of the skulls throughout the continent, and in particular localities much more frequently; among the ancient Peruvians for example in 6.81 per cent. This is far more frequently than in other races, the highest being the Negro, which offers 2.65 per cent, while the Europeans yield but 1.19. The presence of the bone is due to a persistence of the transverse occipital suture, which is usually closed in fetal life. Hence it is a sign of arrested development, and indicative of an inferior race.

The majority of the Americans have a tendency to meso- or brachycephaly, but in certain families, as the Eskimos in the extreme north and the Tapuyas in Brazil, the skulls are usually decidedly long. In other instances there is a remarkable difference in members of the same tribe and even of the same household. Thus among the Yumas there are some with as low an index as 68, while the majority are above 80, and among the dolichocephalic Eskimos we occasionally find an almost globular skull. So far as can be learned, these variations appear in persons of pure blood. Often the crania differ in no wise from those of the European. Dr. Hensell, for instance, says that the skulls of pure-blood Corcados of Brazil...corresponded in all points to those of the average German.

The average cubical capacity of the Native American skull falls below that of the white, and rises above that of the black race. Taking both sexes, the Parisians of today have a cranial capacity of 1448 cubic centimeters; the Negroes 1344 c.c.; the American Indians 1376. But single examples of Indian skulls have yielded the extraordinary capacity of 1747, 1825, and even 1920 c. c., which are not exceeded in any other race....

Beyond all other criteria of a race must rank its mental endowments. These are what decide irrevocably its place in history and its destiny in time....But the final decision as to the abilities of a race or of an individual must be based on actual accomplished results, not on supposed endowments. Thus appraised, the American Indian certainly stands higher than the Australian, the Polynesian or the African, but does not equal the Asian....

While these facts bear testimony to a good natural capacity, it is also true that the receptivity of the race for a foreign civilization is not great. Even individual instances of highly educated Indians are rare; and I do not recall any who have achieved distinction in art or science, or large wealth in the business world.

B. INTELLIGENCE TESTS "PROVE INDIANS TO BE MENTALLY INFERIOR, 1931

Until his death in 1939, psychologist Thomas R. Garth stood at the top of his discipline as an expert on the American Indian. After completing his Ph.D. at Columbia University, Garth directed numerous expeditions to study Indians, and as late as 1937, he served the Government as a specialist on Indian education. In his 1931 book, Race Psychology, *Garth set down his conclusions on racial differences in intelligence. Using various tests on intelligence and racial characteristics, Garth found Indians to be intellectually inferior. In addition, he concluded that "mix bloods" were more intelligent than "full bloods," with intelligence "tending to increase with the degree of white blood."*

The first use of the Binet Scale for the measurement of intelligence in race psychology was made by Alice C. Strong in columbia, S.C., on a group of Negroes, and by Rowe in Michigan who studied a group of whites and Indians with the Binet. In all these studies the performance of the whites was superior to that of the Negroes and Indians....

So far as we know the only use of the Binet with Indians was made by Helen M. and E. C. Rowe. They used the Goddard form on 268 Indians in an Indian school in comparison with 547 whites, all in Michigan, in grades running from kindergarten through the eighth grade. Their results were reported in 1914 by E. C. Rowe in terms of relative mental age. He says that 94% of the Indian children were mentally below the whites. At that time the I.Q. was not in general use.

So, unfortunately, we are unable to give Binet I.Q.'s for Indians, since no study is available in which they are supplied. We shall have to make use of the group I.Q.'s obtained from such tests as the National Intelligence Test and the Otis Intelligence Test. The Indian subjects of these tests have been largely the students in the United States Indian schools and were tested in Oklahoma, Colorado, New Mexico, and South Dakota. They are fairly representative of all tribes of Indians, such as Sioux, Cherokee, Arapahoe, Navajo, Ute, and Pueblo, and are the descendants of those who in early days before the advent of the white man, lurked in the forests, stalked the plains, or followed agricultural pursuits in the Southwest.

Much of the testing reported on Indians has been done by Garth and students under his direction. With the National Intelligence Test, Garth *et al.* obtained a median group I.Q. of 68.6 for 1,050 full-blood Indians of the fairly representative tribal population above mentioned. For a group of 1,000 full bloods with the Otis Intelligence Test they obtained a median group I.Q. of 70.4. This makes in all 2,650 full bloods with a group I.Q. of around 69. Another group I.Q. of 72.5 for full bloods not attending the United States Indian schools but attending the public schools along with white children was reported by Garth and Garrett.

As to the I.Q.'s of mixed blood Indians, they are found to be higher than those of full bloods, tending to increase with the degree of white blood. As we have said, Garth *et al.* found a positive correlation of 0.42 for degree of white blood and I.Q. as obtained by the National

Intelligence Test with 765 subjects. The I.Q. of one-quarter bloods was 77, of half bloods, 75, and of three-quarter bloods 74. Hunter and Sommermeir found a positive correlation of 0.41 between degree of white blood and Otis intelligence score using a group of mixed bloods....

Disregarding the I.Q.'s of the immigrant groups, which we do not believe are measures of the average of the groups in their home lands, the racial I.Q.'s as found are: whites, 100; Chinese, 99; Japanese, 99; Mexicans, 78; southern Negroes, 75; northern Negroes, 85; American Indians, full blood, 70. If one says that what is fair for one is fair for another, then regardless of environmental difficulties, the Chinese and Japanese score so nearly like the whites that the difference is negligible. Certainly they possess a quality which places them in a class beyond the Negro, the Mexican in the United States, and the American Indian, whatever that is. Perhaps it is temperament which makes the latter groups unable to cope with the white man's test. Again, it is barely possible they cannot take the white man's seriousness seriously....

The number of superior individuals in these groups is small to be sure. Of 1,272 Negroes there are 96, to express it in numbers, who are as good as or better than the average white. There are 90 Mexicans out of 1,004 and 75 Indians out of 667 who are seen to do as well as or better than the white median performance. Regardless of race and though few in number, they make a small group which intelligent people must recognize, though it might be wished they were more numerous.

IV. THE INDIAN AMERICAN HISTORY

Although they were virtually exterminated by whites in less than three centuries, Native Americans rarely received the sympathy of professional chroniclers of the American past. In reviewing his country's history, the president of Harvard declared in 1896 that America's principal contribution to civilization was in the abandonment of war as a means of settling disputes. The Indians provided no contradiction for President Charles Eliot because these "Stone-Age" men had to be "resisted and quelled by force... (and) could not be assimilated...or even reasoned with."

Likewise, most writers of American history who touched on Indian relations believed that the related wars should be treated as unique experiences. Professor Walker Prescott Webb, in his classic history of *The Great Plains* (1931), concluded that "so far as the Indian goes, the historical problem comes down to the single issue of his ways in war," which forced "white men to save one bullet for themselves." Thus, "brutal and implacable foe," "unassimilable aborigine," and "inferior savage" were all assumed to be acceptable synonyms for the Indian by most historians. James Truslow Adams in his *The Epic of America* (1931) claimed that the Indians' nervous systems "were unstable and...of a markedly hysterical make-up...cruel and revengeful....They were childishly lacking in self-control." Obligated to comment on the Aztec civilization, Adams relied on reports "by early writers" to emphasize the Aztecs' "ghastly" cruel religion, which made use of human sacrifices. This emphasis on Indian cruelty--especially as manifested during the frontier wars--runs through virtually all early American history books. And these early historians were not likely to discuss the impact of government policies on Indian people. Settling the land with white pioneers was the main focus of these books, and the Indian danger was usually treated as one of the hazards on the frontier along with other natural dangers of a wild, uncivilized, and unfriendly land.

A. FRANCIS PARKMAN EXPLAINS THE INDIAN CHARACTER, 1851

Although Francis Parkman's epic history of Pontiac's conspiracy and the Indian War was first published in 1851, it retained its popularity for future generations. The Boston-born, Harvard-educated Parkman was convinced the Indian was doomed to extinction by the advancing tide of white civilization, and while he willingly admitted certain noble qualities, it was the "dark, cold, and sinister" side of his Indians he chose to emphasize.

Nature has stamped the Indian with a hard and stern physiognomy. Ambition, revenge, envy, and jealousy are his ruling passions; and his cold temperament is little exposed to those effeminate vices which are the bane of milder races. With him revenge is an overpowering instinct; nay, more, it is a point of honor and a duty. His pride sets all language at defiance. He loathes the thought of coercion; and few of his race have ever stooped to discharge a menial office. A wild love of liberty, an utter intolerance of control, lie at the basis of his character, and fire his whole existence. Yet, in spite of this haughty independence, he is a devout hero-worshipper; and high achievement in war or policy touches a chord to which his nature never fails to respond. He looks up with admiring reverence to the sages and heroes of his tribe; and it is this principle, joined to the respect for age springing from the patriarchal element in his social system, which, beyond all others, contributes union and harmony to the erratic members of an Indian community. With him the love of glory kindles into a burning passion; and to allay its cravings, he will dare cold and famine, fire, tempest, torture, and death itself.

These generous traits are overcast by much that is dark, cold, and sinister, by sleepless distrust, and ranking jealousy. Treacherous himself, he is always suspicious of treachery in others. Brave as he is--and few of mankind are braver--he will vent his passion by a secret stab rather than an open blow. His warfare is full of ambuscade and stratagem; and he never rushes into battle with that joyous self-abandonment, with which the warriors of the Gothic races flung themselves into the ranks of their enemies. In his feasts and his drinking bouts we find none of that robust and full-toned mirth, which reigned at the rude carousals of our barbaric ancestry. He is never jovial in his cups, and maudlin sorrow or maniacal rage is the sole result of his potations.

Over all emotion he throws the veil of an iron self-control, originating in a peculiar form of pride, and fostered by rigorous discipline from childhood upward. He is trained to conceal passion, and not to subdue it. The inscrutable warrior is aptly imaged by the hackneyed figure of a volcano covered with snow; and no man can say when or where the wild-fire will burst forth. This shallow self-mastery serves to give dignity to public deliberation, and harmony to social life. Wrangling and quarrel are strangers to an Indian dwelling; and while an assembly of the ancient Gauls was garrulous as a convocation of magpies, a Roman senate might have taken a lesson from the grave solemnity of an Indian council. In the midst of his family and friends, he hides affections, by nature none of the most tender, under a mask of icy coldness; and in the torturing fires of his enemy, the haughty sufferer maintains to the last his look of grim defiance.

His intellect is as peculiar as his moral organization. Among all savages, the powers of perception preponderate over those of reason and analysis; but this is more especially the case with the Indian. An acute judge of character, at least of such parts of it as his experience enables him to comprehend; keen to a proverb in all exercises of war and the chase, he seldom traces effects to their causes, or follows out actions to their remote results. Though a close observer of external nature, he no sooner attempts to account for her phenomena than he involves himself in the most ridiculous absurdities; and quite content with these puerilities, he has not the least desire to push his inquiries further. His curiosity, abundantly active within its own narrow circle, is dead to all things else; and to attempt rousing it from its torpor is but a bootless task. He seldom takes cognizance of general or abstract ideas; and his language has scarcely the power to express them, except through the medium of figures drawn from the external world, and often highly picturesque and forcible. The absence of reflection makes him grossly improvident, and unfits him for pursuing any complicated scheme of war or policy.

Some races of men seem molded in wax, soft and melting, at once plastic and feeble. Some races, like some metals, combine the greatest flexibility with the greatest strength. But the Indian is hewn out of a rock. You can rarely change the form without destruction of the substance. Races of inferior energy have possessed a power of expansion and assimilation to which he is a stranger; and it is this fixed and rigid quality which has proved his ruin. He will not learn the arts of civilization, and he and his forest must perish together.

B. WHY AMERICA SHOULD BELONG TO ARYANS, NOT INDIANS, 1894

Geologist and dean of Harvard's Lawrence Scientific School, Professor Nathaniel S. Shaler, in editing his 1894 two-volume The United States of America, *explained in the first chapter why America was aptly suited to be the home of the great northern Aryan race. In the course of his discussion, he was forced to deal with the Native American who had lived in this country long before any white man appeared. Shaler concluded that the Indian's culture had been vastly exaggerated and that he had not advanced above the level of savagery. In fact, the inferior Indian was fortunate the superior white race did not practice genocide or slavery as other conquering races had.*

We have now to consider the reason why our North American Indians, who have evidently been so long upon a continent well fitted for the uses of civilized men, have failed to advance beyond the primitive condition of men. We cannot fairly attribute this retardation in their social development to an original lack of intellectual capacity. On the whole, these people seem to have more than the usual measure of ability which is found among savages....

The greatest difficulty which our people have encountered in dealing with the conditions presented by the central portion of the continent has arisen from the presence of the Indians in that field. Although the wars with the aborigines were often sanguinary and always harassing, the most serious obstacles were not those of a military sort. It has always proved easy to overcome the armed resistance of the savages, but always extremely difficult to make any satisfactory disposition of them. Although at no time has the population of these native folk north of the Rio Grande exceeded three hundred thousand souls, their habits were such as to require a great extend of land for their subsistence. In general, it may be said that the Indian needs from one to three square miles of land for the support of each of the members of his tribe. If confined within a smaller area, at least until he has adopted the agricultural habit, he is sure to become restless and predatory. Thus it has come about that our people have adopted the rather curious plan of confining these savages within large reservations, around which the tide of civilization has soon closed. In time these great areas given over to savagery have proved to be exceedingly inconvenient, whereupon the tribes were forced to move westward on to lands which were by new treaties devoted to their use....

Although much of the criticism which has been directed against our administration of Indian affairs is doubtless well founded, few of the critics perceive how almost insuperable are the difficulties of dealing with an indigenous people having the qualities of this native American race. Centuries of experience have taught us that these folk are, from the point of view of our civilization, essentially untamable. In general, they can not take up the burden of our Anglo-Saxon civilization, or even accommodate themselves to our ways of living. Here and there, though rarely, some of the tribes, particularly those of the more southern parts of the country, when the more desperate element of the population has been weeded out by war and the blood somewhat commingled with that of the whites, have become soil-tillers, and thereby ceased to be troublesome to the state. The choice before our people in dealing with this indomitable folk lay between a method of extermination, such as has been practiced in other lands, and something like the system which we have adopted. A cruel-minded race such as the Romans would have made short work of the Indian problem. Each war would have been one of extermination, and the primitive tribes would have been slain or enslaved, and thus removed from the field. The difficulties which we have encountered in dealing with the Indians have been in large measure due to the fact that even when exasperated by conflicts with them our frontier people have retained a large share of the just and humane motives which are characteristic of our race. They have recognized the fact that our own people were the invaders of the Indian's realm, and there has been an element of the apologetic in their treatment of the natives each time they came to make peace with them.

Although the foregoing sketch of the conditions which determined the fitness of this country to the uses of our race is inadequate, it may serve to show the reader how great and admirable was the fortune which gave this broad and fruitful land as the field for the development of our people. It is clear that it is better suited for the needs of the northern Aryans than any other extensive territory which has ever come into their possession. From their first scanty holding on its shores they have extended their empire with a swiftness and certainty which of itself shows how well suited the land was to their needs, and how well they were themselves suited to the inheritance.

C. A POPULAR HIGH SCHOOL HISTORY TEXT EXAMINES INDIAN PROBLEMS

Normally a considerable period of time elapses before minority images that first appear in scholarly monographs are incorporated into textbooks for young people; unfortunately, it often takes just as long to eliminate these images from elementary and secondary school texts after they have been discredited by a new generation of scholars. For example, one still widely used elementary social studies text informs its young readers that "a pioneer settles on land where only savages have lived before." The ethnocentrism of such a view is obvious, but still often the rule. In the following passage, *the authors' patronizing attitude is apparent in their attempt to explain the ineptness of reservation Indians and their need to take on the life style of the white majority. Syracuse University's Ralph Volney Harlow was a well-known textbook author for both secondary and college students and his* Story of America, *co-authored with Herman Noyes, went through seven editions between 1937 and 1964, when the following passage appeared.*

In 1887, the government tried a new approach. Congress enacted the Dawes Act which provided for dividing up among individuals the reservation lands owned by the tribes in common. Any Indian who wished could get 160 acres for nothing. Many took advantage of the opportunity and became self-supporting. Civilized Indians were also granted citizenship.

The Indians who chose to remain on the reservations under the guardianship of the government made little progress. Poverty and disease continued to weaken the tribes. Education was made compulsory for Indian children in 1891; but since Congress appropriated only small amounts of money for Indian schools, many children still received little or no education. Many Indians seemed to lack both energy and the training necessary for success in the white man's world.

Nevertheless, there are encouraging signs that the Indian is at last gradually taking his proper place as an independent American....In 1924 full citizenship was granted to all Indians. More recently, Congress has taken important steps to encourage them to be self-reliant. Money is being provided for health, education, and vocational training, and some effort is being made to establish industries near Indian lands to provide jobs. Advice and financial assistance are also being given to individual Indians who want to seek better opportunities in some of our large cities. On the whole, the Indian's future looks brighter today than it has for many years. However, friends of the Indians are often critical of the haste with which government supervision is being withdrawn.

[Editor's note: this concludes the selections taken from In Their Place}

EVA MARTINEZ, *THE WHITENING OF AMERICA*

Eva Martinez is a thirty-six-year-old American Indian of the Ottawa tribe. She is a part-time university student, a full-time coordinator of a program to establish university scholarships for minorities, and the mother of five children. Martinez believes that modern industrial societies have much to learn from the cultural strength of Native Americans and from their traditional comprehension of man's interrelationship with all living things. She also reminds us that from the very beginning Indians have been practicing environmentalists

It is almost impossible to make an Indian feel a sense of personal guilt for walking the face of the earth. Whites always seem to feel guilty about one thing or another; it's an integral part of their culture and certainly part of their Christian religion. If you want to make an Indian feel bad, you can show him what is happening to the environment. We may not be the ones who are destroying the forests and the waters but just being alive at this time is a great wrong for us because we see the terrible things that have been done to mother earth.

We are a very ancient group of people, much older than the groups who make up most of modern society. Who is to say that new methods are always an improvement on the old? If something worked for thousands of generations, perhaps one should try to understand why it did so. Think of it as a kind of recycling process; each new generation must recycle the old without destroying it. In the West, the tendency has long been to replace the old with the new without really examining the full ramifications of what is often a destructive process.

Westerners fall into an ethnocentric predicament of their own making. Think, for example, of the power of words. Most Americans talk about the Western world and the non-Western world, as if one were the norm and the other is somehow what's left over. What would such people think of a world made up only of Indians and non-Indians. Would Anglos go around saying, "Hello, my nationality is non-Indian"?

We are said to be a nomadic people, but one must understand that in the proper context. Whites move all over the place in search of a better job, even from continent to continent, but no one calls them a nomadic people. Indians moved to a new area for what today would be called environmental reasons, to let the old hunting grounds replenish themselves. Indians knew that if we permanently destroyed what we needed to live, we too would soon be dead. So we moved on before endangering the old hunting grounds. The Indian women were always more environmentally conscious than the men who spent most of their time out hunting. The women would go on two-day scouting excursions looking for new areas. They would then give a report on what the weather, water, and land were like.

We should learn from one another's culture. There is the famous old story of the Christian missionary going on to the reservation to spread the word of his God. All the elders sat politely and listened to his sermon. After the Christian missionary finished, one of the elders told him how interesting his story was, and that, in return, he would like to tell the missionary the Indian's explanation of life. Of course, that was not why the missionary came to the reservation. Whites have always expected us to learn from them, but they have seldom considered the possibility of learning from us. Many years ago there was a white doctor who did try to learn from us. He lived in the Upper Peninsula of Michigan and spent his entire professional life writing down the numerous ways Indians used natural remedies to cure various sicknesses. He filled countless notebooks on how we used plants, berries, minerals, and herbs, but when he died back in the 1920's, his family was so embarrassed with this "unscientific" collection that they destroyed his notebooks.

Culture teaches us who we are without having to teach us. No Ottawa Indian has to take a course in Ottawa 101 to learn who he is. Is it really progress that most youngsters in so-called modern countries have to go to school to learn the story of their people? And if the schools cannot tell them, where will they hear this invaluable story? Certainly not from television, the politicians, or their peers. For Indians, this is the function of our elders who have accumulated the wisdom of the ages. And because we believe that all life is a never-ending circle these lessons are much more self-evident to the young when they hear them from their elders.

We do not separate our bodies or souls from the earth. Physically one can but not mentally. When an Indian is out in nature, he is not just staring up at a beautiful piñon tree; he realizes this is what gives us all life. This is part of the circle of life that is so different from the Judaic-Christian view that life is linear. For us, time is a circle, marked by the four seasons, and we are a part of that continuous circle as
are all other things in nature. So for us life doesn't go forward or backwards but is a process of continuous renewal.

We simply do not question our elders. We don't even question not questioning them. It's just understood. Yet, they are not harsh disciplinarians. It's just the way we do things. What the eldest says the youngest understands. If an elder sees that a youngster does not understand, he will try many different ways to make him do so. Sometimes he will physically take a child outside and make him touch something until he does understand. My grandmother was blind when she was old, and she would touch me and ask if I understood. She would touch my eyes, not my mouth, and then she knew that I understood. Elders speak softly, and they do not talk down to children. I think that's why Indian young people are very mature, very understanding, and very knowledgeable. The key is being raised without fear. Everything seems so simple and obvious. This lack of complexity is why no Indian young people go into the field of science.

Just recently my teen-age daughter asked me, "Mom, why do some of the white moms fall apart when their daughters yell back at them? You never do that." I asked her what I would do. She
said, "You'd set us straight." And that's true, because we learn that when we are young. She doesn't even realize that she already knows these lessons because they were learned so naturally. She's with her grandmother one moment, sister the next, and then with younger girls. Even though she is a teen in her mixed up years, there's no confusion as to her female role. Most white teenagers do not know where they are at that point in their maturation process because they are receiving so many mixed signals from television, magazines, advertisements, music, and, above all, their friends.

The elders also teach us at a young age that we will one day venture into the spirit world, and that we have to prepare for this. They teach us that everything around us is important and that we have to understand and respect this. None of this is said with fear of the spirit world but with happiness. So we are taught to take part in inexplicable happenings. When you grow up in a non-Indian world, this often seems incomprehensible. Non-Indians with whom I work simply don't understand or care, and they think that unexplainable happenings make no sense. This is true even though their own Christian religion is filled with so much dogma, including many references to miracles, that must be taken on faith.

We do have many prophecies. The greatest of them is the prophecy of purification, that one day all men will regain their understanding of the importance of the earth. This prophecy can be found in the Hopi and Iroquois legends and most certainly in those of many other tribes. Every Indian child knows this prophecy. One day the time will come when the imbalance between the environment and nature will have passed the point of no return. Indians do not accept this as a doomsday prophecy but as something more fundamental. For example, if you have cancer, and you have to have this painful surgery to have this ugly malignancy removed, Indians would look at the successful removal as the Day of Purification. So on this day all people on earth will decide they can no longer take the poisoning of our earth mother. At that point we shall recycle the earth. This is our greatest prophecy, and it will include all people, working together in harmony.

I've been asked over and over, "Why do you people seem so strong, even stoical, about the future. You don't even seem to be afraid of dying." It's all very simple. I'm always looking for the safest way to turn back to the earth. You look forward to death, which means you've been a good person and lived a good life so that one day you will die without a struggle. You will die feeling free and at one with your surroundings. Death is a kind of honor. I don't mean it's an honor to go out and be killed tomorrow, but it's an honor to be part of the ceremony of becoming at one with mother earth. Naturally, we hate to see somebody die, but as long as the tribe goes on, it is not a permanent kind of mourning. Above all, the circle of life must remain intact. If it is broken, the tribe is endangered.

We insist on dying with dignity. Most Indians, including myself, do not have any health insurance, so we cannot afford health care. This means when we are sick we have to appeal to government agencies for help, but rather than being humiliated by insensitive bureaucrats, many of us who live in white society simply go back to the reservation and die in quiet dignity.

It is this very strength in our culture that is also its greatest weakness. When we are thrown into a hostile environment, this early training is no longer applicable. There is the example of the role of basketball on many reservations, especially in the Southwest and the West. Young Indians are tremendous players, and several of the reservation teams have won high school state championships. These young boys are fearless and clearly excel in the fluidity, speed, and grace of the sport. Many of them have won scholarships to universities, but seldom if ever do they complete their degree. The change of environment is simply too great, and they do not adjust. Soon they are back on the reservation, and many of them sink into lives of alcoholism and poverty. What happened to these young basketball players is what happens to so many of our people when they are stripped of the underpinnings of their heritage. Of course, this also happens to many non-Indian young people who are rootless, without direction, and unable to cope.

In the 1960's certain Indian groups confronted white Americans with the reality of each other's history. Many whites did not want to listen, but some young, idealistic ones did, and especially whose who were fighting their own battles against the establishment. Many of them found a peace they could not find in their own society. In the beginning these experiments were often superficial, including the use of drugs, but those who went deeper found we are a peaceful people who could offer them an inner serenity they had not experienced before. Like us, they developed a special contempt for psychiatrists who would diagnose human problems in personal terms, and they came to understand the relationship between mental illness, air and water pollution, and the destruction of the forests. Every traditional Indian understands the interconnectedness of man, mind, and nature, and because of this understanding we believe it is not we who are maladjusted but the external world the West has created and defined for itself. This needs to be changed if people are to find peace.

Today there are once again increasing numbers of non-Indians attending our powwows, and they are not just standing around the trading tables buying. They're listening and they're enjoying the dancing, and they are welcome to do so by the Indian elders as a sign of togetherness and peace. Everybody takes care of everyone else at the powwows. A child, for example, is totally safe there, away from the distractions of television, materialism, and non-Indian peer pressure. Our children do not say, "Hey, I don't want to go to the Powwow. I want to stay home and watch my favorite television show." We go as a family, and what happens in one weekend can last an entire month.

We will continue our struggle to return to the strength of the circle. We know that too many of our people are poverty-stricken and have a high alcohol and suicide rate. We know that too many of us have fallen victim to the ills of contemporary society. We now have a rehabilitation movement which doesn't use psychoanalysis or medication. It's the turning back to what once made us strong and whole. The drumming of the circle in the powwow is symbolic of this process. The drums bring back our past as do our prayers and our songs, to remind us that only our age-old traditions can make us feel at one with ourselves, our past, mother earth, sister sky, and grandmother moon. Of course, it is not only today's Indians who are alienated from themselves, each other, and their surroundings. This a sickness of modern man.

FREDERICK DOUGLASS, *MY BONDAGE AND MY FREEDOM, 1855*

Frederick Douglass (1817-1895) became the best known African-American of the nineteenth century. Born a slave, he escaped to freedom in 1838 and became the leading black voice among the abolitionists. Many whites doubted that the eloquent and literate Douglass could have ever been a slave, but his autobiographical writings quickly dispel the notion that slavery could not have been so evil if it could produce a man such as Frederick Douglass. In the brief selection below, taken from his 1855 My Bondage and My Freedom, *Douglass decides to return to the plantation to confront Covey, the brutal slave-breaker from whom he has previously run away. It is out of this encounter that Douglass later concluded, "Those slaves who whipped easiest were whipped most."*

Sandy [a fellow slave] now urged me to go home, with all speed, and to walk up bravely to the house, as though nothing had happened. I saw in Sandy too deep an insight into human nature , with all his superstition, not to have some respect for his advice; and perhaps, too, a slight gleam or shadow of his superstition had fallen upon me. At any rate, I started off toward Covey's, as directed by Sandy. Having, the previous night, poured my griefs into Sandy's ears, and got him enlisted in my behalf, having made his wife a sharer in my sorrows, and having, also, become well refreshed by sleep and food, I moved off, quite courageously toward the much dreaded Covey's. Singularly enough, just as I entered his yard gate, I met him and his wife, dressed in their Sunday best--looking as smiling angels--on their way to church. The manner of Covey astonished me. There was something really benignant in his countenance. He spoke to me as never before; told me that the pigs had got into the lot, and he wished me to drive them out; inquired how I was, and seemed an altered man. This extraordinary conduct of Covey, really made me begin to think that Sandy's herb had more virtue in it than I, in my pride, had been willing to allow; and, had the day been other than Sunday, I should have attributed Covey's altered manner solely to the magic power of the root. I suspected, however, that the *Sabbath*, and not the *root*, was the real explanation of Covey's manner. His religion hindered him from breaking the Sabbath, but not from breaking my skin. He had more respect for the *day* than for the *man*, for whom the day was mercifully given; for while he would cut and slash my body during the week, he would not hesitate, on Sunday, to teach me the value of my soul, or the way of life and salvation by Jesus Christ.

All went well with me till Monday morning; and then, whether the root had lost its virtue, or whether my tormentor had gone deeper into the black art than myself, (as was sometimes said of him,) or whether he had obtained a special indulgence, for his faithful Sabbath day's worship, it is not necessary for me to know, or to inform the reader; but, this much I *may* say ,--the pious and benignant smile which graced Covey's face on *Sunday*, wholly disappeared on *Monday*. Long before daylight, I was called up to go and feed, rub, and curry the horses. I obeyed the call, and I would have so obeyed it, had it been made at an earlier hour, for I had

brought my mind to a firm resolve, during that Sunday's reflection, viz: to obey every order, however unreasonable, if it were possible, and, if Mr. Covey should then undertake to beat me, to defend and protect myself to the best of my ability. My religious views on the subject of resisting my master had suffered a serious shock, by the savage persecution to which I had been subjected,
and my hands were no longer tied by my religion. Master Thomas's indifference had severed the last link. I had now to this extent "backslidden" from this point in the slave's religious creed; and I soon had occasion to make my fallen state known to my Sunday-pious brother, Covey.

Whilst I was obeying his order to feed and get the horses ready for the field, and when in the act of going up the stable loft for the purpose of throwing down some blades, Covey sneaked into the stable, in his peculiar snake-like way, and seizing me suddenly by the leg, he brought me to the stable floor, giving my newly mended body a fearful jar. I now forgot my *roots*, and remembered my pledge *to stand up in my own defense*. The brute was endeavoring skillfully to get a slip-knot on my legs, before I could draw up my feet. As soon as I found what he was up to, I gave a sudden spring, (my two day's rest had been of much service to me,) and by that means, no doubt, he was able to bring me to the floor so heavily. He was defeated in his plan of tying me. While down, he seemed to think he had me very securely in his power. He little thought he was--as the rowdies say--"in" for a "rough and tumble" fight; but such was the fact. Whence came the daring spirit necessary to grapple with a man who, eight-and-forty hours before, could, with his slightest word have made me tremble like a leaf in a storm, I do not know; at any rate, *I was resolved to fight,* and, what was better still, I was actually hard at it. The fighting madness had come upon me, and I found my strong fingers firmly attached to the throat of my cowardly tormentor; as heedless of consequences, at the moment, as though we stood as equals before the law. The very color of the man was forgotten. I felt as supple as a cat, and was ready for the snakish creature at every turn. Every blow of his was parried, though I dealt no blows in turn. I was strictly on the *defensive*, preventing him from injuring me, rather than trying to injure him. I flung him on the ground several times, when he meant to have hurled me there. I held him so firmly by the throat, that his blood followed my nails. He held me, and I held him.

All was fair, thus far, and the contest was about equal. My resistance was entirely unexpected, and Covey was taken all aback by it, for he trembled in every limb. "*Are you going to resist, you scoundrel?*" said he. To which, I returned a polite "*yes sir*;" steadily gazing my interrogator in the eye, to meet the first approach or dawning of the blow, which I expected my answer would call forth. But, the conflict did not long remain thus equal. Covey soon cried out lustily for help; not that I was obtaining any marked advantage over him, or was injuring him, but because he was gaining none over me, and was not able, single handed, to conquer me. He called for his cousin Hughes, to come to his assistance, and now the scene was changed. I was compelled to give blows, as well as to parry them; and, since I was, in any case, to suffer for resistance, I felt (as the musty proverb goes) that "I might as well be hanged for an old sheep as a lamb." I was still *defensive* toward Covey, but *aggressive* toward Hughes; and, at the first approach of the latter, I dealt a blow, in my desperation, which fairly sickened my youthful assailant. He went off, bending over with pain, and manifesting no disposition to come within my reach again. The poor fellow was in the act of trying to catch and tie my right hand, and while flattering himself with success, I gave him the kick which sent him staggering away in pain, at the same time that I held Covey with a firm hand.

Taken completely by surprise, Covey seemed to have lost his usual strength and coolness. He was frightened, and stood puffing and blowing, seemingly unable to command words or blows. When he saw that poor Hughes was standing half bent with pain--his courage quite gone--the cowardly tyrant asked if I "meant to persist in my resistance." I told him "*I did mean to resist, come what might;*" that I had been by him treated like a *brute*, during the last six months; and that I should stand it *no longer*. With that, he gave me a shake, and attempted to drag me toward a stick of wood, that was lying just outside the stable door. He meant to knock me down with it; but, just as he leaned over to get the stick, I seized him with both hands by the collar, and, with a vigorous and sudden snatch, I brought my assailant harmlessly, his full length, on the *not over* clean ground--for we were now in the cow yard. He had selected the place for the fight, and it was but right that he should have all the advantages of his own selection.

By this time, Bill, the hired man, came home. He had been to Mr. Hemsley's, to spend the Sunday with his nominal wife, and was coming home on Monday morning, to go to work. Covey and I had been skirmishing from before daybreak, till now, that the sun was almost shooting his beams over the eastern woods, and we were still at it. I could not see where the matter was to terminate. He evidently was afraid to let me go, lest I should again make off to the woods; otherwise, he would probably have obtained arms from the house, to frighten me. Holding me, Covey called upon Bill for assistance. The scene here, had something comic about it. "Bill," who knew *precisely* what Covey wished him to do, affected ignorance, and pretended he did not know what to do. "What shall I do, Mr. Covey," said Bill. "Take hold of him--take hold of him!" said Covey. With a toss of his head, peculiar to Bill, he said, "indeed, Mr. Covey, I want to go to work." "*This* is your work," said Covey; "take hold of him." Bill replied, with spirit, "My master hired me here, to work, and *not* to help you whip Frederick." It was now my turn to speak. "Bill," I said, "don't put your hands on me." To which he replied, "My God! Frederick, I ain't goin' to tech ye," and Bill walked off, leaving Covey and myself to settle our matters as best we might.

But, my present advantage was threatened when I saw Caroline (the slave-woman of Covey) coming to the cow yard to milk, for she was a powerful woman, and could have mastered me very easily, exhausted as I now was. As soon as she came into the yard, Covey attempted to rally her to his aid. Strangely--and, I may add, fortunately--Caroline was in no humor to take a hand in any such sport. We were all in open rebellion, that morning. Caroline answered the command of her master to "*take hold of me*," precisely as Bill had answered, but in *her*, it was at greater peril so to answer; she was the slave of Covey, and he could do what he pleased with her. It was *not* so with Bill, and Bill knew it. Samuel Harris, to whom Bill belonged, did not allow his slaves to be beaten, unless they were guilty of some crime which the law would punish. But, poor Caroline, like myself, was at the mercy of the merciless Covey; nor did she escape the dire effects of her refusal. He gave her several sharp blows.

Covey at length (two hours had elapsed) gave up the contest. Letting me go, he said,--puffing and blowing at a great rate--"now, you scoundrel, go to your work; I would not have whipped you half so much as I have had you not resisted." The fact was, *he had not whipped me at all*. He had not, in all the scuffle, drawn a single drop of blood from me. I had drawn blood from him; and, even without this satisfaction, I should have been victorious, because my aim had not been to injure him, but to prevent his injuring me.

During the whole six months that I lived with Covey, after this transaction, he never laid on me the weight of his finger in anger. He would occasionally, say he did not want to have to get hold of me again--a declaration which I had no difficulty in believing; and I had a secret feeling, which answered, "you need not wish to get hold of me again, for you will be likely to come off worse in a second fight than you did in the first."

Well, my dear reader, this battle with Mr. Covey,--undignified as it was, and as I fear my narration of it is--was the turning point in my "*life as a slave.*" It rekindled in my breast the smoldering embers of liberty; it brought up my Baltimore dreams, and revived a sense of my own manhood. I was a changed being after that fight. I was *nothing* before; I was A MAN NOW. It recalled to life my crushed self-respect and my self-confidence, and inspired me with a renewed determination to be A FREEMAN. A man, without force, is without the essential dignity of humanity. Human nature is so constituted, that it cannot *honor* a helpless man, although it can *pity* him; and even this it cannot do long, if the signs of power do not arise.

He only can understand the effect of this combat on my spirit, who has himself incurred something, hazarded something, in repelling the unjust and cruel aggressions of a tyrant. Covey was a tyrant, and a cowardly one, withal. After resisting him, I felt as I had never felt before. It was a resurrection from the dark and pestiferous tomb of slavery, to the heaven of comparative freedom. I was no longer a servile coward, trembling under the frown of a brother worm of the dust, but, my long-cowed spirit was roused to an attitude of manly independence. I had reached the point, at which *I was not afraid to die.* This spirit made me a freeman in *fact*, while I remained a slave in *form.* When a slave cannot be flogged he is more than half free. He has a domain as broad as his own manly heart to defend, and he is really "*a power on earth.*" While slaves prefer their lives, with flogging, to instant death, they will always find christians enough, like unto Covey, to accommodate that preference. From this time, until that of my escape from slavery, I was never fairly whipped. Several attempts were made to whip me, but they were always unsuccessful. Bruises I did get, as I shall hereafter inform the reader; but the case I have been describing, was the end of the brutification to which slavery had subjected me.

W. E. B. DUBOIS, *THE SONG OF THE SMOKE* (1899)

W. E. B. DuBois (1868-1963) was one of America's most prolific writers and most uncompromising voices for racial justice. Trained at Fisk, Harvard, and Berlin Universities, DuBois worked as a historian, sociologist, essayist, novelist, poet, biographer, and editor. The bibliography of his complete works covers forty-five pages. In 1900 he announced, "The problem of the Twentieth Century is the problem of the color line." Nine years later he helped found the NAACP and became the long time editor of its magazine, The Crisis. *In* The Song of the Smoke *DuBois clearly enunciates his belief that "black is beautiful."*

THE SONG OF THE SMOKE

I am the smoke king.
I am black.
I am swinging in the sky.
I am ringing worlds on high:
I am the thought of the throbbing mills,
I am the soul of the soul toil kills,
I am the ripple of trading rills,

Up I'm curling from the sod,
I am whirling home to God.
I am the smoke king,
I am black.

I am the smoke king.
I am black.
I am wreathing broken hearts,
I am sheathing devils' darts;
Dark inspiration of iron times,
Wedding the toil of toiling climes
Shedding the blood of bloodless crimes,

Down I lower in the blue,
Up I tower toward the true,
I am the smoke king,
I am black.

I am the smoke king,
I am black.

I am darkening with song,
I am hearkening to wrong'
I will be as black as blackness can,
The blacker the mantle the mightier the man,
My purpl'ing midnights no day dawn may ban.

I am carving God in night,
I am painting hell in white.
I am the smoke king.
I am black.

I am the smoke king,
I am black.

I am cursing ruddy morn,
I am nursing hearts unborn;
Souls unto me are as mists in the night,
I whiten my blackmen, I beckon my white,
What's the hue of a hide to a man in his might!
Hail, then, grilly, grimy hands,

Sweet Christ, pity toiling lands!
Hail to the smoke king,
Hail to the black!

Paul Dunbar, *WE WEAR THE MASK* (1895)

Paul Dunbar (1872-1906) was a novelist and short-story writer, but his turn-of-the-century poems made him the best-known African-American poet since the renowned eighteenth-century Phyllis Wheatley. His We Wear the Mask *touches a constant theme in black literature: playing the role white America expected of blacks.*

WE WEAR THE MASK

We wear the mask that grins and lies,
It hides our cheeks and shades our eyes,
This debt we pay to human guile;
With torn and bleeding hearts we smile,
And mouth with myriad subtleties.

Why should the world be otherwise,
In counting all our tears and sighs?
Nay, let them only see us, while
We wear the mask.

We smile, but, O great Christ, our cries
To Thee from tortured souls arise.
We sing, but oh, the clay is vile
Beneath our feet, and long the mile;
But let the world dream otherwise,
We wear the mask.

Claude McKay, *IF WE MUST DIE* (1922)

Jamaican born Claude McKay (1890-1948) became one of the great poets of the Harlem Renaissance, that great flowering of black artistic achievement that exploded in the 1920s. His If We Must Die *is a clarion call to action against injustice. Consider the popularity this poem might have achieved if it had been written by a white poet and directed against an external enemy rather than a black man who was directing his wrath at his fellow Americans.*

IF WE MUST DIE

If we must die, let it not be like hogs
Hunted and penned in an inglorious spot,
While round us bark the mad and hungry dogs,
Making their mock at our accursed lot.
If we must die, O let us nobly die,
So that our precious blood may not be shed
In vain; then even the monsters we defy
Shall be constrained to honor us though dead!
O kinsmen! we must meet the common foe!
Though far out numbered let us show us brave,
And for their thousand blows deal one death-blow!
What though before us lies the open grave?
Like men we'll face the murderous, cowardly pack,
Pressed to the wall, dying, but fighting back!

Langston Hughes, *DEAR DR. BUTTS* (1953)

Translator, poet, essayist, historian, editor, playwright, short-story writer, novelist, the works of Langston Hughes (1902-1967) fill some forty-five volumes. Hughes insisted his one central purpose in writing was "to explain and illuminate the Negro condition in America." His Dear Dr. Butts *story below features Jesse B. Simple, a favorite character of Hughes, whose untutored wisdom exposes profound truths. In this piece, Jesse deplores white America's constant willingness to identify his "Negro leaders."*

"Do you know what has happened to me?" said Simple

"No."

"I'm out of a job."

"That's tough. How did that come about?"

"Laid off--they're converting again. And right now, just when I am planning to get married this spring, they have to go changing from civilian production to war contracts, installing new machinery. Manager says it might take two months, might take three or four. They'll send us mens notices. If it takes four months, that's up to June, which is no good for my plans. To get married a man needs money. To stay married he needs more money. And where am I? As usual, behind the eight-ball."

"You can find another job meanwhile, no doubt."

"That ain't easy. And if I do, they liable not to pay much. Jobs that pay good money nowadays are scarce as hen's teeth. But Joyce says she do not care. She is going to marry me, come June, anyhow--even if she has to pay for it herself. Joyce says since I paid for the divorce, she can pay for the wedding. But I do not want her to do that."

"Naturally no, but maybe you can curtail your plans somewhat and not have so big a wedding. Wedlock does not require an elaborate ceremony."

"I do not care if we don't have none, just so we get locked. But you know how womens is. Joyce has waited an extra year for her great day. Now here I am broke as a busted bank."

"How're you keeping up with your expenses?"

"I ain't. And I don't drop by Joyce's every night like I did when I was working. I'm embarrassed. Then she didn't have to ask me to eat. Now she does. In fact, she insists. She says, 'You got to eat somewheres. I enjoy your company. Eat with me.' I do, if I'm there when she extends the invitation. But I don't go looking for it. I just sets home and broods, man, and looks at my four walls, which gives me plenty of time to think. And do you know what I been thinking about lately?"

"Finding work, I presume."

"Besides that?"

"No. I don't know what you've been thinking about."

"Negro leaders, and how they're talking about how great democracy is--and me out of a job. Also how there is so many leaders I don't know that white folks know about, because they are always in the white papers. Yet *I'm* the one they are supposed to be leading. Now, you take that little short leader named Dr. Butts, I do not know him, except in name only. If he ever made a speech in Harlem it were not well advertised. From what I reads, he teaches at a white college in Massachusetts, stays at the Commodore when he's in New York, and ain't lived in Harlem for ten years. Yet he's leading me. He's an article writer, but he does not write in colored papers. But lately the colored papers taken to reprinting parts of what he writes--otherwise I would have never seen it. Anyhow, with all this time on my hands these days, I writ him a letter last night. Here, read it."

Harlem, U.S.A.
One Cold February Day

Dear Dr. Butts,

I seen last week in the colored papers where you have writ an article for The New York Times *in which you say America is the greatest country in the world for the Negro race and Democracy the greatest kind of government for all, but it would be better if there was equal education for colored folks in the South, and if everybody could vote, and if there were not Jim Crow in the army, also if the churches was not divided up into white churches and colored churches, and if Negroes did not have to ride on the back seats of busses south of Washington.*

Now, all this later part of your article is hanging onto your but. *You start off talking about how great American democracy is, then you* but *it all over the place. In fact, the* but *end of your see-saw is so far down on the ground I do not believe the other end can ever pull it up. So me myself, I would not write no article for no* New York Times *if I had to put in so many* buts. *I reckon maybe you come by it naturally, though, that being your name, dear Dr. Butts.*

I hear tell that you are a race leader, but I do not know who you lead because I have not heard of you before and I have not laid eyes on you. But if you are leading me, make me know it, because I do not read the New York Times *very often, less I happen to pick up a copy blowing around in the subway, so I did not know you were my leader. But since you are my leader, lead on, and see if I will follow behind your* but--*because there is more behind that* but *than there is in front of it.*

Dr. Butts, I am glad to read that you writ an article in the New York Times, *but also sometime I wish you would write one in the colored papers and let me know how to get out from behind all these* buts *that are staring me in the face. I know America is a great country* but--*and it is that* but *that has been keeping me where I is all these years. I can't get over it, I can't get under it, and I can't get around it, so what am I supposed to do? If you are leading me, lemme see. Because we have too many colored leaders now that nobody knows until they get from the white papers to the colored papers and from the colored papers to me who has never seen hair nor hide of you.* Dear Dr. Butts, *are you hiding from me--and leading me, too?*

From the way you write, a man would think my race problem was made out of nothing but buts. But *this,* but *that, and, yes, there is Jim Crow in Georgia* but--. *America admits they bomb folks in Florida*--but *Hitler gassed the Jews. Mississippi is bad*--but *Russia is worse. Detroit slums are awful*--but *compared to the slums in India, Detroit's Paradise Valley is Paradise.*

Dear Dr. Butts, Hitler is dead. I don't live in Russia. India is across the Pacific Ocean. And I do not hope to see Paradise no time soon. I am nowhere near some of them foreign countries you are talking about being so bad. I am here! And you know as well as I do, Mississippi is hell. There ain't no but *in the world can make it out different. They tell me when Nazis gas you, you die slow. But when they put a bomb under you like in Florida, you don't have time to say your prayers. As for Detroit, there is as much difference between Paradise Valley and Paradise as there is between heaven and Harlem. I don't know nothing about India, but I been in Washington, D.C.. If you think there ain't slums there, take your* but *up Seventh Street late some night, and see if you still got it by the time you get to Howard University.*

I should not have to be telling you these things. You are colored just like me. To put a but *after all this Jim Crow fly-papering around our feet is just like telling a hungry man,* "But *Mr. Rockefeller has got plenty to eat." It's just like telling a joker with no overcoat in the winter time, "But you will be hot next summer." The fellow is liable to haul off and say, "I am hot now!" And bop you over your head.*

Are you in your right mind, Dear Dr. Butts? Or are you just writing? Do you really think a new day is dawning? Do you really think Christians are having a change of heart? I can see you now taking your pen in hand to write, "But just last year the Southern Denominations of Hell-Fired Salvation resolved to work toward Brotherhood." In fact, that is what you already writ. Do you think Brotherhood means colored to them Southerners?

Do you reckon they will recognize you for a brother, Dr. Butts, since you done had your picture taken in the Grand Ballroom of the Waldorf-Astoria shaking hands at some kind of meeting with five hundred white big-shots and five Negroes, all five of them Negro leaders, so it said underneath the picture? I did not know any of them Negro leaders by sight, neither by name, but since it says in the white papers that they are leaders, I reckon they are. Anyhow, I take my pen in hand to write you this letter to ask you to make yourself clear to me. When you answer me, do not write no "so-and-so-and-so but--.*" I will not take* but *for an answer. Negroes have been looking at Democracy's* but *too long. What we want to know is how to get rid of that* but.

Do you did me, Dear Dr. Butts?

Sincerely yours,

Jesse B. Simple

Mari Evans, *BLACK JAM FOR DR. NEGRO* (1966)

Mari Evans' Black Jam for Dr. Negro *deals with the same theme as did Langston Hughes'* Dear Dr. Butts, *but her more graphic language reflects the increasing impatience of the 1960's.*

Black jam for dr. negro

Pullin me in off the corner to wash my face an
cut my afro turn
my collar
down
when that ain't my
thang I
walk heels first
nose round an tilted
up
my ancient
eyes
see your thang
baby
an it aint
shit
your thang
puts my eyes out baby
turns my seeking fingers
        into splintering fists
messes up my head
an I scream you out
your thang
is whats wrong
        an you keep
        pilin it on rubbin it
        in
        smoothly
        doin it
        to death
what you sweatin
baby your
                guts
puked an rotten
waitin
to be defended

Richard Wright, *THE ETHICS OF LIVING JIM CROW* (1937)

Richard Wright's (1908-1960) autobiographical Black_Boy *(1945) and* Native Son *(1940), a searing naturalistic treatment of Bigger Thomas, an inhabitant of Chicago's black ghetto, are two of the finest novels about what it mean to be black in white America. Born in Mississippi, Wright gradually moved northwards and finally to France in his search for a society where it was possible to live in dignity and freedom. "The Ethics of Living Jim Crow" is from his first important collection of stories,* Uncle Tom's Children, *and relates the lessons he was early taught "in how to live as a Negro."*

I.

MY FIRST LESSON in how to live as a Negro came when I was quite small. We were living in Arkansas. Our house stood behind the railroad tracks. Its skimpy yard was paved with black cinders. Nothing green every grew in that yard. The only touch of green we could see was far away, beyond the tracks, over where the white folks lived. But cinders were good enough for me and I never missed the green growing things. And anyhow cinders were fine weapons. You could always have a nice hot war with huge black cinders. All you had to do was crouch behind the brick pillars of a house with your hands full of gritty ammunition. And the first woolly black head you say pop out from behind another row of pillars was your target. You tried your very best to knock it off. It was great fun.

I never fully realized the appalling disadvantages of a cinder environment till one day the gang to which I belonged found itself engaged in a war with the white boys who lived beyond the tracks. As usual we laid down our cinder barrage, thinking that this would wipe the white boys out. But they replied with a steady bombardment of broken bottles. We doubled our cinder barrage, but they hid behind trees, hedges, and the sloping embankments of their lawns. Having no such fortifications, we retreated to the brick pillars of our homes. During the retreat a broken milk bottle caught me behind the ear, opening a deep gash which bled profusely. The sight of blood pouring over my face completely demoralized our ranks. My fellow-combatants left me standing paralyzed in the center of the yard, and scurried for their homes. A kind neighbor saw me, and rushed me to a doctor, who took three stitches in my neck.

I sat brooding on my front steps, nursing my wound and waiting for my mother to come from work. I felt that a grave injustice had been done me. It was all right to throw cinders. The greatest harm a cinder could do was leave a bruise. But broken bottles were dangerous; they left you cut, bleeding, and helpless.

When night fell, my mother came from the white folks' kitchen. I raced down the street to meet her. I could just feel in my bones that she would understand. I knew she would tell me exactly what to do next time. I grabbed her hand and babbled out the whole story. She examined my wound, then slapped me.

"How come yuh didn't hide?" she asked me. "How come yuh always fightin'?"

I was outraged, and bawled. Between sobs I told her that I didn't have any trees or hedges to hide behind. There wasn't a thing I could have used as a trench. And you couldn't throw very far when you were hiding behind the brick pillars of a house. She grabbed a barrel stave, dragged me home, stripped me naked, and beat me till I had a fever of one hundred and two. She would smack my rump with the stave, and, while the skin was still smarting impart to me gems of Jim Crow wisdom. I was never to throw cinders any more. I was never to fight any more wars. I was never, never, under any conditions, to fight *white* folks again. And they were absolutely right in clouting me with the broken milk bottle. Didn't I know she was working hard every day in the hot kitchens of the white folks to make money to take care of me? When was I ever going to learn to be a good boy? She couldn't be bothered with my fights. She finished by telling me that I ought to be thankful to God as long as I lived that they didn't kill me.

All that night I was delirious and could not sleep. Each time I closed my eyes I saw monstrous white faces suspended from the ceiling, leering at me.

From that time on, the charm of my cinder yard was gone. The green trees, the trimmed hedges, the cropped lawns grew very meaningful, became a symbol. Even today when I think of white folks, the hard, sharp outlines of white houses surrounded by trees, lawns, and hedges are present somewhere in the background of my mind. Through the years they grew into an overreaching symbol of fear.

It was a long time before I came in close contact with white folks again. We moved from Arkansas to Mississippi. Here we had the good fortune not to live behind the railroad tracks, or close to white neighborhoods. We lived in the very heart of the local Black Belt. There were black churches and black preachers; there were black schools and black teachers; black groceries and black clerks. In fact, everything was so solidly black that for a long time I did not even think of white folks, save in remote and vague terms. But this could not last forever. As one grows older one eats more. One's clothing costs more. When I finished grammar school I had to go to work. My mother could no longer feed and clothe me on her cooking job.

There is but one place where a black boy who knows no trade can get a job, and that's where the houses and faces are white, where the trees, lawns, and hedges are green. My first job was with an optical company in Jackson, Mississippi. The morning I applied I stood straight and neat before the boss, answering all his questions with sharp yessirs and nosirs. I was very careful to pronounce my *sirs* distinctly, in order that he might know that I was polite, that I knew where I was, and that I knew he was a *white* man. I wanted that job badly.

He looked me over as though he were examining a prize poodle. He questioned me closely about my schooling, being particularly insistent about how much mathematics I had had. He seemed very pleased when I told him I had had two years of algebra.

"Boy, how would you like to try to learn something around here?" he asked me.

"I'd like it fine, sir," I said, happy. I had visions of "working my way up." Even Negroes have those visions.

"All right," he said. "Come on."

I followed him to the small factory.

"Pease," he said to a white man of about thirty-five, "this is Richard. He's going to work for us."

Pease looked at me and nodded.

I was then taken to a white boy of about seventeen.

"Morrie, this is Richard, who's going to work for us."

"Whut yuh sayin' there, boy!" Morrie boomed at me.

"Fine!" I answered.

The boss instructed these two to help me, teach me, give me jobs to do, and let me learn what I could in my spare time.

My wages were five dollars a week.

I worked hard, trying to please. For the first month I got along O.K. Both Pease and Morrie seemed to like me. But one thing was missing. And I kept thinking about it. I was not learning anything and nobody was volunteering to help me. Thinking they had forgotten that I was to learn something about the mechanics of grinding lenses, I asked Morrie one day to tell me about the work. He grew red.

"Whut yuh tryin' t' do, nigger, get smart?" he asked.

"Naw, I ain' tryin' t' git smart," I said.

"Well, don't, if yuh know whut's good for yuh!"

I was puzzled. Maybe he just doesn't want to help me, I thought. I went to Pease.

"Say, are yuh crazy, you black bastard?" Pease asked me, his gray eyes growing hard.

I spoke out, reminding him that the boss had said I was to be given a chance to learn something.

"Nigger, you think you're *white*, don't you?"

"Naw, sir!"

"Well, you're acting mighty like it!"

"But, Mr. Pease, the boss said . . ."

Pease shook his fist in my face.

"This is a *white* man's work around here, and you better watch yourself!"

From then on they changed toward me. They said good-morning no more. When I was just a bit slow in performing some duty, I was called a lazy black son-of-a-bitch.

Once I thought of reporting all this to the boss. But the mere idea of what would happen to me if Pease and Morrie should learn that I had "snitched" stopped me. And after all the boss was a white man, too. What was the use?

The climax came at noon one summer day. Pease called me to his work-bench. To get to him I had to go between two narrow benches and stand with my back against a wall.

"Yes, sir," I said.

"Richard, I want to ask you something," Pease began pleasantly, not looking up from his work.

"Yes, sir," I said again.

Morrie came over, blocking the narrow passage between the benches. He folded his arms, staring at me solemnly.

I look from one to the other, sensing that something was coming.

"Yes, sir," I said for the third time.

Pease looked up and spoke very slowly.

"Richard, Mr. Morrie here tells me you called me *Pease*."

I stiffened. A void seemed to open up in me. I knew this was the show-down.

He meant that I had failed to call him Mr. Pease. I looked at Morrie. He was gripping a steel bar in his hands. I opened my mouth to speak, to protest, to assure Pease that I had never called him simply *Pease*, and that I had never had any intentions of doing so, when Morrie grabbed me by the collar, ramming my head against the wall.

"Now, be careful, nigger!" snarled Morrie, baring his teeth. "I heard yuh call 'im *Pease*! 'N' if yuh say yuh didn't, yuh're callin' me a *lie*, see?" He waved the steel bar threateningly.

If I had said: No, sir, Mr. Pease, I never called you *Pease*, I would have been automatically calling Morrie a liar. And if I had said: Yes, sir, Mr. Pease, I called you *Pease*, I would have been pleading guilty to having uttered the worst insult that a Negro can utter to a southern white man. I stood hesitating, trying to frame a neutral reply.

"Richard, I asked you a question!" said Pease. Anger was creeping into his voice.

"I don't remember calling you *Pease*, Mr. Pease," I said cautiously. "And if I did, I sure didn't mean ..."

"You black son-of-a-bitch! You called me *Pease*, then!" he spat, slapping me till I bent sideways over a bench. Morrie was on top of me, demanding:

"Didn't yuh call 'im *Pease*? If yuh say yuh didn't, Ill rip yo' gut string loose with this bar, yuh black granny dodger! Yuh can't call a white man a lie 'n' git erway with it, you black son-of-a-bitch!"

I wilted. I begged them not to bother me. I knew what they wanted. They wanted me to leave.

"I'll leave," I promised. "I'll leave right *now*."

They gave me a minute to get out of the factory. I was warned not to show up again, or tell the boss.

I went.

When I told the folks at home what had happened, they called me a fool. They told me that I must never again attempt to exceed my boundaries. When you are working for white folks, they said, you got to "stay in your place" if you want to keep working.

II.

My Jim Crow education continued on my next job, which was portering in a clothing store. One morning, while polishing brass out front, the boss and his twenty-year-old son got out of their car and half dragged and half kicked a Negro woman into the store. A policeman standing at the corner looked on, twirling his night-stock. I watched out of the corner of my eye, never slackening the strokes of my chamois upon the brass. After a few minutes, I heard shrill screams coming from the rear of the store. Later the woman stumbled out, bleeding, crying, and holding her stomach. When she reached the end of the block, the policeman grabbed her and accused her of being drunk. Silently, I watched him throw her into a patrol wagon.

When I went to the rear of the store, the boss and his son were washing their hands at the sink. They were chuckling. The floor was bloody and strewn with wisps of hair and clothing. No doubt I must have appeared pretty shocked, for the boss slapped me reassuringly on the back.

"Boy, that's what we do to niggers when they don't want to pay their bills," he said, laughing.

His son looked at me and grinned.

"Here, hava cigarette," he said.

Not knowing what to do, I took it. He lit his and held the match for me. This was a gesture of kindness, indicating that even if they had beaten the poor old woman, they would not beat me if I knew enough to keep my mouth shut.

"Yes, sir," I said, and asked no questions.

After they had gone, I sat on the edge of a packing box and stared at the bloody floor till the cigarette went out.

That day at noon, while eating in a hamburger joint, I told my fellow Negro porters what had happened. No one seemed surprised. One fellow, after swallowing a huge bite, turned to me and asked:

"Huh! Is tha' all they did t' her?"

"Yeah. Wasn't tha' enough?" I asked.

"Shucks! Man, she's a lucky bitch!" he said, burying his lips deep into a juicy hamburger. "Hell, it's a wonder they didn't lay her when they got through."

III.

I was learning fast, but not quite fast enough. One day, while I was delivering packages in the suburbs, my bicycle tire was punctured. I walked along the hot, dusty road, sweating and leading my bicycle by the handle-bars.

A car slowed at my side.

"What's the matter, boy?" a white man called.

I told him my bicycle was broken and I was walking back to town.

"That's too bad," he said. "Hop on the running board."

He stopped the car. I clutched hard at my bicycle with one hand and clung to the side of the car with the other.

"All set?"

"Yes, sir," I answered. The car started.

It was full of young white men. They were drinking. I watched the flask pass from mouth to mouth.

"Wanna drink, boy?" one asked.

I laughed as the wind whipped my face. Instinctively obeying the freshly planted percepts of my mother, I said:

"Oh, no!"

The words were hardly out of my mouth before I felt something hard and cold smash me between the eyes. It was an empty whisky bottle. I saw stars, and fell backwards from the speeding car into the dust of the road, my feet becoming entangled in the steel spokes of my bicycle. The white men piled out and stood over me.

"Nigger, ain' yuh learned no better sense'n tha' yet?) asked the man who hit me. "Ain' yuh learned t' say *sir* t' a white man yet?"

Dazed, I pulled to my feet. My elbows and legs were bleeding. Fists doubled, the white man advanced, kicking my bicycle out of the way.

"Aw, leave the bastard alone. He's got enough," said one.

They stood looking at me. I rubbed my shins, trying to stop the flow of blood. No doubt they felt a sort of contemptuous pity, for one asked:

"Yuh wanna ride t' town now, nigger? Yuh reckon yuh know enough t' ride now?"

"I wanna walk," I said, simply.

Maybe it sounded funny. They laughed.

"Well, walk, yuh black son-of-a-bitch!"

When they left they comforted me with:

"Nigger, yuh sho better be damn glad it wuz us yuh talked t' tha' way. Yuh're a lucky bastard, 'cause if yuh'd said tha' t' somebody else, yuh might've been a dead nigger now."

IV.

Negroes who have lived South know the dread of being caught alone upon the streets in white neighborhoods after the sun has set. In such a simple situation as this the plight of the Negro in America is graphically symbolized. White strangers may be in these neighborhoods trying to get home, they can pass unmolested. But the color of a Negro's skin makes him easily recognizable, makes him suspect, converts him into a defenseless target.

Late on Saturday night I made some deliveries in a white neighborhood. I was pedaling my bicycle back to the store as fast as I could, when a police car, swerving toward me, jammed me into the curbing.

"Get down and put up your hands!" the policemen ordered.

I did. They climbed out of the car, guns drawn, faces set, and advanced slowly.

"Keep still!" they ordered.

I reached my hands higher. They searched my pockets and packages. They seemed dissatisfied when they could find nothing incriminating. Finally, one of them said:

"Boy, tell your boss not to send you out in white neighborhoods after sundown."

As usual, I said:

"Yes, sir."

V.

My next job was a hall-boy in a hotel. Here my Jim Crow education broadened and deepened. When the bell-boys were busy, I was often called to assist them. As many of the rooms in the hotel were occupied by prostitutes, I was constantly called to carry them liquor and cigarettes. These women were nude most of the time. They did not bother about clothing, even for bell-boys. When you went into their rooms, you were supposed to take their nakedness for granted, as though it startled you no more than a blue vase or a red rug. Your presence awoke in them no sense of shame, for you were not regarded as human. If they were alone, you could steal sidelong glimpses at them. But if they were receiving men, not a flicker of your eyelids could show. I remember one incident vividly. A new woman, a huge, snowy-skinned blonde, took a room on my floor. I was sent to wait upon her. She was in bed with a thick-set man; both were nude and uncovered. She said she wanted some liquor and slid out of bed and waddled across the floor to get her money from a dresser drawer. I watched her.

"Nigger, what in hell you looking at?" the white man asked me, raising himself upon his elbows.

"Nothing," I answered, looking miles deep into the blank wall of the room.

"Keep your eyes where they belong, if you want to be healthy!" he said.

"Yes, sir."

VI.

One of the bell-boys I knew in this hotel was keeping steady company with one of the Negro maids. Out of a clear sky the police descended upon his home and arrested him, accusing him of bastardy. The poor boy swore he had had no intimate relations with the girl. Nevertheless, they forced him to marry her. When the child arrived, it was found to be much lighter in complexion than either of the two supposedly legal parents. The white men around the hotel made a great joke of it. They spread the rumor that some white cow must have scared the poor girl while she was carrying the baby. If you were in their presence when this explanation was offered, you were supposed to laugh.

VII.

One of the bell-boys was caught in bed with a white prostitute. He was castrated and run out of town. Immediately after this all the bell-boys and hall-boys were called together and warned. We were given to understand that the boy who had been castrated was a "mighty, mighty lucky bastard." We were impressed with the fact that next time the management of the hotel would not be responsible for the lives of "trouble-makin' niggers." We were silent.

VIII.

One night, just as I was about to go home, I met one of the Negro maids. She lived in my direction, and we fell in to walk part of the way home together. As we passed the white night-watchman, he slapped the maid on her buttock. I turned around, amazed. The watchman looked at me with a long, hard, fixed-under stare. Suddenly he pulled his gun and asked:

"Nigger, don't yuh like it?"

I hesitated.

"I asked yuh don't yuh like it?" he asked again, stepping forward.

"Yes, sir," I mumbled.

"Talk like it, then!"

"Oh, yes, sir!" I said with as much heartiness as I could muster.

Outside, I walked ahead of the girl, ashamed to face her. She caught up with me and said:

"Don't be a fool! Yuh couldn't help it!"

This watchman boasted of having killed two Negroes in self-defense.

Yet, in spite of all this, the life of the hotel ran with an amazing smoothness. It would have been impossible for a stranger to detect anything. The maids, the hall-boys, and the bell-boys were all smiles. They had to be.

IX.

I had learned my Jim Crow lessons so thoroughly that I kept the hotel job till I left Jackson for Memphis. It so happened that while in Memphis I applied for a job at a branch of the optical company. I was hired. And for some reason, as long as I worked there, they never brought my past against me.

Here my Jim Crow education assumed quite a different form. It was no longer brutally cruel, but subtly cruel. Here I learned to lie, to steal, to dissemble. I learned to play that dual role which every Negro must play if he wants to eat and live.

For example, it was almost impossible to get a book to read. It was assumed that after a Negro had imbibed what scanty schooling the state furnished he had no further need for books. I was always borrowing books from men on the job. One day I mustered enough courage to ask one of the men to let me get books from the library in his name. Surprisingly, he consented. I cannot help but think that he consented because he was a Roman Catholic and felt a vague sympathy for Negroes, being himself an object of hatred. Armed with a library card, I obtained books in the following manner: I would write a note to the librarian, saying: "Please let this nigger boy have the following books." I would then sign it with the white man's name.

When I went to the library, I would stand at the desk. hat in hand, looking as unbookish as possible. When I received the books desired I would take them home. If the books listed in the note happened to be out, I would sneak into the lobby and forge a new one. I never took any chances guessing with the white librarian about what the fictitious white man would want to read. No doubt if any of the white patrons had suspected that some of the volumes they enjoyed had been in the home of a Negro, they would not have tolerated it for an instant.

The factory force of the optical company in Memphis was much larger than that in Jackson, and more urbanized. At least they liked to talk, and would engage the Negro help in conversation whenever possible. By this means I found that many subjects were taboo from the white man's point of view. Among the topics they did not like to discuss with Negroes were the following: American white women; the Ku Klux Klan; France, and how Negro soldiers fared while there; French women; Jack Johnson; the entire northern part of the United States; the Civil War; Abraham Lincoln; U. S. Grant; General Sherman; Catholics; the Pope; Jews; the Republican Party; slavery; social equality; Communism; Socialism; the 13th and 14th Amendments to the Constitution; or any topic calling for positive knowledge or manly self-assertion on the part of the Negro. The most accepted topics were sex and religion.

There were many times when I had to exercise a great deal of ingenuity to keep out of trouble. It is a southern custom that all men must take off their hats when they enter an elevator. And especially did this apply to us blacks with rigid force. One day I stepped into an elevator with my arms full of packages. I was forced to ride with my hat on. Two white men stared at me coldly. Then one of them very kindly lifted my hat and placed it upon my armful of packages. Now the most accepted response for a Negro to make under such circumstances is to look at the white man out of the corner of his eye and grin. To have said: "Thank you!" would have made the white man *think* that you *thought* you were receiving from him a personal service. For such an act I have seen Negroes take a blow in the mouth. Finding the first alternative distasteful, and the second dangerous, I hit upon an acceptable course of action which feel safely between these two poles. I immediately--no sooner than my hat was lifted--pretended that my packages were about to spill, and appeared deeply distressed with keeping them in my arms. In this fashion I evaded having to acknowledge his service, and, in spite of adverse circumstances, salvaged a slender shred of personal pride.

How do Negroes feel about the way they have to live? How do they discuss it when alone among themselves? I think this question ca be answered in a single sentence. A friend of mine who ran an elevator once told me:

"Lawd, man! Ef it wuzn't fer them polices 'n' them ol' lynch-mobs, there wouldn't be nothin' but uproar down here!"

ARCHIE WILLIAMS, *OLYMPIC CHAMPION*

Archie Williams was a college sophomore when he won the 400 meter dash in Berlin in 1936. Earlier that same year he had set a world record of 46.1 in that event, a mark that would stand until well after World War II. Williams was one of the ten men on the U.S. Olympic team who were referred to in the Nazi press as America's "black auxiliaries," a term reflecting the Nazi belief in Aryan supremacy and black inferiority. But much to the chagrin of the Germans, these "black auxiliaries," led by Jesse Owens, outscored every national track and field team, including their fifty-six Caucasian teammates. Archie Williams holds degrees in mechanical engineering from the University of California, Berkeley; in aeronautical engineering from the Air Force Engineering School at Wright-Patterson Field; and in meteorology from UCLA. He also holds a commercial pilot's license with an instructor's rating and a teaching certificate from the University of California, Riverside. Modest to a fault, his self-effacing remarks fail to disguise a man possessed of extraordinary curiosity, quick wit, and a penetrating intelligence.

That moment of victory was just something that proved that I could do something. Most young guys go through life not sure of what they're doing. You study, and you say, "Well, I can read, and I can write and do math and probably do this and that," but here was something that I did. And I guess that the whole world saw it. I can't say that I filled up with emotion when the flag went up and all that. I got a big thrill out of it, but it wasn't like the end of the world because I've got to think about the guy who almost won. Maybe I just had a step on him. People say, "Well, gee, just think, you were the greatest in the world." I say, "Bullshit. I just beat everybody who showed up that day." How about some guy down in Abyssinia chasing those lions for a living or getting chased by them? He could probably come in and kick my ass without even taking a deep breath. Forget about being the greatest in the world. You just beat the ones who showed up that day. Everybody asks me how I prepared for the Olympics. I didn't. I was preparing to get a degree in mechanical engineering because nobody in my family had ever gone to college. They weren't pushing me, but this was something I wanted to do, a goal that I had. I lived about a mile from Berkeley, so I could walk to school. In those days there weren't any scholarships. Nowadays a guy goes to Cal because they give him a better free ride; in our days we went because a Cal man with his big "C" was something. You'd say, "Boy, I wish I could be one of those kinds of guys." The kids saw it more that way then. They didn't see athletes as the guy slam- dunking or spiking the ball. They saw a guy as an athlete, pure and simple. They didn't see athletics as a way to big bucks. It was just an end to itself. To me athletics were fine so long as I got my lessons. And it was tough, man. I wasn't that smart. So I had to bust my ass. I lot of times wouldn't even get a hot shower because I'd be in the lab until 5 p.m. and everybody else would be home. And I'd have to work out, come in, and take a cold shower. But I don't regret it. It was great. I picked engineering because I liked aviation and I liked flying. I wanted to be a flyboy. I used to make model planes, and I finally thought, if you want to get into aviation, you got to get in on the engineering part of it, and so I signed up for that. It was kind of a challenge, I guess. When I went to Berkeley, I went to my couselor, and the guy said, "What do you want to take?" I said, "I want to take engineering." He said, "Are you kidding? Be serious. You ain't got a chance. Why don't you be a preacher or a real estate man or something?" I said, "Look, man, sign me up. Let me worry about that." Then at the end of my studies, sure enough, the big companies like General Motors or General Electric would come on campus to interview seniors and this same counselor told me he wanted me to take interviews even though he and I knew they weren't going to hire any black engineers. Those big corporations just weren't hiring black people. They weren't, and who else would? Look, I had a job one summer making five dollars a week chopping weeds for the East Bay Water Company. Later I thought about working as an engineer for them. And I talked to the guy down there, but he said, "Sorry about that." In college they had a student branch of the American Society of Mechanical Engineers. But forget it. I couldn't even be a goddam Boy Scout. I went to Sacramento to the state contest because I used to make these model planes with a bunch of my white friends, and I couldn't stay in the YMCA. And guess who the guy was at the desk who turned me down? A Filipino! So I had to stay in a flop house. It really hurt the friends I was with because it never occurred to them that this was the way it was. But I'm not bitter. It's just the way it was then.

I got into sports kind of by accident. As a kid, I wasn't that good in other sports, but I could run pretty fast, so I tried track. Even in high school I wasn't that great. I don't recall winning any races. I finished high school during the depression and there were no jobs, so a friend of mine said to me, "Hey, we're not doing anything. Let's go back to school." I asked him, "What do you mean?" He said, "We can go to San Mateo J. C. and at least have something to do since we can't find any jobs." So we went down there. At San Mateo I found out I had to take trigonometry and physics so I could enroll in a regular four-year college to become a mechanical engineer. I also went out for track, just because everybody else was doing it. I started running pretty good, and the coach said, "I think you might have a good career when you go on to a four-year school." His name was Tex Bird, and he did more than talk about running; he talked about life, and he gave me some good principles to go by. And in the process my times started to come down to where he felt I could go to Berkeley and make the team. And so I did.

At Berkeley I ran into a super coach, Brutus Hamilton, who himself had been an Olympian in the decathlon. In fact, he was a super athlete because he also got a baseball offer from the New York Yankees and he had been the all-service boxing champion. And besides that he was--and many people didn't know this--an English teacher and quite a philosopher. I think he had more to do with whatever success I had, not only on the track but in life, than anyone else I can think of. Oh, I can tell you a lot about Brutus Hamilton. I can't recall a single time when he spoke in anger to me or any of the other fellows. He was always gentle; he was always positive; he was always constructive; it was always, "How can you do it better, and not, "Why did you do that?" or, "What's wrong with you?" None of that kind of stuff. It was always positive. He always made you feel like you meant something to him. With that in mind, any time you did something that wasn't good you felt like you were letting him down. Some people said he was too soft, that he should have been a hard-nosed disciplinarian, but he got stuff out of people that other guys wouldn't have got. For instance, me. I wouldn't have done for other people what I would do for him because he never put the pressure on. He felt that any pressure was self-imposed. He said, "You can be what you want to be, and I can't make you do it. I can't run for you. So just get out there and do the best you can."

Brutus Hamilton was Glenn Cunningham's coach and Bob Kiesel's, too. Kiesel was a sprinter on the winning 1932 relay team. All of us felt the same way. It was more like he was our dad. He had coached at the University of Kansas and then came out here to Berkeley; I think it was 1931 or 1932. I've still got letters that he wrote; they're almost like poetry. He'd talk about things from life. You know, you never see grown men cry. We were over there in Berlin. He went along as a coach, and he missed his family so much that I saw him break down and cry one night. It made me cry too.

I can't remember him even talking about anything like technique. He'd just take what you had and polish it up for you and say, "Work on this." There were times when he'd come up to you and say, "Hey, you look like you're tired. Do you really feel tired or bored?" Then he'd say, "Go home. I don't want to see you for a week." And I'd say, "But coach, I need..." He'd say, "Get the hell out of here. Go." He could feel what you were feeling. He was not a religious man in any formal sense, although he could quote the Bible, but you'd have to take it from there. He wouldn't push anything like this Jerry Falwell. He was just a great man. He was an inspiration.

Actually, I was a walk-on at Berkeley. No one even knew I was there until track season. That first spring I was only running 49.7 or something like that. In fall track I got it down to about 48.5: then the next spring things just started happening. It seemed like every meet I'd knock a half second off. I didn't have any illusions about being that great. My real hero was a guy named Jimmy LuValle who later got third in the Olympic 400 meters. He was from UCLA, and I saw him win the NCAA in 1935. I was way up in the bleachers, and I thought, "I'd sure like to run that good." I never dreamed that I would.

Anyway, my times in the spring of 1936 started coming down. It's kind of hard to believe, but every time I'd run my time would get a little bit better. I won the PAC 8 with 46.8, which was a record for that meet at the time. Then the papers started writing me up, asking, "Can he do it?" I thought, "I don't know. I can try."

Then they had the Pacific AAU at Stanford, and I got down to 46.3, which was getting close. And the next week we went to Chicago for the NCAA, and guess what? 46.1. Right out of a clear sky. I still don't believe it. And the funny part of it is you never know when it's going to happen because this was in a trial heat, no pressure. All I had to do was be in the first four. I was just floating along. I remember it was a one-turn race at the University of Chicago and the tape was in front of a gate and one inch past this gate was a cement sidewalk. When you were running down the home stretch, you could see that cement. They say I let up a little bit, but I don't know if I did or not. Who knows?

But, anyway, that got me in the book with a world record. You know, it's a funny thing. Have you ever heard of biorhythms? Okay, my students are always kidding me about my biorhythms. I always do theirs on the computer so they always were telling me to do my own. One day just for the fun of it I did, and on the day that I set that record of 46.1 everything was perfect, one of those picture book situations. But in the Olympics it was just the opposite.

Everything was for shit. You can take it anyway you want.

The final trials for the '36 team were at Randalls Island, New York. The temperature was 100 degrees. Boy, it was hot, but I won. There was so much excitement. Here's a dumb kid who'd never been out of California and in New York City with all these big athletes. I thought, "What am I doing here?" It was kind of like a dream. I remember Ben Eastman. I had worked out with Ben just before we went back East, and it just happened that to go to the finals we had to share a taxi and Ben said, "Hey, I'll pay for the ride." Every time I see him now I say, "Well, Ben, I still owe you for that taxi ride." It's funny what you remember about those things.

Then we hopped on the ol' boat. In those days they didn't have any 747s. One thing I had to watch was eating. A bunch of young kids and all of us finely tuned and well trained. Well, you get on that big ship, and the first thing they do is start feeding you. They have before breakfast sweet rolls, and then they had breakfast off the menu. Before this we'd been eating in the Automat. And then came lunch and tea break, then supper, and at 10 o'clock at night you could come down and pig out, just to top things off. I imagine I picked up about eight or nine pounds.

I noticed that on board ship they were very careful to put all the black guys in one compartment--"Well, you guys want to be with your own kind"--that kind of crap. My roommate was a guy I had to compete against--Jimmy LuValle. I don't think it ever occurred to them that there might be some heavy psyching involved. Of course, I was too dumb to get psyched out.

Running styles had changed by the time I was running the 400 in the Olympics. You didn't run hard, coast, and run hard again. That was like running an 800 meters. At least when I ran, if you had an outside lane, you didn't know what was going on until you got in that last straightaway, and so you couldn't afford to play games. You had to kick it and get out there. You got to know your pace, that you were not burning it all up all at once, that you were still keeping up with it because when you come out of that final turn, it's really a shocker to look up and see that you're not in the lead.

I'll tell you the biggest worry I had in that damn race in Berlin was whether or not I was going to step out of my lane just before the last straightaway because all the lines are crossing there. It's confusing, and you're tired anyway, and you're trying to run. I guess I did all right because I didn't get disqualified. But I was never quite sure whether I stayed in my lane or not.

Everything is different now. We actually ran the first 220 yards faster than the second 220. I understand nowadays that someone like Lee Evans would probably run the second 220 faster. It's kind of hard to compare what we did with what they're doing now because the training is much more rigorous today. In fact, these guys train all the time. We trained four days a week, with weekends off. These guys today train every day, twice a day sometimes. They do weight training and exercises that nobody ever thought of in my time.

I picked the 440 because I didn't like long distances. I liked sprinting, but I wasn't that fast. I was pretty good. I could run 21.2 in the 220, which would get you about a third or fourth. But it was my coach who said, "I really think your race is the quarter mile because of your temperament."

I didn't like races like the 880 where you had to jockey around for position and mess around. I liked to kick it full throttle and let it fly. That's just the way I am; whereas, some guys, like John Woodruff, liked to mess around, jockey for position, go in and out.

John Woodruff was good. You know he was only a freshman in the Olympics. I was a sophomore. He beat everybody. Big ol' gawky kid, he ran the weirdest race. Ran the first lap in 60.5 and the second in 50.5.

He won the IC4A about four times in both the 440 and the 880. He really didn't have any competition. He was in a class by himself. I was just a flash in the pan; whereas, he was Mr. Consistency. He's a legend.

We had some characters in those days. Spec Towns, for instance. Well, I'm not going to tell you about him. We used to call him Lil' Abner. He'd been in the National Guard and he'd wear these ol' G.I. boots. He's the only guy in the world who would take his cigar, put it down on the starting block, run a race and then come back for it. I don't know whether he ever lit it or not. He was just a lot of fun.

We pulled a good one on Spec in a meet in Oslo after the Olympics. He had just broken the world record in the 110-meter high hurdles. He ran it in something like 13.7. That was an unheard of time then. Well, that night we got some guy to call him on the phone and say, "Mr. Towns, we're very sorry to tell you that your record will not count because there were only nine hurdles on the track." For awhile he was really shook up, but the next day somebody told him the truth.

I knew Glenn Cunningham. He was a hard worker--real dedicated. Remember that as a child he had been in a bad fire, and I think he even had some toes missing. In any case, that guy really had to warm up a lot for his races. In fact, I would warm up with him, and when we'd finish warming up I'd say, "Hell, that's my workout." God, this guy would just run laps and laps and sprints and everything. He had a nice sense of humor. A really serious guy but he could also joke around. In fact, he discovered that my left leg was an inch longer than my right one. He was great on rub downs because he had to do it for himself. He was giving me this rub down and he says, "Relax." And I said, "Goddamn it, I am relaxed." So he shook my legs and called for the coach to come and see that my left leg was about an inch longer than my right. He said, "God, you're a freak."

Another guy was Jack Torrence. There's a guy who, if they'd made the shot-put ring about a foot bigger, would have thrown that goddamn thing a hundred feet. Or if they would have let him have a six pack before the meet. He had the record of 57 feet, which in those days was almost like 80 feet would be now. He didn't do so well in Berlin, though. I think he only finished fifth. Mack Robinson was just a junior college sprinter that nobody was watching. I think he took third in the trials, but he came through like a champ in the finals. He finished second to Jesse in the 200. You know, he's Jackie Robinson's brother. He's kind of a quiet guy. He didn't have too much to say. Just went out there and did his job.

Cornelius Johnson was another character. Ol' Corny was a great psycher. He could clear 6.6 in his sweats. In fact, he'd never take his sweats off. In those days you didn't have this flop thing. You had to muscle your way over the bar. He'd kick way over the bar and just psych everybody out. He was from Compton J.C., and he was funny. I remember one night after the Olympics we all went to Berlin and we had a few drinks and ol' Corny was doing pretty good. We jumped in this taxi but we didn't have enough money to pay. So we passed the hat, but ol' Corny always slept through those things.

Corny's gone now and so are a lot of the guys. The whole sprint relay team is dead. Foy

Draper got killed in the war; and Ralph, Jesse, and Wykoff died in the last few years.

Ralph Metcalf was the senior spokesman for us blacks. He was a little older, a lawyer, and a beautiful man. He looked out for me. He told me what to do and where to go. He was a very polished guy. He later became a congressman from Illinois. In the 1932 Games he got euchred out of the 200 meter gold. After the race it was discovered that he had run two yards farther than anyone else. He got second to Eddie Tolan. But Ralph only said, "Well, that's life." He was very studious. I think he got his Ph.D. at USC or UCLA, and then he taught at Dillard University in New Orleans. When I was on my way to Tuskegee during the war, I went through New Orleans and stayed with him. I can remember that we went out to play golf on a little ol' dinky golf course. He was the kind of guy you wanted for a friend. You could go to him for advice.

What can I say about Jesse Owens? What can I say about God? He was just a nice guy. He kind of kept to himself a little bit. Of course, there was always someone after him for interviews or pictures. I got to know him pretty well; in fact, he still owes me five dollars. But I don't want it that bad. I'll wait. All I can say is he was a nice guy, a good friend. I used to train with him, and it was like running against a deer. We'd run wind sprints, which was good for me because I got the finest there was for an example. The main thing was that everything was effortless for him.

How would he do today? He'd probably jump over this guy's head--what's his name?--Carl Lewis--because Jesse never trained for the long jump. He'd go out and run through the pit a few times. That's why in Berlin he almost fouled out. I watched him in the NCAA in 1935. He ran the 220, ran over to the long jump pit to check if anybody had come close to his 26.1 or whatever it was, and then ran back to the start to set a world record in the low hurdles. He was running against a guy named Slats Hardin who, next to Jesse, was probably the greatest low hurdler in the world. It kind of hurt to see a guy like Slats, who was the epitome of form, and here comes Jesse who didn't know which foot to jump with. He'd just zoom over--shitty form--but fast. I'm glad he didn't try the 440. I was always reminding him what a tough race it was. I kept telling him, "It'll kill you."

After the Olympics I went on this tour with Jesse Owens and a group of guys to Sweden, Denmark, and Finland. We landed in Oslo, and there was this big banner saying, "Welcome Jesse Owens." But Jesse wasn't there because Eddie Cantor had gotten hold of him and told him to come back before everybody else. He promised Jesse this nightclub tour and that he'd make millions. So Jesse jumped on a boat and went home. Well, we get off this airplane in Oslo and there's this "Welcome Jesse" banner, and everybody asks, "Where's Jesse?" "Well, he ain't coming," says somebody. They said, "What do you mean, 'He ain't coming?' Do you see that goddamn sign? He's gotta come." "Sorry, he ain't coming." This one guy goes in the plane looking through the seats and up in the cockpit and finally says, "I know. You're Jesse Owens." And I said, "No I ain't. No I ain't." But he says, "Yes you are. Yes you are." So I said, "Okay." And I signed Jesse's name and walked away.

I save all the articles that say why there are so many black sprinters. Actually it's not that there are so many black sprinters; it's just that the white people take it for granted so they say, "I'm not even going to bother with it." And they don't. Let me tell you this. Jesse was such a phenomenon that after the '36 Games they decided to do a physiological profile on him. Guess what? He turned out to be a Norwegian. All these stereotypes, you know, about the heel bone, your skull being this thick, and liking to tap dance. I have a funny joke I tell about this racial thing. They had two black guys on a re-run of *That's Incredible* the other night. Did you see it? Yeah, the one guy was seven-foot tall and couldn't slam-dunk, and the other one had car insurance. So much for stereotypes.

I got a big kick out of Germany. Here's a twenty-one-year-old kid who'd never been out of California. Hell, I didn't even know where Germany was. The German people did just what you'd expect. They'd rub our skin to see if it would come off. But the people were themselves. I didn't know that much about Hitler or what he was doing. In fact, as far as I was concerned, they were just friendly, warm people who were happy to have us there.

Remember a guy named Gene Venzke from Pottstown, Pennsylvania? He used to run the mile. He was one of the guys who used to run in the Garden all the time. Well, Gene Venzke and I were both interested in planes. There was an airport right near the Olympic village, so one day he said, "Let's go over and take a peek at those planes." We crawled under this fence and someone yells, "Halt!" Well, it was Hogan's Heroes time. We got the hell out of there. Then we saw this plane go by--whoosh. I'd never seen a plane that fast before. I asked one of the Germans, "What kind of plane was that?" "Dat's a mail plane," he said. Well, shit, that was an ME 109. I never saw a plane that fast before. And they were only supposed to be flying gliders. That was the fastest glider in the world.

In the actual Games they crammed all of our heats together in two days. I ran the first heat at 10 o'clock in the morning. The second was at 2:30. The next day the semis were at 3:30 and the finals at 5:00. So you didn't have much time to think about it. My coach told me, "Don't get cute out there. You don't have to win every heat, but why not do it? If you don't, you'll fool around out there and think you'll just get a cheap second or third. But that is a good way to wind up in the bleachers." So each race was a kind of final. There's no sense in saving it for something that wasn't going to happen. In every heat you were running against some guy you never saw before. And I just wanted to keep the game honest; otherwise the first thing you know you're saying, "Who he? Where'd he come from?"

One thing about the whole thing was that we were having a lot of fun. We were serious, of course, but it didn't seem to me, and not to the other guys either, that it was going to be the end of the world if we didn't win. That's one thing I notice about these meets I go to nowadays. Nobody's smiling. Everybody's grim. It's like these prize fighters psyching each other out. We'd clown around--kid around--even with the guys we were racing against. We always had jokes going on. And that's what my coach, Brutus Hamilton, said: "This is nothing but a lot of fun. And if it ever gets to the point where it isn't fun, quit." That's why he used to ask us how we felt and then sent us home if we didn't feel good.

It's a funny thing. USC was always our biggest rival. Ol' Dean Cromwell was the coach there, and he always had athletes backed up. They were stacked up like cords of wood. They had a guy named Al Fitch, a sprinter from Huntington High School. Al was running 9.6 and 21.5 while still in high school. Well, Cromwell says, "You know, Al, if you come to USC I think I can make a sprinter out of you." Shit, he could already beat anybody they had.

And once you started to win, all these guys would ask, "Hey, what do you eat?" Well, actually, I ate anything 'cause I knew my coach would run it off of me. But I'd give these guys a line of shit. They'd ask, "Do you eat honey?" "Yea." "Do you drink milk?" "No." They made some kind of mystique out of it.

I didn't try to psych out my competition. Oh, sometimes I'd limp a little bit. They'd ask, "How you doing?" And I'd groan a bit. Like I said, it wasn't that big of a thing. It sounds like I'm being trite about it, but that's a fact. We felt good. I never saw a guy fall down and cry when he lost or anything. Guys now beat the ground and everything. I think that's why we got more out of it.

Another thing was. The average guy on that '36 team was a college kid. I was just a sophomore. Jesse was, I think, a senior. So was Dave Albritton. All of us were college guys. The average age was probably twenty-one or twenty-two; whereas nowadays, what are they? What's Moses? Twenty-seven or twenty-eight? And the weightmen? Thirty, thirty-five? What it amounts to today is it takes that long to be as good as these guys are. With us it was different. I didn't even dream about the Olympics in the beginning of 1936. I knew they were going to happen, and a guy says, "Hey, are you going to the Olympics?" I'd say, "Hell, I don't know." And he'd say, "Do you think you can make it?" I'd say, "I don't know." It wasn't something where I had to say, "Gee, I've got to make it." Way down inside, I thought, "Gee, I'd sure like to do it." But I wasn't making any big plans for it. How many guys are going to go out for the Olympics? So, consequently, I wouldn't have been too disappointed if I'd tripped over my wienie and fallen on my face.

In my case, I did what I wanted. I enjoyed going to the Olympics, but then I still had to get back to school. There was no future then for a career in track. I also hurt my leg after the Olympics in a meet up in Sweden. I pulled a muscle which never did get well. The next year I went out, and I didn't even make my letter. I tried, but I pulled the same damn thing twice, so I decided, "That's it." It got to the point that I was so scared that every time I'd run I'd be thinking about it. It held up when it counted, so I got my share out of it so why not let some other guys have it.

I graduated in 1939. That's when I got into this aviation thing. I learned how to fly. As I said before, I knew that General Motors wasn't hiring anybody. The guy who ran the flying school where I learned how to fly--a real nice guy--said, "Hey, you want a job?" I said, "Sure." He said, "I'll give you five dollars a week and one hour's flying time." I worked twelve hours a day, seven days a week, gasing airplanes and what not, but I got to fly. This other kid and I--his name was Andy and he's a chief pilot for Pan Am now--were always sneaking extra hours. We'd get out there early in the morning and we'd be warming those planes up. We'd look around, and we'd just take off and fly around the field once and come in. I built up my flying time to where I finally got my instructor's rating and my commercial license. That was early in 1941. There again, a black guy with a pilot's license and an instructor's rating; he's...well, he's nothing. Even the guy I worked for couldn't hire me as a flying instructor. He'd have lost all his business.

That's when I found out about this program at Tuskegee Institute. They were starting this program down there to train blacks to fly. So I went down there for $200 a month and started teaching flying. I worked there for about a year.

Then Pearl Harbor came along, so I signed up as an aviation cadet. Because they knew about my engineering training, they sent me to U.C.L.A. for a year of meteorology school and I graduated from that. I got my commission as a lieutenant in meteorology; then I went back to Tuskegee to be a weatherman, but they turned me back into a flying instructor, and that's what I did throughout the war. We had our own Army Air Force unit--the Spookwaffe--at least that's what we called it. The regular Army Air Force was segregated. The rumor was, "We'll get these niggers in a bunch of airplanes and let them kill themselves, and that will be that." But the funny part of it was that they skimmed the cream of the crop out of the colleges. We had guys with Ph.D.'s, doctors, all-American football players; these guys were handpicked, so there was no way we were going to flop. One of my students was an ace. Another one became a four-star general.

I stayed in the service after the war. After Truman desegregated the service in 1948, I was sent to Wright Field to the Air Force Engineering School for two years. I got a degree in aeronautical engineering there on top of what I already had. After that I went overseas to Korea, Okinawa, and Japan for three years, flying B-29s and other odds and ends. After that I was stationed in New York where I was staff weather officer to the 22nd Air Division. We had the defense of the whole northeast of the country. We worked out of this so-called bombproof building. Well, one day we were in there, and a goddamn foot came through the roof. The guy was up there fixing the roof on our bombproof building. I finally ended up with the Strategic Air Command in Riverside, California, where I was discharged in 1964. I was a lieutenant colonel.

When I was stationed in Riverside, I thought, "Shit, I'm young; what am I going to do?" So I thought, "Hell, I'll go back and be a teacher." When you're an officer in the Air Force, you're teaching all the time. So I went to the University of California, Riverside. I already had my degree, so I had to take all those square fillers like ed. psych., learning processes, and how to run the overhead projector. Heavy stuff. Oh, you had to fill in the squares. Well, I got the degree and I've been teaching high school ever since.

I passed retirement years ago. At 65 they used to kick you out, but now they can't. If they kick me out, who's going to teach this computer stuff? Hell, I'm good for another ten years.

How do I stay looking so young? Shit, I just buy cheap clothes. No, I just take it easy. You do what you can, and you play it one day at a time. Sports? Well, I jog all the way to the parking lot, and my wife and I walk about ten miles a week. That's good enough. Stay loose. I don't know about these guys that jog. It's kind of self-defeating. I know it would hurt my knees. I find if I just take it easy with everything and get a lot of rest, I'll be okay. As ol' Satchel Paige used to say, "Think clean thoughts and don't look back."

Hanging around these kids does something to you, too. You see the energy, and it kind of transfers. They want things, and I like to feel if I wasn't here things wouldn't be happening. It's a good feeling. Every day something comes up that you haven't thought of before, and the kids will ask you about it, or they'll bring in something new. It's exciting. I may be 72, but I'm not quitting for a long time. The next generation of computers is coming out, and I want to see what they're like. I just feel good about what I'm doing.

William H. Grier and Price M. Cobbs, *BLACK RAGE* (1968)

William H. Grier and Price M. Cobbs were Assistant Professors of Psychiatry at the University of California Medical Center, San Francisco, when they wrote Black Rage *in 1968. Each also had his private practice in psychiatry. This book is about the rage felt by African Americans trying to cope in a hostile environment. Unfortunately, time has little changed the authors' analysis. African Americans still must struggle "to find an identity, a sense of worth, to relate to others, to love, to work, and to create," as Senator Fred R. Harris wrote in his* Forword *to this edition. The selection below deals with the psychological barriers confronting young black males in their search for manhood.*

Acquiring Manhood

Jimmy

Jimmy was a twelve-year-old boy whose rapid growth had left him gawky and uncomfortable. He sat slumped in a chair, trying to conceal his ill-fitting clothes. His face was jet-black, and his expressions ranged from somber to sad. Whether relating stories of home, school, or the streets, he disguised his true feelings. At twelve he had learned one of his first lessons--always play it cool. As much as possible, he worked to hid his inner life.

One day he stared long and hard at his fist and said: "I want to hit a white man." For once, the therapist could sense an uncensored outpouring of feelings. Then Jimmy frowned, started another sentence, and began to cry.

The anger was welcome, if unexpected, but the comment was surprising. In over three months of weekly visits, the boy had never directly mentioned white people. There had been allusions to trouble at school with boys who were not "bloods" and once he talked of his father's job at a can factory, where there were few Negroes. But Jimmy had never spoken in terms of racial feelings or problems. He had never directly felt antagonism from a white person, but when his anger spilled over, he chose that target.

He was a quiet, introverted boy who found it difficult to talk for fifty minutes. He would smile in acknowledging something pleasant, but generally he seemed to feel despair. His emotions were expressed in terms of stubbornness and obstinacy. If he felt threatened, he became passive and silent and in this manner opposed anything he did not want to do or say. This was his means of dealing with any authority, whether a teacher in school or a parent. Though he had an above-average intelligence, he was doing poorly in school. There were important things he would not do or forget to do, and his grades suffered. In talking about his life, Jimmy was vague. He had trouble seeing anything in his life as definite, with any form or shape.

One thing in his life was clear. He saw his father as weak and powerless. However much his father threatened, cajoled, or beat him, Jimmy always knew that the man was playing a role.

His father was a large man, lighter in color than his son, and grossly overweight. He dressed in rumpled suits, wrinkled shirts, and greasy ties. In some of the early family sessions, he would interrupt to complain of his various ailments. He spoke of an ulcer that was always "acting up." Mr. B. "played at" (this was Jimmy's phrase) being the minister of a storefront church, in addition to his full-time job at the factory. From an early age, Jimmy was aware that his father could never "stand up." He had heard his mother say it and he observed it himself. One of the boy's few delights was in recalling an occasion when his father cringed and sent his wife to the door to handle a bill collector. Many of Jimmy's friends did not have their fathers living at home, but he was certain that those fathers, in the same situation, would have acted the same way.

Mrs. B was a short, dark woman with an attractive but worried face. She was neat and "fixed up" and openly compared her appearance with her husband's usually disheveled state. She did not hide her contempt for him. She constantly undermined his feeble attempts to relate to Jimmy. She was the dominant figure in the house, and she assumed this position as an unwanted burden, as something about which she had no choice. She would alternate between understanding Jimmy and dramatically washing her hands of everything.

In terms of individual psychopathology, Jimmy can be matched with thousands of teenage boys of every race and ethnic background. He is responding to his puberty with restlessness and feelings he cannot articulate directly. He is angry with his father and alternately attracted to and repelled by his mother. Every therapist has seen many Jimmys. What is different about him is that he is black and is experiencing what every black boy in this country must undergo. His personality and character structure, his emotional assets and liabilities, are being shaped as much by his blackness as by his personal environment.

Jimmy is beginning to realize that he has no power and, like his father, will not get it. At his age the concepts are misty, but he realizes that his father and the fathers of his friends are lacking something. He has had few, if any, traumatic incidents with whites. There have been no overt acts of discrimination. The family has lived in a ghetto, and all their socialization has been within that framework. But Jimmy is part of a historical legacy that spans more than three hundred years. He lives in a large city but he shares his insight with every black child in every city in this country. He must devise individual ways to meet group problems. He must find compensations, whether healthy or unhealthy. There must be a tremendous expenditure of psychic energy to cushion the shock of learning that he is denied what other men around him have. When he states his desire to attack a white man, he consciously acknowledges his wish to attack those who keep him powerless.

Both theories of personality development and clinical experience attest to the troubled path from childhood to manhood. The young man must have developed a fine expertise in making his way in a complex and ambiguous social organization. Under the most favorable signs it is a difficult task and society must turn its most benign and helping face to the young aspirant. And once the game is mastered a certain flexible readiness is required because the rules are constantly being changed.

Thus the black boy in growing up encounters some strange impediments. Schools discourage his ambitions, training for valued skills is not available to him, and when he does triumph in some youthful competition he receives compromised praise, not the glory he might expect. In time he comes to see that society has locked arms *against* him, that rather than help he can expect opposition to his development, and that he lives not in a benign community but in a society that views his growth with hostility.

For the black man in this country, it is not so much a matter of acquiring manhood as it is a struggle to feel it his own. Whereas the the white man regards his manhood as an ordained right, the black man is engaged in a never-ending battle for its possession. For the black man, attaining any portion of manhood is an active process. He must penetrate barriers and overcome opposition in order to assume a masculine posture. For the inner psychological obstacles to manhood are never so formidable as the impediments woven into American society. By contrast, for a white man in this country, the rudiments of manhood are settled at birth by the possession of a penis and a white skin. This biological affirmation of masculinity and identity as master is enough to insure that, whatever his individual limitations, this society will not systematically erect obstructions to his achievement.

Throughout his life, at each critical point of development the black boy is told to hold back, to constrict, to subvert and camouflage his normal masculinity. Male assertiveness becomes a forbidden fruit, and if it is attained, it must be savored privately.

Manhood must always be defined for the setting in which it occurs. A man in a Siberian village may be very different from a man in a Chicago suburb. Biologically they share the same drives and limitations, but their societies may decree totally different roles. Manhood in this country has many meanings, but a central theme is clear. Men are very early taught that they have certain prerogatives and privileges. They are encouraged to pursue, to engage life, to attack, rather than to shrink back. They learn early that to express a certain amount of aggression and assertion is manly. Every playground, every schoolyard is filled with boys fighting and attacking, playing at being grown up. The popular heroes in this country are men who express themselves aggressively and assertively....

> *Mr. R. was a writer who presented himself for treatment in his mid-fifties. In his younger days he had enjoyed success and a certain amount of adulation in white society. Throughout the course of treatment he presented a picture of culture and refinement. His trouble was that several years earlier he had lost the spark of creativity and his writing ceased. He made frequent resolutions to resume writing, but this motivation never matched his ambition.*
>
> *It developed that he was afraid to compete with white men as a writer. Whatever he wrote, his obsessional fears dictated that somewhere someone who was white had written something better. He was a defeated and despairing man when he entered treatment. He had, however, a delicious secret which he used as comfort when he was most depressed.*

His face would crease with a smile when he recounted his numerous affairs as a young man. In all his life he never doubted his ability to outperform a white man sexually. He told how he had "banged, many white women." He sometimes spoke of himself as a deformed man or as a cripple, but sex was the one area in which he felt completely adequate.

The mythology and folklore of black people is filled with tales of sexually prodigious men. Most boys grow up on a steady diet of folk heroes who have distinguished themselves by sexual feats. It is significant that few, if any, of these folk heroes are directing armies or commanding empires. Dreams must in some way reflect reality, and in this country the black man, until quite recently, had not been in positions of power. His wielding of power had been in the privacy of the boudoir.

To be sure, black men have sexual problems. They may have impotence, premature ejaculation, and the entire range of pathology which limits and distorts sexual life. Such ailments have the same dynamic origins in men of all races. But where sex is employed as armament and used as a conscious and deliberate means of defense, it is the black man who chooses this weapon. If he cannot fight the white man openly, he can and does battle him secretly. Recurrently, the pattern evolves of black men using sex as a dagger to be symbolically thrust into the white man.

A black man who was an orderly in a hospital had an eighth-grade education and felt himself inadequate in most endeavors. If called upon to perform a new duty, he would reflect for a moment and feel dumbstruck. One evening an attractive young nurse made seductive overtures to him. At first he was not convinced that she was serious but thought she was playing a game. When he discovered that she meant it, he took her to bed with a vengeance. During the weekly therapy hour he would elaborate and expand on his feats. One central fact became more and more clear. He was able to state very directly that every time he possessed the girl sexually, he was making up for having sat on the back of the bus and having endured numberless humiliations. He was getting revenge for generations of slavery and degradation.

One of the constant themes in black folklore is the "bad nigger." It seems that every community has had one or was afraid of having one. They were feared as much by blacks as by whites. In the slave legends there are tales of docile field hands suddenly going berserk. It was a common enough phenomenon to appear in writings of the times and to stimulate the erection of defenses against this violent kind of man.

Today black boys are admonished not to be a "bad nigger." No description need be offered; every black child knows what is meant. They are angry and hostile. They strike fear into everyone with their uncompromising rejection of restraint or inhibition. They may seem at one moment meek and compromised--and in the next a terrifying killer. Because of his experience in this country, every black man harbors a potential bad nigger inside him. He must ignore this inner man. The bad nigger is bad because he has been required to renounce his manhood to save his life. The more one approaches the American ideal of respectability, the more this hostility must be repressed. The bad nigger is a defiant nigger, a reminder of what manhood could be.

Cultural stereotypes of the savage rapist-Negro express the fear that the black man will turn on his tormentors. Negro organizations dread the presence of the bad nigger. White merchants who have contact with black people have uneasy feelings when they see a tight mouth, a hard look, and an angry black face. The bad nigger in black men no doubt accounts for more worry in both races than any other single factor.

Granting the limitations of stereotypes, we should nevertheless like to sketch a paradigmatic black man. His characteristics seem so connected to employment that we call it "the postal-clerk syndrome." This man is always described as "nice" by white people. In whatever integrated setting he works, he is the standard against whom other blacks are measured. "If they were all only like him, everything would be so much better." He is passive, nonassertive, and nonaggressive. He has made a virtue of identification with the aggressor, and he has adopted an ingratiating and compliant manner. In public his thoughts and feelings are consciously shaped in the direction he thinks white people want them to be. The pattern begins in childhood when the mother may actually say: "You must be this way because this is the only way you will get along with Mr. Charlie."

This man renounces gratifications that are available to others. He assumes a deferential mask. He is always submissive. He must figure out "the man" but keep "the man" from deciphering him. He is prevalent in the middle and upper-middle classes, but is found throughout the social structure. The more closely allied to the white man, the more complete the picture becomes. He is a direct lineal descendant of the "house nigger" who was designed to identify totally with the white master. The danger he poses to himself and others is great, but only the surface of passivity and compliance is visible. The storm below is hidden.

> *A leading Negro citizen came to a therapy session with his wife, who was suffering from a severe and intractable melancholia. She had several times seriously attempted suicide. The last attempt was particularly serious. She was angry with her husband and berated him for never opening up and exposing his feelings.*
>
> *For his part, the husband remained "nice." He never raised his voice above a murmur. His wife could goad him, but he was the epitome of understanding. He was amenable to all suggestions. His manner and gestures were deliberate, studied, and noninflammatory. Everything was understated. During the course of treatment he was involved in several civil rights crises. His public life was an extension of his private one, and he used such words as "moderation" and "responsibility." His entire life was a study in passivity, in how to play at being a man without really being one.*

It would be easy to write off this man as an isolated passive individual, but his whole community looks upon his career as a success story. He made it in the system to a position of influence and means. And it took an aggressive, driving, determined man to make it against the odds he faced. We must ask how much energy is required for him to conceal his drive so thoroughly. And we wonder what would happen if his controls ever failed.

Starting with slavery, black people, and more particularly black men, have had to devise ways of expressing themselves uniquely and individually and in a manner that was not threatening to the white man. Some methods of giving voice to aggressive masculinity have become institutionalized. The most stylized is the posture of "playing it cool."

The playing-it-cool style repeats itself over and over again in all aspects of black life. It is an important means of expression and is widely copied in the larger white culture. A man may be overwhelmed with conflict, threatened with an eruption of feelings, and barely maintaining his composure, but he will present a serene exterior. He may fear the eruption of repressed feelings if they bring a loss of control, but an important aspect of his containment is the fear that his aggression will be directed against the white world and will bring swift punishment. The intrapsychic dynamics may be similar in a white man, but for the black man it is socially far more important that the facade be maintained.

Patients have come for treatment who have had one or two visits with a variety of psychiatrists, psychologists, and social workers. In many cases they were written off as having no significant pathology or as being "poor patients." The importance of the cool style is apparent when one realizes the cost and suffering required to maintain it. Those who practice it have raised to a high art a life style which seems a peculiarly black contribution to adaptation in this society.

Several decades ago, observers were impressed by the black community's adulation of Joe Louis. They were a starved and deprived group, but, even so, their deification of him seemed all out of proportion. In retrospect, there is an explanation. In the ring he was the picture of fury. As he demolished foe after foe, every black man could vicariously taste his victory. If his victims were white, the pleasure was even greater. He symbolized assertiveness and unbridled aggression for the black man. In watching him or reading about him, an entire community could find expression through him of inhibited masculine drives. As others have entered professional sports in later years, the heroes have served a similar purpose. Educated and sophisticated Negroes also participate in this hero worship, since all black men swim in the same sea..

> *A black man in treatment kept reaching for a memory. He finally recalled watching a fight on television, at a time when a black coed, Authurine Lucey, was integrating the University of Alabama. The contest was between a black and white fighter. During the bout he kept hearing someone shout: "Hit him one for Authurine." Even after he had forgotten the fight, the phrase kept returning to his mind, "Hit him one for Authurine." It became his battle cry. Whenever he was pressed, the thought would come again and again in an obsessional fashion. He then began to talk of his own repressed aggression and the pieces of the puzzle began to fit, and the obsession receded.*

When all the repressive forces fail and aggression erupts, it is vital that we ask the right questions. The issue is not what caused the riots of the past few years--that is clear to any man who has eyes. Rather, we must ask: What held this aggression in check for so long and what is the nature of this breached barrier. Dare anyone try to reconstruct it?

During recent riots there was a wry saying in the ghetto. "Chuck can't tell where it's going to hit next because we don't know ourselves." And it was a fact. The most baffling aspect to rioting in Newark, Detroit, and Watts was the complete spontaneity of the violence. Authorities turned to "responsible" Negro leaders to calm the black rebels and the Negro leaders did not know where to start. They were confronted with a leaderless mob which needed no leader. Every man was a leader--they were of one mind.

The goods of America, piled high in the neighborhood stores, had been offered to them with a price tag that made work slavery and made balancing a budget a farce. The pressure was ever on parents to buy a television set, to buy kitchen appliances and new cars. The available jobs paid so poorly and the prices (plus interest) of goods were so high that if one made a purchase he as entering upon years of indebtedness.

The carrot held in front of the ghetto laborer is the consumer item--the auto, the TV, and the hi-fit set. If the poor black man falls into place in America, he takes whatever job is offered, receives minimal pay, purchases hard goods at harder prices, and teeters from insolvency to bankruptcy in the ghetto.

Exhausted, he was offered a stimulant in the form of the civil rights law. When it became clear that they were nothing more than words from Washington, he kicked over the traces. He took a short cut. Instead of working for a lifetime to buy a piece of slum property which might fall at any moment and which he would likely never own anyway--instead of this treadmill, he burned it down. Instead of working for years to pay three times the usual cost of a television set, he broke a window and stole it. Instead of the desperate, frustrating search to find out which white man was friendly and which was hostile, he simply labeled them all the enemy. There never seemed to be a great deal of difference between friends and enemies anyway. So in a spontaneous blast he burned up the ghetto. And the wrong question continued to be asked: Why a riot in Detroit, where conditions were so good?

The worst slum and the best slums are very close together compared with the distance separating the world of black men and the world of whites. At bottom, America remains a slave country which happens to have removed the slave laws from the books. The question we must ask is: What held the slave rebellion in check for so long?

Henry Vance Davis, *AN AFRICAN-AMERICAN PERSPECTIVE ON THE REAGAN-BUSH YEARS AND BEYOND* (1992)

Born and raised in Highland Park, Michigan, Henry Davis is a forty-six-year-old professor of history who is convinced that most universities are neither prepared nor committed to educating those Americans classified as unprepared or unsuited for higher learning. Those so identified are usually minorities or poor or both, and Davis takes sharp issue with critics who would blame the victims for society's own inability or unwillingness to serve all Americans. Davis warns that America's very well-being depends on her willingness to extend economic, educational, and political opportunities to those now excluded. Davis also regrets the loss of the "father-layer" in the black community which traditionally gave young African-American males the support system they so badly needed during their formative years. Finally, Davis suggests that the experiences of African-Americans have great relevance for oppressed people throughout the world.

The experiences of African-Americans should serve as an example to oppressed people everywhere. Regardless of whether they are oppressed because of color, race, religion, or social condition, they can gain from our experience. Our political leaders and the media, of course, would never suggest such a thing, and neither would our educators. But sometimes it comes through. People the world over know Martin Luther King's "I Have a Dream" speech. But there's a lot more that could be learned. The leaders of our civil rights movement should be traveling all over the world to help those who are still dominated by power elites. It is important for everyone to know about African-Americans who have succeeded in spite of this country's many restrictions. Refections on my own life and career may offer some insights into the kind of information the African-American perspective can offer.

I have often thought about why I decided on a career in education because I really don't remember people pushing me to make something of myself. I always knew that because I came from a low-income African-American family, there were severe restrictions put on my American Dream even though I believed I could overcome enough of those restrictions to do what I wanted. My people saw the American Dream as a good job where there was something green attached. My mother did support my desire to go to college, but she died when I was thirteen. While my family gave me many valuable things, a family tradition of education was not one of them. I was the first person on either my mother or father's side of the family to graduate from college.

After high school I worked for Chrysler at the Dodge Main plant until I got my ninety days in which entitled me to join the union. My dad suggested that I stay, but I went off to Ferris State University instead. Most of my friends stayed home and went to Highland Park Junior College, but that didn't fit my image of what a college campus should be. Ferris did. It had grass.

I did not start college with the idea of being a great student. I figured I would stay in college a few years and then would sign a contract to play professional baseball. I eventually came into education through the back door when I decided there was more to interest me in college than I had previously thought.

More than a thirst for education, my community gave me a sense of worth. For whatever reason, the young people I grew up with were very strong-willed individuals, who refused to accept what the system expected of African-Americans. I remember a couple of friends and I would get together regularly and dance and sing and call ourselves "Bucks." As I look back on it, it was a kind of ritual that was our way of doing what our ancestors did as they passed into manhood. We shared and believed in this ritual and had faith we could do it together. We thus got strength from each other. We also got strength from what I call the "father-layer," the adult African-American males who took a "you-family" attitude towards young people in the community.

The city has changed since we had our little group. There are still people who are making it, but fewer than when I was young, and that is largely because the community support group I had is fast disappearing. Those who would make up this father-layer have been discredited, "de-balled" if you will, by welfare, schools, police, television, the friend of the court, and the courts themselves. They are constantly characterized as irresponsible, alcoholic, addicted to drugs, crime-prone, unable to keep a job, and having nothing to offer society. And especially during serious economic recessions, like we are now having, when nobody can get a job, the system condemns black males for being unemployed and having little money and paints them as having babies and leaving their families. So the system actually encourages many young blacks not to identify with this father-layer.

But this scenario leaves a gaping hole in the low-income black community. The wisdom, support, and control of the father-layer are sacrificed. This is particularly destructive to young African-American males. When the neighborhoods are flooded with dope, young African-American males are left along to decipher the complexities of a drug culture. The system now utilizes many sophisticated methods of appearing to support the community when it really does not. Without the father-layer operative, young Black males are left alone to interpret the system's clever and hostile ploys. For example, Reagan and Bush's appointment of conservative blacks who will do their bidding is meant to convince all of us that inadequate social and educational programs and high unemployment would not be real problems in the inner cities if people would just pull themselves up by their bootstraps, like the HNIC's (Head-Nigger-In-Charge) they hold up did. The father-layer would help youth know who their friends and role models should be. Without the wisdom of the community's father-layer young brothers and sisters are put in terrible jeopardy.

Perhaps most damaging is the system's uninterrupted assault on the spirit. There is a spirit in young black males that is essential to their mental health. When I was growing up, we used to have a saying in my neighborhood: "Ass kicking before dishonor." We never wanted to be punks, and punk does not refer to one's sexual preference. We always stood up for what we believed. This embraces a certain kind of coming of age that I think all male homo sapiens on earth go through. But in this country the system threatens or curtails African-American males' coming of age. Beginning in schools, teachers and administrators become increasingly frightened of young blacks and begin treating them with hostility. They fear these youngsters will become overly aggressive, and might get out of control, so they continuously come down on them. When this happens, the child becomes confused and needs direction, and there's no place where he can better get that help than from an adult male who has already gone through this experience. But if the youngster has bought into society's negative characterization of older black males, he will not respect them, and he has nowhere to turn.

I used to listen to an old wino who lived around the corner from me who made it his business to tell me when I was doing wrong. I knew he was a wino, and I also knew he made his money picking up garbage, but I respected him, because that's the way my society was structured. He could tell me to act like I had some sense and I would do so. If I hadn't respected him, I would not have paid any attention to him. These older males no longer pass on their wisdom to young brothers and sisters. There's no one there to tell them, "Hey, I've been there already, now listen, this is what it's all about." These older men have been thoroughly discredited, but they have not been replaced. The young people try to figure it out for themselves, but it's too confusing, and, as a result, not as many of them become successful as when I was young.

The major contribution of the father-layer to young black males is the sharing of these coping skills. But because the layer is described as pathological or as the helpless victim of an omnipotent system of oppression, it is dismissed as a viable source of information, insight, and wisdom into how to become a healthy, strong black man. Again, the black-man-boy has no where to turn save to the black-outlaw-male or the white-black-male; each alternative is deadly, one physically, the other spiritually.

We must work to restore the father-layer to its rightful position of respect in the low-income black community. Obviously this will require that the low income father-layer be supported and developed, and, perhaps not so obviously, it will require that comparatively high-income African-American males assert themselves and protect their culture, not only in the community but also in their business and educational settings as well. Those educated, well-placed blacks who allow themselves to degrade members of the low-income father-layer and abandon the positive aspects of the culture they came from in the face of their white colleagues do themselves, their community, their white colleagues, and ultimately their society a great disservice.

A glance at blacks in higher education provides an example of one aspect of this problem. When the black in black educators gets lost in the higher education system, whites have no chance of becoming bicultural--that is, understanding how to operate in and communicate across cultures--and their resultant blindness restricts the effectiveness of even those with the best intentions. A friend recently told me about his problems with a white psychologist. He had a problem which he felt stemmed from racism in the work place. A black psychologist immediately understood the situation, but he no longer works there. His replacement is a white psychologist who wants to blame childhood abuse for my friend's problem.

The source of the white psychologist's blindness is his lack of understanding of the black culture. The black community has used physical force to communicate with its children for generations. Most successful blacks of my friend's generation will tell you they are thankful for the discipline and love they received, often at the end of a stick. A black psychologist would not think twice about the use of the "rod" in the raising of a child. It would take much more than that to constitute abuse. Yet the white psychologist, perhaps having read too much Dr.

Spock, is convinced and bent on convincing my friend that his problem was not caused by work-place harrassment, but brought out by it, and that his real problem stems from the whippings he received as a child.

Why do I hold Blacks in higher education partially at fault? This white psychologist may be as prejudice-free as America allows him to be, but he most likely grew up in a white environment. If so, only during his higher education would he have been likely to have interacted with articulate blacks. But if those blacks shrank from the task of educating their colleagues about the reality of the black experience in America, that white psychologist has little chance of seeing the world through eyes other than his own little prisms, and his black clients have little chance of receiving help from him on race-related issues. Too many of us who manage to get an education and earn relatively high incomes fail to insist that the whites we interact with listen to and respect the perspective of our culture. We fail to educate our white colleagues to the realities of being black in America. As the poet Bama cries, "Dammit! Stop and think, maybe she had a right to have a drink."

As long as the relatively high income blacks turn their backs on the low-income, father-layer, thereby credentializing the pathology and helplessly oppressed stereotype, whites will have little chance of seeing or treating African-Americans in general and low-income, father-layer blacks in particular with the respect they deserve. And until African-Americans who have "made it" treat the father-layer with respect, the black child will stand alone trying to ferret through the stereotype before he can learn to love and respect that brother around the corner who might hold the key to his healthy future.

We are at a critical time in education. Today's educational leaders of predominantly white colleges and universities are woefully ignorant about educating African-Americans and other minorities. They work to drive people like me out of higher education even though we can communicate where they cannot.

The universities are not ready to implement the kinds of changes necessary to deal with this challenge. For instance, they are grudgingly ready to deal with a certain kind of black professor, but they are not ready to deal with another kind. I can remember after I had been in the university for a while, I looked at certain kinds of black professors, and I turned my back on higher education rather than be like them. *House niggers.* I couldn't be that! No way! I would rather work in a factory than be a punk, because I still believe in "ass-kicking before dishonor." Some of the kids who come out of the ghetto cannot feel comfortable in a situation where there is nobody they can respect.

If predominantly white colleges and universities could accept a wider range of black professors, they could educate a wider range of black students. This is about inclusion--and expansion. The BAM (Black Action Movement) strike at the University of Michigan in 1970 was not just about getting more blacks students into the university, but getting different kinds of black students in. Since then, universities have paid lip service to this, but they really have done very little. University administrators and professors announce they are all for multi-culturalism, equity, and diversity, but then they compete for the same pool of two-parent, middle-class, suburban-educated black kids. Nobody has the guts really to accept the challenge of educating that portion of black America that is most numerous.

After the so-called riots of the sixties, universities did take some young people out of the inner cities who were not formally prepared. Of course, the universities were also not prepared;

yet, many of those kids made it. Today fewer African-Americans are coming out of the ghettos into the university (despite the fact that more are graduating from high school and with higher GPAs and test scores), but the university, like America itself, assuages its guilt by pointing to the good middle-class black kids who are graduating. What is often forgotten is that the parents of many of these black kids were, like myself, representatives of the disenfranchised under-class of the 1960's and '70's that was the first generation to go to college in comparatively large numbers.

Universities are very good at manipulating numbers. They love statistics that indicate such and such percentage of students will not get through the university because they are unprepared rather than focusing on those who beat the odds. Educators have decided that the attrition rate for unprepared African-American students is now so high that they can better serve the African-American community, the university, and the country if they go back to bringing in only the so-called "better-prepared" student.

But statistics can also contradict such thinking. For example, because of BAM the University of Michigan brought in a lot of so-called "unprepared" students, and their attrition rate was not noticeably higher than that for blacks fifteen years later when only so-called qualified African-Americans were entering the university. But what has changed tragically over the past years is that the university is graduating about half as many black students as it did in the mid-seventies, and this is true for students with bachelors, masters, and Ph.D. degrees. This in turn means there are many fewer educated blacks who can reach back and bring more folks in. If you ask an administrator what has happened, he will point to what he calls "race-neutral" criteria that he uses for admittance. But if these policies result in fewer and fewer blacks being able to get a university education, you have a classic case of institutional racism. And what is going on at the University of Michigan is happening all across the country; in fact, since Dr. Charles Moody became vice provost for minority affairs in 1987, the University of Michigan has been doing better than most of its counterparts.

If the system were really serious about multi-culturalism and educating all of its people, it would enthusiastically grasp the challenge of educating all segments of society and implement the changes that would allow educational institutions to teach these kids rather than taking the first opportnity to tell everyone that such programs are not working. Of course, we have had twelve years of Reagan and Bush to deal with, a factor which must be considered.

Blacks were not taken in by Reagan the way whites were. We saw Reagan for what he was, and that was as true of ghetto blacks as it was for black intellectuals and activists. I never thought of Reagan as anything but a rich white boy who felt it was his job to take from the poor and give to the rich. That's why he was selected by his party, that's what he did when he got in office, and that's why so many of those people still love him. I can remember for years I could not keep Nixon and Reagan separated. I would be talking about one and use the name of the other. There simply was no difference in my subconscious. The trickle-down theory was not difficult to see through; it was just that we did not know what to do about it. One of the things that helps blacks live through presidential administrations such as Reagan's is that such experiences tend to galvanize the community to resist such policies. If nothing else, we have been awakened by the Reagan years. I think middle-class blacks now feel more of an urgency to give something back to the community than they did during the early 1980's.

Reagan also exploited the fact that White America gets tired of working for equity and reform. He told folks what they wanted to hear: that everything was all right and that there was no reason for anyone to feel guilty about not doing more for those less fortunate than themselves. In reality, whites knew Reagan was ignoring minorities and the poor, but they wanted to escape any sense of responsibility.

Government leaders have long been able to convince whites that they were somehow separate and superior to blacks. At the same time these leaders were also quite willing to exploit whites. The Vietnam War was a classic example. Johnson and Nixon were killing off thousands of black and white Americans, but, except for a few radicals, white America did not understand this. The same thing is true about automotive jobs in Detroit today. When one of the big three decides to close plants in the U.S. and reopen them in third-world countries where they do not have to pay a living wage, both white and black Americans lose their jobs. Jesse Jackson's political campaigns were so frightening to the power elite precisely because they spoke to this issue. He made his appeal to farmers, unionists, whites, blacks--people who began to realize there were certain kinds of problems they all shared in common regardless of color. Whites stepped outside their conventional voting organizations to embrace Jesse because he talked about issues that cut to the quick of all people's lives, but particularly those outside the power structure. Charles Henry's little book, *Jesse Jackson*, does a thoughtful analysis of this phenomenon.

I really do believe that as African-Americans go so will America as a whole. Our condition will be the gauge for the amount of inclusion or exclusion that the country settles on in the future. If it settles too much on exclusion, we're going to have very volatile times.

America must open up her society in order for it to compete on a world level. Most Americans do not realize that much of what they have accomplished in the past happened in a different world than the one we presently live in.. We now live in the global village, and America cannot isolate herself. The level of education and general awareness of blacks and other minorities is vastly different. Minorities do know what time it is, and so the old games will not work the way they so often did in the past when it was primarily manipulation and power. Power will still be all-important, but in the future it must operate on the basis of information that is accurate and correct, and this information must rise to the top rather than being selected from the top. America must tap this underdeveloped reservoir of talent among its dispossessed to find a brighter future.

At the moment, we seem to be going in the opposite direction, but that is precisely why I say as African-Americans go so will America. Blacks have always been in the vanguard of trying to buck the trend of exclusion. Given the demographics of the twenty-first century, one of the things the power elite will have to do is open up society or they will have to try to be even more exclusive. That may mean some of us might have to be kicked out of the system, but what is a guy like me going to do when he gets kicked out? Am I going to say, "Oh, well, I couldn't get in the system so I'll just go back doing what I used to do." Or am I going to say, "I'm going to burn this micky-ficky down." I think there are many economically, socially, educationally, and politically disenfranchised blacks who are going to say, "Hey, I'm not going to be 'trickle down.' I'm going to be dealt with differently." America will then be confronted with the kind of conflict that will threaten her economic dominance. To a certain extent, that's what happened after the urban riots of the 1960's. Disgruntled blacks were interfering with the capitalistic health of the country, so a few reforms had to be implemented. But under Reagan and Bush, white Americans no longer saw this need. They were told there would be enough for everyone if we just allowed the rich to get richer. African-Americans knew this was nonsense, but, now, so do many whites.

The American "stealocracy," if only for selfish reasons, will come to realize that it has to cut its losses. It will have to say, "All right, we have to open things up and try to give people a fair share so that we can keep as much of what we have stolen as possible or else we might lose it all." The wealthy power structure of the United States is facing the same question as South Africa is. Either you give up some of what you stole and share it and go from there or you risk losing it all.

I am an optimist. I am optimistic despite what Reagan and Bush and even the universities have tried to do. Perhaps it's being a Baptist preacher's son that makes me believe that God wants right to win out in the end. My feeling is that we are going to find a way to get more people involved and to have less of the money concentrated within the top one or two per cent of the people.

The immediate facts do not seem to indicate that we are moving in the direction of inclusion, but that's the bottom line. Is society going to open up or is it going to become even more restrictive? If it opens up, we will make it as a country and as a world. If it closes up further, we will have turmoil. When you think about it, the best part of American history is the opening up of the country to the formerly dispossessed. And that is precisely what we must return to.

H. RAP BROWN, *DIE NIGGER DIE*

H. Rap Brown was one of the most outspoken of the many bright, young black students who in the 1960's became increasingly impatient with the slow progress of the civil rights movement, and who sought more militant means to freedom. Shortly after entering Southern University in Louisiana at the age of fifteen, he became involved in the Student Nonviolent Coordinating Committee (SNCC), and in 1967 became its chairman. SNCC's dangerous and frustrating efforts to register black voters in Mississippi led Brown to conclude, "Every action that we are involved in is political, whether it is religious artistic, cultural, athletic, governmental, educational, economic, or personal." Brown was often arrested for his civil rights' activities, and the following letter was written from jail in New Orleans, Louisiana, February 21, 1968.

February 21, 1968

Being a man is the continuing battle of one's life and one loses a bit of manhood with every stale compromise to the authority of any power in which one does not believe.

No slave should die a natural death. There is a point where caution ends and cowardice begins.

For every day I am imprisoned, I will refuse both food and water.

My hunger is for the liberation of my people.

My thirst is for the ending of oppression.

I am a political prisoner, jailed for my beliefs (that Black people must be free). The government has taken a position true to its fascist nature--those they cannot convert, they must silence. This government has become the enemy of mankind.

This can no longer alter our path to freedom. For our people, death has been the only known exit from slavery and oppression. We must open others.

Our will to live must no longer supersede our will to fight, for our fighting will determine if our race shall live. To desire freedom is not enough. We must move from resistance to aggression, from revolt to revolution.

For every Orangeburg, there must be 10 Detroits.

For every Max Stanford and Huey Newton, there must be 10 racist cops.

And for every Black death there must be a Dien Bien Phu.

Brothers and sisters, as well as all oppressed people, you must prepare yourselves both mentally and physically, for the major confrontation is yet to come. You must fight. It is the people who in the final analysis make and determine history, not leaders or systems. The laws to govern you must be made by you.

May the deaths of '68 signal the beginning of the end of this country. I do what I must out of the love for my people. My will is to fight. Resistance is not enough. Aggression is the order of the day.

Note to america

America, if it takes my death to organize my people to revolt against you,
And to organize your jails to revolt against you,
And to organize your troops to revolt against you,
And to organize your children to revolt against you,
And to organize your God to revolt against you,
And to organize your poor to revolt against you,
And to organize your country to revolt against you,
And to organize Mankind to rejoice in your destruction and ruin,
Then, here is my Life!
But my Soul belongs to my people.
Lasima Tushinde Mbilashaka (We Shall Conquer Without a Doubt)

Yours in Revolution,
H. Rap Brown

James Baldwin, *AN OPEN LETTER TO MY SISTER, MISS ANGELA DAVIS*

James Baldwin's (1924-1989) novels and essays focus on the search for identity, love, and understanding in a hostile world. An idealist who was constantly disillusioned, and who constantly fled this country to live in less-restrictive Europe, Baldwin became one of America's sharpest critics. Angela Davis was a young professor of philosophy at the University of California, Los Angeles, when she was arrested for allegedly helping a black prisoner escape. Baldwin's letter to her as she waited trial is a searing indictment of white America's ignorance of its tortured past, but it is also a salute to a new generation of blacks who could no longer accept the racist world of their parents.

November 19, 1970

Dear Sister:

One might have hoped that, by this hour, the very sight of chains on black flesh, or the very sight of chains, would be so intolerable a sight for the American people, and so unbearable a memory, that they would themselves spontaneously rise up and strike off the manacles. But, no, they appear to glory in their chains; now, more than ever, they appear to measure their safety in chains and corpses. And so, *Newsweek*, civilized defender of the indefensible, attempts to drown you in a sea of crocodile tears ("It remained to be seen what sort of personal liberation she had achieved") and puts you on its cover, chained.

You look exceedingly alone--as alone, say, as the Jewish housewife in the boxcar headed for Dachau, or as any one of our ancestors, chained together in the name of Jesus, headed for a Christian land.

Well, since we live in an age in which silence is not only criminal but suicidal, I have been making as much noise as I can, here in Europe, on radio and television--in fact, have just returned from a land, Germany, which was made notorious by a silent majority not so very long ago. I was asked to speak on the case of Miss Angela Davis, and did so. Very probably an exercise in futility, but one must let no opportunity slide.

I am something like twenty years older than you, of that generation, therefore, of which George Jackson ventures that "there are no healthy brothers--**none at all**". I am in no way equipped to dispute this speculation (not, anyway, without descending into what, at the moment, would be irrelevant subtleties) for I know too well what he means. My own state of health is certainly precarious enough. In considering you, and Huey, and George and (especially) Jonathan Jackson, I began to apprehend what you may have had in mind when you spoke of the uses to which we could put the experience of the slave. What has happened, it seems to me, and to put it far too simply, is that a whole new generation of people have assessed and absorbed their history, and, in that tremendous action, have freed themselves of it and will never be victims again. This may seem an odd, indefensibly impertinent and insensitive thing to say to a sister in prison, battling for her life--for all our lives. Yet, I dare to say, for I think that you will perhaps not misunderstand me, and I do not say it, after all, from the position of a spectator.

I am trying to suggest that you--for example--do not appear to be your father's daughter in the same way that I am my father's son. At bottom, my father's expectations and mine were the same, the expectations of his generation and mine were the same; and neither the immense difference in our ages nor the move from the South to the North could alter these expectations or make our lives more viable. For, in fact, to use the brutal parlance of that hour, the interior language of that despair, he was just a nigger--a nigger laborer preacher, and so was I. I jumped the tract but that's of no more importance here, in itself, than the fact that <u>some</u> poor Spaniards became rich bull fighters, or that some poor black boys became rich--boxers, for example, that's rarely, if ever, afforded the people more than a great emotional catharsis, though I don't mean to be condescending about that, either. But when Cassius Clay became Muhammed Ali and refused to put on that uniform (and sacrificed all that money!) a very different impact was made on the people and a very different kind of instruction had begun.

The American triumph--in which the American tragedy has always been implicit--was to make black people despise themselves. When I was little I despised myself, I did not know any better. And this means, albeit unconsciously, or against my will, or in great pain, that I also despised my father. <u>And</u> my mother. <u>And</u> my brothers. <u>And</u> my sisters. Black people were killed each other every Saturday night out on Lanox Avenue, when I was growing up; and no one explained to them, or to me, that it was <u>intended</u> that they should; that they were penned where they were, like animals, in order that they should consider themselves no better than animals. Everything supported this sense of reality, nothing denied it; and so one was ready, when it came time to go to work, to be treated as a slave. So one was ready, then human terrors came, to bow before a white God and beg Jesus for salvation--this same white God who was unable to raise a finger to do so little as to help you pay your rent, unable to be awakened in time to help you save your child.

There is always, of course, more to any picture than can speedily be perceived and in all of this--groaning and moaning, watching, calculation, clowning, surviving, and outwitting, some tremendous strength was nevertheless being forged, which is part of our legacy today. But that particular aspect of our journey now begins to be behind us. The secret is out: we are men.

But the blunt, open articulation of this secret has frightened the nation to death. I wish I could say, "to life," but that is much to demand of a disparate collection of displaced people still cowering in their wagon trains and singing "onward Christian Soldier." The nation, if America is a nation is not in the least prepared for this day. It is a day which the Americans never expected or desired to see, however piously they may declare their belief in progress and democracy." These words, now on American lips, have become a kind of universal obscenity: for this most unhappy people, strong believers in arithmetic, never expected to be confronted with the algebra of their history.

One way of gauging a nation's health, or of discerning what it really considers to be its interests--or to what extent it can be considered a nation as distinguished from a coalition of special interests--is to examine those people it elects to represent or protect it. One glance at the American leaders (or figure heads) conveys that America is on the edge of absolute chaos, and also suggests that future to which American interests, if not the bulk of the American people, appear willing to consign the blacks. (Indeed, one look at our past conveys that,) It is clear that for the bulk of our (nominal) countrymen, we are all expendable. And Messrs. Nixon, Agnew, Mitchell, and Hoover, to say nothing, of course, of the *Kings' Row* basket case, the winning Ronnie Reagan, will not hesitate for an instant to carry out what they insist is the will of the people.

But, what in America, is the call of the people? And who, for the above-named are the people? The people, whoever they may be, know as much about the forces which have placed the above-named gentlemen in power as they do about the forces responsible for the slaughter in Vietnam. The will of the people, in America, has always been at the mercy of an ignorance not merely phenomenal, but sacred, and sacredly cultivated; the better to be used by a carnivorous economy which democratically slaughters and victimized whites and blacks alike. But most white Americans do not dare admit this (though they suspect it) and this act contains mortal danger for the blacks and tragedy for the nation.

Or, to put it another way, as long as white Americans take refuge in their whiteness--for so long as they are unable to walk out of this most monstrous of traps--they will allow millions of people to be slaughtered in their name, and will be manipulated into and surrender themselves to what they will think of--and justify--as a racial war. They will never, so long as their whiteness puts so sinister a distance between themselves, their own experience and the experience of others, feel themselves sufficient human, *sufficiently worthwhile*, to become responsible for themselves, their leaders, their country, their children, of their fate. They will perish (as we once put it in our black church) in their sins--that is, in their delusions. And this is happening, needless to say, already, all around us.

Only a handful of the millions of people in this vast place are aware that the fate intended for you, Sister Angela, and for George Jackson, and for the numberless prisoners in our concentration camps--for that is what they are--is a fate which is about to engulf them, too. White lives, for the forces which rule in this country, are no more sacred then black ones, as many and many a student is discovering, as the white American corpses in Vietnam prove. If the American people are unable to contend with their elected leaders for the redemption of their own honor and the lives of their own children, we, the blacks, the most rejected of the Western children, can expect very little help at their hands: which, after all is nothing new. What the Americans do not realize is that a war between brothers, in the same cities, on the same soil, is not a racial war but a civil war. But the American delusion is not only that their brothers all are white but that the whites are all their brothers.

So be it. We cannot awaken this sleeper, and God knows we have tried. We must do what we can do, and fortify and save each other--we are not drowning in an apathetic self-contempt, we do feel ourselves sufficiently worthwhile to contend even with inexorable forces in order to change our fate and the fate of our children and the condition of the world. We know that a man is not a thing and is not to be placed at the mercy of things. We know that air and water belong to all mankind and not merely to industrialists. We know that a baby does not come into the world merely to be the instrument of someone else's profit. We know that democracy does not mean the coercion of all into a deadly--and, finally, wicked--mediocrity but the liberty for all to aspire to the best that is in him, or that has ever been.

We know that we the blacks, and not only we, the blacks, have been, and are, the victims of a system whose only fuel is greed, whose only god is profit. We know that the fruits of this system have been ignorance, despair, and death, and we know that the system is doomed because the world can no longer afford--if, indeed, it ever could have. And we know that, for the perpetuation of this system, we have all been mercilessly brutalized, and have been told nothing but lies, lies about ourselves and our kinsmen and our past, and about love, life, and death, so that both soul and body have been bound in Hell.

The enormous revolution in black consciousness which has occurred in your generation, my dear sister, means the beginning or the end of America. Some of us, white and black, know how great a price has already been paid to bring into existence a new consciousness, a new people, and unprecedented nation. If we know, and do nothing, we are worse than the murderers hired in our name.

If we know, then we must fight for your life as though it were our own--which it is--and render, impassable with our bodies the corridor to the gas chamber. For, if they take you in the morning, they will be coming for us that night.

Therefore: peace.

Brother James

Larry Neal, *NEW SPACE/THE GROWTH OF BLACK CONSCIOUSNESS* (1970)

Born in Atlanta and raised in Philadelphia, Larry Neal was formerly Arts Editor of Liberator Magazine *and co-editor, with LeRoi Jones, of the literary anthology,* Black Fire. *In the brief excerpt below from* The Black Seventies, *he describes the awakening black consciousness that was so prevalent in the 1960s.*

It was a squeeze really. Sometimes, in some places, it looked like we weren't gonna make it. But we squeezed through, just like we have been squeezing through for decades. Only this time there was a little more light at the end of the tunnel. Some of us saw God, and seriously began the work of freeing ourselves. The benevolent demon imprisoned within us broke loose, and manifested himself. The Black Spirit asserted itself collectively, and with obvious effects everywhere throughout the country. We were forced, as never before, to make explicit our desire to determine the nature and the course of our lives. In short, we demanded self-determination. What the full implications of this demand are, we do not know yet. One thing is clear, though. As we move into the seventies, many of the things that concerned us in the early sixties are no longer as important as we once thought they were. We fought for the right to eat a meal in some cracker restaurant in the deep South, but now that that right has been assured by the Federal Government, black people are no longer interested in such things. Perhaps it was the victory itself that turned us off. Perhaps it was the acute awareness that finally what we wanted was not the cup of coffee in the cracker restaurant, but something more substantive than that. If we could get it, we wanted the land that the restaurant was built on. We wanted reparations. We wanted power. We wanted Nationhood.

Power became the central issue. Essentially, it has always been the central issue; but for so long we were caught up in symbols. We found ourselves reacting to the most obvious manifestations of white racism while failing very often, to penetrate the core of the problem. When we cut past the bullshit, it became evident that even though the victories of the civil rights movement were legitimate, noteworthy, and necessary, they did not address themselves to the central problem of the black man in America. We came to understand that the simple acquisition of those rights which abstractly belong to all citizens of the United States would in no fundamental manner alter the oppressive situation in which we found ourselves. And that situation is essentially one of powerlessness. . . .

For example, take the concept of "Black Consciousness." When the thing got really going, black people in different places developed unique and often contradictory attitudes towards it; they operated out of the principle along a variety of different styles. Some people joined the Muslims. Some people stopped eating certain foods. Other people, just as sincere as the first group, began to relish those very same tabooed foods. Some people put on African clothing. Most wore naturals. Some wore brighter colors. Some raised hell in school. Some left their white wives and husbands. Some joined RAM or the Black Panther Party. Some dug B. B. King, and some dug Coltrane. But shit. *It was all good and on time*. It was collective motion/energy that could be harnessed and organized.

At times one would walk the streets and feel it in the air--black people asserting that they were each the bearers of an ethos. The beautiful became more beautiful; the black woman assumed more of her rightful place in the psyche of black artists; brothers greeted each other warmly. This was especially true after some catastrophic upheaval like Newark or Watts. Black people spoke to each other in strange tongues which they did not understand, but yet spoke well. Harlem, blighted and dope ridden, oozed an atmosphere of love and concrete spirituality. Black consciousness manifested itself collectively and resolutely upon large segments of the black community. What we are faced with now is the mature shaping of this consciousness. That is, we long to be comfortable with it, to gird ourselves for the long struggle that certainly lies ahead. Black consciousness is necessary and good only if it allows more light, more understanding of the complex struggles in which we find ourselves. But we must emphasize that it is impossible for a people to struggle and win without a sense of collective consciousness....

Under the leadership of Dr. King, the civil rights struggle took place on an essentially moral plane. Black people tried to convince white people of the essentially ethical nature of the struggle. It was the ethical principle that informed the concept of non-violence. It was the young people of SNCC who de-emphasized the ethical aspects of the concept, and began to use it as a tactical weapon. But whether or not we agree with the philosophy of non-violence is not the question. What is important here is that this means of liberation was shaped out of the black man's spiritual legacy. Black people are the last remaining "Christians" in America. In the South, where the movement began, most of the black population are devout Christians. And the minister is very often the only form of leadership existing in many communities.

We know the historical reason for this. But we must understand that people can only work with the tools and the concepts that are available to them. Therefore, the expressive mode of the civil rights movement was spirituals, gospels, and folk songs. These modes of expression spring most immediately from southern black culture.

Had the struggle been born in the North, the modes of expression would have been quite different. In substance, the struggle would have been far more brutal and disruptive in its early phases. It would have been less concerned with the ethic preached by King and other black southern leaders. Where the black leadership in the South expressed itself in the language of Christianity, radical northern leaders expressed themselves in a quasi black nationalistic rhetoric.

King's rhetorical devices, poetic and chock full of imagery, grew primarily out of the symbology of the black church service. On the other hand, Adam Clayton Powell expressed himself in the rhetoric of the street corner speakers--speakers who were spawned by a long history of urban mass movements beginning with Marcus Garvey, and coming through to the labor movement of the thirties and forties.

In the South, the preachers have always been the leaders of a large segment of the black community. Often, they took political positions that were not always in the best interest of the community. But sometimes they were in the forefront of militant action, as it was then perceived. Many of them gave their churches over to civil rights activists, and suffered for it. Many of them were lynched or burned out for aiding in the struggle. The movement would have not been successful, on any terms, if it had not attempted to shape and utilize the living culture of the people. Those of us who are engaged in the current struggle for self-determination and for Nationhood must understand this, and move to make this consciousness of ourselves an integral part of everything that we do. . . .

About 1962, many young blacks began to seek another direction, one that they believed would more militantly set about achieving true freedom for black people. These were primarily urban youth who had recognized the need for action, but were decidedly alienated from the movement in the South. Some had been involved with the radical white left where, in the process of reading Marx and Lenin, they came to realize that despite the importance of these theoreticians to late nineteenth and early twentieth century revolutionary thought, they were still confronted with the necessity of developing their own theories of social change. As a result of this observation, they found themselves squeezed between the pallid liberalism of the integrationists and the pseudo-scientific jargon of the white left. Therefore, they had to turn inward on their most immediate historical experiences in order to construct a meaningful concept of social change.

In doing so, they found that throughout Afro-American history there had always existed a persistent, though fragmented, sense of nationalism. They came to feel that somehow previous generations of black activists and radical thinkers had not fully utilized this feeling; this group ethos tugs at all black people regardless of their social standings. It was clear that, however you cut it, every person of African descent, living in America, had to at sometime come to grips with *Blackness*. And further, there was something metaphysical about it--this confrontation with ourselves.

And the questions, many questions: Who was this Marcus Garvey the old "race men" often spoke of? Why did he have so many followers? Why did his organization fail? Who was W. E. B. Du Bois? Why was he against Garvey? Why didn't Monroe Trotter join the NAACP? What is the NAACP? Who did they represent? What is Africa to me? What is my Name? Why do our women straighten their hair? Where are we going? Why William Delaney, Edward Blyden, Poppa Singleton, Malcolm X? How could they exist in America? If integration was not the answer, what is? There are millions of black people in the world; what is our relationship to them? Why our music, our dance, our talk, our attitudes? . . .

America is in fact two nations, one Black, one White. That is what the nationalists began to say. Not only were there two nations, one was a colony:

> *The American Negro shares with colonial peoples many of the socio-economic factors which form the material basis for present day revolutionary nationalism. Like these peoples of the under-developed countries, the Negro suffers in varying degree from the hunger, illiteracy, disease, ties to the land, urban and semi-urban slums, cultural starvation, and the psychological reactions to being ruled over by others not of his kind. He experiences the tyranny imposed upon the lives of those who inhabit under-developed countries. In the words of a Mexican writer, Enrique Gonzales Pedrero, under-development creates a situation where that which exists "only half exists," where countries are almost countries, fifty per cent nations, and a man who inhabits these countries, is a dependent being, a sub-man. Such a man depends "not on himself but on other men and other outside worlds that order him around, counsel and guide him like a newly born infant."*

These statements are found in a remarkable essay written by Harold Cruse entitled, "Revolutionary Nationalism And The Afro-American." It is significant because it provided the young nationalists organizing in SNCC and RAM (Revolutionary Action Movement) with the first theoretical explanation of why they were nationalists, non-Marxist, and anti-integration.

Further, Cruse pinpointed the particular malaise affecting the Negro leadership:

> *Large segments of the modern Negro bourgeoisie have played a continually regressive "non-national" role in Negro affairs. Thriving off the crumbs of integration, these bourgeois elements have become de-racialized and de-cultured, leaving the Negro working class without voice or leadership, while serving the negative role of class buffer between the deprived working class and the white ruling class elites. In this respect, such groups have become a social millstone around the necks of the Negro working class--a point which none of the militant phrases that accompany the racial integration movement down the road to "racial attrition" should be allowed to obscure.*

If what Cruse was saying is true, then any course to black liberation that is not nationalistically oriented is doomed to failure. It would have to imply also that the civil rights movement, so helplessly locked into the notion that America is a democracy, is finally leading black people down the path to ethnocide--leading them towards cultural annihilation. And since we had turned inward on ourselves, and glimpsed what we considered to be the inner potential of our people, we were frightened by the concepts of the integrationists. Not merely intellectually in disagreement with them but frightened, if you can dig it. So much so, that in order to preserve something of our private selves, many of us refused to even talk to white people. We had to withdraw to get this thing together that had risen before us in all of its truth:

We want a nation controlled by the black people. Yeah, that's what we want. Everything else is cool: no discrimination in housing, fair employment, more black teachers and schools, greater medical aid, more blacks on television and in films, black studies programs; the whole fucking lot was all cool. But we want a *nation.* In spite of all the theories and the arguments against it. We want a nation. We want our children to see a place governed by the sensibilities and highest attitudes of black people. We don't want to rear them to utilize their blackness as a weapon against a death-centered and inhuman culture. We want them to be comfortable in the knowledge of themselves, and not a set of reactions to white people. Therefore nationalism, with all of its contradictions, proposed itself to us.

Ralph Ellison, *PROLOGUE FROM THE INVISIBLE MAN* (1952)

Trained as a musician at Tuskegee Institute, a trip to New York and a meeting with Richard Wright inspired Ralph Ellison to try his hand at fiction. After publishing several essays and short stories, he wrote Invisible Man, *which won the National Book Award for Fiction in 1953 and which a 1965 Book Week pool of critics, authors, and editors judged "the most distinguished single work" published in America since 1945. The naturalistic and semi-autobiographical novel dramatizes the surreal and "invisible" journey of an Afro-American seeking success, friendship, and himself in a world that is insane and irrational.*

I am an invisible man. NO, I am not a spook like those who haunted Edgar Allan Poe; nor am I one of your Hollywood-movie ectoplasms. I am a man of substance, of flesh and bone, fiber and liquids--and I might even be said to possess a mind. I am invisible, understand, simply because people refuse to see me. Like the bodiless heads you see sometimes in circus sideshows, it is as though I have been surrounded by mirrors of hard, distorting glass. When they approach me they see only my surroundings, themselves, or figments of their imagination--indeed, everything and anything except me.

Nor is my invisibility exactly a matter of a bio-chemical accident to my epidermis. That invisibility to which I refer occurs because of a peculiar disposition of the eyes of those with whom I come in contact. A matter of the construction of their *inner* eyes upon reality. I am not complaining, nor am I protesting either. It is sometimes advantageous to be unseen, although it is most often rather wearing on the nerves. Then too, you're constantly being bumped against by those of poor vision. Or again, you often doubt if you really exist. You wonder whether you aren't simply a phantom in other people's minds. Say, a figure in a nightmare which the sleeper tries with all his strength to destroy. It's when you feel like this that, out of resentment, you begin to bump people back. And, let me confess, you feel that way most of the time. You ache with the need to convince yourself that you do exist in the real world, that you're a part of all the sound and anguish, and you strike out with your fists, you curse and you swear to make them recognize you. And, alas, it's seldom successful.

One night I accidentally bumped into a man, and perhaps because of the near darkness he saw me and called me an insulting name. I sprang at him, seized his coat lapels and demanded that he apologize. He was a tall blond man, and as my face came close to his he looked insolently out of his blue eyes and cursed me, his breath hot in my face as he struggled. I pulled his chin down sharp upon the crown of my head, butting him as I had seen the West Indians do, and I felt his flesh tear and the blood gush out, and I yelled, "Apologize! Apologize!" But he continued to curse and struggle, and I butted him again and again until he went down heavily, on his knees, profusely bleeding. I kicked him repeatedly, in a frenzy because he still uttered insults though his lips were frothy with blood. Oh, yes, I kicked him! And in my outrage I got out my knife and prepared to slit his threat, right there beneath the lamplight in the deserted street, holding him in the collar with one hand, and opening the knife with my teeth--when it occurred to me that the man had not *seen* me, actually; that he, as far as he knew, was in the midst of a walking nightmare! And I stopped the blade, slicing the air as I pushed him away, letting him fall back to the street. I stared at him hard as the lights of a car stabbed through the darkness. He lay there, moaning on the asphalt; a man almost killed by a phantom. It unnerved me. I was both disgusted and ashamed. I was like a drunken man myself, wavering about on weakened legs. Then I was amused: Something in this man's thick head had sprung out and beaten him within an inch of his life. I began to laugh at this crazy discovery. Would he have awakened at the point of death? Would Death himself have freed him for wakeful living? But I didn't linger. I ran away into the dark, laughing so hard I feared I might rupture myself. The next day I saw his picture in the *Daily News*, beneath a caption stating that he had been "mugged." Poor fool, poor blind fool, I thought with sincere compassion, mugged by an invisible man!

Most of the time (although I do not choose as I once did to deny the violence of my days by ignoring it) I am not so overtly violent. I remember that I am invisible and walk softly so as not to awaken the sleeping ones. Sometimes it is best not to awaken them; there are few things in the world as dangerous as sleepwalkers. I learned in time though that it is possible to carry on a fight against them without their realizing it. For instance, I have been carrying on a fight with Monopolated Light & Power for some time now. I use their service and pay them nothing at all, and they don't know it. Oh, they suspect that power is being drained off, but they don't know where. All they know is that according to the master meter back there in their power station a hell of a lot of free current is disappearing somewhere into the jungle of Harlem. The joke, of course, is that I don't live in Harlem but in a border area. Several years ago (before I discovered the advantages of being invisible) I went through the routine process of buying service and paying their outrageous rates. But no more. I gave up all that, along with my apartment, and my old way of life: That way based upon the fallacious assumption that I, like other men, was visible, Now, aware of my invisibility, I live rent-free in a building rented strictly to whites, in a section of the basement that was shut off and forgotten during the nineteenth century, which I discovered when I was trying to escape in the night from Ras the Destroyer. But that's getting too far ahead of the story, almost to the end, although the end is in the beginning and lies far ahead.

The point now is that I found a home--or a hole in the ground, as you will. Now don't jump to the conclusion that because I call my home a "hole" it is damp and cold live a grave; there are cold holes and warm holes. Mine is a warm hole. And remember, a bear retires to his hole for the winter and lives until spring; then he comes strolling out like the Easter chick breaking from its shell. I say all this to assure you that it is incorrect to assume that, because I'm invisible and live in a hole, I am dead. I am neither dead nor in a state of suspended animation. Call me Jack-the-Bear, for I am in a state of hibernation.

My hole is warm and full of light. Yes full of light. I doubt if there is a brighter spot in all New York than this hole of mine, and I do not exclude Broadway. Or the Empire State Building on a photographer's dream night. But that is taking advantage of you. Those two spots are among the darkest of our whole civilization--pardon me,--our whole *culture* (an important distinction, I've heard)--which might sound like a hoax, or a contradiction, but that (by contradiction, I mean) is how the world moves: Not like an arrow, but a boomerang. (Beware of those who speak of the *spiral* of history; they are preparing a boomerang. Keep a steel helmet handy.) I know; I have been boomeranged across my head so much that I now can see the darkness of lightness. And I love light. Perhaps you'll think it strange that an invisible man should need light, desire light, love light. But maybe it is exactly because I *am* invisible. Light confirms my reality, gives birth to my form. A beautiful girl once told me of a recurring nightmare in which she lay in the center of a large dark room and felt her face expand until it filled the whole room, becoming a formless mass while her eyes ran in bilious jelly up the chimney. And so it is with me. Without light I am not only invisible, but formless as well; and to be unaware of one's form is to live a death. I myself, after existing some twenty years, did not become alive until I discovered my invisibility.

That is why I fight my battle with Monopolated Light & Power. The deeper reason, I mean: It allows me to feel my vital aliveness. I also fight them for taking so much of my money before I learned to protect myself. In my hole in the basement there are exactly 1,369 lights. I've wired the entire ceiling, every inch of it. And not with fluorescent bulbs, but with the older, more-expensive-to-operate kind, the filament type. An act of sabotage, you know. I've already begun to wire the wall. A junk man I know, a man of vision, has supplied me with wire and sockets. Nothing, storm or flood, must get in the way of our need for light and ever more and brighter light. The truth is the light and light is the truth. When I finish all four walls, then I'll start on the floor. Just how that will go, I don't know. Yet when you have lived invisible as long as I have you develop a certain ingenuity. I'll solve the problem. And maybe I'll invent a gadget to place my coffee pot on the fire while I lie in bed, and even invent a gadget to warm my bed--like the fellow I saw in one of the picture magazines who made himself a gadget to warm his shoes! Though invisible, I am in the great American tradition of tinkers. That makes me kin to Ford, Edison and Franklin. Call me since I have a theory and a concept, a "thinker-tinker." Yes, I'll warm my shoes; they need it, they're usually full of holes. I'll do that and more.

Now I have one radio-phonograph; I plan to have five. There is a certain acoustical deadness in my hole, and when I have music I want to *feel* its vibration, not only with my ear but with my whole body. I'd like to hear five recordings of Louis Armstrong playing and singing "What Did I Do to Be so Black and Blue"--all at the same time. Sometimes now I listen to Louis while I have my favorite dessert of vanilla ice cream and sloe gin. I pour the red liquid over the white mound, watching it glisten and the vapor rising as Louis bends that military instrument into a beam of lyrical sound. Perhaps I like Louis Armstrong because he's made poetry out of being invisible. I think it must be because he's unaware that he is invisible. And my own grasp of invisibility aids me to understand his music. Once when I asked for a cigarette, some jokers gave me a reefer, which I lighted when I got home and sat listening to my phonograph. It was a strange evening. Invisibility, let me explain, gives one a slightly different sense of time, you're never quite on the beat. Sometimes you're ahead and sometimes behind. Instead of the swift and imperceptible flowing of time, you are aware of its nodes, those points where time stands still or from which it leaps ahead. And you slip into the breaks and look around. That's what you hear vaguely in Louis' music.

Once I saw a prizefighter boxing a yokel. The fighter was swift and amazingly scientific. His body was one violent flow of rapid rhythmic action. He hit the yokel a hundred times while the yokel held up his arms in stunned surprise. But suddenly the yokel, rolling about in the gale of boxing gloves, struck one blow and knocked science, speed and footwork as cold as a well-digger's posterior. The smart money hit the canvas. The long shot got the nod. The yokel had simply stepped inside of his opponent's sense of time. So under the spell of the reefer I discovered a new analytical way of listening to music. The unheard sounds came through, and each melodic line existed of itself, stood out clearly from all the rest, said its piece, and waited patiently for the other voices to speak. That night I found myself hearing not only in time, but in space as well. I not only entered the music but descended, like Dante, into its depths, And *beneath the swiftness of the hot temp there was a slower tempo and a cave and I entered it and looked around and heard an old woman singing a spiritual as full of Weltschmerz as flamenco, and beneath that lay a still lower level on which I saw a beautiful girl the color of ivory pleading in a voice like my mother's as she stood before a group of slaveowners who bid for her naked body, and below that I found a lower level and a more rapid temp and I heard someone shout:*

"Brothers and sisters, my text this morning is the 'Blackness of Blackness.'"

And a congregation of voices answered: "That blackness is most black, brother, most black . . ."

"In the beginning . . ."

"At the very start," they cried.

" . . . there was blackness . . ."

"Preach it . . ."

". . . and the sun . . ."

"The sun, Lawd . . ."

". . . was bloody red . . ."

"Red . . ."

"Now black is . . ." the preacher shouted.

"Bloody . . ."

"I said black is . . ."

"Preach it, brother . . ."

". . . an' black ain't . . ."

"Red, Lawd, red: He said it's red!"

"Amen, brother . . ."

"Black will git you . . ."

"Yes, it will . . ."

"Yes, it will . . ."

". . . an' black won't . . ."

"Naw, it won't!"

"It do . . ."

"It do, Lawd . . ."

". . . an' it don't."

"Halleluiah . . ."

". . . It'll put you, glory, glory, Oh my Lawd, in the WHALE'S BELLY."

"Preach it, dear brother . . ."

". . . an' make you tempt . . ."

"Good God a-mighty!"

"Old Aunt Nelly!"

"Black will make you . . ."

"Black . . ."

". . . or black will un-make you."

"Ain't it the truth, Lawd?"

And at that point a voice of trombone timbre screamed at me, "Git out of here, you fool! Is you ready to commit treason?"

And I tore myself away, hearing the old singer of spirituals moaning, "Go curse your God, boy, and die."

I stopped and questioned her, asked her what was wrong.

"I dearly loved my master, son, she said.

"You should have hated him," I said

"He gave me several sons," she said, "and because I loved my sons I learned to love their father though I hated him too."

"I too have become acquainted with ambivalence," I said. "That's why I'm here."

"What's that?"

"Nothing, a word that doesn't explain it. Why do you moan?"

"I moan this way 'cause he's dead," she said.

"Then tell me, who is that laughing upstairs?"

"Them's my sons. They glad."

"Yes, I can understand that too," I said.

"I laughs too, but I moans too. He promised to set us free but he never could bring hisself to do it. Still I loved him . . ."

"Loved him? You mean . . .?"

"Oh yes, but I loved something else even more."

"What more?"

"Freedom."

"Freedom," I said. "Maybe freedom lies in hating."

"Naw, son, it's in loving. I loved him and give him the poison and he withered away like a frost-bit apple. Them boys woulda tore him to pieces with they homemade knives."

"A mistake was made somewhere," I said, "I'm confused." And I wished to say other things, but the laughter upstairs became too loud and moan-like for me and I tried to break out of it, but I couldn't. Just as I was leaving I felt an urgent desire to ask her what freedom was and went back. She sat with her head in her hands, moaning softly; her leather-brown face was filled with sadness.

"Old woman, what is this freedom you love so well?" I asked around a corner of my mind.

She looked surprised, then thoughtful, then baffled. "I done forgot, son. It's all mixed up. First I think it's one thing, then I think it's another. It gits my head to spinning. I guess now it ain't nothing but knowing how to say what I got up in my head. But it's a hard job, son. Too much is done happen to me in too short a time. Hit's like I have a fever. Ever' time I starts to walk my head gits to swirling and I falls down. Or if it ain't that; it's the boys; they gits to laughing and wants to kill up the white folks. They's bitter, that's what they is . . ."

"But what about freedom?"

"Leave me 'lone, boy; my head aches!"

I left her, feeling dizzy myself. I didn't get far.

Suddenly one of the sons, a big fellow six feet tall, appeared out of nowhere and struck me with his fist.

"What's the matter, man?" I cried.

"You made Ma cry!"

"But how?" I said, dodging a blow.

"Askin' her them questions, that's how. Git outa here and stay, and next time you got questions like that, ask yourself!"

He held me in a grip like cold stone, his fingers fastening upon my windpipe until I thought I would suffocate before he finally allowed me to go. I stumbled about dazed, the music beating hysterically in my ears. It was dark. My head cleared and I wandered down a dark narrow passage, thinking I heard his footsteps hurrying behind me. I was sore, and into my being had come a profoundly craving for tranquility, for peace and quiet, a state I felt I could never achieve. For one thing, the trumpet was blaring and the rhythm was too hectic. A tom-tom beating like heart-thuds began drowning out the trumpet, filling my ears. I longed for water and I heard it rushing through the cold mains my fingers touched as I felt my way, but I couldn't stop to search because of the footsteps behind me.

"Hey Ras," I called. "Is it you, Destroyer? Rinehart?"

No answer, only the rhythmic footsteps behind me. Once I tried crossing the road, but a speeding machine struck me, scraping the skin from my leg as it roared past.

Then somehow I came out of it, ascending hastily from this underworld of sound to hear Louis Armstrong innocently asking,

What did I do
To be so black
And blue?

At first I was afraid; this familiar music had demanded action, the kind of which I was incapable, and yet had I lingered there beneath the surface I might have attempted to act. Nevertheless, I know now that few really listen to this music. I sat on the chair's edge in a soaking sweat, as though each of my 1,369 bulbs had everyone become a klieg light in an individual setting for a third degree with Ras and Rinehart in charge. It was exhausting--as though I had held my breath continuously for an hour under the terrifying serenity that comes from days of intense hunger. And yet, it was a strangely satisfying experience for an invisible man to hear the silence of sound. I had discovered unrecognized compulsions of my being--even though I could not answer "yes" to their promptings. I haven't smoked a reefer since, however; not because they're illegal, but because to *see* around corners is enough (that is not unusual when you are invisible). But to hear around them is too much; it inhibits action. And despite Brother Jack and all that sad, lost period of the Brotherhood, I believe in nothing if not in action.

Please, a definition: A hibernation is a covert preparation for a more overt action.

Besides, the drug destroys one's sense of time completely. If that happened, I might forget to dodge some bright morning and some cluck would run me down with an orange and yellow street car, or a bilious bus! Or I might forget to leave my hole when the moment for action presents itself.

Meanwhile I enjoy my life with the compliments of Monopolated Light & Power. Since you never recognize me even when in closest contact with me, and since, no doubt, you'll hardly believe that I exist, it won't matter if you know that I tapped a power line leading into the building and ran it into my hole in the ground. Before that I lived in the darkness into which I was chased, but now I see. I've illuminated the blackness of my invisibility--and vice versa. And so I play the invisible music of my isolation. The last statement doesn't seem just right, does it? But it is; you hear this music simply because music is heard and seldom seen, except by musicians. Could this compulsion to put invisibility down in black and white be thus an urge to make music of invisibility? But I am an orator, a rabble rouser--Am? I *was*, and perhaps shall be again. Who knows? All sickness is not unto death, neither is invisibility.

I can hear you say, "What a horrible, irresponsible bastard!" And you're right. I leap to agree with you. I am one of the most irresponsible beings that ever lived. Irresponsibility is part of my invisibility; any way you face it, it is a denial. But to whom can I be responsible, and why should I be, when you refuse to see me? And wait until I reveal how truly irresponsible I am. Responsibility rests upon recognition, and recognition is a form of agreement. Take the man whom I almost killed: Who was responsible for that near murder--I? I don't think so, and I refuse it. I won't buy it. You can't give it to me. He bumped *me*, *he* insulted *me*. Shouldn't he, for his own personal safety, have recognized my hysteria, my "danger potential"? He, let us say, was lost in a dream world. But didn't *he* control that dream would--which, alas, is only too real!--and didn't *he* rule me out of it? And if he had yelled for a policeman, wouldn't I have been taken for the offending one? Yes, yes, yes! Let me agree with you, I was the irresponsible one; for I should have used my knife to protect the higher interests of society. Some day that kind of foolishness will cause us tragic trouble. All dreamers and sleepwalkers must pay the price, and even the invisible victim is responsible for the fate of all. But I shirked that responsibility; I became too snarled in the incompatible notions that buzzed within my brain. I was a coward . . .

But what did I do to be so blue? Bear with me.

THE AUTOBIOGRAPHY OF MALCOLM X

When The Autobiography of Malcolm X *appeared in 1965, just after Malcolm himself was assassinated in his fortieth year, it created an intellectual firestorm. Most young African Americans embraced it emotionally and intellectually. Some older and middle-class blacks were uncomfortable with its strident tones, Black Muslim religion, and its rejection of the integrationist struggle. White readers were uncomfortable, but fascinated. Yet, everyone recognize* The Autobiography of Malcolm X *to be an extraordinary story of a man who, as the book's cover put it, "rose from hoodlum, thief, dope peddler, pimp...to become the most dynamic leader of the Black Revolution.* The Autobiography *is all of that, and more. It is an American classic of a man and a people's struggle for freedom and cultural independence. Below are the first few pages from* The Autobiography of Malcolm X.

When my mother was pregnant with me, she told me later, a party of hooded Ku Klux Klan riders galloped up to our home in Omaha, Nebraska, one night. Surrounding the house, brandishing their shotguns and rifles, they shouted for my father to come out. My mother went to the front door and opened it. Standing where they could see her pregnant condition, she told them that she was alone with her three small children, and that my father was away, preaching, in Milwaukee. The Klansmen shouted threats and warnings at her that we had better get out of town because "the good Christian white people" were not going to stand for my father's "spreading trouble" among the "good" Negroes of Omaha with the "back to Africa" preachings of Marcus Garvey.

My father, the Reverend Earl Little, was a Baptist minister, a dedicated organizer for Marcus Aurelius Garvey's U.N.I.A. (Universal Negro Improvement Association). With the help of such disciples as my father, Garvey, from his headquarters in New York City's Harlem, was raising the banner of black-race purity and exhorting the Negro masses to return to their ancestral African homeland--a cause which had made Garvey the most controversial black man on earth.

Still shouting threats, the Klansmen finally spurred their horses and galloped around the house, shattering every window pane with their gun butts. Then they rode off into the night, their torches flaring, as suddenly as they had come.

My father was enraged when he returned. He decided to wait until I was born--which would be soon--and then the family would move. I am not sure why he made this decision, for he was not a frightened Negro, as most then were, and many still are today. My father was a big, six-foot-four, very black man. He had only one eye. How he had lost the other one I have never known. He was from Reynolds, Georgia, where he had left school after the third or maybe fourth grade. He believed, as did Marcus Garvey, that freedom, independence and self-respect could never be achieved by the Negro in America, and that therefore the Negro should leave America to the white man and return to his African land of origin. Among the reasons my father had decided to risk and dedicate his life to help disseminate this philosophy among his people was that he had seen four of his six brothers die by violence, three of them killed by white men, including one by lynching. What my father could not know then was that of the remaining three, including himself, only one, my Uncle Jim, would die in bed, of natural causes. Northern white police were later to shoot my Uncle Oscar. And my father was finally himself to die by the white man's hands.

It has always been my belief that I, too, will die by violence. I have done all that I can to be prepared.

I was my father's seventh child. He had three children by a previous marriage--Ella, Earl, and Mary, who lived in Boston. He had met and married my mother in Philadelphia, where their first child, my oldest full brother, Wilfred, was born. They moved from Philadelphia to Omaha, where Hilda and then Philbert were born.

I was next in line. My mother was twenty-eight when I was born on May 19, 1925, in an Omaha hospital. Then we moved to Milwaukee, where Reginald was born. From infancy, he had some kind of hernia condition which was to handicap him physically for the rest of his life.

Louise Little, my mother, who was born in Grenada, in the British West Indies, looked like a white woman. Her father was white. She had straight black hair, and her accent did not sound like a Negro's. Of this white father of hers, I know nothing except her shame about it. I remember hearing her say she was glad that she had never seen him. It was, of course, because of him that I got my reddish-brown "mariny" color of skin, and my hair of the same color. I was the lightest child in our family. (Out in the world later on, in Boston and New York, I was among the millions of Negroes who were insane enough to feel that it was some kind of status symbol to be light-complexioned--that one was actually fortunate to be born thus. But, still later, I learned to hate every drop of that white rapist's blood that is in me.)

Our family stayed only briefly in Milwaukee, for my father wanted to find a place where he could raise our own food and perhaps build a business. The teaching of Marcus Garvey stressed becoming independent of the white man. We went next, for some reason, to Lansing, Michigan. My father bought a house and soon, as had been his pattern, he was doing free-lance Christian preaching in local Negro Baptist churches, and during the week he was roaming about spreading word of Marcus Garvey.

He had begun to lay away savings for the store he had always wanted to own when, as always, some stupid local Uncle Tom Negroes began to funnel stories about his revolutionary beliefs to the local white people. This time, the get-out-of-town threats came from a local hate society called The Black Legion. They wore black robes instead of white. Soon, nearly everywhere my father went, Black Legionnaires were reviling him as an "uppity nigger" for wanting to own a store, for living outside the Lansing Negro district, for spreading unrest and dissension among "the good niggers."

As in Omaha, my mother was pregnant again, this time with my youngest sister. Shortly after Yvonne was born came the nightmare night in 1929, my earliest vivid memory. I remember being suddenly snatched awake into a frightening confusion of pistol shots and shouting and smoke and flames. My father had shouted and shot at the two white men who had set the fire and were running away. Our home was burning down around us. We were lunging and bumping and tumbling all over each other trying to escape. My mother, with the baby in her arms, just made it into the yard before the house crashed in, showering sparks. I remember we were outside in the night in our underwear, crying and yelling our heads off. The white police and firemen came and stood around watching as the house burned down to the ground.

My father prevailed on some friends to clothe and house us temporarily; then he moved us into another house on the outskirts of East Lansing. In those days Negroes weren't allowed after dark in East Lansing proper. There's where Michigan State University is located; I related all of this to an audience of students when I spoke there in January, 1963 (and had the first reunion in a long while with my younger brother, Robert, who was there doing postgraduate studies in psychology). I told them how East Lansing harassed us so much that we had to move again, this time two miles out of town, into the country. This was where my father built for us with his own hands a four-room house. This is where I really begin to remember things--this home where I started to grow up.

After the fire, I remember that my father was called in and questioned about a permit for the pistol with which he had shot at the white men who set the fire. I remember that the police were always dropping by our house, shoving things around, "just checking" or "looking for a gun." The pistol they were looking for--which they never found, and for which they wouldn't issue a permit--was sewed up inside a pillow. My father's .22 rifle and his shotgun, though, were right out in the open; everyone had them for hunting birds and rabbits and other game.

After that, my memories are of the friction between my father and mother. They seemed to be nearly always at odds. Sometimes my father would beat her. It might have had something to do with the fact that my mother had a pretty good education. Where she got it I don't know. But an educated woman, I suppose, can't resist the temptation to correct an uneducated man. Every now and then, when she put those smooth words on him, he would grab her.

My father was also belligerent toward all of the children, except me. The older ones he would beat almost savagely if they broke any of his rules--and he had so many rules it was hard to know them all. Nearly all my whippings came from my mother. I've thought a lot about why. I actually believe that as anti-white as my father was, he was subconsciously so afflicted with the white man's brainwashing of Negroes that he inclined to favor the light ones, and I was his lightest child. Most Negro parents in those days would almost instinctively treat any lighter children better than they did the darker ones. It came directly from the slavery tradition that the "mulatto," because he was visibly nearer to white, was therefore "better."

My two other images of my father are both outside the home. One was his role as a Baptist preacher. He never pastored in any regular church of his own; he was always a "visiting preacher." I remember especially his favorite sermon: "That little *black* train is a-comin' . . . an' you better get all your business right!" I guess this also fit his association with the back-to-Africa movement, with Marcus Garvey's "Black Train Homeward." My brother Philbert, the one just older than me, loved church, but it confused and amazed me. I would sit goggle-eyed at my father jumping and shouting as he preached, with the congregation jumping and shouting behind him, their souls and bodies devoted to singing and praying. Even at that young age, I just couldn't believe in the Christian concept of Jesus as someone divine. And no religious person, until I was a man in my twenties--and then in prison--could tell me anything. I had very little respect for most people who represented religion.

It was in his role as a preacher that my father had most contact with the Negroes of Lansing. Believe me when I tell you that those Negroes were in bad shape then. They are still in bad shape--though in a different way. By that I mean that I don't know a town with a higher percentage of complacent and misguided so-called "middle-class" Negroes--the typical status-symbol-oriented, integration-seeking type of Negroes. Just recently, I was standing in a lobby at the United Nations talking with an African ambassador and his wife, when a Negro came up to me and said, "You know me?" I was a little embarrassed because I thought he was someone I should remember. It turned out that he was one of those bragging, self-satisfied, "middle-class" Lansing Negroes. I wasn't ingratiated. He was the type who would never have been associated with Africa, until the fad of having African friends became a status-symbol for "middle-class" Negroes.

Back when I was growing up, the "successful" Lansing Negroes were such as waiters and bootblacks. To be a janitor at some downtown store was to be highly respected. The real "elite," the "big shots," the "voices of the race," were the waiters at the Lansing Country Club and the shoeshine boys at the state capitol. The only Negroes who really had any money were the ones in the numbers racket, or who ran the gambling houses, or who in some other way lived parasitically off the poorest ones, who were the masses. No Negroes were hired then by Lansing's big Oldsmobile plant, or the Reo plant. (Do you remember the Reo? It was manufactured in Lansing, and R. E. Olds, the man after whom it was named, also lived in Lansing. When the war came along, they hired some Negro janitors.) The bulk of the Negroes were either on Welfare, or W.P.A., or they starved.

The day was to come when our family was so poor that we would eat the hole out of a doughnut; but at that time we were much better off than most town Negroes. The reason was we raised much of our own food out there in the country where we were. We were much better off than the town Negroes who would shout, as my father preached, for the pie-in-the-sky and their heaven in the hereafter while the white man had his here on earth.

I knew that the collections my father got for his preaching were mainly what fed and clothed us, and he also did other odd jobs, but still the image of him that made me proudest was his crusading and militant campaigning with the words of Marcus Garvey. As young as I was then, I knew from what I overheard that my father was saying something that made him a "tough" man. I remember an old lading, grinning and saying to my father, "You're scaring these white folks to death!"

One of the reasons I've always felt that my father favored me was that to the best of of my remembrance, it was only me that he sometimes took with him to the Garvey U.N.I.A. meetings which he held quietly in different people's homes. There were never more than a few people at any one time--twenty at most. But that was a lot, packed into someone's living room. I noticed how differently they all acted, although sometimes they were the same people who jumped and shouted in church. But in these meetings both they and my father were more intense, more intelligent and down to earth. It made me feel the same way.

I can remember hearing of "Adam driven out of the garden into the caves of Europe," "Africa for the Africans," "Ethiopians, Awake!" And my father would talk about how it would not be much longer before Africa would be completely run by Negroes--"by black men," was the phrase he always used. "No one knows when the hour of Africa's redemption cometh. It is in the wind. It is coming. One day, like a storm, it will be here."

I remember seeing the big, shiny photographs of Marcus Garvey that were passed from hand to hand. My father had a big envelope of them that he always took to these meetings. The pictures showed what seemed to me millions of Negroes thronged in parade behind Garvey riding in a fine car, a big black man dressed in a dazzling uniform with gold braid on it, and he was wearing a thrilling hat with tall; plumes. I remember hearing that he had black followers not only in the United States but all around the world, and I remember how the meetings always closed with my father saying, several times, and the people chanting after him, "Up, you mighty race, you can accomplish what you will!"

I have never understood why, after hearing as much as I did of these kinds of things, I somehow never thought, then, of the black people in Africa. My image of Africa, at that time, was of naked savages, cannibals, monkeys and tigers and steaming jungles.

My father would drive in his old black touring car, sometimes taking me, to meeting places all round the Lansing area. I remember one daytime meeting (most were at night) in the town of Owosso, forty miles from Lansing, which the Negroes called "White City." (Owosso's greatest claim to fame is that it is the home town of Thomas E. Dewey.) As in East Lansing, no Negroes were allowed on the streets there after dark--hence the daytime meeting. In point of fact, in those days lots of Michigan towns were like that. Every town had a few "home" Negroes who lived there. Sometimes it would be just one family, as in the nearby county seat, Mason, which had a single Negro family named Lyons. Mr. Lyons had been a famous football star at Mason High School, was highly thought of in Mason, and consequently he now worked around that town in menial jobs.

My mother at this time seemed to be always working--cooking, washing, ironing, cleaning, and fussing over us eight children. And she was usually either arguing with or not speaking to my father. One cause of friction was that she had strong ideas about what she wouldn't eat--and didn't want *us* to eat--including pork and rabbit, both of which my father loved dearly. He was a real Georgia Negro, and he believed in eating plenty of what we in Harlem today call "soul food."

I've said that my mother was the one who whipped me--at least she did whenever she wasn't ashamed to let the neighbors think she was killing me. For if she even acted as though she was about to raise her hand to me, I would open my mouth and let the world know about it. If anybody was passing by out on the road, she would either change her mind or just give me a few licks.

Thinking about it now, I feel definitely that just as my father favored me for being lighter than the other children, my mother gave me more hell for the same reason. She was very light herself but she favored the ones who were darker. Wilfred, I know, was particularly her angel. I remember that she would tell me to go out of the house and "Let the sun shine on you so you can get some color." She went out of her way never to let me become afflicted with a sense of color-superiority. I am sure that she treated me this way partly because of how she came to be light herself.

I learned early that crying out in protest could accomplish things. My older brothers and sister had started to school when, sometimes, they could come in and ask for a buttered biscuit or something and my mother, impatiently, would tell them no. But I would cry out and make a fuss until I got what I wanted. I remember well how my mother asked me why I couldn't be a nice boy like Wilfred; but I would think to myself that Wilfred, for being so nice and quiet, often stayed hungry. So early in life, I had learned that if you want something, you had better make some noise.

Not only did we have our big garden, but we raised chickens. My father would buy some baby chicks and my mother would raise them. We all loved chicken. That was one dish there was no argument with my father about. One thing in particular that I remember made me feel grateful toward my mother was that one day I went and asked her for my own garden, and she did let me have my own little plot. I loved it and took care of it well. I loved especially to grow peas. I was proud when we had them on our table. I would pull out the grass in my garden by hand when the first little blades came up. I would patrol the rows on my hands and knees for any worms and bugs, and I would kill and bury them. And sometimes when I had everything straight and clean for my things to grow, I would lie down on my back between two rows, and I would gaze up in the blue sky at the clouds moving and think all kinds of things.

At five, I, too, began to go to school, leaving home in the morning along with Wilfred, Hilda, and Philbert. It was the Pleasant Grove School that went from kindergarten through the eighth grade. It was two miles outside the city limits, and I guess there was no problem about our attending because we were the only Negroes in the area. In those days white people in the North usually would "adopt" just a few Negroes; they didn't see them as any threat. The white kids didn't make any great thing about us, either. They called us "nigger" and "darkie" and "Rastus" so much that we thought those were our natural names. But they didn't think of it as an insult; it was just the way they thought about us

One afternoon in 1931 when Wilfred, Hilda, Philbert, and I came home, my mother and father were having one of their arguments. There had lately been a lot of tension around the house because of Black Legion threats. My father had taken one of the rabbits which we were raising, and ordered my mother to cook it. We raised rabbits, but sold them to whites. My father had taken a rabbit from the rabbit pen. He had pulled off the rabbit's head. He was so strong, he needed no knife to behead chickens or rabbits. With one twist of his big black hands he simply twisted off the head and threw the bleeding-necked thing back at my mother's feet.

My mother was crying. She started to skin the rabbit, preparatory to cooking it, but my father was so angry he slammed on out the front door and started walking up the road toward town.

It was then that my mother had this vision. She had always been a strange woman in this sense, and had always had a strong intuition of things about to happen. And most of her children are the same way, I think. When something is about to happen, I can feel something, sense something. I never have known something to happen that has caught me completely off guard--except one. And that was when, years later, I discovered facts I couldn't believe about a man who, up until that discovery, I would gladly have given my life for.

My father was well up the road when my mother ran screaming out onto the porch. "*Early! Early!*" She screamed his name. She clutched up her apron in one hand, and ran down across the yard and into the road. My father turned around. He saw her. For some reason, considering how angry he had been when he left, he waved at her. But he kept on going.

She told me later, my mother did, that she had a vision of my father's end. All the rest of the afternoon, she was not herself, crying and nervous and upset. She finished cooking the rabbit and put the whole thing in the warmer part of the black stove. When my father was not back home by our bedtime, my mother hugged and clutched us, and we felt strange, not knowing what to do, because she had never acted like that.

I remember waking up to the sound of my mother's screaming again. When I scrambled out, I saw the police in the living room; they were trying to calm her down. She had snatched on her clothes to go with them. And all of us children who were staring knew without anyone having to say it that something terrible had happened to our father.

My mother was taken by the police to the hospital, and to a room where a sheet was over my father in a bed, and she wouldn't look, she was afraid to look. Probably it was wise that she didn't. My father's skull, on one side, was crushed in, I was told later. Negroes in Lansing have always whispered that he was attacked, and then laid across some tracks for a streetcar to run over him. His body was cut almost in half.

He lived two and a half hours in that condition. Negroes then were stronger than they are now, especially Georgia Negroes. Negroes born in Georgia had to be strong simply to survive....

PART III - AMERICANS AND ANTI-COMMUNISM

It is a battle to the death--either Communism must die, or Christianity must die, because it is actually a battle between Christ and anti-Christ.

Reverend Billy Graham, 1954

I killed more people tonight than I have fingers on my hands. I shot them in cold blood and enjoyed every minute of it. I pumped slugs in the nastiest bunch of bastards you ever saw.... They were Commies, Lee. They were Red sons-of-bitches who should have died long ago.

Mickey Spillane,
One Lonely Night, 1951

Remember, there was once a Congress in which they had a committee that would investigate even one of their own members if it was believed that that person had communist involvement or communist leanings. Well, they've done away with those committees. That shows the success of what the Soviets were able to do in this country with making it unfashionable to be anti-communist.

President Ronald Reagan, 1987

Ours is a divided empire in which certain ideas and emotions and actions are of God, and their opposites are of Lucifer. It is as impossible for most men to conceive of a morality without sin as of an earth without sky.

Arthur Miller, *The Crucible*, 1954

The Equal Rights Amendment is about a socialist, anti-family political movement that encourages women to leave their husbands, kill their children, practice witchcraft, destroy capitalism and become lesbians.

Reverend Pat Robertson , 1992

INTRODUCTION

A political critic once announced, "If we didn't have Communists, we would have been forced to invent them." Unable to blame themselves, Americans have long blamed scapegoats for both domestic and foreign problems. President Calvin Coolidge once proclaimed that the perfection of our history proved that God had personally invented America. Another defender of the faith insisted that God gave the world one last chance and called it America. And historian Richard Hofstadter concluded, "We are the only country that was born to perfection and then aspired to progress." This popular notion of America being God's last, best experiment (evidence can readily be found in most any presidential inaugural address) has made it difficult for many Americans to accept or correct possible internal weaknesses in our system, particularly in terms of our political, social, and economic practices. We prefer to blame corrupt or misguided individuals within the country or some evil external force when things go wrong. For example, in the eighteenth and nineteenth centuries we often accused Catholic priests ("emissaries of the Pope") of undermining our sacred institutions. In the late nineteenth and early twentieth centuries older Americans accused the so-called "New Immigrants" from Southern and Eastern Europe of weakening family values and destroying their homogeneous social fabric. But Communists, both individually and collectively, real and imagined, at home and abroad, have been America's favorite twentieth-century whipping boy.

Communists have posed both a real and imagined threat beyond our borders. After World War I, the United States worried lest the Bolshevik tide engulf a war-weary Europe and the world beyond. The same concern influenced many of our post-World War II policies, leading directly to our involvement in both the Korean and Vietnam Wars. After the fall of Nationalist China in 1949, America faced a new Communist enemy in the People's Republic of China; in fact, it took us over two decades to stop referring to that nation as "Red China." Recent events in the Soviet Union indicate that our inordinate, four-decade fear of Communist military dominance was highly exaggerated; yet, during the Reagan years we tripled our defense spending.

Our fear of Communism has had an enormous impact on our social, economic, and political policies and actions since World War II. It has forced us into two wars, resulting in the deaths of over 100,000 Americans and hundreds of thousands of Asians. It has cost the nation billions of dollars in defense spending, the total bill for which has yet to be paid. It has forced the government into the kinds of hard financial choices that have blocked needed social, education, and peacetime research programs and the desperately needed rebuilding of our crumbling infrastructure. Finally, it has resulted in a massive and debilitating national debt which has alarmingly weakened our ability to compete with Germany and Japan for world markets.

There have, of course, always been Communists in the United States, but their numbers have been minimal and any real threat to our basic institutions largely nonexistent. This reality, however, did not prevent the United States from experiencing the three major Red Scares addressed in Part III:

1) Red Scare of 1919-1920

Triggered by the successful Bolshevik revolution in Russia, America launched a government-sponsored crusade against radicals within our own boundaries. Led by Attorney General A. Mitchell Palmer and a young subordinate named J. Edgar Hoover, state and federal officials, as well as private interests, attacked immigrants, labor unions, minorities, and reformers, while generally violating civil and human rights. Selections by Robert K. Murray, Jack Miller, and William Patterson and the poem *Bol-She-Veek* are reflections on this first Red Scare and its aftermath.

2) The Cold War and McCarthyism

Winston Churchill's 1946 announcement that an Iron Curtain was descending around the world, behind which the Soviet Union was planning worldwide conquest and domination, initiated a cold war that not only dictated huge peacetime military expenditures but also made possible demagogues like Joe McCarthy and J. Edgar Hoover who exploited popular fears for personal and political gain. The Reverend Billy Graham discovered that Communists made good devils, as did author Louis Bromfield. Other selections in Part III make it clear how pervasive anti-communism was in the American popular culture of the 1950's.

3) Ronald Reagan and the Evil Empire

President Reagan successfully revived the postwar fear of Communism by exaggerating the Soviet military buildup. In so doing, he and Secretary of Defense, Casper Weinberger, were able to triple the defense budget. To gain popular support, Reagan called forth the old clichés, including labeling the USSR "the evil empire."

Robert K. Murray, *RED SCARE*

Robert K. Murray, Professor of American History at Pennsylvania State University, published his highly-acclaimed Red Scare, 1919-1920: A Study in National Hysteria *(McGraw-Hill) in 1964. Unquestionably, McCarthyism and our Second Red Scare greatly influenced this highly critical study of the 1919-1920 era. The opening pages of Murray's monograph, quoted below, could just as well have been written about the 1950s.*

In connection with the writing of his spectacular multi-volume history of the fall of Rome, Edward Gibbon once remarked that the most distressing task for any historian is to chronicle the death of a great nation. What is even more distressing is to describe the convulsions of a great nation which, while alive, is in the process of losing its soul.

In 1919 America's soul was in danger. It was in danger not merely because of the nation's refusal to accept its moral responsibilities, or solve intelligently its economic problems, or shun the pitfalls of unbridled self-interest. Primarily it was in danger because the nation was deserting its most honored principles of freedom -- principles which had made it great and which had given it birth.

Nowhere was this fact more obvious than in the social scene of 1919. The war was largely to blame. During the conflict the demand for absolute loyalty had permeated every nook and cranny of the social structure. Independent agencies, such as the National Security League and the American Defense Society, together with the government-sponsored American Protective League, had converted thousands of otherwise reasonable and sane Americans into super-patriots and self-styled spy-chasers by spreading rabid propaganda which maximized the dangers of wartime sabotage and sedition. Supposedly these agencies represented the nation's first line of defense against wartime subversive activity. But by the close of the war they actually had become the repository of elements which were much more interested in strengthening a sympathy for economic and political conservatism than in underwriting a healthy patriotism. Under the guidance of their leaders, these organizations often used "Americanism" merely to blacken the reputation and character of persons and groups whose opinions they hated and feared.

In this connection, the activity of the governments Committee on Public Information was especially significant under the chairmanship of George Creel, it had preached patriotism to the American public by means of the written word, spoken word, motion picture, signboard, and poster, and had so directed its propaganda that "every printed bullet might reach its mark." The public press had followed in the pattern set by the committee and the net result had been an indoctrination of hate, prejudice, and 100 percent Americanism on a colossal scale. As Frank Cobb, editor of the New York *World*, later claimed: "Government conscripted public opinion as they conscripted men and money and materials. Having conscripted it, they dealt with it as they dealt with other raw recruits. They mobilized it. They put it in charge of drill sergeants. They goose-stepped it. They taught it to stand at attention and salute."

Under such circumstances the free play of opinion and the opportunity for independent action had practically ceased to exist. The home front, unable personally to lay hands on the hated

Huns, had made scapegoats of the "draft-dodger," the "slacker," and anyone else who did not conform. Teachers in certain areas had been forced from their jobs for making allegedly unpatriotic statements to their classes about the causes of the war. In some states, the teaching of the German language had been outlawed from the public schools because of its possible subversive influence. Wagnerian selections had all but disappeared from the repertoire of the nation's musicians. In self-defense, towns and individuals with German names had appealed to the courts for relief and Schmidts became Smiths while Berlins became Bellevilles. For a time there had been congressional talk of passing a "no strike" law in order to compel greater labor cooperation than already existed, and in the nation at large men had been beaten and tarred and feathered for failure to buy war bonds or support Red Cross drives. Conscientious objectors such as the Mennonites, Dunkards, and Quakers had been subjected to even worse indignities, while political objectors to the war had been particularly persecuted and scorned.

Meanwhile both the state and federal governments had sought to enforce loyal conduct by passing a mass of sedition and espionage legislation. Most of these wartime laws were still in effect in 1919 and served as a constant reminder that animosity to nonconformity was still very much the vogue. Of these laws, the three passed by the federal Congress were particularly significant to the 1919 scene.

The first was the Espionage Act of 1917 which, while primarily directed at treason, was so constructed and interpreted that it covered much lesser disloyal activity. This law made it a crime, punishable by a $10,000 fine and twenty years in jail, for a person to "...convey false reports or false statements with intent to interfere with the operation or success of the military or naval forces of the United States or to promote the success of its enemies...or attempt to cause insubordination, disloyalty, mutiny, or refusal of duty, in the military or naval forces of the United States, or...willfully obstruct recruiting or enlistment service..."

The second piece of legislation was the Sedition Act of 1918, which dealt more directly with the problem of sedition per se. The law prohibited a person, under pain of $10,000 and twenty years' imprisonment, to "...utter, print, write, or publish any disloyal, profane, scurrilous, or abusive language about the form of government of the United States, or the Constitution of the United States, or the uniform of the Army or Navy of the United States, or any language intended to ...encourage resistance to the United States, or to promote the cause of its enemies..."

The third in this series was of a slightly different character since it was designed to curb the activities of nonconforming aliens who were thought to be a particular threat to the nation. Passed in October 1918, this law decreed that all aliens who were anarchists or believed in the violent overthrow of the American government or advocated the assassination of public officials were henceforth to be excluded from admission into the United States. The law further provided that "...any alien who, at any time after entering the Untied States, is found to have been at the time of entry, or to have become thereafter, a member of any one of the classes of aliens (above mentioned)...shall upon warrant of the Secretary of Labor, be taken into custody and deported..."

In spite of the nation's desire for a rapid return to peace, it was obvious the American public of 1919 was still thinking with the mind of a people at war. Many prosecutions, already begun on the basis of the acts mentioned above, were just coming before the courts and served to remind the nation of the existence of disloyalty. Returning soldiers, evidencing an intense love of country, added to the excitement by howling for the immediate and summary punishment of all such nonconformity. To the 1919 public the German was still a barbarian capable of committing any atrocity, while those who had sympathized with him or who had even slightly opposed the war were equally depraved. Indeed, anyone who spoke with an accent or carried a foreign name, German or otherwise, remained particularly suspect as American superpatriots continued to see spies lurking behind every bush and tree. Still in existence were the National Security League, the American Defense Society, and other such patriotic organizations which in order to live now sought to create new menaces. In short, insofar as the 1919 social mood was concerned the nation was still at war.

It was in the midst of this confusing, intolerant, and irresponsible atmosphere that the Great Red Scare occurred. The taproots of this phenomenon lay embedded in the various events growing out of the Bolshevik Revolution of November 1917. Denying most of the principles that older governments had been founded to secure and advancing the idea of world-wide proletarian revolution, the Bolshevik experiment was destined from the very beginning to represent one of the most crucial problems facing the world both during and after the war.

Losing little time in indicating their lack of interest in capitalist wars, the Bolsheviki concluded a separate peace with Germany in March 1918 and took Russia out of the conflict. Falsely believing that this proved the movement was actually German controlled, the allies, with the United States participating, intervened in Russia to reactivate the eastern front against Germany and thereby eliminate the source of Bolshevik power. In spite of such action, the Bolshevik power remained and indeed became more aggressive. In March 1919 the Third International was formed to serve as a spearhead for a global proletarian revolution, and it seemed to be having some success. In early 1919 Germany was racked with revolution, the situation in Poland and Italy was uneasy, and Hungary actually established a soviet regime.

From the beginning the American public was shocked by the Bolsheviki's disregard for the traditional and considered their separate peace with Germany a great betrayal. The nation then watched apprehensively as the Red Scourge moved westward into Europe. Patriotic societies, meanwhile, consistently denounced the Bolshevik as a counterpart of the dreaded Hun, and the press circulated such exaggerated information about the Bolshevik reign in Russia. Naturally, economic conservatives eagerly seized upon bolshevism's danger in order to further their own campaign of stifling political and economic liberalism. The net result was the implantation of the Bolshevik in the American mind as the epitome of all that was evil.

On the other hand, great sympathy was immediately forthcoming from many American radicals for the Russian revolution and some openly advocated a similar upheaval in this country. In September 1919 two domestic Communist parties were formed and while the movement remained very small, its noise more than compensated for its size. These American Communists held parades and meetings, distributed leaflets and other incendiary literature, and issued revolutionary manifestoes and calls for action.

In an intolerant postwar year in which people were still conditioned to the danger of spies and sabotage, these domestic Bolsheviki seemed particularly dangerous. As labor unrest increased and the nation was treated to such abnormal events as general strikes, riots, and the planting of bombs, the assumption that the country was under serious attack by the Reds found a wide acceptance. In the long run, each social and industrial disturbance was received as prima-facie evidence of the successful spread of radicalism. Even the temporary instability arising from demobilization and reconversion, and the many justified protests concerning high prices, were traced to the Reds.

As a result, exaggerated conclusions were reached concerning the size and influence of the movement. Indeed, never before had the nation been so overwhelmed with fear. It is understandable. Because of its waning faith, its political and moral irresponsibility, and its monetary abandonment of high ideals, the nation had been susceptible as never before, Harassed by the rantings and ravings of a small group of radicals, buffeted by the dire warnings of business and employer organizations, and assaulted daily by the scare propaganda of the patriotic societies and the general press, the national mind ultimately succumbed to hysteria. As one English journalist described the prevailing scene: "No one who was in the United States as I chanced to be, in the autumn of 1919, will forget the feverish condition of the public mind at that time. It was hag-ridden by the spectre of Bolshevism. It was like a sleeper in a nightmare, enveloped by a thousand phantoms of destruction. Property was in an agony of fear, and the horrid name 'Radical' covered the most innocent departure from conventional thought with a suspicion of desperate purpose. 'America,' as one wit of the time said, 'is the land of liberty -- liberty to keep in step.'"

Thus, continued wartime intolerance, postwar industrial unrest, the lack of statesmanlike leadership, and the ill-fated quest for a false normalcy paid pernicious dividends. Fortunately, the Great Red Scare soon subsided, but not before the forces of reaction implicit in the 1919 economic political, and social environment achieved their goal. Civil liberties were left prostrate, the labor movement was badly mauled, the position of capital was greatly enhanced, and complete antipathy toward reform was enthroned. In this respect, the Red Scare served as the major vehicle on which the American nation rode from a victorious war into a bankrupt peace.

Jack Miller, *THE EVERETT MASSACRE, 1916*

Jack Miller's story is a good example of America's long-time fear of radical leftists and laborites,and its willingness to use violence against them. In this case, the target was the Industrial Workers of the World, a radical labor union popularly known as the Wobblies. The following is from Bud and Ruth Schultz's It Did Happen Here: Recollections of Political Repression in America (1989).

The violence of company police, deputized vigilantes, and local and state police, frequently acting as employer agents, made the efforts to unionize American workers a risk to life and safety. Sometimes, violent events were so outrageously brutal that they came to be known in labor history and lore as massacres.

May 30, 1937--the Memorial Day Massacre. A thousand persons gather in support of striking steel workers at Republic Steel's South Chicago mill. Men, women, and children assemble for a parade to the plant. Suddenly, there is a roar of gunfire. Then uniformed police charge with nightsticks and tear gas. Ten are dead. Scores are wounded.

April 20, 1914--the Ludlow Massacre. Striking miners, evicted from their company-owned homes, live in a tent colony at Ludlow, Colorado. During the night, company gunmen and members of the National Guard drench the tents with oil, set them afire, and machine-gun the miners and their wives and children as they try to escape. Thirteen children, a woman, and five men die that Easter night.

March 7, 1932--the Dearborn Massacre. Unemployed auto workers begin a hunger march to the Dearborn, Michigan, plant of Ford Motors to present petitions to get their jobs back. From a bridge and the roadside, they are met with fire hoses, tear gas, and then the pistols of the Dearborn police and Ford's private security force. Three men are killed. Retreating workers are sprayed with machine-gun fire. Another is killed, and many lie wounded on the ground.

November 5, 1916--the Everett Massacre. The Puget Sound ferry-boat Verona *docks at Everett, Washington, with more than two hundred Wobblies on board. Before they can step ashore, a hail of gunfire from Sheriff McRae and his deputies leaves five known dead and others lost in the waters of the sound. The Industrial Workers of the World, the Wobblies, faced assaults from state and local police throughout the West, where they organized lumber, mining, and farm workers. Jack Miller, a vigorous and enthusiastic Wobbly at ninety-five, is the last living survivor of the Everett Massacre*

I was a volunteer organizer for the United Mine workers in 1908, 1909. The United Mine Workers didn't want the operators to know what was going on, so it was very clandestine. I was an agitator, really, and it was just as dangerous then to do something like that as it was to belong to the Wobblies. I was either told to get out, or was escorted out, or sometimes rather forcibly expelled from every coal-mining camp in that Cumberland Valley division of Virginia.

Two of us would go into the camp as partners. When we got there, we wouldn't "know" each other whatsoever. I was the one who did the talking. Then, if I didn't appear in front of the company store between five-thirty and six o'clock in the evening, my partner's job was to find out where I was. He usually knew where to look first, down in the little calaboose. We were taught how to defend ourselves in the "justice" courts, because if they got hold of a union agitator, they loved to throw the book at him. Even a vagrancy charge could lead to eleven months and twenty-nine days.

The year Halley's comet was here, 1910, I became a Billy Sunday convert. He had great powers of description. He was a master of slang and would use it in all his sermons. He had a choir made up of all the best voices in Danville, led by that great conductor Fred Fisher. Then he had a building--it must have been two hundred fifty feet long by fifty feet wide--with just benches. That was the tabernacle I was converted in.

Billy Sunday had come for six weeks, and I heard him every night he preached. And honestly, I was fool enough to be quite sincere in this. They organized a young men's Bible class, and I was elected president. Well, if anybody had asked me to quote a verse from the Bible, I could have said, "Jesus wept," but I wouldn't have been sure of any other.

I started to study the Bible. The first chapter of Genesis didn't go down so bad. It seemed to me a reasonable story people would tell about creation. No orders, no rules were laid down except to "be fruitful and multiply." And I was quite willing. Then I started to read the second chapter of Genesis, and right away this plain creator had disappeared entirely. It opened up by calling him *Lord* God and *King* God. And rules began coming down on us like snowflakes in a Dakota blizzard.

I went back to the church and asked them questions. They'd say, "You have to pray for better pay. You have to pray for greater faith." Finally I got sore. "Listen, if I'm going to teach the Bible, I have to have some of these things that seem unreasonable explained, or I'm not going to do it." They said, "That's no attitude at all for a Christian." Well, I told them what they could do. I remember later, during the Palmer raids, Billy Sunday said, "Put radicals on ships of stone, with sails of lead, and make Hell the first port of call." That, I suppose, was the good Christian spirit.

I hit the road shortly afterward and wound up in Calgary. Now, I didn't know beforehand that you better have your stake made if you were going to spend a winter in Canada. There were very few jobs and, boy, was it cold and shivery! I was partnering with a guy in what they called a "crumborium," where people slept on shelves for fifteen cents a night and were sure to become lousy.

I felt like a big hunk of nothing, a lost soul with no place to go, no reason for existence. Then some Wobbly said to me, "Hey, Jack, let's get in here and listen to this Socialist spout off. We'll be out of the cold, anyhow." So we went in. That night the Socialist was starting a series of six weekly lectures based on the book *From Nebula to Man*. I took those six lectures and was so impressed that I joined the Socialist Party. My education was carried on jointly by the Socialists and the IWW. They had a long hall. On one side the Wobblies met, and on the other side the Socialists met. They had a table sitting out there with literature from both organizations.

If they got anybody who they thought was interested--and they saw I listened to everything attentively--right away they would label him a "student." They had no mercy on me. Four or five of them would get around that little table, with me facing them, either the IWW or the Socialists. They would throw questions at me that I had no idea how to answer. They told me it was my duty to find the answers. Well, I got a very good grounding in Marx. I also got Darwin, the various sciences, and a little smidgen of astronomy--enough to arouse my curiosity. From that time on, I was a student.

Down in Minot, North Dakota, my real education commenced. They were building a normal school there. The contractor just thought he had everything his own way, with all the harvest hands unemployed and hungry, waiting for work. But a few Wobblies got in there and organized a strike. Then, bingo! The city and the county officials declared war on the strikers, and they had a free speech fight on their hands.*

Well, I thought, "You're a hell of a rebel if you haven't had your baptismal, your first free speech fight. You better go up there and take part in it." That night I got on a freight train. When it stopped at Minot, I knew enough to dodge the authorities. I stayed in a big bin off in the coal yard till daylight.

Then I went down Main Street. They were paving it with wooded blocks and had them piled up alongside the curb. No free speechers were there yet, so I jumped up on one of those piles and said, "Friends, comrades, and fellow workers!" I didn't know what else I was going to say, but I didn't have to worry about it. Two cops came and dragged my off.

I asked, "Am I under arrest?"

They said, "No."

I said, "Don't you think you'd better take your hands off me?"

"Well, you can't talk up there."

"Why? Is it against the United States Constitution?" So they let go of me, and I went down a ways, and I got up on the blocks again. A few seconds later, there were five or six of them, all ganging up on me. Oh, I was a bloody sight! I got a scalp wound, and the blood came down my arm. I started to wipe the blood off with my hand and smeared it all over my clothes. Two ladies came up to the cops. One said, "You should be ashamed of yourself, mercilessly beating this man." I don't know why, but that turned the tide. Those people who had been indifferent to the Wobblies or against them began heaving bricks down at these uniformed policemen. They took me to the can, and I was there until the free speech fight was settled.

That same year, I was in the harvest field. I joined Local 400 of the Agricultural Workers Union. We were fighting for four dollars a day in wages. Now I was ready for the IWW. I'd been trying to get a card all through Kansas. They had a branch open in Omaha, so I went in there, and Albert Prashner signed me up. I got my card on July 12, 1916, made out to Jack Leonard. My full name is John Leonard Miller, but that was too much of a handle for a Wobbly.

I stopped there to rest a day or two, and then went on to Council Bluffs. There were twenty-one of us who took possession of a flat car attached to a freight train right there in theyards. When the head brakeman came through, he tried to collect money from us for the privilege of riding "his" train. When we refused, he invited us to unload. We told him he

*The IWW's organizing campaigns were often met with police harassment and city ordinances that forbade the Wobblies to make speeches in public streets or parks. The IWW resisted the restrictions by organizing free speech fights that brought hundreds of Wobblies to the offending town or city to exercise their rights: as soon as one soapbox orator was arrested, another would quickly take the speaker's place, until the jails were filled and the local police and the court system were strained to the breaking point.

didn't own the train, to go back and do the job he was paid for. He swung a big braking stick and hit the guy sitting next to me. As the stick went past, I grabbed hold of it, jerked it out of his hands, and threw it into the swamp. He put down more feet than a centipede, running for help. Pretty soon he came back with the flame crew, the switchmen--everybody came. They were rather reluctant about it, but the brakeman started telling me what he was going to do to me.

I said, "I know you're big enough and dirty enough to do what you say. There's just one trouble--you don't have the guts to try it." He weighed about two hundred pounds, and I was skinny enough to haunt a house. I showed a lot of courage and not much judgment. But I had had a little experience as a wrestler, and there was swamp down there where his strength wouldn't count. I made up my mind that we were going to wind up in that swamp, and he was going to be on the bottom.

He put his head down, just as I hoped he would, and came in swinging. I put my knee under his chin, and then I hip-locked him. I threw him over, and we went down there, rolling in the swamp together. Then I gave that extra heave to put him on the bottom. We were in shallow water, but it was soft mud, and he couldn't get a purchase to get out of it. Every time he started to say something, I shoved his head under the water. And boy, that guy got seasick right there, a thousand miles from the ocean.

Later that afternoon, without any molestation, we got another freight train over to the Missouri Valley, where we did some harvesting. I was carrying what we called the "rigging," the IWW credentials. I signed up fifty IWWs--that was no trick in those days--and was winding up the harvest and threshing at Chester, Montana. Some Wobbly came through: "All footloose rebels head for the free speech fight at Yakima."

The snow was on the ground already, and it was cold. That night it was thirty below zero, and we had to cross the summit where it got down to forty or fifty below. But these enthusiastic Wobblies, not knowing what they were up against, wanted to go right then. I said, "You better wait for good weather." No, they wouldn't do it. Well, I made them gather up enough food to last for a couple of days. We had one thin blanket between the six of us, so we exercised as much as we could to keep our blood in circulation. It was a terrible journey, but we made it to Washington. We got to Yakima one day late.

There, they suggested we go to Seattle and report for the Everett free speech fight. The shingle weavers were on strike in Everett. The sheriff, Don McRae, and his drunken deputies would take the strikers out to the woods, beat them up, and run them out of town. Don McRae took his orders from the Commercial Club. The Commercial Club was run by the lumber trust. And all these groups were organized against the shingle weavers.*

Well, the IWW always went to the rescue, especially of small unions. They would support them financially and give them help on the picket line. They opened up an office for the lumber workers. There was a speakers' corner in Everett, at Hewitt and Wetmore streets, where all sorts of groups spoke. But when the IWW came, they passed an emergency ordinance, overnight, that there would be no more speech making there.

On October 30, 1916, forty-one of us left Seattle on the ferry boat, the *Verona*, intending to exercise our freedom of speech at Hewitt and Wetmore. We were met at the dock by Don McRae and his deputies. I saw Don McRae about twenty-five times, and I believe he was sober

*Shingle weavers were the sawyers, filers, and packers who worked as a crew to produce red cedar shingles. After 1900, mill technology introduced saws that made this a very dangerous and bloody occupation. The Shingle Weavers Union became the largest and strongest union in Everett.

on only two of those occasions. They took us off the boat and into a warehouse on the dock. I remember Don McRae saying, "Hah, I don't think these boys will come to Everett again."

Some fellow worker said, "Well, sheriff, we're only up here in pursuance of our constitutional right." "To hell with the Constitution," said McRae, the sheriff of Snohomish county. "You're in Everett now."

They loaded us into private cars and took us out to Beverly Park. Never at any time in Beverly Park did I hear the word "arrest" used. So we were not under arrest. We were right beside the interurban tracks. At least a hundred of McRae's deputies were lined up on each side of the roadway, armed with every kind of cudgel: billy clubs, baseball bats, ax handles, rifles. They ran us through that gauntlet, one at a time.

One of them said to me, "Oh, my God, if I knew what they were going to do, I'd never have come out here." I looked at him, and I remember saying, cold and unemotional, "Well, listen, mister, you can't ply in shit without getting your hands dirty." I had nothing but contempt for those guys who made a living from something like that, people so lowdown they would have to get up on a high stepladder to shake hands with a snake.

I saw three men go through. Now it was my turn. I made up my mind: By God, I'm going to go through that standing up, or they'll have to drag me. I was just determined. I walked down to that first pair. They tried to shove me off balance, but I guarded against that. Both of them had big long clubs. When one of them swung, I ducked and stepped by quickly to the next. I got by him, using the same trick. The third one--now, don't ask me why I was wearing a necktie that night--grabbed me by the necktie, and I felt a blow come on the top of my head and another under my eye. I didn't remember another thing until I came to, down at the end of the line. I know there was a long lapse of time because I had been the fourth man to walk the gauntlet, but by now nearly everybody else was through.

Things began to register. They said, "Run, you son of a bitch, run!"

I said, "I can't run."

"Run anyhow!" And they forced me across the sharp blades of the cattle guard. Thirty-one of us were treated at the hospital for injuries that we'd received because we wanted to exercise our right of free speech.

We decided that next Sunday a whole boatload of us would go up to Everett in daylight. We were going to hold that meeting up at Hewitt and Wetmore. Abe Rabinowitz, a delightful character with a sense of humor, said, "They may kill us, but they can't eat us. We're too tough for that." Abe was killed that day.

Practically everybody on the *Verona* was a Wobbly. There were so many of us that some followed in a second boat, the *Calista*. It was a two-hour run, and we sang all the way. We sang songs like "Hold the Fort" and "Solidarity." We were singing when the *Verona* whistled, coming into Everett. When the boat came to the dock, as many as could left the cabin to get out. There must have been a hundred or more men on the little forward deck. I was cold, so I'd been down below the freight deck, behind the galley. I came up on the port side in time to see everything of importance and hear everything of importance.

I saw Don McRae standing there with one hand in the air and the other on his belt, near his pistol. His belly wasn't hard to see. He called out to the boat, "Who's your leader?"

The reply came from the boat: "We are all leaders!"

He said, "You can't land here."

Someone said, "The hell we can't!" And at that McRae turned to face the deputies with a hand up in the air as if he were signaling. A single shot came first, followed by a volley. Now, all of the people on that forward deck, in that momentary panic, rushed to the starboard side. And the boat sharply listed. A railing broke, and several men went into the water. I guess nobody will ever know how many fell in. I know for sure than only one got back on the boat. Some people on the dock wanted to launch rowboats to rescue those in the water. They were not allowed to do it by those drunken bastards, the deputies who were shooting at the men swimming in the water and shooting toward the boat. Volley after volley came out in continuous fire off the dock.

After the shooting started, I went back down below. I saw Billings and Ben Legg go past the galley and into the engine room, where they found the engineer hiding behind the boilers. They pulled a gun on him. I could see this, but I couldn't hear it--there was too much shooting and screaming. Then I saw the engineer come up toward the engines. Shortly after that I felt the boat move. That's what saved the lives of the rest of us. As soon as that boat started moving, somebody went to find the captain. There were fourteen bullets that went through the port window by the wheel, any of which could have hit him. They found the captain in his quarters, hiding behind the safe with a mattress over his head. After we were out of immediate range, he took the wheel, and we turned around.

We had no first aid. The wounded just had to suffer it out till we got to Seattle. We couldn't save either one of the guys who died on the way back. Then we met the *Calista*. Jim Thompson, the most convincing speaker we had, the man who invented the clenched fist, was on that boat, along with some of the other speakers. We told them, "For Christ's sake, keep away from Everett! They're nuts up there." One of the important things we did was to turn that boat around.

In Seattle, we were met by the militia. They took us from the old Coleman Dock and marched us up Fourth Avenue. If you go along Fourth Avenue today, under the viaduct, you'll find an old boarded-up building. It's the old city hall. They booked us, put us on the elevator a few at a time, and sent us to the jail on the fifth floor. Our wounded went to the floor just below us. The city hospital was down there.

They had so many of us in one tank that there wasn't room for all of us to lie down on the floor. We finally managed to lie in a row with our heads against the wall. The second row would lie with their head and shoulders on the hips of those in the first row. The third row would lie with their head and shoulders on the second row. That way we made room for all of us, but of course it was awful inconvenient to turn over or do anything else. That was the way they housed us for three days.

Word had come down from Everett that we were to have bread and coffee once a day. That's all we got to eat until we were sufficiently organized to "build a battleship." And when the IWW built battleships, they were quite different from those that were built down at the waterfront.

To build this one, we got in the middle of the floor, twenty of us, and joined arms at the elbows. Then, on the count of three, we jumped as high as we could and all came down in one place. You take twenty people who average a hundred fifty pounds and you have a three-thousand-pound battering ram. It wasn't long before the other fellows around there wanted to join in the fun. We had everybody in that tank at that one place, all those feet coming down there at once. One, two, three, boom!

In a little while, they got wise in the other tanks to what we were doing and started to do the same thing. Finally, we got synchronized. The vibration could be felt all through the building. No building was ever made to stand such a stress as that. The first thing they did was come up and say, "You guys cut that out, or we'll turn the fire hose on you."

Somebody from our crew said, "Hurry up, or we'll soon have a hole in the floor for the water to go through." When that threat didn't work, they appealed to our "better nature." "You got comrades down in the hospital below. Some of them are almost dying, and this noise up here is going to kill them."

One of us said, "Don't you believe it. If those fellow workers hear us fighting up here, they'll get up out of their damn beds and join us."

Pretty soon they called the chief of police, and he brought the mayor, Hi Gill. Hi Gill said, "What are you complaining about?" By this time, somebody had pushed me up ahead. I said, "They're feeding us bread and coffee once a day." Gill turned to the jailer: "Who gave that order here?"

"It came from Everett."

He said, "Since when is the sheriff of Snohomish County running the city jail in Seattle? I want these men fed regular jail fare now." And he sent out for a good hot meal right then.

When they wanted to finger the IWW leaders, they put this Pinkerton stoolie and two others in a special cell with a four-inch opening. We couldn't see in, but they could see out. As we walked by them, they chose the "leaders" by putting up two fingers through the hole for "no" and three for "yes." I had been in the IWW for four months as a rank-and-file member. Yet I was picked as one of the "leaders." Happy Sopel, who had been in so many free speech fights and had been clubbed up so much that he wasn't mentally right, was one of the "leaders." There was a sixteen-year-old kid who was one of the "leaders." At least two who were picked were not even IWW members.

The prosecutor charged seventy-four of us who were fingered with first-degree murder of a deputy, Jefferson Beard. They took forty-one of us up to the Everett jail. The other thirty-three followed later. The age of the Wobblies in prison there ranged from the sixteen-year-old boy to men approaching sixty. There were migratory workers and resident workers; and some of them had worked at so many different jobs and at such a variety of crafts that I honestly believe that, given the tools and materials, they could have built a city complete with all utilities.

The jailers had been used to turning one prisoner against another by playing favorites. But we had no more than got into the jail when we organized. Every week we would elect a different committee of three, and they were the only ones who would speak to the jailer. Oh, yes, we were human beings. There were differences of opinion and some quarreling, but let any issue arise between any one of us and the jailers, then we were at once united and all personal differences forgotten.

The first clash we had was because they were feeding us worse slop than farmers threw their hogs. Our breakfast in the morning was moldy, half-cooked mush. One time, they fed us some beans that were sour. During the night, we were all seized with cramps and diarrhea. We only had one toilet and some buckets for all of us. Do you know what that means, one toilet on the floor for seventy-four people with diarrhea?

We took the rest of the sour beans and plastered the wall of the brand-new jail with them. It made an awful mess. Then someone found that there was about three-quarters of an inch slack in the locking mechanism on our doors. So all twenty men on each side of the corridor threw their weight against this slack until nine of the ten doors were forced open. Then we bent the bars back with blankets rolled into rope, so the doors could never be locked again while I was there. That was our second "battleship." There were no two Wobbly battleships built the same way. From then on, we got pretty good grub.

We asked for a change of venue. They didn't fight it very hard because we were ready to prove that the two judges in Everett were down on the dock with McRae on November fifth. Then twenty-five of us, who were to be witnesses, were moved back to the Seattle jail.

On International Labor Day, 1917, people from all over the world were coming to Seattle. The Russian Revolution had just come into being, and many of them were going through Seattle and Vladivostok to get there. That May Day morning, they all congregated down at the Wobbly Hall, marched out through the main part of town, and went up to Mount Pleasant Cemetery, where three fellow workers killed on the *Verona* were buried.

Coming back, they headed to the King County jail at the top of Profanity Hill, where the twenty-five of us were incarcerated. They came marching up that hill. We felt the sounds before they became recognizable as such. Then we could tell from the cadence, somebody was singing. A minute later, when they came into good hearing, we could make out the air; it was the "Internationale," a good revolutionary song in those days. They were singing it in four distinct languages. We answered back from inside the jail with an IWW song. Back and forth we sang to each other until dark. That was one of the greatest thrills I ever had.

Under the law in the state of Washington, we could choose separate trials. Just imagine how long it would take and how much it would cost them, one trial at a time, for seventy-four cases. The state started with the trial of Thomas H. Tracy. The prosecution went first. They had a witness, A Judas among us, who was supposed to put the finger on Tracy as the killer. Instead, when they asked if he had seen anyone armed on the *Verona*, he pointed to someone other than Tracy. "There is the man," he said. After examination of scores of prosecution witnesses, no one was sure who had killed the deputy we were accused of doing in. We were convinced he had stopped a bullet fired by his own side.

Billings testified that he used his gun to force the engineer to move the *Verona* back from the dock, away from the volley of bullets. When George Vanderveer, our lawyer, asked him why he carried a gun on November fifth, he told of his beating at Beverly Park. Billings said, "I didn't intend to let anybody beat me up like I was beaten on October thirtieth." I was called to the stand to verify that Billings and Legg had gone and forced the engineer, who had left us at the mercy of McRae, to back the boat out.

It was a coincidence. That damned figure five kept going through everything. We brought back five dead men on the *Verona*. It happened on the fifth of November. The trial started on the fifth of the month. It finally came to an end on May 5, 1917, with the acquittal of Thomas H. Tracy. With Snohomish County broke, they dropped the charges on the rest of us and turned us loose. No one was ever charged with the murders of the Wobblies.

You lock a man up for the length of time we were in jail and that's not so funny. There's far more bad things that happen than good. And if you let go of yourself, you could go crazy. You could come out with such an embittered hatred that your life would be miserable from then on. But we were a bunch of determined and spirited Wobblies. We laughed lest we weep.

BOL-SHE-VEEK

(Published in *Public*, July 19, 1919)

I mustn't call you "Miky"
and you mustn't call me "wop,"
For Uncle Sammy says it's wrong
and hints we ought to stop;
But don't you fret, there's still
one name that I'm allowed to speak,
So when I disagree with you I'll call
you Bol-she-vik! veek! veek!
It's a scream and it's a shriek;
It's a rapid-fire response to any
heresy you squeak.

You believe in votes for women? Yah!
the Bolsheviki do.
And shorter hours? And land reforms?
They're Bolshevistic, too.
"The Recall" and other things like that,
are dangerous to seek;
Don't tell me you believe 'em or I'll
call you Bolshevik!
Bolshevik! veek! veek!
A reformer is a freak!
But here's a name to stop him, for it's
like a lightning streak.

William Patterson, *THE MAN WHO CRIED GENOCIDE*

Born in 1891, William L. Patterson first gained national notoriety in 1931 when he defended the Scottsboro boys, nine young black men who had been accused of raping two white women on a train. The young men were quickly sentenced to die, convicted in an Alabama court whose proceedings were far from those guaranteed by the U.S. Constitution. William Patterson spent over fifty years as a member of the Communist party and as a lawyer always willing to defend the downtrodden, regardless of race, religion, or color. The Foreword *from* The Man Who Cried Genocide: an Autobiography *(International Publishers, 1971) gives an introduction to his life, followed by his description of his involvement in the infamous Sacco-Vanzetti Case, an involvement that resulted in his joining the American Communist Party.*

FOREWORD

In these pages I look back over nearly eight decades of my life, in an attempt to record one Black man's journey through the jungles of bigotry in this land. I am not unaware of my own relative good fortune -- I did not get enough formal education to acquire a law degree, and I have found fulfillment in family, friends, associates and in work. Nevertheless, I have never been able to escape or forget the pervasive racism that poisons the air. Son of a slave mother who had made her hazardous and heroic way from the South of her bondage to the West Coast, I could no more evade the clash with racism than a fish could live out of water.

My color and my family's poverty made the attainment of a law degree an arduous task -- interrupted by a variety of jobs, including several voyages abroad as a seaman. Later, practicing law in the teeming streets of Harlem, I got the full impact of the brutal treatment perpetrated upon the Black people -- and its ravages. I found I could not in good conscience continue in the practice of law for personal profit, and before long I had embarked on another educational process -- one that was to prepare me to serve in the crucial civil rights and political struggles of our time.

As it happened, it was in the historic campaign to save two white men, Sacco and Vanzetti, that I first joined actively with the progressive men and women who were participating in the struggle. My closest associates, it turned out , were Communists, and I began to sense that the conscience of man has no color. My cumulative indignation at racial injustice was augmented by this spectacle of class injustice. How implacably the Commonwealth of Massachusetts wreaked its vengeance against a poor shoemaker and a fish peddler -- because they dared to be radicals! Ignoring the outraged cries of millions of decent people throughout the world, ignoring the lack of evidence to prove their case, the state and the prosecutors put two Italian workers to death. And the world marvelled at the courage and dignity with which they met their fate.

It began to dawn on me that the schools I had attended were not in the slightest concerned about the basic causes of injustice or racial persecution. Indeed, they dealt in euphemisms and misinformation. A great majority of journalists, officials, politicians, authors -- sharing the comforts and immunities of the ruling class -- were apologists locked into the conspiracy to obscure the trust about the persecution of Black men, their history, their contributions to America. Few writers understood the destructive impact of racism on both the Black and the white people of our country, threatening its very survival.

With the help of my new progressive and Communist friends, I began to explore the roots of society's most rampant diseases -- racism and exploitation. They lay deep in the imperative for continuing profit and power among those who controlled our economy, our legal system, our government. As time went on, it became crystal-clear to me that the horrors of color persecution and poverty could only be fully grappled with in a struggle against the economic and social forces that had spawned them. In my special concern with the oppression of Black men and women, I felt it was essential to achieve unity between Black and white workers -- nothing was more certain than that the powers that be were concerned with preventing that unity at all costs.

If, in these pages, I direct my sharpest barbs against racism, it is because I could not get away from it---it was my constant and unwanted companion. How could I possibly speak dispassionately of the crimes committed in its name? But the military-industrial-governmental complex lays heavy burdens on other minority peoples as well as on white workers, turning them, periodically or chronically into jobless, homeless expatriates in a land of plenty. To me, the only hope lay in socialism -- the only system that had shown itself capably of ending the terrible contradictions of a profit society. When I saw that the Communist Party was taking the lead in the struggle for the rights of minorities and of labor, exposing the role of imperialism in conquest and war, I found that my constant concern with the racist issue became an integral part of the broader struggle for human rights everywhere.

If Uncle Sam has made my color the dominating factor in my personal story and the central theme of this book, I have been far from a stranger to all the other struggles for justice of this half-century. The number of years one man has lived, his intellectual growth, his political dedication are, however, not alone decisive -- fierce, persistent and relentless battle by all who want freedom and love justice must be waged unremittingly. The cumulative damage sustained by the bodies and minds of people too long abused must be mitigated, must be exposed. New an insidious form of lynching, of genocide creeping in through the back door even when some small degree of progress has been achieved and token opportunities won.

In defending the victims of oppression and legal lynching during the 1930's and 40's, the organizations with which I was identified became deeply involved in a long procession of campaigns--some of them of world-wide impact. The Scottsboro Boys, Willie McGee, the Martinsville Seven, uncounted "little Scottsboro cases" absorbed our energies as we worked to get the facts before the public, to develop the mass action without which legal justice was a will-o'-the-wisp. Cases like these, under the aegis of either the International Defense or later, the Civil Rights Congress, which I headed, occupied my life during these years.

We had lived through the depression of '29, with its evictions, rent strikes, Hoovervilles, hunger marches--in all of which I and my Party took an active part--organizing, teaching, writing, publishing, speaking. Through these crowded days, through the months and years of inquisitions and jailings and abuse, I continued to study the science of Marxism-Leninism both here and in the Soviet Union and to deepen my understanding of the class struggle.

The period ushered in by the defeat of Hitler and his racist myths of blond Aryan supremacy marked one of the great turning points of history. Millions of people in Europe and Asia gained their political freedom; the victory of the Allies (with the immeasurable contribution in lives and treasure from the Soviet Union) seemed to prepare the way for a better era. The United Nations was established with its aim to "reaffirm faith in fundamental rights, in the dignity and worth of the human person, in the equal rights of men and women."

The trial of the German war criminals had been held; for the first time in history the instigators of an aggressive war were placed in the dock as criminals. The Black soldiers who had helped smash the Hitler war machine and the Blacks at home felt there was some hope that the myths of white superiority were on their way out. A good part of the content of Justice Jackson's opening address to the UN about the Nazi war criminals could apply equally to the racists in our own country.

But the Black soldiers were soon disillusioned; even while still in uniform, they were lynched when they demanded recognition and respect for their constitutional rights. Black workers were the first to be fired, and their protests were stifled by the stark terror incited by the tycoons who controlled big business and the media of propaganda. And to administrative branch of the government, the judiciary nor the legislature ever made any serious effort to defend the victims.

The civil rights fights of the post World War II era were in many cases linked with these protest struggles and with the efforts made by various defense organizations and groups to protect the lives of Black men, women and youth victimized by false accusations of rape and other crimes. No Black man could expect even a semblance of legal justice in or out of the South (nor could union organizers nor civil rights workers). (One of the tactics of our struggle was confirmed beyond all doubt -- legal defense was almost useless in itself, since officers of the law were so often implicated in the indiscriminate murder of Black men in the South. It was proved beyond doubt that mass indignation and protest action had to be mobilized in overwhelming degree to make any dent at all in the solid front of blind bigotry. Such demonstrations do not guarantee a people's justice, but without them the hope is slim indeed.)

These methods were, of course, the forerunners of today's sit-ins, strikes, protest marches, peace rallies. Few organizations would now plan a campaign that did not include mass protests in various forms. The social forces engaged in fiercely fought civil rights battles of the 1940's and 1950's still confront each other. At stake in many a legal battle there still is the liberation of the Black man, his very survival, as harsh sentences, prohibitive bail, naked murder are metered out to the militants.

The cry of genocide is raised once again, as it was in 1951 by the Civil Rights Congress, under whose aegis Paul Robeson led a delegation to present the petition, *We Charge Genocide: The Crime of Government Against the Negro People* to the Secretariat of the UN in New York, while I did the same to the UN General Assembly then meeting in Paris. The petition was a detailed documentation of hundreds of cases of murder bombing, torture of Black nationals in the United States. It dealt unsparingly with "mass murder on the score of race that had been sanctified by law" and it stated "never have so many individuals been so ruthlessly destroyed amid so many tributes to the sacredness of the individual."

We live in a land into whose development the blood and sweat of millions of Black men have, for centuries, been poured. As slaves, these men made cotton king, felled forests, built railroads and cities. Now their children must spend their lives in slums and ghettos. They have never been permitted to enjoy the feeling of belonging to the nation their fathers helped to build and mold. Americans by birth and historical development, they will accept nothing less than equality for all.

Crispus Attucks, a Black freeman, was one of the first to die for liberty. Black slaves and freemen fought under George Washington and Lafayette throughout the Revolutionary War. "Give us this day," their children say, "the equality of rights we have won on blood-drenched battlefields, fighting for those who now rule this country. Give us this day the inalienable rights denied us as human beings and the civil rights denied us as citizens."

In 1976 this country will celebrate the 200th anniversary of its independence. Will we celebrate it as one national or as a nation with the majority of Blacks still psychologically and economically enslaved, and the great majority of whites dehumanized by their own prolonged acceptance and participation in this monstrous wrong?

Unless there is equality of opportunity and rights for all, the "law and order" of ruling class America becomes tyranny; the protest actions of those who are denied their rights are called "lawlessness," and their suppression becomes the order of the day. The constitutional basis for a legal struggle for redress of grievances is destroyed, and the ghettos into which the exploited, oppressed Black and other minorities have been herded become occupied territory on which every known degradation can be grafted.

An ideological struggle is being waged throughout the world for the minds of men; the fight against racism becomes an integral part of the fight for peace and freedom throughout the world. The socialist sector of the world has proven how ignorance and poverty can be overcome for the millions, and devotes its energies to trying to build a society in which there will be an end to war and racism and exploitation.

Today, as liberation struggles multiply throughout the world, we still live in the shadow of the atomic bomb; Vietnam, one of the cruelest wars in the history of the United States, robs our people of resources needed desperately to heal the sick, educate our children, house our homeless -- while it engages in the genocidal destruction of the Indochinese peoples. The issues have been more sharply drawn; we see on all hands the collapse of public and private services and the pollution of our continent. We see our country's plots to thwart peoples' revolutions wherever they raise their heads, to make the whole earth subject to its domination. But the enemy is not invincible. The youth of the land and the oppressed more and more reject the false and murderous standards foisted upon them; the socialist states act as a powerful counterbalance to imperialist depredations.

But it was never more imperative that we direct our energies through organized political channels. Millions of our fellow-Americans are still entrapped in the web of white supremacy, as well as in the illusion that the Unites States fights wars only in defense of democracy. The majority of such people can still be won for the fight against racism and imperialism -- especially if they are made to realize that their own interests are more and more jeopardized by unemployment, inflation, suppression of dissent as a result of these policies.

May the record of my experiences in this battle add some useful first-hand evidence from one man who was deeply involved. The government and its institutions still belong of right to the people, as Abraham Lincoln said. But they must take it over. If I have dwelt largely upon my identity as a Black man profoundly concerned with the agony of my race, it is because I know that a decisive part of the rebellion against tyranny will emanate from the most oppressed.

Born out of struggle, they have an affinity with all who fight for the liberation of mankind.

So I hope I have brought you some news of the battle as it was waged for half century--in preparation for the greater struggles which are as inevitable as the dawn.

New York, November 1970.

SACCO AND VANZETTI -- A TURNING POINT

One of the regular visitors to our law office was Richard B. Moore, a wise and learned man. He called my attention to the way in which the political contributions and gains of Black men during the Civil War and Reconstruction were wiped from the slate of history. He pointed out how racism demolished the new constitutional provisions. Moore forced me to seek answers to some basic questions: How could the political gains be restored, consolidated? Who in society would undertake the monumental task involved?

On each visit, Moore presented one legal case after another in which the law was used to deny the Black man his constitutional rights. He proved how futile it was for a Black American to rely solely on U.S. laws--administered and manipulated by racists--as liberating instruments. What he said made sense: Those who sit in the judicial seats of the mighty, deciding today's crucial problems on the basis of ancient precedents, can seldom decide in favor of progress: the search for precedents leads them to those decisions by which the ruling class has established its power.

Moore then began jogging my conscience about what he called the legal lynching being prepared for Nicola Sacco and Bartolomeo Vanzetti, two Italian workers whose execution by the State of Massachusetts was nearing. As an oppressed Black fellow-American, Moore argues, I should be interested. I decided I had no other alternative: I had either to join the battle for the lives of two innocent Italians or to ignore my kinship with these men.

I had come to the crossroads. Every step along the capitalist road seemed to lead to the swamp of moral and political corruption. The first stop on "freedom road" was Boston, Massachusetts, where thousands of concerned and earnest men and women were fighting to save two white working men whose ideology threatened the status quo. In another part of the country, the setting might have been a tree with stout limbs and a rope all ready for a Black man who would "dance on air." As a Black man and as a member of the human family, I was compelled to join the Sacco-Vanzetti freedom fighters.

Along with the millions of immigrants pouring into the United States during the early years of this century were two young Italians -- Vanzetti was 20, Sacco, eighteen. both young men were poor, both hoped to find in America something of that dream of prosperity and freedom that made this country in those days the magnet for the downtrodden of the world. Both men were dedicated to working-class solidarity and all that was humanist in the traditions of their former homeland. They loved people, they had sympathy and understanding of workers' problems in the United States. And they never hesitated to come to the aid of a neighbor in trouble or of workers fighting against the brutal exploitation then practiced in the factories along the Eastern seaboard.

Vanzetti loved to read. He knew Dante's work, the pride of Italian literature. He loved Puccini's music. His mind was always reaching out to grasp the deeper meanings of life, to understand why in a country as rich as ours workers were driven to exhaustion while others did nothing but clip coupons; why racial hatred and discrimination existed against their Black brothers.

If Vanzetti had little formal education, he read widely -- Marx, Charles Darwin, Leo Tolstoy, Victor Hugo, Maxim Gorky, Emile Zola and scores of others. "I learned," he was to write later, while he was in his death cell in Charlestown prison, "that class-consciousness was not a phrase invented by propagandists, but was a real, vital force, and that those who felt its significance were no longer beasts of burden but human beings."

Sacco and Vanzetti became friends during World War I. Rather than go to war to kill their fellow-workers, they had joined a group of anarchists who went to live in Mexico for the duration of the war. Their friendship continued when they returned to Massachusetts.

In the police files there was quite a dossier under the designation "agitators" concerning these two men. Vanzetti had led a strike at a cordage factory for which he was blacklisted. Sacco had raised money to fight frame-ups, he had walked picket lines, had been arrested for demonstrating. Both were very active in the defense of the foreign-born, who were at that time the targets of a sweeping witch-hunt, under the guidance of U.S. Attorney General A. Mitchell Palmer and J. Edgar Hoover. The two friends had organized protest meetings, raised defense money, distributed handbills. They were often followed by spies hired by the federal government.

A protest meeting that Sacco and Vanzetti were organizing for May 9, 1920 never came off. On May 5 they were arrested, charged with dangerous radical activities. But even the authorities must have felt this an insufficient charge, for they added another -- they associated them with a payroll robbery at South Braintree, Mass., on April 15, 1920, in which two guards had been killed.

At their trial, Judge Webster Thayer, who presided, revealed at every turn his marked hatred for the two Italians. Every effort was made by the press and the authorities to whip up mass mob hysteria. The courtroom was surrounded with extra guards, and everyone entering it was searched. Suborned witnesses calmly lied on the stand, with the knowledge, undoubtedly, that even if they were charged with having given perjured testimony they would go free. On July 14, 1921, a jury pronounced Sacco and Vanzetti guilty and they were sentenced to be executed. But the fight to save them was to go on for six years, and the marching feet of the protestors shook cities all around the world.

The trial was to reveal to millions the class nature of justice in the United States. It was a mockery of the word "justice"--no less than had been the trials of hundreds of Blacks who fought for their rights. The Massachusetts State Supreme Court disgraced itself by turning down the appeal. When, in order to quiet the mounting indignation, Governor Alan T. Fuller appointed three of the state's most "distinguished" men (A. Lawrence Lowell, president of Harvard; Samuel Stratton, president Massachusetts Institute of Technology and Robert A. Grant, a Retired probate judge), they went along with the frame-up.

I was not surprised. For, after all, who were Sacco and Vanzetti? Poor immigrants, members of a national minority that had not yet established any political power; no aura of prestige or heroism surrounded them as they moved to the front of the state of history; they had been virtually unknown; they were anarchists but there was no anarchist movement.

It was three years since a working-class government, in alliance with the peasantry, had come into power in Russia; socialism, which had been haunting Europe since 1848, now had flesh and blood; it had a voice in the councils of nations. In the effort to enlist the support of the working class in the war, the capitalist rulers, under pressure, made promises of a better life. After the war, workingmen all over the world were calling for the redemption of these promises. They were prepared to fight for a better life.

The situation was worst of all for Negroes; it was also bad for other minorities; the differences were only those of degree. In the labor markets the Italian was a rung above the Black man. Because he was dark-skinned and a South European, he was catalogued below the Anglo-Saxon, the Scandinavian and other Western Europeans.

I have sketched in this background to emphasize my identification of the victimized Sacco and Vanzetti with the poor and exploited everywhere and with my own betrayed people. I was standing on the threshold of understanding that the struggle of the Blacks was inseparable from the class struggle.

In *The Case of Sacco and Vanzetti*, Felix Frankfurter had written: "By systematic exploitation of the defendants' alien blood, their imperfect knowledge of English, their unpopular social views and opposition to war, the District Attorney invoked against them a riot of political passion and patriotic sentiment; and the trial judge connived at -- one had almost written 'cooperated in' -- the process."

Here was the challenge I had evaded when the Mooney case came into my life. Would I sidestep it again? Or would I face up to the challenge? What Frankfurter called "alien blood" might well have been"black skin". Although the attack on Mooney was an attack on the trade unions and on all oppressed people, he himself did not associate his persecution with the injustices perpetrated on Black people. The case against the two Italians was an attack on the foreign-born, the members of a minority, designed to create fear and prejudice among native-born Americans, to discredit the influence that revolutionary ideas might have on the working class--perhaps especially on the Black masses.

I discussed these questions with my partners. Both men were deeply moved by what I said, but they were of the opinion that any effort on our part in behalf of the accused men would wreck the fortunes of our firm. Dyett and Hall were looking forward to a future in which they might receive high posts from the Democratic party political machine. They did not want to become involved in unorthodox crusades.

The final argument was: "Pat, those guys are Communists! The freedom you talk about is beyond me. I want to be free; if the other guy does, let him earn it like I expect to."

If Communists were to be denied constitutional rights because they were Communists, and Negroes were to be denied those rights because they were Blacks, where would political persecution end? Would only those who were white and Anglo-Saxon and who accepted the gospel of the rulers of the United States be entitled to the protection of the Constitution? If so, the Constitution became the property of only those with economic and political power.

I called meetings in the office. To these came young lawyers, doctors, even members of the clergy, but most of them were against my position. Among those with whom I now discussed the case were a number of leading Black Communists -- Richard Moore, Cyril Briggs, Otto Huiswood, Lovett Fort Whitman, and Grace Campbell. Grace was a magnificent Black women, a school teacher, who had been dismissed because of her political views. These friends talked to me, strengthened my morale with plenty of facts. The powerful writing of Art Shields in the *Daily Worker* also affected me deeply. I was convinced I had to use my profession as a weapon for freedom. If this case were won, that victory in itself would be a blow in behalf of all those seeking equality of rights.

History records the final fight for Sacco and Vanzetti and how it rallied the support of good people around the world. In Paris, London, Madrid, Havana, Mexico City, Buenos Aries, Bombay and Moscow, there were massive rallies. Of course, those who led them were accused of being Communists. Romain Rolland, George Bernard Shaw, Albert Einstein, John Galsworthy, Martin Anderson Nexo, Sinclair Lewis, H.G. Wells and hundreds of other world citizens sent impassioned pleas for their lives, as did Eugene Debs and Anatole France. Were all of these distinguished men following the lead of Communists? I did not believe it.

Vanzetti himself had called for unity in the struggle of white and Negro and for white support of the Negroes' political demands. His position was far more advanced than that of most American labor leaders and that of the American Federation of Labor.

In May 1926, Vanzetti wrote to the International Labor Council as follows: "I repeat, I will repeat to the last, only the people, our Comrades, our friends, the world revolutionary proletariat, can save us from the powers of the capitalist reactionary hyenas, or vindicate our names and our blood before history....

"There are some who think that our case is a trial for a common crime; that our friends should contest our innocence but not turn the case into a political issue, because it would only damage us. Well, I could answer to them all that our case is even more than a political case; it is a case of class war in which our enemies are personally interested to lose us -- not only for class purposes but for personal passions, resentments and fears..."

I decided to go to Boston.

It would have been unwise for me to go alone. I was not known outside Harlem and I would have been lost in the zealous but largely disorganized forces in, or hurrying toward, Boston. There was one direction in which I could turn.

The International Labor Defense, a working-class organization, had been a party to the creation of a Sacco-Vanzetti Emergency Defense Committee; Vito Marcantonio was its president. This fearless lawyer and humanitarian was later to serve with distinction in Congress. Communists, too, were an accepted and conspicuously active part of the committee, which was organizing people to go to Boston. I went down to the ILD office and signed up for the trip.

Rose Baron, the head of the defense committee, greeted me warmly and was one of the people who accompanied me on the trip. She and a jovial Communist leader, Alfred Wagenknecht, made sure that stops for lunch and other needs were made where I would not be refused and insulted because of my color. I made a mental note of that and vowed never to forget it. It was an evidence of sensitivity that touched me. I was being made part of a great struggle without the slightest trace of prejudice.

We arrived in Boston in the evening and drove to Hanover Street, where an office of the defense committee was located. There was just time to wash and get a bite to eat before assignments to cover meetings were handed out. I was assigned to speak at a meeting covered by Paxton Hibben, one of America's outstanding liberals. Other speakers included Ella Reeve Bloor--Mother Bloor--a revolutionary spirit of amazing energy and wisdom, known from coast to coast as one of the great fighters for human rights. There was also Mike Gold, one of the most noted writers on the Left, an editor of the *Masses* and author of *Jews Without Money*.

I was to learn more about Mike. He was seeking a new way of life, a new America, and he believed that he saw in socialism the goal through which all he dreamed of would be attained. Both his prose and his poetry were dedicated to the revolutionary path of struggle. Mike was a friend of Claude McKay, Langston Hughes, Jean Toomer, and other Negro writers whose voices carried overtones of militancy.

On the platform Mike Gold was a deeply earnest speaker. He drew a parallel between the great mass of Jewish immigrants and the Italians, who were also newcomers to the promised land. He read the famous poem of Emma Lazarus telling of the "huddled masses yearning to breathe free" and of the Goddess of Liberty "lifting her lamp beside the golden door." Mike told the story of the Jew and the Italian as garment workers, and his description of their common plight showed how most of the rosy promises had been broken. He called attention to my presence on the platform and spoke of its significance. Then I was called upon to speak.

The plea for unity which I voiced contained a somewhat different message. I tried to show why I had come to Boston to throw myself into the case of Sacco and Vanzetti. I wanted to help unify America in opposing the persecution of these two members of a minority group; I wanted to associate the struggle for their lives with that which Negroes had waged to save their sons and daughters, condemned to ostracism and worse for the crime of being born Black.

Mother Bloor, following me, linked the arrest, trial and conviction of Sacco and Vanzetti with the Palmer raids and the rise of J. Edgar Hoover. Thousands of men had been arrested; hundreds of the foreign-born, who had been welcomed so long as they accepted the ideology of capitalism, were now being deported. But, she pointed out, the slander of the U.S. Department of Justice against the Communists had failed to stampede the American people. The effort to whip up anti-Red hysteria even against Sacco and Vanzetti had fallen flat.

The meeting was a milestone for me. After accepting Mike Gold's invitation to share his room, the next day I was assigned to the picket line on Boston Common. On the Common stood a statue of Crispus Attucks, a Black man who was said to have been the first man to die in the Revolutionary War. I looked into the bronze face and thought what a great and far-sighted American this Black man had been! It was doubtful that this former slave could read -- but he could think. He was against slavery and for the independence of this land. He must have seen in the Revolution a step toward the ending of slavery.

Among others in that picket line were Edna St. Vincent Millay, Clarina Michelson, John Dos Passos, John Howard Lawson and my new friends, Mike Gold and Mother Bloor. Had I been brought forward because of my color? No matter, I was proud to be there. To many of the liberals I know I was something of a curiosity--Negroes were not regarded as an organic part of the progressive people of the land. Was that our fault or theirs? Perhaps it was only a result of centuries of miseducation, of lies that maligned Black men and denied the great role they had played and could play in the battle for freedom.

It was not long before the attack came. Soon, beside the picket signs reading "Save Sacco and Vanzetti," other signs were held up, "Down with the Communists," "Lynch the Reds." These were Boston's hoodlums mobilized by the police, and believing the most slanderous of the lies. Then came the cops themselves -- mounted and afoot -- the city's upholders of law and order.

A notable passage in Upton Sinclair's *Boston*, a semi-fictionalized account of the Sacco-Vanzetti affair, gives this description of that day's events on the Common:

"There was John Dos Passos, faithful son of Harvard, and John Howard Lawson, another one of the 'New Playwrights' from Greenwich Village. There was Clarina Michelson, ready to do the hard work again, and William Patterson, a Negro lawyer from New York, running the greatest risk of any of them, with his black face not to be disguised. Just up Beacon Street was the Shaw Monument, with figures in perennial bronze, of unmistakable Negro boys in uniforms, led by a young Boston blueblood on horseback; no doubt Patterson had looked at this, and drawn courage from it....

"The trooper speeds on; he has spied the black face, and wants that most of all. The Negro runs, and the rider rears the front of his steed, intending to strike him down with the iron-shod hoofs. But fortunately there is a tree, and the Negro leaps behind it; and a man can run around a tree faster than the best-trained police-mount -- the dapper and genial William Patterson proves it by making five complete circuits before he runs into the arms of an ordinary cop, who grabs him by the collar and tears off his sign and tramples it in the dirt, and then starts to march him away. 'Well," he remarks sociably, 'This is the first time I ever see a nigger bastard that was a communist.' The lawyer is surprised, because he has been given to understand that that particular word is barred from the Common. Mike Crowley was so shocked, two weeks ago, when Mary Donovan tacked up a sign to a tree: 'Did you see what I did to those anarchistic bastards? -- Judge Thayer.' But apparently the police did not have to obey their own laws."

But it was not the policeman's name-calling that surprised me--I expected that, law or no law. It was the source of the policeman's annoyance that set me thinking, the fact that he had never before seen a black Communist. I pondered this situation. The National Association for the Advancement of Colored People had never sought to align the political struggles of the Negro people with those of another group. They had sought to draw white men into court campaigns which they had organized and led in behalf of Negroes. But they had mounted no political campaign, participated in no mass demonstrations and had confined themselves to legal action. The Garvey movement, of course, was strictly a separatist movement. In it, the Negro rejected his heritage in America, won in labor and blood.

Now the cop had seen something new. He had seen a Black man concerned with the legal persecution of white Americans who were foreign born--this Negro had to be something special. Nothing less than "a Communist bastard."

The patrol wagon came, and the police of Boston now found themselves confronted with another dilemma. They had a Black man to take to the Joy Street station house along with a white woman, Clarina Michelson. But they could not allow him to ride on the inside of a patrol wagon with a white woman. So I was walked to the jail; and, of course, I was not permitted to share a cell with a white American. The other men with whom I had marched on the picket line made a fight to have me changed over to the pen they were in, but this was no go in Boston, the cradle of the American Revolution.

We were all bailed out and immediately went back to the picket line. I suppose if we had not been so close to the tragic outcome, we would have laughed at our jailers. They were acting in mechanical obedience to the racist teaching that was the only brand of democracy that made sense to them.

The creative artists were the backbone of the picket line. The learned professors and the leaders of organized labor were missing. America's labor leaders were to permit the framed Italians to go to the electric chair without mobilizing for the life-and-death struggle. The absence of the NAACP could be understood, as could that of the Urban League and the Garveyites. But how explain labor? Thousands in the rank and file fought for Sacco and Vanzetti; almost no officials.

Powers Hapgood, a brilliant young Harvard graduate, was everywhere, speaking and agitating. Three times he had been arrested, each time returning to the picket line upon his release. The fourth time he was shunted by a police captain to a psychopathic ward.

It usually took at least ten days to get in and out of Boston's psychopathic ward. The police did not hesitate to send people there who were obnoxious to them. Hapgood was held for only one day. After my third arrest the same captain threatened that if I were arrested again he would take care of me in the same manner--no doubt with jim crow accessories. My presence in Boston was becoming a positive annoyance.

Arthur Garfield Hays, one of the country's best civil liberties lawyers, handled the affair in court. He was the legal adviser to most of those arrested, and it was his opinion that I had better not get arrested again. My new friends agreed, and so I stayed off the picket lines.

Shortly after midnight, August 22, 1927, the Commonwealth of Massachusetts executed Nicola Sacco and Bartolomeo Vanzetti. Who could doubt that it was at the behest of those industrialists who wanted to do away with anything that seemed "communistic" to them, and that they were aided and abetted by the Department of Justice and the Supreme Court? And everything was done in accordance with law and order.

I stood in the crowd outside the Charlestown prison, as close to the gates as the hundreds of armed guards would permit. The lights in the prison windows dimmed three times, ending our last hopes.

For me, the world had changed. American reaction had won a victory of the bodies of two men, but its effort to stampede the people had ended in utter failure. In every capital and large city of the world there were mass protest meetings. Men everywhere around the globe came together -- unbelieving. They stood in the market squares of little Italian towns; they packed the streets not only in Paris, New York, Berlin and London but in provincial towns along the Rhine, in the Alps, along the Mediterranean, in Rocky Mountain mining camps, and on the pampas of Argentina. Hundreds of thousands went on strike, in New York, Pennsylvania, Colorado, Illinois, New Jersey. Police clashed with a throng of 50,000 gathered in New York's Union Square; there were similar gatherings in Chicago and Philadelphia. Communists led these demonstrations.

Most of my Negro friends couldn't see the political significance of all this! Japanese labor leaders sent a deputation to the American Embassy in Tokyo. In the Soviet Union there were hundreds of meetings, and in Latin America there were tens of protest rallies. If there were none in the ghettos of America, I think I knew the reason why: The thinking of our people had been ghettoized; they had been alienated from their white fellow-workers. They had been made to feel themselves apart from the general stream -- inferior.

I returned to New York and the office of Dyett, Hall and Patterson, but the fact that Sacco and Vanzetti had been executed stayed in my mind. They would have no more to say and yet what they had said would live with me forever. My faith in the law as a weapon of democracy in the Untied States was gone. I could not practice law again, at least not as I had before. The prestige that came to the Black lawyer came too often at the expense of his people's rights and of his own integrity.

I reread Vanzetti's testimony to the white American jury that had condemned him to death. It was a document that few columnists had paid attention to, with the honorable exception of Heywood Broun. In it Vanzetti scathingly analyzed and dissected our society; he exposed the class character of those who were to murder him and his comrade. I cannot refrain from quoting some passages:

"...I teach over here men who is with me. The free idea give any man a chance to profess his own idea, not the supreme idea...but to give a chance to print and education, literature, free speech...

"I could see the best men, intelligent, education, they had been arrested and sent to prison and died in prison for years and years without getting them out, and Debs, one of the great men in his country, he is in prison, still away in prison, because he is a socialist. He wanted the laboring class to have better conditions and better living, more education...(so he gets) prison. Why? Because the capitalist class...they don't want our child to go to high school or college or Harvard College...they don't want the working class educated; they want the working class to be low all the time, be under foot, and not be up with the head...

"So that is why I love people who labor and work and see better conditions every day develop, makes no more war. We no want fight by the gun and don't want to destroy young men. The mother been suffering for building the young men...No war for the civilization of men. They are war for business, million dollar comes on the side...

"That is why my idea I love Socialists. That is why I like people who want education and living, building, who is good, just as much as they could. That is all."

That was Vanzetti's testimony -- a small part of it. And just before the sentence had been passed, when he was asked whether he had anything further to say, he replied:

"This is what I say: I would not wish a dog or a snake the most low and unfortunate creature of the earth -- I would not wish to say of them what I have had to suffer for things that I am not guilty of. I am suffering because I am a radical and indeed I am a radical: I have suffered because I am an Italian, and indeed I am an Italian: I have suffered more for my family and for my beloved than for myself; but I am so convinced to be right that if you could execute me two times and I could be reborn two other times, I would live again to do what I have done already.

" I have finished. Thank you."

The speaker belonged, as he himself has so magnificently said, "to nations."

The significance of the case was tremendous. Sacco and Vanzetti belonged to white and Black, Italian, German, English, Jew, Russian, American -- they belonged to progressive mankind. That was why the ruling-class scavengers did them to death. This kind of belonging led to unity. Success in the people's cause lay in unity in the struggle of the world oppressed.

The more I thought of the beautiful words Vanzetti had spoken, the more clearly I saw that some of the eloquent and articulate intellectuals who had been my fellow-protestors had not grasped the essential meaning of my presence in Boston. They saw me only as a Black man who, out of common decency, had come to help rescue these brave men who were fighting for a better America. I hope I was that, but the dominant feature of the step I had taken was political not moral.

Certainly I was more than the "dapper" figure which Upton Sinclair had drawn to represent me in his novel. Mike Gold and Ella Reeve Bloor had, of course, seen me for what I thought I was -- a new link in a chain that would help hold the progressive forces of our country together and bring white and Black *en masse* to see the mutuality of their interests. I had come back to New York as from a university--but a people's university. Far from being a graduate student, it was the beginning and not the end of the course. I would follow another road of struggle. My law career had come to an end.

The last words spoken by Vanzetti rang in my ears: "If it had not been for these things, I might have lived out my life talking at street corners to scorning men. I might have died, unmarked, unknown, a failure. Now we are not a failure. This is our career and our triumph. Never in our full life could we hope to do such work for tolerance, for justice, for man's understanding of men as now we do by accident. Our words -- our lives -- our pains -- nothing! The taking of our lives -- the lives of a good shoemaker and a poor fish peddler -- all! That last moment belongs to us -- that agony is our triumph!"

Lewis H. Carlson, *THE HOLLYWOOD HEARINGS* (1947)

From its inception in 1938, the House Committee on Un-American Activities devoted most of its investigative energies to ferreting out domestic communists, and its "official" hearings anticipated the many governmental investigations that marked the Second Red Scare. The Committee often planned its investigations to embarrass liberal organizations and individuals at odds with its own narrow, conservative views; hence, labor unions, civil rights workers, peace organizations, liberal politicians, New Deal programs, and leftists everywhere became their targets. But the Committee was equally interested in publicity, and the 1947 Hollywood Hearings brought the Committee its greatest notoriety. It mattered little that the proceedings turned out to be farcical; the Committee had its headlines, and it was headlines that fanned the flames of the Red Scare and created an atmosphere a Joe McCarthy could exploit just a few years later. The following is from J. Parnell Thomas and the House Committee on Un-American Activities, 1938-1948 *(Unpublished Ph.D. Dissertation, Michigan State University, 1967).*

Unquestionably the Hollywood hearings brought the House Committee on Un-American Activities the greatest amount of publicity it had yet received in its stormy nine-year career. J. Parnell Thomas was also brought into the public limelight as never before.

The committee had long showed an inordinate interest in the film industry. As early as 1938, *Life* magazine carried a feature article complete with Martin Dies' allegation that Hollywood was a "hotbed" of Communist activities and pictures of suspected film stars. In 1940 the motion-picture industry was investigated in a series of closed hearings which, according to August Raymond Ogden, "were a credit neither to the committee nor the manner in which they were conducted." In 1945, when the committee was between chairmen, John Rankin forced a renewal of committee interest in Hollywood. The Mississippi Democrat announced that he had received reports that "one of the most dangerous plots ever investigated for the overthrow of this government has its headquarters in Hollywood." However, John Wood, upon his appointment to the chair, made it clear that he did not share Rankin's zeal for hunting subversives in Hollywood, and the investigation was shelved until Thomas became chairman.

One of the eight points in the committee program which Thomas had announced in late 1946 was a proposed investigation of Hollywood. There seemed little doubt that he expected that such an undertaking would bring the committee and himself considerable success, and, as he later told the author, he reserved the preliminary investigation for his own personal attention.

Certainly the anticipated publicity played a role in the chairman's decision to launch the Hollywood investigation, and during the course of the hearings he was most zealous in his press releases. Also the fact that these hearings were allowed to die out when the press was no longer either favorable or particularly interested seemed to support this contention. Then too there was the opportunity to connect the government with the making of certain films which supposedly favored something other than the American way of life. Finally there was something in the man himself that must have made these hearings most appealing to him. Since his earliest days in the New Jersey State Assembly he had exhibited a keen sense for the dramatic, and his long years on the committee had made him appreciate the drama that could surround a spectacular investigation. Surely the vision of a Hollywood setting adorned with some of movieland's brightest stars and presided over by himself must have seemed almost irresistible as J. Parnell Thomas prepared for his greatest role. . . .

The Hollywood Hearings, Washington D.C.

The nine-day Washington hearings earned the committee and J. Parnell Thomas their most sensational coverage. In an atmosphere of a Hollywood first-nighter, the newsreel and television cameras covered the movements of the great and near great of Hollywood as they paraded through the witness box. The *Washington Post* called it "the show of the year," and indeed it was as the committee, in the words of Max Lerner, "tried to track down the footprints of Karl Marx in movieland."

The hearings opened with a lengthy, and rather arbitrary, statement by Thomas. The chairman not only emphasized the magnitude and importance of the task facing the committee, but also the very real danger which he felt the committee had already uncovered in Hollywood:

> *With such vast influence over the lives of American citizens as the motion-picture industry exerts, it is not unnatural--in fact, it is very logical--that subversive and undemocratic forces should attempt to use this medium for un-American purposes.... That Communists have made such an attempt in Hollywood and with considerable success is already evident to this committee from its preliminary investigative work.*

Thomas also used the opportunity to censure some of his old enemies and to present his general views on the Communist movement:

> *The problem of Communist infiltration is not limited to the movie industry. That even our Federal Government has not been immune from the menace is evidenced by the fact that $11,000,000 is now being spent to rid the Federal service of Communists. Communists are also firmly entrenched in control of a number of large and powerful labor unions in the country.... Communists for years have been conducting an unrelentless (sic) 'boring from within' against American democratic institutions. While never possessing a large numerical strength, the Communists nevertheless have found that they could dominate the activities of unions or other mass enterprises in this country by capturing a few strategic positions of leadership.*

He concluded his opening remarks with the usual promise that the hearings would be "fair and impartial...all we are after are the facts." Nothing was said about what the committee would do with "the facts" except, of course, to expose this latest menace to our national well-being.

The committee strategy soon became apparent. Chairman Thomas allowed Stripling to direct the testimony of several leading Hollywood personalities who then told of Communist activity in the movie industry. These friendly witnesses included such top ranking producers as Jack L. Warner, Louis B. Mayer, and Walt Disney; such directors as Sam Wood and Leo McCarey; writers such as Rupert Hughes and Morrie Ryskind; and, above all, such famed actors as Robert Taylor, Gary Cooper, George Murphy, Ronald Reagan, and Adolph Menjou. Included also were Lela Rogers, the mother and manager of Ginger, and the writer, Ayn Rand, two ladies who had long been waging their personal crusade against communism. On the other hand, several film-land personalities suspected of Communist propaganda activities were subpoenaed. They were asked specific questions, which, when they refused to answer, were answered for them by the committee's own investigator, Louis Russell.

The first few days of hearings were taken up by the committee's attempt to show how the Communists had introduced propaganda into Hollywood films, with four pictures receiving special notice. The first witness to testify was Jack L. Warner. Warner generously offered the use of the family savings to establish "a pest-removal fund...to ship to Russia the people who don't like our American system of government and prefer the communistic system to ours." But Warner was not so cooperative when it came to one of his films, *Mission to Moscow*, which the committee was citing as an example of Communist propaganda in a Hollywood picture:

> *If the making of* Mission to Moscow *in 1942 was a subversive activity, then the American Liberty ships which carried food and guns to Russia and the American naval vessels which convoyed them were likewise engaged in subversive activities. The picture was made only to help a desperate war effort and not for posterity.*

Mr. Warner was trying to judge his film in the light of the time in which it was made, but the committee had seldom showed a willingness to evaluate anything in its true time perspective. This became ludicrously obvious when Stripling asked Warner, "Well, due to the present conditions in the international situation, don't you think it was rather dangerous to write about such a disillusionment as was sought in that picture?" Unfortunately, Warner and several of the producers who followed him had not been as farsighted as the committee would have preferred, and the fact that the government might have encouraged such pictures to create a better understanding with one of our wartime allies continued to be evaluated in cold-war terms.

On subjects other than his own movies Warner was quite willing to tell the committee what it wanted to hear. He testified that writers did try to inject lines of propaganda into scripts and that he had fired them for this. He also claimed that ninety-five percent of the attempted Red infiltration into Hollywood was through the Screen Writers Guild. The latter organization would take up a great deal of the committee's time, and membership in which would usually be considered an indication of un-American behavior.

On the afternoon of the first day Samuel Grosvenor Wood, an independent producer-director of some thirty years, testified on alleged Communist attempts to infiltrate the Screen Directors Guild. Wood had been the first president of the Motion Picture Alliance for the Preservation of American Ideals, an organization aimed at thwarting the Communists in the movie industry to which many of the friendly witnesses belonged. Wood, though obviously sympathetic to the aims of the committee, denied that the Communists were exercising any degree of influence in the making and producing of movies; however, he did provide a new twist to the investigation when he suggested that the Communists were trying to "unsell America" by not writing patriotic American themes into their movies. In the forthcoming days Chairman Thomas would often interrupt the testimony to ask the witness if he did not think that Hollywood should make more movies showing the "American way".

Wood provided a note of levity when he was asked by Stripling how one identified a Communist: "If you wanted to drop their rompers you would find the hammer and sickle on their rear ends, I think." This was scarcely the kind of testimony that would make the committee's case against Hollywood more convincing; yet Thomas had only praise for Wood's testimony:

> *Mr. Wood, to use the slang expression, you really lay it on the line. If the great, great majority of persons in industry, labor, and education showed the same amount of courage that you show we would not have to worry about communism or fascism in this country. In other words, you've got guts.*

Louis B. Mayer followed Wood on the stand. Mayer and his film "Song of Russia" were examined, as the committee tried once again to cite a specific example of Red propaganda. *Song of Russia*, which the *New York Times* called "a harmless musical film containing more things American than Russian," starred Robert Taylor and Tschaikowsky's music, a rather ungainly combination. In the spring hearings Taylor had supposedly testified that the government had held up his commission and entrance into the navy until he made this movie. Thomas had cited this as a glaring example of government pressure on the movie industry.

Mayer denied that there had been any government interference, and later he submitted a letter from the Office of War Information to the Department of the Navy which stated that MGM Studios had asked for a delay in the induction of Taylor to permit the completion of the picture. The letter went on to say that the Office of War Information believed that the script would serve a useful purpose in the war effort and that the film "had no political implications, being designed to acquaint the American people with the people of one of our Allied Nations."

Robert Taylor's own testimony, given two days later, must have been an embarrassment to the committee chairman. The film star now confessed that he did not think that *Song of Russia* was made at the suggestion of the government, and he admitted that he had not been forced to make the picture. Again too the committee looked foolish when it allowed one of its special investigators, H. A. Smith, to ask Mayer if the picture showed conditions as they existed in 1947. As the movie was filmed in 1943, this was highly unlikely.

To finish his defense of *Song of Russia*, Mayer cited several reviews from some leading papers:

> *New York Post*: A pretty little romance with a made-in-America back-drop of Russia...cozy, clean, luxuriously musical film.
>
> *London Daily Sketch*: ...turned out to be strictly an American anthem.

Washington Post: It is one film about Russia which will probably be little assailed as propaganda.

New York Herald Tribune: Russia itself has all too little to do with *Song of Russia.*

This scarcely sounded like the pro-Russian film that Chairman Thomas had earlier cited as an example of a subversive Hollywood picture produced under White House pressure, and to refute Mayer's testimony he now called one of the committee's own film critics to the stand. Ayn Rand qualified not only as a movie expert, but the fact that she had lived in Russia until 1926 made her an acceptable judge of that country, though one would have thought of an earlier period than the one in which the committee was interested.

Miss Rand was vehemently anti-Communist, a fact that seemed to cloud her judgment on the subject. She insisted that the very picture of the hammer and sickle in the *Song of Russia* made her so sick that she could not understand how "native Americans" permitted this. The fact that the movie showed happy Russian children and smiling Russian people was also cited by her as proof of the film's unreliability. Such an allegation resulted in the following exchange between Committeeman McDowell and Miss Rand:

Mr. McDowell: You paint a very dismal picture of Russia. You make a great point about the number of children who were unhappy. Doesn't anybody smile in Russia anymore?

Miss Rand: Well, if you ask me literally, pretty much no.

Mr. McDowell: They don't smile?

Miss Rand: Not quite that way, no. If they do, it is privately and accidently. Certainly it is not social. They don't smile in approval of their system.

Miss Rand's final objection to the film was that it had not attacked the Soviet Union as she felt any "honest" American film should, a point with which Chairman Thomas readily agreed.

So ended the first day of the fall hearings. Four rather entertaining witnesses had been heard, two movies were examined for subversive content, and the newspapers had their headlines. But it was only the beginning.

The committee heard three witnesses on the second day, and all three willingly testified on the significant inroads the Communists were making into the movie industry. The first, Adolph Menjou, was another self-styled expert on un-American activities who had not only studied the workings of Communism abroad but who had also determined "its probably effects on the American people if they (sic) ever gain power here." Menjou testified to the Communist propaganda in certain movies, but he admitted that it was difficult to recognize because "it was so subtle that it was never obvious;" nor was he more specific when asked if he actually knew any Communists:

Mr. Menjou: I know a great many people who act an awful lot like Communists....

Mr. Stripling: As an actor, Mr. Menjou, could you tell the committee whether or not an actor in a picture could portray a scene which would in effect serve as propaganda for communism or any other un-American purpose?

Mr. Menjou: Oh, yes, I believe that under certain circumstances a communistic director, a communistic writer, or a communistic actor even if he were under orders from the head of the studio not to inject communism or un-Americanism or subversion into pictures, could easily subvert that order, under the proper circumstances, by a look, by an inflection, by a change in the voice. I think it could be easily done. I have never seen it done, but I think it could be done.

The fact that Menjou admitted he had never seen an example of what he was describing but only "thought" it could be done was scarcely the kind of proof the committee should have been seeking; likewise, Menjou's later comment that anyone applauding or listening to Paul Robeson should be ashamed of his Americanism brought no challenge from the committee. After stating that he was quite sure that Stalin had poisoned Lenin, Menjou concluded his testimony with the promise to move to Texas if the Reds came "because the Texans would kill them on sight."

John Charles Moffitt followed Menjou to the stand. Unlike Menjou, who admitted that the only real Communist he had ever met had been the Russian ambassador to England, Moffitt had seen Communists everywhere. Moffitt had been a motion picture reviewer for Esquire magazine and as such he qualified as one of the reliable critics on the subject of subversive films which the committee had promised.

Moffitt's testimony extended all the way from Hollywood to New York. He statistically declared that "forty-four out of one hundred of the best plays produced on Broadway from 1936 through the season of 1946 have contained material to further the Communist Party line....233 other plays produced during the same period favor the party line." No specific examples were offered; and the witness, under Stripling's gentle prodding, admitted that he had read only the condensed versions in the *Burns Collection of Ten Best Plays*; and as to the other 233 plays cited he confessed that he had not read them all. Moffitt later volunteered that the number of novels "that contained the Communist line during that same period is not complete but the proportions are the same or worse than those of Broadway."

When Moffitt finally returned to the subject of Hollywood, it was to explain how the Communist line was so subtly interjected into pictures. He claimed that he had heard John Howard Lawson, a member of the Screen Writers Guild, give the following lecture to aspiring young actors:

It is your duty to further the class struggle by your performance. If you are nothing more than an extra wearing white flannels on a country club veranda, do your best to appear decadent; do your best to appear to be a snob; do your best to create class antagonism. If you are an extra on a tenement street do your best to look down trodden, do you best to look a victim of existing society.

But when asked about who was responsible for such behavior during the actual filming, Moffitt seemed at a loss:

> *I think that many a time an actor plays that five minutes without knowing the significance of what he is doing. I think on many occasions--I think on practically every occasion that I know of the producer, both the associate producer and the studio heads, was in complete ignorance of what was done. I think very often the director may not know.*

Indeed, in the last analysis it seemed that only Mr. Moffitt and the writer who perpetrated the deed knew what was happening, and this appeared harmless enough. It was remarkable that an individual so lacking in subtlety in his own character could be so adroit at discovering the subversive nuances in the actual films.

The final witness of the day, Ruppert Hughes, testified about a different kind of Communist subversion. Hughes, a screen writer, insisted that no anti-Communist pictures could be made because of the fear of "a conspiracy to wreck the theaters, put stinkpots in the theaters, parade in front, picket them, and everything else." When Hughes claimed that the directors who might have produced anti-Communist pictures were thus scared into silence, he was interrupted by an eager Thomas:

> *Mr. Hughes, you may have brought in a new point that we have not had given to us before, and that is the main reason why the producers do not show anti-Communist films, because of the fear they would have that the Communists would go there and disrupt the audience in the theater and in that way they would not make any money as a result of showing these pictures.*

The next day Committeeman Richard Nixon, referring back to the Hughes testimony, made a telling rebuttal to this type of argument and effectively brought it to an end:

> *If those tactics--the stench bomb, the pickets and the usual tactics which are used by the Communists when they don't like what is going on in the theater, or in any kind of a building--were used, wouldn't that be the finest advertising that a motion picture could get and wouldn't that probably make the picture from the standpoint of the public acceptance?*

Unfortunately Nixon attended few of these hearings on Hollywood. His abilities at cross-examining could have been put to effective use; but, as Thomas later told the author, Nixon felt rather uncomfortable with the committee investigating one of his state's most important industries.

Hughes' final comment on personal liberties brought a fitting close to another hectic and confusing day: "I am the utmost believer in tolerance there ever was, but it is not tolerance to permit people to do things to destroy tolerance."

The third day of the hearings pretty much followed the pattern of the first two. Four sympathetic witnesses were heard, but little in the way of new evidence was added. Stripling continued to handle the major share of the questioning with the other committee members interrupting from time to time to make comments or to pose questions of their own. Thomas too seemed content to let Stripling handle the testimony of the friendly witnesses; the chairman would wait for those of a more hostile nature before giving Stripling much of a helping hand; for the time being he was content to handle the press releases. The hearings were carried on the front pages of most papers, and here it was the chairman who was quoted, not his chief counsel.

A good example of this occurred in the October 22 papers. This was the day after the Menjou-Moffitt-Hughes testimony. Menjou did have his picture on the front pages of the *Washington Post* and the *Chicago Tribune*, but the headlines belonged to Thomas. The chairman had stated that the committee would soon produce evidence that "at least seventy-nine persons in Hollywood" had engaged in subversive activity. In addition, he promised a surprise witness for the following week with evidence on how data on an Army supersonic plane had fallen into Communist hands through a Hollywood literary agent. Even the *New York Times* seemed excited about such disclosures, and its page-one headline read "Seventy-Nine in Hollywood Found Subversive, Inquiry Head Says;" and the subheadline added "Evidence of Communist Spying Will Be Offered Next Week, Thomas Declares." It mattered not that the "surprise witness" turned out to be the committee's own Louis Russel and that his information had been known to the FBI for years; the committee and its chairman had their headlines, and with his promise of greater future disclosures Thomas had adroitly diverted the public's attention from the immediate hearings which had certainly been somewhat less than convincing.

Robert Taylor was the main attraction as the committee went into its third day of hearings. As already noted, Mr. Taylor was a rather confused witness on the subject of whether the government had actually intervened in his *Song of Russia*. The rest of his testimony also suffered from inconsistency. It appeared that Taylor was only ready to take his cues at committee direction, but when these became confused so did Mr. Taylor:

> *Mr. Stripling: Mr. Taylor, do you consider that the motion picture primarily is a vehicle of entertainment and not of propaganda?*
>
> *Mr. Taylor: I certainly do. I think it is the primary job of the motion-picture industry to entertain; nothing more, nothing less.*
>
> *Mr. Stripling: Do you think the industry would be in a better position if it stuck strictly to entertainment without permitting political films to be made, without being so labeled?*
>
> *Mr. Taylor: I certainly do.*

The above testimony was given in reference to alleged Communist attempts to subvert the film industry. When it came time for some Thomas-approved propaganda, Mr. Taylor was forced to contradict himself:

> *Mr. Thomas: Mr. Taylor, are you in favor of the motion-picture industry making anti-Communist pictures giving the facts about communism?*

Mr. Taylor: Congressman Thomas, when the time arrives--and it might not be long--when pictures of that type are indicated as necessary, I believe the motion-picture industry will and should make anti-Communist pictures. When that time is going to be I don't happen to know but I believe they should and would be made.

Robert Taylor had often been publicized as one of the chairman's prize witnesses, but the inadequacy of his testimony made it increasingly evident that Thomas had picked a weak star for top billing. Taylor had proved especially embarrassing with his about-face on the issue of government pressure, and he ended his testimony by confiding to a *New York Times'* reporter that he had never knowingly worked with a Communist.

The last two witnesses of the day did not take up much of the committee's time. Howard Rushmore was an ex-Communist who had served as film critic for the *Daily Worker* and was quite willing to testify on Communist intentions in Hollywood. He did force the committee to take notice when he insisted that the Communist party considered that ninety-nine percent of the actors were "political morons," a statistic that seemed to take on some substance in view of much of their testimony.

Morrie Ryskind provided a bit of comic relief at the end of another exhausting day. Ryskind felt he qualified as an expert on the workings of the Communist movement because, among other reasons, he and his wife had been duped into joining and contributing to Communist-front organizations. He later admitted that "you'd have to be deaf and dumb not to know there are Communists in Hollywood. And even then if you used your nose, you'd know the odor was still there." But other than his admission of his own culpability little new was added.

The fourth day of the hearings saw more of Hollywood's finest parade through the witness stand, and once again all proved to be friendly witnesses. Robert Montgomery, Gary Cooper, George Murphy, and Ronald Reagan headed-up Thursday's all-star cast.

Robert Montgomery, though strongly anti-Communist, testified that the Communists had never dominated the Screen Actors Guild; George Murphy likewise defended the Actor's Guild though he did advocate outlawing the Communist party and the making of anti-Communist films; Ronald Reagan, then the president of the Screen Actors Guild, acknowledged that he had "heard" from reliable sources that certain members of the Guild were Communists. Reagan followed this with a warning which seemed curiously out of step with his own willingness to repeat hearsay evidence:

I hope that we are never prompted by fear or resentment of communism into comprising any of our democratic principles in order to fight them. The best thing to do in opposing those people is to make democracy work.

Gary Cooper tried to be of help to the committee when he testified that he had turned down quite a few scripts because he "thought they were tinged with Communist ideas;" but, even with Thomas encouraging him, he could not recall any specific examples.

One of the most striking things about the entire hearings was the fact that these Hollywood stars were considered experts on the workings of communism by Thomas and the committee. Each of them was asked for his opinion on the proposed legislation to outlaw the Communist party. In response to just such a question from the chairman, Gary Cooper candidly manifested how unqualified he was to venture any kind of an opinion on the subject of communism:

> *I think it would be a good idea, although I have never read Karl Marx, and I don't know the basis of communism, beyond what I have picked up by hearsay. From what I hear, I don't like it because it isn't on the level. So I couldn't possibly answer that question.*

It also became increasingly evident that most of these actors, even with Stripling or Thomas leading them through a well-worn script, were curiously out of their element when on the stage of the Committee on Un-American Activities.

On Friday Mrs. Lela Rogers, the mother and manager of Ginger, and the loudest feminine voice in the Motion Picture Alliance for the Preservation of American Ideals, provided the committee with some testimony which left no doubt about her own anti-Communist convictions. She testified that one of the screen writers whom she knew to be a Communist was Clifford Odets. When asked on what she based her accusation, she replied, "I have here a column of Mr. O. O. McIntyre, datelined January 8, 1936, in which Mr. McIntyre says Mr. Clifford Odets, play writer, is a member of the Communist party. I never saw that denied."

Mrs. Rogers also took Odets to task for writing and directing the screen version of *None But the Lonely Hearts* When McDowell asked for specific examples of Communist propaganda in the movie, Mrs. Rogers' answer, though lengthy, was a classic in its hazy ambiguity and its tortured syntax:

> *I can't quote the lines of the play exactly but I can give you the sense of them. There is one place in which--it is unfair, may I say, to take a scene from its context and try to make it sound like Communist propaganda, because a Communist is very careful, very clever, and very devious in the way he sets the film.*
>
> *If I were to give you a line from that play straight out you would say, 'What is wrong with that line?' unless you knew that the Communist is trying in every way to tear down our free-enterprise system, to make the people lose faith in it, so that they will want to get something else--and the Communists have it waiting for them.*
>
> *I will tell you of one line. The mother in the story runs a second-hand store. The son says to her, 'You are not going to'--in essence, I am not quoting this exactly because I can't remember it exactly--he said to her, 'You are not going to get me to work here and squeeze pennies out of little people poorer than I am.'*
>
> *Now, laid upon the background of--that's the free-enterprise system--trade, and we don't necessarily squeeze pennies from people poorer than we are. Many people are poorer and many people are richer.*

As I say, you find yourself in an awful hole the moment you start to remove one of the scenes from its context.

If Mrs. Rogers was getting herself into "an awful hole," the committee did not seen to notice, and her advice too was solicited on the subject of outlawing the Communist party:

Well, I would suggest that the Congress of the United States immediately enact such legislation as will preserve the Bill of Rights to the people for whom it was designed.

When she also tried to explain how the Communists could be so effective in Hollywood when they comprised only about one percent of the movie population, she engaged in the following interesting exchange with Committeeman Richard Vail:

Mr. Vail: But, in other words, to be effective on the Hollywood scene wouldn't you imagine that they have to have greater numerical strength, greater than one percent.

Mrs. Rogers: You are thinking like an American, sir.

Mr. Vail: That is the way I like to think.

Mrs. Rogers: That is right, and you should, and that is why it is so hard for the Americans to understand.

That Thomas and his committee could, with complete sincerity, present such a witness was remarkable in itself, but the fact that they accepted her testimony almost without challenge seemed even more extraordinary. Committeeman McDowell summed it up when he called Lela Rogers "one of the outstanding experts on communism in the United States, and particularly in the amusement industry;" but, pathetically enough, it was her industrious testimony that seemed amusing.

The last of the sympathetic notables was Walt Disney. He had testified before the committee on previous occasions and it knew what to expect. Disney told of Communists trying to organize his studio workers who, according to Mr. Disney, were opposed to any attempts at such pressure. Disney too had an interesting way of judging one's Americanism as in the following case concerning one of his employees he had recently fired:

I looked into his record and I found, number one, that he had no religion; and, number two, that he had spent considerable time at the Moscow Art Theater studying art direction or something.

So ended the parade of stars. They had testified that there were Communists in Hollywood, and some of them had found the Reds to be a real and active threat to the film industry and to the country as a whole. But most of them, while willing to testify to their own anti-Communist feelings, either denied that the Communists had made any real headway in the film industry, or through their testimony they gave clear evidence that they did not know enough about the subject to comment thereon. It must have been evident to Thomas and the committee that they would have to do more to convince the American people, and, accordingly, the next step was to put on the stand some of the individuals suspected of being part of the Communist conspiracy in movie-land. . . .

RICHARD M. NIXON, *ALGER HISS AND THE COMMUNIST CONSPIRACY IN WASHINGTON, 1950*

*Richard M. Nixon was a freshman Congressman from California when he gained his first national headlines as a member of the House Committee on Un-American Activities. Nixon investigated the claims of a former Communist named Whittaker Chambers who claimed that Alger Hiss, a top State Department official, had passed him top secret documents when both were members of the Party. In 1950, Hiss was found guilty of perjury, but only because the statute of limitations on espionage had expired. More than four decades later, Hiss still maintains his innocence, a claim seemingly supported in 1992 when a former top Russian KGB officer insisted that Hiss had never spied for the Soviet Union. The following excerpts are from Nixon's speech celebrating the conviction of Hiss and warning his countrymen that there were certainly other security risks President Truman and his Administration were ignoring. Just two weeks later, Senator Joseph McCarthy delivered his infamous Wheeling, West Virginia, speech on the same subject; in fact, much of the senator's information, and not a little of his language, had been clearly lifted from Nixon's address to Congress (*Congressional Record, *81st Cong., 2nd Sess.).*

In the first place, the conspiracy which existed was amazingly effective. Chambers turned over to the Committee and the Justice Department hundreds of pages of confidential and secret documents form the State Department and other Government agencies. The theft of documents in this quantity would in itself be sufficient to cause us grave concern. But Chambers testified that on at least 70 different occasions the members of his espionage ring had obtained a similar amount of documents for transmittal to Soviet agents....

Mr. Peurifoy, Assistant Secretary of State in charge of Security, and Mr. Sumner Welles, ...testified that a foreign agent having in his possession even one of the many documents which Chambers turned over to the Government could have broken our secret code. This meant, in other words, that the foreign agents who obtained these documents from Chambers broke the American code and were reading all of our confidential communications with foreign governments during that critical period immediately preceding the Hitler-Stalin pact.

The second point we should not forget is that a great number of people other than Mr. Hiss were named by Chambers as being members of his espionage ring. A run-down of the various positions held by the members of the ring indicates the effectiveness with which the conspiracy was able to infiltrate into vital positions, both in Government and in industry. Mr. Chambers' contacts included: Four in the State Department; two in the Treasury Department; two in the Bureau of Standards; one in the Aberdeen Arsenal; a man who later became general counsel of the CIO; one in the Picatinny Arsenal; two in the Electric Boat Co.; one in the

Remington Rand Co.; and one in the Illinois Steel Co.

It is significant that the individuals named, almost without exception, held positions of influence where they had access to confidential and secret information. The tragedy of the case is that the great majority of them were American citizens, were graduates of the best colleges and universities in this country, and had yet willingly become members of an organization dedicated to the overthrow of this Government....

It was after 1943, that Mr. Hiss was Secretary of the Bretton Woods Conference, went to Yalta with President Roosevelt and acted as Secretary of the UN Conference at San Francisco. It is inconceivable that those who were responsible for appointing him to these high positions, where he had the opportunity to do untold damage to his country by transmitting confidential information to the Soviet Government which they could use in their negotiations with us, were not aware of the charges which had been made.

It will be claimed that at this time we were allies of the Soviet Union and had no reason to suspect that they would engage in espionage against us. But let me say at this point that there is no question whatever but that the top officials of our Government were aware of the fact that the Russians were engaging in espionage activities against us even while they were our allies. The testimony of General Groves before the Committee on Un-American Activities in 1948 on that point is significant. I quote the testimony:

> *Mr. Stripling (Counsel for HUAC). General Groves, did you ever report the efforts of the Russian agents to obtain information regarding atomic development to the President of the United States?*
>
> *General Groves: Yes*
>
> *Mr. Stripling. When was that?*
>
> *General Groves: It would have to be in 1944. It was contained in a report to the President which President Roosevelt read in my presence and the matter was discussed with me. This was just before he left for Yalta. It was brought to the attention of President Truman in the first report that was made to President Truman after he took office, which was as soon after his taking office as the Secretary of War could make an appointment, and on that occasion the written memorandum was read by Mr. Truman.*

In other words, concrete information concerning Communist espionage activities in this country was in the hands of both President Roosevelt and President Truman and still no action was taken to check the Chambers' charges against officials who held high positions in the Government at that time....

There is one thing that I have learned in my service on the Committee on Un-Americans Activities, and that is that the Communists will lie about almost everything but they do not lie to each other about the members of the espionage and underground organizations of which they themselves are members.

They know who their people are.

What was done when this shocking information came to the attention of the officials of our State Department, and the President of the United States? You would think now that Mr. Hiss would be confronted with Mr. Chambers and that the mystery would be cleared up, but instead Mr. Hiss continued to serve in high positions in the State Department until he resigned in January 1947 to take a position as head of the Carnegie Foundation for International Peace. In that connection it is significant to note that when trustees of the Carnegie Foundation questioned Mr. Hiss' former associates in the State Department as to his suitability for that position, he received completely unqualified recommendations on all sides. There was no hint whatever that any question had been raised concerning his loyalty to this Nation.

To complete this story of inexcusable inaction upon the part of administration officials to attack and destroy this conspiracy, let me review briefly the conduct of the President and the Department of Justice during the investigation of this case by the Committee on Un-American Activities. On August 5, the day Mr. Hiss first appeared before the committee and denied the charges which had been made against him, the President threw the great power and prestige of his office against the investigation by the committee and for Mr. Hiss by declaring that the hearings of the committee were simply a "red herring."

In other words the "red herring" statement was made in direct reference to the Alger Hiss case.

That same day, he issued a Presidential directive which ordered all administrative agencies of the Government to refuse to turn over any information relating to the loyalty of any Government employee to a congressional committee. This meant that the committee had to conduct its investigation with no assistance whatever from the administrative branch of the Government. Included in this order was, of course, the FBI, who, by reason of that fact, was unable to lend assistance to the committee....

The President had referred to the case as a "red herring" and did so even after the indictment. The Secretary of State, Mr. Acheson, before his confirmation, declared his friendship for Mr. Hiss and the implication of his declaration was that he had faith in his innocence. Two justices of the Supreme Court, Mr. Frankfurter and Mr. Reed, in an unprecedented action, appeared as character witnesses for Mr. Hiss. Judge Kauffman, who presided at the trial stepped off the bench and shook hands with these defense witnesses, one of many of his actions during the trial in which he showed his obvious bias for the defendant. The wife of the former President of the United States, Mrs. Roosevelt, on several occasions during the two trials, publicly defended Mr. Hiss in her news columns. Among the high Government officials who testified in his behalf were Mr. Philip Jessup, then President Truman's ambassador at large in Europe, and now the architect of our far-eastern policy; the Governor of Illinois, Mr. Stevenson; Judge Wyzski of the United States District Court, Boston; Judge Magruder, chief justice of the circuit court of appeals, Boston, and Francis B. Sayre, Assistant Secretary of State.

I have mentioned the individuals who have come to Mr. Hiss' defense, because this is an outstanding example of how effectively the conspiracy was concealed and how far it was able to reach into high places in our Government to obtain apologists for its members.

Why was it that administration officials persisted in their refusal to act through the years, even when substantial evidence of espionage activities was brought to their attention? A number of reasons have been suggested for this failure.

It has been said that the Soviet Union was an ally of the United States and that therefore we should take a charitable attitude toward those administration officials who failed to act when the evidence was presented to them. But Mr. Chambers first presented his information to Mr.

Berle during the period of the Hitler-Stalin pact when it could not be said, under any stretch of the imagination, that the Soviet Union was an ally of this country. Nor can anyone possibly justify the obstructive policies followed by administration leaders even as late as 1948 when the Committee on Un-American Activities was attempting to bring all the facts out into the open and when our announced national policy was to contain communism abroad if not at home.

On the other extreme, there are some who claim that administration officials failed to act because they were Communist or pro-Communist. I do not accept this charge as a fair one as applied at least to the great majority of those officials who could and should have acted on the evidence which was laid before them through the years.

The reason for their failure to act was not that they were disloyal, but this in my opinion makes that failure even more inexcusable.

What was happening was that administration leaders were treating the reports of Communist espionage on a "politics-as-usual" basis. It is customary practice for any administration, be it Republican or Democrat, to resist the disclosure of facts which might be embarrassing to that administration in an election. This is a statement of fact though, of course, I do not mean to justify that practice, regardless of the nature of the skeleton in the political closet.

Because they treated Communist infiltration into our American institutions like any ordinary petty political scandal, the administration officials responsible for this failure to act against the Communist conspiracy rendered the greatest possible disservice to the people of the Nation.

It is essential that we learn the tragic lessons which the Hiss case has so vividly portrayed, and develop a policy which will reduce the possibility for the existence and successful operation of such a conspiracy in the future. I have some recommendations to make along those lines, most of which are not new, but which I reiterate because I feel that they are essential to our national security.

First. Above all, we must give complete and unqualified support to the FBI and to J. Edgar Hoover, its chief. Mr. Hoover recognized the Communist threat long before other top officials recognized its existence. The FBI in this trial did an amazingly effective job of running down trails over 10 years old and in developing the evidence which made the prosecution successful.

I note in the papers this morning that the National Lawyers Guild has again launched an all-out attack against the FBI. The character of the guild is well illustrated by the fact that 5 of the lawyers for the 11 convicted Communists in New York City, who were cited by Judge Medina for contempt of court because of their disgraceful conduct, are prominent members of the Lawyers guild. Let me say just this: That when the National Lawyers Guild or any similar organization is successful in obtaining an investigation of the FBI and access to its records, a fatal blow will have been struck against the protective security forces of this Nation. I am sure that the Members of the House will join with me in resisting such an attack and in supporting the finest police organization which exists in a free Nation today. [Applause.]

Second. Time will not permit me to discuss all the steps which should be taken in the field of legislation if we are adequately to control and expose the Communist conspiracy in this country. But the very least that should be done during this session of Congress is to extend the statute of limitations on espionage cases from 3 to 10 years. The fact that an espionage agent is able to conceal his activities so effectively that he is not apprehended until after the statutory period had elapsed makes the crime even more infamous and serious in nature. Our present laws are totally inadequate to deal with the new types of espionage which have been developed so effectively by the Communists.

Third. The Committee on Un-American Activities should receive the whole-hearted support of the House. It is well recognized that had the committee not been in existence, the Hiss conspiracy might never have been exposed.

Let me say at this point that I know the Members of this House are aware of the fact that membership on the Committee on Un-American Activities should not be sought by any person who desires to avoid probably the most unpleasant and thankless assignment in the Congress. I trust that Members from both sides will join together in supporting that committee and its members in the years to come, and in seeing to it that it gets the authority and the funds to conduct honest, intelligent, and fair investigations of Communists and other subversive groups in this country.

Fourth. It is necessary that we completely overhaul our system of checking the loyalty of Federal employees. Mr. Hiss would have passed the present loyalty oaths with flying colors. The loyalty checks are based primarily on open affiliations with Communist-front organizations. Underground Communists and espionage agents have no open affiliations and it is therefore almost impossible to apprehend them through a routine loyalty investigation under the President's order. Serious consideration should be given to changing the entire approach under the loyalty order and placing the program on a security risk rather than loyalty basis. In this way, where there is any doubt about an individual who has access to confidential information, that doubt can be resolved in favor of the government without the necessity of proving disloyalty and thereby reflecting on the character of a possibly loyal but indiscreet Government employee.

Fifth. Most important of all, we must develop and put into effect an extensive educational program which will teach the American people the truth about communism as well as the truth about democracy. The tragedy of this case is that men like Alger Hiss who come from good families, are graduates of our best schools, and are awarded the highest honors in Government service, find the Communist ideology more attractive than American democracy.

This is a serious reflection on our educational system, and it is essential that we remedy the situation if we are to survive as a free people. The statement of Mr. John Foster Dulles when he commented upon the Hiss verdict last Saturday is particularly pertinent:

> *The conviction of Alger Hiss is human tragedy. It is tragic that so great promise should have come to so inglorious an end. But the greater tragedy is that seemingly our national ideals no longer inspire the loyal devotions needed for their defense.*

Five years ago, at the time of the Dumbarton Oaks Conference in 1944, when Alger Hiss served as director of our secretariat, the number of people in the world in the Soviet orbit was 180,000,000, approximately the population of the Soviet Union. Arrayed on the anti-totalitarian side there were in the world at that time, in 1944, 1,625,000,000 people. Today there are 800,000,000 in the world under the domination of Soviet totalitarianism. On our side we have

540,000,000 people. There are 600,000,000 residents of United Nations countries which are classified as neutral, such as India, Pakistan, and Sweden. In other words, in 1944 before Dumbarton Oaks, Teheran, Yalta, and Potsdam, the odds were 9 to 1 in our favor. Today, since these conferences the odds are 5 to 3 against us.

The great lesson which should be learned from the Alger Hiss case is that we are not just dealing with espionage agents who get 30 pieces of silver to obtain the blueprint of a new weapon--the Communists do that, too--but this is a far more sinister type of activity, because it permits the enemy to guide and shape our policies; it disarms and dooms our diplomats to defeat in advance before they go to conferences; traitors in the high councils of our own Government make sure that the deck is stacked on the Soviet side of the diplomatic table.

America today stands almost alone between communism and the free nations of the world. We owe a solemn duty, not only to our own people but to free peoples everywhere on both sides of the iron curtain, to expose this sinister conspiracy for what it is, to roll back the Red tide which to date has swept everything before it, and to prove to peoples everywhere that the hope of the world lies not in turning toward totalitarian dictatorship but in developing a strong, free, and intelligent democracy.

Senator Joe McCarthy, *WHEELING WEST VIRGINIA SPEECH* (1950)

Joe McCarthy held two presidents hostage and an entire nation paralyzed with fear for four long years. Revisionist historians have since questioned whether McCarthy individually was as important to the Second Red Scare as liberals have insisted. They correctly conclude that the Red witch hunts started well before McCarthy exploded on the national scene in 1950, and that McCarthy simply exploited the hysteria of his times. Such revisionists, however, tend to downplay the many careers and lives needlessly ruined by McCarthy, and the damage he did to labor unions, civil rights, education, government agencies, and religious institutions. It all started with his Republican Day Address in Wheeling, West Virginia, on February 9, 1950, in which McCarthy claimed to have in his hands the names of 205 known members of the Communist Party who were then still employed in the State Department and who were spying for the Soviets. When asked to produce his evidence, McCarthy changed his figures and definitions considerably, but what mattered were his extraordinary accusations which were carried in every major newspaper in the country. Ironically enough, the Wheeling speech was not recorded and McCarthy produced no notes. What follows below is a moderated version which he later inserted into the Congressional Record. (81 Cong., 2nd Sess., 1954-1957).

Five years after a world war has been won, men's hearts should anticipate a long peace, and men's minds should be free from the heavy weight that comes with war. But this is not such a period--for this is not a period of peace. This is a time of the "cold war." This is a time when all the world is split into two vast, increasingly hostile armed camps--a time of a great armaments race...

Today we are engaged in a final, all-out battle between communistic atheism and Christianity. The modern champions of communism have selected this as the time. And, ladies and gentlemen, the chips are down--they are truly down....

Six years ago, at the time of the first conference to map out the peace--Dumbarton Oaks--there was within the Soviet orbit 180,000,000 people. Lined up on the anti-totalitarian side there were in the world at that time roughly 1,625,000,000 people. Today, only 6 years later, there are 800,000,000 people under the absolute domination of Soviet Russia--an increase of over 400 percent. On our side, the figure has shrunk to around 500,000,000. In other words, in less than 6 years the odds have changed from 9 to 1 in our favor to 8 to 5 against us. This indicates the swiftness of the tempo of Communist victories and American defeats in the cold war. As one of our outstanding historical figures once said, "When a great democracy is destroyed, it will not be because of enemies from without, but rather because of enemies from within."...

The reason why we find ourselves in a position of impotency is not because our only powerful potential enemy has sent men to invade our shores, but rather because of the traitorous actions of those who have been treated so well by this Nation. It has not been the less fortunate or members of minority groups who have been selling this Nation out, but rather those who have had all the benefits that the wealthiest nation on earth has had to offer --the finest homes, the finest college education, and the finest jobs in Government we can give.

This is glaringly true in the State Department. There the bright young men who are born with silver spoons in their mouths are the ones who have been the worst....In my opinion the State Department, which is one of the most important government departments, is thoroughly infested with Communists.

I have in my hand 57 cases of individuals who would appear to be either card carrying members or certainly loyal to the Communist Party, but who nevertheless are still helping to shape our foreign policy...

I know that you are saying to yourself, "Well, why doesn't the Congress do something about it?" Actually, ladies and gentlemen, one of the important reasons for the graft, the corruption, the dishonesty, the disloyalty, the treason in high Government positions--one of the most important reasons why this continues is a lack of moral uprising on the part of the 140,000,000 American people. In the light of history, however, this is not hard to explain.

It is the result of an emotional hang-over and a temporary moral lapse which follows every war. It is the apathy to evil which people who have been subjected to the tremendous evils of war feel. As the people of the world see mass murder, the destruction of defenseless and innocent people, and all of the crime and lack of morals which go with war, they become numb and apathetic. It has always been thus after war.

However, the morals of our people have not been destroyed. They still exist. This cloak of numbness and apathy has only needed a spark to rekindle them. Happily, this spark has finally been supplied.

As you know, very recently the Secretary of State proclaimed his loyalty to a man guilty of what has always been considered as the most abominable of all crimes--of being a traitor to the people who gave him a position of great trust. The Secretary of State in attempting to justify his continued devotion to the man who sold out the Christian world to the atheistic world, referred to Christ's Sermon on the Mount as a justification and reason therefore, and the reaction of the American people to this would have made the heart of Abraham Lincoln happy.

When this pompous diplomat in striped pants, with a phony British accent, proclaimed to the American people that Christ on the Mount endorsed communism, high treason, and betrayal of a sacred trust, the blasphemy was so great that it awakened the dormant indignation of the American people.

He has lighted the spark which is resulting in a moral uprising and will end only when the whole sorry mess of twisted, warped thinkers are swept from the national scene so that we may have a new birth of national honesty and decency in government.

Mickey Spillane, *MIKE HAMMER AND THE REDS* (1951)

With 24 books and sales in excess of 130 million, Mickey Spillane is quantifiably America's most successful writer. Clearly aimed at an adolescent male audience of whatever chronological age, Spillane's books were short on complexities but long on violence, individualism, and simple solutions. One Lonely Night *was the best-selling novel of 1951, and the segment below helps explain why. Joe McCarthy was then hot on the trail of domestic Communists who allegedly were subverting the country, and Mike Hammer was eager to help the senator complete his work.*

You know what, Lee, I killed more people tonight than I have fingers on my hands. I shot them in cold blood and enjoyed every minute of it. I pumped slugs in the nastiest bunch of bastards you ever saw and here I am calmer than I've ever been and happy too. They were Commies, Lee. They were red sons-of-bitches who should have died long ago, and part of the gang who are going to be dying in the very near future unless they get smart and take the gas pipe. Pretty soon what's left of Russia and the slime that breeds there won't be worth mentioning and I'm glad because I had a part in the killing.

"God, but it was fun! It was the way I like it. No arguing, no talking to the stupid peasants. I just walked into that room with a tommy gun and shot their guts out. They never thought that there were people like me in this country. They figured us all to be soft as horse manure and just as stupid."

J. Fred MacDonald, *THE COLD WAR AS ENTERTAINMENT IN 'FIFTIES TELEVISION*

During the 1950s, television became America's most popular form of entertainment, and, as media historian J. Fred MacDonald indicates, its programming often reflected the Communist-bashing of the day. "Seeing is believing," and television "certified" what so many Americans already believed--that the Communists were a real and present danger right in their own backyards. The following was published in the Journal of Popular Film and Television, *1978.*

Television emerged as America's prime medium of entertainment and information at exactly the moment the nation became deeply embroiled in the Cold War. Postwar America was forced to adapt video to its social reality at the same time it was experiencing the anxieties of the East-West confrontation, fighting a limited war in Korea, and learning to live with John Foster Dulles' diplomatic philosophy of "brinkmanship," "massive retaliation," and the "liberation of captive peoples." Within this tense atmosphere TV was assimilated and became the most important vehicle through which citizens learned the latest developments in a rivalry which, in simplified terms, matched good Democracy against evil Communism. In this historical coincidence, the Cold War of the 1950s became America's first "television war."

As a persistent aspect of its dissemination of the news, television brought the international struggle into millions of homes nightly. In news, documentary, discussion, and similar types of actuality programming, the Cold War became a familiar phenomenon. Yet, such non-fiction shows were limited in how they could present the Cold War. Tied to fact and the presentation of actual events, news programs could not effectively illustrate emotional ramifications such as the nature of the enemy or the consequences of defeat. These ambiguous qualities were best handled through literary and theatrical techniques. Therefore, for the more flamboyant images of the East-West battle, it is to entertainment programming that one must turn. In doing so, it becomes apparent that throughout the 1950s TV plunged the nation into a bath of Cold War cliches and fear--an inundation of propagandistic images urged public thought to support unquestioningly the policies of the United States government.

No entertainment series did more to champion anti-Communist than *I Led 3 Lives*. The show was based on Herbert A. Philbrick's best-selling account of his nine years as an FBI agent who was posing as a member of the Communist Party. The producer of the program, Frederic W. Ziv, was not unfamiliar with such topical material. In 1952 he had syndicated a popular radio series, *I Was a Communist for the FBI*, which was drawn from the exploits of Matt Cvetic, another FBI counterspy.

On TV, *I Led 3 Lives* enjoyed great success. It was released to syndication in 1953 and ran for 117 half-hour episodes. As late as the 1970s it was still being shown on local domestic stations. Throughout the series, Richard Carlson appeared as the FBI agent whose heroics seemed to be saving the United States from impending collapse. A typical show might involve Red plans to introduce a new low-cost narcotic to American youngsters, an attempt by the

Communists to steal top secret information, or a plot to incite labor unrest by spreading hate-filled pamphlets to factory workers. Occasionally, Philbrick might even be ordered by the Party to a foreign country--certainly outside the legal jurisdiction of the Federal Bureau of Investigation--where he invariably caused FBI intentions to defeat Communist goals.

The world of *I Led 3 Lives* was a threatening one in which Philbrick was balanced between subversive Reds intent upon destroying the American way of life, and the demands of an FBI "plant" secretly struggling to thwart and expose these diabolical ends. Each weekly victory meant "eliminating one more threat to our national security." Each Philbrick triumph was the result of American character and morality besting the deceit and general malevolence of "the Red underground." And in case viewers missed the immediacy of Philbrick's martyrdom, each week Carlson reminded viewers that this was for real:

> *This is the story, the fantastically true story, of Herbert A. Philbrick who for nine frightening years did lead three lives--average citizen, high-level member of the Communist Party, and counterspy for the Federal Bureau of Investigation. For obvious reasons the names, dates, and places have been changed. But the story is based on fact.*

Like most entertainment programs with Cold War themes, *I Led 3 Lives* never discussed the East-West issues in rational terms. It offered no explanation of why adult Americans joined the Communist Party. It never honestly discussed the effectiveness of subversion in the United States, nor did it explain the degree to which the CPUSA was infiltrated by other FBI agents. Viewers encountered instead a classic morality tale in which the forces of Good always won, but the forces of Evil were never fully vanquished.

Interestingly, the series appears to have been supervised to a degree by the Bureau. Carlson admitted to an interviewer in 1954 that all scripts were taken from fact with the approval of the FBI. According to the actor, this was a necessary procedure "since we play pretty fast and loose with the Bureau throughout the show."

Although Philbrick occasionally left the country as part of his Red assignments, he was almost always a domestic operative. Working abroad to protect American values, however, was a vast array of patriotic undercover agents which entertained viewers throughout the decade. Often these spies were government agents. In *Passport to Danger*, Cesar Romero portrayed Steve McQuinn, a diplomatic courier whose duties for the State Department took him to such cities of intrigue as Sofia, Belgrade, Berlin and Istanbul. *The Man Called X* and *David Harding, Counterspy* had been successful radio shows before coming to television. And the Cold War so affected the old radio series, *The Falcon*, that when it appeared on TV in 1955, its hero, Mike Waring, had ceased to be a private detective and was now an agent of U.S. intelligence laboring against international evil.

Such Cold War heroes were frequently military intelligence officers. And often these series were said to be based upon actual military records. *Pentagon, U.S.A.* was a short-lived series in 1953 which concerned cases from the criminal investigation files of the United States Army. In 1958, *Behind Closed Doors* was purportedly based on the experiences and records of Rear Admiral Ellis M. Zacharias, deputy chief of naval intelligence during World War II. Despite Zacharias' achievements in the war, the series had a pointedly Cold War theme. Here stories concerned such activities as the attempt by American spies to plant a listening device in the Russian Embassy in London, arranging the defection of a Russian Air Force lieutenant, helping the anti-Communist Czech underground, and preventing the assassination of world leaders such as King Hussein of Jordan and Marshal Tito of Yugoslavia.

Espionage was a popular theme. It was even featured in historical series like *O.S.S.*, which focused on the Office of Strategic Services, the forerunner of the Central Intelligence Agency, during World War II. And *I Spy*, an anthology program hosted by Raymond Massey, presented spy stories from Biblical times to the present.

The degree to which the fears of the Cold War had become the grist of popular entertainment was strikingly evidenced in a trade advertisement in *Variety* in January, 1956. Here the syndicators of *The Man Called X* purchased two full pages to trumpet the relevance of their property. "Now! TV's Most Colorful Man of Mystery!" proclaimed one banner headline. "C.I.A. Vital to U.S. Policy Makers," and "Spy Stories Always Great Entertainment," suggested others. Most pointedly, the ad announced that "Secret agents have molded our destiny." To drive home the point that *The Man Called X* was pertinent to, and exploitive of, the real fears of Americans in the 1950s, the advertisement grimly accentuated the necessity of spies.

> Survival of any nation today, in the event of an attack by an enemy power, may be directly in proportion to its advance "intelligence," or knowledge of that enemy...disposition of land, sea, and air power, hidden targets, weak points, concentration of physical resources, defenses, stamina of its people, intentions, plans, and capacities of its government.

The program, itself, was the quintessential Cold War spy series. Produced by Frederic W. Ziv for the 1955-56 season, the program featured Barry Sullivan as Ken Thurston, "code name X," whose activities took him behind the Iron Curtain to aid the cause of world freedom. In a stentorian voice the narrator proclaimed that "These are the stories of America's intelligence agents, our country's first line of defense." In the opening of one show--a drama in which Thurston arranged the defection of a prominent East European ballerina--the thrust of all espionage series was succinctly summarized: protect Americans, aid free people around the world, and thwart the war-threatening goals of international Communism.

TV images of American spies were not limited to professional intelligence operatives. Supplementing the military and governmental agents were those patriotic citizens involved in overseas on the U.S. side of the Cold War. *Biff Baker, U.S.A.*, a CBS presentation in the 1952-53 season, concerned a businessman whose import-export affairs took him and his wife all over the world. While closing deals for his company, Baker invariably would do a little spying for his country. Baker melded in his personality the ethnic of capitalism and the spirit of patriotism. The series was so effective that business organizations criticized it for leaving the impression that all American businessmen working abroad were spies.

Baker and his wife were convincing. When blocked by an East European official, he could be blunt--as he was when he told a Czech military officer, "I'll go over your head, all the way to Moscow!" He could be decisive. In one episode, while vacationing in Austria he had no second thoughts in destroying a secret Communist radio station which had been jamming broadcasts from the Voice of America. And that escapade he carried out "in the name of all people who seek freedom beyond the Iron Curtain." Baker could also be brave, as he was the time he aided a French plantation owner fighting off a murderous band of Vietminh rebels outside Saigon. "Anything's possible with these fanatics," warned the Frenchman. Baker apparently agreed as he quipped, "I'm not partial to pink."

The spectrum of these citizen-spies ranged from Steve Mitchell, the hero of *Dangerous*

Assignment, who worked for a private intelligence agency that always supported American foreign policy goals, to the central character of *China Smith*, a vagabond Yankee drifting from Hong Kong to Kuala Lumpur, instinctively fighting Communist because it was inherently evil. In *The Hunter* the hero was a sort of international playboy, but a patriot, who at a moment's notice could leave a tennis match at Wimbleton and jet to Rumania to help an anti-Communist informer, or leave an art display in Germany and sneak into Prague to help the Czech underground. A favorite type for these series was the newspaperman. In this vein was *Foreign Intrigue*, syndicated from 1951 to 1955. Also important was *Crusader*, a series which in 1955 featured Brian Keith as Matt Anders, an international journalist who fought for scoops and world security concurrently.

If the milieu of the professional spy was intriguing, the private-citizen-as-secret-agent was downright compelling. All the fears and frustrations of the era could be transferred onto the shoulders of this hero. Here was a forthright picture of a man acting out his nationalistic convictions. Moving through a shadowy Hungarian street, dodging Polish border guards, making fools out of Russian military officials, stamping out Red guerrilla movements--in activities like these the powerless average viewer could project himself, through the citizen-spy, into the international struggle. In this manner, characters such as Matt Anders and Biff Baker became modern-day Minute Men, temporarily laying aside professional commitments to aid in the defense of social freedom.

Because they were amateurs, these non-professional spies usually happened upon their weekly suspenseful involvement. In the episode of *Foreign Intrigue* aired August 27, 1953, it was in pursuit of a news story in East Berlin that journalist Bob Cannon came to help a rocket scientist defect to the West. Matt Anders just happened to be a passenger on a Polish airplane when it was hijacked at gunpoint to Hamburg and freedom. Even when Biff Baker was approached by American government officials and asked to do a little espionage work, he seemed ignorant of the implications of doing such favors.

There was nothing serendipitous, however, about the propaganda impact of these series. They all strongly asserted the anti-Communist position in the Cold War. Never doubting the political and moral rightness of their activities, these heroes acted to bring American justice to the unjust world. Casual and affable on one hand, they stood resolutely against Communist terror--and they always emerged as winners. Nowhere was this message of Americanism more strongly stated than in the written preamble which rolled across the TV screen at the beginning of each episode of *Crusader*:

> Crusader *records the struggle of democratic people against the enemies of freedom and justice at home and abroad. These are the stories of people who have been helped by the many great organizations which are dedicated to bringing truth to those who are fed lies, light to those who live in darkness, protection to those who live in fear.*

Inherent in most of these Cold War adventure programs was an image of the world, outside the United States, as wretched and unsettled. Those clinging to the notion that a post-war united world of free and equal nation states found little solace in such series. Crime, espionage, poverty and generalized dispiritedness permeated the stories in shows like *Orient Express* and *Terry and the Pirates*. Scenes in such programs often showed bombed-out cities or starving characters, this to American viewers grown used to the middle-class, suburban happiness depicted in series like

Father Knows Best, The Adventures of Ozzie and Harriet, and *77 Sunset Strip*. Relative to a cholera epidemic in Libya, primitive farming techniques in Pakistan, or political revolution in southeast Asia the United States was a fat, contented place. In the words of the hero of *The Hunter*, it was "a place at the end of the rainbow where even the toothpaste is green." Thus, viewers within "fortress America" were tempted by Cold War TV to envision the rest of the world as backward and brutal. And within this context, television also assured citizens that they were being protected.

During the Cold War religion was a critical theme in much of the nation's popular culture. Movies, music, radio and the print media produced many successful products with religious messages. Television, too, presented spiritual programming; and often it was aired in primetime. Frequently such television shows struck their own blows for the United States in the East-West conflict. The fundamental depravity explaining all Red actions was alleged to be atheism inherent in Communism. If there was brutality within the Soviet Union and its satellites, it was explained as the result of Godless ideology. If Communists were threatening world peace, it was because atheism had no respect for God and His worshippers.

Conversely, such programs stressed that suppression of the Eastern European peoples was suppression of the Christian faith. They suggested that Providence, however, was on the side of the downtrodden--even the "captive" Russian people--and would eventually destroy the perfidious Red empire. In its own way, television conveyed the message that the strength of the anti-Communist position was in its alliance with the Divine.

Such themes appeared in a range of programs. In *Navy Log, Victory at Sea*, or other military series images of praying soldiers and sailors illustrated the religious nature of the American armed forces. A dramatic production such as "Cardinal Mindszenty," which appeared on *Studio One* on May 3, 1954, related the plight of the Hungarian prelate who for many years escaped Communist prisons by gaining sanctuary in the American Embassy in Budapest.

Two popular anthology series which utilized Cold War religious material were *TV Reader's Digest* and *Cavalcade of America*. In "The Boy Who Walked to America," *Cavalcade of America* in January 1956, blended religion and anti-Communism in a story about a Korean boy who hitchhiked to America. After a plane flight from his homeland to Japan, the lad became the ward of an Army chaplain who eventually secured permission for the child to emigrate to Father Flanagan's Boys Town in Omaha, Nebraska. This mixture of a sweet child seeking American freedom, and a loving priest arranging for his move to the United States underscored the vile nature of an enemy who would cause a child such anguish.

Sunday-morning religious programs often related anti-Communist stories. Series like *Lamp Unto My Feet, The Catholic Hour, Religious Town Hall* and *Look Up and Live* addressed ideas of freedom, patriotism, spiritual fulfillment within a religious nation, and escape from behind the Iron Curtain. The most zealous program of this sort, however, was *Zero-1960*.

Zero-1960 was produced by the Blue Army of Our Lady of Fatima. It debuted in May 1957 and was nationally syndicated until 1960. The Blue Army was a decade-old organization which sought to end Communism through moral opposition. The show was named after the year in which the full message of the miracle of Fatima, partially revealed in 1917, was anticipated. The series seemed to worry less about expected holy messages than about the spectre of atheistic Communism.

This was a stark political-religious presentation. The opening telecast set the pace for the series as Roman Catholic Bishop Cuthbert O'Gara, a missionary in China, told how the Chinese Communists had stripped him naked before his parishioners and had dragged him through the city streets. By 1958 the program handled topics such as the imminent spiritual and political revolutions in the Soviet Union, the possibility of annihilation in a Red-precipitated nuclear war the confessions of a former Soviet commander and the resistance by American Blacks to the lure of Communism. In its last season, *Zero-1960* had become a religious discussion series presenting celebrities like the President of the Philippines discussing Communism in Southeast Asia, and the Chairman of the House Committee on Un-American Activities speaking on Red spies in the United States.

More consistently and more grimly than other religious shows, *Zero-1960* championed the cause of anti-Communism. But its line of argument was not incompatible with the Cold War values found in other religious and non-religious series. And, scheduled as it was on Sunday mornings--a spot in the typical TV log that was filled with spiritual programs and public service presentations about the armed forces--Church and State seemed to complement and legitimize each other.

The appearance of spiritual series in network evening hours illustrates the strategic position religion assumed in the Cold War era. *Crossroads*, an ABC dramatic program between 1953 and 1956, treated the experience of clergymen. Although it avoided the open politics found in many Sunday-morning programs, it did promote a responsible and humane image of religious institutions, as well as reflecting the importance of faith in the personal lives of most citizens.

If *Crossroads* was politically restrained, Bishop Fulton J. Sheen's *Life is Worth Living*, was the most aggressively anti-Communist program in primetime TV. Sheen came to ABC in the early 1950s, and by the Fall of 1953 his program was being aired on more than 130 stations. Even into the 1960s Sheen, the Bishop of Rochester and director of the World Mission Society for the Propagation of the Faith, appeared in a syndicated series.

Sheen was a chronically outspoken foe of Communism. During the Depression he had written hostile essays on such topics as "Communism and Religion," "The Tactics of Communism," and "Liberty Under Communism." In this latter tract, published in 1937 as a response to the promulgation of the Soviet Constitution, Sheen enunciated ideas which had not changed by the time he entered television two decades later:

There is no liberty under Communism, because there is no Spirit. Liberty comes from the rational soul; that is why cabbages have no liberty.... Liberty for them [Communists] exists only when the citizens desire what the State desires, and do what the dictators order, and think only what the Party thinks.... Such is the liberty of dogs under the lash of their masters, and the liberty of cuckoos in cuckoo clocks, or the liberty of prisoners in prison.... Such are the "rights" granted to the slaves of Red Dictatorship under the new Red Constitution.

On *Life Is Worth Living* Bishop Sheen lectured the nation on matters of general moral uplift as well as Cold War politics. In talks punctuated only by how flowing satin robes and a blackboard on which he made chalk drawings, he left no doubt where he stood concerning the East-West confrontation. Sheen questioned the motives of those Americans who refused to tell Congressional investigators whether they had ever been members of the Communist Party. "Any good citizen, if asked by Congress if he were a member of Murder, Inc., would immediately deny it," he told viewers in one show. "Why is it, then, that some of our citizens insist on their constitutional rights when asked if they are Communists?" Sheen attacked Communists for having "perverted the notion of brotherhood into world imperialism," and for "denying God, denying morality, denying conscience, but keeping confession and guilt." Perhaps the most publicized Sheen program occurred on February 24, 1953, when the Bishop spoke on the projected "Death of Stalin." When the Soviet leader unexpectedly died nine days later, some suggested that Sheen's words might have been responsible.

In Bishop Sheen's view, the United States was to be more than the policeman of the globe--it was the new savior of the world by divine appointment. "America is at the crossroads--the crossroads of the starving world. It sees the world being crucified by Communism," he announced to an audience in 1953. "The long arm of Providence is reaching out to America, saying "Take up the cross of all the starving people of the world. Carry it'." Sheen was also forthright in explaining the future he envisioned for the United States. As he pontificated on one program,

> We have already saved the world from the swastika, which would cross out the cross and make a double cross. Now we must save the world from the hammer and sickle: the hammer that crucifies, and the sickle that cuts life like immature wheat that it may never be one with the Bread of Life.

Cold War fears were often disseminated through the dramatic programming television offered in the 1950s. In feature films, made-for-TV films, and live dramas the political values of the decade were incorporated into American electronic entertainment. Networks and local stations faced a dilemma in dealing with many movies produced during World War II. At that time the Soviet Union was an ally in the war against Nazi Germany. Hollywood films had frequently paid homage to this alliance by turning out wartime movies praising the Russians. In the Cold War, however, this patriotism was considered subversive, and TV stations had to be careful about which wartime pictures they aired.

Films such as *Mission to Moscow* and *Song of Russia* were of questionable loyalty, according to the Cold War mentality. Some stations even worried about *Ninotchka*, the Greta Garbo feature from 1939 which actually satirized Communist dogma. The extent to which anti-Communist fears could carry television was seen in the TV version of *The North Star*--an RKO production in 1943 written by Lillian Hellman. The original movie was a sympathetic treatment of the bravery of a Russian peasant village in resisting brutal Nazi invaders. Before it came to television, however, it was edited to diminish praise of the Russians and was retitled *Armored Attack*. More strikingly, the film was given a new, contemporary ending--footage of Russian tanks suppressing the Hungarian Revolution in 1956, while a narrator reminded viewers that despite the heroism of the Russian peasants, Communist leaders were as brutal now as the Germans had been in World War II. It was an act of classic Cold War paranoia.

Dramas produced exclusively for television approached the issue of Communism early but cautiously. This was especially true because the outbreak of the Korean War in June 1950 left TV without governmental guide lines--as they had been available in World War II--explaining how to portray the Reds. The first series to present an editorialized position on Communism was *Cameo Theater* in its play, "Line of Duty," aired July 26, 1950.

The play concerned revolt in a European country against twenty years of Communist tyranny. At the time of the telecast, however, *Variety* remarked that the issue was not clear-cut. Many in the television industry were concerned that an attack on Communism might precipitate a demand from the CPUSA for equal time to rebut the charges. This was an especially sensitive matter in 1950, an election year, for according to Section 315 of the Communications Act of

1934, if one candidate for public office were granted facilities, equal opportunity had to be afford all candidates.

These concerns did not intimidate all broadcasters. When radio station WLIZ (Bridgeport, Conn.) refused to sell time to the Communist Party in 1950, Senator William Benton announced his support for the ostracism. According to Paul Porter, former head of the Federal Communications Commission, such a ban was justified because "in this particular period...such a broadcast would tend to incite the community," and because Reds were not legitimate candidates--they were most likely exploiting the law "for the purpose of confusion."

The precedent set by *Cameo Theater* made anti-Communism a popular subject for dramatic production, live and on film, during the so-called "Golden Age" of TV drama. If one considers the Spring and Summer of 1953 as typical, the following list of programs establishes clearly that Cold War messages were prevalent:

--"Somewhere in Korea," *The Web* (May 3): UN soldiers escape North Korean POW camp.

--"The Jewel," *Ford Theater* (May 28): postwar amnesia victim.

--"Counterplot," *Your Play Time* (June 14): American journalist tortured by Reds to get phony confession.

--"Malaya Incident," *Ford Theater* (June 18): love blooms as land owner fights Red guerrillas in Malaya.

--"Jetfighter," *Plymouth Playhouse* (June 28): Yank pilot in trouble over Russian zone of Germany.

--"Bilshan and the Thief," *General Electric Theater* (July 5): refugee learns American patriotism from a thief.

--"The Mascot," *Suspense* (July 7): American army deserter plans to become dictator of Mediterranean island.

--"The Traitor," *Fireside Theater* (September 1): Yank POW spies for Koreans against fellow American prisoners.

--"Two Prisoners," *Armstrong Circle Theater* (September 8): liberated POW has readjustment problems.

As the decade progressed, anti-Communism became more lavish and more expensive. "The Plot to Kill Stalin," was well received on *Playhouse 90* in September 1958. "Darkness at Noon," on *Producers' Showcase* in May 1955, and "1984" on *Studio One* in September 1953 were famous anti-Communist novels here dramatized for American audiences. But "The Vanished" on *Armstrong Circle Theater* in April 1958, was based on the less-renowned book, *I Was a Slave in Russia.*

The plight of American soldiers in Korean prisoner-of-war camps was treated in two *United States Steel Hour* productions--"P.O.W." in October 1953, and "The Rack" in April 1955. Even the prestigious Rod Serling lent his writing talent to the crusade with "Forbidden Area." This was a *Playhouse 90* program in October 1956, which concerned an Air Force saboteur and a sneak atomic attack on the United States set for Christmas eve. This was not, however, one of Serling's triumphs, as one critic blasted him for carelessly creating an "overall feeling [that] was one of inciting to hysteria by thinking in terms of H-Bombs, B-52s and submarines."

The recurrent message of Cold War television came across loudly and clearly: the American way-of-life was being threatened by totalitarian Communist aggressors, and in order to survive the United States--with leadership coming primarily from the government through its espionage agencies and its armed forces--would have to root out subversives at home, outmaneuver enemy agents overseas and win over the uncommitted and enslaved populations of the world through generosity, efficiency, bravery and strength. It was a tall order. But it was accomplished each time culture heroes like Herb Philbrick, Biff Baker, China Smith, or Steve Canyon won another battle against Red perfidy.

Like the fearful nation it helped to create, the American television industry was gripped, itself, by Cold War distrust. Throughout the 1950s producers, networks and advertising agencies maintained "blacklists" of people suspected of leftist sympathies. Actors, writers, directors, and producers found their TV careers terminated or severely curtailed because of alleged political transgressions. Conversely, those not cited on blacklists were often reluctant to undertake TV projects which questioned Cold War cliches. This muddled situation was accurately described in an article in the *London Times* in October 1954, that assailed the ominous "climate of fear" in American television which "strips the medium of so much reality and truth."

What was missing in all this turmoil was a persistent, rational discussion of the issues in the East-West struggle--an intelligent dialogue through which honest information might have challenged propaganda. Instead, the result was a nation of patriotic, trusting citizens left underinformed and fearful. It was a citizenry which in the next decade was hardly in a position to criticize its political and military leaders when they began to slide inexorably into that tragic anti-Communist war in Asia.

Louis Bromfield, *THE TRIUMPH OF THE EGGHEAD* (1952)

Novelist Louis Bromfield was typical of those who used McCarthyism and the Red Scare to go after their political, social, and intellectual enemies. Bromfield knew the quickest way to discredit an individual or a movement was to tar it with a red brush. In the following article, Bromfield attacks Franklin Roosevelt, Harry Truman, social reformers, one-worlders, pinko professors, and "egg-heads," all of whom he classifies as degenerate liberals." His classic definition of an "egghead" was often applied to Adlai Stevenson, the Democrat whom Dwight Eisenhower defeated for the presidency in 1952. This article was published in The Freeman, *December 1, 1952.*

What honest, intelligent and informed citizen answering in a national poll today would want to be called a *liberal*? Perhaps not one in fifty. Yet less than a generation ago the term was complementary and even laudatory. It implied intelligence, knowledge, good will and, above all, deep concern for the development of one's fellow-men -- for the flowering of the individual into complete and varied expression of his talents, abilities and capacity for living a full life. *Liberal* was an honorable word, born of the ideas of the French Revolution and the brilliant and enlightened eighteenth century which was followed in Europe and the world by a great upsurge in the intellectual, spiritual and material welfare of man.

What has happened to the meaning and the dignity of the word? A great deal that is worth examination, I think. Part of the degradation has arisen simply from the cold, impartial, inexorable march of history. A great deal more has arisen from the type of person who, since the arrival on the world scene of Franklin D. Roosevelt, has debased the original meaning and implications of the word itself. I see Mr. Roosevelt merely as a date marker and not as an example of a true liberal, in either the antique or the immediate sense of the word.

History will find Mr. Roosevelt difficult to label properly. He was, above all, an extremely shrewd politician, not on the ward level of Mr. Truman, but on the level of Alcibiades and the Gracchi--like himself, sons of privilege who espoused the cause of the theoretical mob. As such he may also serve as a symbol and a key to the degradation of the honorable word, for he frequently used *liberalism* not as a goal or an ideal as Jefferson and Franklin used it, but shrewdly as a means toward an and--the end of political power. Probably this condition more than any other, together with Roosevelt's unquestioned talents and influence as an occasional demagogue, brought about the suspicion and the lack of repute which now surround the word.

Roosevelt gave the *liberals* their great chance. During his long tenure of office they flocked into Washington in droves. There were a million of them and they shared a million ideas of how to save the nation and bring *pâté de foi gras* to the Hottentots. Their variety was great. It ranged from men like Henry Morgenthau, Henry Wallace, Leon Henderson, Harold Ickes, Francis Biddle and Harry Hopkins to the little professors who left one or another obscure bush college in order to take, overnight, positions of great authority and power. It did not matter that these men had had little or no experience or that some of them approached the level of mental unbalance known as *crackpotism*. They were all *liberals*--in wholesale lots.

What no one observed at the time and what only time has made clear is that virtually none of these *liberals* was liberal in the great tradition of the eighteenth century. They were, almost without exception, watered-down Marxists, which is just another name for Fabian Socialists. The exceptions were the concealed Communists. Few of them were concerned with the spirit of man or his cultural advance or his development as a rich and rounded individual capable of a fine and rewarding life. Their concerns were almost entirely material, exactly as all Marxian philosophy is material. Their flaming ideal was "security," by which at the price of a man's soul he turned everything over to government in the persons of men who were frustrated or psychopathically unsound or sentimental with the sadistic and vengeful sentimentality of the Soviet commissar who shoots your mother for your own good and the common good. They treated mankind as if it were a large lump of dough to be molded into shape by the confused and pushing fingers of those who, however lacking in experience, were persuaded beyond all argument that they knew best.

They dealt, all of them, either in terms of lachrymose sentimentality or shriveled academic abstractions; and the world has found out again and again that mankind is not an abstraction but an infinite variety of glands, of temperaments, of ambitions and desires. Empires and small nations have gone to ruin again and again on the assumption that mankind was an abstraction. We are beginning to find it out all over again, and not only in Russia which continues to provide a tyrannical suppression of liberties and a peculiar artistic and scientific sterility, as well as one of the world's lowest living standards--to the perpetual confusion of the materialist Marxists and Fabian Socialists....

All of this material philosophy was handmade for the acquisition of vast political power. You could buy votes with pensions, with subsidies, with mass favors to such furies as organized labor and the farm bloc down to the lowest level of our citizenry, and when I say *lowest* I am not thinking in terms of material income but in terms of ignorance, lack of thrift, degeneracy, shiftlessness and actual viciousness. According to the New Deal politicians no such qualities existed among our people. People with such characteristics were merely *unfortunate* and could be saved by a government handout which in turn demanded their votes and every sort of bureaucratic control. You could not buy the votes of these elements by espousing such things as education, or honor in government, or freedom of the will and the spirit. Marx knew that long ago. The knowledge is inherent in every sentence of Das Kapital ....

But the materialists and the defeated Truman politicians do not share responsibility alone with the bedraggled remnants of Mr. Roosevelt's hordes for the degradation of the once honorable word *liberal*. They, together with the Marxists, have thrown out of the window that noble word *honor* by which man has painfully lifted himself by his bootstraps over centuries of time. Let me suggest that you make your own list of the great liberals of history and then check the word *honorable* against their names. You will find that *honor* was of first importance and consideration to these men. Who can say that of the new *liberal*? Who can say it of Hiss or even of most of those who befriended him? Honor is held in simple contempt among our faded Marxian carbon-copy *liberals*.

The sentimentalist, the secluded professor in his tower of tarnished bargain-priced ivory, and the hysterically emotional have all done their share to make the word *liberal* seem to designate someone who is disappointed, or frustrated, frivolous, sloppy or shallow. These include the fuzzy-minded who burst into tears when they hear that the State is not able to thrust caviar down the throat of a Georgia Woolhat or a Mississippi Redneck, who would probably throw it up quickly in disgust as some of them threw up Mrs. Roosevelt's costly and futile cooperative settlements. Among these are the *liberals* who would bring about the millennium through decree. In a sense they are the first cousins of the psychopathic reformer who would force people to attend revival meetings under the threat of the lash. The difference is merely one of degree. Neither intellect nor logic, prime characteristics of the true liberal, plays any role in their activities.

In this horrible mess our leading *liberals* have been in this country, as they have been consistently in Europe, the best agents of communism and of the Russian Soviet government. Anyone with a knowledge of our history for the past ten years could name at random a score of men called *liberals* who have achieved far more in behalf of Communists Russia and against the good of this nation that any Communist, however prominent, either here or in Europe. Of what menace or importance are Gerhardt Eisler or William Z. Foster or all the Hollywood *Reds* as compared to the few *liberals* who have largely molded our propaganda and foreign policy during the past ten years?

Stalin should reward them well. But if he gained control here, he would round them up as the vanguard for the nearest camp, as he did with the *liberals* in the satellite countries.

The Communist Party and it maneuvers have in this country been a failure, save perhaps in the cases like that of Hiss in which they accomplished evil through direct corruption. Not as much can be said of the *liberals* at Yalta, at Potsdam, in China and all of Asia. They have made the way easy for Russian aggression, while smugly believing that they were wiser and more generous and nobler than the average sound citizen. They have been dupes, duped less by the outright influence of Stalin and his fellow-men than by their own confusion, smugness and muddled thinking. In these times such men are dangerous, supremely dangerous to the whole of the nation and of the world. History is writing down the record, and each day the story becomes a little clearer to the American people.

For a long time thoughtful men have been seeking a word to describe these remote products of Middle-European socialism who kidnapped and tarnished the word *liberal*, and during the recent political campaign the word miraculously appeared out of the common sense, the wisdom and the instinct of the people themselves. It was a process, a birth which has happened again and again in history. Immediately the word received the virtually universal and spontaneous acceptance accorded a new word for which a long and profound need has been experienced.

The word is *egghead*. In the periodical revision of the dictionary I have no doubt that the word "egghead" will be included and that it will be defined something like this:

> *Egghead*: A person of spurious intellectual pretensions, often a professor or the protégé of a professor. Fundamentally superficial. Over-emotional and feminine in reactions to any problem. Supercilious and surfeited with conceit and contempt for the experience of more sound and able men. Essentially confused in thought and immersed in mixture of sentimentality and violent evangelism. A doctrinaire supporter of Middle-European socialism as opposed to Greco-French-American ideas of democracy and liberalism. Subject to the old-fashioned philosophical morality of

> Nietzsche which frequently leads him into jail or disgrace. A self-conscious prig, so given to examining all sides of a question that he becomes thoroughly addled while remaining always in the same spot. An anemic bleeding heart.

The recent election demonstrated a number of things, not the least of them being the extreme remoteness of the egghead from the thought and feeling of the whole of the people.

President Ronald Reagan, *EVIL EMPIRE SPEECH* (1983)

The anti-communism pushed by President Reagan in the 1980s did not remotely resemble the earlier two Red Scares. At no time did the President or leading members of his administration mention the threat of domestic Communists, although Reagan did warn of misguided secularists seeking a nuclear freeze. No, this time it was the "Evil Empire" itself that posed the problem. Reagan was not the first President to use the military threat of communism as a pretext for seeking increased defense spending, but no other President did it so successfully. Reagan convinced the country and Congress that we were jeopardizing our national security by falling dangerously behind the Soviets in military preparedness. Longstanding fears of communism prevented the kind of careful scrutiny that such a claim deserved; instead, President Reagan managed to triple defense spending during his eight years in office. President Reagan delivered the following remarks to a convention of evangelical Christians in Orlando, Florida, on March 8, 1983.

This Administration is motivated by a political philosophy that sees the greatness of America in you, her people, and in your families, churches, neighborhoods, communities -- the institutions that foster and nourish values like concern for others and respect for the rule of law under God.

Now I don't have to tell you that this puts us in opposition to, or at least out of step with, a prevailing attitude of many who have turned to a modern-day secularism, discarding the tried and time-tested values upon which our very civilization is based.

No matter how well-intentioned, their value system is radically different from that of most Americans.

And, while they proclaim they are freeing us from superstitions of the past, they have taken upon themselves the job of superintending us by government rule and regulation. Sometimes their voices are louder than ours, but they are not yet a majority....

But whatever sad episodes exist in our past, any objective observer must hold a positive view of American history, a history that has been the story of hopes fulfilled and dreams made into reality. Especially in this century. America has kept alight the torch of freedom --not just for ourselves but for millions of others around the world....

During my first press conference as President, in answer to a direct question, I pointed out that as good Marxists-Lenists the Soviet leaders have openly and publicly declared that the only morality they recognize is that which will further their cause, which is world revolution.

I think I should point out I was only quoting Lenin, their guiding spirit, who said in 1920 that they repudiate all morality that proceeds from supernatural ideas or ideas that are outside class conceptions; morality is entirely subordinate to the interests of class war; and everything is moral that is necessary for the annihilation of the old exploiting social order and for uniting the proletariat.

I think the refusal of many influential people to accept his elementary fact of Soviet doctrine illustrates an historical reluctance to see totalitarian powers for what they are. We saw this phenomenon in the 1930s; we see it too often today. This does not mean we should isolate ourselves and refuse to seek an understanding with them.

I intend to do everything I can to persuade them of our peaceful intent; to remind them that it was the West that refused to use its nuclear monopoly in the '40s and '50s for territorial gain and which now proposes 50 percent cuts in strategic ballistic missiles and the elimination of an entire class of land-based, intermediate-range nuclear missiles.

At the same time, however, they must be made to understand we will never compromise our principles and standards. We will never give away our freedom. We will never abandon our belief in God.

And we will never stop searching for a genuine peace. But we can assure none of these things America stands for through the so-called nuclear freeze solutions proposed by some. The truth is that a freeze now would be a very dangerous fraud, for that is merely the illusion of peace. The reality is that we must find peace through strength.

I would agree to a freeze if only we could freeze the Soviets' global desires. A freeze at current levels of weapons would removed any incentive for the Soviets to negotiate seriously in Geneva, and virtually end our chances to achieve the major arms reductions which we have proposed. Instead, they would achieve their objectives through the freeze.

A freeze would reward the Soviet Union for its enormous and unparalleled military buildup. It would prevent the essential and long-overdue modernization of United States and allied defenses and would leave our aging forces increasingly vulnerable. And an honest freeze would require extensive prior negotiations on the system and numbers to be limited and on the measures to insure effective verification and compliance....

A number of years ago, I heard a young father, a very prominent young man in the entertainment world, addressing a tremendous gathering in California. It was during the time of the cold war, and communism and our own way of life were very much on people's minds. And he was speaking to that subject. And suddenly, though, I heard him saying "I love my little girls more than anything." And I said to myself, "Oh, no, don't. You can't--don't say that." But I had underestimated him. He went on: "I would rather see my little girls die now, still believing in God, than have them grow up under communism and one day die no longer believing in God."

Yes, let us pray for the salvation of all of those who live in totalitarian darkness, pray they will discover the joy of knowing God. But until they do, let us be aware that while they preach the supremacy of the state, declare its omnipotence over individual man, and predict its eventual domination of all peoples of the earth -- they are the focus of evil in the modern world....

If history teaches anything, it teaches: Simple-minded appeasement or wishful thinking about our adversaries is folly--and it means the betrayal of our past, the squandering of our freedom.

So I urge you to speak out against those who would place the United States in a position of military and moral inferiority....

So in your discussions of the nuclear freeze proposals, I urge you to beware the temptation of pride--the temptation blithely to declare yourselves above it all and label both sides equally at fault, to ignore the facts of history and the aggressive impulses of an evil empire, to simply call the arms race a giant misunderstanding and thereby remove yourself from the struggle between right and wrong, good and evil....

PART IV - VIETNAM

Someone had blundered
Theirs not to make reply,
Theirs not to reason why,
Theirs but to do and die

Alfred, Lord Tennyson
The Charge of the Light Brigade

Vietnam represents the cornerstone of the Free World in Southeast Asia, the keystone to the arch, the finger in the dike. Burma, Thailand, India, Japan, the Philippines, and obviously Laos and Cambodia are among those whose security would be threatened if the red tide of Communism overflowed into Vietnam.

Senator John F. Kennedy, 1956

We are not going to send American boys 9 or 10,000 miles away from home to do what Asian boys ought to be doing for themselves.

President Lyndon Johnson, 1964

Conscientious objection must be reserved only for the greatest moral issues, and Vietnam is not of this magnitude.

Henry Kissinger, 1969

Everything I read and heard about the war violated my deepest patriotism, my pride in what this country stood for in the world, until I resolved that the American thing to do was to oppose the war.

James Quay, Conscientious Objector

And so, quite naturally, once again to war...to secure the necessary access to the world marketplace.

William A. Williams, historian, 1972

The mature and sensitive people of this country must realize that their freedom of protest is being exploited by avowed anarchists and communists who detest everything about this country and want to destroy it.

Vice President Spiro Agnew, 1969

There have been many explanations of how we got into the Vietnam War....But all explanations come back to one. It was the result of a long series of steps taken in response to a bureaucratic view of the world.

John Kenneth Galbraith,
How to Control the Military, 1969

The Executive can bootstrap the nation into any war by sending one American soldier into hostile territory....The Vietnam War escalated in precisely this context.

Legal Brief, *Berk v. Laird*, 1970

I ain't a'marchin' anymore.

Phil Oches, folksinger

INTRODUCTION

No one was neutral about the Vietnam War, at least not after it began to occupy the media's attention in the late 1960's. It was "hell in a small place," as one correspondent described it, a war in which the United States dropped more bombs than did the Allies during all of World War II. The casualties were enormous: 58,000 Americans lost their lives, as did hundreds of thousands of Vietnamese. The after-effects have been equally devastating. More than 60,000 veterans have committed suicide since the withdrawal of American troops in 1973. The Vietnam War drove one President from office and forced another to remain "hunkered" down in his command post in Washington. The war was also fought on the home front, tearing apart families, friends, religious congregations, and public institutions. It was our longest war, and it cost us the good will of most of the world's people, including many who had long admired our democratic ideals.

Walter LaFeber and John Garry Clifford examine the historical policies that led us into war. In 1965, President Johnson reneged on his 1964 campaign promise not to send American boys and called for a moral crusade to end Communism in Southeast Asia. In 1971, President Nixon, as had Kennedy and Johnson before him, tried to explain to newsmen why his policies would end the war and lead to a lasting peace. Television critic Michael Arlen assesses the effect a "living-room war" had on Americans back home.

The most moving and sensitive comments on the war not surprisingly come from those who were on the front lines. Lynda Van Devanter describes what witnessing daily mayhem and death did to the young nurses who cared for the wounded. Van Devanter has collected many of the poems nurses wrote to express their frustration, grief, and permanent hurt. Vietnam veteran Bill Ehrhard publishes his own searing poetry, as have many other soldiers. Front-line soldiers such as Brian "Doc" Koss and John Erdos relate what the war did to them.

When the home front became a cauldron of dissent, Vice President Spiro Agnew labeled such activity "Impudence in the Streets," and Chicago's Mayor Richard Daley defended his use of force against demonstrators at the 1968 Democratic Convention, one of whom was Bradford Lyttle. Tom Hayden and the radical Students for a Democratic Society did their own name-calling, but their 1962 Port Huron Statement still reflected the idealism of the Kennedy years. Another idealist was James Quay who explains why he became a Conscientious Objector. Essayist Norman Podhoretz still sees the war as a necessary struggle against "the evils of Communism," but William L. Griffen and John Marciano suggest the war has different lessons to impart.

Vietnam was clearly our most unpopular war, and it was the only one we ever lost. The scars still run deep and many questions remain unanswered: Should we have been there at all? What were our objectives and could we have achieved them? Did we lose our innocence or did we lose something even more significant? Did the dominos tumble after we were driven out of Vietnam? And, finally, how did the defeat affect our subsequent foreign policy?

Walter LaFeber, AMERICA, RUSSIA, AND THE COLD WAR

Walter LaFeber, Professor of History at Cornell University, is one of America's best known diplomatic historians. In the short selection below, taken from his America, Russia and the Cold War, *he explains why President John F. Kennedy decided to involve the United States militarily in Southeast Asia.*

The missile crisis did not advance Kennedy's "Grand Design" for Europe, but it tragically accelerated the American rush into Vietnam. Key Washington policy makers assumed that the one result of the October confrontation was a nuclear standoff between the two superpowers. Both had clearly indicated their reluctance to use nuclear force. The United States had won primarily because Khrushchev unwisely challenged Kennedy in the Caribbean, where American conventional naval power was decisive. Within months, both sides were discussing the easing of Cold War tensions. If the assumption was correct that the two great powers mutually feared each other's nuclear arms, then, the Kennedy administration concluded, the leaders of the emerging nations might feel that they had considerable opportunity to play West versus East, or, as in Southeast Asia and Africa, to undertake revolutionary changes without fear that either the United States or Russia would be able to shape these changes. If nationalist leaders acted on these beliefs, the newly emerging world could become increasingly unmanageable, perhaps dangerously radical from Washington's point of view. Such a view meshed perfectly with the other American fear that the communist policy line of support for (but not direct involvement in) "wars of liberation" had been established in 1960-1961 precisely to exploit the emerging nationalism. The New Frontiersmen dedicated themselves to shattering "wars of liberation" with such nationalist movements. Vietnam would be used as the example.

The President also focused on Southeast Asia because he hoped to discipline what he believed to be the expansiveness of Communist China. In 1949-1950 Kennedy, then a member of the House of Representatives, had joined Republicans in denouncing the Truman administration for supposedly "losing" China. He softened these views during the 1950s, but in preparing to run for the presidency in 1960 he was reluctant to consider disavowing the use of nuclear weapons: "I wonder if we could expect to check the sweep south of the Chinese with their endless armies with conventional forces?" After the missile crisis, Kennedy summarized his position in a conversation with Andre Malraux, French cultural affairs minister. Assistant Secretary of State for European Affairs William R. Tyler has described this talk:

> *[Kennedy] wanted to get a message to de Gaulle through Malraux . . . that really there was no reason why there should be differences between us and France in Europe, or between us and our European Allies, because there was no longer a likely Soviet military threat against Europe [since the Cuban missile crisis]. . . . But the area where we would have*

problems in the future . . . was China. He said it was so important that he and de Gaulle and other European leaders should think together about what they will do, what the situation will be when China becomes a nuclear power, what will happen then. . . . This was the great menace in the future to humanity, the free world, and freedom on earth. Relations with the Soviet Union could be contained within the framework of mutual awareness of the impossibility of achieving any gains through war. But in the case of China, this restraint would not be effective because the Chinese would be perfectly prepared, because of the lower value they attach to human life, to sacrifice hundreds of millions of their own lives, if this were necessary in order to carry out their militant and aggressive policies.

The missile crisis and the Berlin confrontation in 1961 also reinforced the administration's belief that it knew how to threaten to apply or, if necessary, actually apply conventional military power to obtain maximum results. White House officials joked that poor John Foster Dulles had never been able to find a suitable war for his "massive retaliation"; these pragmatic Kennedyites, however, had apparently solved the great riddle by perfectly matching power to crisis. One false premise ultimately wrecked this self-satisfaction: in Berlin and Cuba the Russians had backed down (Castro, noticeably, had been willing to fight to keep the missiles); in Vietnam the United States dealt with nationalist Vietnamese who, like Castro, had much to win by continuing to fight against apparently overwhelming American firepower.

This fatal flaw did not clearly appear in 1962-1966. On the contrary, during the autumn of 1962 the President's policies seemed to be proved correct during the brief war between India and China. India provoked the war during a border dispute over territory more important to the Chinese than to the Indians. The Chinese attacked with devastating force, destroying both the myth of Indian power and the American hope that India could serve as a cornerstone in the containment of China. The Chinese carefully occupied only some of the disputed territory, voluntarily withdrawing from other conquered areas. On November 20 Prime Minister Nehru urgently asked Kennedy for aid. An American aircraft carrier moved across the southern Pacific toward India, but before it could become a factor the crisis ended. Some Washington policy makers nevertheless drew the false conclusion that the Chinese had backed down only after receiving warnings from the United States and, independently of the American move, from Russia.

Kennedy's advisors displayed similarly unwarranted confidence in their ability to control power in late 1962 when they decided to turn Laos into a pro-American bastion. They thereby helped destroy the Geneva Agreements which the United States had solemnly signed in midsummer 1962. Under the agreements, all foreign troops were to withdraw from Laos. The communist Pathet Lao were to joint neutralist Souvanna Phouma's coalition government. American military advisors, indeed, began to leave, but the Central Intelligence Agency stepped up the supplying of the Meo tribesmen, an effective guerrilla army operating behind Pathet Lao lines.

In April 1964, however, a right-wing coup in Vientiane made Souvanna only a figurehead leader. The Pathet Lao retaliated with an offensive that threatened to conquer the entire Plain of Jarres. The United States then began initially small but systematic bombing raids on Laos, which Washington carefully tried to keep secret. To save a supposedly pivotal domino, the Kennedy-Johnson advisors confidently escalated their application of power. The actual result, however, was that at the very time the United States escalated its commitment to South Vietnam, the key area of Laos became uncontrollable and formed an open channel for aid to the National Liberation Front in South Vietnam.

In 1962-1963 the assumptions that would govern American policies in Vietnam fell into place. First, Vietnam was vital to American interests because, in John F. Kennedy's words of 1956, "Vietnam represents the cornerstone of the Free World in Southeast Asia, the keystone to the arch, the finger in the dike. . . . Her economy is essential to the economy of all of Southeast Asia; and her political liberty is an inspiration to those seeking to obtain or maintain their liberty in all parts of Asia--and indeed the world." As Kennedy emphasized in his May 25, 1961, address to Congress, the battle of "freedom versus tyranny" was being waged in newly emerging areas such as Vietnam. While belittling the foreign policies of the previous administration, the Kennedy advisors gulped down whole the Eisenhower "domino" theory. More precisely, the Dulles and Eisenhower formulation of the 1950s remained valid because, without an open Southeast Asia for its raw materials and markets, Japan, essential to the entire American strategic policy in the western Pacific, would have to turn toward its traditional market of China.

Second, the Kennedy administration assumed that China not only was to be isolated but, as some thought it had been in India, militarily disciplined. Both the Chinese and the Russians were to be taught that "wars of liberation" were not possible in areas the United States considered vital to its own interests. Third, the missile crisis, the India-China conflict, and the emerging Laotian situation gave the administration confidence in its ability to escalate military power while keeping it under control. Because of McNamara's work, moreover, the military power was available. For the first time in their history, Americans entered war with a great army at the ready, a force created by self-styled "realists" who, in the tradition of Forrestal and Acheson, believed that they could ultimately shape world affairs with American firepower.

These assumptions--the validity of the domino theory (particularly its economic implications for Japan), the century-old American fear of a "Yellow Peril," and the belief held by American liberal spokesmen that, as children of Niebuhr, they knew the secrets of using military force effectively--these governed the Kennedy administration as it moved deeper into Vietnam.

In 1962 Secretary of Defense McNamara had observed, "Every quantitative measurement we have shows we're winning this war." Some factors in Southeast Asia, however, could not be computed. Twelve thousand American military personnel were involved in the conflict, yet the Viet Cong continued to gain ground. The strategic hamlet program, geared to secure the countryside, was failing despite, or perhaps because of, the determination of the Diem regime. The peasants disliked being forced to leave their homes and to be resettled elsewhere, particularly by a government that had condemned any meaningful land reform program. "No wonder the Viet Cong looked like Robin Hoods when they began to hit the hamlets," one civilian American official remarked. Viet Cong successes mounted despite their kidnapping and brutal murdering of village and hamlet officials.

Kennedy's hope of reversing the situation rested on the ability of Diem's government to wage a successful military campaign while stabilizing South Vietnam's political situation.

Saigon's military capability was dramatically called into question on January 2, 1963, in the village of Ap Bac, approximately fifty miles from Saigon. A small Viet Cong force was surrounded by a Vietnamese unit that was ten times larger, but despite the demands of American advisors to attack, the South Vietnamese refused. The Viet Cong then methodically shot down five American helicopters, damaged nine more, killed three Americans, and disappeared. Apparently only United States soldiers had the will to fight in Vietnam, but Kennedy carefully pointed out after one fire fight between Viet Cong and American personnel that the United States forces in Vietnam were not "combat troops," and that if the situation changed, "I, of course, would go to Congress." He was not prepared to do this in 1963. Nor was the White House even prepared to inform adequately the Congress and the public.

With an American presidential election little more than a year away, and his own belief that in 1964 his main challenge would come from the right wing of American politics, Kennedy carefully threw the best possible, even if misleading, light on Vietnamese affairs. American newspaper correspondents who candidly reported Diem's failures were rewarded either with Kennedy's unsuccessful attempt to give one critical correspondent a "vacation" from Vietnam, or with rejoinders to their questions like the one given by Admiral Harry Felt, commander of American forces in the Pacific: "Why don't you get on the team?" In 1963 there was a widening abyss between the actual situation in Vietnam and the self-assurance of the Kennedy administration that it could manipulate military power to control nationalist revolutions.

By late summer 1963 the abyss was so wide that it could no longer be covered. Throughout the early part of the year, Diem, with the assistance of his brother Nhu Dinh Diem and Madame Nhu, ruthlessly suppressed domestic opposition. When Washington protested the Nhu's activities, Diem and his brother openly objected to this pressure. The beginning of the end for Diem and Nhu occurred on May 8, when Diem's troops shot into a crowd of Buddhists who were celebrating Buddha's birthday by waving religious flags, thereby violating the regime's rule that forbade the exhibit of any banner but the government's. The firing climaxed years of bitterness between the Roman Catholic regime of Diem and the Buddhists, who comprised more than 80 percent of the country's population. Many Buddhist leaders wanted no part of the war, no part of any foreign intervention in their nation, and no part of the Diem regime. They represented a new, potentially radical nationalism that neither the Diem regime nor the American officials in Vietnam could understand, let alone cope with. In June Buddhist-led anti-government riots spread through Saigon. Diem retaliated by raiding Buddhist pagodas. Several Buddhists burned themselves to death in public protest, an act that Madame Nhu sarcastically welcomed as a "barbecue show." Students in normally quiet schools and universities joined the Buddhists. Diem confronted a full-scale rebellion.

The Kennedy administration's confusion in dealing with the revolutionary situation became glaringly evident during the crisis. While continuing to announce that the military program was going well, the White House attempted to push Diem into making necessary domestic reforms by cutting off relatively small amounts of military and economic aid. That move, however, was sufficient to encourage anti-Diem elements in the army. On November 1 and 2, with, at least, the knowledge and approval of the White House and the American ambassador in Saigon, Henry Cabot Lodge, a military junta captured Diem and his brother. Within hours the two men were shot and the junta assumed power. Three weeks later President Kennedy was assassinated in Dallas, Texas.

President Lyndon B. Johnson, ***PEACE WITHOUT CONQUEST*** **(1965)**

During his 1964 campaign for re-election, President Johnson promised not "to send American boys...to do what Asian boys ought to be doing for themselves." By 1965 he had clearly changed his mind. Using a questionable attack on an American destroyer in the Bay of Tonkin for his justification, Johnson greatly escalated our involvement in the war. In the following speech delivered on April 6, 1965 at Johns Hopkins University, Johnson invoked lofty moral arguments to support his decision. Privately he admitted, "The only thing I know to do is more of the same and do it more efficiently and effectively."

Tonight Americans and Asians are dying for a world where each people may choose its own path to change.

This is the principle for which our ancestors fought in the valleys of Pennsylvania. It is the principle for which our sons fight tonight in the jungles of Vietnam.

Vietnam is far away from this quiet campus. We have no territory there, nor do we seek any. The war is dirty and brutal and difficult. And some 400 young men, born into an America that is bursting with opportunity and promise, have ended their lives on Vietnam's steaming soil.

Why must we take this painful road?

Why must this Nation hazard its ease, and its interest, and its power for the sake of a people so far away?

We fight because we must fight if we are to live in a world where every country can shape its own destiny. And only in such a world will our own freedom be finally secure.

This kind of world will never be built by bombs or bullets. Yet the infirmities of man are such that force must often precede reason, and the waste of war, the works of peace.

We wish that this were not so. But we must deal with the world as it is, if it is ever to be as we wish.

The world as it is in Asia is not a serene or peaceful place.

The first reality is that North Vietnam has attacked the independent nation of South Vietnam. Its object is total conquest.

Of course, some of the people of South Vietnam are participating in attack on their own government. But trained men and supplies, orders and arms, flow in a constant stream from north to south.

This support is the heartbeat of the war.

And it is a war of unparalleled brutality. Simple farmers are the targets of assassination and kidnapping. Women and children are strangled in the night because their men are loyal to their government. And helpless villages are ravaged by sneak attacks. Large-scale raids are conducted on towns, and terror strikes in the heart of cities.

The confused nature of this conflict cannot mask the fact that it is the new face of an old enemy.

Over this war--and all Asia--is another reality: the deepening shadow of Communist China.

The rulers in Hanoi are urged on by Peking. This is a regime which has destroyed freedom in Tibet, which has attacked India, and has been condemned by the United Nations for aggression in Korea. It is a nation which is helping the forces of violence in almost every continent. The contest in Vietnam is part of a wider pattern of aggressive purposes.

Why are these realities our concern? Why are we in South Vietnam?

We are there because we have a promise to keep. Since 1954 every American President has offered support to the people of South Vietnam. We have helped to build, and we have helped to defend. Thus, over many years, we have made a national pledge to help South Vietnam defend its independence.

And I intend to keep that promise.

To dishonor that pledge, to abandon this small and brave nation to its enemies, and to the terror that must follow, would be an unforgivable wrong.

We are also there to strengthen world order. Around the globe, from Berlin to Thailand, are people whose well-being rests, in part, on the belief that they can count on us if they are attacked. To leave Vietnam to its fate would shake the confidence of all these people in the value of an American commitment and in the value of America's word. The result would be increased unrest and instability, and even wider war.

We are also there because there are great stakes in the balance. Let no one think for a moment that retreat from Vietnam would bring an end to conflict. The battle would be renewed in one country and then another. The central lesson of our time is that the appetite of aggression is never satisfied. To withdraw from one battlefield means only to prepare for the next. We must say in southeast Asia--as we did in Europe--in the words of the Bible: "Hitherto shalt thou come, but no further."

There are those who say that all our effort there will be futile--that China's power is such that it is bound to dominate all southeast Asia. But there is no end to that argument until all of the nations of Asia are swallowed up.

There are those who wonder why we have a responsibility there. Well, we have it there for the same reason that we have a responsibility for the defense of Europe. World War II was fought in both Europe and Asia, and when it ended we found ourselves with continued responsibility for the defense of freedom.

Our objective is the independence of South Vietnam, and its freedom from attack. We want nothing for ourselves--only that the people of South Vietnam be allowed to guide their own country in their own way.

We will do everything necessary to reach that objective. And we will do only what is absolutely necessary.

In recent months attacks on South Vietnam were stepped up. Thus, it became necessary for us to increase our response and to make attacks by air. This is not a change of purpose. It is a change in what we believe that purpose requires.

We do this in order to slow down aggression.

We do this to increase the confidence of the brave people of South Vietnam who have bravely borne this brutal battle for so many years with so many casualties.

And we do this to convince the leaders of North Vietnam--and all who seek to share their conquest--of a very simple fact:

We will not be defeated.

We will not grow tired.

We will not withdraw, either openly or under the cloak of a meaningless agreement.

We know that air attacks alone will not accomplish all of these purposes. But it is our best and prayerful judgment that they are a necessary part of the surest road to peace.

We hope that peace will come swiftly. But that is in the hands of others besides ourselves. And we must be prepared for a long continued conflict. It will require patience as well as bravery, the will to endure as well as the will to resist.

I wish it were possible to convince others with words of what we now find it necessary to say with guns and planes: Armed hostility is futile. Our resources are equal to any challenge. Because we fight for values and we fight for principles, rather than territory or colonies, our patience and our determination are unending.

Once this is clear, then it should also be clear that the only path for reasonable men is the path of peaceful settlement.

Such peace demands an independent South Vietnam--securely guaranteed and able to shape its own relationships to all others--free from outside interference--tied to no alliance--a military base for no other country.

These are the essentials of any final settlement.

We will never be second in the search for such a peaceful settlement in Vietnam.

There may be many ways to this kind of peace: in discussion or negotiation with the governments concerned; in large groups or in small ones; in the reaffirmation of old agreements or their strengthening with new ones.

We have stated this position over and over again, fifty times and more, to friend and foe alike. And we remain ready, with this purpose, for unconditional discussions.

And until that bright and necessary day of peace we will try to keep conflict from spreading. We have no desire to see thousands die in battle--Asians or Americans. We have no desire to devastate that which the people of North Vietnam have built with toil and sacrifice. We will use our power with restraint and with all the wisdom that we can command.

But we will use it.

This war, like most wars, is filled with terrible irony. For what do the people of North Vietnam want? They want what their neighbors also desire: food for their hunger; health for their bodies; a chance to learn; progress for their country; and an end to the bondage of material misery. And they would find all these things far more readily in peaceful association with others than in the endless course of battle. . . .

We often say how impressive power is. But I do not find it impressive at all. The guns and the bombs, the rockets and the warships, are all symbols of human failure. They are necessary symbols. They protect what we cherish. But they are witness to human folly.

A dam built across a great river is impressive.

In the countryside where I was born, and where I live, I have seen the night illuminated, and the kitchens warmed, and the homes heated, where once the cheerless night and the ceaseless cold held sway. And all this happened because electricity came to our area along the humming wires of the REA [Rural Electrification Administrative]. Electrification of the countryside--yes, that, too, is impressive.

A rich harvest in a hungry land is impressive.

The sight of healthy children in a classroom is impressive.

These--not mighty arms--are the achievements which the American Nation believes to be impressive.

And, if we are steadfast, the time may come when all other nations will also find it so.

Every night before I turn out the lights to sleep I ask myself this question: Have I done everything that I can do to unite this country? Have I done everything I can to help unite the world, to try to bring peace and hope to all the peoples of the world? Have I done enough?

Ask yourselves that question in your homes--and in this hall tonight. Have we, each of us, all done all we could? Have we done enough?

We may well be living in the time foretold many years ago when it was said: "I call heaven and earth to record this day against you, that I have set before you life and death, blessing and cursing: therefore choose life, that both thou and thy seed may live."

This generation of the world must choose: destroy or build, kill or aid, hate or understand.

We can do all these things on a scale never dreamed of before.

Well, we will choose life. In so doing we will prevail over the enemies within man, and over the natural enemies of all mankind. . . .

James Quay, *LIFE, LIBERTY, AND THE RIGHT TO PROTEST*

Born into a conventional American family, James Quay was expected "to do his duty," as his father before him had done during World War II. But young Quay chose to become one of the Vietnam War's 170,000 Conscientious Objectors. What follows is his transformation from a young, conservative, West Point applicant to a dissident who, invoking the moral lessons of the Nuremberg Nazi Trials, refused to do his government's bidding.

I can't recall exactly when the war in Vietnam finally attracted my attention. I remember a few snapshots from the early years: a Buddhist monk protesting against the South Vietnamese government, seated in the lotus position and burning like a torch; the overthrow and assassination of premier Ngo Dinh Diem three weeks before President Kennedy was assassinated; the alleged attack on U.S. destroyers in the Gulf of Tonkin in August 1964. But Vietnam in general and these events in particular felt remote when I arrived in LaFayette in the fall of 1964. I was supposed to register at my local selective service board when I turned 18-September 26, 1964-but I forgot. In fact, I didn't go for three weeks, but it was no big deal. I never considered not registering, and they did not think my being late meant anything. That wouldn't be true later.

My family were middle-of-the-road Republicans. I favored Nixon over Kennedy in the 1960 election and found good things to say about Barry Goldwater four years later. My junior year in high school, I applied to become a candidate to West Point, the U.S. Military Academy, and took and passed all the necessary tests. I changed my mind before the selection was made, because the only degree offered at West Point was a B.A. in science, and I didn't want to limit my options. I already had an inkling that West Point might be confining in other ways, but I don't remember having any moral objection to entering the military. As it was, I never had to decide: my congressman selected me only as first alternate and I went to Lafayette College instead.

My father had enlisted in 1941 trusting that what his government was telling him about his war was true. That trust between the American government and its people was one of the earliest lies offered of the Vietnam war. I can't take time to document all the lies here, but I remember confronting a State Department official who spoke at Lafayette in 1967 or 1968 with some of them. "Look," he told me, " I admit you've been lied to in the past, but you've simply got to believe us now." The lies continued.

Despite the difficulty in gaining an accurate picture about events so far away, it became clear to me that enormous destruction was being visited upon the people of North and South Vietnam, so that finally, whether Vietnam was two countries or one, whether Ho Chi Minh was a communist aggressor or a nationalistic hero, I felt the destruction was incompatible with any proper American objective. Later, during the Tet Offensive of 1968, an American artillery officer said of the village of Ben Tre, "We had to destroy it in order to save it." That sentence crystallized what many came to feel about the war. If we were destroying South Vietnam in order to save it in the name of freedom, what and who would be left to be free?

What provoked my private reservation into public opposition was an incident at Lafayette. When an official from the South Vietnamese embassy came to speak at Marquis Hall in May 1967, a dozen people I knew stood peacefully in front of the building with signs that read "Stop the Bombing." I regret I was not one of them. For this, they were surrounded by hundreds of fraternity boys and bombarded for hours with water, ink, and verbal abuse. The campus police were strangely absent. A rally was organized to support the right of free speech: my first demonstration was for the First Amendment.

Everything I read and heard about the war violated my deepest patriotism, my pride in what this country stood for in the world, until I resolved that the American thing to do was to oppose the war. I wrote to my congressman and received polite replies urging me to support the President. I joined The Committee Against the Crime of Silence and put my name on record at the United Nations as opposing my government's war in Vietnam. I wrote editorials for the *Lafayette* and took part in demonstrations. Today, the mention of anti-war demonstrations conjures pictures of mighty throngs of people choking the streets of major cities and chanting slogans, but at the beginning it was different. I remember joining a dozen other students and faculty members on Saturdays in the town square of Easton to stand for one hour of silent witness, protesting the war. The people who passed us were not always friendly: we were reminding them of unpleasant events far away, and many mistook our opposition to the war as opposition to the country. One Sunday I handed out leaflets at a Methodist church and then attended the worship service, only to hear myself denounced as a "tool of the Moscow line" by the minister. It was the beginning of my education into the nature and power of governmental authority.

You see, at the beginning, I thought persuading my fellow citizens would be easy. All Americans were being lied to by their government, so all we had to do was discover the truth, reveal what was really going on in Vietnam, and the American people would rise up and demand that their government stop the war. But I came to see that the reason many Americans supported the war wasn't because they had analyzed the government's policy and approved it, but simply because they trusted whatever their government said about the war and refused to believe their government's authority should be opposed. How could the country that had saved the world from Hitler now be fighting an immoral war? In arguments repeated in homes all over the country, objections to the war were met with the reply: "The President knows more than we do. This is a democracy. We have to support the President."

Fortunately for me and for all anti-war protestors, this country was created out of resistance to governmental authority. The Declaration of Independence, after all, tells every American that the time may come when it is not only his right to rebel against his government, but his duty. The tradition of conscientious objection to war is even older, arriving with the first Quakers in 1635. James Madison, one of the architects of the U.S. Constitution, proposed making objection to war a constitutional right. It was defeated, but so were all proposals for national conscription for the first generation of this country's existence. In short, conscientious objection is as American as cherry pie.

In the spring of 1967 I told my parents that I was planning to become a conscientious objector. I remember that my parents were concerned but not opposed--mostly I think they were baffled. In a journal that I kept at the time, I noted my father's silence. I was rejecting the course of action he had taken in World War II and he could not help me. He could show me how a man does what his government asks of him: he could not show me how to oppose that government. But my father did me a great kindness: he knew a member of the local draft board, and from that day in 1967 until the board made its decision a year later, my father made a point not to mention my case to his friend. Though I was making a choice he would not have made, he allowed me to make my own decision and face its consequences without angry threats or benign interference. I had friends who were not so lucky.

"I can understand the anguish of the younger generation," Henry Kissinger told an interviewer in 1969. "They lack the models, they have no heroes, they see no great purposes in the world. But conscientious objection is destructive of society...Conscientious objection must be reserved only for the greatest moral issues, and Vietnam is not of this magnitude." Kissinger could not be more mistaken. It was only by actively opposing the war and choosing to be a conscientious objector that I was able to find role models I could admire, to discover a new group of heroes to replace John Wayne, and to join my small individual efforts to one of the greatest purposes of this or any other time-peace.

My claim to conscientious objector status was not based on traditional religious beliefs. In fact, I had been interviewed by the Lafayette alumni magazine in an article on campus religious life and quoted as an example of an agnostic. Until 1965, you could only be released from military service if you could demonstrate that your opposition to participation in war was by reason of "religious training or belief." But in 1965 the Supreme Court had ruled that a person could not be denied C.O. status simply because he did not belong to an orthodox religious sect. It was enough, the high court ruled, if the belief which prompted your objection occupied the same place in your life as the belief in a traditional deity occupied in the life of a believer. I have only just discovered that the Court's opinion cites several authors that I had read in a freshman religion course at Lafayette, among them, theologian Paul Tillich:

> *And if the word [God] has not much meaning for you, translate it, and speak of the depths of your life, of the source of your being, of your ultimate concern, of what you take seriously without any reservation. Perhaps, in order to do so, you must forget everything traditional that you have learned about God.*

I knew I objected to the war in Vietnam. What I had to discover was the ultimate source of that objection and describe it for myself and for the five ordinary Americans that comprised draft board #90 in Allentown, Pennsylvania, in the space provided on Special Form 150. That form asked: " Describe the nature of your belief which is the basis of your claim and state whether or not your belief in a Supreme Being involves duties which to you are superior to those arising from any human relation." Though I would phrase things differently today, I find I still essentially believe what I wrote 17 years ago:

> *I affirm that love and justice are the essence of a Supreme Being and that every human being is divine in that he has love and justice within him to some degree. I sincerely believe that the principles of love and justice with which men have constructed their gods and their government reside in each man. I affirm the divinity of every human being. The more a man demonstrates these two*

divine attributes in his daily living, the more divine he himself will become.

Because I believe that from man all awareness and order comes, because I believe that each man is a divine being striving to become more divine, and because I believe that divinity manifests itself only through the love and justice of human relationships, I believe that human relationships are the highest relationships. Therefore there are no duties which to me are superior to those arising from human relations.

The Vietnam War and the draft of men to fight that war forced hundred of thousands of young men to ask themselves what values they were willing to suffer and die for, at an age when they are just learning to think for themselves about such matters. Those who had to take that choice discovered the Authority they were willing to obey, be it the authority of family, church, public opinion, or government. To use Tillich's phrase, in choosing we learned what our ultimate concerns were, the nature of the gods we worshiped. For many, the consequences of their choice were harsh and lasting. Some of us found out that our Gods were lifeless idols. Some of us found out that our Gods were very much alive.

As I worked on Special Form 150 in early 1968, the government indicted Dr. Benjamin Spock and others for counseling young men to resist the draft. The USS Pueblo was seized by North Korea. The Tet Offensive brought an end to the American optimism about the war. In March, peace candidate Eugene McCarthy nearly defeated Lyndon Johnson in the New Hampshire primary. Robert Kennedy announced his candidacy for President. I filed for conscientious objector status on the first day of spring, 1968. No one knew it, but old men, women, and children had just been massacred by American soldiers at My Lai. Two week after that Martin Luther King was assassinated in Memphis. Three weeks later, while students occupied the President's Office at Columbia, at a small demonstration on my campus, a young man had his head grazed by a pellet shot from a local fraternity. I graduated in late May. A week later, my fiancee and I went to New York City to look for an apartment. That night peace candidate Robert Kennedy was assassinated in Los Angeles.

It felt as though the country were having a nervous breakdown.

I did not know what I would do if the draft board refused my claim to C.O. status. I did know I would not enter the armed forces. I felt I was prepared to go to prison rather than flee to Canada, but fortunately I never had to find out. On June 14, Flag Day, my draft board informed me that I had been classified "1-O" (Conscientious Objector). I was further informed that they did not expect to receive any call for draftees until that fall, which meant I could sit it out and possibly not be called. Instead I volunteered for two years alternate service as a case worker with the New York City Department of Social Services, who assigned me a caseload of families in central Harlem. All around me, young men were going to war and to prison; I did not want to avoid service on a technicality. So I became one of the 170,000 men who were granted conscientious objector status during the Vietnam War and one of 96,000 who completed the two years' alternative service.

There is a figure who haunted me then: Adolph Eichmann, a Nazi who helped coordinate the trains that carried Jews to the death camps during World War II. He fled to Argentina after the war, but in 1961 the Israeli secret police located and kidnapped him to Israel. He stood trial in Jerusalem for his role in the murder of thousands of Jews, even though, he protested, he had never personally killed a Jew. A political theorist named Hannah Arendt covered the trial for the *New Yorker* magazine and in a subsequent book, entitled *Eichmann in Jerusalem: A Report on the Banality of Evil*, explored the question of how six million human beings could be systematically killed by other human beings. What we learned is that something as abominable as the Holocaust is not accomplished by villains--there are not enough villains in the world to accomplish such horrors. No, the terrible news of that book is that crimes of this magnitude are only possible when ordinary men and women do what they're told. What Arendt found at the heart of Eichmann's deeds was--nothing. In Arendt's words, he was "thoughtless," he literally had no thoughts of his own that mattered, rather he acted in accordance with the thoughts of others.

Eichmann, like the Nazis who were tried by the Allied immediately after World War II, defended himself by saying that he was simply following orders. But at the trial in Nuremberg, the Allied judges ruled that the fact that a person acted under the orders of his government or a superior did not relieve him of responsibility, provided a moral choice was possible. All along the chain of command that led from Hitler to the death camps were ordinary people like Eichmann who were just following orders. While I do not equate the war in Vietnam, destructive of life as it was, with the Nazi Holocaust, I came to see that the Americans, too, could be content to follow orders, unmindful of the devastating impact their ordinary actions here at home had on others far away. This discovery disturbed me then; it disturbs me still.

In November 1969 my wife and I went to Washington, D.C. to join the March Against Death. In subfreezing temperatures we marched with candles from the Washington Memorial to the White House with 40,000 others, each with the name of an American killed in Vietnam around our necks. At the end of the march, each of us stood on a small wooden platform and shouted that name at the White House:

GLENDON WATERS

All I knew about Glendon Waters was that he was from Texas. I know now that he was killed in July 1967--about the time I began protesting the war--and that his name is on the Vietnam Veteran's Memorial.

Why are those names so moving? Why do visitors to the Memorial reach up and touch the names? Why do I, after 15 years, still remember a name I spoke once and whose owner I never knew? Because a name brings the person closer, makes it easier to remember that casualty figures contain the final news about a particular being, a lover, a son, a father, a brother, whose death brought terrible grief to his family. Often mere numbers make us numb. We must try hard not to become numb. So "Glendon Waters" is what I say instead of 59,000 dead. Glendon Waters died in Vietnam.

We have to break the cycle of men like Glendon Waters. I believe that means breaking the cycle of unquestioning obedience to authority, as I have suggested. It means fashioning a new model of manhood. And finally, it means we have to imagine more concretely and sympathetically the lives of others. In the movie *Hearts and Minds*, we are shown a former Air Force pilot who sits on his porch. We have heard him describing how insulated he was in his air-conditioned B-52 cockpit from the death and destruction he caused below. He tells us that he did not drop napalm but that he dropped worse: CBUs (cluster bomb units), bombs that explode sending nearly 200,000 steel balls one-quarter inch in diameter into human beings unfortunate enough to be nearby. He tells us that the has a three-year-old son and that now, if he tried to imagine the feelings of a Vietnamese father seeing his three-year-old hit by the bombs he dropped...

Well, he can't finish the sentence, he breaks down under the horror of that vision. Now that he has a son, he can imagine what it would be like. He can imagine concretely the human dimensions of the damage he inflicted so thoughtlessly before. If he had been encouraged to imagine this before he climbed into his plane, before he entered the Air Force, if 18-year-old boys were forced to consider the consequences of their actions as soldiers, if those at home were forced to imagine what we ask our soldiers to do, they might be more reluctant to leave and we more reluctant to send them off to kill.

I have a son, eight years old, named Jesse, and a daughter, three named Jenny. I held them both within minutes of their birth. I love them more than I love my own life. I cannot imagine any cause that would justify their deaths. And I cannot imagine any cause that would justify the deaths of someone else's children. Yet that is what modern warfare means. In Vietnam, Cambodia, Laos, Biafra, Angola, Iran/Iraq, Afghanistan, El Salvador, Nicaragua, soldiers have not just killed soldiers; willingly or unwillingly, knowingly or unknowingly, they have killed women and children. There is no cause noble enough to justify the deaths of innocent women and children. None.

Opposition to killing must begin before the war begins. The crucial moment in the passage from civilian life to military life is called "induction." That word come from the Latin meaning "to be led into." At a certain point, you are asked to take a step forward. You can't be forced to take that step and no matter how many others step forward with you, it is step only you can take or refuse to take. Once you take that step you enter a world where you are expected to obey all lawful commands given to you, no matter what your personal objections might be. I can understand the courage that it takes to obey, especially when you consider that such obedience might ultimately cost you your life.

That is the step I refused to take. While I felt my country had the right to require service of me, I denied it the right to order me to kill other human beings. That is a step I hope that all of us might one day refuse to take.

BRIAN "DOC" KOSS, MEDIC

The most dramatic stories of war are always told by the soldiers themselves, and Vietnam, with its many published oral histories, made this fact graphically clear to the reading public. As a medic, "Doc" Koss saw the worst of war, and the tortured memories followed him home before he finally was able to control them with the support of his fellow veterans.

The folks back home couldn't know how it really was. I once talked to a bunch of college students, and I'm telling 'em about wading through body parts, and stuffing body bags. I was really getting into detail. These kids had never heard any of this, and all these eyes were staring at me. They were like, "Whoa, this couldn't have happened." I was telling them how we flew into the jungle to pick up some wounded. They had cut just enough trees so a helicopter could land and pick up the wounded. The only way we could get to them through this 150-foot, triple canopy jungle was to go straight down, pick them up, and go straight out. If something happened, you were shit out of luck. The first helicopter that went in got shot down, so then there was no place to land. We sent another helicopter in to rescue the crew, and they also got shot up. They made it out, but they didn't get the crew from the first helicopter. Then some three infantrymen, another medic, and I went in. We stayed the night and tried to secure the area and patch guys up as best we could. That was a hairy night. Shit was flying that night; I was probably as scared as you can get. There were a lot of casualties, and we had to go through the bodies. These guys had been overrun and had been in hand-to-hand combat. They were all chopped up. There is just no way to describe it. It's impossible to describe, but we spent two days just going through the remains trying to put those bodies together. I remember a colonel coming on the radio and yelling at us to get with the program, that it just wasn't that important to get the right body in the right bag, or even the right parts together. We were just supposed to send something home. We got so mad. We could have been court-martialed for the shit we said to this guy on the radio, and just because we believed that Joe Smith should have his own two arms and legs when we sent him home.

The officers measured our success in Vietnam through the body count. This was the their chance to make rank, so we killed as many as we could. There was no territory to gain. They would turn in their monthly report of the number killed, and if they killed enough, they eventually earned another bar or star. That's how they judged their performance, but that's a hell of a way to fight a war.

I was being stupid when I got wounded. I only had three weeks left on my tour, and I didn't have to go out on that last patrol. But at the time only three of our six medics were available, and I couldn't see saying, "Hey, you go take my place." If something then happened, you would have to live with it the rest of your life. We all felt that way, so I went out there anyway, but as I look back on it, it really was kind of stupid.

One of our night patrols got trapped in an ambush. The NVA set up speakers and played bugles like they were going to charge. Then it was rockets and mortars for three hours. Next came the sappers with satchel charges, and then came the human wave. It was a hairy,

hairy night. The next day they sent us out to recover bodies and look for wounded. We got out there but there were no bodies, just a trail of blood and propaganda leaflets which told us to follow the trail of blood. We knew that was really dumb....What the hell were we going to find? But we did, and we got hit with some really heavy shit. We were lucky that we had some helicopters nearby that we called in to spray the jungle. Everybody got screwed up. I got hit with some shrapnel from a rocket propelled grenade. But my biggest injury was from the concussion because it hit so close to me. It hit on a hill behind me and lifted me right up off the ground.

The only one who wrote me on any regular basis was my mom. My dad wrote me one letter the whole time I was in country. My brother and sister probably wrote me once a month, but my mom wrote me three or four times a week. But I could never tell her what was really going on so she had no idea of what I had been going through. Even though my father didn't write, I wrote him at his business so mom wouldn't see it. I told him what was actually going on. One time he wrote back after I had told him some really bad stuff, and said, "They can't do that, that's against the Geneva Convention." Then I quit writing him entirely. He asked mom why I quit writing. He was just not in touch with reality. I wanted to ask him, "Are you listening to what I'm saying?" After I got home, anytime I would start talking, he would start telling his war stories about World War II and didn't want to hear mine. It was kind of tough, and he would have been the one guy I could talk to because he had been through a war. I did write to some of my friends, but I never heard anything.

But there were a lot of good times in Vietnam, especially the brotherhood you felt with a lot of the other guys. One thing I tell everybody is that after a few months in Vietnam you're no longer serving your county, you're there doing what you can for your buddies. Whatever you do that someone else might consider heroic, you're doing to save someone else's life or you're doing it because he's depending on you to do it. Someone's shooting at you, but instead of ducking, you're out there running around trying to save somebody.

The bonds we established over there are hard for anyone else to understand. Just think of the closest friend you've ever had in civilian life, but he will be nowhere as close as we were. When you're constantly close to death, you get very close. I had guys tell me things that were just plain ridiculously embarrassing, things they would never tell anybody else. And this bond followed us even after we came home. This one guy called me out of the clear blue, some fifteen years after we had served together. He wanted me to come up to Minnesota and visit him. I told my boss at work that I had to go. When I got there we just gave each other the biggest hug. It was great. The years may have changed the way he looked, but he was still the same guy--and we were still tight.

The adjustment to civilian life was tough. My mom had no idea what I had been going through so she treated me exactly the same as before, not realizing that I had changed--that I had *really* changed. That was true of many of us. One of my vet buddies told me about starting out the door one night after returning home, and his parents asked him where he was going. He said, "Out." And they said, "Don't forget, you have to be home by midnight." He still had a curfew. His parents just had no idea what he had gone through.

I got very involved with drugs after coming home, especially after my mom died. I smoke tons of marijuana, I mean I smoked a *lot* of marijuana. I more or less used it as a way to numb my feelings. I became isolated from almost everything. My exciting time was when

I took my daughters out to the woods and taught them how to survive. They would want to go to the mall or something, but I would say, "Let's go out to the woods. I'll teach you how to survive." The woods was the only place I felt at home. I didn't want to take them to the mall, that was for sure. I didn't want to go where there were any people. So I spent most of their childhood just hiding in the house.

I was one of the first vets the VA recognized as having PTSD (Post Traumatic Stress Disorder). I had to go to the VA hospital and have a physical and an interview with their psychiatrist. I ended up getting a 10% disability benefit. But in the long run, that wasn't so good because it kept me from getting jobs I should have gotten. I wanted to be a mailman. It's a good job, good money, and not much stress. But I didn't get that job because of a letter that the VA sent the Postal Service which mentioned my meeting with the VA psychiatrist. I thought that meeting should have been confidential. After having read that report, I wouldn't have hired me either.

When I came back from Vietnam I was anti-everything. I was angry. And I was bitter. I was a completely different person. But slowly I healed, and I changed. I eventually became president of a veterans' group. I now march in parades; in fact, I'm now commander of the color guard. That's a big change. I still remember this parade in Kalamazoo the year before I got involved with the Vietnam Veterans of America. It might have been about 1984. It was the first national parade in this country for Vietnam veterans, and it happened in *my* hometown. I didn't even want to go. I thought, "Nah, I don't want to be a part of this." But my wife talked me into it. Just as we were getting ready to leave, she said, "Put you army shirt on; let 'em know." So I put my fatigue shirt on. I was just standing there watching the parade when the first guys came by and saw me standing there. They grabbed me and said, "Come on brother." I went out there, and I didn't even make it a block before I was crying. I had these huge tears rolling down my face. It was unbelievable. People were watching us, and they were clapping and yelling: "Hey, it's all right guys!" It was an outpouring of emotion from the people watching and from those of us marching. Everything was so positive. It was just incredible! Unbelievable! It was the same feeling I had when I visited the Vietnam Memorial in Washington. It's the best memorial there. A very impressive, fitting tribute. I had trouble looking up at the specific names, but it was a healing thing to walk by it. I probably walked by it fifty times. I just walked from one end to the other.

Lynda Van Devanter, *HUMP DAY*

Lynda Van Devanter served as a nurse in Vietnam and later wrote of her experiences in Home Before Morning: The True Story of an Army Nurse in Vietnam. *In the following passage she describes what is meant by "Hump Day," but more important is her unforgettable description of what taking care of the horribly wounded and dying did to the psychological well-being of the nurses in Vietnam.*

It was a few days before my hump day, the exact middle of my tour when I would be "over the hump." I was lost in a heavy sleep under my bed when the phone started ringing. The sound was more impossible to ignore than the rockets that had driven me there a couple of hours before. Still half asleep I listened to the words "More casualties, Van. We need you in surgery."

By the time I arrived in the operating room, I was alert, with my senses at their peak. I changed immediately to scrub clothes and reported to the head nurse for my assignment. Her short red hair was wild, the front of her scrub dress blood-stained. A mask dangled from her neck. "There's a bad one in the neuro room," she said. "I need you to pump blood in there." The neuro room was one of the places I usually tried to avoid. Head wounds were so messy and this one would undoubtedly be bad. But even knowing that, I was totally unprepared for the sight that awaited me when I stepped through the entrance.

Leading to the operating table was the largest trail of blood I had ever seen. I tried to walk quickly through it but slipped. When I regained my balance, my eyes were drawn to the gurney, where several people were transferring the wounded soldier from the green litter to the table. Three intravenous lines ran from bags of blood to his body, one in his jugular vein and one in each arm. The lower portion of his jaw, teeth exposed, dangled from what was left of his face. It dragged along the canvas litter and then swung in the air as he was moved from the gurney to the table. His tongue hung hideously to the side with the rest of the bloody meat and exposed bone. When he was on the table, Mack Shaffner, the facial surgeon, dropped the lower jaw back into place. One of the medics kicked the gurney to the side. It rolled across the room and banged into the wall.

I held my breath to keep from getting sick. For a moment, I was glued to the spot. I had already been through six months of combat casualties, plenty of them gruesome; I thought I had gotten used to it all, but they kept getting worse. I didn't think I could handle this one.

But the shout of the anesthesiologist, Jim Castelano, snapped me out of my trance. "The son of a bitch is drowning in blood," he screamed. "Somebody help me get a fucking airway in him." My training and instincts moved me into action for a tracheotomy. I raced across the room and ripped a prepared instrument pack out of the cabinet, quickly removed the layers of heavy cottonwrap from the tray and placed it on a Mayo stand and rolled it to him. Scalpels, clamps, sponges, forceps, retractors, scissors, metal trach tube.

A gurgling came from the soldier's throat. Jim's hands were quick. "Don't you dare die, you mutherfucker." With two fingers, he felt for the space between the cricoid and thyroid cartilage. "Give me a knife, Van." He made a vertical incision to get through the skin, and a horizontal one between the cartilage. Blood spurted from the neck. Then he pushed the scalpel handle into the space and turned it sideways to open the hole. "Trach tube."

I handed him a crescent-shaped hollow metal tube, which he immediately shoved into the hole. He pulled out the tube guide and more blood shot from the opening. There was an ugly metallic coughing sound as the soldier bucked for breath.

"Suction!"

I brought the suction machine and some clear plastic sterile tubing. Jim forced the suction catheter into the trachea. Immediately, red blood and mucus were sucked through the clear tube. Then it stopped.

"Come on, asshole, cooperate!" Jim pulled the catheter out. A long-black string of clotted blood hung from the end. With a sponge he wiped it away before forcing the catheter back into the trachea. More blood and mucus. He retracted the catheter once more. "Breathe, damn you!"

A barely audible sound escaped.

"That's it, soldier, come on." We connected the oxygen line to the trach tube and Jim started using an airbag to regulate the boy's breathing.

I immediately moved into position to help Mack, who was already grabbing instruments from the trach tray to clamp off the largest bleeders in the face and jaw. Meanwhile, the scrub technician set up the sterile field of linens and instruments.

Once the largest bleeders were tied off, Mack put on his gown and gloves and began to repair the damage. Now I fully realized what the head nurse meant when she told me I was needed to pump blood. The soldier was bleeding so fast that three IV lines were not enough.

"No blood pressure, " Jim yelled. "Keep that blood pumping and get another IV into him."

I replaced the empty hanging blood bags with new ones and then started a fourth line in his left leg.

"The stethoscope is broken. Van, get me another one."

"Get the crash cart, Van, in case he arrests."

"Who stole my goddamned tape?"

"Van, more towels for his head."

In the middle of the confusion, the neurosurgeon who had replaced Bubba came into the room. He looked at the soldier on the table and shook his head. His face was red. "Who the fuck woke me up for this dork?"

"The brain doesn't look too damaged," Mack answered.

"You're wasting your time."

"We can fix him," Max insisted. "Just give me a chance."

"Bullshit," the neuro guy answered. "That sucker's going to die and there's not a fucking thing you can do." He stormed out of the room.

Mack yelled after him. "We're going to need your help as soon as we stop the bleeding." "You can call me when you're ready," the neurosurgeon said, "and not a minute before." It was a moment when we all sorely missed Bubba. If he had been here, he would have stayed with us through the night to offer any possible assistance in pulling the soldier through. Unfortunately, not all neurosurgeons were as helpful.

When the circulating nurse arrived, my sole job became pumping blood, while Mack fought against the odds. After a while, I turned it into a routine: Start at the neck, take down the empty bag of blood, slip a new one into the pressure cuff, pump the cuff, rehang it, and check the temperature in the blood warmer. Then go to the left arm and repeat the process. Next the left leg and finally the right arm. Then start at the neck and repeat the entire sequence. It took about twenty-five minutes to make a round of him.

As Mack and the scrub tech clamped and cauterized the blood vessels, little puffs of smoke rose from what was once the soldier's face. The smelling of burning flesh filled the room.

Following every second and third time around the soldier, I changed the IV tubing because the two blood filters were getting thick with clots. Since we only had two blood warmers, I had to run the other lines through buckets of warm water to raise the temperature. When the buckets started to cool, I changed the water. It was all just another simple job where I could turn off my mind and try to forget that we were working on a person.

But this one was different. The young soldier wasn't about to let me forget.

During one of the circuits around the table, I accidentally kicked his clothes to the side. A snapshot fell from the torn pocket of his fatigue shirt. The picture was of a young couple--him and his girlfriend, I guessed--standing on the lawn in front of a two-story house, perhaps belonging to her parents. Straight, blond and tall, he wore a tuxedo with a mixture of pride and discomfort, the look of a boy who was going to finish the night with his black tie in his pocket, his shirt open at the neck, and his cummerbund lying on the floor next to the seat. She, too, was tall, and her long brown hair was mostly on top of her head, with a few well-placed curls hanging down in front of her ears. A corsage of gardenias was on her wrist. Her long pastel gown looked like something she had already worn as a bridesmaid at her cousin's wedding, and it fit her in a way that showed she was quickly developing from a girl into a woman. But the thing that made the picture special was how they were looking at each other.

I could see, in their faces, the love he felt for her, and she for him, a first love that had evolved from hours of walking together and talking about dreams, from passing notes to each other in history class, from riding together in his car with her sitting in the middle of the front seat so they could be closer.

On the back of the picture was writing, the ink partly blurred from sweat: "Gene and Katie, May 1968."

I had to fight the tears as I looked from the picture to the helpless boy on the table, now a mass of blood vessels and skin, so macerated that nothing could hold them together. **Gene and Katie, May 1968**. I had always held the notion that, given enough time, anything could be stopped from bleeding. If you kept at it, eventually you would get every last vessel. I was about to learn a hard lesson.

I pumped 120 units of blood into that young man, yet as fast as I pumped it in, he pumped it out. After hours of work, Mack realized that it was futile. The boy had received so much bank blood that it would no longer clot. Now, he was oozing from everywhere. Slowly, Mack wrapped the boy's head in layers of pressure dressings and sent him to post-op ICU to die.

Gene and Katie:May 1968. While I cleaned up the room I kept telling myself that a miracle could happen. He could stop bleeding. He could be all right. Nothing was impossible. **Please, God, help him.** I moved through the room as if in a daze, picking up blood-soaked lines, putting them into a hamper, trying to keep myself busy. Then I saw the photograph again. It was still on top of the torn bloody fatigue shirt. A few drops of blood were beaded on the edge of the print. I wiped them off and stared.

This wasn't merely another casualty, another piece of meat to throw on the table and try and sew back together again. He had been real. **Gene.** Someone who had gone to the prom in 1968 with his girlfriend, **Katie.** He was a person who could love and think and plan and dream. Now he was lost to himself, to her, and to their future.

When I finished making the room ready for the next head injury--the next young boy--I walked to post-op to see Gene. His bandages had become saturated with blood several times over and the nurses had reinforced them with more rolls of gauze, mostly to cover the mess. Now, his head seemed grotesquely large under the swath of white. The red stains were again seeping through. I held his hand and asked if he was in pain. In answer he squeezed my hand weakly. I asked him if he wanted some pain medication, and he squeezed my hand again. All the ICU patients had morphine ordered for pain, and I asked one of the nurses to give Gene ten milligrams intravenously, knowing that, while it would relieve his pain, it would also make him die faster. I didn't care at that point; I just wanted him to slip away quickly and easily.

The drug went to work immediately. As his respiration slowed and his grip became weaker, I imagined how it would be back in his hometown. Some nameless sergeant would drive an Army-green sedan to the house where Gene's parents lived. The sergeant would stand erect in his dress uniform, with his gold buttons glinting in the morning sun and bright ribbons over his left breast pocket. Perhaps a neighbor would see him walking past a tree in the front yard, one that Gene used to climb before the war; perhaps a little boy would ride his bicycle along the sidewalk and stop near the house to catch the impressive stranger stride confidently up the stairs and to the door. And when the mother and father answered the knock, no one would say a word. They would both know what had happened from the look on the sergeant's face.

And Katie? She would probably find out over the phone.

I ran my finger over the edge of the picture before putting it into the envelope with his other possessions. Then I walked outside, sat on the grassy hill next to post-op, and put my head in my hands.

I wouldn't cry, I told myself. I had to be tough.

But I knew a profound change had already come over me. With the death of Gene, and with the deaths of so many others, I had lost an important part of myself. The Lynda I had known before the war was gone forever.

I was off the next day, so I hitched a helicopter ride to Cam Ranh Bay. I had to see Barbara. I had to talk with her, to talk with someone who knew me before all this began. I had to try to make sense of it, to perhaps recall something from our past that could make me laugh, that could make me remember something other than war. I wanted to talk like we did on our cross-country trip, to look back on the pranks of nursing school and to dream about a future when the war would be over and we would each be married, living in our nice houses with our loving husbands and kids.

Was it all a fantasy? You bet your ass it was. I knew now that life would never be like that, but there was no law about dreaming.

When I reached Cam Ranh, I helped the helicopter crew and hospital staff to move some wounded from the chopper. Then I went to find Barbara.

A new woman was living in Barbara's room and she seemed annoyed at me for disturbing her sleep. When I told her I was Barbara's best friend, she told me that Barbara had been transferred to an evac hospital in the Mekong Delta. I got a sick feeling as I walked back to the chopper pad. It would be impossible for me to get transportation all the way down to the Delta.

I caught a chopper back to Pleiku that afternoon. I had a feeling I would never see her again.

I didn't cry.

I just felt empty.

December 7, 1969, was the twenty-eighth anniversary of the Japanese attack on Pearl Harbor. It was also my hump day. I envied my father's generation for their "moral war."

> *Hi, Lynda, this is your father with the tape recorder again. I'm sure you know that December 7th was one of the most memorable days in history. Early Sunday morning, I got my usual Pearl Harbor call from Tom Gladstone. You've heard me say time and again that on the real Pearl Harbor Day, Mom and I were with Maureen and Tom when the news broke. We were at war.*
>
> *From what we read in the papers and see on television and from the little snatches we get from you, I know things are anything but pleasant over there where you are. I know it's a real sacrifice for you and all these kids. But I'll tell you one thing: It makes me walk ten feet tall when I tell them that my little gal's right over there at the front.*

Although we had spend the previous days under a lot of pressure, my hump day was fairly routine--a few belly wounds, some chest cases, a missing limb or two, and not more than a couple of expectants. I worked a scheduled twelve-hour shift. The time moved quickly.

After work, Jack and a group of friends took me to the Air Force Officers Club for dinner. We watched a Filipino USO show--a rock band and some dancers who were supposed to be sexy--and everyone had a few drinks. I hadn't been drinking for the previous month or so, but that night I had two rusty nails. The second was probably a mistake. I was only half through it when the tears started rolling down my face. By the time I was finished, I was visibly shaken and sobbing quietly. I couldn't stop.

As I looked around the club, all I could see was Gene, the young bleeder we had lost a few nights earlier. **Gene and Katie, May 1968.** Then, when his face was gone, I began seeing all of them--the double and triple amputees, boys with brain injuries, belly wounds, and missing genitals. I could see the morgue and hundreds of bodies strewn haphazardly; the face of eighteen-year-old kids racked with pain as they lay dying. There were seventeen-year-old kids who probably hadn't had a chance to make love who had lost their penises. There were others who were not old enough to shave who had their faces burned off. There were married fathers who were blinded and would never see their children. Or who were paralyzed and would never be able to throw a ball, run along a trail, or even lift a pencil. They were all with me in that room.

I tried to force them out of my mind.

For a moment, I did.

Then all the images came crashing back on me. I lost control and became hysterical.

My friends tried to soothe me. They could not.

Finally, they took me back to my hooch and left me alone with Jack. He offered me comfort. I wouldn't accept it. I became a wild person, sobbing and shaking uncontrollably. "I want my mother. I want my father," I screamed. "I want to go home! Vietnam sucks! We don't belong here! This is wrong! I want Barbara! The whole thing is wrong! I hate it! I hate it!" I kept screaming the same things again and again. Each time Jack would approach me, I would kick him away.

He called Coretta for help. She had gone through a similar episode months before and knew what to do. She understood.

When she came into the room, Coretta leaned against the far wall, asking me questions and quietly saying things to comfort me. Eventually, she came close enough to touch me. She sat on the bed and put her arms around me, rocking me and whispering in my ear while I spent the night bawling.

Around five in the morning, I passed out from exhaustion and slept for the next twenty-four hours. After I awoke, I felt numb. I threw away the rhinestone flag I had previously worn on my uniform and found myself feeling nothing.

Christmas in Vietnam. They say the star in the east is only a flare over Camp Enari. After Christmas, I turned my numbness and sorrow into anger:

Dear Mom and Dad,

I don't know where to start except to say I'm tired. It seems that's all I ever say anymore. Thank you both for your tapes and the little goodies in the Christmas packages. Christmas came and went marked only by tragedy. I've been working nights for a couple of weeks and have been spending a great deal of time in post-op. They've been unbelievably busy. I got wrapped up in several patients, one of whom I scrubbed on when we repaired an artery in his leg. It eventually clotted and we did another procedure on him to clear out the artery--all this to save his leg. His name is Clarence Washington. I came in for duty Christmas Eve and was handed an OR slip for Clarence-above-knee amputation. He had developed gas gangrene. The sad thing was that the artery was pumping away beautifully. Merry Christmas, kid, we have to cut off your leg to save your life. We also had three other GIs die that night. Kids, every one. The war disgusts me. I hate it! I'm beginning to feel like it's all a mistake.

Christmas morning I got off duty and opened all my packages alone. I missed you so much, I cried myself to sleep. I'm starting to cry again. It's ridiculous. I seem to be crying all the time lately. I hate this place. This is now the seventh month of death, destruction, and misery. I'm tired of going to sleep listening to outgoing and incoming rockets, mortars, and artillery. I 'm sick of facing, every day, a new bunch of children ripped to pieces. They're just kids--eighteen, nineteen years old! It stinks! Whole lives ahead of them--cut off. I'm sick to death of it. I've got to get out of here.

I'm so glad that Steve finally got out. He was lucky to have made it through a year in this hellhole without getting seriously wounded. I never got to talk to him, but I understand the bitterness in his letters home, now, in a way I couldn't when I first got here. When I finally got someone in his unit on the phone the other day, they said he'd just left for Saigon to catch his Freedom Bird. With any luck, he's somewhere over Japan about now, and free from this green suck. How I envy him. I found out a couple of weeks ago that Barbara has been transferred to a unit near where Steve was. I've written her few times but gotten no answer, and the phone lines in her area are utterly awful, so I haven't been able to reach her. I hope she is okay. I just heard another chopper come in. I better go. They need me in the OR.

Peace,
Lynda

WOMEN POETS OF THE VIETNAM WAR

DUSTY

There is nothing more intimate than sharing someone's dying with them. When you've got to do that with someone and give that person, at the age of nineteen, a chance to say the last things they are ever going to get to say, that act of helping someone die is more intimate than sex; it is more intimate than childbirth, and once you have done that you can never be ordinary again.

Dusty, Army Nurse, Vietnam, 1987

By Dusty. From Visions of War, Dreams of Peace: Writings of Women in the Vietnam War. Edited by Lynda Van Devanter and Joan A. Furey. Warner Books, New York, 1991. Reprinted by permission of the editor.

THE BEST ACT IN PLEIKU, NO ONE UNDER 18 ADMITTED

I kissed a Negro, trying to breathe life into him.
When I was a child--back in the world--
the drinking fountains said, "White Only."
His cold mouth tasted of dirt and marijuana.
He died and I put away the things of a child.

Once upon a time there was a handsome, blond soldier.
I grabbed at flesh
combing out bits of shrapnel and bits of bone
with bare fingers.

A virgin undressed men,
touched them in public.
By the time I bedded a man
who didn't smell like mud and burned flesh
He made love and I made jokes.

Sharon Grant, 1982

By Sharon Grant. From Visions of War, Dreams of Peace: Writings of Women in the Vietnam War. Edited by Lynda Van Devanter and Joan Furey. Warner Books, New York, 1991. Reprinted by permission of the editor.

A BOOM, A BILLOW

While waiting for a plane to DaNang
I watched American bombers a mile away.
The uninvolved objectivity with which I stared at the sleek
jets,
their wings slipping back in fiercely powerful lines,
confused and disturbed me.
The jets swooped down,
then up quickly,
to circle and swoop once more.
A boom.
A billow of dark gray smoke.
Napalm.

That afternoon I met a boy at the Helgoland hospital ship.
He sought me out because I came from Quang Ngai,
his ancestral home.
He had no nose,
only two holes in the middle of his face.
His mouth was off to the side.
One eye was gone;
there was a hollow in his forehead above the other.
Most of the rest of his body was the same.
One hand was partly usable,
the fingers of the other soldered to his wrist.
Napalm.

Lady Borton, 1972

THE COFFEE ROOM SOLDIER

I walked into the coffee room for a cup of brew.
The push was over and I needed energy to re-group
for the next assault on our forces
and on my senses.

I initially stepped casually over his shattered body
laid out, unbagged, on the coffee room floor
out of the way
thinking, where would I find them next:
in my bed?

I turned with cup in hand and ascertained the damage.
His chest wall blown away, exposing the internal organs
An anatomical drawing.
Dispassionately I assessed his wound
and sipped from my cup.

I then saw his face
that of a child in terror
and only hours ago
alive as I
or maybe I was dead as he,
because with another sip, a cigarette and a detached analysis
I knew I could no longer even feel.

I stepped out and grabbed a mop and pail
so we would stop slipping in the blood on the R&E floor
bagged the extra body pieces and the coffee room soldier
re-stocked supplies, then went outside to watch the sunrise,
alone and destitute of tears.

Penny Kettlewell, 1990

By Penny Kettlewell. From Visions of War, Dreams of Peace: Writings of Women in the Vietnam War. Edited by Lynda Van Devanter and Joan A. Furey. Warner Books, New York, 1991. Reprinted by permission of the editor.

SEVENTEEN SUMMERS AFTER VIETNAM

eyes closed, lying on a Maine beach
listening to the ocean, sound of
choppers coming in. Flashback.
Alpha Bravo Charlie
composites of a dream

Whiskey Yankee Zulu
phantasms of the expendable lives
of my generation wasted in the mad, hysterical,
heroined, "don't mean nuthin" nights
of I Corps. GODDAMIT, I WANNA KNOW WHY

seventeen summers after Vietnam
choppers still coming in, carrying
George Bush, heading for a landing
on his lawn at Kennebunkport, why

seventeen summers after Vietnam
the cast of characters, hardly changed
tomorrow, a photo op for the press
still the same rich white boys, on a lawn.

Mary Pat O'Connor, 1990

By Mary Pat O'Connor. From Visions of War, Dreams of Peace: Writings of Women in the Vietnam War. Edited by Lynda Van Devanter and Joan A Furey. Warner Books, New York, 1991. Reprinted by permission of the editor.

KNOWING

("Recent research indicates Dioxin
is the most potent toxin ever studied."
--news report, September 1987)

I watched the helicopters
flying slowly north and south
along the DaNang river valley,
trailing a grey mist
which scattered the sun
in murky rainbows.
I never wondered if I knew
all I ought to know
about what they were doing.

I knew that it was called
defoliation,
that the spray would destroy
the hiding places of snipers
and ambushing guerrillas.
I did not know to ask:
at what price?

Every evening
the sunset choppers arrived
filled with soldiers burning
from jungle fevers:
malaria, dengue, dysentery.
We took them directly
to the cooling showers,
stripped their wet
dirt encrusted uniforms
as we lowered their temperatures
and prepared them for bed.
I did not ask where they had been,
whether they or the uniforms I held
had been caught in the mist,
whether defoliation
had saved their lives.
I did not know to ask.

I knew part of the price
when nine other women

By Marilyn McMahon. From Visions of War, Dreams of Peace: Writings of Women in the Vietnam War. Edited by Lynda Van Devanter and Joan A. Furey. Warner Books, New York, 1991. Reprinted by permission of the editor.

who had watched the helicopters
and seen the mist
talked of their children:
Jason's heart defects, and
Amy's and Rachel's and Timothy's.
Mary's eye problems.
The multiple operations
to make and repair digestive organs
for John and Kathleen and little John.
How lucky they felt
when one child was born healthy
whole.
How they grieved
about the miscarriages
one, two, three, even seven.
Their pain, their helplessness,
their rage when
Marianne died of leukemia at 2,
and Michelle died of cancer at 2 1/2.
Their fear of what might yet happen.

I knew more
when I watched my parents
celebrate their fortieth
wedding anniversary,
four children, three grandchildren
sitting in the pews.
I knew what I would never know
what the poisons and my fears
have removed forever from my knowing.
The conceiving, the carrying of a child,
the stretching of my womb, my breasts.
The pain of labor.
The bringing forth from my body of a new life.

I choose not to know
if my eggs are
misshapen and withered
as the trees along the river.
If snipers are hidden
in the coils of my DNA.

Marilyn McMahon, 1988

John Erdos, *GRUNT*

John Erdos was not anxious to go into the military and certainly not to Vietnam. He had a decent paying job and was purchasing his own home. But he went, and became a "Grunt," the foot soldier who had to do the dangerous, dirty work in Vietnam. Erdos is bitter about many of his war experiences, and his feelings are undeniably typical of so many who fought there.

It's not always clear who goes off to fight and who does not. It was 1967 when I got my welcoming letter from Uncle Sam. I had heard so much about our young guys running off to Canada or hiding in schools to stay out of the military that I thought I would talk to the local recruiter about not going. I told him I was buying a house and would lose everything I had worked for if I had to go. He told me my personal problems were of no concern to him. He also told me if I didn't volunteer, I would be an infantry foot soldier over there stomping rice patties. I didn't like the sound of that. He said my only alternative was to enlist. He promised if I signed up with him I would get a whole extra year of schooling. Being a naive country boy, I figured a man in uniform wouldn't lie to me, so I signed up. Of course, he just wanted my body in the military to fulfill his recruiting quota.

We were indoctrinated to believe we were going over there to protect the citizens of South Vietnam and to preserve their freedoms from the communist aggressions of North Vietnam and China. We believed what we were told. That's all you could do. We didn't know any better.

I later came to believe we were sent there to protect the megabuck millionaires who had investments over there. The people there sure didn't like us. We were foreign soldiers coming into their own back yard. We Americans wouldn't like that. The Vietnamese gave us the feeling we really weren't wanted there. All they wanted from us was the great all-American dollar. They would do anything for that, but once they found they couldn't get any money or food or supplies from you, they wouldn't have anything to do with you; in fact, they would avoid you like the plague.

It seemed like many people back home didn't want us to win. The guys who made the bullets and equipment--the government--it was just like they didn't care about us. Once you were over there, you were just a number. It was all so unemotional. And when I came home from Vietnam, it seemed like the guys who ran to Canada, or who successfully avoided the draft some other way, had all the jobs. Not even the government had jobs for us. Nobody seemed to care about us.

Nobody can understand what it was like in Vietnam who wasn't there. I have seen a lot of Hollywood films about war, and they don't even come close. There was a TV series called *China Beach*, or something like that. I used to watch it. They made a soldier's life in 'Nam seem like a nine to five job. They'd portray guys going out into the bush in the morning, then coming back in the afternoon to put on their civilian clothes and go out and boogie in the nearest town. Believe me, it was nothing like that. That program was a joke, but I used to watch it.

I got to Vietnam in January of 1968. In February, the Viet Cong launched a massive offensive. If you survived, you were a veteran, even though you had only been there a month.

I was a radio mechanic. We had to know how to fix everything, because there could be no break in the chain of communications. We didn't have much support. In fact, our base camp tents, and almost everything else, had to be put up on blocks because there was usually a foot of water on the ground. It was just a swamp. The tent they gave us to sleep in had all this green fungus growing on the inside because the weather was so hot and humid. You could put your finger through the tent in practically any spot because it was so rotten. The outside of it would get baked and the inside would rot.

You would always take a pair of dry socks with you wherever you went because whenever you got five minutes to sit down, you would take off your old wet socks, rinse them out in dirty rice patty water, and lay them over your shoulder so they could get somewhat dry for the next time you got a chance to sit down. Your feet would shrivel right up. You learned all this from experience, because no one told you to change your socks. The first time I had my boots on for three days in a row, I peeled my socks off, and the sole of my foot peeled right off with them. Then I limped around for six weeks with no skin on the bottom of my feet.

We were always wet, either from sweat or water. There were little rivers and marshes you had to ford across. There weren't any boats or bridges. You always tried to keep your ammo dry by holding it over your head. That's when the Vietnamese liked to hit you--right in broad daylight when you were neck deep in mud. So we had to put a guy on each side of the river, armed and ready while we forded the rivers and marshes. When you got to the other side, you had to peel off your clothes and pick off the leeches. I don't know how they could get in there that fast, but they sure liked to hook onto you. Then in the jungles you would get wood ticks all over you. They were everywhere. You couldn't touch anything without getting ticks.

The mosquitoes were also terrible. As soon as the sun would start to go down, it got dark real fast because of the millions and millions of mosquitoes that would take flight from the grass and the jungle. It seemed like the whole country was encased in a black cloud rising from the grass.

We were always harassed by snipers. They would disrupt your sleep and disrupt your life any way they could. They always knew the best times to hit you. They knew us Americans so very well. They knew that in the morning, we got up and wanted to eat. So we would all be standing behind the truck that tossed out the C-Rations. They would then throw mortars at us, and everyone would scramble. After I went through this once, I decided not to stand in any more lines. Whenever I saw a group of GIs standing around talking, I would walk the other way. I learned to avoid all groups because that's where they would target their mortars or hand grenades.

You always had to watch for booby traps. If the Viet Cong left a plain trail through the jungle, you would want to stay off it. You'd never walk down an obvious trail because it would always be booby-trapped. I would rather walk through the stuff that was so thick it wore you out to go a couple of hundred yards. Those jungle vines were just like you'd see in the old Tarzan movies. It was so dark that when you stepped out into the sun light again, you had to stand there for five or ten minutes, just to let your eyes get reaccustomed to the light. The Viet Cong also knew that was a good time to hit us.

A lot of the booby traps were made out of stolen American ammo that wouldn't fit in their guns. Some of the traps were really simple. When you were a kid, you played "kick the can." Well, you'd be walking down the trail and see a can. I don't know what possessed you to do it, but you would kick the can. They would have taken one of our C-Ration cans we had thrown away and put a grenade in it, pull the pin so that if you kicked the can, the grenade rolled out, and kaboom. It was very primitive, but very effective. They would take any live rounds they found and put them in a piece of bamboo and drive a nail up to where the firing pin was. They would bury these right in the trail. If you stepped on one of them, it would put a nice whole in your foot or blow it right off. Either way you would be out of commission, and that's what they wanted. It takes two guys to take care of one wounded until the Choppers got there; then, it ties up even more men.

The Viet Cong would put river clay on the roads. When it got wet, it was like putting two or three inches of grease on top of a highway. Our trucks would slip right off into the ditch. We also lost several trucks from road mines. We used to put sand bags against the floor boards, so that the scrap metal that came through wouldn't get you so bad. Sometimes they used plastic explosives that little kids had probably stolen from us.

You just couldn't trust anyone. Everyone dressed and looked the same. "Charlie," as we called him, was a farmer during the day and a soldier at night. He led two entirely different lives. At night he put away his hoe, picked up his rifle, and began shooting at us for sport or something. They must have figured that if they kept us up all night, we would be too tired to go on patrol the next day. We would fire back, and the next morning we would send out a search patrol to see how many VC we had killed. We wouldn't find any bodies because they would have dragged them off. That was supposed to discourage us because here we had lost five or six of our guys, but we couldn't find any enemy bodies.

Some of the guys would develop a hatred for the Vietnamese. You kind of acquired that after you lost a few close friends. You would see them in the day time, and they would come up and slap you on thc back and say, "You Number One GI." Then a couple of nights later you'd shoot a sniper and you'd discover you were looking at the body of the guy who called you "Number One GI." I guess we should have told him, "Hey, I'm number one at a rifle too."

The military leaders always wanted a body count. Got to have those bodies. Unless you got a body count, it was like you failed: "What happened to you? What's the matter? Didn't you shoot?" It was kind of a mental way to break us. It didn't work on me, but I know a lot of guys felt bad about not getting a count, because maybe they had just lost a best buddy or something like that.

When I first got in Vietnam, nobody wanted to know your name, because they didn't want buddies. Buddies cause pain. After you saw some guy lose his best buddy, you didn't want any close friends. I just sort of kept to myself. Oh, I did have one good friend--Callus Herbert from Green Bay, Wisconsin. He was the kind of guy you could trust your back to. You never had to question whether he would be there, and I hope he felt the same way about me, because I always did back him up on anything.

I wasn't over there trying to be a hero. I was no John Wayne. When those rockets came flying over our heads, I was always the first one down. The other guys used to joke about it. They would say, "Hey, I just saw a furrow of dirt. That must've been ol' John." I would just plow in like a mole, keeping my head low.

We would go out on what were called "Search and destroy" missions. For political reasons the name later was changed to "search and seizure." We would go into these small villages. You quickly learned that if there were no children around, you better be on guard, because it was probably an ambush. We walked into villages that maybe had only ten huts in them. They lived in these grass huts with no doors on them. Pigs and cows, or whatever they had, just roamed in and out. It was like stepping back in time into a *National Geographic* layout. We were supposed to make friends with the people--get to know the village chieftains and barter with them. We would trade cigarettes and C-Rations, and they would give us a dead chicken or something. It was a public relations type of thing. You couldn't eat what they gave you. As soon as we were out of sight, we would throw it away or stomp it into the mud so we didn't offend them.

We were also supposed to be helping the South Vietnamese soldiers, the ARVN. They tried to integrate them with us, but that didn't work because our guys didn't trust them, and with good cause. It was not just a racial thing. You really could not trust them. We would say, "Okay, you go over there and do a search on that village, and we'll go over here and search." They would go through their village and never get shot at or find any arms. A few days later we would go through the village they supposedly had searched, and snipers would start shooting at us, and we'd find all kinds of arms everywhere. That really made us think, "What are we here for?" It didn't make a lot of sense.

It was all very confusing because you didn't know who was the enemy and who was not. How can you fight something that is not there during the day, but at night seems to be everywhere. You were not authorized to shoot them during the day unless they shot at you first. If you did shoot and kill one, you could be brought up on charges and sent to Leavenworth for murder. It was a ridiculous situation. In all the old war movies I used to watch as a kid, it was never like this. This was a new game--definitely a new game.

If we had wanted to, we could have gone through Vietnam with our armor and our skill. We could have started right off at the very southern tip of the peninsula and within 30 to 60 days we could have swept the entire country, right up to the feet of Ho Chi Minh himself in the North. It would have been all over, if they would have let us do it, but we were supposed to be there to keep the peace. They just wouldn't let us go in there and do our job.

On some of our missions guys would pick marijuana and bring it back with them. They would hide it in their packs and bring it in. When they were pulling bunker duty, they would dry it right in the bunkers. I saw plenty of guys get goofy on marijuana, and a couple of them gave up their lives for it. They just didn't care.

I didn't see any sense in drugs. There were these little huts where I think they were smoking opium. They looked like a little outside privy. If you went in there, someone had to drag you out when your time was up. I never got into that kind of stuff. I didn't even get drunk. I like to drink beer, but you would never want to get drunk, because you don't want to get caught off guard. It was a whole year of tenseness. You just can't believe how tense it was. Sometimes you were so tired of being scared, you wished somebody would shoot you, just so you could get away from that mess.

One of the scariest things was when we had to call in artillery. If we were out of range of our fire base, an officer would sometimes call in naval artillery. I can remember one time this silly lieutenant called in artillery from the USS New Jersey which was at least 35 miles away from us in the Gulf of China. It shot 16 mm shells, and that was much more frightening than sniper fire. Those shells sounded like a Volkswagen flying over your head at two or three hundred miles an hour. They were landing a couple of hundred yards from us, and when they landed, the concussion just lifted you right out of the mud. There you were lying face down in the mud with your fingers in your ears hoping they would not land right on top of you.

We had second lieutenants who didn't have enough training to be Boy Scout leaders, let alone squad leaders out in the jungle. Some of the biggest pansies I've ever met in my life were officers. They were scared, and instead of saying, "Come on follow me," they were standing behind us saying, "Go on men." It was pretty sad. Most of the officers on the front lines were young and inexperienced. You seldom saw the higher ranking officers. They were somewhere else.

It was the same kind of thing with military discipline. They would try to make us do everything their way. They'd tell us when to go to bed, when to wake up, what to eat, and what line to stand it. All this was supposed to build good military discipline, but I looked at it differently. I figured they were training us to get killed: "Okay, today it's your turn to go out there and get shot. Just stand in line. Then, we'll bring up ten more." I didn't think much of that. Pretty soon you just worked for your own survival. That was the game plan I built up for myself. I just wanted to keep going, stay alive, and come home in one piece.

I remember getting sprayed with agent orange. You could look up and see the air force guys standing in the doors of their C-131's. They were dressed up like space cadets, with masks on and everything. They would come in maybe a couple of hundred feet off the ground, and spray all around our area to keep the foliage down. It was like being out in a mist. They covered you with it. But if they didn't defoliate, you would have to go out there whacking that stuff down in the hot sun. You had to keep your field of fire clear so you wouldn't be attacked by a human wave of Viet Cong at night. Agent Orange didn't seem to bother me, but there were some guys who claimed it gave them a headache or some other problem. I still don't have any children, but I don't know if that's got anything to do with Agent Orange.

Most of the Grunts in Vietnam were from poor or non-college backgrounds. We had one guy there who never had to do anything, and I couldn't understand it. Then one day I saw his records, and they had *PI* stamped all over them. I asked one of the clerks what *PI* meant, and he told me, "Political Influence." He was a white guy from California who was related to some important political figure there. He made his rank automatically, but the rest of us had to work for our stripes. We were the worker bees. We were the ones without political influence. We were supposed to do what they told us, and not ask any questions.

There were other kinds of politics as well. I had an acting first sergeant who didn't like me. My battalion commander kept putting me in for promotions and medals and stuff like that. I got hit with shrapnel so he put me in for a purple heart. Then he put me in for promotion to sergeant. Well, this acting first sergeant called me in and said, "If anybody gets anything from this company, I'm going to do the giving." When the battalion commander saw me a couple days later, he asked me where my stripes were. I told him what the sergeant had said. He really reamed out that sergeant, but that just made him madder than ever. I did get my promotion, but I didn't get paid again from October of 1968 until February of 1969, when I got home. That sergeant just shipped my records out of there.

Coming home was tough. After surviving all that crap over there, we had to face more of it at home. I remember flying into an air base in California. We were circling for our landing, and one of the guys looked out the window and said, "Hey, look, they've got a parade down there for us. It must be a welcome home party." It turned out to be a bunch of protesters.

They called us "baby killers" and all that, like we wanted to go over there and kill babies. I couldn't believe it. All those people smoking their wacky tobacco and wearing their flowers and long hair. I thought, "Geez, that's what we went over there for--so these fools can stay here at home, not knowing what life is all about." They were demonstrating about stuff they knew nothing about. It was unfair and detrimental to us. I didn't like the war either, but I didn't firebomb draft boards and stuff like that. I figured if I was not too good for war, they shouldn't be either. I didn't want to go over there, and I didn't volunteer. I didn't say, "Hey, send me over there so I can shoot somebody." The whole thing was disgusting so you didn't talk about it much. You just wanted to forget.

After getting out, I would be filling out a job application, but when I came to the part asking whether or not I was a veteran, I didn't know what to write. Sometimes I would just leave it blank. Those who had never been in Vietnam figured if you weren't a baby killer you were a drug addict or some kind of homicidal maniac. The first couple of months I was home, I would pick up the local paper and read, "Vietnam Veteran Comes Home from Service, Shoots wife and Children." These articles never mentioned that the guy might also have been a Baptist or a Rotarian or a member of the UAW. Always the articles or the TV news emphasized that the guy was a veteran. People looked at you like you just came out of a mental institution. You could see it on their faces: "Hey, you better watch this guy; he might unload any second now and go on a killing spree." It was a weird feeling when your own people look at you this way.

My wife says I was changed by Vietnam, but I personally don't feel that different. I can remember waking up in cold sweats, and my pillow would be soaked. I would have to get up and have a cigarette; then, I would be all right for the rest of the night. Just bad dreams I guess. The dreams gradually faded away. I started getting more involved with my work and other interests and that helped. I found out the more I worked, the less time I had to dream. You go to sleep when you're tired, and you feel a lot better for it.

My outlook is different on certain things. I never used to be interested in history. I now want to know where we are going as a nation. When I was a kid, I never cared who discovered America or anything like that, but now I want to know. I sure hope we learned something from the Vietnam War, but I don't think the right people felt the pain. The political and miliary leaders never really felt the lives lost because of their stupid planning and operations. It was like they thought, "Well, I'm just learning how to play war so we have to expect to lose so many guys until we learn how to do it right." Our lives didn't mean anything to them, but they did to us. While they sat back here and said, "Well, that didn't work so let's try this," we were over there asking, "What are you fools doing to us?" You just can't replace human lives. You don't know how many Einsteins died over there. The guy who might have found the cure for cancer might have been one of them. You just don't know how many great human beings never made it back from Vietnam.

I visited the Vietnam Memorial, but I just couldn't handle it. I started to read some of the names, but I couldn't go any further because I didn't want to see any names I knew. I left and sat on a park bench. It's black marble, a good color to fit the occasion I guess. I don't know. I just hope the Memorial weighs on all those fat cats up there in the Pentagon. I hope it makes them think about all the people's lives they disrupted--and ended. I hope it weighs on their shoulders. I know one thing. I would never get caught in that situation again. I would run to Canada first. I would be the first in line to get out of here. Of course, if the threat were here at home, and we had to defend our own land, I would stay and fight, but that was not the case in Vietnam.

John Garry Clifford, *CHANGE AND CONTINUITY IN AMERICAN FOREIGN POLICY SINCE 1930*

University of Connecticut diplomatic historian John Garry Clifford chronicles the ever changing explanations political leaders offered to explain our escalating involvement in Vietnam. Clifford also suggests that LBJ in particular and governmental bureaucrats in general were often isolated from the realities that surround their policies. Finally, Clifford is highly critical of bureaucratic language that obfuscates rather than illuminates national policy. The following is from James T. Patterson, ed., Paths to the Present.

Although it is too early to determine, the Vietnam war may well prove to have been both the logical culmination of American foreign policy since 1945 and a turning point comparable to that of World War II. Certainly on a perceptual level, in the way Americans viewed the world, the war set in motion changes that became obvious by 1970. On an institutional level, in the way government agencies connected with foreign policy defined their goals and procedures, the evidence of change by the early 1970s was less marked. One thing became certain: the options available to American diplomatists were more varied than at any other time since the fall of France in 1940.

Vietnam, which Senator John F. Kennedy described in 1956 as the "cornerstone of the Free World in Southeast Asia, the Keystone to the arch, the finger in the dike," was the logical, if erroneous, culmination of Cold War perceptions. The "lessons" of the past were constantly invoked. "If we don't stop the Reds in South Vietnam," said Lyndon Johnson, "tomorrow they will be in Hawaii, and next week they will be in San Francisco." Former Undersecretary of the Air Force, Townsend Hoopes, described the thinking of Dean Rusk: "In his always articulate, sometimes eloquent, formulations, Asia seemed to be Europe, China was either Stalinist Russia or Hitler Germany, and SEATO was either NATO or the Grand Alliance of World War II." If these analogies seemed somewhat strained, intended more for public persuasion than for internal conviction, the leaders in Washington all subscribed to the belief--unquestioned since Pearl Harbor--that aggression must be deterred. Vietnam became a test of America's will. "I don't need to remind you of what happened in the Civil War," Johnson told a press conference in 1967. "People were here in the White House begging Lincoln to concede and to work out a deal with the Confederacy when word came of his victories. . . . I think you know what Roosevelt went through and President Wilson in World War I. . . . We are going to have this criticism. We are going to have this difference. . . . No one likes war. All people love peace. But you can't have freedom without defending it. . . . We are going to do whatever it is necessary to do to see that the aggressor does not succeed."

But who was the aggressor in Vietnam? The Soviet Union? As the "quagmire" deepened, observers noted that Soviet supplies indeed helped the "enemy," but that Moscow was not master-minding a world-wide Communist conspiracy. The Sino-Soviet split became so evident by the mid-1960s that even the most militant Cold Warriors had to take notice. Perhaps the "enemy" was China, and Dean Rusk conjured up the frightening image of a billion Chinese armed with hydrogen bombs. But even after President Nixon's trips to Moscow and Peking in 1972, the war continued. The suggestion persisted that it was a *civil* war, an internal conflict between two versions of Vietnamese nationality, but this reality did not gibe with Cold War perceptions. Not enough was known in Washington about the fundamental differences in Asian societies, and belief in the Domino Theory came easily, along with visions of armed Communist hordes. Bureaucrats did not want to change their perceptions. James C. Thomson, a White House consultant during the early 1960s, recalls a conversation in March of 1964 with an Assistant Secretary of State. "But in some ways, of course, it *is* a civil war," Thomson said. "Don't play word games with me!" the official snapped.

Bureaucratic style contributed significantly to the tragedy. Part of it derived from technological superiority, which in turn gave rise to a "can do" philosophy. At one extreme, in Walter LaFeber's phrase, was "General Curtis LeMay's notion that Communism could best be handled from a height of 50,000 feet." At a more sophisticated level was the conviction that no matter how resilient the enemy proved, the United States could work its will through "smart" bombs, search and destroy tactics, electronic barriers, superior air power, or sheer economic momentum. A crazy sense of bloodlessness began to emerge. "Every quantitative measurement we have shows we're winning this war," McNamara stated in 1962. Statistics proliferated--infiltration rates, weapons-loss ratios, aircraft sorties rates, expended ammunition tonnages, allied troop contributions, enemy "body counts," friendly casualties. Bureaucratic jargon ("free fire zones," "surgical" air strikes, "Threshold of pain," "slow squeeze") obscured the reality of flesh being mangled, villages devastated, ecology ruined. Describing the gradual pressure imposed by the "Rolling Thunder" bombing campaign, one State Department official said: "Our orchestration should be mainly violins, but with periodic touches of brass."

This armchair atmosphere could not be dispelled by battle reports or occasional trips to Saigon. A process of self-hypnosis seemed at work. David Halberstam has told the story of Daniel Ellsberg's return from a tour of duty in Vietnam and his attempts to tell presidential adviser Walt Rostow how badly the war was going. "No, you don't understand," said Rostow. "Victory is very near. I'll show you the charts. The charts are very good." "I don't want to see any charts," Ellsberg replied. "But, Dan, the charts are very good," Rostow insisted. Similarly, James Thomson has described his shock on returning to Harvard after several years in the State Department. He suddenly realized that "the young men, the flesh and blood I taught and saw on these university streets, were potentially some of the numbers on the charts of those faraway planners. In a curious sense, Cambridge is closer to this war than Washington."

The imperviousness of official Washington from external dissent contributed to the debacle. The smugness that came with access to classified information was partly responsible. The experts knew the facts, the critics did not. Internal dissenters were rarer and somehow safer to government leaders. President Johnson used to greet Bill Moyers rather affectionately: "Well, here comes Mr. Stop-the-Bombing." And when the war protest became especially shrill in 1966 and 1967, Johnson, who had followed the experts into the morass, displayed his furious temper. Dissenters, he said, were "nervous Nellies," "chickenshit." "I'm the only President you have," he would say. "Why don't you get on the team?" When hawks like Bundy and McNamara began to waver, Johnson sarcastically called the former "George McBundy" and unceremoniously nominated the latter to head the World Bank. This presidential temperament reinforced the natural bureaucratic tendency to remain silent so as not to lose one's effectiveness. Townsend Hoopes has described Vice-President Hubert Humphrey's abortive dissent in 1965: "His views were received at the White House with particular coldness, and he was banished from the inner councils for some months thereafter, until he decided to 'get back on the team.'" Not until the Tet offensive of early 1968 did effective criticism penetrate the Oval Office, and then it took someone of the stature of Dean Acheson to shake Lyndon Johnson. "With all due respect, Mr. President," said the mustachioed Dean of Middletown, "the Joint Chiefs of Staff don't know what they are talking about." When the Senior Advisory Group on Vietnam corroborated Acheson's estimates a few weeks later, the President's plaintive reaction underlined the extent to which policy had been made in a vacuum. "What did you tell them that you didn't tell me?" he asked his staff. "You must have given them a different briefing."

Momentum was another reason for escalation. The men in Washington may have thought they controlled events, but in actuality the genii of war were beyond control. For all their sophisticated technology, for all their favorable statistics, for all their "can do" spirit, American leaders never understood the extent to which decisions closed options previously available, making other decisions almost inevitable. Moreover, policy decisions often resulted from compromise, as in the case of the Kennedy administration sending military advisers to South Vietnam in 1961, notwithstanding the Taylor-Rostow report which recommended 8,000 troops. These compromises represented the usual adjustment of differences between the various agencies involved: the Saigon embassy, CIA, the State Department, the White House Staff, and the Joint Chiefs. Once advisers were committed, however, pressure rose for increasing their numbers.

Similarly, in the winter of 1964-65, certain "dovish" planners in the State Department who were strongly opposed to bombing the North urged instead that ground forces be sent to the South. They thought such a move would increase bargaining leverage against the North and be a prod for negotiations. At the same time, military men determined not to fight another "land war" in Asia were calling for the air-strike option. Still other civilians seeking peace wanted to bomb Hanoi into early peace talks. Within eight months all factions were disappointed: there was a costly and ineffective air campaign against the North, a mushrooming ground commitment in the South, and negotiations farther away than before. Each step also added greater weight to the military's demands. As soon as the Army's mission had changed from advising to saving Saigon, it was inevitable that the Joint Chiefs should press for escalation. Each service had its special panaceas, and under a tacit agreement the Joint Chiefs usually spoke in unison. McNamara then scaled down their demands. The result: escalation. Even after Nixon began withdrawing ground forces in 1969, military pressure to "protect" these troops resulted in decisions to invade Cambodian sanctuaries, to mine the harbors of Haiphong and Hanoi, and to resume aerial bombardment of the North at ever-increasing rates.

Vietnam brought about an "agonizing reappraisal" in American foreign policy far more searching than anything John Foster Dulles had envisaged in the 1950s. Dissent in American wars was not a new phenomenon. New England Federalists had opposed the War of 1812, abolitionists had protested the Mexican War, and Mugwumps and anti-imperialists had been vocal in 1898. Generally these dissenters were relatively small in number, well educated, respectable (usually upper class WASP), and quite orthodox in the way they protested--pamphlets, petitions, rallies, letter writing campaigns, efforts in behalf of anti-war candidates. The Vietnam war protest was different. The movement had enough diversity to include such heterogeneous spokesmen as Norman Mailer, Muhammed Ali, Abby Hoffman, John Kenneth Galbraith, George Kennan, Jane Fonda, Joan Baez, Jeannette Rankin, Martin Luther King, Robert Kennedy, Timothy Leary, Dick Gregory, and Noam Chomsky. Protest went from genteel teach-ins, to Senator Eugene McCarthy's brash campaign for the Democratic nomination in 1968, to marches on Washington, moratoria, and violent attempts by revolutionary groups to bring the war "home" to America. Protest literature ranged from the witty to the obscene.

People opposed the war for different reasons. Some still clung to the Cold War arguments for containment, but denied that the doctrine applied to Asia, or particularly to Vietnam. Others saw the war as killing reform at home, diverting attention from desperate conditions in the cities and in race relations. A less articulate group protested the deaths of American soldiers in Asian jungles, but seemed willing to permit American aircraft to drop billions of tons of bombs on yellow peoples. Others blamed President Johnson. "We've got a wild man in the White House," said Senator McCarthy. "A desperate man who was likely to get us into war with China," warned Senator Albert Gore of Tennessee.

More and more, protest occurred because of a moral revulsion to the war. Reaction to napalm bombing and "defoliation," horror at the destruction of the city of Hue in order to "save" it, incredulity at the My Lai massacre and the shootings of students at Kent State and Jackson State in 1970--all these events called into question the ethical standards of American policy. Confused about the identity of the aggressor in Vietnam--the Viet Cong? Hanoi? China?--more and more Americans came to agree with Walt Kelly's possum, Pogo: "We have met the enemy and they are us."

By the late 1960s this moral revulsion, fueled by the obvious *practical* failure of the American effort, had prompted a reassessment of long-held assumptions. One State Department official complained in 1966: "There is a considerable sort of feeling of unhappiness here that elements in the population that used to be thought of as our 'natural constituency' are not doing yeoman service for the Department now. We do have a constituency of sorts--the Foreign Policy Association, the Council on Foreign Relations, and all the other groups like that. These people have helped us all along for years, with the United Nations, the Marshall Plan, NATO, Korea, and all the others. But they are not helping us with the American public on the Vietnam issue. When they come to town to be briefed on Vietnam, they do not leave with marching orders, as they used to." When Dean Acheson told President Johnson that the generals did not know what they were talking about, he was also serving notice that the foreign policy consensus in existence since World War II had shattered. Another symbolic confrontation occurred in the spring of 1970 following the Cambodia invasion, when a group of prominent academicians, headed by Richard Neustadt, visited Henry Kissinger and recanted their support for executive predominance in foreign policy. These defections did not mean that Nixon could not count on continued support from the "silent majority," that Congress suddenly cut off military appropriations, or that the Navy decided to convert its aircraft carriers into hospital ships. What did emerge was an eventual repudiation of the Vietnam war by a majority of the so-called "foreign policy public." "What the hell is an Establishment for, if it's not to support the President," Kissinger complained. The reaction was especially strong among academicians. The political scientist Bruce Russett wrote: "Vietnam has been to social scientists what Alamogordo was to the physicists. Few of those who have observed it can easily return to their comfortable presumptions about America's duty, or right, to fight in distant lands."

If one accepts the premise that statesmen make decisions based in part on their perception of past "lessons," then a positive result of the Vietnam debate was the searching reassessment of recent diplomatic history by historians. Sometimes polemical, often brilliant, always provocative, the "revisionist" historians of the Cold War explicitly challenged the assumptions that undergirded American foreign policy in the years after World War II. Not all of their arguments, such as the suggestion that the atomic bombs were dropped in 1945 more with an eye to postwar relations with Russia than because of a desire to defeat Japan quickly, have been accepted. Nor have all "revisionists" agreed with one another. Nevertheless, their writings altered the way scholars look at the recent past. The Cold War was no longer viewed as a brave American response to unprovoked Soviet aggression, but rather as a series of actions and reactions analogous to a scorpion and a tarantula trapped in a bottle. Some revisionists emphasized American economic goals in the postwar world, the desire for multilateral trade, and contrasted this "open door" mentality to the state-trading system of the Russians. Other scholars stressed the prevalence of "myths" in Washington, exaggerated fears of foreign aggression and fears of right-wing critics at home. Still others highlighted America's tendency to oppose revolution abroad under the cloak of anti-Communism. A few scholars, most notably Bruce Russett, have questioned the necessity for intervening in World War II against Hitler. Even isolationism has received a favorable hearing. George Kennan was not alone when he announced in 1966: "I find myself in many respects sort of a neo-isolationist."

Why have these new perspectives not permeated the foreign affairs bureaucracy? Aside from the obvious answer that presidents and generals do not read many scholarly books, the main reason the Vietnam war continued until 1973 was, as political scientists are quick to point out, that fundamental changes in government policy occur only incrementally. Whatever the "lessons" drawn by scholars from Vietnam, the Navy will continue to insist on aircraft carriers and missile submarines. The Army will undoubtedly deplore My Lai, but only slowly reassess the futility of fighting a guerrilla enemy with modern technology. The Air Force may well conclude that the "lesson" of Vietnam came with the heavy bombing raids of December 1972, and that the worst mistake of the war was to shackle air power. So long as the annual defense budget totals more than eighty billion dollars, the possibility of another Vietnam through bureaucratic inertia exists. Even the State Department, reportedly "dovish" on Vietnam after Dean Rusk left office, continued to be staffed by senior officers who joined the foreign service in the 1940s and 1950s. Perceptions within government do not change as quickly as those on the outside, especially under presidents who are determined not to be the first to lose a war.

Even bureaucracies develop cracks occasionally. The classic response of a frustrated bureaucrat is the leak. Leaks are not rare phenomena, and they are usually accepted as a standard part of the political process, especially evident during the annual "battle of the budget" when institutional interests struggle for their slice of pie. Sometimes, however, leaks originate with obscure officials and have disturbing consequences for official Washington, as in 1941 when isolationist Army officers leaked mobilization plans to the *Chicago Tribune*, or in the 1950s when Joe McCarthy had his anonymous informants in various branches of government. Then, in 1971, came the publication of the Pentagon Papers in the *New York Times*.

Handsome and articulate Daniel Ellsberg may well personify the idea of the Vietnam war as a perceptual watershed in American foreign policy. An academic who grew to maturity in the Dulles era, worked for the Pentagon, wrote papers for RAND, and even served a voluntary tour as a Marine officer in Vietnam, Ellsberg was a true believer until he saw firsthand the destruction wrought by American policies. His disenchantment deepened when Secretary McNamara assigned him to the team that researched and wrote the Pentagon Papers. So convinced was Ellsberg that the war had been a mistake and, furthermore, that the so-called "quagmire" was less the result of blundering than conscious manipulation, that he became committed to overthrowing the Cold War consensus he had so eagerly served. Failing to persuade top officials like Henry Kissinger to end the war, Ellsberg finally leaked the Pentagon studies to the *Times* in the expectation that public opinion would be transformed.

The results were not what Ellsberg expected. Public attention focused on the sensational circumstances of the publication, not on what the Pentagon Papers revealed, as if to suggest that Americans, inured to massive bombing and killing of civilians, were unwilling to dredge their consciences and ask how aggressive war had been launched. Richard Nixon's landslide victory over George McGovern, as well as the subdued reaction to the resumption of bombing after the election, further pointed to a public reluctance to reassess the rationale behind Vietnam.

That is, until Watergate. What began as a "third-rate burglary" with negligible effect on the 1972 presidential campaign exploded into a crisis with large, if undefined, consequences for American foreign policy. According to two analysts, "Prince Watergate kissed the sleeping Congress, reinforcing its mood of independence and altering the political balance between the President and the politicians at the other end of Pennsylvania Avenue." Moreover, notwithstanding Senator Howard Baker's focus on how much the President knew about Watergate, and when, the revelations at the Ervin Committee hearings in 1973 threw into question the whole set of government procedures designed to maintain "national security." Wire-taps, secret tapes, "plumber's units," the contention that the President can violate the Bill of Rights in behalf of national security, the view that dissenters are "enemies"--all became part of the public debate. Despite contradictory testimony, it seemed clear that Watergate was an indirect result of the Nixon administration's extreme reaction to radical protest, as well as to internal leaks such as Ellsberg's. Thinking itself under siege, the administration regarded groups like the Weathermen as greater threats to "national security" than Soviet SS-9 missiles. For the first time since 1941 the power of the chief Executive to act unilaterally in foreign policy was seriously challenged by Congress. By halting the bombing of Cambodia in August 1973 and passing the War Powers Act over the President's veto a few months later, Congress began a long overdue reappraisal of foreign policy.

Historians cannot predict the future. To suggest, however, that changes in American assumptions about the world began in the 1960s and that Watergate and Vietnam accelerated these changes, is not presumptuous. The "lower profile" of American involvement abroad, as proclaimed by the Nixon Doctrine, will result in "lower" perceptions about American power and responsibilities. The intellectual capital that financed the Marshall Plan, NATO, and Korea was expended in Southeast Asia in the 1960s. The Nixon-Kissinger policies of detente toward the Soviet Union and the People's Republic of China have in themselves altered Cold War patterns. Do these changes signal a return to the isolationism of the 1930s, as defenders of the Vietnam war sometimes suggested? In the sense that domestic needs will not automatically take second place to foreign policy, or that Congress will not rubber-stamp executive initiatives, these changes do reflect some of the concerns of the Stimson-Hoover era. Nevertheless, the huge foreign policy bureaucracy spawned by World War II and the Cold War will remain, and it will take time for new perceptions to become embedded. Public opinion, decidedly noninterventionist in Asia because of the failure of the ground war in Vietnam, may well permit intervention by means of naval and aerial bombardment in future crises. The renewal of war between Israel and the Arab states in the fall of 1973, combined with the Arab embargo of oil, raised the prospect of American intervention in the Middle East, and with it the possibility of a Soviet-American confrontation. Like all previous empires in decline, the United States will retreat reluctantly.

Nevertheless, Vietnam and Watergate have left an ambivalence which allows room for cautious optimism. As the political scientist Robert W. Tucker has observed, Pearl Harbor and the Berlin Blockade will not be automatic reference points for the coming generation of "foreign policy elites." Rather, memories of My Lai and the Cuban Missile Crisis will be much sharper. "Never again," a slogan which the Army brought out of the Korean War, ought to remain a convenient watchword. The waning of anti-Communism as a political issue, as well as the need to combat industrial pollution, to conserve energy, to revitalize public transportation, and to obtain public health insurance, should tend to "lower" profiles and "cool" American foreign policy. Gradually, one may predict, the traditional American mission of erecting a "city on the hill": and solving domestic problems will take precedence over building "democratic" governments in remote areas of the world.

John Quincy Adams said it well more than 150 years earlier:

> *Wherever the standard of freedom and Independence has been or shall be unfurled, there will her [America's] heart, her benediction and her prayers be. But she goes not abroad in search of monsters to destroy. . . . She well knows that by once enlisting under other banners than her own, were they even the banners of foreign independence, she would involve herself beyond the power of extrication. . . . The fundamental maxims of her policy would change from* liberty *to* force.

President Richard Nixon, ***A CONVERSATION WITH THE PRESIDENT ABOUT FOREIGN POLICY*** **(1970)**

*Richard Nixon was elected in 1968 in part because of his promise to end the war in Vietnam. It took him five years. Like his predecessors, he promised to bring about an independent, non-Communist South Vietnam, but he also began the gradual withdrawal of American troops and the turning over of the war to the South Vietnamese army. To help his "Vietnamization" policy Nixon greatly escalated the bombing of civilian targets, including North Vietnam and neutral Cambodia, and launched a program of "pacification" of the South Vietnamese countryside which often included the assassination of recalcitrant political leaders. In the selection below, Nixon attempts to convince a group of television newsmen, as had Kennedy and Johnson before him, that his military tactics would help end the war and win a lasting peace (*Public Papers of the President of the United States, Washington, D.C., Government Printing Office, 1971).

Mr. (HOWARD K.) SMITH: Mr. President, one of the things that happened in the Senate

last week was the rescinding of the Gulf of Tonkin resolution by the Senate. Mr. Katzenbach, in the previous administration, told the Foreign Relations Committee that resolution was tantamount to a congressional declaration of war. If it is rescinded, what legal justification do you have for continuing to fight a war that is undeclared in Vietnam?

THE PRESIDENT: First, Mr. Smith, as you know, this war, while it was undeclared, was here when I became President of the United States. I do not say that critically. I am simply stating the fact that there were 549,000 Americans in Vietnam under attack when I became President.

The President of the United States has the constitutional right--not only the right, but the responsibility--to use his powers to protect American forces when they are engaged in military actions, and under these circumstances, starting at the time I became President, I have that power and I am exercising that power.

MR. SMITH: Sir, I am not recommending this, but if you don't have a legal authority to wage a war, then presumably you could move troops out. It would be possible to agree with the North Vietnamese. They would be delighted to have us surrender. So that you could--

What justification do you have for keeping troops there other than protecting the troops that are there fighting?

THE PRESIDENT: A very significant justification. It isn't just a case of seeing that the Americans are moved out in an orderly way. If that were the case, we could move them out more quickly, but it is a case of moving American forces out in a way that we can at the same time win a just peace.

Now, by winning a just peace, what I mean is not victory over North Vietnam--we are not asking for that--but it is simply the right of the people of South Vietnam to determine their own future without having us impose our will upon them, or the North Vietnamese, or anybody else outside impose their will upon them.

When we look at that limited objective, I am sure some would say, "Well, is that really worth it? Is that worth the efforts of all these Americans fighting in Vietnam, the lives that have been lost?"

I suppose it could be said that simply saving 17 million people in South Vietnam from a Communist takeover isn't worth the efforts of the United States. But let's go further. If the United States, after all of this effort, if we were to withdraw immediately, as many Americans would want us to do--and it would be very easy for me to do it and simply blame it on the previous administration--but if we were to do that, I would probably survive through my term, but it would have, in my view, a catastrophic effect on this country and the cause of peace in the years ahead.

Now I know there are those who say the domino theory is obsolete. They haven't talked to the dominoes. They should talk to the Thais, to the Malaysians, to the Singaporans, to the Indonesians, to the Filipinos, to the Japanese, and the rest. And if the United States leaves Vietnam in a way that we are humiliated or defeated, not simply speaking in what is called jingoistic terms, but in very practical terms, this will be immensely discouraging to the 300 million people from Japan clear around to Thailand in free Asia; and even more important it will be ominously encouraging to the leaders of Communist China and the Soviet Union who are supporting the North Vietnamese. It will encourage them in their expansionist policies in other areas.

The world will be much safer in which to live.

MR. SMITH: I happen to be one of those who agrees with what you are saying, but do you have a legal justification to follow that policy once the Tonkin Gulf Resolution is dead?

THE PRESIDENT: Yes, sir, Mr. Smith, the legal justification is the one that I have given, and that is the right of the President of the United States under the Constitution to protect the lives of American men. That is the legal justification. You may recall, of course, that we went through this same debate at the time of Korea. Korea was also an undeclared war, and then, of course, we justified it on the basis of a U.N. action. I believe we have a legal justification and I intend to use it.

MR. [ERIC] SEVAREID: Mr. President, you have said that self-determination in South Vietnam is really our aim, and all we can ask for. The Vice President says a non-Communist future for Indochina, or Southeast Asia. His statement seems to enlarge the ultimate American aim considerably. Have we misunderstood you or has he or what is the aim?

THE PRESIDENT: Mr. Sevareid, when the Vice President refers to a non-Communist Southeast Asia that would mean of course, a non-Communist South Vietnam, Laos, Cambodia, Thailand, Malaysia, Singapore, and Indonesia. That is the area we usually think of as Southeast Asia.

This is certainly something that I think most Americans and most of those in free Asia and most of those in the free world would think would be a desirable goal.

Let me put it another way: I do not think it would be in the interest of the United States and those who want peace in the Pacific if that part of the world should become Communist, because then the peace of the world, the peace in the Pacific, would be in my opinion very greatly jeopardized if the Communists were to go through that area.

However, referring now specifically to what we are doing in Vietnam, our aim there is a very limited one, and it is to provide for the South Vietnamese the right of self-determination. I believe that when they exercise that right they will choose a non-Communist government. But we are indicating--and incidentally, despite what everybody says about the present government in South Vietnam, its inadequacies and the rest, we have to give them credit for the fact that they also have indicated that they will accept the result of an election, what the people choose.

Let us note the fact that the North Vietnamese are in power not as a result of an election, and have refused to indicate that they will accept the result of an election in South Vietnam, which would seem to me to be a pretty good bargaining point on our side.

MR. [JOHN] CHANCELLOR: Mr. President, I am a little confused at this point because you seem in vivid terms to be describing South Vietnam as the first of the string of dominoes that could topple in that part of the world and turn it into a Communist part of the world, in simple terms.

Are you saying that we cannot survive, we cannot allow a regime or a government in South Vietnam to be constructed that would, say, lean toward the Communist bloc? What about a sort of Yugoslavia? Is there any possibility of that kind of settlement?

THE PRESIDENT: Mr. Chancellor, it depends upon the people of South Vietnam. If the people of South Vietnam after they see what the Vietcong, the Communist Vietcong, have done to the villages they have occupied, the 40,000 people that they have murdered, village chiefs and others, the atrocities of Hue--if the people of South Vietnam, of which 850,000 of them are Catholic refugees from North Vietnam, after a blood bath there when the North Vietnamese took over in North Vietnam--if the people of South Vietnam under those circumstances should choose to move in the direction of a Communist government, that, of course, is their right. I do not think it will happen. But I do emphasize that the American position and the position also of the present Government of South Vietnam, it seems to me, is especially strong, because we are confident enough that we say to the enemy, "All right, we'll put our case to the people and we'll accept the result." If it happens to be what you describe, a Yugoslav type of government or a mixed government, we will accept it.

MR. CHANCELLOR: What I am getting at, sir, is, if you say on the one hand that South Vietnam is the first of the row of dominoes which we cannot allow to topple, then can you say equally, at the same time, that we will accept the judgment of the people of South Vietnam if they choose a Communist government?

THE PRESIDENT: The point that you make, Mr. Chancellor, is one that we in the free world face every place in the world, and it is really what distinguishes us from the Communist world.

Again, I know that what is called cold war rhetoric isn't fashionable these days, and I am not engaging in it because I am quite practical, and we must be quite practical, about the world in which we live with all the dangers that we have in the Mideast and other areas that I am sure we will be discussing later in this program.

But let us understand that we in the free world have to live or die by the proposition that the people have a right to choose.

Let it also be noted that in no country in the world today in which the Communists are in power have they come to power as a result of the people choosing them--not in North Vietnam, not in North Korea, not in China, not in Russia, and not in any one of the countries of Eastern Europe, and not in Cuba. In every case, communism has come to power by other than a free election, so I think we are in a pretty safe position on this particular point.

I think you are therefore putting, and I don't say this critically, what is really a hypothetical question. It could happen. But if it does happen that way we must assume the consequences, and if the people of South Vietnam should choose a Communist government, then we will have to accept the consequences of what would happen as far as the domino theory in the other areas.

MR. CHANCELLOR: In other words, live with it?

THE PRESIDENT: We would have to live with it, and I would also suggest this: When we talk about the dominos, I am not saying that automatically if South Vietnam should go the others topple one by one. I am saying that in talking to every one of the Asian leaders, and

I have talked to all them...,and every one of them to a man recognizes...that if the Communists succeed, not as a result of a free election--they are not thinking of that--but if they succeed as a result of exporting agression and supporting it in toppling the government, then the message to them is, "Watch out, we might be next."

Michael Arlen, *THE LIVING-ROOM WAR*

Michael Arlen was the television critic for the New Yorker *when, between 1966 and 1968, he wrote a series of articles analyzing how television was transmitting the war to the folks sitting home in the comfort of their living rooms. Keep in mind that many military and political leaders still believe we lost our willingness to fight in Vietnam because of television's portrayal of the war.*

I read in the paper a while back that sixty percent of the people in this country get most of their news about the Vietnam war from television, so for the past couple of weeks I've been looking, with admirable regularity, at the evening news shows put on by the three networks, to see what sort of Vietnam coverage the viewers are being given. If my own experience is any guide, I'd say that sixty percent of the people in this country right now know more about the "weather picture" over major metropolitan areas than they could ever wish to know and a good deal less about Vietnam than might be useful. For example, in a random selection last week, CBS (*The CBS Evening News*, with Walter Cronkite) ran a three-minute film that showed a Marine company breaking off an unsuccessful engagement with some North Vietnamese (the Marines had been trying to get them off the top of a hill), that included a moving, emotional scene of wounded soldiers (ours) being helped, stumbling and limping, across a ravine, and that closed with a short interview with an out-of-breath, bright-eyed, terribly young Marine sergeant who said that it had been a tough fight but the Marines would push them off the hill tomorrow--they always did. ABC, which has its evening news show at 5:45 in the afternoon, didn't have any film on Vietnam (although it often does) but instead had a few minutes' account by Peter Jennings of the results of another Marine operation--Operation Irving (Operation *Irving*?) --a statement about a cessation of bombing in the demilitarized zone, and the latest battle-casualty statistics. NBC (*The Huntley-Brinkley Report*) had a three-minute film of some of our soldiers helping several dozen South Vietnamese out of an Air Force plane that had just returned them from a Vietcong prison camp. The former prisoners seemed (as one might imagine) in pretty miserable condition, and there were numerous closeups of scrawny limbs and of mournful, undernourished faces. Our own men looked strangely large, healthy, and compassionate. CBS, again, showed a five-minute film of a company of South Vietnamese troops on patrol coming under Vietcong sniper fire. The technical quality of the film, as of NBC's, seemed remarkably good. You could see a handful of soldiers, under cover of some trees, firing into a line of trees that appeared to be several miles away. The rifle fire sounded clear and sharp. The camerawork was expert and agile. There was a sequence, very close up, of an American adviser asking someone over a field telephone to send in a couple of armed helicopters. You could hear everything the adviser said (he seemed calm and matter-of-fact, and he too was terribly young). Then there were more scenes of soldiers, crouching and standing, firing toward the distant line of trees, and later, up in the sky, far in the distance, the two helicopters. At the end, CBS correspondent Morley Safer came on to say that there had probably been only three or four Vietcong snipers, that nobody knew whether or not the southern troops had killed them, and that was the way it often was in Vietnam.

That's the way it often is with television's reporting of the war, and it's hard to know what to make of it. The technique that goes into the filming--to say nothing of the arrangements for getting the stuff out of the field and into Saigon and over here to the networks within thirty hours--is often extraordinarily good. But what it all adds up to seems not nearly good enough, and when I write "seems" I mean "seems," because I certainly don't have any shimmering private vision of how this war ought to be reported. I do know, though, that the cumulative effect of all these three- and five-minute film clips, with their almost unvarying implicit deference to the importance of purely military solutions (despite a few commentators' disclaimers to the contrary), and with their catering (in part unavoidably) to a popular democracy's insistent desire to view even as unbelievably complicated a war as this one in emotional terms (our guys against their guys), is surely wide of the mark, and is bound to provide these millions of people with an excessively simple, emotional, and military-oriented view of what is, at best, a mighty unsimple situation. I don't for a moment suggest that the networks should stop showing film of men in combat--although I can't say I completely agree with people who think that when battle scenes are brought into the living room the hazards of war are necessarily made "real" to the civilian audience. It seems to me that by the same process they are also made less "real"--diminished, in part, by the physical size of the television screen, which, for all the industry's advances, still shows one a picture of men three inches tall shooting at other men three inches tall, and trivialized, or at least tamed, by the enveloping cozy alarums of the household. I should add that the networks don't always run combat footage in their Vietnam news reports; now and then they have human-interest stories (about a Vietnamese village, or an Army medic helping Vietnamese children), some of which are fine, if rather too smooth, and once in a very great while they'll come up with a whole program devoted to Vietnam. Saturday before last, in fact, I was all set to watch a show called "ABC Scope: The War in Vietnam" ("A report on Operation Market Time: the Navy and Coast Guard's attempt to stop the smuggling of Vietcong supplies and weapons"), but when the time came for it they showed us Jim McKay instead, standing in front of a gray screen and reading aloud the scores of all the college football games that had taken place since the fall of Constantinople. Then, on Sunday, NBC came along with a weekly program called *Vietnam Report*, which sounds good on paper, but which, the week I saw it, consisted in its entirety of Senator Fulbright expressing his views on Vietnam for about thirty minutes. I suppose I shouldn't knock as earnest an undertaking as this, especially when I think of Jim McKay and all those football scores, but it seems to me that Senator Fulbright's views on Vietnam are fairly well known by now, and that NBC, by having him repeat them at this time, was trying rather too evidently to appear as the Giant Communications Network Not Afraid to Air the Voice of Dissent but without incurring any bruises, or even any personal discomfort, in the role. Senator Fulbright was accompanied on the program by an NBC correspondent, Robert McCormick, who fed him some bland, leading questions about the "wisdom of our involvement," etc., and then appeared to vanish into thin air while the Senator uncoiled his opinions. (He was against our "involvement.") It all sounded very safe and institutional, and rather like a rerun.

On balance, it seems to me that CBS has probably been doing the best job lately of reporting on Vietnam, because in addition to having some especially enterprising photographer-reporter crews in Vietnam it has Eric Sevareid in Washington. Mr. Sevareid came on the other evening at the end of the seven-o'clock news and spoke for a few minutes about the political significance of recent military actions in the Mekong Delta, and I thought it was the most useful and intelligent few hundred words about the war I'd heard in two weeks of listening to television news reports...

Summertime now, or very nearly. Kids already gabbling about the last day of school. Women walking down East Eighty-sixth Street in those jouncy cotton dresses. Connecticut suntans. Air-conditioning in Schrafft's. *Daktari* reruns on the television, *Lassie* reruns. *Gilligan's Island* reruns. *Star Trek* reruns. Lots of baseball. (Not much doing on television in the good old, mythic old American summertime.) The other Saturday, just back from a trip, and for some reason conscious more pointlessly than ever of that miserable war, I made a mental note to watch, at five o'clock that afternoon, an NBC program called *Vietnam Weekly Review* for whatever it might have to offer, and went outside (it was a nice day--warm, sunny, full of the first hints of summer's dust and laziness, of all those hammocks one will never swing in), toward Fifth Avenue and the park, past which close to one hundred thousand men, women, and children were marching as part of a "Support Our Boys in Vietnam" parade. Lots of people in the streets. Lots of American Legion posts. Lots of those Catholic high-school bands. A flatbed truck went by full of teamsters, many of them holding aloft placards reading, "It's Your Country! Love It Or Leave It!" The Putnam County John Birch Society went by, singing "America the Beautiful". An American Legionnaire went by in a wheelchair, carrying a placard reading, "Victory over Atheistic Communism." The crowd applauded. Somewhere up toward Ninety-sixth Street a band was playing "The Yellow Rose of Texas". Children all around me clutched American flags and looked the way children usually do, with or without flags.

I went back home at ten to five, got out a beer, turned on the TV set. There was a baseball game in progress on NBC. (No *Vietnam Review* that week.) Not a bad game, either. Clendenon hit a long ball in the tenth and wrapped it up for Pittsburgh. I forget who was playing Pittsburgh, but you could look it up. From Fifth Avenue, two blocks away (you could hear it through the open window), a band was finishing up "The Marine Corps Hymn," then started "Sister Kate." Sometimes I wonder what it is that the people who run television think about the war. I'm sure they think about it. Everybody thinks about it. I'm sure they care a lot. (At times, I even picture them sitting around in the Communications Club after hours, brows furrowed in meditation, their tumblers of brandy and Perrier water barely sipped at. Finally a voice is raised. "Well, hang it, Fred. I think Tom Hayden speaks for all of us . . .") Perhaps one is unfair. Perhaps not. In any case, there are good men who work for television trying to tell us about the war. For example, the other Monday night, a little after seven, Walter Cronkite peered out at us pleasantly from the TV screen, said, "Today's Vietnam story in a moment," and then there we were, via film that had been taken twenty-six hours earlier, eighteen miles south of the DMZ, watching a Marine scout detail that had been sent out to look for North Vietnamese encampments. The film began routinely, with the CO briefing his patrol leaders (a sequence that always seems to be staged, although it probably isn't), and then we were watching a small group of men on their way up a thickly wooded hill ("They went up to investigate the distant voices," said the on-the-scene correspondent), and heard the sound of faraway small-arms fire, and suddenly men were running here and there in front of the camera, the small-arms fire became louder and more intense, and once again--in our living room, or was it at the Yale Club bar, or lying on the deck of the grand yacht *Fatima* with a Sony portable TV upon our belly?--we were watching, a bit numbly perhaps (we have watched it so often), real men get shot at, real men (our surrogates, in fact) get killed and wounded. At one point in the film, a mortar round fell near the cameraman, and for a couple of seconds the film spun crazily until it (and he) got straightened out again, and then we were looking, through the camera, at a young man--a boy, surely no more than nineteen or twenty--square-jawed, handsome, All-American, poised there on the side of the hill, rifle held in close to him, waiting on the side of the hill for the signal to move up to where the shooting was, and afraid. In the background, you could hear machine guns firing and the voice of the platoon sergeant, a deep-voiced Negro, calling, "Git on up there! Git! Git!" And the boy stayed there for several moments in the camera's eye, his own eyes staring straight ahead, his face so full of youth, fear, bravery, whatever else, until he finally moved up. One thinks of how one's memories of those other wars (wars one didn't fight in) exist for the most part frozen in the still photographs of the great war photographers--Robert Capa's picture of the Spanish Loyalist falling on the Catalonian hillside, Eugene Smith's Marine face down on the beach at Tarawa, Margaret Bourke-White's St. Paul's Cathedral against the blitz, David Duncan's Marines advancing through the Korean mud. Vietnam is different, to be sure. Not quite so "exciting." Not quite so photogenic. But it seems to me that Kurt Volkert, the man who held and worked that camera, who caught the meaning of that face, is one of the best journalists of the war, and one could probably say the same for many of the other cameramen covering Vietnam for the American networks.

Another afternoon not long ago, I watched a routine film clip, this one taken by Vo Huynh, a Vietnamese who works for NBC, about a military engagement in the South: scenes of men moving in to attack, and attacking--with one heart-rending sequence of a young soldier being carried out, his leg apparently smashed, screaming to his comrades, "It hurts! It hurts!" The special qualities of courage, energy, and strange, tough sensitivity that made men like Robert Capa so good at what they did--so good because so useful, so useful because they went in there (Capa's great pictures of the second wave at Omaha Beach were so blurred that you could barely make out the faces) and tried to show us what it was really like--are qualities that don't exist to any lesser degree in men like Kurt Volkert and Vo Huynh. They too seem to be trying to show us what it's like--at least, what the small, small corner allotted to them is like--and Lord knows there are mighty few other people on television who seem to be trying.

Vietnam is often referred to as "television's war," in the sense that this is the first war that has been brought to the people preponderantly by television. People indeed look at television. They really look at it. They look at Dick Van Dyke and become his friend. They look at a new Pontiac in a commercial and go out and buy it. They look at thoughtful Chet Huntley and find him thoughtful, and at witty David Brinkley and find him witty. They look at Vietnam. They look at Vietnam, it seems, as a child kneeling in the corridor, his eye to the keyhole, looks at two grownups arguing in a locked room--the aperture of the keyhole small; the figures shadowy, mostly out of sight; the voices indistinct, isolated threats without meaning; isolated glimpses, part of an elbow, a man's jacket (who is the man?), part of a face, a woman's face. Ah, she is crying. One sees the tears. (The voices continue indistinctly.) One counts the tears. Two tears. Three tears. Two bombing raids. Four seek-and-destroy missions. Six administration pronouncements. Such a fine-looking woman. One searches in vain for the other grownup, but, ah, the keyhole is so small, he is somehow never in the line of sight. Look! There is General Ky. Look! There are some planes returning safely to the *Ticonderoga*. I wonder (sometimes) what it is that the people who run television think about the war, because *they* have given us this keyhole view; we have given them the airwaves, and now, at this critical time, they have given back to us this keyhole view--and I wonder if they truly think that those isolated glimpses of elbow, face, a swirl of dress (who *is* that other person, anyway?) are all we children can really stand to see of what is going on inside that room.

Vo Huynh, admittedly, will show us as much of the larger truth of a small battle and of a wounded soldier as he is able to, and CBS, as it did some nights ago, will show us a half-hour special interview with Marine Corps General Walt, which is nice of CBS, but there are other things, it seems, that make up the Vietnam war, that intelligent men *know* make up the Vietnam war--factors of doubt, politics, propaganda, truth, untruth, of what we actually do and actually don't do, that aren't in most ways tangible, or certifiably right or wrong, or easily reducible to simple mathematics, but that, even so (and even now), exist as parts of this equation that we're all supposedly trying so hard to solve--and almost none of them get mentioned. It seems almost never to get mentioned, for example, that there's considerable doubt as to the effectiveness of the search-and-destroy missions we watch so frequently on television. (The enemy casualty figures seem to be arbitrarily rigged, and the ground we take isn't anything we usually plan to keep.) It seems almost never to get mentioned, for example, that there's considerably doubt as to the actual efficacy of many of the highly publicized (on TV, as elsewhere) sweeps into territory that, if you read the fine print, you realize the enemy has often already left, and presumably will come back to when we, in turn, have gone. It seems rarely to get mentioned that there has been considerable doubt as to the effectiveness of our bombing, or that an air force that can't always hit the right village certainly can't avoid killing civilians when it bombs power plants in Hanoi. It doesn't seem to get mentioned, for example, that we are using "anti-personnel" weapons such as the Guava and the Pineapple more than the military appears to want to admit, or that any people who drop their tortures from planes flying at five thousand feet are likely to be regarded as no less accomplices than if they had stood in person in some village square and driven little slivers of metal, at high velocity, into the flesh of other human beings. It doesn't seem to get mentioned, for example, that "anti-personnel," "delivering hardware," "pacification mission," and "nation building" are phrases, along with "better dead than Red," that only a people out of touch with the meaning of language could use with any seriousness. It doesn't seem to get mentioned, for example, that when a senior member of the administration states that he sees no reason for thinking we will have to send more troops to Vietnam this year he is probably not telling the truth, and that the fact of his probably not telling the truth is now more important than the fact of the troops. It doesn't seem to get mentioned--Well, enough of that. It is summertime now, or nearly. My kids were squabbling over bathing suits this morning, and who will learn to sail and who to ride. In summertime we cook outdoors a lot, play coronary tennis, drink, watch pretty sunsets out across the water. This summer, I will almost certainly perfect my backhand, write something beautiful (or very nearly), read *Finnegans Wake*, or something like it. This summer--already the streets outside seem quieter, more humane. A car rolls softly over a manhole cover--a small clank. All those quiet streets, all those brave middle-class apartments--and what lies beneath those manhole covers? Wires? Cables? Dying soldiers? Dying children? Sounds of gunfire? Screaming? Madness? My television set plays on, talking to itself--another baseball game, in fact. Juan Marichal is pitching to Ron Hunt. Hunt shifts stance. Marichal winds up. The count is three and two.

SOLDIER POETS OF THE WAR

A CONCISE HISTORY OF THE VIETNAM WAR: 1965-1968

The air in the room is dark and greasy
as a city slicker's hair. LBJ reaches out
and finds what he wants. The balls are
small,
easily cupped in his hand. So he knows
he's right when he says, "I've got the
bastard
by the nuts and I won't let go
till he yells uncle." It is only later,
after Lyndon gets blue in the face,
that he knows he's made a mistake.

Ron Weber

A BLACK SOLDIER REMEMBERS

My Saigon daughter I saw only once
standing in the dusty square
across from the Brink's BOQ/PX
in back of the National Assembly
next to the ugly statue of
the crouching marines facing
the fish pond the VC blew up
during Tet.

The amputee beggars watch us.
The same color and the same eyes.
She does not offer me one of the
silly hats she sells Americans and
I have nothing she needs but
the sad smile she already has.

Horace Coleman

A DOWNED BLACK PILOT LEARNS TO FLY

"now that the war is over
we'll have to kill each other again
but I'll send my medals to Hanoi
and let them make bullets if
they'll ship my leg back and
if they mail me an ash tray
made from my F4C they can keep
the napalm as a bonus. Next time
I'll wait and see if they've declared
war on me--or just America

Horace Coleman

TIME ON TARGET

We used to get intelligence reports
from the Vietnamese district offices.
Every night, I'd make a list
of targets for artillery to hit.

It used to give me quite a kick
to know that I, a corporal,
could command an entire battery
to fire anywhere I said.

One day, while on patrol,
we passed the ruins of a house;
beside it sat a woman
with her left hand torn away;
beside her lay a child, dead.

When I got back to base,
I told the fellows in the COC;
it gave us all a lift to know
all those shells we fired every night
were hitting something.

W. D. Ehrhart

MAKING THE CHILDREN BEHAVE

Do they think of me now
in those strange Asian villages
where nothing ever seemed
quite human
but myself
and my few grim friends
moving through them
hunched
in lines?

When they tell stories to their children
of the evil
that awaits misbehavior,
is it me they conjure?

W. D. Ehrhart

THE INVASION OF GRENADA

I didn't want a monument,
not even one as sober as that
vast black wall of broken lives.
I didn't want a postage stamp.
I didn't want a road beside the Delaware
River with a sign proclaiming:
"Vietnam Veterans Memorial Highway."

What I wanted was a simple recognition
of the limits of our power as a nation
to inflict our will on others.
What I wanted was an understanding
that the world is neither black-and-white
nor ours.

What I wanted
was an end to monuments.

W. D. Ehrhart

STILL LATER THERE ARE WAR STORIES

Still later there are war stories
for those who think of us, not as we were

Randall Jarrell

1

Another buddy dead.
There is enough dying--
Gary Cooper will
ride up, slow and easy
slide off his horse
without firing a shot
save us all.

It is a matter of waiting.
We grow old counting the year
in days, one by one
each morning, ritual marks
once more, one less--
the plane has yet to land

2

Down freeways, past federal cemetery flags
half masted, dark green lawn,
the watered rows of stone--I could have
come home--November five--to a decade
recounting days since, another
waiting above jungle trails
for then we hope never to see--
field hospital beds, orthopedic surgeons
saving lives, fifteen minutes away.....

Daily boy scout excursions
through brush so thick
one hour hacking brings you
twenty feet closer to home,
down a new tropic trail. The jungle
loaded, nobody
comes away in one piece.

D. F. Brown

AFTER OUR WAR

After our war, the dismembered bits
--all those pierced eyes, ear slivers, jaw splinters,
gouged lips, odd tibias, skin flaps, and toes--
came squinting, wobbling, jabbering back.
The genitals, of course, were the most bizarre,
inching along roads like glowworms and slugs.
The living wanted them back, but good as new.
The dead, of course, had no use for them.
And the ghosts, the tens of thousands of abandoned
souls
who had appeared like swamp fog in the city streets,
on the evening altars, and on doorsills of cratered
homes,
also had no use for the scraps and bits
because, in their opinion, they looked good without
them.
Since all things naturally return to their source,
these snags and tatters arrived, with immigrant
uncertainty,
in the United States. It was almost home.
So, now, one can sometimes see a friend or a famous
man talking
with an extra pair of lips glued and yammering on his
cheek,
and this is why handshakes are often unpleasant,
why it is better, sometimes, not to look another in the
eye,
why, at your daughter's breast thickens a hard keloidal
scar.
After the war, with such Cheshire cats grinning in our
trees,
will the ancient tales still tell us new truths?
Will the myriad world surrender new metaphor?
After our war, how will love speak?

John Balaban

THOUGHTS BEFORE DAWN
for Mary Bui Thi Khuy, 1944-1969

The bare oaks rock and snowcrust tumbles down
while squirrels snug down in windy nests
swaying under staffs above the frozen earth.
The creaking eave woke me, thinking of you
crushed by a truck thirteen years ago
when the drunk ARVN lost the wheel.

We brought to better care the nearly lost,
the boy burned by white phosphorus, chin
glued to his chest; the scalped girl;
the triple amputee from the road-mined bus;
the kid without a jaw; the one with no nose.
You never wept in front of them, but waited
until the gurney rolled them into surgery.
I guess that's what amazed me most.
Why didn't you fall apart or quit?

Once, we flew two patched kids home,
getting in by Army chopper,
a Huey Black Cat that skimmed the sea.
When the gunner opened up on a whale
you closed your eyes and covered your ears
and your small body shook in your silk ao dai.
Oh, Mary. In this arctic night, awake in my bed
I rehearse your smile, bright white teeth,
the funny way you rode your Honda 50, perched
so straight, silky hair bunned up in a brim hat,
front brim blown back, and dark glasses.
Brave woman, I hope you never saw the truck.

John Balaban

IN CELEBRATION OF SPRING

Our Asian war is over; others have begun.
Our elders, who tried to mortgage lies,
are disgraced, or dead, and already
the brokers are picking their pockets
for the keys and the credit cards.

In delta swamp in a united Vietnam,
a Marine with a bullfrog for a face,
rots in equatorial heat. An eel
slides through the cage of his bared ribs.
At night, on the old battlefields, ghosts,
like patches of fog, lurk into villages
to maunder on doorsills of cratered homes,
while all across the U.S.A.
the wounded walk about and wonder where to go.

And today, in the simmer of lyric sunlight,
the chrysalis pulses in its mushy cocoon,
under the bark on a gnarled root of an elm.
In the brilliant creek, a minnow flashes
delirious with gnats. The turtle's heart
quickens its taps in the warm bank sludge.
As she chases a frisbee spinning in sunlight,
a girl's breasts bounce full and strong;
a boy's stomach, as he turns, is flat and strong.

Swear by the locust, by dragonflies on ferns,
by the minnow's flash, the tremble of a breast,
by the new earth spongy under our feet:
that as we grow old, we will not grow evil,
that although our garden seeps with sewage,
and our elders think it's up for auction--swear
by this dazzle that does not wish to leave us--
that we will be keepers of a garden, nonetheless.

John Balaban

AFTER THE VIETNAM WAR

sometimes
on windless night
when the moon glows
like a tv set in a dark room
the vietnam dead rise

bodyless heads arms & legs
skitter down pock marked roads
like great hordes
of mutilated rats
in the villages
small dark women kneel
on the dirt floors
of huts

they cut their black hair
rub ashes on foreheads
their cries are almost human

Steven Ford Brown

PORT HURON STATEMENT (1962)

In 1962 Tom Hayden and several of his University of Michigan friends founded the Students for a Democratic Society. SDS *later became nationally known for its radical, even violent, anti-war activities and for its insistence on revolutionary social and economic change. But its initial Port Huron statement reflected the idealism of the Kennedy years and the authors' own moderate desire to reform from within the system.*

INTRODUCTION: AGENDA FOR A GENERATION

We are people of this generation, bred in at least modest comfort, housed now in universities, looking uncomfortably to the world we inherit.

When we were kids the United States was the wealthiest and strongest country in the world; the only one with the atom bomb, the least scarred by modern war, an initiator of the United Nations that we thought would distribute Western influence throughout the world. Freedom and equality for each individual, government of, by, and for the people--these American values we found good, principles by which we could live as men. Many of us began maturing in complacency.

As we grew, however, our comfort was penetrated by events too troubling to dismiss. First, the permeating and victimizing fact of human degradation, symbolized by the Southern struggle against racial bigotry, compelled most of us from silence to activism. Second, the enclosing fact of the Cold War, symbolized by the presence of the Bomb, brought awareness that we ourselves, and our friends, and millions of abstract "others" we knew more directly because of our common peril, might die at any time. We might deliberately ignore, or avoid, or fail to feel all other human problems, but not these two, for these were too immediate and crushing in their impact, too challenging in the demand that we as individuals take the responsibility for encounter and resolution.

While these and other problems either directly oppressed us or rankled our consciences and became our own subjective concerns, we began to see complicated and disturbing paradoxes in our surrounding America. The declaration "all men are created equal..." rang hollow before the facts of Negro life in the South and the big cities of the North. The proclaimed peaceful intentions of the United States contradicted its economic and military investments in the Cold War status quo....

Our work is guided by the sense that we may be the last generation in the experiment with living. But we are a minority--the vast majority of our people regard the temporary equilibriums of our society and world as eternally-functional parts. In this is perhaps the outstanding paradox: we ourselves are imbued with urgency, yet the message of our society is that there is no viable alternative to the present. Beneath the reassuring tones of the politicians, beneath the common opinion that America will "muddle through," beneath the stagnation of those who have closed their minds to the future, is the prevailing feeling that there simply are no alternatives, that our times have witnessed the exhaustion not only of Utopias, but of any new departures as well....

Some would have us believe that Americans feel contentment amidst prosperity--but might it not better be called a glaze above deeply-felt anxieties about their role in the new world? And if these anxieties produce a developed indifference to human affairs, do they not as well produce a yearning to believe there *is* an alternative to the present, that something *can* be done to change circumstances in the school, the workplaces, the bureaucracies, the government? It is to this latter yearning, at once the spark and engine of change, that we direct our present appeal. The search for truly democratic alternatives to the present, and a commitment to social experimentation with them, is a worthy and fulfilling human enterprise, one which moves us and, we hope, others today. On such a basis do we offer this document of our convictions and analysis: as an effort in understanding and changing the conditions of humanity in the late twentieth century, an effort rooted in the ancient, still unfulfilled conception of man attaining determining influence over his circumstances of life....

THE STUDENTS

If student movements for change are still rarities on the campus scene, what is commonplace there? The real campus, the familiar campus, is a place of private people, engaged in their notorious "inner emigration". It is a place of commitment to business-as-usual, getting ahead, playing it cool. It is a place of mass affirmation of the Twist, but mass reluctance toward the controversial public stance. Rules are accepted as "inevitable," bureaucracy as "just circumstances," irrelevance as "scholarship," selflessness as "martyrdom," politics as "just another way to make people, and an unprofitable one, too.". . .

Tragically, the university could serve as a significant source of social criticism and an initiator of new modes and molders of attitudes. But the actual intellectual effect of the college experience is hardly distinguishable from that of any other communications channel--say, at a television set--passing on the stock truths of the day. Students leave college somewhat more "tolerant" than when they arrived, but basically unchallenged in their values and political orientations. With administrators ordering the institution, and faculty the curriculum, the student learns by his isolation to accept elite rule within the university, which prepares him to accept later forms of minority control. The real function of the educational system--as opposed to its more rhetorical function of "searching for truth"--is to impart the key information and styles that will help the student get by, modestly but comfortably, in the big society beyond.

THE SOCIETY BEYOND

Look beyond the campus, to America itself. That student life is more intellectual, and perhaps more comfortable, does not obscure the fact that the fundamental qualities of life on the campus reflect the habits of society at large. The fraternity president is seen at the junior manager levels;

the sorority queen has gone to Grosse Pointe; the serious poet burns for a place, any place, to work; the once-serious and never-serious poets work at the advertising agencies. The desperation of people threatened by forces about which they know little and of which they can say less; the cheerful emptiness of people "giving up" all hope of changing things; the faceless ones polled by Gallup who listed "international affairs" fourteenth on their list of "problems" but who also expected thermonuclear war in the next few years; in these and other forms, Americans are in withdrawal from public life, from any collective effort at directing their own affairs.

The very isolation of the individual--from power and community and ability to aspire--means the rise of a democracy without publics. With the great mass of people structurally remote and psychologically hesitant with respect to democratic institutions, those institutions themselves attenuate and become, in the fashion of the vicious circle, progressively less accessible to those few who aspire to serious participation in social affairs. The vital democratic connection between community and leadership, between the mass and the several elites, has been so wrenched and perverted that disastrous policies go unchallenged time and again.

POLITICS WITHOUT PUBLICS

The American political system is not the democratic model of which its glorifiers speak. In actuality it frustrates democracy by confusing the individual citizen, paralyzing policy discussion, and consolidating the irresponsible power of military and business interests.

A most alarming fact is that few, if any, politicians are calling for changes in these conditions. Only a handful even are calling on the President to "live up to" platform pledges; no one is demanding structural changes, such as the shuttling of Southern Democrats out of the Democratic Party. Rather than protesting the state of politics, most politicians are reinforcing and aggravating that state. . . .

THE ECONOMY

We live amidst a national celebration of economic prosperity while poverty and deprivation remain an unbreakable way of life for millions in the "affluent society," including many of our own generation. We hear glib references to the "welfare state," "free enterprise," and "shareholder's democracy" while military defense is the main item of "public" spending and obvious oligopoly and other forms of minority rule defy real individual initiative or popular control. Work, too, is often unfulfilling and victimizing, accepted as a channel to status or plenty, if not a way to pay the bills, rarely as a means of understanding and controlling self and events. In work and leisure the individual is regulated as part of the system, a consuming unit, bombarded by hard-sell, soft-sell, lies and semi-true appeals to his basest drives. He is always told that he is a "free" man because of "free enterprise." . . .

The Military-Industrial Complex

The most spectacular and important creation of the authoritarian and oligopolistic structure of economic decision-making in America is the institution called "the military-industrial complex" by former President Eisenhower--the powerful congruence of interest and structure among military and business elites which affects so much of our development and destiny. Not only is ours the first generation to live with the possibility of world-wide cataclysm--it is the first to experience the actual social preparation for cataclysm, the general militarization of American society. . . .

Since our childhood these two trends--the rise of the military and the installation of a defense-based economy--have grown fantastically. The Department of Defense, ironically the world's largest single organization, is worth $160 billion, owns 32 million acres of America and employs half the 7.5 million persons directly dependent on the military for subsistence, has an $11 billion payroll which is larger than the net annual income of all American corporations. Defense spending in the Eisenhower era totaled $350 billions and President Kennedy entered office pledged to go even beyond the present defense allocation of 60 cents from every public dollar spent. Except for a war-induced boom immediately after "our side" bombed Hiroshima. American economic prosperity has coincided with a growing dependence on military outlay--from 1911 to 1959 America's Gross National Product of $5.25 trillion included $700 billion in goods and services purchased for the defense effort, about one-seventh of the accumulated GNP. . . .

TOWARD AMERICAN DEMOCRACY

Every effort to end the Cold War and expand the process of world industrialization is an effort hostile to people and institutions whose interests lie in perpetuation of the East-West military threat and the postponement of change in the "have not" nations of the world. Every such effort, too, is bound to establish greater democracy in America. The major goals of a domestic effort would be:

1. America must abolish its political party stalemate.

2. Mechanisms of voluntary association must be created through which political information can be imparted and political participation encouraged.

3. Institutions and practices which stifle dissent should be abolished, and the promotion of peaceful dissent should be actively promoted.

4. Corporations must be made publicly responsible.

5. The allocation of resources must be based on social needs. A truly "public sector" must be established, and its nature debated and planned.

6. America should concentrate on its genuine social priorities: abolish squalor, terminate neglect, and establish an environment for people to live in with dignity and creativeness.

Bradford Lyttle, *THE DEMOCRATIC CONVENTION DEMONSTRATIONS, 1968*

Bradford Lyttle's The Chicago Anti-Vietnam War Movement *originated as a graduate school paper; as such, and in spite of the author's obvious pacifist sympathies, it attempts to objectify "The Days of Rage" that surrounded the 1968 Democratic Convention. What follows is a day-by-day, blow-by-blow description of the battles that took place between Mayor Richard Daley's Chicago police force and the thousands of anti-war demonstrators who came to Chicago to protest the Democratic Party's nominating convention and its support of the Vietnam War.*

August 18, contingents of demonstrators, most of them Yippies, began arriving in Chicago, Rennie Davis and Tom Hayden discussed demonstration tactics with demonstrators near the Lincoln Park fieldhouse, and the Chicago Police Department assigned a surveillance unit to the park.

August 19-20, in Lincoln Park, Mobe marshals conducted training sessions in karate, judo, and "washoi," or "snake dancing," a street formation that Japanese militants claimed was effective against police attacks.

August 22, Jerome Johnson, a 17-year-old American Indian from Sioux Falls, S.D., was shot and killed by police at North Avenue and Wells St. The police claimed that the youth had been fleeing the scene of a robbery, and had failed to halt when ordered to.

Friday, August 23, the Yippies revealed their candidate for President at Civic Center Plaza. Pigasus, an "obnoxious, horrible" pig, ran on a platform of "garbage." The police quickly "arrested" him, and turned him over to the Humane Society. They arrested Jerry Rubin and five other Yippies, too.

By the afternoon of Saturday, August 24, there were 2,000 demonstrators in Lincoln Park. At 6:00 p.m., a crowd of 600 gathered northwest of the park fieldhouse and started a bonfire. Police announced a curfew and cleared the park at 11:00 p.m. The ousted demonstrators gathered on Wells St. and discussed the situation.

Sunday, August 25, the first severe violence broke out at Lincoln Park. Early in the afternoon, several hundred demonstrators marched from Lincoln Park to Grant Park. Many later returned to Lincoln Park. By mid-afternoon, a crowd of several thousand had assembled near the Lincoln Park horse ring and concession stand.

Shortly after 5:00 p.m., Yippies tried to drive into the park a flatbed truck that they hoped to use as a stage for their Festival of Life. Police stopped the truck, and arrested a man who stood in front of the truck trying to prevent it from being moved. They then arrested a youth who was urging the crowd to sit in front of a police squadron van, and take away the police's guns. The crowd grew ugly, and the police retreated to the west of the park. They then arrested a girl who said she was the arrested youth's girlfriend, and wanted to be with him. The surrounding crowd surged into the police lines. Officers began clubbing. A melee ensued. Reinforcements came to the aid of the police, and the demonstrators and police separated. Many officers then removed their nameplates.

In the evening, fire trucks accompanied by police entered the park to extinguish several bonfires. A crowd jeered the firemen and officers, and threw things at them. A crowd of more than 100 surrounded about a dozen policemen who were standing with their backs against a wall of the fieldhouse. People in the crowd taunted the police. When the crowd moved in, the officers charged three times, clubbing fiercely and indiscriminately.

Starting about 8:30 p.m., the police broadcast warnings about the 11:00 p.m. curfew. Most of the people voluntarily left the park. At about 11:00 p.m., helmeted and motorcycle police drove a crowd of approximately 600 demonstrators out of the park to the west. More than 200 demonstrators remained on the eastern edge of Stockton Drive.

The part of the crowd that left the park proceeded to Eugenie Triangle (at the intersection of Clark, LaSalle and Eugenie Streets), and then surged along LaSalle. At North Ave., their numbers had grown to about 2,000, and they were blocked by a line of police. The police told them to get off the street. The people then took to the sidewalks to the east and west, and milled about.

At the Wells-North intersection, police knocked down and kicked a man who had failed to move. The crowd then dispersed, many people returning to Lincoln Park, which the police permitted them to re-enter.

Another large group of demonstrators marched south on LaSalle St., blocking vehicular traffic and tipping over trash cans. When police blocked an intersection, they detoured east and west. Police finally blocked this group at the Michigan Ave. bridge over the Chicago River. Officers clubbed demonstrators who tried to cross the bridge, and attacked a press photographer. The crowd finally dispersed, and filtered back to Lincoln Park and the Old Town area. Several store and car windows were smashed, and other damage was done during the demonstration.

Near midnight, about 100 officers cleared the park a second time. Motorcycle units accompanied the skirmish line. Demonstrators pelted the police with bottles and rocks, and shouted abuse. Police used their batons against newsmen who wouldn't leave the scene.

Officers then charged a crowd of demonstrators near Stockton Drive. The mass of struggling people clogged traffic on the drive. Some police and demonstrators shouted insults at each other. The crowd retreated to the west parking lot adjacent to Clark St., saw that the officers weren't following them, and moved back. One observer described the behavior of the crowd this way:

> *The thing about this crowd was that since it thrived on confrontation it behaved in a way much different than any other crowd I've ever seen. During racial riots, the police would break up the crowd and the crowd would stay broken up. It might regroup in another place but rarely would it head back for direct confrontation with its assailants.*
>
> *This was a most unusual crowd. This time...the police would break people's heads but the crowd would not run away. What it would do would...regroup and surge back to the police and yell more epithets, as much as saying: "Do it again."*

Police charged again, this time driving the people into Clark St. Several people were knocked down and hurt. Some demonstrators fought hand-to-hand with the police. A reporter was beaten.

Police then threw tear gas canisters into the crowd of demonstrators. Many demonstrators ran to Eugenie Triangle, where they mixed with other demonstrators and cars to completely clog traffic. Some police yelled "Kill the commies." Some demonstrators shouted, "Kill the pigs!" Some demonstrators threw rocks at the police. Motorists honked their horns. Confusion and cacophony reigned.

The police formed another skirmish line and drove the people south along Clark St. At about the 1700 block, some policemen began clubbing people in the retreating crowd. Police hurled gas canisters and clubbed newsmen and women. Finally, the crowd dispersed and the violence subsided.

Distressed by the violence that had occurred Sunday night in their neighborhood, clergymen of the North Side Cooperative Ministry met Monday morning and discussed the situation. They decided on two main actions. In the afternoon, they held a press conference at which they said that Chicago had been turned into a "police state." Also, they decided that when the evening curfew came they should try to act as "buffers" between the police and demonstrators. Acting on their consciences, ministers either would go into the park, or remain on its periphery.

Early Monday morning, Tom Hayden and anti-war activist Wolfe Lowenstein were arrested in Lincoln Park while they were discussing plans for a march from the park to the Conrad Hilton. Hayden was charged with obstructing police, resisting arrest, and disorderly conduct.

Immediately after these arrests, Rennie Davis led a march of 4-500 out of the park south toward police headquarters to protest the arrests. The march reached its objective and demonstrated at the headquarters without being stopped or attacked.

Late in the afternoon, a melee broke out in Grant Park at the statue of Civil War General Logan, across from the Hilton Hotel. A number of activists who were part of a parade of several hundred people on their way to police headquarters to protest Hayden's and Lowenstein's arrests, draped Vietcong flags on the statue, and climbed on it. Officers drove and pulled them off the statue, breaking one boy's leg. The police then formed a skirmish line and cleared the area. Some paraders carried signs calling the police pigs, and some shouted insults. A newsman reported seeing police beat a girl.

Starting about 9:00 p.m., groups as large as 1,000 or more roamed Old Town streets, throwing bottles and rocks, and causing some damage to cars. Police policy was to keep marches from the downtown area. Using their clubs and exchanging insults with the demonstrators, police dispersed the groups.

Later in the evening, a crowd of perhaps 1,500 began a march south on Wells St. Occupying the center of the street, the people blocked traffic. Also, some rocks and bottles were thrown and windows broken. When the march turned east at Division St., club-wielding police drove it back. Officers also attacked several reporters, news photographers, and onlookers.

Near 11:00 p.m., people in Lincoln Park constructed a barricade of picnic tables and trash baskets between the Garibaldi statue and a snow fence near the concession stand. Demonstrators raised revolutionary flags at the barricade. Some shouted insults at the police.

Poet Allen Ginsberg tried to calm the crowd of about 1,000 by chanting "OM."

The police broadcast an order to clear the park. Instead of dispersing, the crowd behind the barricade built up to 2-3,000. The police donned gas masks and passed out 20-30 riot and shotguns. Fire Department light trucks illuminated the scene.

Shortly after midnight, a patrol car approaching from the west was surrounded by the crowd. Some demonstrators attacked the car with rocks and bottles shouting "Get the police car!", and, "Kill the cops!" The battered car finally escaped.

At 12:27 a.m., the police lobbed gas and smoke bombs into the crowd and accompanied by the light trucks advanced on the barricade. Officers clubbed indiscriminately. A seminarian received multiple lacerations of the head and a skull fracture. A woman was beaten and thrown into a pond. Police threw a cyclist returning from work into the pond. Other officers knocked down a news photographer.

By 12:45 a.m., the clearing operation was complete. Most of the demonstrators were along Clark St., where many shouted and threw things at the police. Clouds of gas distressed and angered people in the crowds jamming the Eugenie and Old Town triangles.

After sporadically attacking the crowd, the police set up skirmish lines and drove the people north and south on Clark St., and up and down the side streets, gassing and clubbing freely. Newsmen, onlookers, and local residents were among those attacked. Demonstrators retaliated with insulting epithets and by throwing and breaking things. Violent incidents continued until about 2:00 a.m.

Mobe activities were the only demonstrations that went on late Monday and Tuesday morning and afternoon. Acting independently, a group of pacifists organized a nonviolent demonstration. From the time that they first heard about plans for demonstrations at the convention, several pacifists on the East Coast, including members of New England CNVA, and A Quaker Action Group (AQUAG), had been worried about the likelihood of violence. They asked David Finke if he could arrange a conference early in convention week to explore what might be done to increase the likelihood of nonviolent demonstrations. Finke set up the conference for Monday evening at McGiffert House, on the University of Chicago campus. About 60 people attended, among them Ross Flanagan (AQUAG), Tom Hayes (Episcopal Peace Fellowship), Otto Liljenstolpe, Staughton Lynd, Kale WIlliams, and Ron Young (FOR). Monday evening and Tuesday morning at Quaker House, the conference agreed on plans for a nonviolent demonstration that involved a Tuesday morning service at a near northside church, a walk to the Amphitheater, and a 24-hour vigil or picket.

The demonstration took place, largely as planned. At 1:00 p.m., Staughton Lynd and Kale Williams led a press conference to announce the program. Ross Flanagan and Tom Hayes spoke at the meeting in the church. About 200 people wearing black sashes, including a number of clergymen, then began the march. They carried a banner that said, "We Mourn Suppression of Human Rights: --Vietnam,--Czechoslovakia,--Chicago." The march proceeded along Michigan Avenue, where a number of television interviews were taken, and passed the police headquarters at 11th Street. As the march progressed, people joined it, until there were more than 1,000 in the parade. At 39th and Halsted, police blocked the march. The marchers then established a picket line and vigil....

Demonstrations not organized by pacifists resumed Tuesday. Near noon, two marches to the Polish Consulate to protest Poland's participation in the invasion of Czechoslovakia took place. According to the police, one group was not "Lincoln Park hippies."

Later in the day, Lincoln Park area clergymen and residents formed the Lincoln Park Emergency Citizens' Committee, sent a delegation to the police, and asked that people be allowed to sleep in the park. The police refused the request.

An NSCM delegation told the police that members of their group planned to hold a vigil in the park Tuesday night, even if it meant committing civil disobedience.

Crowds of several hundred gathered in the park in the afternoon. Allen Ginsberg continued his chanting sessions.

At 7:00 p.m., about 1,500 people listened to speeches by Bobby Seale and Jerry Rubin.

At 7:30 p.m., police attacked, maced, and dispersed a march of more than 500 on Clark St. At 8:10 p.m., 200 marched to the Chicago Transit Authority bus barn at Clark and Schubert to support a busmen's strike against alleged discrimination in the Transit Workers' Union. Later joined by another support march, the combined group was involved in several incidents involving strike-breaking bus drivers and police.

Other marches of several hundred went south and west. At 10:35 p.m., about 1,000 people moved out of Lincoln Park toward The Loop and Grant Park. They reached their destination without a confrontation with the police.

Shortly after midnight, despite pleas from clergymen, officers swept Lincoln Park again, using gas freely. Police broke the windows of several cars bearing "flower power" stickers that were parked on Clark near Lincoln and Wells, and moved the cars away. Police then gassed crowds at Clark St. Some of the gas blew east and incapacitated motorists on Lake Shore Drive. Hundreds of people jammed the intersection of Lincoln, Wells, and Clark, some shouting obscenities and throwing rocks, bottles and other missiles at the police. Several squad cars were damaged. Police chased and beat demonstrators, and threatened several local residents who were only onlookers.

Without a search warrant, badges or nameplates, a group of officers invaded an apartment in Old Town, held its student occupants at gunpoint, and searched it. On departing, they allegedly took a camera, cash, and other valuables....

(Tuesday) evening at the Coliseum, almost 3,000 attended an "un-birthday party" to mark Lyndon Johnson's 60th birthday. Speakers who condemned the police included Dick Gregory, David Dellinger, Allen Ginsberg, Jean Genet, William Burroughs, and Terry Southern. Phil Ochs, The Fugs, Home Juice, and The Popular Worm were among the entertainers.

At about 11:00 p.m., Mobe co-chairman Sidney Peck asked the crowd to join those in front of the Hilton to help protest the beating of kids there. Shortly before midnight, approximately 2,000 people left the Coliseum and marched to Grant Park. They soon were joined by a large group that had been driven out of Lincoln Park. Eventually, the crowd in Grant Park numbered about 5,000. Many were abusive and threw things at the police.

Initially indecisive about how to deal with the Grant Park group, the police finally told the demonstrators that they could remain in the park east of Michigan Avenue. This concession pleased the crowd, and, as the night progressed, the demonstrators became less and less boisterous. Some lit bonfires. Peter, Paul and Mary sang from an improvised stage. Several clergymen conducted religious services....

Wednesday, August 28, proved the climax of the demonstrations. The one event for which the city had granted a permit was an afternoon rally at the old bandshell on the south end of Grant Park. I attended the rally, and wrote a report of it which is the basis of the following account:

"The rally was scheduled for 1:00 p.m., but people were slow in arriving. A large group of Yippies came in from Lincoln Park about 1:30. By the time the rally began, at about 2:00 p.m., there probably were no more than 6,000 people present.

"Police handed out a flier asking those at the rally to cooperate with them. The leaflet said that the rally had been authorized, but not a march to the Amphitheater. People attempting to march would be subject to arrest.

"As the rally's program started, platoons of blue helmeted police gathered on the west side of the crowd. After the rally had been in progress about half an hour, a large number of young people suddenly turned around and began to shout and gesture defiantly toward the Field Museum. Cries of "Pigs!" and "Oink! Oink!" went up. A line of National Guardsmen had formed along the south side of the park, and Guardsmen could be seen standing on the roof of the Field Museum. Soon, however, the crowd quieted, and turned back to the speakers.

"A number of speakers at the rally denounced police brutality in terms that couldn't help but antagonize the police standing nearby. An exception was Carl Strock, a young man who had recently returned from working with the AFSC in South Vietnam. He suggested that it was more revolutionary to ask the police to join the anti-war movement than to call them pigs.

"After the rally had been underway for about an hour, someone lowered the American flag on the west side of the bandstand to half mast. A roar went up from the crowd. For a few minutes the flag fluttered at half mast. Then it was pulled down and disappeared completely. This seemed to set off the police, for a group of about 40 drove into the crowd near the flagpole, hitting many people with clubs. They arrested, among others, the man who had pulled down the flag, and Rennie Davis. They clubbed Davis on the head, giving him a wound that required many stitches.

"As the police and crowd milled about, the situation became uglier and uglier. A full-scale onslaught by all the police seemed imminent. Then, the police who had attacked drew back from the crowd and regrouped to the northwest. Demonstrators shouted, threw things, including rocks, and advanced toward the police. A policeman threw a teargas bomb that was promptly picked up and thrown back. The crowd shouted in delight.

"Within a few minutes, another group of police formed a wedge and drove into the center of the crowd, penetrating well into the rows of benches. Many people were clubbed. Benches were tossed about. Again, there was wild disorder, and we expected an attempt to disperse the entire meeting. However, these police too soon withdrew, and within a short time both platoons that had attacked were marched across the Inner Drive, well away from the demonstrators. David Dellinger, who was chairing the rally, said that the authorities had promised him that there would be no more attacks on the assembly. Looking at the hurt demonstrators and broken benches around them, the crowd was, by and large, skeptical.

"People reacted differently to the situation, and to what seemed another, imminent police onslaught. A first aid team gave competent care to a youth with a gashed head. Jim Peck sat beneath a lamp post with a STOP WAR sign, prepared to remain there no matter what happened. One youth leader helped break up benches, so that demonstrators could use pieces of the benches as clubs. Other activists counselled against fighting with the police.

"The speakers became more militant, denouncing the police and Mayor Daley. Norman

Mailer apologized for not planning to be in the march to the Amphitheater that was scheduled to follow the rally. He said that he had to return to New York City to meet a writing deadline. Dick Gregory spoke at length. He was militant, provocative, humorous, and utterly courageous, ringingly denouncing Daley and police brutality before hundreds of angry policemen. Allen Ginsberg led the crowd in the Hindu chant "OM," with the intent, he said, of soothing nerves and inspiring courage....

"The situation remained static for about 20 minutes. Then, the police began a series of savage charges and sweeps that produced most of the bloodshed. The main objective of the police seemed to be to clear Michigan Avenue, but sometimes they attacked the people in front of them so fiercely that chaos and turbulence resulted, rather than an orderly withdrawal. In one widely reported incident, police drove in from three sides to trap about 50 people against the Hilton Hotel shop windows. The struggling people had no route of escape, and the officers clubbed them repeatedly."

"A window finally broke. *Rights in Conflict* has this description of the incident:

> *With a sickening crack, the window shattered, and screaming men and women tumbled through, some cut badly by jagged glass. The police came after them.*
>
> *"I was pushed through by the force of large numbers of people," one victim said. "I got a deep cut on my right leg, diagnosed later by Eugene McCarthy's doctor as a severed artery....I fell to the floor of the bar. There were 10 to 20 people who had come through....I could not stand on the leg. It was bleeding profusely.*
>
> *A squad of policemen burst into the bar, clubbing all those who looked to them like demonstrators, at the same time screaming over and over, "We've got to clear this area." The police acted literally like mad dogs looking for objects to attack.*
>
> *A patrolman ran up to where I was sitting. I protested that I was injured and could not walk, attempting to show him my leg. He screamed that he would show me I could walk. He grabbed me by the shoulder and literally hurled me through the door of the bar into the lobby....*
>
> *I stumbled out into what seemed to be the main lobby. The young lady I was with and I were both immediately set upon by what I can only presume were plain clothes police....We were cursed by these individuals and thrown through another door into an outer lobby." Eventually, a McCarthy aide took him to the 15th floor...*
>
> *In the heat of all this, probably few were aware of the Haymarket's advertising slogan: "A place where good guys take good girls to dine in the lusty, rollicking atmosphere of fabulous old Chicago...."*

Mobe co-chairman Sid Peck was one of those beaten by the police. He suffered a broken finger, dislocated shoulder, and possibly a cracked skull.

My report continues: "On other occasions, groups of police would pursue and club individual demonstrators.

"Many in the crowd heaped verbal abuse on the police. Pigs! and Fascists! were popular shouts. Masses of demonstrators would raise their arms in the fascist salute and chant Sieg Heil! Following each police onslaught and withdrawal, youngsters would approach and curse violently at them....

Wednesday night, while "The Battle of Michigan Avenue" was in full swing, Jane Kennedy was in the MCHR's headquarters in the Church Federation Building on Michigan Avenue. She recalls this experience:

> *Somebody in the Church Federation was monitoring the police radio and they heard on the police radio that the police were saying, "come on, let's get all those medical people there on Michigan!"...So they came up to me and said listen...And we had at that point many people in there who had been bloodied, who were vomiting sometimes from the tear gas, or whatever it was that they threw at us; sometimes from the sheer fright--it was just inconceivable--people were in a state of shock because here was the government, our government, beating us up, and I said, "Oh, my God! I cannot let the police come in here."--because we had passed out these little leaflets that said if you're ill, and you need some medical help, come to this address....And many of those people had come. Now, when you do something like that, then the assumption is that you are assuming responsibility for their safety. And I could not allow the police to come up and beat them up some more. It would not be my living up to my part of the responsibility. So I said to my co-chairman who was Irene Turner, "Well, I'm going to go down in front of the door. I'm going to try to prevent them from coming up stairs." Of course, she didn't want me to do it, but I said I must do this. So somehow or other she sent word out to the Church Federation I was going to stand in front of the door and try to stop them from coming up...and, of course, the beautiful thing that happened was I was standing there--I didn't know what I was going to do; I'm not violent. I was going to try to explain to them how they couldn't come up or something--and so I was standing at the doorway and all of a sudden I was in a crowd. I was all by myself when I started and all of a sudden I was almost being crowded to the second row of this fairly large doorway. I saw all these nice people with their Roman collars; all the ministers from the Church Federation standing with me. And so it apparently was just the right--you talk of symbols!--just the right thing, because three unmarked cars of helmeted police pulled up to the doorway, and the car doors opened and they looked up at us from their seats in the cars, and all they saw was this whole group of clergymen with all of their accouterments on. Well, they kind of had one foot out the car doors and they began talking with one another in the three cars, and they stood for a moment, and then they looked back and the clergymen waved to them and said, "Everything's OK here officers!" And so they very slowly and reluctantly got back in their cars and drove off.*

Television cameras mounted on the Hilton's marquee had a full view of "The Battle of Michigan Avenue." As the savage police charges took place, demonstrators chanted, "The whole world is watching."

During the battle the Democratic Party was nominating its candidates at the Amphitheater. TV pictures of police attacking the demonstrators, which were delayed for about an hour because a telephone workers' strike had shut down transmission lines, reached Amphitheater TV sets just as Senator Abraham Ribicoff of Connecticut was nominating George McGovern. Outraged, along with other delegates, by the police attacks on demonstrators, Ribicoff said, "With George McGovern, we won't have Gestapo tactics in the streets of Chicago." An uproar followed, in which Mayor Daley shouted abusively at Ribicoff. Ribicoff replied, "How hard it is to accept the truth. How hard it is." A motion to adjourn the Convention was overruled. Just before midnight, the delegates gave the nomination to Hubert Humphrey.

After midnight, McCarthy and McGovern delegates caucused to discuss their defeat. Many had seen TV clips of the violence on Michigan Avenue. The delegates collected $2,500 bail money for arrested demonstrators, and decided to hold a candlelight procession from Randolph to the Hilton. At 3:00 a.m., after being bussed to their starting point, some 600 people, carrying lighted candles in Coca-Cola cups, began walking three abreast to the Hilton. The police cooperated with the march. One demonstrator in Grant Park shouted over a bullhorn, "Those candles mark the wake of the Democratic Party." The Grant Park crowd cheered when they heard about the $2,500 bail collection....

Early Friday morning, August 30, the police decided that objects thrown on them from Hilton Hotel windows had come from a 15th floor suite. Police and several Guardsmen then invaded the suite, which was registered in the names of Harvard economist John Kenneth Galbraith and two other McCarthy supporters. A party was in progress. When the police tried to clear the suite, scuffles broke out between the police and McCarthy supporters. One supporter was clubbed for allegedly trying to hit a policeman with a table. Another was roughed up after he called the police an uncomplimentary name. Before leaving, the police evicted approximately 50 people from the floor. Senator McCarthy arrived shortly afterwards, and soothed his people. The incident received heavy press coverage and commentary....

Supplement 7 of *Rights in Conflict* reports that, in all, 668 people were arrested during the Convention demonstrations. 66.2% were between 18 and 25 years of age, and 32.6% were students. 43.5% were out of state. 52.5% were from Chicago and its suburbs. These figures contradicted the Daley administration's contention that most of the demonstrators were "outside agitators."...

MAYOR RICHARD DALEY AND THE CITY OF CHICAGO DEFEND THEIR POLICE, 1968

Mayor Richard Daley responded angrily when critics of his handling of the demonstrators at the 1968 Democratic Convention accused him of running a police state. During his nominating speech for George McGovern, Connecticut's Senator Abraham Ribicoff even accused Daley of "Gestapo tactics in the streets of Chicago." This was too much for Daley who cursed and shook his fist at Ribicoff from his seat in the convention, all of which was duly recorded by the networks' television cameras. Daley lumped the demonstrators together as terrorists seeking to topple the government. What follows are Mayor Daley's statement to the delegates of the Convention defending the actions of his police and an excerpt from the City of Chicago's official report on the "Confrontation." (The Strategy of Confrontation: Chicago and the Democratic National Convention, *published by the City of Chicago, September 6, 1968).*

A STATEMENT BY MAYOR RICHARD J. DALEY TO THE DELEGATES OF THE DEMOCRATIC NATIONAL CONVENTION, AUGUST 29, 1968

On behalf of the City of Chicago and its people and the Chicago Police Department I would like to issue this statement and I expect that in the sense of fair play it will be given the same kind of distribution on press, radio and television as the mob of rioters was given yesterday.

For weeks and moths the press, radio and television across the nation have revealed the tactics and strategy that was to be carried on in Chicago during the convention week by groups of terrorists.

The intention of these terrorists was openly displayed. They repeatedly stated that they came to Chicago to disrupt the national political convention and to paralyze the city.

They came here equipped with caustics, with helmets and with their own brigade of medics. They had maps locating the hotels and the routes of buses for the guidance of terrorists from out of town.

To protect the delegates and the people of Chicago from this planned violence the city worked with the Secret Service, the Federal Bureau of Investigation, the Department of Justice and other agencies directly involved in the maintenance of law and order. In every instance the recommendations of both the Kerner and Austin reports were followed--to use manpower instead of firepower.

The newspapers stated specifically that the terrorists were planning to use those who were opposed to the present Vietnam policy as a front for their violence. It was also pointed out that they would attempt to assault, harass and taunt the police into reacting before television cameras. Fifty-one policemen were injured. Sixty percent of those arrested did not live in Illinois.

In the last two days we have seen the strategy of these announced plans carried on in full and the whole purpose of the city and the law enforcement agencies distorted and twisted.

One can understand how those who deeply believe in their cause concerning Vietnam would be deeply disappointed but to vent their disappointment on the city and law enforcement agencies--that these dissenting groups and television could be used as a tool for their purposes of calculated disruption and riot, is inexcusable.

In the heat of emotion and riot some policemen may have over-reached but to judge the entire police force by the alleged action of a few would be just as unfair as to judge our entire younger generation by the actions of this mob.

I would like to say here and new that this administration and the people of Chicago have never condoned brutality at any time but they will never permit a lawless violent group of terrorists to menace the lives of millions of people, destroy the purpose of this national political convention, and take over the streets of Chicago.

CONCLUSION

(Official Report of the City of Chicago, September 6, 1968)

This report is offered not as a defense of the City of Chicago but primarily in an effort to point out the nature and strategy of confrontation as it was employed in Chicago.

We have examined what actually transpired in the city as well as what had been forecast and threatened this for the week.

The leaders of the dissident movement are nationally known agitators who had arrived fresh from triumphs at Berkeley and Columbia. Their publicly stated purpose in coming to Chicago was twofold. The immediate object was to disrupt the Convention and the City. Their ultimate goal, also publicly proclaimed, was to topple what they consider to be the corrupt institutions of our society, educational, governmental, etc., by impeding and if possible halting their normal functions while exposing the authorities to ridicule and embarrassment. They are anxious to destroy these institutions, but it is unclear as to what replacements they envision, as Senator Daniel Inouye of Hawaii observed in the Convention's Keynote address when he asked "what trees do they plant?"

The dual goals of immediate disruption and ultimate destruction were pursued in Chicago against the government under the guise of a protest against the war in Vietnam. This promised to be a very successful ploy since, as debates at the Convention demonstrated, everyone wants peace and disagreement occurs only over methods.

In spite of such attractive bait, the guerrilla or psychological warfare tactics which were employed by these revolutionaries erupted in few serious incidents, the main one being an eighteen minute encounter in front of the Hilton Hotel. As is so often the case, the trusting, the innocent, and the idealist were taken in and taken over. The news media, too, responded with surprising naivete and were incredibly misused. Indeed, any success the revolutionaries achieved in their ultimate objective of fomenting hatred and ridicule among the citizenry against the authorities was in large part attributable to the almost totally sympathetic coverage extended by reporters to the revolutionary leaders and more understandably, to the attractive idealistic but unwary young people who unwittingly lent them assistance and camouflage.

For us in Chicago, the aftermath will involve investigations and assessment of the performance of governmental officials, police and military units, radio, television and newspapers. We are concerned about injured newsmen, injured policemen, injured civilians, injured protesters, and injured reputations; but most of all we are concerned about the lack of public awareness of the significance of the departing words of the Yippie and "Mob" leaders, "We won" and "The revolution has begun."

It seems clear that a nucleus of adult trouble makers avowedly seeking a hostile confrontation with the police will be engaging in the same activities detailed in this report in other cities and towns across the nation. They have announced their intention "to create 200 to 300 Chicagos." All who believe in the essential desirability of our present form of government are challenged to find the best response to what is frequently a violent and revolutionary attack upon our institutions--a response at once effective yet consistent with the dignity and freedom of each and all our citizens.

Norman Podhoretz, *WHY WE WERE IN VIETNAM*

The editor of Commentary *magazine, Norman Podhoretz has remained one of the most uncompromising supporters of the Vietnam War. Although admitting the government did not always conduct the war effectively or even intelligently, Podhoretz remains convinced that such wars are necessary to roll back the evils of communism. The following excerpt is from his* Why We Were in Vietnam.

Stupid though the American way of war no doubt was in the political context of Vietnam--where it served to arouse the hostility of the very people whose "hearts and minds" were being courted and whose support was a necessary ingredient of victory--it could not reasonably be considered immoral. Nor could it even be considered extraordinarily brutal. Writing in 1970, not, obviously, to defend the United States, but out of the expectation that things might yet get worse both in Vietnam and elsewhere, Daniel Ellsberg warned his fellow activists in the antiwar movement that "an escalation of rhetoric can blind us to the fact that Vietnam is...no more brutal than other wars in the past--and it is absurdly unhistorical to insist that it is. . . ."

Even granting to writers like the sociologist Peter L. Berger that "the war was marked by a distinctive brutality...flowing in large measure from its character as a war of counterinsurgency," Ellsberg's point was so obviously true that it poses a difficult intellectual problem. One can easily enough understand how the young of the 1960s--who were in general notoriously deficient in historical knowledge or understanding, and who therefore tended to look upon all the ills around them, including relatively minor ones, as unique in their evil dimension--would genuinely imagine that never in all of human experience had there been anything to compare in cruelty and carnage with the war in Vietnam. But how did it happen that so many of their elders and teachers, who did have historical perspective and had even lived through two earlier and bloodier wars, should have taken so "absurdly unhistorical" a view of Vietnam? The answer is, quite simply, that they opposed--or had turned against--the American effort to save South Vietnam from Communism. Being against the end, they could not tolerate the very means whose earlier employment in Korea and in World War II they had not only accepted but applauded.

In World War II, as Lewy says, "despite the fact that the Allies...engaged in terror-bombing of the enemy's civilian population and generally paid only minimal attention to the prevention of civilian casualties--even during the liberation of Italy and France--hardly anyone on the Allied side objected to these tactics." The reason was that "the war against Nazism and fascism was regarded as a moral crusade in which the Allies could do no wrong. . . .

So, too, with the Korean War, in which practically all the major population centers were leveled, dams and irrigation systems were bombed, napalm was used, and enormous numbers of civilians were killed. Yet there was no morbidly fascinated dwelling on those horrors in the press, and very little moral outrage expressed. For the Korean War was seen as an extension of World War II not merely in the strategic sense of representing a new phase in the resistance to aggression through the principle of collective security, but also in being part of a moral crusade against Communism. As such it was a continuation of the struggle against totalitarianism, whose first battles had been fought and won in the Second World War.

The fact that this aspect of the Korean War was rarely emphasized in the official pronouncements, which tended to dwell upon the strategic element, does not mean that it was considered less important. It means rather that it was taken so entirely for granted as to need little if any explicit stress. The consensus of the period was that Communism represented an evil comparable to and as great as Nazism. This was the feeling in the country at large, and it was even the prevalent view within the intellectual community where Communism was regarded--not least by many who had earlier embraced it--as the other great embodiment of totalitarianism, the twentieth century's distinctive improvement upon the despotisms and tyrannies of the past. In one of the most influential books of the Korean War period, *The Origins of Totalitarianism*, Hannah Arendt brought Nazism and Communism together under the same rubric as systems of total control (in contrast to the traditional despotisms which exercised lesser degrees of domination over the individuals living under them). Indeed, Arendt went even further, arguing that Hitler, for all his anti-Communist passion, had looked admiringly to Lenin and Stalin for lessons in the practical implementation of his own brand of totalitarianism.

To go to war in order to contain the spread of Communism was therefore on the same moral plane as going to war against Nazism had been, "and those who fought such a war could do no wrong" either. "There was hideous bloodletting in Korea," wrote Richard H. Rovere in 1967, "and few liberals protested it"; he himself...celebrated the Korean War as "a turning point in the world struggle against Communism." Having then believed that "we had obligation" to go to the aid of the government in South Vietnam when it was threatened by a combination of internal and external Communist aggression, by 1967 he had come to feel that the American role was indefensible. "People who used to say there are things worse than war now say there are things worse than Communism and that the war in Vietnam is one of them." Rovere himself was clearly one of those people, and their number was now legion. It was because they no longer thought that Communism was so great an evil that they saw the American war against it as a greater evil than it truly was, either by comparison with other wars, or more emphatically, in relation to the political system whose extension to South Vietnam the war was being fought to prevent.

Here then we arrive at the center of the moral issue posed by the American intervention into Vietnam.

The United States sent half a million men to fight in Vietnam. More than 50,000 of them lost their lives, and many thousands more were wounded. Billions of dollars were poured into the effort, damaging the once unparalleled American economy to such an extent that the country's competitive position was grievously impaired. The domestic disruptions to which the war gave rise did perhaps even greater damage to a society previously so self-confident that it was often accused of entertaining illusions of its own omnipotence. Millions of young people growing to maturity during the war developed attitudes of such hostility toward their own country and the civilization embodied by its institutions that their willingness to defend it against external enemies in the future was left hanging in doubt.

Why did the United States undertake these burdens and make these sacrifices in blood and treasure and domestic tranquillity? What was in it for the United States? It was a question that plagued the antiwar movement from beginning to end because the answer was so hard to find. If the United States was simply acting the part of an imperialist aggressor in Vietnam, as many in the antiwar movement professed to believe, it was imperialism of a most peculiar kind. There were no raw materials to exploit in Vietnam, and there was no overriding strategic interest involved. To Franklin Roosevelt in 1941 Indochina had been important because it was close to the source of rubber and tin, but this was no longer an important consideration. Toward the end of the war, it was discovered that there was oil off the coast of Vietnam and antiwar radicals happily seized on this news as at least providing an explanation for the American presence there. But neither Kennedy nor Johnson knew about the oil, and even if they had, they would hardly have gone to war for its sake in those pre-OPEC days when oil from the Persian Gulf could be had at two dollars a barrel.

In the absence of an economic interpretation, a psychological version of the theory of imperialism was developed to answer the maddening question: *Why are we in Vietnam?* This theory held that the United States was in Vietnam because it had an urge to dominate--"to impose its national obsessions on the rest of the world," in the words of a piece in the *New York Review of Books*, one of the leading centers of antiwar agitation within the intellectual community. But if so, the psychic profits were as illusory as the economic ones, for the war was doing even deeper damage to the national self-confidence than to the national economy.

Yet another variant of the psychological interpretation, proposed by the economist Robert L. Heilbroner, was that "the fear of losing our place in the sun, of finding ourselves at bay,...motivates a great deal of the anti-Communism on which so much of American foreign policy seems to be founded." This was especially so in such underdeveloped countries as Vietnam, where "the rise of Communism would signal the end of capitalism as the dominant world order, and would force the acknowledgement that America no longer constituted the model on which the future of world civilization would be mainly based."

All these theories were developed out of a desperate need to find or invent selfish or self-interested motives for the American presence in Vietnam, the better to discredit it morally. In a different context, proponents of one or another of these theories--Senator Fulbright, for example--were not above trying to discredit the American presence politically by insisting that *no* national interest was being served by the war. This latter contention at least had the virtue of being closer to the truth than the former. For the truth was that the United States went into Vietnam for the sake not of its own direct interests in the ordinary sense but for the sake of an ideal. The intervention was a product of the Wilsonian side of the American character--the side that went to war in 1917 to "make the world safe for democracy" and that found its contemporary incarnations in the liberal internationalism of the 1940s and the liberal anti-Communism of the 1950s. One can characterize this impulse as naive; one can describe it, as Heilbroner does (and as can be done with any virtuous act), in terms that give it a subtly self-interested flavor. But there is no rationally defensible way in which it can be called immoral.

Why, then, were we in Vietnam? To say it once again: because we were trying to save the Southern half of that country from the evils of Communism. . . .

In May 1977, two full years after the Communist takeover, President Jimmy Carter--a repentant hawk, like many members of his cabinet, including his Secretary of State and his Secretary of Defense--spoke of "the intellectual and moral poverty" of the policy that had led us into Vietnam and had kept us there for so long. When Ronald Reagan, an unrepentant hawk, called the war "a noble cause" in the course of his ultimately successful campaign to replace Carter in the White House, he was accused of having made a "gaffe." Fully, painfully aware as I am that the American effort to save Vietnam from Communism was indeed beyond our intellectual and moral capabilities, I believe the story shows that Reagan's "gaffe" was closer to the truth of why we were in Vietnam and what we did there, at least until the very end, than Carter's denigration of an act of imprudent idealism whose moral soundness has been so overwhelmingly vindicated by the hideous consequences of our defeat.

William L. Griffen and John Marciano, *TEACHING THE VIETNAM WAR*

After studying the treatment of the Vietnam War in twenty-eight high school textbooks, Griffen and Marciano conclude that the treatment of the war presented to students is censored and inaccurate. The texts, they say, contain falsehoods that make any rational analysis of the war impossible. Textbooks repeat the government's rationale for America's involvement in Vietnam without questioning the issues that were used to justify the decision. The texts never acknowledge the legitimacy of the Vietnamese efforts to drive the United States out of Vietnam or put the American position in the context of previous efforts at colonialism in Asia. The atrocities committed by the military in the war are never discussed. The texts are part of the big lie by which the establishment that controls the schools is able to deny its responsibility for what was done to the Vietnamese people by the military. The texts, they conclude, make another Vietnam possible as long as the capitalists who control the schools and their teaching materials never question the dominant class's position on either Vietnam or the Cold War. Another generation, they believe, is being prepared for another Vietnam by the way history is taught in the American public schools. The following is from the authors' Teaching the Vietnam War.

Textbooks offer an obvious means of revealing hegemony in education. By hegemony we refer specifically to the influence that dominant classes or groups exercise by virtue of their control of ideological institutions, such as schools, that shape perceptions of such vital issues as the Vietnam War. Through their pretensions of neutrality and objectivity and through their suppression of data and alternative views, textbooks further the hegemonic process by establishing the "parameters which define what is legitimate, reasonable, practical, good, true and beautiful." Within history texts, for example, the omission of crucial facts and viewpoints limits profoundly the ways in which students come to view historical events. Further, through their one-dimensionality textbooks shield students from intellectual encounters with their world that would sharpen their critical abilities. Despite the disclaimers of those who make a false separation between the world of textbooks and schools, and the world of public issues such as the Vietnam War, there is in reality a vital connection between the two. Noam Chomsky has commented on this connection:

> *...as American technology is running amuck in Southeast Asia, a discussion of American schools can hardly avoid noting the fact that these schools are the first training ground for the troops that will enforce the muted, unending terror of the status quo of a projected American century; for the technicians who will be developing the means for extension of American power; for the intellectuals who*

can be counted on, in significant measure, to provide the ideological justification for this particular form of barbarism and to decry the irresponsibility and lack of sophistication of those who will find all of this intolerable and revolting.

The treatment of the Vietnam War in American textbooks serves as one means by which schools perform their larger social functions. Their most basic function is to obtain an uncritical **acceptance** of the present society, thus hindering rational analyses of conflicts such as Vietnam. Martin Carnoy of the Center of Economic Studies, Stanford University, argues that the schools thus serve as "colonialistic" institutions designed to maintain the capitalist structure, allowing "powerful economic and social groups **acting in their common self-interest"** to " influence...schooling to further their own ends." This hegemonic domination is "eminently reasonable" once we understand the class nature and control of American society and education.3 Similarly, the textbook examination of the Vietnam War is eminently reasonable once we understand the role it plays in the larger social functions of schooling.

Jonathan Kozol, author of the prize-winning educational work, *Death at an Early Age*, argues:

The government is not in business to give voice to its disloyal opposition...School is in business to produce reliable people, manageable people, unprovocative people, people who can be relied up to make the correct decisions, or else nominate and elect those who will make the correct decisions for them.

The textbooks we examined rarely raise the disloyal and controversial questions necessary to understand the origins and nature of the Vietnam War. Even those textbook authors who are seemingly critical of America's role in the war question it only within a very narrow framework. They rarely raise a fundamental point about the larger purposes of the war, and hence rarely encourage students to attempt a truly critical examination of it.

In *Pedagogy of the Oppressed*, exiled Brazilian educator Paulo Freire discusses education within the context of domination to indoctrinate individuals into an unquestioning acceptance of social reality. While Freire bases his educational views on the assumption that all persons have the potential to look critically and creatively at their world and can learn to comprehend and change oppressive conditions, he is nonetheless acutely sensitive to the manipulation of thc educational process in order to maintain the hegemonic power of the dominant class. The textbook authors are aiding this indoctrination. They are prime examples of what Paul Baran call the "intellect worker," which he defines as "the faithful servant, the agent, the functionary, and the spokesman for the capitalist system. Typically, he takes the existing order of things for granted and questions the prevailing state of affairs solely within the limited area of his immediate occupation." The authors of these textbooks have taken this society and the official U.S. position on the war for granted; it has not been assumed, not rationally investigated. They have not examined the fundamental nature of the war, nor the social, economic, and political contradictions that brought it about.

It is not surprising that textbooks have served this role, in that they must reinforce, not critically questions, the larger political goals of the educational system. There is no conspiracy at work; it is merely that the texts must serve the primary purpose-which is to have the students support U.S. foreign policies rather than consider them critically and possibly reject them. It is also clear that the hegemonic parameters established by the texts excludes from inquiry any consideration that the liberation struggle of the Vietnamese was a justifiable one against a foreign invasion aided by native clients forces and leaders. Such an interpretation is evasive, offering no more than a consolidated construct, a homogenous view of historical events. Rather than undertake the difficult task of self criticism which might expose their underlying premises on American society, foreign policy and the Vietnam War to impart a comprehensive, honest picture of the conflict, the authors and publishers of those texts have adopted what Chomsky terms "a pragmatic attitude...that is, an attitude that one must 'accept,' not critically analyze or struggle to change, the existing distribution of power, domestic or international, and the political realities that flow from it."

The textbooks' examination of the Vietnam War is similar to the treatment of other vital issues in American history. Morgart and Mihalik, sociologists of education, have analyzed the role of social science and educational materials in the treatment of labor unions and the working class and conclude that in addition to the actual class-biased socialization of certain behavior for students, schooling also fosters a "cognitive socialization" regarding the prevailing ideological positions. Thus both the experience of schooling and the content of materials, such as these texts, allow teachers and students to avoid or obscure questions central to a critical understanding of American society and foreign policy. Morgart and Mihalik argue that what is at work in the schools is a narrowing of the field of investigation: "This regulation of ideas-which by the way needn't be an all or nothing kind of totalitarian regulation-can be affected by that which **is** learned and that which **is not** learned."

The crucial issue here is the judgment students and teachers will make about the Vietnam War in American history. Chomsky has defined the educational import of this issue when he writes that the same forces who attempted imperial domination of Vietnam, and who "suffered a stunning defeat," will now attempt to explain this defeat to the American people who are "a much less resilient enemy." He argues that the "prospects for success are much greater. The battleground is ideological, not military." Our examination of these textbooks forces us to share his deep concern.

Chomsky states that the intelligentsia (the intellect workers) will play a key role in attempting to see that no "wrong lessons" are learned from the war or from the resistance to it. "It will be necessary to pursue the propaganda battle with vigor and enterprise to reestablish the basic principle that the use of force by the U.S. is legitimate, if only it can succeed." Given the present analysis found in the textbooks, it is highly unlikely that in the near future textbook authors will seriously consider his conclusion on the purpose of the conflict. They "may concede the stupidity of American policy,and even it savagery, **but not the illegitimacy inherent in the entire enterprise."** From our investigation, we conclude that it would be extremely naive to expect this position to get much of a hearing in American schools. To pursue this line of reasoning would necessarily lead to a critical assessment of American domestic and foreign policy, and a reassessment of the basic purposes and functions of education itself.

The textbooks reveal the meager extent to which critical thinking emerges in historical material; to the extent that it does in schools, we must thank teachers who have gone far beyond the apologetic nature of these textbooks. The texts rationalize and affirm the official U.S. view, rarely placing the assembled facts in the context of a reasoned and rigorous examination. Their judgment on the war is invariably one of tactics, not of ends or purposes. As Noam Chomsky asks, "could we have won? Other questions might be imagined. Should we have won? Did we have a right to try? Would an American victory have been a tragedy of historic proportions? Were we engaged in a criminal aggression?" Such heretical thoughts have been obscured by these texts. Thus the educational dialogue on the war can continue in a technically "free" manner because the parameters of dialogue have been safely restricted.

The textbooks do not call into question any of the major premises of American foreign policy, premises that formed the foundation of he Vietnam War, that Chomsky argues are shared by both doves and hawks. What are these premises? "The U.S. government is honorable. It may make mistakes, but it does not commit crimes. It is continually deceived and often foolish...but it is never wicked. Crucially, it does not act on the basis of perceived self-interest of dominant groups, as other states do." To expect schools to use materials that call into question the honor and veracity of the U.S. relations with the rest of the world is asking much of education and textbooks. It is asking the schools to subvert their present function: to integrate students into the logic of the system.

Chomsky is correct: It would be foolish to expect the schools " to deal directly with contemporary events." He argues, however, that an effort could be made to analyze critically past imperialist efforts, such as the Philippines deceptions." It is not unreasonable to expect this critical examination to happen to some degree, but judging from the textbooks we examined, the extent to which it occurs is rare. Tragically, many teachers and students have examined such epic events in the American history of the Vietnam War with little rational understanding of the root causes or its relevance to present U.S. actions, such as involvement in Third World liberation struggles in Southern Africa, Latin America and the Middle East.

Consider Chomsky's overall assessment of the war:

> *The American record...can be captured in three words: lawlessness, savagery and stupidity- in that order. From the outset, it was understood,and explicitly affirmed...that the U.S. "intervention" in South Vietnam...was to be pursued in defiance of any legal barrier to the use of force in international affairs...Lawlessness led to savagery, in the face of resistance to aggression. And in retrospect, the failure of the project may be attributed, in part, to stupidity.*

The bitter reality is that the texts we examined never consider that this assessment might be accurate, or **even that it is a position which could be investigated rationally and then rejected.** Those in dominant class positions in America, who were ultimately responsible for the invasion of Vietnam and the deception and contempt directed at the American people, will do all they can to frustrate such an investigation. They are well aware that such knowledge carries with it profound implications for public policy; that a critically informed understanding of the Vietnam War will undermine their hegemonic domination, particularly if students emerge from our schools with a healthy distrust of the government, its role in Vietnam, and present and future foreign adventurers.

Generations of educators, many of them uncritical and seduced by the "Big Lie" of the dominant class, have labored to keep such a critical inquiry from the schools and the textbooks. The possibility of opening the debate on the Vietnam War in the schools rests not only with those who understand the real tragedy of Vietnam, but with those who are willing to fight for truthful history in the schools.

SOME FINAL THOUGHTS

When we began this project, we had no illusions of discovering any fundamental analysis of U. S. policy in Vietnam. We found instead that the basic purposes of U. S. policy were avoided, and thus the "critical" views that emerge do so within a carefully limited framework.

The twenty-eight textbooks present a political spectrum from the conservative-hawk position, which dominates the earlier texts (1961-68), to a middle of the road apologists' perspective, which dominates the later ones.(1970-78). The conservative-hawk view is basically that of the U.S. standing firm against the Communists who were invading free South Vietnam. Reflecting the Cold War mentality of the 1950s, these texts often argue that the invasion was instigated and directed by the Chinese and the Russians. The later texts avoid this simplistic view; rather, they emphasize a new outside agitator, the North Vietnamese, with China and the Soviet Union now providing material aid and moral support. The conservative-hawk parrots the then prevailing official view on the domino theory, while the later texts move away from this perspective, yet continue to avoid any possible suggestion that the domino theory was in fact simply a justification.

The middle of the road texts embrace the more sophisticated "Quagmire" thesis, in which the United States became involved out of honorable motives but became entangled in a war that could neither be understood nor won despite the best of intentions. The textbooks thus exclude, **even as a valid thesis for examination**, the position that the conflict was a logical extension of imperialist policies that first brought the United States to China, to the Philippines and Korea; that our efforts in Vietnam were simply a continuation of earlier French colonialism. The perspective of such historians as Gabriel Kolko, who argues that there is overwhelming evidence of "how devious, incorrigible,and beyond the pale of human values America's rulers were throughout this epic event in U.S. history," remains outside the limits of debate.

While the earlier texts view South Vietnam as a free nation under attack by the Communists, the later view freely admits the corrupt nature of the Diem family and successive regimes, but in a manner that shows no real insights, sheds no real light, on the motives in supporting such regimes. The later texts reveal a pathetic tale of the kind-hearted but stumbling American giant who was trapped and manipulated by South Vietnamese allies, wishing to help but held back by the likes of Diem, Ky, and Thieu.

A consistent use of biased language describes NLF-DRV actions and motives, while U. S. premises and tactics are presented either in benevolent or technical-military terms. Thus the Viet Cong and the Communists terrorized the people to gain their support (although it is admitted in later texts that they had **some** support among the people because of the excesses of the Diem regime), while the U. S. actions are framed in terms of massive firepower, strategic hamlets, protective reaction, and "search and destroy" operations. Nowhere is it suggested that the U.S. tactics, including defoliation, search and destroy missions, and civilian bombing raids, were inherently terroristic, clearly war crimes as defined by the Nuremberg Tribunal. Nowhere is it suggested that the Vietnamese who fought against the United States were principled and dedicated, as opposed to the officially supported parade of businessmen, generals, landlords, war profiteers, and pimps. There is no recognition of the view that in this war the United States might have been "the [enemy] of men who are just, smart, honest, courageous and **correct**."

Twenty-eight textbooks examined the most bitter conflict in recent American history without calling into question a single fundamental premise surrounding the conflict. The limited margin of debate and dissent was maintained, safe from attacks upon the integrity of our leaders, or upon the nation itself. American high-school students, teachers , and parents could read these textbooks without **considering** the possibility that they lived in a nation that had committed the most blatant act of aggression since the Nazi invasions of World War II.

PART V - THE STRUGGLE OVER POPULAR MUSIC

Music produces a kind of pleasure which human nature cannot do without.

Confucius, c. 500 B.C.

All music is folk music. I ain't never heard a horse sing a song.

Louis Armstrong, 1971

Music is a higher revelation than philosophy.

Ludwig Van Beethoven, 1810

Rock music is the most brutal, ugly, vicious form of expression...sly, lewd--in plain fact, dirty [a] rancid smelling aphrodisiac...martial music of every delinquent on the face of the earth.

Frank Sinatra, 1957

The only sensual pleasure without vice.

Samuel Johnson, 18th century

The art of the prophet, the only art that can calm the agitations of the soul; it is one of the most magnificent and delightful presents God has given us.

Martin Luther, 16th century

A safe kind of high.

Jimi Hendrix

Rock and Roll is a communicable disease.

New York Times, 1956

Without music life would be a mistake.

F. W. Nietzsche, 1889.

Rock and Roll is phony and false and sung, written, and played for the most part by cretinous goons.

Frank Sinatra

Jazz is the expression of protest against law and order, the bolshevik element of license striving for expression in music.

Anne Shaw Faulkner,
*Ladies Home Journa*l, 1921

Thus it came to pass that jazz multiplied all over the face of the earth and the wriggling of bottoms was tremendous.

Peter Clayton and Peter Gammond, 1966

Present day swing music, the Big Apple Dance, and orchestra jam sessions are responsible for increasing the use of marihuana, both by dance band musicians and by the boys and girls who patronize them.

Federal Narcotics Supervisor Joseph Bell, 1938.

The best way to get to knowing any bunch of people is to go and listen to their music.

Woody Guthrie, 1975

I don't know anything about music--in my line you don't have to.

Elvis Presley

I write as a sow pisses.

Wolfgang Amadeus Mozart

I believe rock can do anything- it's the ultimate vehicle for everything. It's the ultimate vehicle for saying anything, for putting down anything, for building up anything, for killing and creating.

Pete Townshend

Music is an incitement to love.

Ancient Roman Proverb

I declare that the Beatles are mutants. Prototypes of evolutionary agents sent by God endowed with a mysterious power to create a new human species--a young race of laughing freemen.

Timothy Leary

We're more popular than Jesus Christ now.

John Lennon, 1966.

Much of today's popular music is complex and exciting...But in too many of the lyrics, the message of the drug culture is purveyed. We should listen more carefully to popular music, because at its best it is worthy of serious appreciation, and at its worst it is blatant drug-culture propaganda.

Vice President Spiro Agnew, 1970.

The universal language of mankind.

Henry Wadsworth Longfellow

Rock music has one appeal only, a barbaric appeal, to sexual desire... Young people know that rock has the beat of sexual intercourse. Picture a thirteen-year-old boy sitting in the living room of his family home doing his math assignment while wearing his Walkman headphones or watching MTV...(his) body throbs with orgasmic rhythms; whose feelings are made articulate in hymns to the joys of onanism or the killing of parents; whose ambition is to win fame and wealth in imitating the drag-queen who makes the music. In short, life is made into a nonstop, commercially prepackaged masturbational fantasy.

University of Chicago Professor Allan Bloom
The Closing of the American Mind, 1987.

We are all gifted. That is our inheritance.

Ethel Waters, on black singers, 1954.

The popular song is America's greatest ambassador.

Sammy Cahn, 1984.

INTRODUCTION

America's greatest contribution to world culture in the twentieth century is its popular music. People who share with Americans no common cultural traditions play, listen, and dance to some form of American music. In Tibet, bootleg tapes of Motown are for sale in the marketplace in Lahasa. An orchestra specializing in big band music survived the Chinese Cultural Revolution and is performing again in Shanghai. Rap artists perform on German MTV. Whether it is jazz, blues, big band, Nashville, heavy metal, or rock and roll, American music is the universal language of our time.

American music says feel good, lighten up, and get down. It is party music. It is the great democratic art of the century. It teaches us that we can all dance together.

The French were the first to discover and appreciate American music. The African-American army band of *James Europe* went to France during World War I with the American Expeditionary Force and entertained the host country with classic jazz. Black Americans played hot jazz in Europe during the 1920's, and many remained there rather than return to the overt racism of their homeland. European composers incorporated jazz rhythms into concert hall music in the twenties. Between the World Wars, Louis Armstrong, Duke Ellington, Benny Goodman and other jazzmen performed throughout Europe to wildly enthusiastic crowds.

With the more recent development of cheap and standardized means of electronic reproduction, American popular music became available to audiences everywhere. Records and tapes could be bought on the black market behind the Iron Curtain, and several Soviet leaders were surreptitious jazz fans. Radio Free Europe's broadcasts reached millions of people in the most remote regions of the communist world. The music guaranteed an audience for the political messages, but the music, not the propaganda, was the great liberalizing weapon in the arsenals of the Cold War.

The electric guitar is arguably the greatest invention of the twentieth century. It provided dissidents a voice the police could not silence. In pre-solidarity Poland, the government outlawed underground clubs which played unregulated rock and roll, but this ban met with widespread popular resistance. Czech president Vaclav Havel has described how native rock bands had to go underground when persecuted by the communist government. Havel insists the state's arrest and imprisonment of a Czech group led to the anti-government solidarity movement that mobilized the Czech resistance. Many of those in the Charter 77 human rights organization are now in the democratic government of Czechoslovakia. Clearly, the globalization of American music was a factor of incalculable importance in subverting the authority of the grim and joyless regimes of Eastern Europe, and, as such, became one of the great revolutionary forces in the modern world.

Ironically, censorship groups in the United States have attacked this most popular of American arts since its origins. From ragtime to rap and hot jazz to hip hop, moral, political and cultural conservatives have condemned every new form of pop music. Critics labeled the 1920's the Jazz Age because they believed the music of the decade caused the decline in the morals and manners of American youth. Every subsequent innovation in musical style, from be-bop in the 40's to rock and roll in the 50's, has been subjected to similar charges. Rock and roll was the alleged cause of juvenile delinquency, crime, drug use, sexual promiscuity and incipient revolution. Ultraconservatives thought the Beatles' music weakened the brain's ability to resist communist indoctrination. The authoritarian regimes in the former communist states tried to censor American popular music for political reasons; the radical right in the United States demanded censorship for moral transgressions. The guardians of public morality have long been convinced that American youth must be protected from the hedonistic, pleasure seeking life style the music advocates. No other democratic art form has been so consistently blamed for corrupting the morals of the country as has American popular music.

The essays that follow trace the debate over the influence of popular music on the nation's moral and political stability. In the articles from *Goldmine*, the authors argue that what is obscene for one generation is acceptable for another. Censorship is inseparable from time and place. Obscenity is often in the eye, ear, or groin of the beholder. Music is not a matter of concern as long as the audience is black or poor, but as soon as the sound is picked up by the kids in the suburbs, it becomes a national problem to be solved through censorship.

Peter Melton, *CENSORED!*

Peter Melton points out that music does indeed influence behavior, but whether it does for good or bad is impossible to determine. The corporations that form the music business fear the power of the censors who believe the music does have a negative impact on the behavior of the young. The music industry for years kept the music for white and black audiences on separate labels, with black music published under "Race" labels. When African-American music crossed over into mainstream white culture in the 1950's, the companies responded with "cover" records. Pat Boone made his fame doing covers of the music of Little Richard and Fats Domino. He called this "sanitizing" the orginal black performer. Sometimes drug songs were blacklisted and sometimes they were not. Now the record industry even puts out two covers for its discs and records, a sanitized version for the mall "family" shops and the cover designed or commissioned by the recording artists. The following article was published in Goldmine, *February 22, 1991..*

The censorship battles in the United States never seem to end. One year it's heavy metal, the next it's rap that's being singled out as a threat to decency and the well-being of young minds. But if history is any kind of reliable barometer, current debates over explicit lyrics may seem as quaint as concerns over whether Elvis Presley's gyrations would corrupt the youth of his America.

Granted, a great many of the recordings made today are considerably more risque than anything attempted by the King. But yesteryear's censors considered their target as much of a threat, and were every bit as serious in their convictions as their counterparts today.

Music has been attacked through the ages because it excited the body as well as the mind. Dances like the Waltz and the Charleston were considered lewd by many in their day, composers Verdi and Mozart had to break taboos to write about subjects considered untouchable in opera.

People today may shake their heads trying to imagine how Mozart's work could ever have been considered obscene. But there are plenty of equally baffling examples in our own century. Consider that although rock 'n' roll is considered the music of rebellion, non-rockers Billie Holiday and Cole Porter made songs that ventured on seldom-touched topics like racism and prostitution. And that long before the FBI investigated what the Kingsmen were singing on *Louie, Louie*, Patricia Norman was thought by many to be putting a well-known obscenity to a catchy tune. And as difficult for the Guns 'n' Roses generation to believe, a group of folk singers named the Weavers were once considered more dangerous than the Rolling Stones.

What consistently gets targeted by the morality judges? Lyrics allegedly about sex, drugs and politics are high on the list. Why was *That Acapulco Gold* singled out as containing objectionable drug references when Brewer and Shipley's *One Toke Over the Line* emerged unscathed in the Top 10? How did Lou Reed's *Walk On The Wild Side*, with its reference to "giving head," get onto the charts unmolested when many radio stations saw fit to bleep the word "crap" from Paul Simon's *Kodachrome*? What constitutes off-color is evidently in the ear of the listener.

Sex, drugs and politics: three subjects that never fail to get a rise out of someone. But Madonna, Prince, the Beatles and Bob Dylan are not pioneers in treating these subjects explicitly. Long before they began making their marks, others had broken ground, and often met with censorship for their troubles.

In 1922, in the decade when the phonograph record first achieved widespread popularity, a blues singer named Trixie Smith recorded *My Daddy Rocks Me* ("With One Steady Roll") for Black Swan records. It was one of the first times "rock" was used on a record as a euphemism for coitus. Risque records eventually became a pretty popular genre in which composers could make full use of their creativity for inventing double entendres. Most of the really risque records were found in blues (then called "race" records) and country music ("hillbilly"); their audiences were most likely to hear these sides in bars or dance joints, and as long as only blacks or poor white were listening to it, nobody else cared much.

Bessie Smith and Jimmie Rodgers perfected the art of the nasty song: hearing *Need a Little Sugar in My Bowl*, *Pistol Packin' Papa* and *Let Me Be Your Side Track* today show their power has not diminished in the decades since they were put on wax.

One of the fun things about reading Nick Tosches' book *Country* is seeing how many artists recorded risque material. Jimmie Davis, co-writer of the standard *You Are My Sunshine*, recorded *Tom Cat and Pussy Blues* in 1932, with lyrics about "cock and pussy," still managed to get elected Governor of Louisiana. Roy Acuff before *Wabash Cannonball* fame, put his voice on *When Lulu's Gone*, which was heavy on the lust ("Oh lordy, bang away my Lulu, bang away good and strong") Gene Autry's young fans might have been startled to hear their hero sing *Wild Cat Mama*, *She's A Hum Dum Dinger* or *She's A Low-Down Mama* before he converted to trail songs.

A few records in this genre were withdrawn, like Hank Penny's *Let Me Play With Your Poodle* on King in 1947, but the smut-song generally died out on its own in the early 1950s, ultimately to be replace in Country 'n' Western by the sorts of subjects C & W is known for today: drinking, gambling, adultery. Normal stuff.

A song didn't have to be about sex to cause trouble. *Gloomy Sunday* was about suicide. In 1936, it was probably the first time a major recording was withdrawn from the market (in this case, by the record companies). Written by Hungarians Lazlo Javor and Rezso Seress, the song caused furor in Europe when it was reported that some people had killed themselves after hearing its lyrics, a lament to a departed loved one. "Gloomy Sunday, with shadows I spend it all, my heart and I have decided to end it all." Because of the hard times in the '30s, this was considered combustible. But Hal Kemp was able to get his version of the song on the market with no trouble in 1936, and it was a hit in the U.S., peaking at #4.

Versions released in the following months by Paul Whiteman, Vincent Lopez and Henry King didn't fare as well, because their nervous record companies had the copies pulled from shelves. Even five years later, in 1941, when Billie Holiday recorded her version, it was considered too risky by Columbia, and it was passed to race label OKeh. The music-as-suicide cause argument later came into fashion by religious groups in the 1970s and '80s, and even got to the courts, in the case of Ozzy Osbourne and Judas Priest, both of whom were ultimately cleared of any wrong-doing.

Billy Holiday also stirred controversy with her 1939 recording of *Strange Fruit.* The song is a vivid indictment of lynching in the South, and was written by Lewis Allen with Holiday in mind. She was initially hesitant about the song, because with lyrics like "Pastoral scene of the gallant South, the bulging eyes and twisted mouth/Scent of magnolia sweet and fresh and the sudden smell of burning flesh." "I was scared people would hate it," she said in *Lady Sings the Blues.* It took courage for a black person to sing such a song in the '30s, but Holiday believed in it, and it is now one of the compositions most identified with her. Columbia passed on *Strange Fruit*, and it was released by the tiny Commodore label. It did well on the sales chart, peaking at #16, but radio wouldn't touch it.

Most censorship has been done by the record companies themselves, not crusaders. They call the shots until the artist can acquire the clout to overrule them. Examples of prior restraint show up in unexpected places.

When Broadway musicals got earthy, as they did in *Showboat* (1927), *Anything Goes* (1934), *Porgy and Bess* (1935), *Kiss Me Kate* (1948), *My Fair Lady* (1956), and *West Side Story* and *New Girl In Town* (both 1957), the record companies made alterations. All had lyrics censored for the soundtrack albums; what was okay on stage wasn't acceptable on turntable.

"Showtunes on disks 'come clean,'" said a 1957 *Variety* article, explaining *West Side Story's* changes coyly " ... a blue Yiddishism (rhymes with cluck) was changed." *Anything Goes* merely had the audacity to refer to the "blue Yiddishism," in Cole Porter's line, "Good authors, too , who once knew better words now use four letter words." The RCA Victor soundtrack with Helen Gallagher has that version, but Columbia's edition with Mary Martin changed it to "three letter words."

Columbia also took liberties with Porter's *Kiss Me Kate* where on "I've Come to Wive It Wealthily in Parua" "goddamn nose" became "goldarned nose." *On The Farm* was the offending song in Bob Merrill's *New Girl In Town*, a musical version of Eugene O'Neill's *Anna Christie*, RCA changed "vicious sons of bitches" to "lecherous, treacherous cousins."

Columbia changed a line in *Get Me To The Church On Time* in *My Fair Lady* from "For God's sake get me to the church on time" to "Be sure to get me to the church on time." *Showboat* and *Porgy and Bess* were altered to remove offensive racial terms.

Every type of music made by blacks has encountered some kind of censorship problem in this country. Rhythm 'n' Blues particularly had the knack of getting bigots outraged, probably because the music appealed to so many young whites. While it is a fact that R & B and its stepchild rock 'n' roll faced everything the forces of censorship could muster and triumphed, there were casualties.

As stupid and venal as things like rock 'n' roll banning on radio stations, jukeboxes, and even entire cities seemed, they had some effects. Some people were intimidated. It may explain Bill Haley's cleanup of *Shake, Rattle and Roll.* The way Jesse Stone wrote it (using the name Charles Calhoun) and Big Joe Turner sang it, it went, " You wear low dresses, the sun comes shining through/I can't believe my eyes, all of this belongs to you." Haley's version went, "You wear those dresses, your hair done up so nice/ You look so warm, but your heart is cold as ice."

Not all record companies were willing to play that self-cleaning game. In 1951, several Los Angeles radio stations decided they would act against "suggestive" records. Records by Decca, Columbia and particularly Capital were banned from playlists. Capitol discs deemed unsuitable were Stan Freberg's *John and Marsha*, Dottie O'Brien's *Four or Five Times* (because of her "inflections") and Dean Martin's *Wham, Bam, Thank You, Ma'am* (because of the title). But Capitol basically ignored the action, with no real harm, to the records. A small victory, but a victory it was.

Radio stations eventually found it was easier to "bleep" the parts of the records judged unsuitable, and in time record companies began providing "clean" version of tunes. Here's what the airways had to aim for, according to a 1939 NBC manual : "Direct allusion to lovemaking, or the use of such words as 'necking,' 'petting' and 'passion' must be avoided...direct reference to drinking, and songs that have to do with labor and national political propaganda are also prohibited on the air."

That's what R & B and rock 'n' roll were up against, that and the Tin Pan Alley composer decrying the degeneration of music, the "citizens committees" designed to keep it out of their turf, the politicians who promise to stop it.

But nobody could stop a piece of recorded dynamite called *Work With Me, Annie* by Hank Ballard and the Midnighters. It was about nothing but sex, and it was raunchy. Even though the title had been changed from the more suggestive *Sock It to Me, Mary* during recording, the lyrics were plain: "Annie, please don't cheat/Gimme all my meat/Oo-oo-wee, so good to me/Work with me, Annie/Let's get it while the gettin' is good." There were many attempts to ban it in 1954, but for every radio station that dropped it from its playlist, the record just kept on selling. *Annie* was an important record because it was unstoppable, and opened the boundaries a little wider.

So it comes as somewhat of an embarrassment that despite *Annie's* triumph, there exists the "radio version" of songs that appear in different form than on market singles and albums. Record buyers have often been startled to find that the song they enjoy on the airwaves is different from the one on the single or the album. The word "damn"--which Clark Gable had successfully delivered on the cinema screen in 1939's famous *Gone With the Wind* moment--was edited from the Kingston Trio's *Greenback Dollar* in 1963 to get stations to play it. Van Morrison's 1967 hit *Brown Eyed Girl* had its "makin' love" removed; the clean version appears on some copies of *Blowing' Your Mind!*

There are plenty of other examples. Simon and Garfunkel's *The Boxer* in 1969 had "whore" removed by many stations; The Beatles' *Ballad of John and Yoko* met a similar fate for it use of "Christ." There's even reportedly an altered version of Roy Orbison's *Oh Pretty Woman* although why that song would need to be sanitized is unclear. There is a radio version of Steve Miller's *Jet Airliner* from 1977, Randy Howards's C&W hit *The All-American Redneck* from 1983, and enough radio stations used sanitized version of 2 Live Crew's *Me So Horny* to make it a hit.

But that's radio. Once a record gets to the stores, it is very rarely withdrawn. But there are exceptions.

There is the case of Screamin' Jay Hawkins. In 1955, he cut a song called *Put A Spell On You* for Grand that was fairly tame. The next year, he signed with OKeh. He did a new version of *Spell* during a recording session in which he consumed a good deal of wine. The wild, drunken version of *Spell* is considered a classic today but Middle America was appalled by Hawkin's groaning and shrieking and it never even made the charts. The protests led OKeh to issue a new version that faded the end of the song quicker, removing the final groans and gasps, but the record still didn't chart. Hawkins himself feels that the song typecast him as a wild man, and he has said he was greeted by pickets everywhere he appeared, citizens concerned that its influence would corrupt innocent young ears.

It wasn't protests that led to two versions of Lloyd Price's #1 single, *Stagger Lee*, in 1958 being released, it was an appearance on *American Bandstand*. After Price's version of the blues standard became a hit, Dick Clark booked him to appear on the show, but asked him to change some lyrics, according to Greil Marcus's *Mystery Train*. The song's theme of gambling and murder was apparently considered too heady for the teens, so the lyrics were changed so that Stagger Lee didn't shoot Billy, and they resolved their differences like two reasonable adults. After the *American Bandstand* appearance, Price's label, ABC, pulled his original version and substituted the new one, which was the way the 45 remained. The original is usually available on Price greatest hit packages.

Politics has often made the powers that be nervous. Expressing one's view can be hazardous, and can make it difficult to get a record out, as Woody Guthrie, Paul Robeson, and blues singer J. B. Lenoir found. The latter did a song called *Eisenhower Blues* that basically went unheard because of its frankness about inequality. (Elvis Costello did a remake on his *King of America* LP).

The Weavers found out how dangerous politics can be. They were dropped by their label, Decca, and blacklisted in 1953 after Pete Seeger and Lee Hays testified on Communist infiltration into the entertainment business. Apparently their testimony was insufficiently patriotic. Other singers also had trouble. Bob Gibson was also blacklisted; Cisco Houston was asked to sign a "loyalty oath" before appearing on TV. He ripped up the paper, but was allowed to go on anyway.

The Weavers were not so lucky. All three TV networks banned their appearances. Other folk performers fired back by boycotting *Hootenanny*, the TV program that had become popular on the strength of the Weavers. The American Civil Liberties Union also joined the defense. (It wasn't *Hootenanny's* only censorship attempt. The Tarriers had trouble getting on the show because they were a racially mixed group, but NBC eventually allowed them to perform.)

1963 was a tough year for folk artists. Bob Dylan, who had one slight -selling album to his credit, was booked on *The Ed Sullivan Show*. During rehearsals Dylan previewed the song he intended to perform, *Talking John Birch Society Blues*. Sullivan thought it was a sharp satire of the hard-right anti-communist group, but CBS lawyers considered the song potentially libelous and asked that Dylan change it. He refused, and walked off the show rather than compromise, a bold move considering how much exposure a Sullivan appearance was worth in those days.

Columbia began wondering how bad the Birch satire was if CBS wouldn't allow it. The label finally decided the song wasn't going on Dylan's second LP, *The Freewheelin'Bob Dylan*, no matter how much the singer, his manager, Albert Grossman, or talent scout John Hammond protested. *Birch* was replaced on the album, along with three other songs Dylan apparently decided to excise: *Let Me Die In My Footsteps*, *Gamblin' Willie's Dead Man's Hand*, and *Rocks and Gravel*. The four cuts did show up on some versions of the album and those copies are among the most valuable rarities ever pressed. As it turned out, *Freewheelin'* was Dylan's commercial breakthrough, and it gave him the clout to release albums as he saw fit.

There were other attempts made to censor folk songs. Peter, Paul and Mary's *Puff The*

Magic Dragon was pegged a "drug song" by many, and Barry McGuire's 1965 folk-rock protest *Eve Of Destruction* inspired several right-wing organizations in California to petition the FCC saying the song violated the "fairness doctrine." (There was a conservative answer song, by a group called the Spokesmen, *The Dawn of Correction*.

Drugs became the focus in the '60s. RCA was worried enough about the word "trips" in Jefferson Airplane's *Running Round This World* that the label removed the song entirely from all but the earliest copies of *Jefferson Airplane Takes Off!* in 1966. It was not the last clash the band and its label would have. RCA disliked the cover of *After Bathing At Baxter's* and was worried that two songs on *Volunteers*, *We Should Be Together*, with its line "Up against the wall, motherfucker." *Eskimo Blue Day*, with its repeated utterance of "shit," would keep some record stores from stocking it. But the band stood fast, and the songs stayed as they were.

Being pegged as drug-influenced hurt a lot of songs. The Byrds *Eight Miles High* in 1966 would have certainly done better on the singles chart had not so many radio stations steered clear of it. Other compositions cited were Dylan's *Rainy Day Women #12 and 35*, Donovan's *Sunshine Superman* and *Mellow Yellow*, the Association's *Along Comes Mary*, the Amboy Dukes' *Journey to the Center of the Mind*, the American Breed's *Bend Me , Shape Me*, the Beach Boys' *Good Vibrations*, Steppenwolf's *Magic Carpet Ride*, the Yardbirds' *Over, Under, Sideways, Down*, and Jimi Hendrix's *Purple Haze*. But even anti-drug songs, like Bloodrock's *DOA* and the Raiders' *Kicks* were attacked in some quarters, and how *Along Comes Mary* or the Fifth Dimension's *Up, Up And Away* were considered drug songs is pretty hard to fathom.

Equally difficult to understand is why *Try It* was banned on many radio stations. The Standells looked like they would have a big hit with the song in 1967, until a Southern California radio magnate named Gordon McLendon seized upon it as an example of sexual depravity polluting the airwaves. He started a campaign against *Try It*, and it worked well enough to deny the song crucial airplay. The Standells' record company, Tower, tried to milk the controversy by proclaiming "Banned!" on the cover of the album, but the band was hurt more than helped. The Ohio Express later had a hit with the song, toning down its sex aspects with a subtle change: The word "action" became "kissing."

In two years' time, things became more explicit, thanks to ground-breaking by the Beatles and Rolling Stones, among others. But Electra wasn't quite ready for musical revolutionaries MC5 in 1969. *On Kick Out The Jams*, the title song was introduced with the immortal phrase, "Kick out the jams, motherfuckers!" The album cover also came with liner notes by White Panther John Sinclair including the same word. After the initial pressing, Sinclair's notes were dropped and "brothers and sisters" adorned "Jams" instead of "motherfuckers."

Sometimes it's hard to even find out whether an album was censored or not. One song on the Mothers of Invention's *We're Only In It For The Money*, *Hot Poop* was apparently changed after its initial release, but the censored versions may be rarer than the original. Some price guides for collectible record albums list other songs as being altered, and Mothers' leader Frank Zappa has said that the record label made extensive changes without consulting him.

At one time, record covers were afterthoughts, slapped together by the record companies with little input from the artists. A picture of the singer or a pretty girl was considered sufficient, But as musicians began gaining more freedom in the '60s, they saw the potential to do something interesting with the 12 x 12 canvas. That freedom led to censorship problems.

Sgt Pepper's Lonely Hearts Club Band is generally credited with being the first rock "concept" cover. But a strong case can be made for *'Yesterday'...And Today*, released on the U.S. market a full year earlier. The tenth Beatles album released by Capital, it was an example of the company's usual treatment of the Fab Four's output, namely, to make two albums of one by padding with singles and B-sides.

And Beatles prepared a cover for *'Yesterday'... And Today*, that no doubts expressed their feelings about the treatment their British albums were getting at the hands of their U.S. label. The "butcher cover" showed the Beatles in white smocks accompanied by hunks of raw meat and dismembered baby dolls, and was pressed and shipped before howls of protest at Capitol forced the company to recall *'Yesterday'* and replace it with a new cover. Many of the originals were destroyed (along with thousands of dollars worth of advertising), but some survived, and others simply had the new covers pasted on top making them the most valuable rarity in rock.

This was not altogether unprecedented- the Rolling Stones' *Now* had been replaced because of some liner notes by Andrew Loog Oldham deemed too provocative by London Records--but it was not something that happened with any regularity. And racy covers were going to become more prevalent.

1966's other censored sleeve was the Mamas and Papas' *If You Can Believe Your Eyes And Ears*. The quartet was pictured in a bathtub, with the bathroom's toilet visible. Dunhill considered the commode a breach of good taste and obscured it in later versions.

The Mamas and the Papas' cover was fairly innocent; not so with Moby Grape's self-titled debut for Columbia in 1967. Drummer Don Stephenson extended his middle finger as his hand rested on a washboard, in the familiar "fuck-off" gesture. The cover was changed to remove the offending digit.

1968 brought a new kind of explicitness to the record cover. Jimi Hendrix's *Electric Ladyland* featured a bevy of nude women, but Reprise refused to allow it. His U.K. label Polydor, did release it, despite protests from many record shops. The Rolling Stones wanted a restroom with graffiti on the front cover of *Beggars Banquet*, but London wanted it changed. While the two sides haggled, the record's release was delayed, hurting sales. The record company finally won, but at a high price: Mick Jagger was stung enough by the incident to form a production company to put more power in the band's hands. By the next year, the Stones had left London Records for more freedom and their own label distributed by Atlantic. (The original *Beggars Banquet* cover has finally been released in the U.S.; it was changed when the Stones catalog was remastered for CD.

But '68 may be remembered most for the cover of John Lennon's and Yoko Ono's *Two Virgins*. The front and back featured the pair in the nude. Lennon had to go to Track records in the U.K., to release it as intended (Tetragrammaton did so in the U.S.) and the nudity was covered with a brown outer wrapper. Covered or not, the album encountered plenty of problems. Some distributors faced obscenity charges for selling it, and 30,000 copies were raided at a New Jersey warehouse.

Nudity also proved a problem for Blind Faith's debut. The shot of the defrocked young girl was altered in America to feature the group on the cover instead.

Cover problems became more frequent in the '70s. Alice Cooper's *Love It To Death* was changed because Cooper's prominent thumb was judged to be too phallic; a year later, in 1972, the band's *School's Out* was seized by government inspectors because the paper panties that were to accompany each LP were flammable. Alice Cooper's manager, Shep Gordon, made sure this bit of news got out to the wire services, where it made a splendid bit of free publicity.

One of the most outrageous covers was by the obscure Mom's Apple Pie, managed by ex-Grand Funk Railroader producer Terry Knight. The sleeve painting on their 1972 debut pictured a mother figure holding a pie with a vagina in it. It wasn't too subtle, and later editions were tamed.

Golden Earring's *Moontan* (1973) featured a nude woman and was later changed; David Bowie's *Diamond Dogs* in 1974 depicted Bowie as half-man, half-dog, with the canine's genitals plainly visible; subsequent editions were airbrushed. Roxy Music's *Country Life* in 1975 featured partial nudity in its two cover models standing in front of foliage. Censored covers feature only the foliage, with the women removed.

Legal problems led to alternations on the Stones' *Some Girls* in '78. Some of the celebrities on the inner sleeve objected, and their photos were removed in subsequent pressings.

Cover censorship is still very much an issue. Some chains, like Wal-Mart, won't handle records it considers outside the boundaries of good taste. Wal-Mart's pressure led Mercury to change the Helmut Newton photograph of a tattoo artist and a woman in a clinch suggesting coitus on the Scorpions' *Love At First Sting* in 1984 to an alternate picturing the band members only. The Scorpions had had a couple of covers changed before; *Virgin Killer's* nude prepubescent girl in 1976 was only issued outside the U.S., and *Lovedrive*, with its outrageous photo of a woman's breast covered with bubblegum, was later changed after the initial issue in 1979. But *Love At First Sting* was the first example of one retailer having enough clout to force a change. It was a sign of things to come.

In 1968, Wal-Mart announced it was deleting albums by AC/DC, Black Sabbath, Judas Priest, Motley Crue, Ozzy Osbourne, David Lee Roth, and comedians Eddie Murphy, Cheech and Chong, and Richard Pryor for cover content and lyrics. (In Roth's case it was because of the album's inner sleeve.) It is no coincidence that since then, many record companies design two covers; what the bands want, and what the shopping malls will allow. In recent years, albums by Poison and Hurricane have received this dual treatment, and Jane's Addiction added a bit of defiance to their "clean" cover of *Ritual De Lo Habitual* by reproducing the First Amendment.

It wasn't just the major label records that had trouble. The Dead Kennedy's *Frankenchrist* caused a furor and led to a trial after its release in 1985. Although the album had a warning sticker informing buyers of the explicit poster by H. R. Giger enclosed inside, the parents of a girl who had bought in a San Fernando Valley record store complained to the California Attorney General. DK's singer Jello Biafra then found San Francisco police searching his apartment, looking for "evidence." The band won, but at a high price. The trial cost the band a lot of money (it didn't have a big conglomerate backing it up) and enough strain to cause its breakup. Although Biafra received help and encouragement from many fellow musicians, the music industry was strangely silent.

In recent years, the industry has begun fighting for its rights. 2 Live Crew received the kind of support they need to fight the censors even though many defending their rights are not enamored of the sexism in their recordings. When rapper Ice-T and his metal band Body Count were attacked in 1992 for their song *Cop Killer*, many rushed to their defense, and some in the music industry paid for newspaper ads criticizing the attempts of police groups to censor the band's recording. Even Body Count's parent label, Time-Warner, stood fast in the face of public denunciation by conservative celebrity Charlton Heston and by President George Bush. But the pressure became too great for the band, and they decided to excise the song from the album. Additionally, the cover art of an African-American with a tattoo reading "Cop Killer" was altered to have it read "Body Count." Such controversies only mark the latest battle in a war of values that shows no signs of abating.

Gillian G. Gaar, *CENSORSHIP YESTERDAY & TODAY--AS AMERICAN AS APPLE PIE*

In the following guest editorial published in Goldmine, *February 22, 1991, Gillian G. Gaar examines recent obscenity controversies and attempts to place them into a historical context. In so doing he dispels the myth that the United States, with its traditionally guaranteed liberties, has long stood in opposition to state censorship.*

Just at the point when it seemed as if rock music had become far too complacent--and corporate--to be considered dangerous anymore, the last year has seen an unprecedented number of attacks on various art forms and means of expression, with a particular focus on rock music and artwork too left-of-center to be deemed "proper." And hey, wasn't it heartening to see that rockmusic could still pack a powerful enough punch to make people nervous? Perhaps that meant the continual sell-out for the almighty dollar hadn't eroded rock's inherent subversiveness after all.

And as it turned out, the hue and cry over rock resulted in relatively little actual damage; 2 Live Crew was acquitted of obscenity charges. Judas Priest was found not guilty of intentionally placing subliminal "suicide" messages on their *Stained Class* album, the mandatory record labeling bill which passed in the Louisiana state legislature was vetoed by Governor Buddy Roemer, similar bills introduced in states across the nation either dropped by the wayside or were withdrawn, and one of the leading proponents of mandatory record labelling, Missouri State Rep. Jean Dixon, was voted out of office in her state's Republican primaries in August.

Not that this means everyone can get nice and comfortable again just because our First Amendment rights have been reconfirmed in this round; further attacks along these lines are sure to follow, if history is any indication. But one of the unexpected benefits of all this activity is that it has pushed people at every level of the music industry, from major label executives to the average consumer, to think about the issue of free speech and reassess their own values. For at its heart, the struggle over censorship is a struggle over ideas--which ideas have the right to be expressed, and who has the right to express them. Are there ideas that are just too dangerous to be expressed, that are actually harmful? If so, does the fact that an idea has been judged as "dangerous" means that it's okay to suppress it? And who can determine whether a specific idea is "dangerous" or not?

This article is not going to try to ascertain that point where ideas move from being simple expressions of one's views to potential motivation for harmful action, or to debate if this is in fact possible (e.g. can listening to a song about murder actually influence a listener to go out and commit the crime?). The intention here is to examine and evaluate the recent attempts at censorship while placing them in their historical context. Censorship is nothing new in the arena of rock or, indeed, in American society itself, despite belief to the contrary. The music industry may have recently issued a poster that states "Censorship is UnAmerican," but in fact censorship is an American as apple pie, and has long been a proud tradition in this country, as any quick scan of U. S. history will tell you; 17 years after adopting the First Amendment, a "family" edition of Shakespeare's work was published in 1818, removing the racier passages penned by the Bard, and we've been divided over what constitutes a "dangerous" idea and if it's okay to suppress it ever since.

The belief that America has always stood in opposition to censorship has its roots in the belief that the country was founded as a democracy "with liberty and justice for all. " A closer look at who that "all" included at the time reveals another story, as performance artist Laurie Anderson pointed out in her keynote address at last year's New Music Seminar, which focused on censorship. "At the time, of course, [the Founding Fathers] didn't see America as a democracy at all," she said. "They founded this country as a republic to be ruled by white male land owners."

In a later part of her speech she spoke further about the inequities that still remain in our country that supposedly values "equality" for all its citizens. "We hate kids. We hate women. We hate black people, gay people, and don't forget the old people; we don't have much use for them either. There are laws that protect the rights of some of these groups, [but] in reality, of course, these laws are hard to enforce, and it's much easier to attack artists who point out these painful realities, especially if these artists are black, female, gay or all of the above."

Anderson's point underscores the charge of racism as a factor in the type of harassment groups like 2 Live Crew or NWA (Niggas With Attitude) have experienced, while white male comics like Andrew Dice Clay and Sam Kinison, whose routines cover similar ground (using "dirty" words and sexist jokes) don't get arrested or receive threatening letters from the F.B.I. Add into this something as basic as the generation gap which results in elders always disparaging anything young people claim as their own, and the fact that a popular art form like rock music has a power of reaching literally millions of listeners, and it's easy to see why rock music has been so consistently and rigorously condemned.

In fact, this condemnation is so consistent, it's possible to take any recent attack on rock or a rock performer, and find some parallel in music history. Midwest radio stations banned records by k. d. lang last year because they disagreed with her vegetarian beliefs; the Weavers were similarly banned from television because of their 'red' leanings. Both Jane's Addiction and Prince faced problems over the cover artwork of their albums; EMI and Capitol Records simply refused to distribute John Lennon and Yoko Ono's album *Two Virgin*, because of its cover. At least 2 Live Crew was able to release their own "clean" versions of *As Nasty At They Wanna Be*, Marianne Faithful had that decision made for her when Australia deleted *Why D'ya Do It?* from *Broken English* before releasing the LP in that country (South Africa saved itself the trouble and just banned it completely).

But now the attacks on rock are somewhat different. It's been popular in recent times to lament the passing of "60s activism," when a generation united itself to speak out against the Vietnam War, among other social causes. But that sense of activism is still alive and well, it's just that conservatives have now adopted those liberal techniques, using their suddenly discovered strength in numbers. Such "grassroots efforts" played a large part in the establishment of the Parents' Music Resource Center (PMRC), a watchdog group that was appalled at the "degeneracy" of rock music in much the same manner that authority figures in the 50s wrote off rock 'n' roll as "a means by which the white man, and his children, can be driven to the level of the nigger."

Founded in 1985 by Susan Baker and Tipper Gore, the group was also known as the

"Washington Wives," because many of the women's husbands were public officials (such as Secretary of State Jim Baker and {then} Senator Albert Gore). Indeed, there was speculation that it was these political connections which enabled the group to get Senate hearing on the alleged dangers of rock music within a year of PMRC's founding.

Shortly after the hearings, the record industry, or , more specifically, the Recording Industry Association of America (RIAA), agreed to voluntarily place "warning" stickers on albums with "explicit" lyrics. There was speculation that the RIAA had caved in so readily because the hearings were held at around the same time that a new blank tape tax bill was making the rounds, and that the record companies were compromising little in restricting what their artists, the most expendable unit in the music industry equation (there's always another one waiting outside your door to get in), could say. For its part, the record industry argued that it opted for voluntary stickering in order to avoid government regulation of such matters, and that it was only adopting the lesser of the two evils.

But there were other options. The RIAA could have stood its ground and refused to give in to what was just a special interest group, which has no legal power of its own. And when the PMRC had insisted that regulations were in order, and that it would continue to fight to get them, the RIAA could have taken the game away for good by insisting that the establishment of an organization like the Motion Picture Association of American (which rates movies), which the industry would oversee, would be the only way to assure consistency. And perhaps the government, faced with the task of having to provide equal regulation for every recorded product on the market (which vastly outnumbers films), would have dropped the matter completely. This route might well have circumvented some of the problems the record industry now faces, for "voluntary" stickering was due to fail from the start.

In the first place, even today you'll find albums containing, for example, swear words, without stickers, which means a zealous PMRC investigator can cite a label for not doing its job. Secondly, it's easy to see that stickering has never been anything but selective enforcement. The albums most likely to be stickered are rap, heavy metal, punk/hard core or comedy LPs. Yet many of the "dangerous" themes present in these explicit records are just as freely expressed in other genres, such as country, rife with substance abuse, physical violence and murder, or classic opera, such as *Madame Butterfly*, in which the title character indulges in sex outside marriage, gives birth to an illegitimate child and eventually commits suicide. This inconsistency has been regularly pointed out by those opposed to labelling, but the PMRC has yet to pass judgment on Hank Williams, Puccini or the Andrew Sisters' Beat Me Daddy, Eight to the Bar, let alone suggest that impressionable minds had better be 18 before they purchase such stuff.

Finally, the lack of a comprehensive system has meant anyone could feel free to join in the game, with some interesting results. A Pacific Northwest record chain decided it would put its own stickers on albums it thought were potentially offensive, regardless of whether the record company had done so or not; they ended up stickering Frank Zappa's *Jazz From Hell* LP, evidently unaware the record is an instrumental album (a buyer for the company later called the situation "an oversight"). And the disagreement over what material can be regarded as "offensive" has surfaced with expected regularity. The Oklahoma legislature considered the mere mention of "nudity" in a lyric as justifying an album's stickering in its labelling bill. And leaving the parameters open to the broadest possible interpretation is what got Judas Priest charged in Nevada, while Ozzy Osbourne has been tried three times over the alleged harmful effect of his song *Suicide Solution*.

Proponents of record labelling have tried to avoid charges of censorship by arguing that warning stickers are only meant to provide a guide for parents, like the MPAA movie ratings. It's a good argument on the surface, but again, due to the lack of an organization assuring uniformity, warning stickers have become far more than a mere "guide." There are record chains which have announced they will not carry **any** album with a sticker for fear of reprisals. Conversely, you may hear of a movie chain not showing a specific film because of its controversial nature, but rarely do you hear of a chain banning all films with, say, an R rating. Even the possibility of an X rating didn't always hinder the release of a film; movies such as Lizzie Borden's *Working Girls* and Pedro Almodovar's *Tie Me UP! Tie Me Down!* were released to critical acclaim at art houses across the country without any rating at all, and the new NC-17 rating adopted by the MPAA should have settled the "X" question for good.

Another difference between album warning stickers and movie ratings is the nature of the offense incurred. The bills pushed into state legislatures would have made it a criminal offense to sell stickered albums to minors. When was the last time you heard of a theater ticket seller or theater manager being arrested for selling a ticket to an R-rated film to a 16-year-old without a parent? This makes it clear that the regulation and enforcement of the sales of stickered albums is regarded in a far more serious light than regulating and enforcing the sales of tickets to rated movies. The laws would also presumably make it an offense to sell without a sticker an album that should have been rated, which is again not the case with films; even though many chains won't take films that haven't been rated by the MPAA there is no law requiring that films must be submitted to the board in order to be shown, and art houses and video stores provide outlets for unrated films to be seen.

But then, why bother with having laws? Harassment can be an equally effective way of stopping the spread of ideas you don't like. It only took the threat of prosecution to induce various chains to pull a stickered product from their shelves. The Dead Kennedys experienced massive legal prosecution over an H. R. Giger poster included in their *Frankenchrist* album, despite the fact that the record carried a warning sticker (so much for the effectiveness of voluntary labelling). A spokesman for the Sound Warehouse chain in Dallas, Texas, says police asked record store personnel to remove 2 Live Crew's *Nasty* from its shelves before any arrests were made because it was believed the record "might" be obscene (the police denied taking such action). When the chain later faced nine misdemeanor charges for selling *Nasty*, it agreed to pull the record from its Dallas County stores, and the charges were quickly dropped.

The rationale that the prohibition of such offensive materials is not censorship but is needed for the "protection" of such oppressed groups as women and children is largely a smokescreen behind with someone like Florida attorney Jack Thompson, the primary crusader against 2 Live Crew in his state, can hide his fear of ideas that differ from his own (a look at the statistics on rape and child abuse in the U. S. shows just how high such "protection" actually ranks on the American agenda). New and different ideas are challenging and can be threatening but their suppression is never an effective ways of dealing with them. In the first place, it can backfire, just as the attempt to curtail the distribution of *Two Virgins* helped make it a highly sought after item (and now one of Lennon's most collectible releases), banning Nasty sparked the record into new life and gave it a substantial number of new sales. And simply pushing the unwanted idea out of sight isn't going to make that idea disappear.

But the most troubling aspect of the censorship push in the music (and art) world in America is that it negates the idea of free choice. If this is to be a country where the Constitution now applies to all of us, not just the white male landowners, we have to accept that if individuals have the right to decide how to lead their own lives, they also have the right to make decisions that we may not agree with. And of course this freedom should work both ways; if Group A has the right to be offensive, you have the right to be offended--and the right to say so.

Laurie Anderson concluded, "For me, this has never really been a First Amendment issue. 2 Live Crew can sing about pussy all they want, and I can do everything short of the law to make their lives as miserable as I can. This is a battle of competing ideas and I consider it part of my job as an artist to make art that competes."

It's only by examining ideas in the light that can tell you how well they'll stack up to reality. And the more ideas out there, the greater chance there is for society to change for the better; it's restricting those choices, and having fewer options, that makes the path even harder to find. And finally, the only way to get your idea heard is not to make those other ideas keep quiet, but to speak up for yourself.

> *First they came for the Communist, and I didn't speak up because I wasn't a Communist.*
>
> *Then they came for the Jews, and I didn't speak up because I wasn't a Jew.*
>
> *Then they came for the trade unionists, and I didn't speak up because I wasn't a trade unionist.*
>
> *And then they came for the Catholics, and I didn't speak up because I was a Protestant.*
>
> *Then they came for me, and by that time no one was left to speak up.*

Pastor Martin Niemoeller

Jeff Tamarkin, ***THE CENSORSHIP DEBATE - FOUR OPINIONS***

Jeff Tamarkin's interviews below with Fank Zappa, Pat Boone and Jennifer Norwood, the Executive Director of the Parents Music Resource Center (PMRC), a group organized by Tipper Gore, wife of vice president Albert Gore, examine the problem of determining whether or not pop is harmful and what should be done about it. Frank Zappa is opposed to censorship. Norwood believes that music one listens to without thinking about it has a much more powerful influence on the hearer than that which forces him to concentrate. To Boone, the fine arts requires an educated listener, pop does not. "People," Boone says, "abuse freedom." To prevent society from becoming anarchistic, he believes censorship is necessary. He would allow the majority to determine what is obscene, and then use the state's police powers to enforce that consensus. This article was published in Goldmine, *February 22, 1991.*

Author's note: Last year I was asked to write an article on the issues of record labeling and censorship in the music industry for a magazine called *Music Alive!*, a publication which is read by hundreds of thousands of junior high school music students. It occurred to me while preparing the article that almost all of the debate over the labeling/censorship issue was being waged by adults, although most of those participants claimed that their main concern was "for the kids."

I conducted interviews with three people during the course of my research, each an outspoken individual on the topic: Frank Zappa, a musician whose name should be familiar to anyone reading this magazine; Jennifer Norwood, the Executive Director of the Parents Music Resource Center (PMRC), an organization which favors voluntary "warning" labeling of certain records by the record companies; and Dave Marsh, editor of the newsletter *Rock and Roll Confidential* and author of several best-selling rock books.

In my interviews I focused on "the kids": how this affected them, if it did at all; what they thought about the issues; and whether this is really about children at all. The article was written from an unbiased standpoint and presented both sides of the debate, asking questions which the students were then to discuss among themselves after reading the article in class.

After the article was published in *Music Alive!* last fall, the magazine received over 1,300 letters from "the kids" in response to the points raised therein. The overwhelming majority of the students writing in said they opposed any form of censorship or labeling of music. They felt they were capable of deciding what music they wanted to listen to, and that, basically, their parents and teachers and government officials had no business trying to tell them what they could or couldn't listen to. Many students said they were unaware that members of the United States and local government, or other political and religious organizations, were even attempting to regulate their listening habits before reading the article.

Wrote Judy Cosentino of Syracuse, New York: "Our parents tell us what to do. We don't need any other adults to tell us what to do."

K. Koneman of Clifton Park, New York, wrote: "Stickering is just not the right way to stop young people from listening to bad music...It will not do any good."

Following are the interviews with Zappa, Norwood and Marsh originally conducted for that article, as well as comments on the subject by Pat Boone, excerpted from the interview which appears elsewhere in this issue.

FRANK ZAPPA - MUSICIAN

***Goldmine*:** Should anything be censored?

Frank Zappa: The first thing you have to remember is that there is no such thing as a dirty word. You also have to remember that people who have a fixation on the existence of dirty words are either superstitious or unfortunate victims of bad mental health. People who have a restrictive attitude toward sex or talking about sex have the same types of problems outlined above.

Just because people fall into a certain age bracket doesn't mean they are smart or even competent. And many of the people who fall into the technical category of parents don't qualify as parents, based on the way in which they conduct themselves. Just because they happened to reproduce by accident, in many instances it begs the issue to call these people parents. They take no responsibility whatsoever for the development of their kids. And it's these irresponsible types who are the ones involved in this debate.

The secret agenda there is that if there is any regulation to be imposed on their unruly offspring they'd rather have government or some religious organizations do it for them so they can go out and do the trivial things they were doing in the past.

***Goldmine*:** Is a 12-year-old capable of knowing what's healthy and what isn't?

Frank Zappa: I don't think that's relevant. If there is no such thing as a dirty word does it make any difference what you hear or what you read? If sex is not bad then what's the problem? A lot of people have been bamboozled by these pressure groups that are trying to make an issue out of this. But nobody has ever asked the basic question: Prove to me that there is such a thing as a dirty word or sex is bad. Where is the actual threat? If there was an actual threat then you might try to come up with a solution for the threat. But in fact there is no threat.

***Goldmine*:** One of your albums, *Jazz From Hell*, was banned by one record chain, and it was an instrumental album. Did they give you a reason?

Frank Zappa: And that's the one I got the Grammy for. When questioned by *Billboard* magazine on why they would ban an instrumental album, a spokesman for the chain of 150 stores said, "Well, it must have something to do with the packing." The packaging happens to be just a photograph of me on the front.

Goldmine: What is your feeling about some of the events that have taken place in Florida and Louisiana in the past couple of years, the arrest of record clerks for selling 2 Live Crew albums and such?

Frank Zappa: They are running neck and neck for the inbred cornpone intellectual capability award in the United States. I happen to think that a lot of these intellectual decisions, since they are coming out of local situations that have gone to state legislatures, you have to assume that inbreeding has played a large part in the development of these policies. Because states elsewhere, where there hasn't been a lot of intermarrying, which tends to deteriorate mental capabilities, don't seem to have the same problem.

Goldmine: Going back to our 12-year-old, should he or she be able to buy a 2 Live Crew album?

Frank Zappa: Absolutely. And I think most 12-year-olds would agree, too. The only ones that wouldn't agree are the one that come from those families that have inflicted some kind of restrictive religious dogma on them. The fact of the matter is, no matter what they're singing about, the net results in terms of transmitting the behavior described to the listener is virtually nil. These guys are talking about what, anal sex? Not too many 12-year-old kids are going to hear a record about anal sex and go out and do it.

The other thing is that the guy who has been persecuting 2 Live Crew (Florida attorney Jack Thompson) is actually fronting for one of these television ministries and its a sham for him to go on the air with a slide under his name that says so-and-so, lawyer. The dangerous thing is that the judge in Florida who wrote the decision that claims the album is obscene used a very interesting wording. He said that the reason the album is obscene is because it induces the listener to filthy thoughts. The problem with that is that if the decision is upheld it creates the groundwork for legislation governing thought control. That's something no state should ever be proud of.

What this is really about is it's a decision that every citizen is going to have to make: Do we want the name of our country to continue to be the United States of America or is it going to be a subsidiary of Iran? Whenever you mix religion and politics and a guy who says he's hearing his instructions from God is running the show and writing the legislation, everybody loses.

What's amazing is that the people who don't buy that keep their mouths shut. In the name of the children these people [the religious/political right] are creating the machinery to hand over to them a world that no American would choose to live in. If the intellectual and oral level of all entertainment in the United States must be reduced to the point where it be deemed safe for a person of seven years or under from a lower middle class white family, which is basically how the rules are constructed here, if everything has to be reduced to that, what do you think the economic future of this country is going to be?

The Republican party likes to say it's the party of Lincoln. Well, it is the party of Lincoln: Lincoln Savings and Loan. There hasn't been anybody from that party that has stood up and said this is un-American, this is wrong. In fact, almost to a man they've voted for all these kinds of restrictive regulations. The Democrats haven't been any better but at least in most instances they haven't initiated it, they just go along.

Goldmine: The PMRC says it only wanted "Parental Advisory" stickers place on records it deemed objectionable. Where does parental guidance fit into this picture?

Frank Zappa: Let's ask ourselves another basic question: If parents are for shit, do you really desire guidance by them? And in many instances the parents are so bad they become politicians. Do we need guidance by them? In the worst instance, the parents become ministers. Do we need guidance by them?

The age of the individual and the fact that the person has reproduced does not give that person the right to dispense legislation for somebody else. I'll bet right now in that 12-year-old bracket, if you took the sum total of the native intelligence of that segment of the population and put it on one side of the scale, and took every parent in American and put it on the other side of the scale, it would either balance out equally or the kids would come out a little bit ahead.

Goldmine: Where do you think we're headed in the censorship wars?

Frank Zappa: Let me say it in TV terms. Remember *Lost In Space*? The famous words, "Danger, Will Robinson"?

JENNIFER NORWOOD - EXECUTIVE DIRECTOR OF THE PARENTS' MUSIC RESOURCE CENTER (PMRC)

Goldmine: What's is the PMRC's agenda today?

Jennifer Norwood: The same as it's always been, we're an education organization. We feel there that there are themes in music that are graphic, that promote destructive health messages to children. We feel that in many cases they reflect problems that are going on in children's lives. There's been a lot of misconception about songs causing children to commit suicide. We're not a part of that argument. It's way too simplistic.

But if you look at what's happening out there, that suicide is the second leading cause of death among adolescents, then you know that it's a real problem and you have to start talking about ways to prevent suicide. When they're talking about suicide prevention they discuss detecting depression and they list all these signs of depression that parents are to look out for, like lack of appetite, giving away personal possessions, and the very easiest sign of depression is the child that's listening to music that reflects the depression. You're not going to be listening to upbeat music if you're feeling suicidal.

So if parents are tuned into the music and talking to their kids about themes in the music they have a real insight into what's really going on in the child's head. So whether or not you want to blame the music you can use the music as a key, as a clue to communicate better what's going on with them. To that end we have been working with adolescent help units and guidance counselors, people who treat troubled adolescents, and trying to get them involved in recognizing and understanding musical themes so they can deal better with the children.

Goldmine: Is music directly responsible for suicide among teens?

Jennifer Norwood: I would never say that one song is directly responsible.

Goldmine: How do you feel about the recent case involving Judas Priest, in which the rock band was being directly blamed for teen suicide? The prosecution claimed that backward masking on their *Stained Class* album caused the two boys to kill themselves.

Jennifer Norwood: We weren't involved with that at all. We're very clear in telling parents that as far as backward masking goes, there's no scientific evidence that the human ear can pick up a message that's been recorded backwards.

Goldmine: The record industry came around to your position and instituted record labeling a few years ago. Yet the PMRC carries on. Did that cooperation change your position at all?

Jennifer Norwood: It doesn't change our position at the present time. There are some people that are going farther than we went in terms of calling for legislation that would mandate labeling, attacking obscenity laws, attacking bands using the obscenity laws. So we're kind of out there trying to deal with that right now.

We're opposed to legislation and have always been opposed. We had a press conference with NARM (National Association of Record Merchandisers) of the retail industry in order to encourage legislators to drop their legislation in favor of the voluntary system. We're also still encouraging the record industry because there are still a number of companies that are not part of the voluntary agreement. We had a press conference with Louisiana Governor Buddy Roemer when he vetoed legislation that had been passed in Louisiana, mandatory labeling legislation., We applauded his veto.

Goldmine: Does the PMRC support the right of individual states to ban records?

Jennifer Norwood: No, we're opposed to legislation altogether. In fact, we called Buddy Roemer when he had the legislation that had passed both the House and Senate on his desk and Mrs. Gore [Tipper Gore, founder and president of the PMRC] had a conversation with him and said she supported any efforts to veto it because voluntary labeling is a much better situation and solution.

Goldmine: Why should records have labels at all?

Jennifer Norwood: Because up until now parents simply haven't been tuned in. A lot of parents today are part of the rock 'n' roll generation., They grew up with rock music in a time when rock music was being attacked by other adults and they are saying, well, I'm not going to make the same mistake.

But when you have things as graphic as 2 Live Crew and Geto Boys, which go much farther than anything like the Beatles or Elvis or any people of that time were doing, parents need to be tuned in. A lot of music today does promote destructive health messages. And whether it's causing destructive behavior or whether it's part of a continuing trend toward children, it has to be addressed.

In fact, the American Medical Association feels so strongly about this that they came out with a statement of concern directed toward the music industry about these messages and also endorsing voluntary labeling. That's a big step; the AMA is an incredibly powerful organization.

Goldmine: What's the difference between record labeling and censorship?

Jennifer Norword: Look censorship up in the dictionary and then ask they question again.

Goldmine: The rap group 2 Live Crew was arrested for performing its music in front of an adult audience. Is that taking things too far?

Jennifer Norwood: The situation surrounding 2 Live Crew is something involving obscenity laws. There are obscenity laws on the books. We aren't encouraging people to target bands with the obscenity laws, it's a different debate entirely. We're trying to promote more information, giving parents accurate information that up until now has really only been available to children. Parents have had to listen to that, go into your room and put on your headset. We're trying to tell them they have to become involved.

Goldmine: Should parents choose the music their children can listen to?

Jennifer Norwood: We're not saying that parents should choose their music for them. To me, the warning label is not going to take the place of good parenting. What it does, for a parent, is it lets them know that there may be something either graphic, violent or promoting drugs and alcohol in that album. The object at that point is not take it away and not to deny the child that music, but to sid down, get the lyrics and talk about it. If it's a song that's promoting violence against women, and you're dealing with a young girl, ask her how she feels about it. If it's a son, ask him how he feels about his sister being treated like that. And get the child to think critically about what's going on in the music and let him go.

Goldmine: Doesn't stickering a record make it more attractive to a child?

Jennifer Norwood: Yeah, well, if you look at the whole debate that's come around television, when it used to be the electronic babysitter, now we're teaching parents ways to communicate with their children with television, to have good programming and bad programming and talk about it when it's graphic and violent. Talk about how it relates to real life and how children deal with it. There's so much of it out there and you can't deny children television or music. They have access to it in numerous ways. We're here to help parents deal with teaching children to think critically and make good choices.

We've been dealing with the issue of bigotry in music, which has really refocused the issue. A lot of people that weren't as concerned about violence take a different approach when it's violence directed toward different minorities. It's bought a lot of new people into the debate.

The whole idea is our culture has a tremendous impact on us, adults and children. We're making the mistake in our society of treating children like miniature adults and they simply don't come into this world with the critical thought process to handle some of the really graphic messages we're sending. One good example of that is a survey that was conducted by a Rhode Island rape crisis center that surveyed sixth to ninth grades and found that a majority thought that rape was okay. The people conducting that survey, when asking more questions, found that the level of sexual violence presented in the media--not just music but also movies and television-- was responsible for that attitude. They see so much of it that it's hard for them to conceive of a situation when it's that wrong. So we have to start looking at the message we're sending to children and how it's affecting them.

Goldmine: do you foresee a time when so-called offensive music will stop being made as a result of your campaign?

Jennifer Norwood: That depends on the demand. If children continue to want sexual, explicit and violent material then the industry will continue to make it. If you look back at the '60s and early '70s there were drug and alcohol messages in so much of popular music and somewhere along the way the producers decided that it wasn't such a good idea to keep doing it. Today you very rarely see any song promoting drugs or alcohol. So hopefully one day it will be the same with bigotry in music, which is something you didn't really have up until a few years ago.

Goldmine: Most critics seem to agree that 2 Live Crew's lyrics are pretty stupid, but still support their right to use them.

Jennifer Norwood: We have to address the fact that they sold two million albums. Some of it is due to the controversy but they sold a million before they were declared obscene. We have to address the fact that children are out there buying this. There is also a level of responsibility when you have a corporate giant that's promoting them and targeting a certain age group. There has to be a level of responsibility there and it all has to come together, not necessarily to eradicate the 2 Live Crew but to recognize the messages that are out there and to help children cope with them.

Goldmine: The PMRC and other people on your side of this issue haven't called out for the stickering of country or opera records. Yet much country music deals with alcohol and adultery and some operas are extremely violent. Why are you targeting rock and rap?

Jennifer Norwood: I don't see why country records shouldn't be stickered. Children do listen to country, and in fact Nashville record companies have agree to be part of the stickering. But to be honest with you, I don't see the point in stickering opera because I don't know anyone under the age of 18 who listens to opera. When it's in the context of a music class you talk about the lyrics and think critically about it. It doesn't influence you.. But if you're listening to the music without thinking about what you're hearing, it has a much stronger impact.

Goldmine: Do you get feedback from the kids themselves? What do they think of the PMRC?

Jennifer Norwood: We get a lot of letters and most of them pretty much say the same thing: you hate my music, you must hate me. I would simply say to them this isn't an indictment of the music. People erroneously attach this issue to just heavy metal and rap. The people that work at PMRC are all very young. I'm 29 and I'm the oldest and we range all the way down to 23 and all of us listen to rock, heavy metal and rap and there's plenty of good and bad. [Ed. note *Goldmine* was unable to confirm Ms. Norwood's age; however, Tipper Gore, for one, is in her early 40s.] I'm not telling children this is good and this is bad and if you listen to this you'll become this, because that's not the way it is.

We all define music and interpret lyrics in a different way. We're just trying to send a message that there are songs out there that are negative and if we look at how much money is put into advertising, music that goes along with advertising, if we look at all the musicians that are donating their time to rock against drugs and anti-suicide messages, then we know that music has an impact. Or else there wouldn't be so many people out there trying to make a positive impact.

We have to recognize that it can also have a negative impact and that if each one of us just takes the time to look at what we're listening to and think about what's being said, and either accept or reject those messages on their own merits, then we'll be much less influenced.

DAVE MARSH - EDITOR, *ROCK & ROLL CONFIDENTIAL*

Goldmine: If you were speaking to a group of kids about the issue of censorship in music, what would you say to them?

Dave Marsh: I would ask whether they think their parents taught them the difference between right and wrong and whether their teachers have, and whether they think they've learned their values from their parents and teachers. The real issue for me is whether parents and teachers give kids their values or whether it's done by rap musicians and pressure groups, whether it's done by heavy metal musicians and government officials' wives.

I think it ought to be parents and teachers. I feel it's very upsetting that people in positions of authority don't have more confidence in kids and parents, and also that they blame kids for a lot of things that have only to do with adults.

One of the things kids have to ask themselves is whether they're being used by certain adults as an excuse and whether adults who spend more time worrying about rock lyrics than they do about whether there's a good music program in their schools are really adults who have a good sense of values themselves.

What this issue comes down to, whether you're 12, 22, or 102, is whether we can have a discussion about this or whether we have to put a label on everybody's forehead and not have it. The first question is, can we talk about this? Then, do we talk about whether there is some objectionable and offensive content in popular culture? Not just music but all kinds of stuff.

Yeah, we need to talk about it a lot more than we have been. On the other hand, can we have that discussion as long as we're pinning label on certain aspects of it? I think the answer is no and that's the reason I've always opposed labeling. I think it censors the discussion.

Then I think you get into the real interesting area of whether it's necessary for everything to be expressed in one way. Not just about lyrics, but also whether all music has to be chromatic, because that's part of what this is about. Some people think this [rock] is not music because it's not what a bunch of people in Europe used to do.

***Goldmine*:** Do kids want their parents telling them what to listen to?

Dave Marsh: I think kids do want their parents to help them decide. My experience as a parent is that kids want lots of guidance. It has to be presented in a way that's open-minded. They don't want anybody to tell them yes or no but they do want information, they do want discussion, they want to know where everybody stands. That might be the only good thing about all this, to the extent that there is some opportunity to discuss this. On the other hand, I think kids are smart enough to know when something is being made a scapegoat.

Goldmine: Should a 12-year-old kid be allowed to buy a 2 Live Crew album?

Dave Marsh: I think it depends on the 12-year-old. I don't think they're all alike. I like to think that my kids, and any kid who's been brought up by parents who pay attention to them have some kind of open relationship with them, have good judgment. Not that they don't make mistakes, but good judgment.

In some respects Luther Campbell and 2 Live Crew are very funny. If you're 12 they're probably funnier than if you're 30. But I wouldn't want to put it into a situation where you say that all 12-year-olds are the same.

PAT BOONE - SINGER

Goldmine: [In this issue's cover story] you talk about Madonna and 2 Live Crew and how you disapprove of the content of their music. A lot of people would agree with you that it's not very good music but still say it has the right to exist and be sold. You used an analogy about Rembrandt and you say that if an artist creates pornographic art it's legitimate art because a true artist created it. But who decides what is art? One of the questions that's been debated is whether it should be up to the government to decide.

Pat Boone: It shouldn't be but it's a curious fact that irresponsibility in use of freedom quite often causes that freedom to be lost. It brings about what is sometimes called a pendulum reactions and we swing from a very permissive society to a repressive one. And a repressive society is brought on because of lack of responsibility of artists or certain people in the society. People abuse the freedom.

Goldmine: A lot of people thought the '50s was a repressive era. Is that what happened then, in your opinion?

Pat Boone: No. I think it was, by comparison , a moral and responsible era. But there are always people who want to push the envelope. They want to be beyond the limits. Like [the late photographer Robert] Mapplethorpe. No question, a great artist, great photographer, sensitive.

But he also had an anarchistic mindset. He didn't like any restrictions and he, obviously being an open homosexual, wanted to glorify homosexual things. And not only homosexual but pedophile things. So he does it in such an artistic way that people, say, hey, this is art, you can't suppress this. Sure, it's art, but it's offensive to a great many people. It's one thing to do it and offer it discreetly and maybe have it come to your house in brown paper wrapping. It's another things to put it on public display with tax money. That's another part of the great hue and cry that can bring strong censorship.

Goldmine: What happened to if you don't like it, don't go see it?

Pat Boone: Don't go see it but a lot of this is being funded by tax money and there are those who say, I think very irresponsibly, we don't care what the public like, this is art and we want public funding to do this even if it outrages the very public that's paying for it, at least the majority of the public.

That's what's finally going to bring about some repressive measures. I will say this about censorship: I feel that some form of censorship is necessary in any form society for the preservation of the society, for the self-interest of the society. And by censorship I mean any kind of majority-approved measure that sets some limits--and I use the traffic light or stop sign on the corner as one expression of that. Censorship is simply the will of the people exercised to defend itself against irresponsibility.

Goldmine: I'm back to the first question: Who decides?

Pat Boone: That's right, and what I say is censorship is necessary and good, healthy as long as it's majority-approved, self-imposed and voluntary. If a society voluntarily imposes restrictions on itself in a majority-approved way, which is always subject to review, then that's healthy. I think we've let things go too far so that the majority thinks it can't do anything.

And it can. I think if people continue to act irresponsibility then an aroused and very concerned majority of people are going to say, hey, wait a minute, these pictures may be artistic but they're showing our kids innocently posed for prurient interests. And it fosters not only child pornography but child abuse.

This is a field I'm involved in, helping people who've been abused as children and already 30 percent, and maybe as high as 50 percent of all the young girls on school playgrounds today --it doesn't matter whether it's low-income, privileged, middle class or whatever--have either already been sexually abused, are being or will be sexually abused before they get into their teens, and quite often by a family member, a father, a stepfather, a brother, an uncle. Something is fostering this--this is far greater than it ever was before. Boys are also being taken advantage of, by older boys and men.

Well, somebody, in order for society to protect itself, is going to say wait a minute, these things are related, we're gonna draw some lines here. And whether people scream First

Amendment or not, we're gonna say you can't step over this line; we're gonna draw an arbitrary line here. And I think what'll have to happen is there'll be some government-appointed people with some width in background, culture, perspective, and this group, which is always subject to review, replacement or whatever, will have to make value judgments.

Norman Lear addressed this some time back, I thought very responsibly, when there was the [Jerry Falwell-led] Moral Majority, when he [Lear] was in the early formation of his People for the American Way [an organization launched by Lear in 1981 which attempted to fight the religious right's attempts to control television programming].

He [Lear] spoke to a whole bunch of TV producers, his own peers, and said," Look, guys, while we don't feel like anybody should tell us what we can and can't produce or write, there are legitimate concerns and there is some irresponsibility and we ought to police our own industry voluntarily before it's forced on us." He saw the handwriting on the wall, he saw that Jerry Falwell's Moral Majority had a valid concern and was gonna do something about it.

He [Lear] set up People for the American Way not only to fight them off but he came to me and asked me to be the voice; he wanted me to be the spokesperson. I said, "Look, have you even met with Jerry Falwell? Do you even know him? I think you and he may share some of the same concerns. Nobody wants to abridge speech or artistic expression but somebody's got to cry out not just for freedoms but responsibility as well. Not only exercise the freedoms but in a sense preserve them."

So he chose to fight. He said, "No, I can't get with him, he'll quote scriptures out of the Bible." When I met with Jerry Falwell I said, "Will you meet with Norman Lear to try and prevent this Armageddon of the airwaves? And would you sit down and talk with him? Maybe you guys can work together to promote responsibility and freedom of speech."

And he said, "Sure, I will. I'll fly anywhere, I'll meet with him." He was willing and offered several times and Lear just wouldn't meet with him; he felt intimated by Falwell.

He [Lear] set up this huge, well-funded organization and they went at it. But he recognized that the public-at-large, and parents, even a lot of responsible kids themselves, are gonna say, "Hey, we don't like being bombarded with profanity and preachments and advertisements for drugs and rampant sex and any kind of perversion. And what can we do? We've lost the freedom from it, how can we regain at least a semblance of freedom from these things?"

One of two things is going to happen. We're either going to just dissolve into a morass of anarchistic and degrading and depraved behavior or somebody somewhere is going to say we've got to draw a line somewhere. Because there' always gonna be those who want to go beyond whatever limits there are.

Goldmine: But what you're talking about, this lack of responsibility, isn't just limited to the music and art worlds. It's representative of what's going on in society. So my question is why there is so much concern over the arts. Why not start at the source rather than the artistic manifestation of what's going on in society?

Pat Boone: I think you're right. But it's more visible there because obviously movies, TV, music, are every place and they're very smartly marketed. And they catch our attention and intrigue us and then you move beyond that into advertising of products and after a while it's just all-pervasive.

Goldmine: But should Jesse Helms and other people in government be the ones to decided what is art and what isn't? That seems to be the real question.

Pat Boone: No, but the trouble is there's almost nobody else in the Senate and in Congress that will take an initiative, take all the verbal abuse. He probably could've been a shoo-in for re-election if it weren't for that issue.

Goldmine: That and abortion. He has some pretty extreme views on that too.

Pat Boone: But in North Carolina he's probably on the winning side of that issue. Harvey Gatt [Helm's opponent in last November's election] got a lot of his funding from the entertainment industry and a lot of support and it made his campaign a lot more palatable and attractive to the general public there. It nearly cost Helms his election.

I don't think he wants to draw the line. It's like the Supreme Court justice who said, " I can't define pornography but I know it when I see it." And if you see pictures of guys kissing each other--I haven't seen this, I've only heard descriptions of it- and you see a picture of some representation of Jesus immersed in urine, I mean, almost anybody will be offended by it. Hardly anybody is going to say it's great art.

People can see the situation but they're afraid to open their mouths. There's very few willing to open their mouths so Jesse Helms took the heat. Even the most biased writers say he sure seems nice to the people he has personal contact with; he does have blacks on his staff so he's not a total bigot. They [writers, *et. al.*] disagree with his position but partly because of the way he's been presented. And of course he does talk in the Old South vernacular.

I agree with you, Jesse Helms shouldn't be the one...no one [should be]. And that's why I say I don't think it should be up to Jack Valenti [president of the Motion Picture Association of America] and that tiny little group to be the arbiters of what's acceptable in the movies either. They are really funded and promoted by the movie industry. It's supposedly policing itself but since all the salaries are paid by the movie industry guess who they're gonna be leaning toward. And Jack Valenti is a personal friend; we've had some personal correspondence about this. I said, "Jack, I wouldn't have lasted six months in your job if by some freaky chance I had been appointed to it."

I would've tried to be the advocate for the public, not for the movie industry. I would've said to the movie industry. "Let's see if we can do some good in our society."

James and Annette Baxter, *THE MAN IN THE BLUE SUEDE SHOES*

Elvis Presley is one of the great revolutionary figures of modern America. His sudden and amazing popularity among youth in the United States and abroad is one of the phenomenonal success stories of our times. James and Annette Baxter's The Man in the Blue Suede Shoes, *published in* Harpers Magazine, *a journal for an educated, middle-class audience, is a serious effort at understanding Presley. The authors regard Elvis as a genuine talent who reflected the Southern mind. Their 1958 appraisal of Elvis's voice and music is still relevant today.*

Ol' Elvis Presley may be a better musician than most people dare to admit--and he might be offering the kids a commodity their parents can't recognize.

As a subject for polemic Elvis Presley has few peers, and too many people have experienced sudden shifts in blood pressure--either up or down--for him to be regarded as anything but an authentic barometer of the times. But, even now that he has been on the national scene for more than two years, he may be telling us more about ourselves than we would care to admit.

Presley's climb to fame, in the winter of 1955-56, followed upon the appearance of that raucous brand of popular music, primitive and heavy-footed, known as rock and roll. Untouched by subtlety, rock-and-roll seemed to signal a total collapse in popular taste, the final schism between a diminishing group sensitive to tradition and the great bulk of those who make entertainment to sell. Suddenly there was Elvis, not merely a manifestation of rock-and-roll, but of lascivious gyrations of the torso that older generations quickly recognized--the classic bump and grind of the strip-teaser. Television compounded the jeopardy: Elvis could come lurching into any living-room, and he did, and the chorus of adolescent shrieks was swelled by shrieks from the parents. The stomping blatancy of "Blue Suede Shoes" and the insinuations of "I Want You, I need You, I Love You" were sufficiently distressing, but the foot-spread stance and the unmistakable thrust-well, "The Pelvis" was going too far.

He went too far in every direction. Elvis was making millions of dollars, owning white Continental Mark II's, getting into fights and reviving sideburns and being prayed over and building a house for his parents. The legend should have swallowed him out of sight, but it was all true--all furthermore, palpably American. He may not actually have arrived for his Army physical in a Cadillac with a Las Vegas show girl and announced that he wanted to be treated just like everyone else--but the story was pure Elvis. Anyway,the gawky, loose-limbed, simple boy from Tupelo, Mississippi, was a genuine *tabula rasa*, on which the American populace could keep drawing its portrait, real and imaginary, and keep rubbing it out.

Admonished that there were those who found his hip-swiveling offensive, Elvis is said to have replied, " I never made no dirty body movements." And this is believable; Elvis moves as the spirit moves him; it all comes naturally. Hormones flow in him as serenely as the Mississippi past Memphis, and the offense lies in the eye of the beholder, not in Elvis's intentions.

By constantly reminding his teen-age listeners of what he so obviously was--a simple boy from Tupelo who had suddenly become famous--Elvis somehow removed the sting from the sexuality that could easily have terrified them. Valentino had to become an exotic in order to keep from frightening the ladies of an earlier era with his own heavy-lidded gaze; Elvis could remain the boy next door. He was even able to capitalize on his innocence: in his television appearances he could find himself flinging a Svengali-like finger out toward his audience and, when they squealed, he couldn't keep from giggling. He was as amused as they were by his idiotic power to hypnotize and, although the spell was on, the curse was off.

But Presley's stunning rapport with his own generation must hinge on something more than the ageless call of the wild. Appealing to the youthful imagination in some way inscrutable to the parents of the teen-agers who worship him, Elvis fills some kind of need that the older generation can't fathom, and more significantly, doesn't feel. Why? Perhaps because they have run out of dreams.

Parents for whom the introduction of television in the late 'forties begat the era of the great giveaway need no dreams--they are already living one. Ranch-style homes, organization-man jobs, and exalted community status have outrun whatever hopes they brought from a meager past, and adults are too delightedly clutching these tangible evidences of a dream-come-true to bother projecting a more fanciful one. Their smartly-executed station-wagon psyches, jauntily upholstered and gleaming trimmed, leave no room for excrescences and irrelevancies. But their offspring, a generation of poor little rich children, whom no part of the postwar bonanza has the power to enthrall, remain desperately in need of an enchanter.

THE MYSTERIOUS SOUTH

To meet this historic contingency Elvis is blessed not only with sex but with authentic Southernness. His primitivism carries conviction; when he intones the monotonous phrases of "I Got a Woman," Southern medium espouses Southern temperament. The range of verbal expression is precisely as limited and as colorful as we feel Elvis's own vocabulary must be. The voice, on the other hand, insisting on the subtlest of shifts in mood and timing, suggests that the man from whom it issues is, like his music, elusive.

The sum of Presley's qualities matches the national image of the Southland. For the South today popularly represents what the West once did: the self-sufficient, the inaccessible, the fiercely independent soul of the nation. With the taming of the West completed, only the deep South retains a comparable aura of mystery, of romantic removal from the concerns of a steadily urbanized and cosmopolized America.

The removal is two-fold: it combines an indifference to grammatical niceties, which the rest of the country benightedly associates with "civilization," with an old confidence in the private, intuitive vision. The rationalism of the "progressive" sections of the nation has always seemed to the Southerner inadequate to penetrate the darker corners of his experience, and these components of the Southern mind are central to the Presley performance.

The adolescent is far more responsive to them than his parents could be. In the backwoods heterodoxies of Elvis he recognizes a counterpart to his own instinctive rebellion. And when Elvis confesses that he's "Gonna Sit Right Down and Cry," the accents of lament are felt as genuine; there's none of the artifice of the torchsinger in his wail. Elvis is for real, and in his voice the teen-ager hears intimations of a world heavily weighted with real emotion.

Most real emotions, the teen-ager knows without coaching, are daily discredited by his parents and teachers. Their own equably democratic temperaments and cheerfully enlightened code of behavior seem to deny the world that Elvis affirms. And the teen-ager, when he pounds convulsively at the sight and sound of Elvis, is pounding for entrance into that more enticing realm.

He is pounding his feet, however; ultimately the music Elvis makes must be given some credit for his popularity. And there is probably an ugly, awesome little truth in the deduction that he is prodigiously gifted. To those attentive to the music itself the most conspicuous feature of Elvis's singing is the versatility with which exploits the tradition of the Negro "blues-shouter." He can shift without apparent strain from the blasting stridency of "Hound Dog" to the saccharine ooze of "I'll Never Let You Go," covering , when called upon, every transitional pose between: the choke--and--groan of "Love Me," the plaintive nasal whine of "How's the World Treating You," the gravel-throated bellow of "Long Tall Sally," or the throb-and-tremolo of "I Got a Woman."

Vocal pyrotechnics he has indeed (to what must be the everlasting despair of his imitators), but they would remain merely curiosities were he not able to manipulate them into an organic whole. His twisting of a tonal quality possesses a diabolical inevitability, and his phrasing is as flawless as it is intricate. Marianne Moore's comment about e.e. cummings--"He does not make aesthetic mistakes"--might with only brief hesitation be applied to Elvis Presley. Elvis has got the beat, and "Don't Be Cruel" will bear scrutiny by any but the most outraged of his captious audience.

LAUGHING AT US

But there is in Presley's delivery something much more subtle and hard to get at. From some fathomless and unstudied depth he has managed, in a whole series of songs, to call forth irony. Elvis is laughing at us, and at himself, without knowing it, and while remaining altogether serious. The throbbing sentimentality is at once wholly fake and sterling pure; listen for it in "I'm Counting on You," or "Trying to Get to You." And so is the pompousness of "One-Sided Love Affair" and the mawkishness of "old Shep." In his interpretation of these songs there are ambiguities that are surely unsuspected even by such an uninhibited and highly sophisticated primitive as Elvis himself.

This neither fish-nor-fowl quality can be a frightening thing to adults, who suppose that they have fully identified themselves in an identifiable environment. But to adolescents, who detest above all the status quo--who want the world to be so limitless in its potentials that they cannot fail to find their changeling selves somehow secure within it--to them it is the throbbing substance of life itself. And when combined with the frenetic pulsations, the hectic, nervous quiverings of rock-and-roll, the rhythms of their own vacillations, it is enough to make Elvis a millionaire.

Whither Presley? When his present public finds itself, as it someday must, demesmerized by time, and when the image-like fascination of Elvis gives way to some new and less inspired teen-age melodrama, what's to become of this young man whose life and legend are by now indistinguishable?

Will Elvis himself be able to salvage a personality from among the accumulated debris of prolonged public exposure? Will he choose one of several paths systematically trodden by the once great: lucratively "advising" the producers of "The Elvis Presley Story," lecturing across the country on the prevention of juvenile delinquency, opening with moderate hoopla a restaurant in Atlantic City, appointing a respectable hack to ghost his memoirs, or posing rakishly for a Chesterfield ad?

Some indication that Elvis has a notion of the responsibility of his mission is his plan for a fifteen-acre Elvis Presley Youth Foundation in Tupelo, reported in *Time*. How far this project may go is uncertain, but if it takes him back to Mississippi for spiritual recuperation from time to time, it will be both good for him and the youth who want him, need him and love him.

THE ROCK IS SOLID

This item featured in the music column of Time Magazine *(November 17, 1957) was typical of music critics' handling of rock 'n' roll in its early years. This particular critic notes wistfully that Elvis and rock 'n' roll seem to be enduring despite the music's lack of artistic value.*

Is the golden glottis gurgling to a stop? Is there a quiver to those rosebud lips, a beginning of wilt to those poodle-wool sideburns? For two years, lovers of peace, quiet and a less epileptic kind of minstrelsy have waited for Elvis Presley and the adenoidal art form, rock 'n' roll, to fade. But knowledgeable disk jockeys and trade bulletins offer such purists little hope. In spite of previously noted tremors, last week rock 'n' roll looked solid as Gibraltar, and Elvis--with a new stomp-and-holler hit, *Jailhouse Rock* (RCA Victor)--was perched right on top.

The new Presley disk hit second place on *Billboard's* authoritative top-tunes listing in its second week on the chart, and by last week Victor claimed to have shipped 2,000,000 copies (total Presley sales of single disks so far: a staggering 28 million). The movie--bred lyrics of *Jailhouse Rock* suggest a powerful argument for penal reform, but not clues to the record's whopping success.

Everybody in a whole cell block
Was dancing to the jailhouse rock...
[Mumble, mumble] crash, boom, bang
The whole rhythm section was a purple gang.

No New Sound. Philosophizes Chicago Deejay Marty Faye on rock 'n roll: "These kids have accepted this twanging guitar, this nasal unintelligible sound, this irritating sameness of lyrics, this lamentable croak. They've picked a sound all their own, apart from anything the adults like. Rock 'n' roll is still as strong as ever,and we'll have to live with it until the kids find a new sound."

For a while last summer, it looked as if the kids might have found one. Calypso jounced and jingled into earshot, but in the end turned out to be loss *lieder*. Industry plotters pegged Hawaiian music for the next turntable fad, but found the kids not in a hula mood. Rock 'n' roll faltered slightly when ballads (*Love Letters in the Sand*, *Tammy*) began catching on again, and a few of the U.S.'s disk jockeys report that ballads are continuing to cut into rock 'n' roll popularity. From staid Boston, WBZ's Bill Marlowe states flatly that "Rock 'n' roll has had it. The teenagers are beginning to look to better music." But in Los Angeles the craze is just as strong as ever, and in Atlanta, jukebox operators and record shop proprietors say that rock 'n' roll is still by far the most popular music.

No Steady Starlets. Elvis, unworried, continues to live off what most parents would agree is the fat of teenagers' heads. As befits a solid citizen (possible 1957 gross, $1 million), he has lately eschewed fist-fights and steady starlets, projected a 15-acre Elvis Presley Youth Foundation in Tupelo, Mississippi, his birthplace.

Living off the fat of the heads. As Elvis gets older (22), he grows more conservative: his favorite vehicle, his handlers report, is not his black Harley-Davidson motorcycle, his royal purple Lincoln Continental, his red Messerschmidt, his yellow Isetta, his pink or his yellow Cadillac, but a sumptuous, black, bankerish Cadillac limousine. If austerity and decorum shroud Presley's personal life, his fans need not worry that the old megalomania is disappearing. His tour manager, explaining that the reason Elvis has not graced TV this season is that no network has met his $100,000-an-hour fee, allowed that "if there were a program of half-hour duration, Elvis might make a concession and take $75,000."

Meanwhile, Elvis has prepared a surprise package for the nation that is likely to be the most serious menace to Christmas since *I Saw Mommy Kissing Santa Claus*. Victor is planning to release an album of Yule songs by Presley, accompanied by guitar and organ, the selections including *Silent Night* and *Santa, Bring My Baby Back to Me.*

John Lardner, *DEVITALIZING ELVIS*

This following article appeared in "Lardner's Week" in Newsweek *(July 16, 1956). Lardner, while quite willing to make fun of Elvis himself, takes Steve Allen to task for doing likewise on "The Steve Allen Show."*

Along with the lively baseball, or rabbit pill, modern civilization has produced the lively vocalist, or rabbit singer. Outstanding among the twitching Carusos of the present day is a chap named Elvis Presley. There is nothing to be said against Elvis--and many people have said it--except that when placed in front of a microphone, he behaves like an outboard motor.

Pardon me. I stand corrected. Professor Klein, the Yale sociologist, who is peering over my shoulder as I write this, asks me to note that what Elvis acts like is a lovesick outboard motor. Well and good. There has been no movement to stabilize or deaden the rabbit ball, and offhand there would seem to be no clear need to stabilize or deaden the rabbit vocalist. Live and let live--that is how most of us boys in the upper crust of sociology look at it. Nonetheless, we all watched with interest last week when one of our number, Steve Allen (who has his own show, as we say in the scientific game), made a public attempt to neutralize, calm, or detwitch Elvis Presley, the lively singer.

Allen did this, one assumes, in what he personally considers the best interests of civilization. For him, it was logical. Civilization today is sharply divided into two schools which cannot stand the sight of each other. One school, Allen's, is torpid and dormant in style; it believes in underplaying, or underbidding, or waiting 'em out. The other, Presley's, is committed to the strategy of open defiance, of confusing 'em, of yelling 'em down. The hips and the Adam's apple, this school believes, must be quicker than the eye.

Each school has its own habits and markings, off stage and on. Members of the lively, or rabbit school tend to wear their sideburns long, if they do not actively bust out in goatees. In private life, they ride motorcycles--or, on especially gay weekends, the motorcycles ride them, the effect being much the same. During public performances, they seldom focus their eyes. The eye, in fact, is a vestigial organ among them, like the necktie and the vermiform appendix. When singing, this species is addicted to splitting or bisecting the notes. As in:

Lo-uving yo-ou e-uternally
Wi-yith a-ull my-igh har-ut!

The Allen or play-it-down school wears its hair much shorter. Like Primo Carnera, the time has *vastus lateralis* was paralyzed, members do not reach when stuck with pins. They play pianos, as being less jumpy than guitars, and sing:

Love yaternally (Sister),
Withal mott. (Now and then adding a casual "Vo-de-o-do" to show you are still there.)

When Allen made his move last week to mute and frustrate Presley, for the good of mankind, the proceedings were instructive, but somewhat saddening. Allen was nervous, like a man trying to embalm a firecracker. Presley was distraught, like Huckleberry Finn, when the widow put him in a store suit and told him not to gap or scratch.

Allen's ethics were questionable from the start. He fouled Presley, a fair-minded judge would say, by dressing him like a corpse, in white tie and tails. This is a costume often seen on star performers at funerals, but only when the deceased has specifically requested it in his will. Elvis made no such request--or for that matter, no will. He was framed.

Later in the experiment, Allen fighting with no holds barred for the survival of the take-it-easy school, made a comic out of Presley, and fed him a couple of torpid punch lines.

"Who was that lady I seen you with last night, Elvis?" said Allen, sticking his thumb in the victim's eye and turning it slowly around.

"That was no lady, that was my git-tar," said Elvis morosely.

Now, I do not claim that that was exactly the gag that was used; but at any rate, it was a gag from which no ordinary twitching vocalist, or rabbit singer, could be expected to recover. Elvis recovered. As he left the hall, more dead than alive, he found the street hip-deep in bobby-soxers. And he bloomed like a rose, they tell me, and writhed again as of old.

Sue Hubell, *THE VICKSBURG GHOST*

Sue Hubell returned to her native Michigan to investigate a series of "Elvis-Sightings" in Vicksburg, a small town not far from Kalamazoo where she grew up. She was not alone. Reporters came from all over the United States and even abroad to investigate the rumors. Such attention was a sure sign that the man and his music had been transformed in the American imagination into something of profound religious meaning. Hubell reported her findings in the New Yorker Magazine *(September 25, 1989).*

The human predicament is typically so complex that it is not altogether clear which lies are vital and what truths beg for discovery.

Daniel Coleman, *Vital Lies, Simple Truths: The Psychology of Self-Deception*

I guess most people found it hard to believe that Elvis Presley didn't die after all but instead is alive and well and shopping at Felpausch's Supermarket, in Vicksburg, Michigan. I know I did when I read about it in the *New York Times* last Fall. The *Times* wasn't on record as saying "THE KING LIVES," or anything like that, but it did report that a Vicksburg woman named Louise Welling had said she'd seen him the year before, in the supermarket's check-out line. Her sighting encouraged Elvins everywhere, many of whom believe that Presley faked his death. It also added an extra fillip to Elvismania, which is part nostalgia and part industry, the industry part consisting of the production of Elvis memorabilia, books, articles, tours, and prime-time TV *docu-dramas*. Fans have made periodic demands for an Elvis postage stamp, and a multimedia musical--*Elvis: A Rockin' Remembrance*--had an Off-Broadway run his summer.

Promotion was what made Elvis Presley. In 1977, the year of his death, his likeness was more widely reproduced than any other save that of Mickey Mouse, and it has been reported that the news of his demise was greeted by one cynic with the words "Good career move!" According to Albert Goldman, the biographer who tells this story, Presley was by then a porky, aging, drug-befuddled Las Vegas entertainer and was getting to be a hard personality to promote. The Presley image shorn of the troublesome real man was easier to market. For example, after the King's death, Presley's manager, Colonel Thomas A. Parker, contracted with a vineyard in Paw Paw, Michigan--a town not far from Vicksburg--to produce a wine called *Always Elvis*. Its label bears a head shot of the entertainer, in a high-collared spangled white shirt, singing into a hand-held microphone. Colonel Parker's own four stanza poem appears on the back of the bottle. Goldman has computed that the poem earned Parker twenty-eight thousands dollars in royalties, "making him, line for line, the best -paid poet in the world." Although the wine is no longer produced, I was able to find a dusty old bottle in my local liquor store. In the interests of journalism, I sampled it. It was an adequate companion to the poem, which closes with the couplet

We will play your songs from day to day
For you really never went away.

In its year-end double issue, *People* ran a story featuring recent photographs of Elvis purportedly taken by readers around the country, each picture as vague and tantalizing as snapshots of the Loch Ness monster. While debates mounted over whether or not Elvis Presley was still alive, I got stuck back there in the part of the *Times* story which said that he was shopping at Felspausch's. By the latter part of the nineteen-fifties, when Elvis arrived to sweep away the dreariness of the Eisenhower years, I was too old to respond to the Dionysian sexual appeal that he had for his teen-age maenads; consequently, I was also unmoved by retro-Elvis. But I did grow-up near Vicksburg. My family lived in Kalamazoo, a bigger town (in which Elvis was also said to have appeared) twelve miles to the north, and we spent our summers at a lake near Vicksburg. My widowed mother now lives at the lake year round, and when I visit her I often shop at Felpausch's myself. I know Vicksburg tolerably well, so when I read the account in the *Times* I strongly suspected that the reporter had been snookered by a group of the guys over at the Mar-Jo's Cafe on Main Street, half a block from Felspausch's, which is on Prairie Street, the town's other commercial thoroughfare. Last June, while I was visiting my mother, I decided to drive into Vicksburg and find out what I could about the Elvis Presley story.

Vicksburg is a pretty village of two thousand people, more or less. A hundred and fifty years ago, when it was first settled by white people, the land was prairie and oak forest. James Fenimore Cooper, who lived in the nearby town of Schoolcraft, wrote about the area in his book *Oak Openings*. It is in Southern Michigan, where the winters are long and gray, and even the earliest settlers complained of the ferocity of the summer-time mosquitoes. Vicksburg's one block commercial section has been spruced up in recent years. There are beds of petunias at the curb edges, and new facades on the nineteenth-century buildings. The carefully maintained Victorian houses on the side streets are shaded by maples big enough to make you think elm. A paper mill, built near a dam that the eponymous John Vickers constructed on Portage Creek for his flour mill, has long provided employment for the local people, but today the village has become something of a bedroom community for commuters to Kalamazoo. Still, it seems very like the place I knew when I used to come to band concerts on Wednesday evenings at the corner of Main and Prairie, during the summers of the nineteen thirties and forties. The band concerts are a thing of the past, but there are other homegrown entertainments, such as one going on the week I was there--the annual Vicksburg Old Car Festival, which is run by Skip Knowles, a local insurance man. The festival has a fifties' theme, and last year, inspired by the commotion that Louise Welling's sighting of Elvis had produced, Knowles added an Elvis-look-alike contest to the roster of events. Knowles has his office in a store-front on Main Street which used to be Matz's Confectionery, where I first discovered lime phosphates (known locally as "green rivers").

And the teen-agers are still bored. While I was in the library going through back issues of local newspapers, two high-school girls introduced themselves to me, saying that they had lived in Vicksburg all their lives and would be happy to talk to me about it. I asked them what they thought about Elvis Presley. They smiled patronizingly and informed me that no one they knew paid any attention to him. "But everything just stands still in Vicksburg," one of them confided. "We go to Kalamazoo on Saturday nights. I can't wait to get out of here and go to college."

Mar-Jo's has stayed the same, too. It has been in the same place for forty years. It was named after Marge Leitner and her partner, Josephine, whose last name no one at the cafe can remember. It is your basic tan place: tan floor, tan walls, tan tables, tan counter. The sign taped to the cash register was new to me. It said:

This Is Not
Burger King
You Get It
My Way
or You Don't
Get It
at All

But the men having coffee together at the big round table near the front windows could have been the same ones sitting there the last time I was in, which was a couple of years ago.

"How's you-know-who?" gray crewcut asks feed-store cap. "Don't see her anymore.

The others guffaw, and one says, "He's taken her clothes."

"What clothes?" feed-store cap shoots back. A ripple of caffeine-fueled laughter circles the table.

Shirley White, a small, wiry woman, has been a waitress at Mar-Jo's for eleven years. Her hair is dark and tightly curled. She is efficient and cheerful. She knows virtually all her customers by name and how they like their coffee, and she banters with all of the others. She gets to work at four-forty-five every morning, so she is usually way ahead of the best the town wits, giving as good as she gets. The coffee-club boys once arranged the kind of prank on her that made me suspect them of the Elvis Presley caper. One of the regulars was a big man who she could deftly unsettle with a clever phrase or two. His invariable riposte was a mumbled "Paybacks are hell." A few years ago, he was on vacation in Florida when her birthday came around, and she had nearly forgotten about him. Mar-Jo's was jammed that day, and no one would tell her why. "Just as I was busiest, this really big monkey walked in," she told me. At least, it was a big guy dressed in a monkey costume, and he kept following me around, getting in my way. I was real embarrassed, and everyone kept laughing. Then a messenger handed me something called an Ape-O-Gram. It had just three words: "Paybacks are hell."

Nearly all the coffee drinkers thought that the Elvis Presley sighting was as funny as the Ape-O-Gram, but no one would own up to having had a hand in making up the story. Louise Welling, it seemed, was a real person, and well known in town. She lived to the east, a few miles outside the village, they told me. "She's different, that's for sure," one of the coffee drinkers said. "No one believes her about Elvis Presley, but we all enjoyed it. Kind of put Vicksburg on the map. Isn't it funny? Elvis Presley wasn't even a very good singer. But I don't think Louise thinks it's funny." They referred me to a woman in town who knew Louise Welling better than they did and lived not far from her.

I went over to see the woman, who had an office in town, and talked to her with the understanding that her name would not be used. "Yes," she said," I guess you could say that Louise is different. Her whole family is different, except for her husband, who works at General Motors. He's real quiet. But she's not crazy or anything. In fact, I think she's real bright. I don't know what to make of her claim that she saw Elvis Presley. She was a big Elvis fan from way back, but she doesn't bring him up or talk about this stuff unless someone asks her. She's a kind woman. She's reliable, too, and I wouldn't hesitate to call her if I had trouble. I'm afraid that after the story came out a lot of people played jokes on her. Made Elvis phone calls. Sent her Elvis letters. I'm pretty sure she's not in it for money. She just seems to think it's an interesting story, and it makes her mad when people don't believe her. Of course, none of us do. I don't know anyone in this town who thinks she really saw Elvis Presley. She was furious with the Vicksburg newspaper because they wouldn't run her story."

It seemed odd to me that the Vicksburg *Commercial* had not used Louise Welling's story-- a story that had made the *New York Times*--so I called up Jackie Lawrence, the owner of the *Commercial*, and asked her to meet me for lunch at Mar Jo's. Jackie Lawrence, a former nurse, is a big woman with curly brown hair, and she talks about Vicksburg, her adopted town. There are, she said, perhaps a dozen loyal Elvis fans in town--people who make pilgrimages to Graceland and would **like** to believe Louise Welling even if they don't.

We studied the daily specials, which were posted on the wall, and I decided to order Ken's Homemade Goulash. Next to the list of specials were snapshots of Ken Fowler, a cheerful young man with a fine brushy mustache, who bought Mar-Jo's two years ago and does a lot of the cafe's cooking. Shortly after he bought the place, he had a birthday, and the regulars, the waitresses, and Ken's wife conspired to bring in a belly dancer. The event was captured on film, and the posted snapshots showed Ken, in apparent embarrassment, on a chair in one corner of the cafe, surrounded by laughing customers as a woman in gold draperies writhes in front of him.

Jackie Lawrence told me that she remembered Louise Welling coming into the newspaper office, which is a few doors down from Mar-Jo's, in March, 1988, six months after the sighting at Felpausch's. At the time of her visit, Mrs. Welling knew that her story would soon be printed nationally, in the *Weekly World News*--and so it was, three months later. (According to Jim Leggett, who is the dean of free-lance tabloid photojournalists and once schemed to drill a hole in Howard Hughes's coffin in order to photograph his face, the *Weekly World News* is not exactly esteemed in the trade. "It prints the flotsam left by the better tabloids," he told me.) Mrs. Welling had wanted the *Commercial* to run her story first, Lawrence said. "She stood right by my desk, trying to tell me all about it. I said to her, 'I'm sorry, I don't have time for this,' and showed her out the door. And if she came in again, I'd say the same thing."

There was only one mention in the *Commercial* of the stir caused by Louise Welling's encounter with Elvis. The winner of Skip Knowles' 1988 Elvis-look-alike contest, a truck driver named Ray Kajkowski, came into the newspaper office a few days after the event to ask for prints of any pictures that might have been taken. While he was there, he kissed Jean Delahanty, one of the *Commercial's* reporters, and she wrote a column about it, which concluded, "Some days are better than others!"

There is no chamber of commerce, as such, in Vicksburg. The town doesn't need one; it has Skip Knowles. I had telephoned Knowles before coming to Vicksburg. "Give me a jingle when you get in," he said. "Maybe we can do lunch." He is a handsome, trim, dark-haired man, and at our lunch a gold chain showed through the open collar of his shirt. There was another gold chain around his wrist. He was born in Atchison, Kansas, he told me, but spent his teen-age years--from 1962-1968--near Detroit, where he developed a passion for cars and for cruising, that cool, arm-on-the-window, slow patrolling of city streets which was favored by the young in those days. His dark eyes sparkled at the memory.

"We had what we called the Woodward Timing Association," he said. "It was made up of the guys that cruised Woodward Avenue. The Elias Big Boy at Thirteen Mile Road and Woodward was the place we'd go. But you know the grass is always greener somewhere else. Well, my ultimate dream was to cruise the Sunset Strip. It wasn't until I got married, in 1969, and went out to California that I got to do that. And I talked to those guys cruising the Strip, and you know what they told me? It was **their** dream to cruise Woodward. He shook his head and laughed. "My wife and I still cruise when we go to a city." He hoped the local people had got cruising down pat for this year's festival, he said, handing me a packet of publicity material and a schedule of festival events. "I had to teach them how to cruise last year, which was the first time we closed off streets for it.

The second annual Elvis-look-alike contest would be held at 9 p.m. Saturday, over on Prairie Street, in the parking lot of the Filling Station, a fast-food restaurant across the street from Felpausch's. Skip Knowles knew a good thing when he had it. Before last summer, he said, the festival had been drawing several thousand people, but each year he had had more trouble getting good publicity. "I can't understand the way they handled the Elvis business over at Felpausch's," he told me. They even refused an interview with the *New York Times*. But I decided to play it for whatever it was worth."

After the first Elvis-look-alike contest, Knowles received a lot of calls from Louise Welling, who wanted to talk about Elvis Presley with him. "I put her off," he said. "She's **really** different. I think she really believes Presley never died." He also received other phone calls and visits. When his secretary told him last fall that a reporter from the *Times* was in his outer office waiting to talk to him, he thought it was just a hoax--a joke like the ones dreamed up at Mar-Jo's. But when he came out the man introduced himself as the paper's Chicago bureau chief and interviewed him about the Elvis contest. Then a producer from Charles Kuralt's show, *Sunday Morning*, called and said he was interested in doing a segment for the show on the impact of the Elvis sighting in Vicksburg, and would anything be going on in Vicksburg around Thanksgiving time? "I told him, 'Look, I'll do **anything** to get you here,'" Knowles recalled. "'If you want me to rent Cadillac limos and parade them up and down Main Street for you to film, I'll get them.' But the TV people never came."

I decided it was time to talk to Louise Welling herself. I couldn't make an appointment with her by telephone, because she had recently obtained an unlisted number, but one midweek morning I took a chance on finding her at home and drove out to see her. The Wellings live in the country, in a modest split-level house on non-split level terrain; this is the sand, flat part of Michigan, too far south for the ice-age glaciers to have sculpted it. Mrs. Welling sometimes works as a baby-sitter, but this morning she was home alone with four of her five children--all of them grown--and Nathan, the four-year-old grandson. Mrs. Welling is a heavy-set woman with closely cropped dark hair and a pleasant face. Her eyes stay sad when she smiles. She touched my arm frequently as we talked, and often interrupted herself to digress as she told me her story. She said that she grew up in Kalamazoo and for a time attended St. Mary's, a

Catholic grammar school there. When she turned sixteen, she was given a special present--a ticket to a Presley concert in Detroit. "Somehow, the fellow who took tickets didn't take mine, so after the first show I was able to move up, and I sat in front during the second, " she said. " And then, toward the end, Elvis got down on his knee right in front of me and spread his arms wide open. Well, you can imagine what **that** would be like for a sixteen-year-old girl." Her voice trailed off, and she fell silent, smiling. I asked her if she had continued to follow his career.

"When I got married, I started having children, and I never though much about Elvis," she said. "After all, I had problems of my own." But then, in 1973, she saw a notice in a throwaway shopping newspaper from Galesburg, a nearby town, saying that Presley would be in Kalamazoo and, although he would not be performing, would stay at the Columbia Hotel there.

"I didn't try to get in touch with him," Mrs. Welling said, adding, with a womanly smile, "I had a husband, and you know how that is." Three years later, however, Presley appeared in concert in Kalamazoo, and she sent flowers to him at the Columbia Hotel, because she assumed that he would be staying there again. She went to the concert, too , and as she remembers it, Elvis announced in the course of it that he had a relative living in Vicksburg. "He said he liked this area," she recalled. "Kalamazoo is a peaceful place. He'd like that. And I think he's living at the Columbia right now, under another name. But they won't admit it there. Every time I call, I get a run-around. You know what I think? I think he has become an undercover agent. He was interested in that sort of thing."

"What year was it that you saw him in concert in Detroit?" I asked. I had read somewhere that Presley had not started touring outside the South until 1956.

"Oh, I don't remember," Mrs.Welling said. "I'm fifty-one now, and I had just turned sixteen--you figure it out."

The arithmetic doesn't work out--nor, for someone who grew up in Kalamazoo, does the Columbia Hotel. The Columbia had its days of glory between the First World War and Prohibition, and it was growing seedy by the forties, when I used to ride by it on my way to school. Its decline continued after I left Kalamazoo, until--according to Dan Carter, one of the partners in a development company that remodelled the hotel to create an office complex called the Columbia Plaza--it became a "fleabag flophouse and for a while a brothel." Carter also told me that in the mid-eighties a rumor arose that Elvis Presley was living there, behind the grand pink double doors on the mezzanine, which open into what was once a ballroom. The doors have been locked for years--the empty ballroom, its paint peeling, belongs to the man who owns Bimbo's Pizza, on the floor below--but that didn't deter Elvins here and abroad from taking pilgrimages to Columbia Plaza. "You'd hear foreign voices out in the hallway almost every day," he said. "Then there was a visit from some people from Graceland--at least, they told us they were from Graceland, and they looked the part--who came by to see if we were making any money off this." They weren't, he said, and today the building's management denies that Elvis Presley, under any name, lives anywhere on the premises.

Mrs. Welling's next good look at Elvis Presley came at Felpausch's in September, 1987. There had been, she told me, earlier hints. In 1979, she had seen a man in the back of the county sheriff's car when the police came to her house to check on the family's dog, which had nipped a jogger. "The man in the back seat was slouched down, and he didn't look well," she said. "I'm sure it was Elvis." A few years later, black limousines began to appear occasionally on the road where she lives. "Now, who around here would have a limo?" she asked. Then she began seeing a man she believes was Elvis in disguise. "He looked real fake," she recalled. "He was wearing new bib overalls, an Amish hat, and a beard that didn't look real. I talked to a woman who had seen the same man, and she said he sometimes wore a false nose. Now, why does he have to bother with disguises? Why couldn't he have said that he needed a rest, and gone off to some island to get better."

A note of exasperation had crept into Mrs. Welling's voice. She showed me a cassette that she said contained a tape that Presley made after he was supposed to have died; in it, she said, he explained why he had faked his death. But when she played it the sound was blurred and rumbly, and I couldn't make out the words. The tape had been issued in 1988, to accompany a book by a woman--with whom Mrs. Welling has corresponded--who put forward the theory that the body buried as Presley's was not his own. The book and another by the same author, which Welling said was a fictional account of a rock star who fakes his death, were lovingly inscribed ("It's hard to take the heat") to Mrs. Welling.

Here is what Mrs. Welling said happened to her in September, 1987. She had just been to eleven o'clock Sunday Mass at St. Martin's church. With Grandson Nathan, she stopped at Felpausch's to pick up a few groceries. Having just celebrated one publicly accepted miracle, she saw nothing strange in the private miracle at the supermarket.

"The store was just about deserted," she said. "There wasn't even anyone at the check-out register when I went in. But in the back aisles I felt and heard someone behind me. It must have been Elvis. I didn't turn around, though. And then, when I got up to the check-out, a girl was there waiting on Elvis. He seemed kind of nervous. He was wearing a white motorcycle suit and carrying a helmet. He bought something little--fuses, I think,not groceries. I was so startled I just looked at him. I knew it was Elvis. When you see someone, you know who he is. I didn't say anything, because I'm kind of shy and I don't speak first. After I paid for the groceries, I went out to the parking lot, but no one was there."

I asked Mrs. Welling if she had told anyone at the time what she had seen. She replied that she had told no one except the author of the Elvis-isn't-dead book, who was very supportive. After that, she and her daughter Linda started seeing Elvis in Kalamazoo--once at the Burger King, once at the Crossroads Shopping Mall, and once driving a red Ferrari. And she said that just recently, while she was baby-sitting and filling her time by listening to the police scanner, she heard a man's voice ask, "Can you give me a time for the return of Elvis?" and heard Presley reply, "I'm here now."

I asked her what her family thought about her experiences. Linda, a pale, blond woman who was sitting off to one side in a dining alcove smoking cigarettes while I talked to her mother, was obviously a believer, and occasionally interjected reports of various Elvis contacts of her own. "But **my** mother thinks it's all nutty," Mrs. Welling said, laughing. "She says I should forget about it. My husband doesn't say much--he's real quiet--but he knows I'm not crazy.

It wasn't until the spring of 1988, Mrs.Welling said, that she started getting in touch with the media. She claims that she didn't bother talking to the people at the Vicksburg newspaper (although Jackie Lawrence remembers otherwise), because "it wasn't an important newspaper." Instead, she tried to tell her story to the *Kalamazoo Gazette* and people at the television station there. No one would take her seriously--except, of course, the author of the Elvis book. After Mrs.Welling had written to her and talked to her on the telephone, a writer for the *Weekly World News* phoned for an interview. Mrs. Welling asked him how he knew about her, but he declined to reveal his sources. In early May, the tabloid prepared the ground for Mrs. Welling's story by running one that took note of the rumor that Presley was living in Columbia Plaza and gave Mrs. Welling's friend a nice plug for her book. Shortly after that the syndicated columnist Bob Greene gave the rumor a push. By that time, the *Kalamazoo Gazette* realized it could no longer ignore Mrs. Welling's phone calls, and in its May 15th issue Tom Haroldson, a staff writer, wrote a front-page story headlined ***ELVIS ALIVE IN KALAMAZOO SAY AREA WOMAN AND NEWS TABLOID***. That was the beginning of Mrs. Welling's fame, but it was not until June 28th that the *Weekly World News* told her whole story. In thousands of supermarkets, the issue appeared with a big front-page picture of Mrs. Welling and a headline in type an inch and a half high proclaiming ***I'VE SEEN ELVIS IN THE FLESH!*** The story began to be picked up by newspapers around the country as a brightener to the increasingly monotonous accounts of the pre-Convention Presidential campaigns. CBS investigated for possible production on *60 Minutes*. Radio stations from coast to coast and as far away as Australia called to interview Louise Welling and anyone else they could find. Kalamazoo's mayor, Edward Annen, reacted to all this by announcing to a *Gazette* reporter, "I've told them that everyone knows this is where he lives and that they should send their residents here to spend tourist dollars to find him."

Funny signs sprouted throughout Kalamazoo and Vicksburg in places of commerce. A rival market of Felpausch's posted one that said, "JIMMY HOFFA SHOPS HERE." A dentist boasted, "ELVIS HAD HIS TEETH CLEANED HERE." At Mar-Jo's, the sign read, "ELVIS EATS OUR MEATLOAF." The folks at Felpausch's, however, were not amused. Cecil Bagwell, then the store's manager, told the *Gazette*, "The cashier who supposedly checked out Elvis that day cannot remember anything about it," and characterized Mrs. Welling as "an Elvis fanatic." Bagwell no longer works at Felpausch's, but I spoke with Jack Mayhem, the assistant manager, who scowled when I brought up the subject. "I won't comment," he said, adding, nonetheless, "We've never given the story to anyone, and we're not going to. All I'll say is that the woman is totally--" and he rotated an extended finger beside his head.

Before I left Mrs.Welling that morning, I asked her why she thought it was that **she** had seen Elvis, when others had not--nor did not even believe her.

"I don't know, but the Lord does," she answered. "I'm a religious woman, and when things like this happen--that we don't understand--it just proves that the Lord has a plan."

The next day, a friend who had heard about my investigations telephoned to tell me that there had been an Elvis sighting just a week or so earlier in Kalamazoo at the delivery bay of the Fader construction company which is owned by her family. She hadn't seen the man herself, she said, but the women in the office had insisted that the truck driver making the delivery was Elvis Presley. I suspected that it might have been Ray Kajkowski, winner of the Elvis-look-alike contest and kisser of Jean Delahanty. This turned out to be true. One Friday evening, at a run-through for the Old Car Festival's cruising event, I was introduced to Kajkowski by Skip Knowles, and Kajkowski confirmed that he had made quite a stir while delivering a shipment of concrete forms to Fader. He gave me his card--he has apparently made a second career for himself as an Elvis impersonator at parties and night clubs--and then he whipped out a pair of mirrored sunglasses, put them on, and kissed me, too. "Young, old fat, skinny, black, white, good-looking, not so good-looking, I kiss them all," he said. "I'm a pretty affectionate fellow. I was raised in a family that hugged a lot."

Ray Kajkowski lives in Gobles, not far from Vicksburg. At forty-one, he is thick-featured, a bit on the heavy side, and looks like--well, he looks like Elvis Presley. He has big sideburns and dyed black hair, which he wears in a pompadour. He went down to Graceland recently with his wife and his two teen-age sons to study the Presley scene and recalls that while he was in the mansion's poolroom a couple came in and the wife took one look at him and collapsed on the floor in a faint.

"When I was growing up, I felt like an outsider," he told me. "I didn't think I was as good as other people, because my dad wasn't a doctor or a lawyer. We were just common folks. I knew about Elvis even when I was a little kid. I didn't pay much attention, though, except that some of my buddies had pictures of Elvis, so we'd trade those to our older sisters and their friends for baseball cards. He laughed.

"I felt like we were invaded when the Beatles came over," he continued. By that time--1963--he was in Central High School in Kalamazoo, and had begun to appreciate Presley's music and to defend it against foreign stars. "I mean, Elvis was a small-town boy who made good. He was just ordinary, and sure, he made some mistakes, just like me or you or any of us. But he went from zero to sixty. He had charisma with a capital *C* and somehow people still know it."

After Presley's death, Kajkowski said, he felt sad and started reading about Elvis and studying his old movies. "Then, in September or October, 1987, right around then, I was at a nineteen-fifties dance in Gobles. My hair was different then, and I had a beard, but there was a fifty-dollar prize for the best Elvis imitator. Fifty bucks sounded pretty good to me, and I watched this one guy do an imitation, and he didn't move or anything, and I thought to myself, I can do better than that, so I got up and entered and won, beard and all. After that, I shaved off my beard, dyed my hair, and started building my act. I do lip-synch to Elvis tapes. I've got three suits now, one black, one white, one blue. My wife does my setups for me and runs the strobe lights. Evenings when we don't have anything else to do, we sit around and make scarves for me to give away. I cut them, and she hems them. When I'm performing, I sweat real easy, and I mop off the sweat with the scarves and throw them out to the gals. They go crazy over them. And the gals proposition me. They don't make it easy. Sometimes they rub up against me, and when I kiss them they stick their tongues halfway down my throat. Once, I went to shake the guys' hands, because I figured it was better to have them on my side. But one big guy wouldn't shake my hand, and later he came over and grabbed me like a grizzly bear and told me to quit it. 'You don't sound like Elvis Presley. You don't look like Elvis Presley. Stop it!' I told him, 'Hey, it's all lip synch! It's just an act! It's entertainment! But I try to keep it under control. My wife's the woman I have to go home with after the act."

I asked Kajkowski if he had ever been in Felpausch's. As a truck driver, he said, he had made deliveries there; occasionally, he even shopped there. But although he owned a motorcycle, he said, he rarely drove it, and he never wore a white motorcycle suit.

I asked him what he made of Mrs. Welling's story.

"Well," he said thoughtfully, "when someone puts another person at the center of their life, they read about him, they think about him, I'm not surprised that he becomes real for that person."

Saturday night, at nine o'clock, Louise Welling is standing next to me in the Filling Station's parking lot--it is built on the site of John Vicker's flour mill--in a crowd that has just seen prizes awarded in the fifties dance concert and is waiting for the beginning of the second annual Elvis-look-alike contest. She is neatly dressed in a blue-and-white checked overblouse and dark pants. Her hair is fluffed up, and she is wearing pretty pink lipstick. She invited me to come to the contest, and told me that although many of the entrants in such affairs didn't come close to Elvis she was hoping that this one would draw the real Elvis Presley out from hiding. "If he came to me in the past, I believe he'll come again," she said. "I hope it will be before I die. If he comes, I'm going to grab him and hold on to him and ask him why he couldn't just be honest about needing to get away for a rest. Why couldn't he just tell the truth? Look at all the trouble he's caused those who love him."

Earlier in the day, I stopped in at Mar-Jo's for coffee. There were lots of extra visitors in the cafe. Ken Fowler had turned on the radio to WHEZ, a Kalamazoo station, which was broadcasting live from out on the street, acting as the festival's musical host. Rock music filled the cafe. Patrons were beating time on their knees, and the waitresses had begun to boogie up and down behind the counter. I asked one of them--a girl named Laurie, who was decked out fifties style with a white floaty scarf around her ponytail--what she made of Mrs. Welling's story. "I think it's kind of fun," she said. "I haven't met the lady, but, you know, maybe she's right. After all, if Elvis never died he has to be someplace."

Mrs. Welling is subdued, as she stands next to me, but all attention--scanning the people, anticipatory. We are in the very back of the good natured crowd, which has enjoyed the nostalgia, the slick cars and the pony tails. She spots Kajkowski and says to me that he's not Elvis but "so far he's the only one here who even looks anything like him."

Skip Knowles is up on the stage, in charge of what has turned out to be a successful event. There have been record-breaking crowds. Six hundred and fifty cars were entered. He has had plenty of media coverage, and he seems to be having a very good time. He calls for the Elvis contest to begin. Ray Kajkowski's act is so good now that he has no competition--he is the only one to enter. I watch him play the crowd. He had told me, "When I first started, I really liked the attention, but now it's just fun to do the show, and, yeah, I do get caught up in it. I like the holding power I have over people. I know how it is to feel left out, so I play to everyone. But I like people in their mid-thirties or older best. I don't like to entertain for these kids in their twenties. The gals back off when I try to drape a scarf around them. I think that's an insult. "Now he's dancing around the edge of the crowd, reaching out to kiss the women, who respond to him with delight and good humor, and then he launches into what Mrs. Welling tells me is "You're a Devil in Disguise." I look at her, and she seems near tears. Her shoulders slump. "I don't like to watch," she says softly, and walks away to gather her family for the trip home.

On my way home,on the morning after the festival, I made one final stop in Vicksburg, on the south side of town, at what is left of Fraser's Grove. For about forty years--until the early nineteen-twenties--Fraser's Grove was one of this country's premier spiritualist centers. In 1883, Mrs. John Fraser, the wife of a well-to-do Vicksburg merchant, turned the twenty-acre woodland into a camp and gathering place for mediums, believers in mediums, and the curious. She had been inspired by a lecture on spiritualism given in a hall on Prairie Street by one Mrs. R. S. Lilly, of Cassadaga, New York, a town in the spiritually fervent "burned-over" district of that state. In the years that followed, Mrs. Fraser became a national figure in seance circles, and another resident of Vicksburg, C. E. Dent, was elected president of something called the Mediums' Protective Union. A group calling itself the Vicksburg Spiritualists was formed shortly after Mrs. Lilly's visit, and it met each Sunday. Its Ladies Auxiliary held monthly chicken dinners (fifteen cents a plate, two for a quarter). On summer Sunday afternoons, people from around this country and abroad packed the campground at Fraser's Grove to talk of materialization and reincarnation and watch mediums go into trances to contact the dead. According to a 1909 issue of the Vicksburg *Commercial*, they debated subjects such as "Is the planet on which we live approaching final destruction, or is it becoming more permanent?" (A follow-up article reports that the Spiritualists opted for permanency.)

Trees still stand in much of Fraser's Grove, although some of them have been cut down to make room for a small housing development. The campground itself has been taken over by the Christian Tabernacle, which makes use of the old camp buildings. Tazzie, my German shepherd, was with me, and I parked at the edge of the grove to let her out for a run before we drove onto the interstate highway. We headed down a dim path, where events passing strange are said to have taken place. The grove produced no Elvis, no John Vickers, not even a phantom band concert or the apparition of Mr. Matz--no spirits at all. But Tazzie did scare up a rabbit, and the oaks were still there, and, untamed through a hundred and fifty generations, so were the mosquitoes.

Ralph J. Gleason, *LIKE A ROLLING STONE*

Published in the prestigious American Scholar *(Autumn, 1967), rock critic and journalist Ralph Gleason defends the music of the sixties as the artistic expression of a generation seeking a romantic sense of self in a society increasingly dominated by impersonal and scientific rationality. Gleason argues that the "pagan" thrust in the music is part of the revolt against the puritan standards of American Society. All people, and especially the young, need to experience the feeling of community denied them in a society committed only to the superiority of rationalism and materialism. His defense of marijuana was also very daring for the times.*

Forms and rhythms in music are never changed without producing changes in the most important political forms and ways.

Plato said that.

There's something happenin' here.
What it is ain't exactly clear.
There's a man with a gun over there tellin' me I've got to beware.
I think it's time we STOP, children, what's that sound?
Everybody look what's goin' down.

The Buffalo Springfield said that.

For the reality of politics, we must go to the poets, not the politicians.

Norman O. Brown said that.

For the reality of what's happening today in America, we must go to rock 'n' roll, to popular music.

I said that.

For almost forty years in this country, which has prided itself on individualism, freedom and nonconformity, all popular songs were written alike. They had an eight-bar opening statement, an eight-bar repeat, an eight-bar reprise. Anything that did not fit into that framework was, appropriately enough, called a novelty.

Clothes were basically the same whether a suit was double-breasted or single-breasted, and the only people who were beards were absentminded professors and Bolshevik bomb throwers. Long hair, which was equated with lack of masculinity in some sort of subconscious reference to Samson, I suspect, was restricted to painters and poets and classical musicians, hence the term "long-hair music" to mean classical.

Four years ago a specter was haunting Europe, one whose fundamental influence, my intuition tells me, may be just as important, if in another way, as the original of that line. The Beatles, four long-haired Liverpool teen-agers, were busy changing the image of popular music. In less that a year, they invaded the United States and almost totally wiped out the standard Broadway show--Ed Sullivan TV program popular song. No more were we "flying to the moon on gossamer wings," we were now articulating such interesting and, in this mechanistic society, unusual concepts as "Money can't buy me love" and "I want to hold your hand."

"Societies, like individuals, have their moral crises and their spiritual revolutions," R. H. Tawney says in *Religion and the Rise of Capitalism*. And the Beatles appeared ("a great figure rose up from the sea and pointed at me and said 'you're a Beatle with an *a* Genesis,'" according to John Lennon). They came at the proper moment of a spiritual cusp--as the martian in Robert Heinlein's *Stranger in a Strange Land* calls a crisis.

Instantly, on those small and sometimes doll-like figures was focused all the rebellion against hypocrisy, all the impudence and irreverence that the youth of that moment was feeling vis-à-vis his elders.

Automation, affluence, the totality of instant communication, the technology of the phonograph record, the transistor radio, had revolutionized life for youth in this society. The population age was lowering. Popular music, the jukebox and the radio were becoming the means of communication. Huntley and Brinkley were for mom and dad. People now sang songs they wrote themselves, not songs written **for** them by hacks in grimy Tin Pan Alley offices.

The folk music boom paved the way. Bob Dylan's poetic polemics, *Blowin' in the Wind* and *The Times They Are A-Changin'*, had helped the breakthrough. Top-40 radio made Negro music available everywhere to a greater degree than ever before in our history.

This was, truly, a new generation--the first in America raised with music constantly in its ear, weaned on a transistor radio, involved with songs from its earliest moment of memory.

Music means more to this generation than it did even to its dancing parents in the big-band swing era of Benny Goodman. It's natural, then, that self-expression should find popular music so attractive.

The dance of the swing era, of the big bands, was the fox trot. It was really a formal dance extended in variation only by experts. The swing era's parents had danced the waltz. The fox trot was only a ritual with only a little more room for self-expression. Rock 'n' roll brought with it not only the voices of youth singing their protests, their hopes and their expectations (along with their pathos and sentimentality and their personal affairs from drag racing to romance), it brought their dances.

"Every period which abounded in folk songs, has, by the same token, been deeply stirred by Dionysian currents," Nietzsche points out in *The Birth of Tragedy*. And Dionysian is the word to describe the dances of the past ten years, call them by whatever name from Bop to the

Twist to the Frug, from the Hully Gully to the Philly Dog.

In general, adult society left the youth alone, prey to the corruption the adults suspected was forthcoming from the song lyrics. ("All of me, why not take all of me," from that hit of the thirties, of course, didn't means all of me, it meant, well....er....)or from the payola-influenced disc jockeys. (Who ever remembers about the General Electric scandals of the fifties, in which over a dozen officials went to jail for industrial illegalities?)

The tv shows were in the afternoon anyway and nobody could stand to watch those rock 'n' roll singers; they were worse than Elvis Presley.

But all of a sudden the *New Yorker* joke about the married couple dreamily remarking, when a disc jockey played "Houn' Dog" by Elvis, "they're playing our song," wasn't a joke any longer. It was real. That generation had suddenly grown up and married and Elvis was real memories of real romance and not just kid stuff.

All of a sudden, the world of music, which is a big business in a very real way, took another look at the music of the pony tail and chewing gum set, as Mitch Miller once called the teen-age market, and realized that there was one helluva lot of bread to be made there.

In a short few years, Columbia and R.C.A. Victor and the other companies that dominated the recording market, the huge publishing houses that copyrighted the music and collected the royalties, discovered that they no longer were "kings of the hill." Instead, a lot of small companies, like Atlantic and Chess and Imperial and others, had hits by people the major records didn't even know, singing songs written in Nashville and Detroit and Los Angeles and Chicago and sometimes, but no longer almost always, New York.

It's taken the big ones a few years to recover from that. First they called the music trash and the lyrics dirty. When that didn't work, as the attempt more recently to inhibit songs with supposed psychedelic or marijuana references has failed, they capitulated. They joined up. R.C.A. Victor bought Elvis from the original company he recorded for Sun Records--("Yaller Sun records from Nashville" as John Sebastian sings it in *Nashville Cats*)--and then bought Sam Cooke, and A.B.C. Paramount bought Ray Charles and then Fats Domino. And Columbia, thinking it had a baby folk singer capable of some more sales of "San Francisco Bay," turned out to have a tiny demon of a poet named Bob Dylan.

So the stage was set for the Beatles to take over--"with this ring I can--dare I say it?--rule the world!" And they did take over so thoroughly that they have become the biggest success in the history of show business, the first attraction ever to have a coast-to-coast tour in this country sold out before the first show even opened.

With the Beatles and Dylan running tandem, two things seem to me to have been happening. The early Beatles were at one and the same time a declaration in favor of love and of life, an exuberant paean to the sheer joy of living, and a validation of the importance of American negro music.

Dylan, by his political, issue-oriented broadsides first and then by his Rimbaudish nightmare visions of the real state of the nation, his bittersweet love songs and his pure imagery, did what the jazz and poetry people of the fifties had wanted to do--he took poetry out of the classroom and out of the hands of the professors and put it right out there in the streets for everyone.

I dare say that with the inspiration of the Beatles and Dylan we have more poetry being produced and more poets being made than ever before in the history of the world. Dr. Malvina

Reynolds--the composer of *Little Boxes*--thinks nothing like this has happened since Elizabethan times. I suspect even that is too timid an assessment.

Let's go back to Plato, again. Speaking of the importance of new styles of music, he said, "The new style quietly insinuates itself into manners and customs and from there it issues a greater force...goes on to attack laws and constitutions, displaying the utmost impudence, until it ends by overthrowing everything, both in public and in private."

That seems to me to be a pretty good summation of the answer to the British rock singer Donovan's question. "What goes on? I really want to know."

The most immediate apparent change instituted by the new music is the new way of looking at things. We see it evidenced all around us. The old ways are going and a new set of assumptions is beginning to be worked out. I cannot even begin to codify them. Perhaps it's much too soon to do so. But I think there are some clues--the sacred importance of love and truth and beauty and interpersonal relationships.

When Bob Dylan sang recently at the Masonic Memorial Auditorium in San Francisco, at intermission there were a few very young people in the corridor backstage. One of them was a long-haired, poncho-wearing girl of about thirteen. Dylan's road manager, a slender, long-haired, "Bonnie Prince Charlie" youth, wearing black jeans and Beatle boots, came out of the dressing room and said, "You kids have to leave! You can't be backstage here!"

"Who are you?" the long-haired girl asked.

"I'm a cop," Dylan's road manager said aggressively.

The girl looked at him for a long moment and then drawled, "Whaaaat? With those boots?"

Clothes really do **not** make the man. But sometimes...

I submit that was an important incident, something that could never have happened a year before, something that implies a very great deal about the effect of the new style, which has quietly (or not so quietly, depending on your view of electric guitars) insinuated itself into manners and customs.

Among the effects of "what's goin' on" is the relinquishing of belief in the sacredness of logic. "I was a prisoner of logic and I still am," Malvina Reynolds admits, but then goes on to praise the new music. And the prisoners of logic are the ones who are really suffering most--unless they have Mrs.Reynold's glorious gift of youthful vision.

The first manifestation of the importance of this outside the music--I think--came in the works of Ken Kesey and Joseph Heller. *One Flew Over the Cuckoo's Nest*, with its dramatic view of the interchangeability of reality and illusion, and *Catch-22*, with its delightful utilization of crackpot realism (to use C.Wright Mill's phrase) as an explanation of how things are, were works of seminal importance.

No one any longer really believes that the processes of international relations and world economics are rationally explicable. Absolutely the very best and clearest discussion of the entire things is wrapped up in Milo Minderbinder's explanation, in *Catch-22*, of how you can buy eggs for seven cents in Malta and sell them for five cents in Pianosa and make a profit. Youth understands the truth of this immediately, and no economic textbook is going to change it.

Just as--implying the importance of interpersonal relations and the beauty of being true to oneself--the under-thirty youth immediately understands the creed patiently explained by

Yossarian in *Catch-22* that everybody's your enemy who's trying to get you killed, even if he's your own commanding officer.

This is an irrational world, despite the brilliant efforts of Walter Lippmann to make it rational, and we are living in a continuation of the formalized lunacy (Nelson Algren's phrase) of war, any war.

At this point in history, most of the organs of opinion, from the *New York Review of Books* through the *New Republic* to *Encounter* (whether or not they are subsidized by the C.I.A.), are in the control of the prisoners of logic. They take a flick like *Morgan* and grapple with it. They take *Help* and *A Hard Day's Night* and grapple with those two beautiful creations, and they fail utterly to understand what is going on because they try to deal with them logically. They complain because art doesn't make sense! Life on this planet in this time of history doesn't make sense either--as an end result of immutable laws of economics and logic and philosophy.

Dylan sang, "You raise up your head and you ask 'is this where it is?' And somebody points to you and says 'it's his' and you say 'what's mine' and somebody else says 'well, what is' and you say 'oh my god, am I here all alone?'"

Dylan wasn't the first. Orwell saw some of it, Heller saw more, and in a different way so did I. F. Stone, that remarkable journalist, who is really a poet, when he described a *Herald Tribune* reporter extracting from the Pentagon the admission that, once the first steps for the Santa Domingo episode were mounted, it was impossible to stop the machine.

Catch 22 said that in order to be sent home from flying missions you had to be crazy, and obviously anybody who wanted to be sent home was sane.

Kesey and Heller and Terry Southern, to a lesser degree in his novels but certainly in *Dr. Strangelove*, have hold of it. I suspect that they're not really a *New Wave* of writers but only a *last wave* of the past, just as is Norman Mailer, who said in his Berkeley Vietnam Day speech that "rational discussion of the United States involvement in Viet Nam is illogical in the way surrealism is illogical and rational political discussion of Adolph Hitler's motives was illogical and then obscene." This is the end of the formal literature we have known and the beginning possibly of something else.

In almost every aspect of what is happening today, this turning away from the old patterns is making itself manifest. As the formal structure of the show business world of popular music and television has brought out into the open the Negro performer--whose incredibly beautiful folk poetry and music for decades has been the prime mover in American song--we find a curious thing happening.

The Negro performers, from James Brown to Aaron Neville to the Supremes and the Four Tops, are on the Ed Sullivan trip, striving as hard as they can to get on that stage and become part of the American success story, while the white rock performers are motivated to escape from that stereotype. Whereas in years past the Negro performer offered style in performance and content in song--the messages from a Leadbelly to Percy Mayfield to Ray Charles were important messages--today he is almost totally style with very little content. And when James Brown sings, *It's Man's World*, or Aaron Neville sings, *Tell It Like It Is*, he takes a phrase and only a phrase with which to work, and the Supremes and the Tops are choreographed more and more like the Four Lads and the Ames Brothers and the McGuire Sisters.

I suggest that this bears a strong relationship to the condition of the civil rights movement today in which the only truly black position is that of Stokely Carmichael, and in which the N.A.A.C.P. and most of the other formal groups, are, like the Four Tops and the Supremes, on an Ed Sullivan tv-trip to middle-class America. And the only true American Negro music is that which abandons the concepts of European musical thought, abandons the systems of scales and keys and notes, for a music whose roots are in the culture of the colored peoples of the world.

The drive behind all American popular music performers, to a greater or lesser extent, from Sophie Tucker and Al Jolson, on down through Pat Boone and as recently as Roy Head and Charlie Rich, has been to sound like a Negro. The white jazz musician was the epitome of this.

Yet an outstanding characteristic of the new music of rock, certainly in its best artists, is something else altogether. This new generation of musicians is not interested in being Negro, since it is an absurdity.

The clarinetist Milton Mezzrow, who grew up with the Negro Chicago jazzmen in the twenties and thirties, even put "Negro" on his prison record and claimed to be more at home with his Negro friends than with his Jewish family and neighbors.

Today's new youth, beginning with the rock band musician but spreading out into the entire movement, into the Haight-Ashbury hippies, is not ashamed of being white.

He is remarkably free from prejudice, but he is not attempting to join the Negro culture or to become part of it, like his musical predecessor, the beatnik. I find this of considerable significance. For the very first time in decades, as far as I know, something important and new is happening artistically and musically in this society that is distinct from the Negro and to which the Negro will have to come, if he is interested in it at all, as in the past the white youth went uptown to Harlem or downtown or crosstown or to wherever the Negro community was centered because there was the locus of artistic creativity.

Today the new electronic music by the Beatles and others (and the Beatles' *Strawberry Fields* is, I suggest, a three-minute masterpiece, an electronic miniature symphony) exists somewhere else from and independent of the Negro. This is only one of the more easily observed manifestations of this movement.

The professional craft union, the American Federation of Musicians, is now faced with something absolutely unforeseen--the cooperative band. Briefly--in the thirties--there were co-op bands. The original Casa Loma band was one and the original Woody Herman band was another. But the whole attitude of the union and the attitude of the musicians themselves worked against the idea, and co-op bands were discouraged. They were almost unknown until recently.

Today almost all rock groups are cooperative. Many live together, in tribal style, in houses or camps or sometimes in traveling tepees, but always **together** as a **group**; and the young girls who follow them are called "groupies," just as the girls who in the thirties and forties followed the bands (music does more than soothe the savage breast!) were called "band chicks."

The basic creed of the American Federation of Musicians is that musicians must not play unless paid. The new generation wants money, of course, but its basic motivation is to play anytime, anywhere, anyhow. Art is first, then finance, most of the time. At least one rock band, the Loading Zone in Berkeley, has stepped outside the American Federation of Musicians entirely and does not play for money. You may give them money, but they won't set a price or solicit it.

This seems to me to extend the attitude that gave Pete Seeger, Joan Baez and Bob Dylan such status. They are not and never have been for sale in the sense that you can hire Sammy Davis to appear, as you can hire Dean Martin to appear, any time he's free, as long as you pay his price. You have not been able to do this with Seeger, Baez and Dylan any more than Allen Ginsberg has been for sale either to *Ramparts* or the C.I.A.

Naturally, this revolt against the assumptions of the adult world runs smack dab into the sanctimonious puritan morality of America, the schizophrenia that insists that money is serious business and the acquisition of wealth is a blessing in the eyes of the Lord, that what we do in private we must preach in public. Don't do what I do, do what I say.

Implicit in the very names of the business organizations that these youths form is an attack on the traditional, serious attitude toward money. It is not only that the groups themselves are named with beautiful imagery: The Grateful Dead, the Loading Zone, Blue Cheer or the Jefferson Airplane--all dating back to the Beatles with an *A*--it is the names of the nonmusical organizations: Frontage Road Productions (the music company of the Grateful Dead), Faithful Virtue Music (the Lovin' Spoonful's publishing company), Ashes and Sand (Bob Dylan's production firm--his music publishing company is Dwarf Music). A group who give light shows is known as the Love Conspiracy Commune, and there was a dance recently in Marin County, California, sponsored by the Northern California Psychedelic Cattlemen's Association, Ltd. And, of course, there is the Family Dog, which, despite, *Ramparts*, was never a rock group, only a name under which four people who wanted to present rock 'n' roll dances worked.

Attacking the conventional attitude toward money is considered immoral in the society of our fathers, because money is sacred. The reality of what Bob Dylan says--"money doesn't talk, it swears"--has yet to seep through.

A corollary of the money attack is the whole thing about long hair, bare feet and beards. "Nothing makes me sadder," a woman wrote me objecting to the Haight-Ashbury scene,"than to see beautiful young girls walking along the streets in bare feet." My own daughter pointed out that your feet couldn't get any dirtier than your shoes.

Recently I spent an evening with a lawyer, a brilliant man who is engaged in a lifelong crusade to educate and reform lawyers. He is interested in the civil liberties issue of police harassment of hippies. But, he said, they wear those uniforms of buckskin and fringe and beads. Why don't they dress naturally? So I asked him if he was born in his three-button dacron suit. It's like the newspaper descriptions of Joan Baez's "long stringy hair." It may be long, but **stringy?** Come on!

To the eyes of many of the elder generations, all visible aspects of the new generation, its music, its lights, its clothes, are immoral. The City of San Francisco Commission on Juvenile Delinquency reported adversely on the sound level and the lights at the Fillmore Auditorium, as if those things of and by themselves were threats (they may be, but not in the way the Commission saw them.) A young girl might have trouble maintaining her judgment in that environment, the Commission chairman said.

Now all this implies that dancing is the road to moral ruin, that young girls on the dance floors are mesmerized by talent scouts for South American brothels and enticed away from their happy (not hippie) homes to live a life of slavery and moral degradation. It ought to be noted, parenthetically, that a British writer, discussing the Beatles, claims that "the Cycladic fertility goddess from Amorgos dates the guitar as a sex symbol to 4800 years B.C."

During the twenties and thirties and the forties--in other words, during the prime years of the Old Ones of today--dancing, in the immortal words of Bob Scobey, the Dixieland trumpet player, "was an excuse to get next to a broad." The very least effect of the pill on American youth is that this is no longer true."

The assault on hypocrisy works on many levels. The adult society attempted to chastise Bob Dylan by economic sanctions, calling the line in *Rainy Day Woman*, everybody must get stoned" (there is a purely religious, even biblical, meaning to it, if you wish), an enticement to teen-agers to smoke marijuana. But no one has objected to Ray Charles' *Let's Go Get Stoned*, which is about gin, or to any number of other songs, from the Kingston Trio's *Scotch and Soda* on through *One for My Baby and One More* [ONE MORE!] *for the Road*. Those are about alcohol and alcohol is socially acceptable, as well as big business, even though I believe that everyone under thirty now knows that alcohol is worse for you than marijuana, that, in fact, the only thing wrong about marijuana is that it is illegal.

Cut to the California State Narcotics Bureau's chief enforcement officer, Matt O'Connor, in a TV interview recently insisting, a' la Parkinson's Law, that he must have more agents to control the drug abuse problem. He appeared with a representative of the state attorney general's office, who predicted that the problem would continue "as long as these people believe they are not doing anything wrong."

And that's exactly it. They do not think they are doing anything wrong, any more than their grandparents were when they broke the prohibition laws. They do not want to go to jail, but a jail sentence or a bust no longer carries the social stigma it once did. The civil rights movement has made a jailing a badge of honor, if you go there for principle, and to a great many people today, the right to smoke marijuana is a principle worth risking jail for.

"Make Love, Not War" is one of the most important slogans of modern times, a statement of life against death, as the Beatles have said over and over--"say the word and be like me, say the word and you'll be free."

I don't think that wearing that slogan on a bumper or on the back of a windbreaker is going to end the bombing tomorrow at noon, but it implies something. It is not conceivable that it could have existed in such proliferation thirty years ago, and in 1937 we were pacifists, too. It simply could not have happened.

There's another side to it, of course, or at least another aspect of it. The Rolling Stones, who came into existence really to fight jazz in the clubs of London, were against the jazz of the integrated world, the integrated world arrived at by rational processes. Their songs, from *Satisfaction* and *19th Nervous Breakdown* to *Get Off My Cloud* and *Mother's Little Helper*, were anti-establishment in a political way. The Stones are now moving, with *Ruby Tuesday* and *Let's Spend the Night Together*, into a social radicalism of sorts; but in the beginning and for their basic first-thrust appeal, they hit out in rage, almost in blind anger and certainly with overtones of destructiveness, against the adult world. It's no wonder the novel they were attracted to was David Wallis' *Only Lovers Left Alive*, that Hell's Angels' story of a teen-age future jungle. And it is further interesting that their manager, Andrew Loog Oldham, writes the essays on their albums in the style of an Anthony Burgess' violent *A Clockwork Orange*.

Nor is it any wonder that this attitude appealed to that section of the youth whose basic position was still in politics and economics (remember that Rolling Stone Mick Jagger was a London School of Economics student, whereas Lennon and McCarthy were artists and writers). When the Stones first came to the West Coast, a group of young radicals issued the following proclamation of welcome:

> *Greetings and welcome Rolling Stones, our comrades in the desperate battle against the maniacs who hold power. The revolutionary youth of the world hears your music and is inspired to even more deadly acts. We fight in guerrilla bands against invading imperialists in Asia and South America, we riot at rock 'n' roll concerts everywhere. We burned and pillaged Los Angeles and the cops know our snipers will return.*
>
> *They call us dropouts and delinquents and draftdodgers and punks and hopheads and heap tons of shit on our head. In Viet Nam they drop bombs on us and in America they try to make us make war on our own comrades but the bastards hear us playing you on our little transistor radios and know that they will not escape the blood and fire of the anarchist revolution.*
>
> *We will play your music in rock 'n' roll marching bands as we tear down the jails and free the prisoners, as we tear down the State schools and free the students, as we tear down the military bases and arm the poor, as we tatoo **BURN BABY BURN!** on the bellies of the wardens and generals and create a new society from the ashes of our fires.*
>
> *Comrades, you will return to this country when it is free from the tyranny of the State and you will play your splendid music in factories run by the workers, in the domes of emptied city halls, on the rubble of police stations, under the hanging corpses of priests, under a million red flags waving over a million anarchist communities. In the words of Breton, **THE ROLLING STONES ARE THAT WHICH SHALL BE! LYNDON JOHNSON--THE YOUTH OF CALIFORNIA DEDICATES ITSELF TO YOUR DESTRUCTION! ROLLING STONES--THE YOUTH OF CALIFORNIA HEARS YOUR MESSAGE! LONG LIVE THE REVOLUTION!!!***

But rhetoric like that did not bring out last January a Human Be-In on the polo grounds of San Francisco's Golden Gate Park the twenty thousand people who were there, fundamentally, just to see the other members of the tribe, not to hear speeches--the speeches were all a drag from Leary to Rubin to Buddah*--just to **BE.**

In the Haight-Ashbury district the Love Generation organizes itself into the Job Co-ops and committees to clean the streets, and the monks of the neighborhoods, the Diggers, talk about free dances in the park to put the Avalon Ballroom and the Fillmore out of business and communizing the incomes of Bob Dylan and the Beatles.

The Diggers trace back spiritually to those British millenarians who took over land in 1649, just before Cromwell, and after the Civil War freed it, under the assumption that the land was for the people. They tilled it and gave the food away.

The Diggers give food away. Everything is Free. So it is with the Berkeley Provos and the new group in Cleveland--the Prunes--and the Provos in Los Angeles. More, if an extreme, assault against the money culture. Are they driving the money changers out of the temple? perhaps. The Diggers says they believe it is just as futile to fight the system as to join it and they are dropping out in a way that differs from Leary's.

The Square Left wrestles with the problem. They want a Yellow Submarine community because that is where the strength so obviously is. But even *Ramparts*, which is the white hope of the Square Left, if you follow me, misunderstands. They think that the Family Dog is a rock group and that political activity is the only hope, and Bob Dylan says, "There's no left wing and no right wing, only up wing and down wing." and also, "I tell you there are no politics."

But the banding together to form Job Co-Ops, to publish newspapers, to talk to the police (even to bring them flowers), aren't these political acts? I suppose so, but I think they are political acts of a different kind, a kind that results in the Hell's Angels being the guardians of the lost children at the Be-In and the guarantors of peace at dances.

The New Youth is finding its prophets in strange places--in dance halls and on the jukebox. It is on, perhaps, a frontier buckskin trip after a decade of *Matt Dillon* and *Bonanza* and the other TV folk myths, in which the values are clear (as opposed to those in the world around us) and right is right and wrong is wrong. The Negro singers have brought the style and the manner of the Negro gospel preacher to popular music, just as they brought the rhythms and the feeling of the gospel music, and now the radio is the church and Everyman carries his own walkie-talkie to God in his transistor.

Examine the outcry against the Beatles for John Lennon's remark about being more popular than Jesus. No radio station that depended on rock 'n' roll for its audience banned Beatles records, and in the only instance where we had a precise measuring rod for the contest--the Beatles concert in Memphis where a revival meeting ran day and date with them--the Beatles won overwhelmingly. Something like eight to five over Jesus in attendance, even though the Beatles charged a stiff price and the Gospel according to the revival preacher was free. Was my friend so wrong who said that if Hitler were alive today, the German girls wouldn't allow him to bomb London if the Beatles were there?

"Nobody ever taught you how to live out in the streets," Bob Dylan sings in *Like a Rolling Stone*. You may consider that directed at a specific person, or you may, as I do, consider it poetically aimed at plastic uptight American, to use a phrase from one of the Family Dog founders.

"Nowhere to run, nowhere to hide," Martha and the Vandellas sing, and Simon and Garfunkel say, "The words of the prophets are written on the subway walls, in tenement halls." And the Byrds sing, "A time for peace, I swear it's not too late," just as the Beatles sing, "Say the word." What has formal religion done in this century to get the youth of the world so well acquainted with a verse from the Bible?

Even in those artists of the second echelon who are not, like Dylan and the Beatles and the Stones, worldwide in their influence, we find it. "Don't You Want Someone to Love," the Jefferson Airplane sings, and Bob Lind speaks of "the bright elusive butterfly of love."

These songs speak to us in our condition, just a Dylan did with "lookout kids, its somethin' you did, god knows what, but you're doin' it again." And Dylan sings again a concept that finds immediate response in the tolerance and the anti-judgment stance of the new generation, when he says, "There are no trials inside the Gates of Eden."

Youth is wise today. Lenny Bruce claimed that TV made even eight-year-old-girls sophisticated. When Bob Dylan in *Desolation Row* sings, "At midnight all the agents and the superhuman crew come out and round up everyone that knows more than they do," he speaks true, as he did with " don't follow leaders." But sometimes it is, as John Sebastian of the Lovin' Spoonful says, "like trying to tell a stranger 'bout a rock 'n' roll."

Let's go back to Nietzsche.

Orgiastic movements of a society leave their traces in music [he wrote]. Dionysian stirrings arise either through the influence of those narcotic potions of which all primitive races speak in their hymns [-dig that!-] or through the powerful approach of spring, which penetrates with joy the whole frame of nature. So stirred, the individual forgets himself completely. It is the same Dionysian power which in medieval Germany drove ever increasing crowds of people singing and dancing from place to place; we recognize in these St. John's and St. Vitus' dancers the bacchic choruses of the Greeks, who had their precursors in Asia Minor and as far back as Babylon and the orgiastic Sacea. There are people who, either from lack of experience or out of sheer stupidity, turn away from such phenomena, and strong, in the sense of their own sanity, label them either mockingly or pityingly "endemic diseases." These benighted souls have no idea how cadaverous and ghostly their "sanity " appears as the intense throng of Dionysian revelers sweeps past them.

And Nietzsche never heard of the San Francisco Commission on Juvenile Delinquency or the Fillmore and the Avalon Ballrooms.

"Believe in the magic, it will set you free," the Lovin' Spoonful sing. "This is an invitation across the nation," sing Martha and the Vandellas, and the Mamas and the Papas, " a chance for folks to meet, there'll be laughin' and singin' and music swingin', and dancin' in the street!"

Do I project too much? Again, to Nietzsche. "Man now expresses himself through song and dance as the member of a higher community; he has forgotten how to walk, how to speak and is on the brink of taking wing as he dances...no longer the **artist,** he has himself become **a work of art."**

"Hail hail rock 'n' roll," as Chuck Berry sings. "Deliver me from the days of old!"

I think he's about to be granted his wish.

* The Be-In speeches by Timothy Leary, the psychedelic guru, Jerry Rubin, the leader of the Berkeley Vietnam Day movement, and Buddah, a bartender and minor figure in the San Francisco hippie movement who acted as master of ceremonies.

Susan Huck, *THE GREAT KID CON*

Susan Huck's The Great Kid Con, *published originally by the ultra-conservative John Birch Society, accuses Ralph Gleason and kindred sympathizers of aiding the communist conspiracy to destroy America. Blinded by their "liberalism," Huck insists such people fail to see that popular music, from the folk songs of Woody Guthrie to the anti-war music of Phil Ochs, is all part of a Marxist plot to radicalize young minds through drugs, sex, and revolution. The article below is from* Review of the News, *(February 11, 1970).*

America seems to remain full of people who consider it pretty paranoid and extremist to note the role of pop records in promoting dissension and rhetoric of "revolution." Yet there is no particular reticence about aims to be found either in the actual words of so many currently "popular" songs, or in the views broadcast by their performers. In fact, the revolutionists--the professionals, that is--flaunt their pop-singer and folk-rock allies as openly as said performers flaunt their Marxism in song and interview.

That bit of Living Theater called the Chicago Conspiracy Trial has even been scored for music as defense strategist William Kunstler parades performing "artists" into the courtroom. He knows that they are not going to be allowed to sing in there, but he is eager to let the younger generation know where some of their idols stand.

On January 22, for example, Judge Julius Hoffman refused to allow Judy Collins to sing for the jury, "Where Have All the Flowers Gone?", which dwells upon the theme of dead soldiers--American dead, of course. Previously Mr. Kunstler, the professional defender of professional revolutionists, had brought to court Phil Ochs, Arlo Guthrie, and "Country Joe" McDonald.

Phil Ochs, to judge by his latest "songbook" does not entertain a single non-communist thought. Kunstler wanted him to sing his masterpiece, "I Ain't Marchin' Any More" (except in leftist demonstrations). "Country Joe" was supposed to perform "Vietnam Rag" for the jury, and Arlo Guthrie, son of Communist Woody Guthrie, offered to run through "Alice's Restaurant." For some reason, Judge Hoffman did not choose to endure revolutionary pop concerts during working hours.

Kunstler was arguing, all the while, that such songs are "directly relevant to the protests during the (Democrat) Convention" the "protests" which erupted into planned rioting and violence in August 1968.

Singer Judy Collins, incidently, helped Jerry Rubin and Abbie Hoffman to form the so-called Youth International Party, or "Yippies," which they all agree was never a "party" nor openly "international." Since its leaders are thirtyish, it may not even be "youthful." But it was a group formed to participate in apparently mindless and zany violence.

But to return to the role of popular music in promoting (they hope) a revolution to destroy America as we know it...you will be glad to know that Ralph J. Gleason, a Berkeley-based music critic, writing for the Drama Review, takes it all very seriously. In the issue of *Drama Review* for Summer 1969 he begins his article, "The Greater Sound," as follows:

> *Today, all over the United States, American young people are being spoken to as revolutionists in words they understand, in a style that makes those words acceptable, and through an invisible medium that old professional politicos have not yet picked up on....It's possible to say that the expression of youth's disaffiliation through pop music merely siphons off rebellious feelings and makes them assimilable and in the long run harmless--but surely this is offset by the fact that unarticulated protest is made specific, and applied to political subjects like Vietnam, for kids in remote towns who wouldn't otherwise know that they are part of a vast movement, or wouldn't connect their discontent to its sources in our social-political setup.*

At least Ralph Gleason is able to see the conscious and sustained effort which is being made--more than can be said for *National Review's* "former" Maoist Philip Abbott Luce, for example. And Gleason, while ritualistically ridiculing the "radical right" (that's us), does state that "they correctly define the Beatles as their enemy." While, unfortunately, Californian Gleason misidentifies California Congressman James Utt as "James Tustin," he does agree with him that rock music and sex education are interconnected campaigns.

Mr. Gleason knows that all this is intended to destroy America as we know it, and he even sounds uneasy about it, like an overage "liberal" overtaken by events. But you see, it couldn't possibly be a *Communist* enterprise. The Ritualistic "liberal mind is closed to that notion!

Nevertheless, critic Ralph Gleason is an informed and, within the limits of his ideological framework, an honest observer of the rock-music politics-and-revolution campaign, and makes a number of very valuable observations.

He knows what the aforementioned "Country Joe" McDonald is talking about when he sings to millions: "Come on mothers through out the land, pack your boys off to Vietnam" (And Gleason is probably quite old enough to know that no such songs were allowed during World War II, when American troops were, as it turned out, dying in order to deliver half of Europe to our wonderful Red "ally," Josef Stalin.)

Unlike *National Review's* Phil Luce, Gleason knows exactly what Grace Slick means when "advising listeners to 'feed your head'"; he knows she's drug-peddling, as usual, and that "once you set up a *situation* (italics ours) in which the sacred tenets of the social fabric are treated as obsolete or irrelevant, anything may be questioned."

He mentions an album by the group calling itself the Mothers of Invention, which he describes as "all-out satirical commentary on American society rivaled only by that of Lenny Bruce," and which has sold 300,000 copies--pointing out that this would be a very respectable number of copies of a book to be sold. Pop records, you see, are a "mass medium." True, they are "invisible" in the sense that the words are heard, then gone, and it takes a little doing to get hold of written copies of them. But that just makes it difficult to wave the actual words under the noses of doubters.

(Incidently, we have found that the printed versions of popular songs are frequently "cleaned-up"--if you listen to the record and compare, you notice the difference right away. And for some weird reason, records with really foul "lyrics" do not seem to be played on AM radio stations, but are sometimes broadcast over FM. A spokesman for the Federal

Communication Commission with whom we spoke could not understand this, since the laws and regulations apply equally to both types of stations. However, he dodged almost instinctively, even while stating that federal law prohibits "obscenity" on the air. "But what is obscenity?" he asked at once. Obviously he didn't know.)

As an example of the sort of "popular" music you are more likely to hear on FM stations, Gleason cites a typical hate America ditty by Buffy Saint-Marie entitled, "My Country Tis of Thy People You Are Dying." (Buffy's people? Yes, maybe we are dying of them.) According to Gleason, "She applies a fundamental Marxist thesis" in this opus.

Another singer, Nina Simone, extols the virtues of self-brain washing; or "change your molecules" as Grace Slick put in our interview for the March 1970 issue of *American Opinion*.

The link-up with the promotion of indiscriminate and public sex, and drug use, is perfectly clear to critic Ralph Gleason. "Stars" of revolutionary rock do not content themselves with merely uttering the hoary four-letter words, or embellishments thereof. Being performers, you see, they have to find ways to flaunt sex as well. Gleason mentions "Jim Morrison of the Doors unzipping..." before a Florida audience and doing what exhibitionists do. There was "Country Joe" cheerleading the kiddies in those easy-to-spell words. Gleason's article was written before "Beatle" John Lennon's id reached full flower. Did you know, dear reader, that for a little over $1,000 you, too, can possess fourteen priceless lithographs of John and his wife Yoko, "performing" on their honeymoon?

As for drugs, there's a tendency to flaunt that,too. The inimitable Dr. Timothy Leary said it out loud in his widely-quoted interview with the *Berkeley Gazette* last year: "Drugs are the most efficient way to revolution." Leary frankly wants to see the entire nation "dropped out" to a complete preoccupation with drugs and sex, and reduced to a primitive tribal existence by the year 2000-- he has made that as clear as his somewhat muddled mind can make anything clear any more. Another overage hippie, Paul Goodman, had expressed his "dream" of the future, years ago, in somewhat the same way--from sea to shining sea, Americans reduced to a Neolithic culture, laboring communally in the pot and poppy fields.

It is interesting to note that, while Grace Slick of the Jefferson Airplane is obviously all for mind-zapping drugs, Ralph Gleason, speaking in her defense, said that she is fighting valiantly against one drug--methadine, or "speed." As the saying goes, "Speed kills." That seems to be the only objection to it. (although other drugs "kill" too). It's hard to imagine what Grace has against "speed." Maybe whoever winds her up feels that enslaved addicts and mind-blown cripples are of more lasting use to the "Movement's" drive to enfeeble America than young people who are merely dead.

Gleason makes another point about drugs, too: **"Lighting a joint(of marijuana) is a revolutionary act,"** Leary says, and there is a deep truth in this, since the act puts the actor outside the law from that time on.

We of the "radical right" have said that too--and we know that this is precisely the intent of the "drug culture." Certainly "liberalizing the marijuana laws" will not solve the problem. It will simply move the playing field further to the left, and the revolutionary Left is already miles out of that ball park, too, now peddling heroin like there's no tomorrow.

Continuing, critic Gleason says:

> *I think that the whole body of rock music,spreading out from the center, with*

> *(Bob) Dylan, the Beatles, and the (Rolling) Stones, involved its audience in an even more fundamental confrontation with society. It says,* **you are, all of you, wrong.** *(Emphasis ours).*

Yes,that's the standard line for the pitifully ignorant young--***Everything*** is rotten about America, so ***everything*** has got to go. Then, out of the shambles, by some miracle only the ignorant and credulous could possibly believe in, there will arise a world of infinite beauty created by drug-sex-and-rock nuts instead of old fuddy-duddies who ***work.***

Lot of people in this country are "fundamentally wrong"- -mainly "liberal" leaders. But it takes a special kind of blinders to conclude that the fundamentally right people are the electric--guitar twangers.

"The radical movement...has always seen music as an arm of the revolution," Gleason observes flatly. "Radical sympathy supported the folk-music revival, beginning with Leadbelly and Woody Guthrie and coming on down to Peter, Paul, and Mary." Gleason fails to note the ideological uniformity of those he mentions, as well as that other resurrected Old Communist, Pete Seeger. Possibly the "folk-music revival" occurred because those boys represented an investment, after all. Gleason thinks that the "radical theoreticians" were late in climbing aboard the boat. Those old-time Communists were aboard the boat the last time it pulled out, too, in the "People's Song" and "Hootenanny" days of the late 'forties. Some of them rode the same boat even in the 'thirties. That's how ***new*** all this is to the unnamed "radical theoreticians" who, according to Gleason, stood back fastidiously from folk-rock because it was "manipulated by perverted money-makers."

It's the radicals who are doing the manipulating; we'll let the "perverted money-makers" term stand. Gleason should have seen that, because in his very next paragraph, alluding once more to the quaint willingness of those supposed capitalists of the record companies to support the Revolution, he says:"...in order to make money, corporate American enterprise will, in a kind of autolysis, allow its own destruction to be preached via a product that is profitable."

Lenin said it more pithily. Something about "the capitalists will sell us the rope to hang them with," if memory serves. But "autolysis" ***is*** , by definition, degenerate.

And, the record companies not only "make money" by spreading the doctrines of Communist revolution in America directly, through their records,they also ***spend*** money supporting the so-called "underground" newspapers which flaunt their porno-political messages to the same audience. They do this mainly through full-page ads designed to convince the gullible that the record companies are beautifully anti-"Establishment," when in fact they are as Establishment as *Time* and *Life*. All the youthful "marks" would have to do would be to visit the home offices of said record companies. They simply drip Establishmentarianism--big glass buildings, "corporate image" all over their reception areas, and filled with offices containing "perverted money-makers" with those famous button-down minds--the kind of minds who think visitors would rather pick up the latest copy of, so help me, *Cash Box* magazine that anything else, if they actually want to read.

It's not at all hard to believe that regular devourers of *Cash Box* are elbowing for first grabs at the young people's fat allowances or skinny paychecks. The first thing these young people had better learn in a hurry is that regular devourers of other kinds of publications are in just as advantageous a position. They'll let the *Cash Box* types keep most of the loot; what they're grabbing for are minds. They want to con these kids into enslaving themselves to drugs, sex and revolution. They want to talk them into destroying their own society and heritage, in the perfectly asinine expectation that some Utopia will spring full-blown from the alliance of old perverts and spoiled brats.

John Buckley, ***COUNTRY MUSIC AND AMERICAN VALUES***

The most popular music in the United States is not rock and roll. It is country music. Since 1970, the audience growth for country music has exceeded that of every other musical style. Because it embraces many of the so-called traditional values, country music enjoys a wide spectrum of popular support, including some of society's most conservative elements. The article below was published in Popular Music and Society *(Vol. 6:4, 1978).*

In recent years, country music has become an increasingly popular form of entertainment. Its audience has been steadily expanding for the last decade and a half. In 1961, only 81 out of 4,400 radio stations in the United States broadcast country music full-time. In 1974, the number had grown to 1,020 out of 6,900 with another 1,450 programming three of four hours of country music a day. Altogether it is estimated that about half of the radio stations in the nation play some country music. There is a country music station in every major market in the United States. Record sales are also increasing. In 1973, slightly more than half of the single records purchased in this nation were country music.

Despite this popularity, much of the public thinks of country music as an artistic and intellectual wasteland. The music has been criticized for being both too vacuous and too reactionary. It is, moreover, often seen as a persuasive medium for the transmission of rural conservatism. Both *The Nation* and the *Saturday Review* have, in recent years, described country music as reinforcing the values of its listeners, while a *Harper's* article concluded that "It is not too far fetched to say the violence of the 1973-'74 truckers' strike was fired, in part, by the Nashville sound."

It is the purpose of this paper to examine the relationship between country music, as expressed in it lyrics, and the values of it audience. It is suggested that country music does not reinforce or alter attitudes. Instead, it offers a symbolic world with which audience members may identify.

Since there is no exact agreement as to what is "country music," only songs are studied which appeared on the *Billboard* "country" charts after January 1, 1973. Some songs recorded prior to 1973 and some songs recorded after 1973, but which did not appear on the *Billboard* survey, are included when particularly as illustrative. *Billboard* surveys are drawn from record sales and radio sales and radio play and, as such, provide a general index of the public's conception of "country." Consequently, some songs of performers such as Kris Kristofferson and Linda Rondstadt are treated as country music while others are not.

It is worth noting that, although banjos and fiddles are still an important part of the "Nashville sound," not all of country music is the stereotyped steel guitars and whining vocal. A number of country recordings have "crossed-over" to the pop charts, becoming hits in two different markets simultaneously. Both country and pop audiences are usually unaware of this process and selectively perceive such songs to fit their preconceived notion as to what is "country". Different groups may listen to the same song for different reasons; country fans enjoy the qualities they identify with "country," and pop fans hear the elements they believe characteristic of "pop." John Denver and Olivia Newton-John, for example have received major awards in both country and pop music in recent years.

Attention is confined to the lyrics for three reasons. First, country music lyrics are meant to be heard. In general, the melody is the more important factor in the selection of material in rock music, while lyrics are the more important consideration in country music. The instrumental is subordinate to the vocal.

Second, the lyrics are unambiguous. Unlike some other musical forms, there are no allegories and no double-meanings. Both performer and audience clearly understand the meaning of a song.

Third, the lyrics are often an attempt at identification. The landscape, people, and situations encountered in country music, unlike much of popular music, are intended to be realistic reproductions of life. That relatively few listeners have experienced some of the situations described in the music (i.e. going to prison, committing murder) is less important than that the music attempts to elicit universally shared emotions. Loneliness, trust, suffering, insecurity, human weakness, and personal dignity are all constant, integral parts of the country idiom.

In order to examine the relationship between country music and audience values, this paper will (1) sketch the characteristic themes of country music, (2) outline the perspectives toward personal and social relations displayed in the music, and (3) describe the country music audience and its relationship to the music.

Country Music Themes

Eight basic themes characterize country music. Sometimes songs contain only a single theme, but, more often, they are crowded with several. The pattern, however, is for one to dominate, while the others assume a subordinate role. Consequently, the central theme of a song determines its classification.

(1) Satisfying and fulfilling love relations. Like popular music,the majority of country songs deal with love. In a content analysis of country songs from selected years, 1960-70, DiMaggio, Peterson, and Escoe found that seventy-five percent of the songs deal with love in its various forms. A minority of these songs treats satisfying and fulfilling male-female relationships.

Such relations are almost always depicted as within the frame-work of marriage. While both sexes are forever "slip'n around" and "hav'n one night stands," there are no hymns celebrating the joys of cohabitation. Songs treat relationships between men and women, not boys and girls. Except for an occasional song reminiscing about an old high-school sweetheart, adolescent courtship is wholly ignored. Songs tell of the relations, good and bad, of adults. Consequently, marriage is a pivotal consideration.

Sex is an integral, but not a dominant, part of satisfactory relationships. The chorus of Charlie Rich's *Behind Closed Doors* suggests the sexual dimension of the relationship while the stanzas describe the public dimension. The same attitude is expressed more concisely by the Ronnie Milsap when he sings, "I'm not just her lover; I'm her friend."

(2) Unsatisfactory love relationships. Easily the single most prominent theme in country music is unsatisfactory love relations. An earlier study of popular music found expressions of romantic discord to be common. In country music, however, the audience not only knows that the singer is unhappy but is candidly told why. If satisfactory male-female relations are equated

with good marriage, then unsatisfactory relations are most often associated with a marriage that is going, or has gone, wrong. One or both partners are unfaithful, weak, or inattentive which leads to divorce, regrets, and, in some cases, repentance.

Sex is a more volatile factor in unsatisfactory relations. It is frequently emblematic of other interpersonal difficulties. Titles such as *Barrooms to Bedrooms*, *I'd Rather Be Picked Up Here Than Be Put Down at Home*, and *Out of My Head and Back Into My Bed* are representative of the emphasis. Male-female relations, in sum, do not go awry because of lack of money or meddling in-laws but because of loneliness, jealousy, and human weakness.

(3) Home and Family. Family relations, while not given anything like the attention devoted to male-female relations, are seen as equally complex. When set in an identifiable locale, these songs are most likely to tell of a farm family and rural life. Typical is David Allen Coe's *Family Reunion*, the narrative of a mountain family gathering to play fiddle tunes. Like many other songs in which the family is sympathetically portrayed, Coe is recalling an earlier time.

Home, however, is also the setting for unhappiness. Life is hard for both parents and children, and the problems encountered are not easily solved. *Rocky Mountain Music*, for example, tells of a father's death, the mother's subsequent illness and bad temper, and a little brother whose mental illness causes him to be "taken away." Like the male-female relationship, the family and home present the individual with a range of experience, some rewarding and some debilitating.

(4) Country. It is no accident that family life is more likely to be better in the country; there is a positive agrarian image in country music. "Country" may be a recognizable physical location, but it is more than this; it is a state of mind, a way of life. "Country is," as Tom T. Hall sings, "workin' for a livin', thinkin' your own thoughts, lovin' your town," but, above all, "country is all in your mind."

(5) Work. Country music does not feature traditional work songs so much as it does songs about work. *The Workin' Man Blues* and *One Piece At A Time* describe dull, repetitive physical labor "with the crew" or "at the factory." There are no songs about school for, as Charlie Daniels notes, "A rich man goes to college/and a poor man goes to work." Work in country music is almost exclusively a male purview. Women are mothers, wives, lovers, barmaids, and truck-stop waitresses. Housework, to be sure, is drudgery, but, with rare exceptions, is discussed only when justifying a love affair.

(6) Individual worth. Country music is rooted in a belief in the worth of an individual. People live lives of quiet dignity, their strength and character not always appreciated by others. They meet and come to terms with, but do not always conquer, blindness, death, poverty, alcoholism, and being orphaned. *MacArthur's Hand*, for example, tells the story of an old man being sentenced for vagrancy. Once decorated for heroism by the General himself, the proud veteran is now destitute. The old man summarizes his case for the judge, "I was fit to fight your wars/Am I not fit to walk your streets?" The quality of the man's life is not measured by his conventional accomplishments but by the content of his character.

(7) Rugged individualism. Not only is the individual important, but he, for it usually is a man, controls his own destiny. As Charlie Daniels boasts, "I ain't ask'n nobody for noth'n if I can't get it on my own." Travel, violence, prison, and drink constitute the world of the rugged individualist. The jobs of these men are more expressions of their personality than sources of income. The cowboy has given way to the trucker as mythic hero, symbolizing self-reliance and

personal independence. The danger, the uniqueness of the life, and the sense of camaraderie are evident in songs such a2s *White Knight* and *Big Mama*. The trucker is answerable only to himself.

Barroom fights, time in jail, wild parties, and getting drunk are seldom glorified as ends in themselves but, instead, as rites of the rugged individualist. They are actions emblematic of a life style.

There are, however, occasional doubts as to whether the life style really brings happiness. Titles such as *Here I am Drunk Again* and lyrics such as "Today I'll face the big fight/But I really had a ball last night" express an ambiguous love-hate relationship for the wild life, albeit a minority one.

(8) Patriotism. Perhaps no aspect of country music has received more attention than its patriotic theme. The aggressive militancy of the Vietnam era, when approximately ten percent of country music dealt with social or political issues,will be discussed later, but, suffice to say here, that contemporary songs are overwhelmingly non-polemical. Indeed, social and political issues have almost entirely disappeared as song topics. Of the eight themes, the patriotic currently receives the least emphasis.

Of course, country performers are not alone in singing about true love, the wild side of life, or love of country. Not all the themes in country music, to be sure, are unique to the idiom. What is unique is the symbolic world that is sketched by these themes. It is peopled almost exclusively by adults in the prime of life. Affairs of significance center around the male. The rural life, which has been recently embraced by other genres, has been a favorite image of country writers for over fifty years. Adolescence is infrequently recalled. College, like business and the professions, is all but non-existent, and work is dull, physical, and unrewarding. Marriage, whether good or bad, is at the center of romantic relations. In this world, people, above all, retain their individuality, whether struggling for control over their own destiny or preserving through inner dignity.

First, although it uses some of the same themes as other genres, only country music features all eight themes described here. These themes form a symbolic world that is endemic to country music. Some aspects of the landscape are found in other musical idioms, but nowhere else are social relationships exactly so constituted.

Second, these themes do not change over time. Writers may fashion new and different ways to present the themes, but the themes themselves remain essentially unchanged year after year. Whether the setting is the railroads, mines, or Harlan County in the 1930's, or highways, factories, and urban bars in the 1970's, the message is the same.

Third, the presence or absence of certain instruments, generally, does not make music country. To be sure, many country songs may be identified by the stylized steel guitars and fiddles. Traditional instruments and instrumentation, however, are not the reliable trademark that they once were. Guitars, fiddles, and banjos have been appropriated by other genres. Some country performers, in turn, added electricity to their instruments and engineering to their voices. At the same time, an increasing amount of recording is done with orchestral accompaniment.

Fourth, the appeal of country music, like other musical idioms, is not always confined to its own listeners. Successful songs may "cross-over," achieving popularity in more than one genre, by attracting a country as well as a non-country audience. Glenn Campbell and Ann

Murray are as much country entertainers as pop celebrities. Some "progressive country" and "country rock" performers, such as Charlie Daniels and Jimmy Buffet, have both a rock and a traditional country following, with each group drawing something different from the music.

Country Music Perspectives

These eight themes unambiguously express daily problems and primal emotions. In addition, song lyrics provide perspectives on the social and personal relations represented in the themes. Perspective is provided when the audience is informed of the singer's attitude toward the primary theme in a song. For example, what is the performer's attitude toward being a trucker? Basically five perspectives appear to characterize country music. Although most perspectives can be, and are, taken toward all eight themes, certain perspectives are more closely associated with particular themes.

(1) Expressive. The performer's purpose in a number of songs is merely to express or describe his/her feelings. An exuberance for life and a need to communicate one's satisfaction undergird the expressive impulse which occurs most frequently in the extremes of rugged individualism and the satisfactory love relationship. Songs like *Dear Woman*, and *I've Got a Winner in You* so obviously disparate from *The Red-neck National Anthem*, spring, nonetheless from a shared desire to glorify life choices.

The need to communicate feelings is also manifest in narrative songs. These three-minute morality plays are most often employed in describing unsatisfactory love relationship or instructing the audience on the importance of individual worth. George Jones and Tammy Wynette's *Gold Rings* follows the prescribed formula, the first verse describing a couple's purchase of a wedding ring in a pawnshop, the second their marriage "later on that afternoon," and culminating in the break-up of the marriage in the third verse. The expressive perspective is common, but not preeminent, in country music.

(2) Utopia. Many of the people who are not happy with their current situation imagine affairs as being, or having been, better at some other times and/or place. If life is somehow insufficient, it was better in some other place or at some other time. *Paradise*, for example, looks back on an agrarian utopia. "A backwoods old town" in western Kentucky is nostalgically recalled as the setting of childhood memories. Its idyllic landscape, however, is a thing of the past since "Mr. Peabody's coal train has hauled it away." While most songs are not so explicit, performers, nonetheless, express an acute awareness that there are conditions which are more desirable than the one in which they currently find themselves. Past and present utopias can be found in most characteristic themes.

Other themes are sometimes also approached from a utopian perspective as, for example, lost love in *The Most Beautiful Girl in the World* and trucking on *Convoy*. The latter song in a saga of a cross-country truck convoy that evades the law and violates the speed limit. Utopias are real or fictive, occurring in the present and the past, but it is singular that there are almost no future utopias in country music. Emmy Lou Harris's *One of These Days*, a general reaffirmation that things will be better in the future, is a rare exception.

(3) Escape and fantasy. Perhaps the most prevalent attitude expressed in country music is escape and fantasy. Sometimes the flight is physical, but more often, it is psychological. It characterizes unsatisfactory male-female relations, rugged individualism, and work. Assignation

is often portrayed as flight from an unsympathetic spouse. Titles such as *Help Me Make It Through the Night*, *She's Helping Me Get Over You*, and *From Woman to Woman* are suggestive of the attitude. Work is confronted with psychological fantasy as well as physical escape. In *Daydreams About Night Things*, Ronnie Milsap, for example, sings, "While my hands make a livin'/My mind's home lovin' you." Fifteen years in the factory have cost Johnny Paycheck his "woman" and given him nothing in return. He fantasizes that he will hit his foreman and walk out, after telling the boss to "take this job and shove it." Much of rugged individualism is also escape and fantasy. The destination is less important than the trip in songs like *Ridin' My Thumb to Mexico*, while the bar, with its attendant drinking and fighting, appears as a refuge from daily problems.

(4) Forbearance. Forbearance, the determination to preserve, is often an indication of individual worth as well as being a perspective that is frequently adopted in family relations. People in these songs do not conjure visions or try to escape into fantasy but confront their problems directly. Like the veteran in *MacArthur's Hand*, they continue to strive, although the tide of events may run against them. When laid-off "down at the factory" before Christmas, Merle Haggard recalls how he had "wanted Christmas to be right for daddy's girl" but now hopes only to "make it through December." He does not recall better days or get drunk, but instead, makes plans for the family's future.

(5) Polarization. Although the polarized perspective is almost entirely absent from contemporary country music, the attitude deserves attention since it played such a prominent role in the songs of the 60's. Polarization is, of course, a rhetorical strategy as well as a perspective, but the concern here is with its function as perspective, with what it suggests about people's attitudes and world view.

Country music has long defended the values of its audience, and its defense has been most aggressive when those values were most seriously challenged. Comparing the advantages of farm and city life as old theme in country music, but the social upheaval of the 1960's, with songs like *I Wouldn't Live in New York City if You Gave Me the Whole Darn Town*, introduced a shrillness seldom heard before. New issues, like the changing role of women, were cast in extremist alternatives. Tammy Wynette, for example, sang the polemical *Love Me, Don't Liberate Me* as well as the more traditional *Stand By Your Man*.

But it was the Vietnam War and domestic dissent that elicited the strongest reaction from country artists. From December 1965 through August 1966, there were always at least four Vietnam songs on the *Billboard* country charts. Most defending the justness of the War and the wisdom of American involvement. The lyrics of these songs, frequently set to martial music, often conveyed a "love it or leave it" tone. By December 1969 and the release of *Okie from Muskogee,* comment was channeled into attacking dissenters, defending traditional American values, and generally ignoring the propriety of American involvement. If some country music frequently presented a polarized perspective during the 1960's, it was reflecting political and social attitudes of the day.

The Country Audience

To say, as some critics have, that country music is "Southern white, working class music" is only partially true. Its following has grown in recent years until, today, it is more national than regional. This is only one characteristic that emerges from a rough profile that it is now possible to draw of the country music audience. It is clear that the average country music fan is increasingly likely to live in the North. Moreover, research indicates that he/she will not be a transplanted Southerner but a native Northerner. This trend enabled radio station WHN in New York City to increase its audience 50 percent within eight months to 1.2 million after adopting an all-country format. The shift is also reflected in record sales. Approximately 10 percent of Loretta Lynn's records are sold in the New York metropolis area. Furthermore, "there is no regional difference between the South and the rest of the nation in the distribution of country music listeners by age, occupation, years of schooling, and family income."

Evidence suggests that the country music audience clusters between the ages of 25 and 49. Country music also has the greatest appeal for the less well educated. As years of education increases, the probability that one will be a country music fan decreases so that high school, and especially grade school graduates are significantly over represented in the country audience.

If country music is no longer a primarily Southern idiom, it remains predominantly working class. It is the rare executive or professional who is a country music fan. More common, but still disproportionately small, are the numbers of fans among the ranks of managers, clerical and sales workers. Peterson and Davis in their 1974 study of *The Contemporary American Radio Audience* point out that "fully 45.5 percent of country music listeners are craftsmen, skilled or semi-skilled workers." They also report that unskilled workers (farm and manual laborers, cooks, porters, bartenders, service workers, etc.) are over represented in the ranks of country fans. The country audience, therefore is concentrated in the "middle income category," earning a family income of between $5,000 and $15,000 in 1975. Few of the very poor or the very wealthy are attracted to country music.

Part of the attraction of country music for this audience would appear to be in the lyrics. Its themes are perspectives reflect common experiences. It is music of identification, written for and about working class adults. Like the people portrayed in the songs, country fans also get married, raise a family, hold a job, take pride in their country as well as confront marital and family problems, illness, and death.

Marriage and family are probably fulcrums of everyday experience. Their real work holds out as much opportunity for personal enrichment as do the fictional jobs of Ronnie Milsap and Johnny Cash. It is not surprising, therefore, that negative perspectives outnumber positive in country music and that any type of future utopia is almost non-existent.

The growth of country music in recent years, however, has attracted increasing numbers of Northerners, urbanites, and even some college students, groups less likely to identify with some traditional country themes. Nonetheless, the music is able to express the values of both its old and new constituencies. That it is able to do this is attributable to the audiences' perception.

Popular culture materials, such as music, may serve different purposes for the same, or different, audiences. It would appear that country music by communication values of newly acquired significance, is mirroring an important portion of Northern urban opinion. As the Program Director for New York City's WHN explains, "There is a back-to-the soil feeling among urbanites now-a-days. People are ecology conscious. They long for simple days when music reflected love and loneliness and death and going to jail, the stuff country music is all about.

Recent converts in Northern cities, then, are attracted by the ability of the music to articulate their problems. They can identify not only with the common themes of marriage, home and family, and individual worth, but they can also appreciate the importance of self-reliance, forbearance, the agrarian lifestyle, and the general emphasis on the quality of life. In this, they are not appreciably different from their counterparts in the South where "apparently, a larger number of working and lower-class urban whites dream of some day resigning from their jobs and moving to the country to earn a living on a small farm."

In sum, the lyrics of country songs reflect the values of its audience. The fictive world created by country music is not the same as the real world of audience members, but it is one they can easily understand and with which they can identify.

David Kennedy, *FRANKENCHRIST VERSUS THE STATE: THE NEW RIGHT, ROCK MUSIC, AND THE CASE OF JELLO BIAFRA*

David Kennedy describes how the state tied up a controversial band in lengthy and expensive litigation.. The Dead Kennedy's Band and its lead singer, Jellow Biafra, were charged with distributing obscene matter to a minor. In this case it was not the music, but a poster by a well known European artist that was included in the album. Although the state failed to prove its charges, the case did result in the break up of the band. Kennedy's article was published in the Journal of Popular Culture *(summer 1990).*

Congress shall make no law respecting an establishment of religion, or prohibiting the free exercise thereof; or abridging the freedom of speech, or of the press; or the right of the people peaceably to assemble, and to petition the government for a redress of grievances.

Constitution of the United States

The First Amendment of the Constitution of the United States I think this is a cost effective way of sending our the message to those people who wish to profit from the distribution of harmful matter to minors that were not going to look the other way and we are going to prosecute.

Assistant L.A. City Attorney, Michael Guarino

The poster speaks for itself: It is art. I don't think [the law] was intended to go after replications of art that have appeared in legitimate arenas.

Carol Sobel, American Civil Liberties Union lawyer on Biafra Case

The poster in question, like Dead Kennedy material and visual art in general, lampoons the conformism of American society. That is preeminently political speech. We know it works because it annoyed the authorities enough to try to intimidate their critics into submission by calling them obscene.

Berry Lynn, Legislative counsel to the national ACLU

On June 2nd, 1986, the eve of municipal elections, the Los Angeles City Attorney's office charged Jello Biafra, lead singer of the punk rock band the Dead Kennedys, and four others, with violating section 313.1 of the California state penal code of "Distribution of Harmful Matter to Minors." The reason for the charge was the inclusion of a poster in their most recent album *Frankenchrist*. If convicted, the defendants would face up to a year in jail and a fine of two thousand dollars. However, the defendants chose to risk personal bankruptcy and fight the charges for the principle of free speech. They realized that the charges were significant because they were the *first* ever to be filed against a record album in the United States. A conviction against any of the five would set a legal precedent affecting all musicians, artists, writers, film makers and performers. Their collective and solitary resolve would bring about one of the key battles this century in the United States in the ongoing struggle between the proponents of censorship and those of free speech. Moreover, the entire episode was a direct outcome of efforts by the political right, in this case, the Parents Resource Music Center, in the United States during the mid-1980's to suppress and censor the range of expression in the rock music industry.

The origins of the trial took root on December 6th, 1985, when fourteen-year-old Tammy Scharwath of Sylmar, California, bought the Dead Kennedys' album *Frankenchrist* from a Wherehouse records store at the Northbridge Fashion Mall. She bought the album for her eleven-year-old brother. The album's shrink-wrap was stickered. The sticker read "Warning: The inside fold-out to this record cover is a work of art by H.R. Giger that some people may find shocking, repulsive, and offensive. Life can be that way sometimes." The mother of the daughter, Mary Ann Thompson, when she saw the poster, agreed and more. She wrote a letter of complaint to the State District Attorney's office where she stated, "The record cover called this art. I call it pornography." The letter was referred to the Los Angeles City Attorney's office where it came in to the hands of the Assistant Los Angeles City Attorney, Michael Guarino.

When Michael Guarino read Mary Ann Thompson's letter and saw the poster, he quickly decided to prosecute. As he later stated, "I didn't feel there was much choice but to prosecute. We have made the distinction that is utterly without socially redeeming importance to minors." Guatino had an agenda for obscenity cases, but on the basis of a single complaint against the Dead Kennedys' poster he decided to prosecute. It was, he said, "A decision to go after more deserving targets."

Thus, on April 15th, 1986, nine police officers, three from Los Angeles and six plain clothsmen from San Francisco were armed with a search warrant to raid Jello Biafra's apartment to acquire three copies of the *Frankenchrist* album and the Giger poster. At 6:30 a.m. they forced their way into Biafra's apartment by breaking a window by the door. Biafra, who had been listening to a record, first heard the officers as they were coming up his stairs. The police claimed that they had knocked and received no answer.

The police quickly acquired the three copies of the album and the poster, and then proceeded to search the apartment for about two hours. Biafra felt that they were looking for weapons or drugs which he said he never touches. The officers also inquired as to the whereabouts of the original poster. They were disappointed when Biafra informed them that the painting was hanging in a gallery somewhere in France. During the search, Biafra remembered one of the LA policemen giving him an odd smile and saying, "Ah, you'll get about a year." When the police finally left, they also took business records of Alternative Tentacles (Biafra's independent record label), an issue of *Maximum Rock 'n' Roll* and some private mail of Biafra's. Later that same day, the warehouse/office of Alternative Tentacles was raided.

On June 2nd, 1986, the eve of local elections, the Los Angeles City Attorney's office charged Jello Biafra, lead singer and songwriter of the Dead Kennedys, Steve Boudreau of Greenworld Distribution, Salvadore Alberti of Alberti Record manufacturing, Michael Bonnano, Manager of Alternative Tentacles, alias Microwave, and Ruth Schwartz of Mordam Records for violating section 313.1 of the California state penal code under "Distribution of Harmful Matter to Minors." If convicted each of the defendants faced a fine of up to $2,000 and year in jail. Wherehouse, the retailer was not charged as it agreed to no longer carry the album. The five defendants chose to fight the charge based upon the First Amendment. The reason that they risked personal bankruptcy is that they realized the significance of the trial. Never before had such charges been filed against a record album in the U.S.

In law, obscenity has two definitions. It can be "immoral," meaning that the object in question is bad in and of itself, or "harmful," meaning that the object can cause bad things to happen. In this legal situation, the contentious material was consider harmful. Californian law defines harmful matter as material which appeals to "prurient interests, i.e., a shameful or morbid interest in nudity, sex or excretion, and is patently offensive to the prevailing standards in the adult community as a whole in respect to what is suitable material for minors and is utterly without redeeming social importance." Given this context, Guarino considered the case to be one of pornography.

However, the defendants and critics viewed the case differently. Biafra bluntly stated, "It's not about pornography, but a political issue." Biafra originally had seen the painting in an issue of *Penthouse*. Thus, he rhetorically asked, "Why didn't they file against *Penthouse*?" Frank Zappa pointed out that what Guarino wanted to do was establish a legal precedent. An inside source on the defense said that "they thought they were going to be dealing with a bunch of blue-haired kids who wouldn't know what they were doing." Moreover, the prosecution thought they would be dealing with people who would be unable to financially defend themselves. Only by Herculean efforts, with the aid of the NO MORE CENSORSHIP Defense Fund, was $55,000 from some eleven hundred donors raised (eventually $75,000). The only high-profile rock artist to come to the aid of the defendants were Frank Zappa and Steve Van Zandt, each of whom contributed one thousand dollars, and Paul Kantner. Most of the money raised was from small donors like a nineteen-year-old English boy who auctioned off his collection of rock memorabilia for eighty pounds or a woman from Yugoslavia who had visited the U.S. in 1962 and sent her two lucky U.S. dollar bills. As Frank Zappa described the situation, "It's a cowardly system, performing a cowardly act, responding to a cowardly parent." Nate Hentoff of *The Village Voice* facetiously, and perhaps foolishly, asked, "How can you charge a person under that law when you don't even know what 'harmful' means?" The statute is so overly broad that the collective speeches of Ronald Reagan could be considered harmful to minors because they teach them not to think." Even the Los Angeles Times called the charges "highly unusual."

The contentious item from which the Dead Kennedys' poster was taken is called *Landscape #20, Where Are We Coming From?* by the noted Swiss surrealist painter H.R. Giger. Giger is best known in America for his Academy award winning design work for the 1980 film *Alien*. The painting itself was widely circulated in Europe and is now presently residing in a private collection in Paris. The work is featured in the art book, 20th Century Masters of Erotic Art which is widely available at public libraries. Biafra spotted the piece in an April issue of Penthouse during the production of the Frankenchrist LP and was immediately struck by it. It was included in the album by agreement with Giger.

The painting depicts ten pairs of disembodied genitalia copulating in a bleak and surreal vista. It is indeed repulsive. But the question is, is it pornographic? Given its style, some observers do not immediately discern the images. It is often viewed unknowingly upside down. One observer thought it was bean sprouts poking out from kidney beans. Another thought, at first, that it was sticks in the mud.

As to the question of whether it was pornographic or not, the two sides were widely divergent. How each side depicts it is indicative of their interpretation of the case; pornography issue or free speech issue. Doug Simmons of The Village Voice stated, "Since none of the works is designed for masturbation I don't see how anyone can call it pornographic." Or said Frank Zappa after his children saw it, "Nobody snuck off to their bedroom to piddle around with it or fetish it for weeks on end--they just looked at it, had a laugh and that was that." In contrast Guarino, said that the poster depicted "dead body parts." Susan Baker of the PMRG stated that "Jello Biafra's poster depicted numerous sets of diseased genitalia engaged in anal intercourse."[1] The logic of Guarino and Baker's descriptions is clearly an attempt to construe that the poster is, as the charges demand, "without redeeming social value."

Jello Biafra pointed out that the poster would never have been included in the album had the band felt that it was harmful or exploitive in any way. For him the poster is explicitly political. "It's the greatest metaphor I've ever seen for consumer culture on parade...The painting portrayed a vortex of exploitation, that vicious circle of greed where one of us will exploit another for gain and wind up looking over our shoulder lest someone do the same to us in return...I felt that we should include this piece of art work as a kind of crowning statement of what the record was trying to say musically, lyrically and visually."

That these charges could be pressed in the middle of the 1980s was not particularly surprising given the attitudes and aspirations of the governing Reagan Administration in Washington. The charges were indicative of the hostility of the Reagan Right to unfettered free speech, particularly that which is critical of its politics, and was an outcome of its very efforts to suppress such free speech. The Right's hostility to rock music in particular dates back to the origins of rock music in the 1950s. Little Richard's early hits were held back and replaced by sanitized white covers. Elvis Presley's pelvis was deemed too lewd for television audiences on the Ed Sullivan show in 1957. Even Cole Porter and his songs "Let's Do It" and "All of You" were condemned as in poor taste. The early sixties saw the Federal Communications Commission set up a study to investigate the lyrics of the song "Louie Louie." A month of scrutiny lead to the memorable conclusion that "the song is unintelligible at any speed."

These attitudes and efforts continue to this day. Since the 1970s, the religious right has taken up the fight to suppress rock music with a vengeance. In the words of television preacher Jimmy Swaggart, it is the devil's music. The ascension of the Reaganites to power in 1980 was efforts against rock music escalate nationally and locally. The U.S. Department of Customs and Immigration began to make it more difficult to obtain the necessary H-1 visas to perform in the U.S. It became necessary for bands to prove "economic viability" by showing substantial "contract guarantees" and "distinguished merit or ability" by providing translated and notarized articles illustrating recognition in their own country and the U.S. For underground bands this was often difficult or impossible. Further examples of this climate of intolerance were the Meese Commission on Pornography with its contentious findings. Allen Sears, an executive of this commission, sent out letters to distributors and retail outlets across the country containing veiled threats about the sale of magazines like Playboy and Penthouse. As a result, the Southland Corporation and its 4,500 stores stopped carrying these magazines. So, too, did some ten thousand other stores who received similar letters. Following a widely broadcasted speech, in which Jimmy Swaggart fulminated against the "new porn" of rock magazines, and meetings with company officials days later, eight hundred Walmart stores pulled some 32 rock-oriented magazines including Rolling Stone and Creem. Swaggart later commented, "I really don't know if their decision was based upon anything I said or not. It may just be coincidental. But I'd be pleased if this kind of filth was taken off the racks in every store in America."

It was in this atmosphere that the Parents Music Resource Centre was founded in May 1985. The PMRC was the brain child of Susan Baker, Tipper Gore, Patsy Hollings, and Pam Hower, all of whom were wives of senators, congressional representatives or, in the case of Susan Baker, Secretary of the Treasury. The initial impetus came from Susan Baker, a "born again Christian," when she became aware of the lyrical content of Prince's "Darling Nikki," a song about masturbation. Within a few weeks these women had mobilized an influential group of seventeen such wives.

Ostensibly, the primary goals of the PMRC are "to educate and inform parents of this alarming new trend...towards lyrics that are sexually explicit, excessively violent or glorify the use of drugs and alcohol...as well as to ask the industry to exercise self-restraint." Ideologically, PMRC was attempting to link rising teenage pregnancy, rape, suicide, drug use and drinking solely to lyrical content of rock music and argue that it is the fundamental factor in bringing about these developments. Yet, they harbor no objection to the lyrical content of opera or country/western, or violence on television. Tipper Gore, in her book, Raising PG Kids in an X-Rated Society, notes "that 56% of music videos were analyzed as containing violence versus 75% of all prime time television." The logic of this contradiction is that it is not the content of rock music per se that is the problem, but how they are ideologically articulated. The PMRC contention is that the lyrical content of rock music is subversive to the values which constitute the fabric of American society. In taking this position, the PMRC are de facto allies, wittingly or otherwise, of the religious right in the United States.

The PMRC was set up in May 1985 with $5,000 in seed money from Mike Love of the Beach Boys (Reagan supporters in 1980) and office space donated by Joseph Coors of the Coors beer empire (well known arch-conservative Reagan fund-raiser). Reverend Jeff Ling is the primary resource person of the organization. A pastor from the New Covenant Fellowship in Manassas, Virginia, he had been preparing and presenting slide shows of sex and violence in rock music for five years. He is the author of most of the PMRC literature. Additionally, the PMRC draws upon research from a religious organization in Pittsburgh called Teen Vision. The promotion and distribution of Tipper Gore's book is done by the 700 Club and the national Religious Booksellers Convention. Nonetheless, PMRC denies any religious connections.

The means by which the PMRC suggests the rock industry "clean up their act" are:

1. Lyrics be printed on album covers.
2. Explicit covers be kept under the counter.
3. A rating system for records similar to that of films being established.
4. A ratings system of concerts.
5. Reassessment of performers' contracts who engage in violence and explicit sexual behavior on stage.
6. media watch by citizens and records companies to pressure broadcasters not to air "questionable talent."

Unfortunately, there are problems with these suggested courses of action. For example, the Dead Kennedys saw their LP In God we Trust Inc. banned by the TransWorld Music Corporation because the lyrics were printed on the album cover. There are two problems with a record-rating system. First, many chain malls have threatened to evict stores carrying restrictively rated albums. Naturally, retailers are reluctant to offer controversial material. Second, the simple logistics of a ratings system are enormous. Every year 250,000 songs are recorded in the United States alone. A rating system for concerts also has two problems. First, most ratings (i.e., those for family) would constitute prior restraint. Second, the effect of a ratings system for concerts is that often promoters will refuse to book rock concerts. Since such a system was made law by the efforts of Henry Cisneros (an old Harvard friend of Albert Gore) of San Antonio, there have been virtually no rock concerts in the city. Although much of their activity results in censorship, PMRC strenuously avoids the label of censors. They cloak their efforts by attempting to equate rock music and pornography, thus making rock music liable to laws governing pornography. Susan Baker comments: "The music industry is on the hot seat. They have suddenly discovered that they are not exempt from the laws that govern our society. Pornography sold to children is illegal, enforcing that is not censorship. It is simply the act of a responsible society that recognizes that some material made available to adults is not appropriate for children." With Regards to the charges against Jello Biafra and the Frankenchrist LP poster, the PMRC released this statement.

> *The PMRC feels that the poster and the Dead Kennedys' album Frankenchrist is a blatant example of pornography and failure to provide truth in packaging. The warning sticker which was placed on the shrink wrap, not on the album itself, claims that the poster is a work of art which some may find repulsive and offensive. This does not relay the explicit nature of the poster and does not adequately warn parents to the contents of the album.The right to consumer information prior to purchasing a product is the time honoured principle in this country. This is clearly a violation of that principle.*

Indeed, the PMRC stated that they are against government intervention and what they seek, are "voluntary agreements" on the part of record companies. But on the issue of government intervention, the PMRC is evasive when it comes directly to what they mean. In Musician, Charles Young interviewed Tipper Gore. On the issue of "government intervention" she refused to be explicit.

CY: Suppose a district attorney in Tennessee decided to indict Prince?

Gore: No, no, no. Just generally.

CY: Just generally you're against government intervention? That's going to do a lot of good for Prince or the Dead Kennedys if they go to jail.
Gore: I'm not going to defend or attack the Dead Kennedys.

The PMRC's distinction between "voluntary agreements" and censorship are nebulous at best and nefarious at heart. Barry Lynn of the national ACLU explains. "They want 'voluntary agreements', not censorship. To label an album is to relay send a message to stores not to sell it and radio stations not to broadcast it. Under these circumstances an artist's freedom of expression isn't worth very much." Reverend Jeff Ling is clearer. "Do I think [explicit music] should be out of the stores? Sure I do. And I think labelling will do that."

The PMRC was set up in May of 1985 and by September of 1985, following a major letter writing campaign of intimidation directed at the Record Industry Association of America and distributors using Congressional letterhead and the signatures of the original seventeen wives, the Senate Commerce Committee opened hearings on "porn rock." The influence of the original seventeen Washington wives was obviously instrumental. No legislation was under consideration before the hearings and it was essentially a media circus which featured ominous and outrageous comments from senators, the acidic wit of Frank Zappa and Dee Snider, a heavy metal vocalist with the band Twisted Sister, and John Denver. Yet despite that lack of legislation, Ira Glasser, the executive director of the ACLU gave this analysis of the purpose of the hearings. "What they are doing is using the threat of legislation to force voluntary compliance. And the threat of legislation does not exist since no such legislation would survive a Constitutional challenge. The only purpose is to try and create self-censorship in the music industry."

There was, however, another story behind the hearings and the threat of legislation. Since 1982, the Recording Industry Association of America had been trying unsuccessfully to pass the Home Audio Recording Act (HR 2911 and S 1739). The core of this act was a special royalty tax on blank tapes of one penny per minute. This translated into 90 cents for a 90 minute tape or $250,000,000 annually! Of this $250,000,000, 90% would go directly to the record companies with the remainder going to artists on the basis of record sales. Fundamentally, this would mean that only a few superstars would profit. Since June 1984, the National PTA (with 5.6 million members) had made similar, though less strident attempts as the PMRC to get some kind of music-labelling system. Their attempts were ignored. However, in May 1985, the PMRC letter to the RIAA received immediate attention. By June 5th Stanley Gorikov, President of the RIAA was meeting with Tipper Gore, Susan Baker and Patsy Hollings in Albert Gore's senatorial offices to discuss the state of rock music and further outline the PMRC's demands. The Senate Commerce Technology and Transportation Committee which hosted the "porn rock" hearings included four husbands of the PMRC wives, including the chairman John C. Danforth. With the threat of legislation on the one hand and the hope of a deal on the other before the RIAA, the results of the "porn rock" hearings were a compromise. The RIAA offered to provide simple labelling for contentious albums; a simple generic "Parents Advisory--Explicit Lyrics." The PMRC had in effect backed down. However, it vowed to review the effectiveness of the labelling system after a year.

Meanwhile, across the United States, thirteen states, with Maryland leading the way, were considering legislation to restrict the diversity and accessibility of rock music. The strategy of these legislators was simple. Maryland State Senator, Democrat Judith Toth explained. "I say (the recording industry) is going to go broke defending themselves. Wait until we start court cases under existing laws. The purpose isn't to win; the purpose is to keep them so tied up that they don't know what hit them." In a nutshell, with or without constitutionally valid law, force the RIAA to undertake self-censorship.

A final comment that must be made about the PMRC and their anti-rock allies is their analysis of lyrics. Certainly, there are tasteless and talentless groups, such as W.A.S.P. or Motley Crue. However, these anti-rock groups display an inability to understand lyrics in context. The most blatant example is, ironically, the Dead Kennedys' single, Nazi Punks Fuck Off, which these groups contend glorifies Nazism. Nothing could be further from the truth. One only has to consider the title of the song. The lyrics of the song condemn nilihilism, warning that it leads to fascism. Moreover, these anti-rock groups display enormous intolerance, subscribe to ridiculous ideas about the dangers of backward masking, and are possessed with the belief that rock music is the reason for all anti-social behaviour. But, as Frank Zappa put it, "To say that rock music is an exclusive cause of anti-social behaviour is not supported by science."

Throughout the deepening chill of the Reagan era, the punk rock of the Dead Kennedys represented the cutting edge of the American Punk scene. Ever since their formation in July 1978, the band has been surrounded by political controversy. The band emerged from the San Francisco scene in July 1978. San Francisco is home to a large gay community and some of the most progressive politics in the country. The truly baptizing political experience of the band was the assassination of Mayor George Moscone and supervisor Harvey Milk in December 1978.

The Dead Kennedys were a very brash, abrasive and humorous band. But above all, they were intensely political. As a political band, they had a basic political project--battling fascism. Their original impetus was regionally based. They saw the politics of Californian Governor Jerry Brown as representing a New Age fascism. The lyrics from their first single *California Uber Alles* illustrates this perfectly.

Carter Power will soon go away
I will be Fuhrer one day
I will command all of you
Your kids will meditate in school

What they feared was the conjunction of the "Me/Yuppie" generation, material wealth, political apathy with an oppressive ideological and state apparatus. The victory of the Reaganites in 1980 altered the focus of their political project and they moved to target the national arena. Appropriately, they reworked their *California Uber Alles* into a pseudo-jazz/punk fusion called *We've Got a Bigger Problem Now*, substituting Ronald Reagan for Jerry Brown. For example, "I am Emperor Ronald Reagan/Born again with fascist cravings/Still you made me president/"etc. The core of all their projects was lampooning consumer culture as it was manifested in status quo politics. They contended this was a vital component of a fascist project. What they sought to do was shock and jolt their audiences from their "complacent consumerist cocoons."

Perhaps their most admirable quality was their unremitting capacity for criticism and their implacable idealism. Consequently, by the end of their career, a large portion of their final LP Bed Time for Democracy (1986) was criticism of the state of the punk rock scene itself in America. Their dissatisfaction with the punk scene and Jello's legal problems brought about the break-up of the band in December of 1986.

To fight the charges against them the defendants quickly mobilized a defense team of attorneys. To head the defense was lawyer Philip Schnayerson. When asked by the defendants to represent them, he agreed, and organized the defense. All the lawyers involved agreed to work just for expenses. Moreover, the ALCU provided assistance in the form of Carol Sorbel.

At the beginning of 1987, the defense team, in conjunction with the Southern Californian chapter of the ALCU, challenged the legal sufficiency of the complaint. This was rejected. An attempt was made to argue that the wording of the statue was too vague and therefore unconstitutional. This was rejected. Finally, a demurrer challenged the application of the law to people other than the point-of-retail sales. This, too, was rejected. On March 13th, 1987, the five defendants entered pleas of "Not Guilty" at their arraignment. Also, a writ requesting a stay-of-the-case was filed with the Appellate Division of the Los Angeles Superior Court and was denied. On June 1st, 1987, almost a year after their arrest, the trial was set for August 11th, 1987.

The prosecution was headed by Guarino. The task which he set for the prosecution was as follows:

1. Prove that the poster appeals to prurient interest.
2. Prove that it would be deemed offensive to minors by the average Californian adult.
3. Prove that it was utterly without redeeming value.

Guarino felt that one legal fact in his favour was that the Supreme Court has said again and again, "It is reasonable to assume that obscenity interferes with the quality of life." Thus, as he explained, "It is not necessary that a harmful act actually resulted. The assumption [that such an act might occur] is legitimized by court rulings."

The defense's case was simple. They were going to argue that the charges violated the defendants' constitutional rights granted by the First Amendment. The key to their strategy would be their efforts to link the poster and the album in thematic unity.

Judge Susan E. Isacoff presided. She was described as relatively young, attractive and very relaxed. Off the record, she made jokes and became known for her affinity for M & M's after lunch. Her performance was eminently capable and very professional.

The contrast between the two benches was great. Prosecutor Guarino was slim, bispectacled, under forty and allegedly bore a resemblance to the television telepathic, The Amazing Kreskin. Ruth Schwartz, one of the accused, was less charitable. "Short, skinney, and looks like a slimey turtle in his ill-fitting suits and glasses...In a nutshell, Guarino is a sarcastic, annoying kind of guy. Our attorneys still claimed him to be intelligent. Maybe this is what makes him such a snake." Nonetheless, it was admitted that he possessed a sharp mind and a wise-cracking style. His only apparent objective fault was his habit of talking down to witnesses. Philip Schnaryerson, the leader of the defense presented a markedly different image. He had dark brown hair and a moustache. He was softer than Guarino, but just as mentally sharp. His mischievous sense of humor was a constant irritation to the prosecutor.

The mood of the court was anything but somber. Lively child custody battles raging in the adjacent court room could often be heard. There was a constant banter between the opposing benches. The public gallery attracted numerous young fans sporting leather, boots and buzz-saw hair styles. On the final day of the court, one of the defense lawyers took a picture of Guarino with a phoney camera which had a pop-out penis.

The first two weeks of the trial were taken up by the resolution of contentious issues between the benches, the admission or the discarding of evidence and jury selection. Those issues which could not be decided by agreement between the benches were decided by Judge Isacoff. The key decision which she rendered was to allow the poster to be considered in the context of the lyrics. This was a vital step for the defense's case. This meant that Guarino had to prove that the entire record was harmful. Later, Guarino admitted that this decision gave the case to the defense on a silver platter.

The process of the admission of evidence proved to be important and very humorous, particularly when the prosecution had to read out the names of such groups as the Fartz, The Crucifucks, Butthole Surfers, The Dicks and Grong Grong from the Alternative Tentacles catalogue. The entire courtroom was giggling. When Guarino reached the Dead Kennedys' single *Too Drunk to Fuck*, he refused to read it out. This brought the house down and he was forced to show it to Judge Isacoff who snickered. However, this humorous episode was important because the end result was that all charges were dropped against all the defendants, except Biafra and Microwave.

The selection of the jury was another tricky process. Ruth Schwartz compared it to the popular game Risk. From an original pool of fifty, a diverse jury was selected. There were eight women and four men. Seven were white, three were black and two were Asian. Their ages spanned from nineteen to seventy-two with the median age at forty. With this final preliminary business finished, the trial proper was about to being. The press now began to show up in force.

On August 23rd, 1987, the trial began with the prosecution's opening statements. Guarino said he sought to "demonstrate a commitment to the law" and prosecute against such material. Moreover, he established the prosecution's position that this was a case about harmful pornography and its distribution to minors. Unveiling the poster to the jury, he said, "This ladies and gentlemen is what harmful matter looks like. You want the definition? Look at the poster." The defense's opening statements were as unremarkable. Schnayerson presented the defense's case that the issue was not pornography, but freedom of speech. He replied to Guarino's depiction of the poster as harmful and without redeeming social value. "Instead of being without redeeming social importance, this is the highest. It is one of the highest of people committed to social causes."

The prosecution called seven witnesses to the stand, including Lt. Carter of the L.A.P.D. who led the raid on Biafra's apartment, the mother, Mary Ann Thompson, and her daughter Tammy Scharwath. Guarino's strategy was simple. Let the poster speak for itself. Thus, he called no expert witnesses. (Later, Tammy said that although the poster was gross, she didn't think that it was harmful.)

The defense chose a different route. They called only three witnesses to the stand and all of them were expert witnesses. The first was Joan Weinstein, an associate professor at the University of Pittsburgh, who Schnayerson hoped would establish the legitimacy of Giger's work in general. This she did. She also tried to link the poster to the songs *Soup is Good Food* and *MTV Get Off the Air*. Guarino countered by challenging Weinstein's credentials for interpreting lyrics and made a case for general lack of morals in Giger's work to which Weinstein objected.

The defense's next witness was Greil Marcus, a highly respected "academic" rock critic. Marcus' purpose was to explain the Dead Kennedys and the poster. He characterized them as satirical, left-wing and committed to battling complacency. But most importantly, "they are a very puritanical band. They are very suspicious of pleasure. The poster reinforces that."

The defense's final witness was Dennis Erokan, publisher and editor of BAM (Bay Area Music) magazine. This was a potentially risky witness for the defense because of the Dead Kennedys' famous BAM awards prank in 1980. However, his testimony indicated that time had healed the would. Ekokan characterized the Dead Kennedys as an angry band and certainly not interested in selling sex. "My feeling is that it is not a sexual message. It is rather repulsive." Guarino, throughout all of the witnesses' testimony, attempted to drive a wedge between the lyrics and the poster. Because of this, more time was spent arguing between the benches than with the actual questioning of the witnesses.

There was general surprise that Biafra was not called to the witness box. Biafra had purchased a suit for the occasion and had been preparing for weeks to testify. He is, however, abrasive, sarcastic and does not mince words with those whom he disagrees with. Schnayerson felt it best that "his music speaks for itself." Guarino was obviously caught off guard by this move by the defense.

Guarino's hasty closing statement urged the jury not to be fooled by the defense's relating the poster to the lyrics. "The distinction between the lyrics and the poster is as distinct as you'll ever see in a court of law." He finished by likening Giger to a psychotic killer. "The poster is 95% devoted to sexual imagery of the grossest kind...The people in the poster have no feeling, no warmth. It's dehumanized sex. That's prurient appeal...Giger sees people as [accused Night Stalker] Richard Ramirez sees people-- as objects. It's okay to hurt them. It's okay to maim them."

The defense's closing statement was divided between Microwave's attorney, Steve Burda, who had said little up to this point, and Schnayerson. Burda reminded the jury that there had been a warning label. He attempted once again to link the poster and the lyrics. "You can't buy the poster without buying the album." He closed emphasizing the trial was not about pornography but the freedom of speech. Schnayerson handed out the lyrics to the jury before he began. "The evidence is that these are committed young people, not purveyors of smut." He went on to discuss recent local events of hardship and related them to the lyrics of Frankenchrist. "Why would people who are concerned with social issues put a poster in an album that would be rotten, be filthy, be smut? They wouldn't do it. That's the answer." He returned to freedom of speech and emphasized for the last time that the trial was about this-- freedom of speech and not pornography.

Guarino's final statement continued to try to drive a wedge between the lyrics and the poster, but he seemed confused. He had been expecting Biafra to take the stand and had presumed that he would not have to make his final statements to the jury until the next day. The defense had been braced for a personal attack, yet none came. Burda passed a note to Schnayerson "If this is the best he can do, we're in good shape."

The jury then retired to decide the verdict. After a few hours they asked for a tape so that they could see if it was possible to hear and understand the lyrics. They were. Oddly, one of the jurors refused to listen and hid in the washroom until the music stopped. Thereafter, the deliberation became very heated and infused with moral overtones. The jury split along generational lines at 5-5 with two undecided. After two official ballots, it swung to 7-5 in favour of acquittal. Finally, on August 27th, 1987, after 36 hours of deliberation, the jury reported to the judge that they were hopeless deadlocked. Guarino immediately requested a re-trial, and said he would try to make clearer the term "harmful." Judge Isacoff denied the request, indicating she did not want to develop a trial and error procedure. She then declared a mistrial. Whereoupon, Biafra let out a yell, jumped up and ran from the courtroom screaming, "We got it." The judge tried to restrain Biafra with the threat of contempt of court, but to no effect. Thereafter, the case was dismissed. As the NMCDF fact sheet proclaimed, Frankenchrist was free!

AFTERMATH

Immediately following the trial, Guarino, who was visibly disappointed, tried to shake Jello Biafra's hand. Biafra refused. But shortly thereafter he did and presented Guarino with Big Black's notorious limited edition LP Songs About Fucking with its gruesome cover. Guarino threw it to the floor and left the building angrily. Meanwhile, Biafra was asked by nine of the jurors for autographed copies of his album which were promptly supplied. Biafra's immediate post-trial comments were, "We learned the lengths that vindictive people will go to just get the legal equivalent of a quick ejaculation" and "Forcing the issue is always worth it. I hope this slams the door on the misuse of judicial power on underground artists with an opposing point of view."

The costs of the trial for Jello Biafra, despite his acquittal, were heavy. He was now heavily in debt. His band had broken up. His marriage had ended. His artistic career was uncertain. He felt that he would have to learn how to write songs again. His comments on the trial. "It was a small but important victory...A lot of people were alerted to the issue by our decision to fight this as openly as we did, but they shouldn't take this as the end of all assaults against the First Amendment and the Constitution...We all have to continue to stay on our toes...This trial was designed to send out the message; Shut Up. Don't say what you want to say. Don't take chances or you could be next."

Michael Guarino intended to pursue other targets and has apparently done so without notoriety. The Reagan tide began to recede. "Porn rock" soon disappeared. The PMRC was still kicking, although no longer with such national vigor. But most importantly, a legal precedent was not established for either side. Essentially, the verdict was a tactical draw and a strategic victory for free speech in its battle against censorship.

POSTSCRIPT

The night of his acquittal Biafra attended the premiere of the independent film Tape Heads. Biafra had a small part as an FBI agent. He sole line near the end of the film when he arrests one of the main characters is, "Remember what we did to Jello Biafra."

1. Susan Baker et al, "First Page of Crusaders," *The Album Network* (July 3, 1987) p. 1.